Pioneer Profiles

A History of Petersburg Settlers

1898-1959

Pioneer Profiles

A History of Petersburg Settlers

1898-1959

Petersburg, Alaska

© 2004 Pioneers of Alaska Igloo 26 and Auxiliary 10

All rights reserved. No part of this publication may be reproduced or used in any form or by any means — graphic, electronic, or mechanical, including photocopying, recording, taping, or information storage and retrieval system — without the written permission of the Pioneers of Alaska Igloo 26 and Auxiliary 10.

ISBN 0-9754257-0-6

Edited by Kathy Pool

Design and Layout by Sandy Hershelman Designs
Port Hadlock, Washington

Cover photo courtesy of Glorianne DeBoer

Table of Contents

Acknowledgments............ 7

Preface...................... 9

Family Stories................ 11

Other Early Settlers........... 368

Epilogue..................... 375

Index........................ 377

Map......................... 380

Photo by Cheney & Johnston of Petersburg, Alaska, 1910-1915.
Alaska State Library, Alaska Purchase Centennial Commission Collection, PCA 20-135

Citizen's Dock
Photo courtesy of Justine Gronseth Morrell

Acknowledgments

The Pioneers have completed our book of Petersburg settlers, 1898-1959. This project has taken us almost three years to complete, from the first contacts made to descendants, urging them to write family reminiscences, to the final editing and printing.

We thank everyone for the time and effort in writing their stories, many of which are being published for the first time.

Although this project reflects the interests of Pioneer Igloo 26 and Auxiliary 10, as well as many community members, we are especially grateful to a few who worked diligently to make this book a reality.

Without the vision of John and Carol Enge, co-chairpersons, this project would not have been undertaken and completed. The idea for this book, and the first of the stories, came from the interviews they conducted for their KFSK radio show, "Pioneer Profiles."

Thanks go to Norman Fredricksen, Darlyne Conn, Bruce and Wendy Westre, and Neil Newlun for the many hours of transcribing stories into digital format, and to Doug Welde for his copying services. Catherine Hanson tackled the enormous job of assembling the many pages into a single format, and Sandy Hershelman and Kathy Pool took the final steps of design, layout and editing.

Thanks to Darlyne Conn and Jean Curry for assembling mailing lists, Norman and Lynda Fredricksen for the cover design, treasurers Lynda Fredricksen and Darlyne Conn for their accounting services, and Carrie Enge for preparing our grant applications.

Consultants Dave Fremming, Marie Darlin and Sue McCallum guided us with their good advice.

We are grateful to our advertisers — Alaskan Glacier Sea Food Co., American Legion Ed Locken Post #14, Hammer & Wikan, Icicle Seafoods, Inc., Lee's Clothing, People's Rexall Drug Store, Petersburg Motors, Sons of Norway, The Trading Union, and Wells Fargo Bank — for financially supporting this project. Generous grants from the Transient Room Tax and the Petersburg Public Library are also appreciated. And lastly, thanks to the Petersburg Masonic Lodge #23, the Pioneers of Alaska Igloo 26 and Auxiliary 10, and Fred and Marjorie File for their additional financial support.

The use of historical photographs from the special collections at the Clausen Memorial Museum, Alaska State Library, the University of Alaska Anchorage Library, the University of Washington Library, and the National Oceanic & Atmospheric Administration have added visually to the book. But, it's been the generous loan, and use, of photographs from the albums of Petersburg's families that has made *Pioneer Profiles* especially appealing.

A special acknowledgement — for the use of previously published material — goes to Don Nelson, author of *Little Norway: The Story of Petersburg*, Jackie O'Donnell, author of *Alaska Panhandle Tales*, and Ruth Sandvik, editor of *Petersburg: Heritage of the Sea*.

The Pioneers of Alaska Igloo 26 and Auxiliary 10 Book Committee

Seated, left to right: Darlyn Conn, Erling Husvik, Doug Welde and Norman Fredricksen.

Standing: Louis Severson, Jim Hammer, Mildred Lewis, John Enge, Carol Enge and Lynda Fredricksen.

This book is dedicated to all of those who have come before...

Preface

The history of an era is best told by the people who lived it...

It has been more than 100 years since the founding of Petersburg on the shores of Alaska's Mitkof Island. The site was chosen for its proximity to the sea, the beauty of the surrounding mountains, and because there were icebergs from nearby glaciers floating by.

Petersburg was founded, settled, and developed in three distinct stages. The first 20 years reflect the true pioneers, who had a vision for the place and what it could become as a fishing center.

The next period of settlement included the arrival of relatives and friends of the original settlers. They were seeking a better way of life and stayed because of the abundance of salmon, shellfish, and halibut. A cold storage was built to make fishing a year-round industry. A city government was formed, a school was built, and several churches were established.

After World War II, Petersburg veterans realized that Petersburg was the place where they wanted to settle and raise their families. Transportation by regular steamship service and small airlines made it more accessible. A communications service, improved harbor facilities, and water and electric power made the community a comfortable place in which to live.

Though Petersburg was born for economic reasons, the stories in our book relate the struggles of the early settlers as they provided for their families. It tells of their labors fishing and logging, and working in the saw mills and on construction sites. The stories relate how they traveled from village to village for work, and how they built their homes from local lumber. The women not only cared for their homes and children, but worked side by side with the men. In many cases, the women ran the businesses.

The history of an era is best told by the people who lived it. Our book records stories of the courage it took to travel to America from their native lands, without knowing the language. It tells of their struggles to build homes and live off the land. It also shares the pleasures of life in Petersburg.

We felt it was important to retain the individual voices of the writers of these biographies. To do so, we edited this book with a light hand.

In compiling this book, we were aware that some early settlers were not included. We tried to contact their descendants. When we could not, we relied on the memories of the town's elders and compiled their reminiscences of certain families. We are sorry if some are missing.

This book evolved as a project of the Archives and Historical Committee of the State Pioneers of Alaska. As members of that committee, we challenged our local organization to record their families' history in Petersburg. Many agreed to write this for their families — thus, our book was born.

The family photos, accompanying many of the articles, are wonderful glimpses into Petersburg's history. We cannot thank all of you enough for sharing those precious memories with us. They are indeed the crowning glory of our book!

John and Carol Enge
Co-chairs
Petersburg Pioneers' Project

Petersburg Harbor

John and Minnie Allen

By Don Nelson

John Allen grew up on the Lummi Indian Reservation near Bellingham, Washington.

As well as can be recalled, Minnie was from the Chicago, Illinois, area. She attended a Roman Catholic school where she studied music. It was there that Minnie met John, and they were married on November 16, 1892.

They came to Petersburg in 1915. John was the acting Postmaster and U.S. Commissioner. John was also a fishing and hunting guide.

The Allens had two children. Their son, John, was later killed in a hunting accident. Their daughter, Mary, was an accomplished pianist, who played for the Sons of Norway dances and the Variety Theatre during the silent films. Mary was also a professional photographer.

John and Minnie moved to Green Rocks where they raised silver foxes and "lived off the land." They were very hospitable. A visit to their home might include a dinner of venison roast, goose tongue, wild cranberry sauce and chess pie.

John Allen

Their local friends drove to Papke's Landing, often in Bert Cornelius' hearse, where they would be met and transported by John in a large flat-bottom boat. Standing up, John would row them across Wrangell Narrows to Green Rocks.

Mary's Lake was a short hike from their log cabin and a favorite swimming and ice skating spot for locals.

John lost his eyesight in his later years. He traveled to Seattle aboard the steamship *Denali*, for the last time in 1952.

Minnie is fondly remembered as the author of the "Humpback Salmon" song.

Minnie Allen

Photo courtesy of Clausen Memorial Museum

"Humpback Salmon"

I like humpback salmon,
Good ole humpback salmon,
Caught by a Norske fisherman.

I like shrimp and shellfish,
They sure do make a swell dish.
I think that halibut is grand!

I don't like T-bone steak,
Caught from a steer in Texas.
But give me fish...
And I don't give a darn if I do pay taxes,

I like humpback salmon,
Good ole humpback salmon,
Caught by a Norske Fisherman.

From *Petersburg: Heritage of the Sea*

American Legion Petersburg Post No. 14

From information compiled by Frederick Nelson, who later became Department Commander of the American Legion for the Territory of Alaska.

American Legion Petersburg Post 14
(Now the Edward Locken Post No. 14)

When Frederick Nelson arrived in Petersburg on December 19, 1919, he was, so far as he knew, the only member of the American Legion in town. At the time, he was a member of Multnomah Post No. 1 of Portland, Oregon.

After contacting several ex-servicemen with the motive of organizing a local post, Nelson inserted an ad in the local newspaper on January 23, 1920, inviting all ex-servicemen to meet at the Town Hall on January 25, 1920. The attendance was so small that the matter was temporarily dropped.

However, when a number of veterans agreed to turn out in their uniforms to participate in the 1920 Fourth of July parade, an application for a post charter was made.

The Petersburg Post No. 14 charter was issued October 1, 1920.

The first Post Commander was Sergeant Paul C. Lacey, operator in charge of the local Signal Corps cable office. The Vice Commander was Dr. H.C. Carothers. The Adjutant was Frederick Nelson, who had worked out all the details for obtaining the charter. There were a total of 22 charter members:

Alva Allen
H.C. Carothers
Carl W. Chenoweth
Arthur W. Crawford
Hugo M. Fredrickson
Charles A. Greenaa
Oscar Granquist
Otto J. Hallin
Joseph D. Hill
Chester M. Holm
James R. Jandorf

Peder Jelle
Chester A. Johnson
Paul C. Lacey
Clarence D. Lawrence
Ed Locken
Chris Mathisen
Frederick Nelson
Olaf S. Olsen
Steinar Sandwick
Louis Vick
L.A. Woodward

Fourth of July parade, 1920
Identifed: Ed Locken (1), Fred Nelson (2), and Doc Carothers (3)

Charles and Jessie Andersen

By Margaret Rehm

Charles G. Andersen was born in July of 1891 on a small island in northern Norway, near Harstad. With a desire to go to the "New World," he left Norway in 1912, promising his mother he would return in five years for a visit. However, in 1917, World War I was being waged and he could not get to Norway. Charlie had registered for the draft and was called into the U.S. Army in 1918. He was sent to Haines, Alaska, for a few months before the armistice was signed and he was subsequently discharged.

Jessie Flett was born in November of 1890 in a small seacoast town, Portknockie, Scotland, north of Aberdeen. She always wanted to "go abroad." That opportunity came when she learned of a lady, with a very young child, needing assistance in getting to Vancouver, B.C. Jessie made that trip with her, leaving Scotland in 1912.

Jessie worked as a domestic in Vancouver for about five years when yet another opportunity to expand her horizons came along. She had a chance to go to Port Walter, Alaska, and work in the fishing industry. It was there that she met Charlie Andersen, who was a crew member on Louie Martens' fishing vessel, which also happened to be in Port Walter.

Hearing there were some Scottish girls from Vancouver arriving, Charlie, and others, went to the dock to greet them.

While Jessie was in Port Walter, a tub of hot water she was carrying dropped on her legs and severely burned her. She was sent to Sitka, and then to Juneau, for care.

The romance continued, as Charlie visited her in both Sitka and Juneau.

Charlie Andersen

Jessie Andersen

Charlie and Jessie were married in August of 1918, in Prince Rupert, British Columbia, at the home of a friend of Jessie's, who was also from Scotland.

The Andersens then made their new home in Petersburg, where Charlie and a friend, John Otness, bought the fishing vessel *Teddy J* and continued in the fishing industry. A few years later Charlie sold his interest in the *Teddy J* and bought a fishing vessel, the *Hazel H*.

Jessie and Charlie were both interested in, and involved in, their community. Jessie was a member of the American Legion Auxiliary, Ladies of the Golden North, Parent-Teacher's Association, Lutheran Ladies Aid, the Hospital Guild, and Eastern Star, where she served as Worthy Matron. Charlie belonged to the American Legion, Masons, and Shriners. He served on the city council and the selective service board.

Neither Jessie nor Charlie had many years of formal schooling. At that time, in their part of the world, education beyond high school was difficult to obtain. However, they gave their children the opportunity for higher education.

Margaret was born in Vancouver B.C., in 1920, and Cecil was born in Petersburg, in 1924. Both graduated from the University of Washington with credentials to qualify for secondary school teaching.

Jessie and Charlie have four grandchildren, all of whom have college degrees. They have seven great-grandchildren, two of whom have college degrees. Charlie passed away in 1967 at the age of 76. Jessie followed in 1991, at the age of 101.

Bert and Helen Anderson

By Berthiel Evens

Bert Anderson was born in Bralanda, Sweden, on January 12, 1914. He lived on the family farm until 1923, when his father returned from the gold rush in Alaska to bring his family to America. The Andersons settled in Oakland, California.

At 20, Bert decided to see Alaska for himself. He and his future brother-in-law, Bob Hill, hitched rides on various boats from San Francisco to Petersburg. The friends fished the 1935 season with Richard Hofstad aboard the F/V *Tango*.

When Bert returned to Oakland, he worked for Standard Oil and bought a 33-foot boat. He and Bob fixed it up and named it the F/V *Helnor* for their future brides, Helen and Norma.

In 1939, they set off from Oakland, California, to fish in Petersburg, Alaska. But they arrived too late for the season.

Bert had to be in Oakland by September 30th for his marriage to Helen Baxter Hill, so they sold the boat to Andy Wikan.

Bert was a World War II veteran, serving in Korea and Okinawa.

In 1949, Bert and Helen came to Petersburg to stay. By now they had two children, Berthiel and Carl.

Bert started fishing with his childhood friend, Bud Olsen, on the F/V *Wave*. He also fished with Don Philbin on the F/V *Progress*, with Erling Thomassen on the F/V *Iceland*, with Ray Thomassen on the F/V *Shirley*, and with Neal MacDonald on the F/V *Jan M*.

In 1959, Bert quit fishing to work construction as a carpenter. He helped build the Blind Slough Fish Hatchery, Crystal Lake Dam, the Petersburg City School and many houses.

In the 1960s, Bert and Helen purchased a lot at Sandy Beach from the Bureau of Land Management and built their home there.

Bert liked to keep chickens, ducks and turkeys. At one time, he owned a cow, and he always had a dog. It was hard to get Bert away from Sandy Beach, because he was always working on his house and caring for his many animals.

Helen and Bert's retirement years were spent doing the things they enjoyed at a more leisurely pace. Bert's illness also took a toll on their time.

Their grandchildren liked spending time with them and hearing the stories Bert told about the bears and porcupines.

Bert passed away in November 1989.

Helen and Bert Anderson

Helen Baxter Hill was born on February 4, 1920, in Oakland, California. She lived there until moving to Petersburg.

She worked a few years for the Employment Service and the Forest Service, waitressed at Winnie's Café, and was the only woman dispatcher at the Petersburg police department. She later worked at Health and Human Services.

Through the years, Helen served on the school board, was a member of the Women of the Moose, Business and Professional Woman, and the Alaska Pioneers.

Helen fondly recalled her greatest contribution to the environment. While building streets in Petersburg, the city crews were running trucks up and down Sandy Beach in front of her home. They were taking loads of sand and causing the devastation that still exists today.

One morning, as she prepared to go to work, she decided she had had enough. She sent a telegram to Governor Egan about what was happening. The governor wasn't in his office, but the message was relayed to him in Sitka.

By midafternoon the trucks were stopped forever. Helen proved that the voice of one citizen can indeed make a difference.

After Helen's husband died, she did some traveling, but was content to enjoy her home. She enjoyed knitting, crocheting, and deck gardening. She also loved walking through her garden in the early morning hours.

Helen passed away in December 2000.

Carl Anderson

By Carol Enge

Carl Anderson was born in Bralanda, Sweden, on May 15, 1918. He immigrated to the United States with his family at the age of 5, arriving at the port of New York aboard the S/S *Stockholm*.

The family settled in Oakland, California, where Carl attended grade school. He was confirmed at St. Paul's Lutheran Church in 1933. He graduated from University High School in 1937.

A lover of the outdoors and adventure, Carl, his brother Bert, and two friends departed from Oakland for Alaska in 1938, aboard a 33-foot boat named the M/V *Helnor*.

Carl was inducted into the Army in November 1941. He served in the Aleutian campaign and received an honorable discharge, as technical sergeant, in August of 1945.

During military leave in 1944, he married Edna "Dollie" Knowlton in Berkeley, California. He returned with her to Petersburg after World War II.

They had two daughters, Carlene and Mary Elin. An infant son, Alfred LeRoy, died at birth.

Carl was employed on a fish tender, and as a machinist and foreman for the Kayler-Dahl Fish Company. He also worked as a carpenter, building and assisting the constructors of the new Petersburg General Hospital.

With his friend Tony Westre, Carl built a cabin at Blind Slough. He and his family spent many enjoyable days there.

Carl spent his last years at the extended care facility at Petersburg Medical Center. He died on October 23, 1996.

Fishing boats in the harbor at Petersburg, no date
Photo by John N. Cobb
University of Washington Libraries, Special Collections, COB129

Olaf and Constance Arness

Provided by Arlene Peterson and Ann Arness Lyons

Olaf Hagen Arness, the second child of Alexander and Radina Arness, was born in Norway, June 4, 1870. He grew tall and strong, enjoying good health all of his life until his last illness. He had a pleasing smile and was good natured and liked by all who knew him.

The Alexander Arness family lived in Norway on a small farm on the banks of a fjord on the shore of the Norwegian Sea. This was at latitude 67 degrees which is approximately the Arctic Circle. They lived in a log house with a barn and outbuildings also of logs, mostly spruce or birch, with sod roofs.

During the winters, Alexander was away from home for months at a time, fishing with his crew off the Lofoten Islands, from his sail-and-oar powered boat.

During the short summer, he and his sons planted and harvested a big garden and two crops of hay. The few acres of land at home did not provide sufficient pasture. In May, the cattle and sheep were driven to the plateaus close to the top of the mountain ranges. With the animals went the eldest daughter. She lived there in a shelter. It was her job to milk the cows twice each day, churn the cream into butter, and make cheese from the skimmed milk. A younger brother also went along.

On May 18, 1883, at the age of 13, Olaf, with his brothers, sisters and his parents, left Norway by ship for America, where Alexander thought his children would have a better chance at a successful life. The family located in Minnesota and took to farming. Since Alexander was a man of considerable means, he could afford to buy passage for his family, and on his arrival, buy a farm with buildings and land already under cultivation. The change, the new life, the new language, the new countryside and the different climate, called for drastic adjustments. The flat open prairies of Minnesota, the hot, scorching sun and dry winds of summer, the snow and howling storms of winter, were a stark contrast to the beautiful, scenic Norway with its mountains, valleys, seas, fjords, and cool climate.

Sorrow, anguish, and homesickness were to torture Alexander for the months and years to come. He wept

The Arness Family, from front left: Alvin, Olaf, baby Thelma, and Constance
Back: Clifford, Octor, Gedskin, and Agnes

openly many a time for his friends and homeland and he missed his life at sea. But he was a religious man and relied on his God to bring him through.

Alexander's wife, Radina, was more stoic and realistic. Because of the many routine household duties, plus bringing up seven children and caring for the animals, she had little time to spend in regret. Radina was strict in the upbringing of the children and expected obedience from each. Playing cards, dancing, and the like were sinful and not tolerated.

The farming operations in Minnesota progressed with more than average success. The original farm expanded. Olaf and his brothers helped with the work on the farm until they reached the age when they became restless and wanted to strike out for themselves. They left the farm, one by one, and took

Olaf and Constance Arness cont'd

up homesteads elsewhere. Olaf located near Crookston, Minnesota, and it was there he met Constance Bjorge. They were married March 24, 1895.

After seven years of diligent work on his own farm and with four children added to his household, Olaf had visions of taking his family to live where there were forests of trees and cool running streams. In 1902, having heard of the gold rush in Alaska, Olaf and Ingvald Bjorge, his brother-in-law, decided to take a trip to Alaska to view the possibilities of settling there.

Back in Crookston, after his Alaska visit, Olaf decided to sell the farm and move to Puget Island on the Columbia River. The nearest town was Cathlamet, where he purchased a small general merchandise business. His wife and older children helped operate the store while he tried fishing, logging, and boat building. Another child was born there. The family consisted of Alvin, Gedskin, Octor, Clifford, and Agnes.

Being of an adventurous nature, Olaf's thoughts eventually turned to visions of the country he had seen passing through Alaska's Wrangell Narrows. He could see a tremendous future there, with all that land waiting to be settled, abundant timber, lakes and rivers, hills and plenty of wild game. In 1909, he sold his interest in the Cathlamet store to his brother Ole. In June of that year, he moved with his family to Mitkof Island on Wrangell Narrows to an area called Scow Bay. (Doyhoff was the U.S. Post Office's name of the area they settled.) Scow Bay got its name from fish scows anchored in the bay or moored to pilings, ready to receive fishermen's catches. Olaf had brought his 36-foot boat with him and used it for fishing for halibut.

Olaf picked out a piece of land which was to become his homestead (official government identity was H.E.S. 138) and they began building a four-bedroom, two-story house. The property was located three miles south of Petersburg, which could be reached by either walking the beaches or by boat. Here in this new home, their seventh child, Thelma Marie, was born on Christmas Day 1911. Olaf bought three cows, a few chickens, and planted a vegetable garden. From then on there was plenty food for all.

Olaf rigged up for logging and tried that for a while, but the expense of rafting the logs to distant mills was too great. He then started a small sawmill of his own in 1912, cutting his own timber. The two miles of sidewalk to the Scow Bay schoolhouse was built with lumber from his mill. With improvements and more machinery, he later cut finished lumber. Olaf supplied the town of Petersburg with lumber to build its Sons of Norway Lodge. He also cut the timbers for the roadway between Scow Bay and Petersburg. Things were looking up. Each year the demand for lumber increased. He supplied the town of Petersburg with all of its street planking, lumber for homes, buildings, and road construction. He cut box lumber for the fish buyers and packers at Petersburg, Wrangell and Juneau; they made boxes to pack and ship frozen fish to Seattle.

In 1941, at the age of 71, he sold his mill to his son Octor and daughter Agnes. It was operated by the Arness family until it burned in 1955. Prior to the fire, Agnes sold her share to Lars Eide of Wrangell, but Octor continued his share of the operation.

In 1948, Olaf and his wife, Constance, took their first extended vacation trip to visit many friends and relatives in Washington, Oregon, California, and Minnesota. It was a memorable trip. As soon as they arrived back home, Olaf began making plans to visit Norway, the land of his birth. However, this was not to be. Olaf, 79, became ill. Sent to Seattle for tests, he was found to be suffering from cancer and six months after returning home, he died November 15, 1949.

Olaf's family and a host of friends felt keenly his disappointment at not being able to fulfill his dream of visiting the place of his birth. He was "one grand person," always ready and willing to help others. Many newcomers to Alaska got their start with his encouragement and by employment in his mill. He had a wonderful helpmate in his wife, Constance, who shared his enthusiasm and willingness to help others. Constance lived in Scow Bay until she entered the Pioneer's Home at Sitka, Alaska. She passed away in Sitka on July 16, 1968, at the age of 94.

Descendants of Olaf and Constance still live in Petersburg. Their son Octor married Florence Hansen and they had two daughters, Arlene and Ann. Arlene's children are Tom Peterson, Christine Rumple, Wendy Piccolo, Virginia Davis, and Ralph Peterson. Ann's children are Debra, Barbara, and James Lyons.

Octor's wife, Florence, died in April 1953. He lived almost another 20 years in his house near the family sawmill at Scow Bay. Octor died in November of 1972.

Ed and Ingeborg Baggen

By Don Nelson

Edgar and Ingeborg (Solem) Baggen arrived in Petersburg about 1906. Ingeborg had emigrated from Kristiansund, Norway. Ed's brother, Martin Baggen, also arrived in town about this time. Ingeborg Baggen had a niece, Emma, who later arrived from Norway and married Ingebright Johnson.

Ed Baggen had a sister, Marie Severson, who came to Petersburg in the early days, but later moved to Wrangell. Baggen also had a brother George, who lived in Juneau. He founded and operated the Samson Tug and Barge Company of Sitka.

Ed was a halibut fisherman and a gillnetter on the Stikine. In 1906, Louis Miller built a small house for the Baggens, located on the south side of Hammer Slough near the current bridge across Nordic. It was the first house built in that locality. Ed had a warehouse in front of the house with a long approach extending out into the creek.

A daughter, Margaret, was born about 1914 and died in the 1918 flu epidemic. She is buried in a marked grave in the cemetery across the Narrows, along with her father.

In 1921, Ed Baggen became ill and died on a fishing boat, on the way to St. Ann's Hospital in Juneau.

Ingeborg went to work first as a janitor in the new school that had been built in 1924. She then was a cook at the hospital. She later worked at the laundry. The upstairs of the Baggen home was rented out, mainly to young immigrants from Norway, who flocked to Petersburg in the early days.

A son, Edgar Irvin, was born May 15, 1913 in Petersburg and graduated from Petersburg High School in 1930. Like many young boys living in Petersburg, Edgar enjoyed duck and goose hunting. He was accompanied on such trips by his hunting dog.

Edgar was also very talented as an artist and a poet. He drew many sketches for the original PTA cookbook. He once constructed a miniature Statue of Liberty for a Fourth of July parade. After completing school in Petersburg, Edgar enrolled in a six-year program in dentistry at the University of Minnesota.

During summer vacations, to earn money for financing his university education, he worked as a cook on fishing boats and on a tender for Standard Oil tankers. He had the reputation of being an excellent cook. No doubt his mother played an important part by passing on her culinary skills.

Edgar became an accomplished ski jumper and was also certified as a ski jumping judge.

After graduating from the University of Minnesota, Edgar returned to Petersburg and opened a dental office on the second floor of the current Gloria Ohmer-Patti Norheim Building on Main Street. This building now houses Pangea and the Diamente.

Ed Baggen

After about four years, he moved to Fairbanks to open another dental practice.

His mother Ingeborg also moved to Fairbanks at this time. (She died there in 1973.)

On May 20, 1941, in Petersburg, Edgar married Mertie Johnson, whose parents were Andrew and Laura Johnson of Petersburg. Four children were born to the Baggens: Wendy Rameriz of Brooklyn, New York; Jill Jensen of Greenwood, California; Laurel Davidson of Fairbanks; and Abe "Eddie" Baggen of Fairbanks.

Edgar practiced his dentistry profession in Fairbanks, until 1975 when he retired. He was very active in Fairbanks civic affairs and was a member and president of the school board for many years. Edgar served two terms in the second and third State Legislature from 1961 to 1964.

Mertie Baggen passed away in 1968. Edgar died in 1991 in Port Orchard, Washington.

Dr. Warren and Ann Bailey

By Carol McMillian

In 1945, Warren Washington (born 1908, Salina, Kansas) and Ann (Hicks) Bailey (born 1917, Malta, Montana) arrived in Petersburg from Ketchikan, on the *North Sea*, with Lynn Ann (born 1941, Portland, Oregon), Carol Lee (born 1943, Portland, Oregon) and Warren Weston (born 1944, Ketchikan, Alaska).

Warren had served as a dentist in the U.S. Coast Guard, in Ketchikan, during WWII from 1943-1945. He purchased the dental practice in Petersburg when he was discharged. His dream had been to establish a dental office on a yacht and service the small towns in S.E. Alaska, but he did not have the means at the time.

He then became so busy in Petersburg that the closest he came to the idea of a traveling office was an annual "Tooth Extraction Clinic" in Kake. The clinic was held for one day at Bell's General Store, with a porcelain display toilet as the dental chair, and Bue Hentze (Petersburg plumber and fishing buddy of Warren's) as the "dental assistant." In exchange for the "free" dental work, the townspeople of Kake outfitted Bue and Dr. Bailey with a boat, motor, and grub for a

Warren Bailey

three-day fishing trip to nearby Kadake Bay, renowned at the time as one of the world's top fly fishing spots for sea-run cutthroat trout.

Warren's dental office was in the old Bank of Petersburg building from 1945 until 1951, when it was moved to the converted detached garage next to the newly acquired family home on "E" Street (now the Lutheran Church Parsonage).

The dental practice served most of mid-S.E. Alaska, providing "24/7" toothache relief for transient fishermen, loggers, and others passing through. Many a quiet night was interrupted by a distressful knock on the door (coincidently, usually after closing hour for the bars) seeking emergency care. Treatment was given and accounts were settled on the spot by the fresh seafood barter system.

In 1946, the Baileys were joined by Ann's parents, Norman Weston (born 1890, Humber Bay, Ontario, Canada) and Eva (Zabell) Hicks (born 1887, Birds Creek, Ontario, Canada) from Bismarck, North Dakota, where Norman had retired as construction engineer for the State of North Dakota.

Ann Hicks Bailey

Dr. Warren and Ann Bailey cont'd

In Petersburg, Norman Hicks became U.S. Commissioner and Customs Officer. The family has copies of a wonderful letter he wrote to his oldest grandchild, Bob Walker, in Butte, Montana, in 1947, detailing his catching and landing of an 85-pound, five-foot-four-inch-long halibut. He had been fishing alone in Frederick Sound from a 12-foot skiff.

The Hicks had a primitive cabin (later, "Lemke's Cabin") on the creek across the Narrows from the Norman Tate home in Scow Bay. They enjoyed many visits from the grandchildren, who had been joined by Norman Edward, born in 1947 at Petersburg General Hospital.

Norman Hicks died at age 59, in early February 1949, after suffering a heart attack in Petersburg.

Eva Hicks and Ann Bailey traveled to Malta, Montana for the interment of his body. During their absence, the Baileys' home on the CAA hill was gutted by a fire that originated in the kitchen.

Warren Bailey was at work on Main Street and Norma Wilder was caring for the children. All escaped the fire safely excepting "Mopsey," the family dog. Mopsey burned and permanently scarred her rump when she went back into the burning house, presumably to look for her "children."

When Ann arrived home on the steamer, unaware of the fire, Warren had the children lined up on the dock to greet her. He was fearful that partial word of the fire might reach Ann en route, and he wanted her to know that everyone was all right. The only clue to Ann that something was amiss was that the four children were dressed in unfamiliar clothing!

The Bailey family was blessed for a short time with a fifth child, Norma Jean, who was born in December 1952, in Petersburg. She was diagnosed with acute leukemia in 1954 and died shortly before her second birthday.

Lynn, Carol, Warren "Butch" and, in front, Norman

In May 1961, Warren Bailey died from a heart attack at the age of 52.

He had been president of the school board. He was also active with the Petersburg Hospital Board, the Alaska Dental Board and Dental Association, as well as the American Legion and Freemasons.

In 1954, Eva Hicks and Ann Bailey were instrumental in the establishment of St. Andrews By-The-Sea Episcopal Church in Petersburg.

After Warren's death, Ann worked for the Forest Service and transferred to Juneau after her family was grown. She retired in 1971 and moved to Point Agassiz with friend Alice Farra. They built a two-story cabin, greenhouses, and extensive gardens. The pair lived off the land and sold plants in Petersburg.

In 1982, Alice Farra became manager of Mountain View Manor. Ann shared the position by running the office, while Alice maintained the building and grounds. Both retired again in 1994.

Alice returned to her original home state of Montana. Ann lived at Mountain View Manor, until her 1996 death from cancer at age 79. While in Petersburg, she was active in Eastern Star, American Legion Auxiliary, BPW, and the library board.

Many wonderful times were passed at Sasby's Point with Vivian and Perry Langley, Norma and Bill Wilder, Don and Slim Pettigrew, and Elmer and Sally Copstad. Bue and Jane Hentze were special friends, as were Mary and Dr. Russell Smith, and Vange and Norman Tate. Later, when Ann and Alice moved to Point Agassiz, a cadre of pioneer-spirited women and men (Virginia Culp, Norma Tenfjord, Patti Norheim, as well as Fran and Spencer Israelson, and Glenn and Martha Reid) were frequent and welcome visitors to the farm. Was there ever a better time and place to grow up? Not hardly!

Farrell and Alda Bennett

By Leeila Jones

Farrell and Alda Bennett came to Alaska in 1943. They left Vancouver, Washington, with their two daughters, Lolita "Rusty" and Leeila "Lee", and arrived in Ketchikan, Alaska aboard one of those wonderful "Princess" ships.

After a year, they moved to Wrangell, where more children, Lanore and Lyle, were added to the family.

In 1951, the family moved to Petersburg where they settled. They bought a home on Wrangell Avenue, which was then known as the Ballard residence.

Farrell worked for Barney White, as a mechanic, on the limited number of cars in Petersburg at that time. He soon could identify each one without looking, as they rattled past our house on the old plank streets of Petersburg.

Eventually, he worked at Pacific American Fisheries (PAF), as a machinist on the canning retorts.

Farrell was also a very active member in the Moose lodge. He was one of the first men, along with Verner Israelson, Bert Anderson, Mel Brady, James Wheeler, Louie Vessel, and others that were instrumental in forming what is now the Loyal Order of the Moose #1092.

Alda worked briefly at the Lillian Shop. She loved the social exposure her work provided and would recall some rather intriguing customers, specifically a group of unique ladies that lived and worked about three miles "out the road." They apparently had an arrangement with the management permitting them to shop after hours, exclusively.

Eventually, Alda left the shop to devote her time to raising Lanore and Lyle.

Rusty had married and was living in Washington State. Lee graduated from PHS, married Trygve Thorsen and lived in Petersburg until 1990.

Betty Pederson, Florence LeRoy, Polly Lee, Marnee Israelson, Mildred Elkins, and others still recall Alda's "back to school" coffee parties celebrating, with a sigh of relief, the end of summer vacation.

After Farrell left PAF, Alda supplemented their income by dressmaking and altering clothes.

In 1956, she began working for the weather bureau as a weather observer. It's interesting to note that the weather observers began in Petersburg many years earlier. From 1924 to 1929, observers worked from the school grounds; from 1929 to 1932, from the Jacob Otness home; from 1932 to 1940, from Wheeler's store; and from 1940 to 1956, from the CAA hill.

Alda's job required "readings" every hour from 6:30 a.m. to 3 p.m., seven days a week. She would walk approximately 25 feet from the back of the house on a boardwalk into the muskeg, to her little white instrument house in every kind of weather imaginable. She would take instrument readings, gauge the cloud cover, compile all the data, and phone her readings into the main office in Juneau. After a while, they went high-tech and gave her an old clackity teletype. All family gatherings and functions revolved around Alda "taking her readings" every hour, and she did this unfailingly for 13 years.

Farrell died in 1971. Alda died in 1997.

Lyle Bennett still resides in Petersburg and owns the Petersburg Gallery and Bennett Vending. Lanore Bennett Rodenburg lives in Murrieta, California, with her husband Bill. Lolita "Rusty" died in 1990. Lee Bennett-Thorsen Jones lives in Juneau.

The Bennett family children, grandchildren, great-grandchildren, and great-great grandchildren, many of whom reside in Petersburg, continue to contribute to its growth and cherish the fundamental small-town values of this wonderful community.

Sing Lee Alley, 1950s

Harold and Ethel Bergmann

By William and Joyce Bergmann

Harold and Ethel Bergmann, together with their two children, Judy and William, first saw Petersburg from the deck of the mail boat *Penguin*. It was August of 1952, and they were aboard the *Penguin* destined for Unimak Island, on the Aleutian Chain, and Harold's first teaching job at the one-room schoolhouse at Nikolski.

During their passage through Wrangell Narrows, they admired the cemetery and clean white houses they could see from the ship.

Harold said that any community that took such good care of their cemetery must take good care of their people, too.

The following year they passed Petersburg again, this time to a different, distant small schoolhouse at Chignik, on the Alaskan Peninsula.

However, that first view of Petersburg was enough for the Bergmanns. In August of 1954, when the mail boat stopped at the northern end of Wrangell Narrows, the Bergmanns descended the ramp, making Petersburg their new home.

When they arrived in Petersburg, they brought along Ethel's mother, Adeline, who worked in Bob Schwartz's Citizen's Steam Laundry. Grandma Adeline was known for her German cooking and her love of playing bingo and cards. Adeline was part of the new wave of old-timers who got to spend their final years in the wonderful Mountain View Manor. Adeline died in 1983.

Ethel and Harold were both born and raised in Wisconsin. Ethel came from the rural community of Appleton. She was born on October 26, 1919, from the marriage of Adeline Ella Eichstedt and Lee Bloomer. The Eichstedts and Bloomers trace their heritage to Germany.

Harold was born and raised in Milwaukee, the oldest son of five children of the union of Arthur Bergmann and Emma Kuehl. Harold's grandparents came from Pomerania, in Prussia.

While growing up, any money Harold earned doing odd jobs after school went to put food on the table for his younger brothers and sister.

Although Ethel and Harold both went to the same high school, they never dated until the late 1930s.

Ethel and Harold were married February 13, 1943, while Harold was on leave from the service. His sister Joyce was the best man at their wedding because all the men were in the service.

Harold spent the war in India as a weatherman. He always felt we lived in a charmed place compared to the abject poverty he observed in India. This influenced him throughout his life; he would always help others who were not so fortunate, whether it was with money or some other type of support.

Ethel became a crane operator during the war.

After the war, they built a house of rammed earth, while Harold was working two jobs — going to the University of Milwaukee and helping to raise a family. Judy was born on September 9, 1944. William was born on October 28, 1947.

Harold and Ethel Bergmann, with young William and Judy, 1952.

Once in Petersburg, Harold began work as a sixth-grade teacher in the old three-story grade school. He was also the speech teacher in the high school.

Harold loved children and had an innate sense of how to get them to learn and think on their own. Although his teaching was often very unconventional, there was hardly a student who sat in his classroom who didn't feel the effects of Mr. Bergmann for the rest of his or her life.

Harold also worked on seine boats during the summer, including Norm Tate's, Arne Trones' and Albie Hofstad's boats.

Ethel was also fishing during the summer. She

and Bernadine Trones teamed up to beach seine at the mouth of Petersburg Creek.

She met Dagmar and Jess Ames, who owned the Yukon Fur Farm, a mink ranch that had several thousand breeding mink at its peak. Like all of the other mink farms in West Petersburg, the scream and smell of mink did not linger over the Ames' ranch. When they decided to leave Petersburg, they offered the ranch to the beach seiner they had befriended and her husband.

college in the fall of 1965, feeding, breeding, and skinning mink would become a lot more work, especially for Harold. So, the dream of having a farm ended. When the last mink was skinned on the Yukon Fur Farm, Ethel ended up with a fur coat.

Many of William's friends, including Norman Bailey, Wayne Peterson, Mark Sandvik, Roger Pederson and Greg Nichols, have memories of feeding the mink or getting chased down the long runways by angry mink, during breeding season. Ethel and William

Tessa, William, Joyce, Ethel and Harold Bergmann on May 17, 1991.

During the 1950s, even though mink ranching in Alaska was in its last throes, the Experimental Fur Farm, which Jim Leekley operated, still had active ongoing studies of mink and other fur bearers.

Jim, recognizing the Bergmann's desire to have a real fur farm, pushed them to get some breeding pairs and start raising mink. The Yukon Fur Farm expanded to 400 breeders after five years, but the fur market was failing. Friendly letters started arriving from the IRS telling Harold and Ethel that "you have to make money or it is called a hobby." Also, with William leaving for

continued beach seining at the mouth of the creek until the fishery was closed.

Ethel and Darlene Coon bought the Star gift shop from Bunny Mathisen in the mid-1960s. The Star was the place to buy that special gift for your loved one before Christmas. The 1-2-3s served in the back room of the Star on Christmas Eve helped lubricate the mind and the pocketbook, helping a husband buy just that perfect piece of jewelry.

Harold returned to Wisconsin during the summers in the mid-1960s to get his master's degree.

Harold and Ethel Bergmann cont'd

Soon after receiving it, he became principal of what was to become the Rae C. Stedman Grade School. He remained its principal until he transferred to Atkasook, Alaska, in 1978. Harold taught school there for one year with his daughter, Judy, before retiring.

Judy remained on the North Slope and taught school in Barrow for about a dozen more years, and then moved to Anchorage. Heidi Jeffers and Gretchen Charles, Judy's daughters, arrived as the first grandchildren in the 1960s.

William married Joyce Wingfield of Enterprise, Oregon, in 1969. Their first daughter, Joan Bergmann, was born in 1970. Amber arrived two years later. Tessa, William and Joyce's third daughter — and Harold and Ethel's last grandchild — was born in 1985.

William fished commercially and graduated from Oregon State University in 1971. He began working, in 1972, as a fisheries manager for the State of Alaska in Petersburg. He continues to manage fisheries around Petersburg to this date. Joyce works as a nurse at Petersburg Medical Center.

Because of their outgoing personalities and their unique lifestyle on Petersburg Creek, Harold and Ethel made friends young and old. Ethel was a fantastic cook, loved to spark up a party and enjoyed gardening. She didn't like to kill things, whether it was a spider, a flower, or a tree.

Ethel and Harold were both instrumental in changing West Petersburg, from a suburb of Petersburg to the City of Kupreanof, a roadless, independent community.

Ethel became the first mayor of Kupreanof and was proud to help set up that community's permanent fund, while other cities were busy spending the oil money that seemed to have no end. Harold later followed in her footsteps as the mayor.

They both loved animals. Numerous dogs, cats, geese, chickens, and ducks roamed the ranch, and some of those pets, plus other unique ones, lived in the house with them at times. They included Elroy the Pig, Gladys the Goat, and Pedro the Attack Rooster.

The most unique thing about living in Petersburg for Harold and Ethel were the friends they made during their years there. Lifelong friends included Hi and Roxy Lee, Oscar and Ruth Sandvik, Bob and Charlotte Schwartz, Eldor and Polly Lee, Andy Mathisen, and many more.

Ethel was very artistic and was involved in the art community for many years. She learned many media, including painting, pottery, metal welding of sculptures, and block printing. She loved having her sculptures in the garden. A metal blue heron stood watch as you walked up the float to the house.

Harold had a radio show on KFSK for years. People would tune in to listen on Saturday mornings. He obtained information for his radio program, while going about his daily routine of shopping, checking the mail, and harassing people on the street.

At any moment, he would pull out a small notebook and pen from his shirt pocket and make notes about life in Petersburg. You had to be careful what you said, or a quote or some outlandish statement about you would be on the radio the following Saturday. Some folks would cross the street when they saw him coming, so they wouldn't be part of the news on Saturday morning. His audience listened because they never knew what the "Mouth of Petersburg Creek" would say about activities in Petersburg, Kupreanof, the world, or possibly about them.

In her later years, Ethel traveled with the Sumdum Women, a gathering of friends that wanted to see the unique sites of Southeast Alaska in style.

In Harold's later years, he took care of Ethel and loved her all the more. Ethel died after a very full life on October 10, 1999.

Harold never quit teaching people and he never stopped saying what he thought.

Harold died on October 31, 2001. Some of his seventh grade students from years before remember him saying that he would die on Halloween, so he could come back and visit them.

**Mink tag
Yukon Fur Farm**

Frank and Annie Bollen

By Beulah Reid Jones

Frank Bollen was born June 7, 1887 in Beaver Township, Republic County, Kansas. After the death of his mother, his father moved the family to the state of Washington, remarried and had two more sons.

Frank met and married Annie, a young woman who was born and raised in Lake Bay, Pierce County, Washington. Annie was born on January 12, 1889.

They had two daughters: Laura Ann, on April 26, 1913, and Elma Mae, on May 31, 1920. Both the girls were born in Seattle.

Frank worked tugboats in the Puget Sound area. In 1923, he moved his family to McNeil Island where he and Captain Tom Torgenson were partners, owning and running the steamboat *Rounder*. Frank was the engineer. They hauled passengers and freight from Steilacoom, Washington, to McNeil Island and all the other islands in the area. The Bollens lived on McNeil Island until 1936, when the government bought the privately owned property from the residents.

It was during these years that Laura "Lollie" met and married Frank Luhr in September of 1929. When they had to move from McNeil Island, Frank and Annie moved to Lake Bay, Washington.

Frank's younger brother, Harry Bollen, had moved to Petersburg with wife Myrtle in 1936. They wanted to try their hand at fishing on the troller *Ava*. Upon hearing of their success, in 1938, Frank and Annie acquired the boat *Lollie Mae*, loaded it with their possessions, left their daughters behind, and set off for Petersburg to troll.

They lived with Harry and Myrtle in a house on what was then known as Front Street. Their daughter Elma joined them for a six-month visit before moving back to Tacoma. Frank and Annie then moved to a very small house belonging to Benny Ventura, located next to the Kolstrand blacksmith shop. In 1946, Frank and Annie purchased the house on the corner of South Nordic and Indian Street. This house was built by Ralph Susort and is currently a rental, owned by Sigred and Harold Medalen.

Frank soon graduated to a larger troller, *AB&G*, and fished the outside waters around Yakobi Island, Icy Point and Cross Sound until his retirement from fishing in 1960. When Annie found too many things for him to do around the house, Frank would make a fishing trip even if the fish weren't biting.

Annie worked in the fish and shrimp canneries of Petersburg to supplement their income. She was also a cook at The Pastime and Recreation, both local restaurants. She had a formidable presence and scared most people away with her sternness, but had a heart of gold when you got through the front she put up. More than one person was able to sweet talk her into fixing dinner for them after the grill had been turned off and cleanup had begun. After retiring from cooking, Annie cared for the three children of Lew Williams Jr., who was the owner of the *Petersburg Press* and mayor of Petersburg at the time.

Annie was an avid gardener. You could find her in the yard from sunup to sundown during the spring and summer months. She sifted soil taken from the empty corner lot next to their house for her flower beds. She found a $10 gold piece in the sifted dirt and gave it to her oldest great-grandchild, Donna Luhr. Annie's sweet peas, dahlias, delphiniums, and gladiolas were her pride and joy.

Her great-grandkids, Don Luhr's children, and the Williams and Medalen kids spent many hours playing at Annie and Frank's house. She let them do things that their mothers frowned on, such as playing in the water and dirt. Grandma Annie would get very upset if a baby-sitter was hired to take care of her great-grandkids, so the Luhr children spent many a night with her and Grandpa Frank.

She would buy clothes for the kids to wear from the Salvation Army, so they wouldn't ruin their play clothes. She would also take them to movies their parents wouldn't dream of seeing. Needless to say, the Luhr children, as well as the neighbors' kids, dearly loved these great-grandparents.

Their daughter, Laura Luhr, stayed home from fishing in 1963 to care for her mother. Annie died quietly at home of pancreatic cancer on August 16, 1963. Frank lived alone, with his parakeet, after Annie's death. His great-grandkids continued to visit him often. Joyce Ann stopped by every day after school when her mother was working. He passed away on January 17, 1970 of pneumonia at Petersburg General Hospital. Both Frank and Annie are interned at the cemetery in Petersburg.

Jim and Edna Brennan

By Jim Brennan III

The Brennan family first came to Alaska in 1870, when James Brennan, a Trinity College of Dublin graduate, Irish revolutionary, and political refugee, came to Washington Territory and then to Wrangell. He went up the Stikine and made a successful strike in the Cassiar gold field. Shortly after his return, his health and finances failed. He died just before his son, James Aloysius "Sam" Brennan was born, in 1873, in Cowlitz Prairie, Washington.

Jim and Edna Brennan

James Aloysius "Sam" Brennan was called Jim, like his father.

In 1893, Jim came to the Ketchikan area and then Wrangell. He worked as a blacksmith at the forerunner to the A.J. Mine in Juneau in 1894. In 1897, Jim worked as a packer over the Chilkoot Trail, earning his grubstake before going on to the great Klondike strike. When mining prospects worsened, Jim left Dawson, traveled down the Yukon River, and joined the gold stampedes at Nome and then Fairbanks.

Returning to Nome, he served as secretary of the miners' union before finally leaving Nome in 1906, long after most of the miners had given up.

After spending several years in Juneau, Jim Brennan came to Petersburg in 1910, with his wife Edna and two small children, Leroy and Dick.

Jim opened a saloon, popularly known as the Bucket of Blood, near the site of Petersburg's present day General Services Building. The saloon featured good liquor, gambling, and pool, except when such activities were prohibited.

During Alaska's "Bone Dry" law, which preceded national Prohibition, Jim adapted. He converted the Bucket of Blood to the "Gilt Edge," with soft drinks, pool, billiards, and cigars. However, Jim had to temporarily close his establishment in 1918, when he was the victim of a trumped-up charge of sedition brought by a corrupt federal prosecutor, as was later proven in legal proceedings.

The false charge arose out of a visit to Petersburg by the Deputy U.S. Attorney and a navy vessel, ostensibly to confiscate a Scow Bay moonshine still and shut down the town's red light business.

When this prosecutor and the naval officers began swilling the evidence and pressuring the ladies for their favors, prior to running them out of town, Jim would not tolerate the hypocrisy and burst through the door with a U.S. Marshal in tow as a witness.

Unfortunately, this earned Jim a completely fabricated charge of pro-Germanic sedition — a very serious criminal allegation in World War I Alaska — from a vindictive prosecutor wielding largely unchecked power.

Jim had to put up everything he owned to make bond, hire a lawyer, and locate the witnesses the prosecutor had run out of Petersburg.

Once the true facts came to light, the charges were dismissed, amidst detailed Juneau newspaper stories regarding the "interesting" developments in the case.

Jim resumed operation of the saloon until it was destroyed by fire in 1951. The bar was well known up and down the coast, partly because of the camaraderie

Jim and Edna Brennan cont'd

of the gold stampede days.

Jim was a strong and bighearted man, who led Norwegians, Natives and other converted Irishmen in annual St. Patrick's Day parades and celebrations, where he usually won the Fat Man's Race.

He made many uncovered loans to those who were down on their luck. He was a founding member of the Arctic Brotherhood and of the Moose Lodge in Petersburg. He served on the city council and on the city committee that first brought electricity to town. He was also active in territorial politics.

Jim Brennan died in 1952.

Edna Brennan was an accomplished writer who wrote a history and description of Petersburg for the first issue of the *Petersburg Progressive*, in 1913. She was also active in the town's first theatrical productions.

Edna suffered ongoing health problems, which required her to live in Port Townsend, Washington, while raising her young boys.

Despite her chronic illness, she lived until 1951.

Jim Brennan in a "Fat Man's Race," an annual St. Patrick's Day event, which Brennan usually won.

Dick and Helen Brennan

By Jim Brennan III

At an early age, Richard F. "Dick" Brennan began helping his dad, Jim Brennan, in the bar, during visits to Petersburg from Port Townsend, Washington. He moved to Petersburg when he got a little older.

In his early teens, Dick became a good card player. He was most accomplished with a pool cue, which was, for a time, his major source of income. This nighttime occupation often caused him to miss early classes, but he nonetheless graduated from Petersburg High School.

Dick completed a year at the University of Washington before the Depression forced him to return to help his family. He became a U.S. Postmaster when he was 23, and retired from the position in 1970.

Over the decades, as Petersburg's mail came increasingly by airplane rather than steamer, Dick gained a reputation for running a friendly, but very efficient, postal service. One of his first employees was Helen Lund, born in Petersburg and valedictorian of her high school class. She was the pretty eldest daughter of Norwegian immigrants, Peder and Anna Lund.

Helen and Dick married in 1934. They raised three children, who graduated from Petersburg High School: Judy in 1957, Molly in 1960, and Jim in 1967.

The Brennan family spent many summers boating together out of Petersburg, first on the *Drake*, then on the *Jaunty*, a 32-foot Monk-designed cruiser.

Former students from across Wrangell Narrows remember boarding the "school boat," every morning and evening, as it traveled between the boat harbor and Kupreanof Island, and some years, Sasby's Point. Dick made this run for 32 years without mishap. He was an active officer of the Petersburg Vessel Owners Association.

The Brennan's family cruiser was somewhat unique at a time when nearly all other sizable Petersburg vessels were commercial fishing boats. The idea of touring Southeast Alaska for the fun of it was still novel. Fishermen friends would ask the purpose of his frequent boating ventures. Dick wanted "to see what's around the next point." Some of these ventures took the family all the way to Puget Sound.

Dick and Helen befriended many trollers and old-timers, residing in bays and coves where ambitious enterprises had once thrived. Dick would strike up conversations with strangers; Helen would turn them into lasting friends. The family's maritime explorations of Southeast Alaska and British Columbia eventually focused on Warm Springs Bay, on Baranof Island, where they renovated a cabin that is still used by the family.

Petersburg friends will remember Dick with a cigarette and whisky Coke in hand, discussing topics to which his open mind, intellectual curiosity, wide-ranging reading and recollections of Southeast's early characters had lately taken him.

Helen was his ever-present reminder that life is supposed to be fun, particularly with another boat trip on their horizon. Rough water crossings, however, were never Helen's idea of fun. Dick and Helen both enjoyed the retelling of the story of one particularly harrowing trip, with the *Jaunty* wallowing in big seas far from shelter, when Helen spontaneously announced she was "taking my kids and getting out of here!"

Dick and Helen Brennan

Dick and Helen moved to Lacey, Washington, when Helen became ill in 1971. After Helen passed away the following year, Dick often returned to Petersburg. He also engaged in intensive foreign travels, including lengthy stays in Mexico and Argentina, where he was fluent in self-taught Spanish. One of his journeys took him to Vienna, Austria, where he became smitten by a spirited Polish woman, Margit Olszewska. They married and lived in Lacey, with Margit's daughter, Klaudia. Dick passed away in 1988.

Dick and Helen's children remained in Alaska. An anthropologist and Glacier Bay/Icy Straits wilderness guide, Judy lives with her husband, Greg Streveler, in Gustavus. Retired, Molly and Ron Crenshaw live in, and boat out of, Juneau. Jim, an attorney, and his wife, Lani, live in Anchorage and boat in Prince William Sound.

The Peter Buschmann Family

Told by August Buschmann. Edited by Ronn Buschmann.

Peter Buschmann, my father, was born in Aure, Norway, on July 31, 1849. His ancestors include primarily ministers, but also architect/builders, fishermen and fisheries-associated businessmen.

Prior to coming to the United States, he had a net-making business, which had fallen upon hard times. The Buschmann fishing nets were made by hand as individual cottage businesses in the Aure district of Norway. The Buschmann family supplied the twines and other supplies and then collected the finished product for transport to market. With the introduction of net-making machinery in Germany, handmade nets were not competitive in the marketplace and this line of business was largely abandoned.

Father caught salmon in small quantities in Norwegian floating traps and sold them wholesale. He was interested in halibut, but I don't remember him fishing for, or selling, them before he came to America.

His primary fishing business was ownership and collaboration in the catching, packing, and processing of herring. His principle processing establishments were in Laurvigen, in Aure, where he had a large herring saltery and other buildings. He also had interests in several trading and salting establishments along the coast of Norway. His small coastal vessels were used in connection with these operations and the production was shipped primarily into Russia. It was the Czar's imposition of an import tax on Norwegian herring, as well as a decline in coastal and Lofoten Island herring stocks, that encouraged Father to look towards a brighter future on the West Coast of the United States.

He reached Tacoma, Washington, with my mother, Petra, and eight children on June 7, 1891. When we first arrived, Father's funds were all but exhausted. My brother, Chris, and I sold newspapers, the *Tacoma News*, on the streets of Tacoma for a short time.

By late summer of 1891, Father had moved the family to a place called Scow Bay, a short distance from Port Townsend, Washington. Chris, Father, and I worked in a salmon and herring saltery operated there by Ragnor Dahl.

Shortly thereafter, having heard of the rich fisheries in Alaska, Father made a voyage in 1891, with John Johnson on the sloop *White Wing*. Having left early fall, he returned on Christmas Eve. The balance of the 1891-92 winter was spent fishing dogfish sharks in Puget Sound and rendering their livers for the high-quality and valuable oil. My brother, Chris, and I helped in this endeavor, which was a profitable, but messy and smelly, business. We also caught halibut and codfish, which we, being mindful of the tides, delivered by rowboat to the town of Everett, some 30 miles distant. We also had a small saltery and smokery for salmon, halibut, and herring, which we operated for several months. The products were sold locally.

Later that winter, we moved to Port Townsend and then on to Fairhaven, Washington. Here, we also operated a small saltery and smokery for salmon, halibut, and herring. These products were sold in the Fairhaven (now Bellingham) area. During the summer of 1892, we helped Father operate a Norwegian-style floating salmon trap on Stuart Island, one of the San Juan group of islands in Puget Sound. We built a small pile-driven salmon trap on the west coast of Lummi Island, near Fairhaven. This was accomplished by building a raft from logs to substitute for a pile-driver scow. We made the gins from hewn piling and used an iron-ringed, small log four feet long, as a hammer, which we hoisted with a hand windlass. Due to the inadequacy of our pile-driving equipment, we could not set the lead far enough into the straits for this trap to be effective on the large run of sockeye salmon passing by. Years later, the famous Allsop salmon trap was installed in the same location with a steam pile-driver. This trap was operated with wonderful success for many years.

In the early spring of 1893, Father and I sailed for Ketchikan, Alaska aboard the steamer *Topeka*, arriving in March. He quickly associated us with Clark and Martin, the owners of a small (55-60-foot) halibut schooner, the *Volunteer*. We spent the next six months fishing and curing halibut and salmon. We caught most of our halibut off Stone Rock and Cape Chacon, which is the south end of Prince of Wales Island. We fletched and salted the halibut in the hold of the vessel until it was full. We then sailed to Ketchikan, where we discharged, repacked, and boxed the halibut for shipment to Seattle by steamer.

There was monthly steamship service in those

The Peter Buschmann Family cont'd

days. Father had arranged for Peter McKinnan, as captain and partner, since Father was not yet a citizen. I signed on as cook and deckhand at 13. We enjoyed a pleasant and interesting summer off the Cape until late August. Thereafter we did most of our fishing in bays and inlets south of Ketchikan, until late September, when we returned to Ketchikan and delivered the schooner back to the owners.

The man in the square frame is the original Peter Thams Buschmann (1762-1845). He was a minister and was responsible for building Prestegarten and other church buildings in the Aure district of Norway. Holding the picture is Johan Christian Buschmann (1762-1845). The young man at his shoulder is Petersburg's Peter Buschmann. The best guess would be that the women are young Peter's sister, mother and grandmother.

Father was always watchful, investigating sites for the future operation of canning and salting establishments. He purchased a large skiff and some halibut gear. We, Father and I, rowed to Loring Cannery, on Naha Inlet, and camped in an old Indian shack across the bay from the cannery. This became our headquarters, and we fished halibut, dogfish, and shark in that area for a couple of months. We salted the halibut and made lubricating oil from the dogfish and shark livers by boiling them in a large tank. Lacquer barrels obtained from the cannery were cleaned and used as oil containers. We shipped more than 50 barrels of oil to Seattle, where the oil was sold for 25 cents a gallon. Our production represented a small fortune in those days.

During the fall of 1893, we fished halibut in the bays and inlets south of Ketchikan. Later that fall, Father located a cannery site on the west side of the mouth of Mink Arm, in Boca de Quadra Inlet, about 40 miles distance from Ketchikan.

During the late fall and early winter of that year, Father, with the assistance of Alfred Magnuson of Victoria B.C., was able to finance the Quadra Packing Company. The purpose of Quadra Packing Company was to build and operate a salmon cannery at this Mink Arm site.

The balance of the winter and early spring saw my father in preparations for the seemingly monumental task of constructing enough of a cannery that he could produce some sort of a salmon can pack by fall. This cannery was built during the spring and early summer of 1894. Substantial packs of about 10,000 cases of salmon were produced during that and later seasons.

All of the salmon were caught in Boca de Quadra Inlet and its tributaries. There were no powerboats in those days, only long oars and a strong back. With this operation as a nucleus, Father established a salting station for mild curing king salmon on the south side of Taku Inlet, across from Taku Glacier, in 1895. Here he packed from 100 to 200 tierces, 800-pound barrels, of mild-cured king salmon each year.

In the spring of 1896, Father located a trade and manufacturing site on the southeast side of the north end of the Wrangell Narrows, Mitkof Island. He organized the Icy Straits Packing Company to finance construction of a salmon cannery and fish processing station at this site. Not only did this location have plentiful salmon runs, but it was close to some of the best halibut fishing grounds in Southeast Alaska.

Father had halibut fishing and shipping in mind, since Alaska steamers from Juneau, Skagway, Sitka, and further westward generally went south through Wrangell Narrows. Another important consideration

The Peter Buschmann Family cont'd

for the halibut fishermen was the fact that floating icebergs, both from the Leconte and Thomas Bay glaciers, drifted into Frederick Sound and often the Wrangell Narrows itself. There was also a substantial herring resource in local waters. Initially, however, Father realized that this location at the north end of Mitkof Island would be a perfect town site. Not only was there an abundance of flat, buildable land and protected harbors, but the surrounding mountains reminded him of the home he had left in Norway. So, it was here that Father intended to put down permanent roots in America.

Shortly after locating the future town site, we built a small shack out of rough-hewn spruce lumber on the deck of the *Annie M. Nixon*. Father, always trying to accomplish many things at once, set us to this task upon leaving Ketchikan, and we were occupied with construction until we arrived at the north end of the Wrangell Narrows. Once there, we set the shack overboard onto some float logs and towed it to shore with a small rowed skiff. He left our friend, Paul (an Indian from the Loring, Ketchikan area) and me with the task of dragging the cabin above high water and building a foundation. They left us with tools and food for several weeks and continued on to the mild curing station in Taku Inlet. This cabin, though I was scarcely able to stand up in it, was sufficient to validate the land claim to the 40-acre trade and manufacturing site which would later become the downtown of the City of Petersburg. Over the next year, as we went about our fishing ventures, we would stop here with additional supplies and equipment.

In 1897, I worked for Father at his mild cure salmon saltery on the south side of Taku Inlet. The saltery was not far from the Taku Glacier, from which hundreds, and at times thousands, of tons of ice broke off into icebergs whenever a steamer close by blew its whistle. This location was unique, as the contour of the solid rock shoreline was almost perpendicular from the bottom up to above the high-water mark where it flattened off to a large shelf on which the saltery was built. No wharf or dock was necessary, since at high tide steamers of a thousand tons or more could land alongside this perpendicular rock wall. Each steamer would tie fast to a large ringbolt at each end and we would unload cargo. Next we would load the 800-pound tierces of mild-cured king salmon by rolling them from the saltery over heavy planks onboard the steamers. During 1897, Father, Mother, my sister, and I celebrated our Fourth of July by making ice cream at the foot of a dead glacier across the inlet, known as Norris Glacier. Father also bought a salmon saltery location in Bartlett Cove, near the entrance of Glacier Bay.

The year 1898 saw a renewed effort to develop the site at the north end of Wrangell Narrows. It was at this time that the original cannery buildings were built. Father also located the store and housing, and established a rough idea of how the town was to be laid out. In 1898, he built a sawmill at the mouth of Mill Slough. Mr. S. L. Hogue contracted for most of the logs cut in the sawmill. This lumber was used to build most of the original cannery buildings and dock. Mr. Hogue did most of his logging across the Narrows from Petersburg and used two yoke of oxen to pull the logs out of the woods.

Father realized that it was best for immigrants to spend a few years in America before settling in Alaska and did not encourage immigrants to come directly to the Mitkof Island site. He did want to encourage the settlement and offered free land to anyone who wished to build a home. Of course, he did sell the lumber and store supplies. My brothers, Chris and Eigil, and myself, put in for, and were granted, 80-acre homesteads near the trade and manufacturing site.

Eigil and Chris spent the winter of 1899 in what was becoming a town at the north end of Mitkof Island. There was additional work on the cannery buildings, and they built the store and cannery superintendent's home, which included a cookhouse and warehousing in the basement. There were built a number of small "China cabins," along banks of the Wrangell Narrows, in which the cannery workers would reside. The first pack of canned salmon was produced summer of 1899. Eigil Buschmann and Jack Kelley alone fished salmon for the cannery with a small beach seine in the bay across the Narrows from Petersburg. At its head was a creek, then called Hange Creek, which was a very good pink salmon stream.

I spent the summer of 1899 at the Bartlett Cove saltery. This would be my first experience as a boss. Glacier Bay has several long arms at the heads of which were large glaciers, including Muir Glacier. On a

The Peter Buschmann Family cont'd

beautiful summer day, I was sitting in our small, modest, log cabin dining room, waiting for the cook to announce lunch. I suddenly felt a very severe and unusual movement; and to my surprise, I saw my steamer trunk moving towards me from across the room. I then realized we were having an earthquake, which lasted several minutes. The cook's helper, a native boy of 12, was as white as a ghost when he ran into the cabin. He had been walking around in the large Indian cemetery located on top of sand dunes behind the camp. While this severe movement was on, he thought the Indians buried there were coming to life. The epicenter was about 170 miles away, close to Yakutat, where I was told three small islands came to the surface as a result.

Ice broken from the glaciers by the earthquake of 1899 formed bergs as large as buildings and jammed into Glacier Bay and Icy Straits, making it dangerous and almost impossible for large steamers to navigate this area for several days. For some time thereafter, steamers often made long detours to escape the many large ice floes while going to and from Juneau and other local ports to the westward. The tender *White Wing,* that generally served our salting station, could not push her way into Bartlett Bay for two weeks; and even after that, it was with difficulty on account of floating ice. We packed about 600 barrels of mostly red salmon there that year, employing Hoonah natives.

Father had an interest in the halibut schooner *Annie M. Nixon*, and in 1895 convinced his partners to convert her from sail to steam. He installed a Captain Hummeland, who operated her from 1895 to spring of 1900, at which time Captain Hummeland became master of the tender *Phillip F. Kelley*. I served as halibut fisherman on the *Annie M. Nixon* part of two winters. She carried four dories and eight fishermen, in addition to captain, engineer, and cook (who was also a deckhand). The gear and dories were not local, but were brought up from Puget Sound when the boats came north in the spring. We fished mostly off Point Ellis and Coronation Island and the eastern shore of Chatham Straits, delivering our catch to Petersburg.

It may be of interest to mention that we used cordwood for fuel in those days and loaded up with cordwood when leaving Petersburg. But when fuel ran short, it was the fishermen's duty to go ashore in some sheltered cove, saw a few trees into cordwood lengths, split these into cordwood size, and lighter the wood to the steamer in our dories. Timber along the shores was plentiful, so fuel was always available.

The winter of 1900 saw increased activity at the township site. My brother, Chris, was established as superintendent of the fisheries operation. My cousin, John Thormodsater, arrived from Norway to take the position of cannery bookkeeper and storekeeper.

Father sent a surveyor from Seattle to help lay out the settlement and provide the government survey for my brothers' and my homesteads. He and my brother, Eigil, became friends. They set about the task of surveying the main street and laying out lots for cannery-built homes on streets south. Father realized that for the community to succeed, there would have to be homes, so that families could settle here. Those members of the cannery crew and any out-of-work fishermen could always find work as carpenters and laborers. After several weeks of hard work, Eigil decided it was time to go hunting. He invited the surveyor, who accepted the invitation. They rowed to Scow Bay, beached the skiff, and set out for a day of hunting. In the early afternoon, the weather changed to a driving snowstorm. The snow continued unabated for a week. The hunters were ill-equipped for spending the night out, but were able to build a fire. Unable to find their way back to the skiff, they found themselves completely lost. The surveyor froze to death the third night. On the morning of the fourth day, Eigil realized he had to get back to civilization or he would follow the surveyor's end. He stumbled out onto the beach early afternoon, found the skiff, and was able to row to a small cabin on Scow Bay, where its inhabitants warmed him up, fed him, and returned him to the superintendent's house.

Following are the names of some of the early employees and settlers, in and around Petersburg: Chris Tweten, storekeeper, and later partner in the Hogue and Tweten store; Knut Hauge, general work and fishing, also toastmaster and speaker on most occasions; Peter Norberg, web foreman and first-class fisherman and web man; Charley Norberg, sawmill foreman and first-class fisherman and web man; Mr. Newhall, carpentry foreman for the cannery and ship's carpenter; and Mrs. Newhall, a charming and hard-

The Peter Buschmann Family cont'd

working lady, who cooked for crew when necessary. Her daughter, Lena, and my brother, Eigil, helped in the dining room at times.

S.L. Hogue, previously mentioned, was a very industrious member of the community. A.H. Sonsthagen was an expert at splitting and mild curing king salmon, and was in charge of that work. Louis Miller was a carpenter. His wife and two children, Richard and Edna, arrived in 1902. Peter and Chris Nilsen took up a homestead across the Narrows, taking in the point and a small bay. They had a boat building shop and built a very comfortable home surrounded by a bountiful garden with flowers, vegetables, and berries. Peter Olsen, Chris Olsen, Peter Jorgensen, Jack Kelley and Mr. Ursin all helped make up salmon seines, gillnets, and herring gear in the spring; and fished during the summer.

Rasmus Enge was also one of the early men at Petersburg. His wife, Anna Enge, was a charming and hard-working lady and a wonderful helpmate for Rasmus. She was always willing to help with cooking, or in the dining room, when necessary. It was Rasmus Enge, his wife, Anna, and some workers that were put ashore at Sitkoh Bay on Chichakof Island in the winter of 1900-1901. Father had previously located a cannery site there and was determined to build a cannery and put up a pack in 1901. They built a 12-foot-by-14-foot cabin; and the group was left with food, supplies, and some building materials in preparation for construction of the cannery and support buildings. The winter, however, proved to be one of the worst in memory, or since, for that matter. The cold north winds precluded further work on the cannery and froze the fresher water at the head of the bay for several miles between the cabin and the deeper salt waters of Peril Straits.

Father sent supplies several times to the group on other conveyances, but they were unable to approach the cannery site due to the ice and turned back. When word of this reached the settlement, Chris (Father was in Washington) sent one of our own boats to the rescue. The Enge group, however, had suffered considerable hardship, both due to the cold weather and lack of food. They were forced to subsist on deer, which fortunately were in good supply. When our tender arrived to the rescue, they could not approach because of the ice. Observing no signs of life, the Captain leaned on the steam whistle, but it was several hours, and after we had landed a rescue party, before we could see the small band of dark figures making their way along the shoreline. After they returned to Petersburg, Chris, and ultimately Father, attempted to interest Rasmus in returning to Sitkoh Bay, but Enge would have no part of their grand scheme. He went to work building salmon nets for the cannery and fishing local herring stocks. Eventually Rasmus acquired boats of his own and built several of the larger buildings in town, including a theatre.

Father sent me to Sitkoh Bay from Petersburg, in charge of a crew and expedition, with orders to build and operate a cannery there that year. Cannery tenders and scows from Petersburg, about 120 miles distant, furnished lumber and supplies during construction. The winter had been severe and unfortunately the ice remained late, which necessitated dragging a substantial portion of the lumber and supplies over the ice until the ice broke up. We built the cannery buildings, as well as the government-required hatcheries in nearby Basket Bay and Pavlov Harbor. The summer was a fruitful one and we packed 60,000 cases of salmon, mostly pinks.

In 1900, a large covered halibut-buying scow was anchored in Scow Bay, where my brother Eigil was in charge for two winters. Here, boxes and other necessities could be had; and the schooners could tie up and conveniently unload and ice their halibut right on the scow, ready for shipment by southbound steamers. This was a great convenience for the halibut schooners and for the cannery tenders *Anna M. Nixon* and *White Wing*. Halibut fishing for part of the winter, when these tenders were not otherwise busy, provided employment for their crews, instead of their being idle during the winter months. The shipping of halibut from Petersburg and the above-mentioned scow was important business in those days. Each boat's halibut catch was iced and boxed separately. It might take a week for the steamer to land at the other ports and take on cargo and then make its way south. If the skipper had made too long a trip, or if the catch was not properly dressed, cleaned, and iced, the fish might spoil before arriving at market. In that case, the boat would receive a bill for the freight instead of payment.

The Peter Buschmann Family cont'd

The alternative was to salt the catch, which could preserve the fish indefinitely, but this product would fetch a lower price in the markets down south.

During the 1901 and 1902 herring seasons, Eigil and Ursin fished and supplied most of the herring used for bait by the halibut fishermen, discharging their catches at the scow in Scow Bay and at Petersburg.

In 1903-1904, Eigil was the agent for Charley Norberg and Chris Tweten on their halibut shipping scow in Scow Bay.

Father built a large dam upland on the creek at the south end of the town. Water was piped to the cannery in stave pipe produced by wrapping cedar staves with iron hoops (the pipe sections were shipped by steamer from the Puget Sound area). These pipes were laid on the ground and drained when the weather turned cold, so as not to burst by freezing. This did much to alleviate what had become a water problem at certain times of the year. There were several taps into the pipe, as it passed through the settlement, so that others had access to this plentiful supply.

A Mr. Ketchum built a small sawmill by a large creek known as Ketchum Creek. The mill was operated by a large overshot water wheel, using water from this creek. It furnished most of the wood for halibut boxes for this area for several years, starting in 1901. The Knutson brothers built a good house and a boat shop across the Narrows, about a mile south of Nelson's. They tried to can halibut in a small way. The product was quite good, but apparently not a financial success.

During the winter of 1901 and spring of 1902, Father and his associates sold all their Alaska interests, then held by Quadra Packing Company, Petersburg Packing Company, and Chatham Straits Packing Company, to a newly organized large company known as the Pacific Packing and Navigation Company. This company, on account of financial difficulties, went bankrupt in 1903. This was a sad experience for us, having received payment for our properties mostly in their common stock that eventually became worthless, and bonds that we later were compelled to sell for five cents on the dollar.

Father died in 1903. Overwhelmed by the fact that the profits from 10 years of work had been lost, and feeling responsible for encouraging friends and associates to invest in what he considered a promising venture, he took his own life. The family, devastated by the loss of their patriarch, sold the recently built Petersburg home and retreated temporarily to Washington State.

My oldest brother, Christian, became general manager for the company that bought most of the bankrupt Pacific Packing and Navigation Company's assets at sheriff's sale. Its name was the Northwestern Fisheries Company. Northwestern Fisheries operated salmon canneries in Bristol Bay, Uyak, Chignik, Kenai, Orca, Dundas Bay, Santa Anna, Hunter's Bay, and Boca De Quadra.

Eigil became superintendent at Boca de Quadra for Northwestern Fisheries Company for a few years. He later became superintendent for Mr. Einar Beyer's cannery operations at Rose Inlet in Southeast Alaska, until Mr. Beyer and associates organized the Southern Alaska Canning Company. At that time, Eigil became general manager for all their Alaska operations, which included the Rose Inlet Cannery. They also built a cannery and saltery at Port Walter and a new cannery in Boca de Quadra.

Eigil familiarized Haakon Friele (Einar Beyer's young nephew from Norway) with the Alaska canned salmon business. Friele was put in charge as superintendent at Port Walter and later at the new Boca de Quadra cannery, where he remained in charge until the Southern Alaska Canning Company discontinued operations in 1921.

Eigil had a good cannery location at Hidden Inlet, on Portland Canal close to the Canadian border, where he later expected to build and operate his own cannery. In 1922, Haakon Friele was able to interest the Great Atlantic and Pacific Tea Company in the canned salmon business. To ensure success, he needed a seasoned and able Alaska manager and a good location on which to build the first cannery. Fortunately, Eigil could supply both. He finally agreed with Friele to sell his cannery site to the Great Atlantic and Pacific Tea Company and become their Alaska manager. This combination of Haakon Friele, who later became an able executive, and Eigil, with his energy and practical fishing and canning experience, worked out exceptionally well for the Great Atlantic and Pacific Tea Company. The Nakat Packing Corporation, a wholly owned subsidiary, operated their Alaska canned

The Peter Buschmann Family cont'd

salmon business.

Eigil built the cannery at Waterfall on Meares Passage, on the west coast of Prince of Wales Island, in 1924/5. At the time, this was the largest cannery in the world. He had initially hoped to power the cannery with hydro-generation from a large stream, just to the north of the cannery, but had to satisfy himself with utilizing this stream for the cannery's fresh water needs. He installed a row of diesel generators to provide power.

Eigil built a substantial superintendent's house at Waterfall and kept wonderful gardens. His family would spend the canning season here. His sons learned the fish business and ran seine boats and trap tenders for the cannery. In 1941, they packed 256,000 cases at the Waterfall cannery alone. The company also had canneries at Union Bay, Ketchikan, Bristol Bay, and Anacortes on Puget Sound. Their total annual pack exceeded 650,000 some years. Eigil continued as their general superintendent until his retirement in 1954.

After Father sold his Alaska cannery and saltery interests in 1901, he sent me to Swanson's Harbor in 1902 to build the first salmon pile trap in Southeastern Alaska, close to Point Couverden on Icy Straits. This trap caught over 1,000,000 salmon that season.

I commenced to build a salmon cannery at Swanson's Harbor that fall and the next spring, but financial difficulties from the sale of securities received for our properties, previously mentioned, prevented us from continuing this venture. We finally were compelled to abandon that dream in late 1903.

In 1904, I operated the *Lincoln*, one of our steamers, with a seine crew, catching herring for the Killisnoo fishmeal plant at Killisnoo. This was an interesting summer as the steamer was ill-equipped for handling nets. In 1905, I contracted to deliver more than 200,000 dog, or chum, salmon to two small sailing ships that had sailed from Japan and anchored in Chaik Bay, Southeastern Alaska. The fish were salted in the holds of these ships and, when loaded, they sailed home to Japan.

I became superintendent for Northwestern Fisheries Company, at Santa Anna, in 1906. In the fall

Peter Buschmann's salmon saltery on the south side of Taku Inlet.
The saltery was not far from the Taku Glacier, from which tons of ice broke off into icebergs.

The Peter Buschmann Family cont'd

of 1906, after the Santa Anna cannery was closed for the winter, I was instructed to proceed to Hunter Bay, located about 165 miles by boat from Santa Anna, on the west coast of Prince of Wales Island, where this company owned another salmon cannery that had been closed for several years. My mission was to determine what repairs to foundations, buildings and machinery were necessary to put this plant into operating condition for the 1907 salmon canning season. I proceeded to Wrangell from the Santa Anna Cannery where I boarded the small local 65-foot passenger boat, the *Ella Rohlfs*. It took me to Hunter Bay Cannery, where I was greeted by the watchman and also by Craig Millar who, associated with his father, had salted salmon bellies in this area for many years. They had sold their Hunter Bay location to the Pacific Steam Whaling Company, which built a cannery there in 1896, one of the oldest in this part of Alaska. Craig had done considerable hunting when time permitted, was an excellent shot, and loved the sport.

I stayed for several days at Hunter Bay Cannery, checking and listing necessary repairs and getting fishing information. When the *Ella Rohlfs* came by again on her regular trip, Craig and I boarded her, bound for Ketchikan. A strong southeasterly was blowing, but its real strength was not realized before we made the turn past Mexico Point, a promontory facing Dixon Entrance and the Pacific Ocean, about 10 miles from Hunter Bay. After we passed Mexico Point into open water, the size of the swells and the velocity of the storm increased. After bucking the storm for about two hours, we were off a point locally known as the Brown Bear. By this time the storm had reached gale proportions and, using all the power this boat's machinery could muster, it became doubtful whether we could make it around Cape Chacon, the southern end of Prince of Wales Island. After another long hour of strenuous bucking against the gale, the decks awash most of the time, we were off Point Nunas, where the course was changed and we were heading for Cape Chacon. This last turn put us in the trough, and the swell and breaking seas were now more on the beam, or broadside. Our boat often rolled her sides under, and the decks were constantly awash. After steering this course for some time, we were finally off the entrance to Nichols Bay, in which there is a beautiful landlocked harbor. The velocity of the gale was increasing and the waters became more and more turbulent between Point Nunas and Cape Chacon from the strong tide rips prevalent there. The captain decided to put the weather "on the stern" and run before the gale into Nichols Bay. This would relieve the passengers from the terrific strain and discomfort they had been subjected to for several hours after passing Mexico Point. We were about 50 miles from Ketchikan and the passengers were delighted to learn of this decision.

With the gale behind us, we were soon anchored in Nichols Bay, where the water was quiet and we could relax comfortably while the gale continued outside the bay. After we had enjoyed a good meal, Craig and I decided to row ashore and try to shoot a deer, since they are fat in the fall and the meat delicious. We borrowed a couple of carbines, put on our boots, slickers, and sou'westers, launched one of the small lifeboats, and pulled ashore, landing on the north and lee side of a peninsula about three-quarters of a mile across. We made our deer calls from small alder limbs, Craig going to the right and I to the left around the shore. When I reached a point about opposite the middle of the peninsula, I went into the woods very cautiously and occasionally blew my deer call.

The spruce and hemlock trees were large and tall and the underbrush was very thick in places. It was difficult at times to see clearly as far as a couple of hundred feet in any direction, since it was raining and the strong gale created a heavy mist. I walked slowly through the underbrush, stopping occasionally to look, listen, and blow my deer call. After a short walk I thought I was about in the center of the peninsula. I was proceeding very slowly in a crouched position, with my rifle always ready for action, when suddenly I heard a shot from my left and immediately realized I had been hit, although there was no pain. I called at the top of my voice, hoping to prevent another shot being fired, not knowing who had shot me. The soft-nosed bullet grazed my left arm just above the wrist, took out part of the bone, went through the flesh of my left leg about an inch and a half above my knee cap, and shattered the stock of my gun.

A minute or two later, Craig came out of the brush. When he realized he had mistaken me for a deer

The Peter Buschmann Family cont'd

and shot me, the expression on his face turned from surprise to alarm. I told him they were only flesh wounds and they did not hurt. Very little blood was flowing, so there was nothing to worry about. After briefly discussing the accident, we wrapped a handkerchief tightly around my leg wound, bandaged the wound on my arm, picked up what was left of my gun, and with Craig supporting me, we walked slowly to the boat.

While walking to the beach, Craig told me he had seen an object through the underbrush and mist that had looked like a deer. Then he had heard a deer call and, after looking very carefully several times, was certain he had seen the head, horns, and neck of a large buck. He first aimed at the hindquarter but when he positively saw the head and neck, he aimed at the neck, since he did not want to shatter the hindquarter and spoil the meat.

After reaching the beach, we boarded our boat and Craig rowed me to the *Ella Rohlfs* anchored a short distance away. After arriving in my stateroom, a basin of warm water was brought up to clean the wounds, but to our surprise there was no medicine on board. We used kerosene as a substitute. A lady passenger was kind enough to loan us her small silk handkerchief, which we used to clean and pull through the leg wound from time to time. We were stormbound at this anchorage for almost two days until the storm was over and we were able to proceed.

When we arrived in Ketchikan, I was taken to a comfortable room in the Stedman Hotel and immediately called Dr. J. L. Myers, who came over and dressed my wounds properly. While Dr. Myers was cutting away the loose flesh in and on both sides of the leg wound where gangrene was setting in, I, for the first time, felt the first pain of any consequence. He said it was lucky we arrived when we had. After a few days of bed rest, I was permitted to walk around on crutches and leave for Seattle. I used the crutches for about two weeks and have felt no ill effects since.

I commissioned the construction of the *Ruth* shortly thereafter, in the fall of 1906, to fish for the Hunters Bay Cannery. She was the first power seine boat in the Alaska salmon fisheries. My brother, Eigil, operated her. I became superintendent of the Hunter Bay cannery in 1907 and continued through 1909.

With her engine, the *Ruth* proved a marked improvement over the rowed and sailed boats used for salmon fishing, and so the next year I built the *Fredelia II*. In 1909, while seining, we lost propulsion. The engine seemed to run perfectly, and the shaft was turning as far as we could see, but the propeller would not turn. We rigged a sail out of two blankets lashed to a pair of oars from our skiff for a mast. With a third oar lashed in the stern for extra steerage, we sailed five miles to the beach, dumped our fish so we could beach the boat to determine the malfunction. A low-tide examination showed we had a broken tail shaft. We refloated the boat and Tom Tenneson, the engineer, and I rowed 45 miles to Ketchikan. We obtained a new shaft and three days later we were back fishing.

In 1910, I built and operated the Kenai Cannery at the mouth of Kenai River on Cook's Inlet, Central Alaska, for the Northwestern Fisheries Company. I must comment on this season's operation, since it was very successful and one of my lucky seasons. Everything progressed like clockwork, which I partly credit to the fact that our departure date from Seattle was Friday, March 13. In Seattle, we loaded the large, four-masted sailing ship, the *Saint Paul*, with lumber, shingles, tinplate for making cans, fuel, groceries, scows, and all other materials necessary to build and operate a salmon cannery.

Eigil, his partner, Tommy Tenneson, and their helpers, had cut and rafted all the piling for our traps and foundations the previous winter, living in tents in below zero weather, close to Seldovia, Alaska. This was a backbreaking job with only hand tools, and having the piles cut and ready was a tremendous help.

The ship sailed from Seattle to Cook's Inlet and, about 10 days later, anchored in deep water several miles off the mouth of the Kenai River. We lightered the lumber, tinplate, and all the other cargo ashore on scows from the ship. We lived in shacks and tents on the beach for the first two or three weeks. The early temperatures were at times down to 15 degrees below zero. The river ice, pushed up by the current to 5 to 15 feet thick, was breaking up on the riverbanks.

We built the bunkhouses, mess house, cannery, warehouse, and other necessary buildings, made our cans, built and located our fish traps, hung our gillnets, filled our cans with salmon, and loaded the ship on its

The Peter Buschmann Family con't'd

return in the late summer. After an absence of five and a half months, we sailed to Seattle, 1800 miles distant, and arrived there the early part of September with over 30,000 cases filled with red salmon. I resigned from the Northwestern Fish Company that fall.

Our share of the financial success of this season allowed my brothers and I to retire the last of Father's debts, which we assumed upon his death. He had guaranteed many of the investments in his fishing ventures and, although the financial failure was due to the ineptitude of the new owners of Father's company, we felt an obligation to repay those who had invested on Father's word.

Since the spring and summer of 1911, I have been on my own. Early in 1911, I organized the Deep Sea Salmon Company and invited Mr. T. C. Mc Hugh to become a stockholder and an officer. I then built and operated our first cannery at Ford Arm, West Chichakof Island, Southeastern Alaska, and canned about 22,000 cases salmon that season. While operating this cannery, I also built and operated a cannery on Goose Bay, Knik Arm, about nine miles north of Anchorage, Alaska, during 1915, but abandoned this cannery after the 1917 season on account of poor quality fish.

I moved the machinery from Goose Bay to Port Althorp, close to Cross Sound, Southeastern Alaska, where I built a modern cannery in the fall of 1917 and spring of 1918. I operated this cannery myself from 1918 until I sold it in 1930. This was a very successful operation and our pack ranged from 75,000 to over 200,000 cases each of the 12 years I operated there, except for the depression year of 1921. For one or two years, this cannery had the largest salmon pack in Alaska. After buying out Mr. McHugh's interest in the Deep Sea Salmon Company, in 1923, I consolidated the operation of the Ford Arm cannery with the Pyramid Packing Company's cannery operations at Sitka and became the largest stockholder. I organized the Peril Straits Packing Company in about 1925. We operated a cannery in Peril Straits with Nick Bez as superintendent. My brothers, Leif and Nick, were minority stockholders. We bought the cannery at Hood Bay and organized the Hood Bay Canning Company with A. P. Wolf, H. A. Fleager, and myself as equal stockholders in 1926. We operated there, with Mr. Wolf as manager, until we sold out to the Bureau of Indian Affairs in 1949. This disposed of the last of my cannery interests in Alaska. During the many years while operating the above-mentioned four canneries, their combined annual pack was about 400,000 cases. We employed from 700 to 800 men and women during the summer months.

After I sold my cannery interests, I still had minority interests in the Sitka Cold Storage Company, which operated a large cold storage plant at Sitka, and the Aleutian Cold Storage Company, which operated a plant at Sand Point, Alaska. I was also part owner in several fish traps operating in Southeast Alaska until fish traps were legislated out of existence in 1959.

Leif was the youngest of Father's children and the only one born in America. He was a very able manager and helped at Port Althorp during the construction and operation of that cannery, except for 1921 and 1922 when he operated a herring saltery and fish meal plant for the Franklin Packing Company on Prince William Sound. Lee Wakefield owned Franklin Packing Company. After the sale of Port Althorp in 1930, Leif purchased a cannery at Skowl Arm on Prince of Wales Island, which he operated very successfully.

My other brother, Trygve, has not been mentioned. He worked as a fisherman in the Alaska fisheries during his vacations while attending high school and the University of Pennsylvania. It was in Petersburg that he met Katherine Bronson, of Wrangell, who later became his wife. He declined to continue in the fisheries and went on to medical school and a successful surgical practice in Seattle.

Peter Buschmann's many descendents now live all over the United States. They are successful doctors, lawyers, engineers, and teachers, among other vocations. A few have stayed in the fisheries.

Peter Most is a Bristol Bay salmon and herring fisherman. Charlie Most fishes Bristol Bay salmon and herring, seines salmon in Southeast Alaska and fishes crab and sardines off the Washington coast. Ronn Buschmann participates in many fisheries in Southeast Alaska and lives with his wife, Deirdre, and three of his four children in Petersburg.

© 2003 Ronn Buschmann. Used with permission.

Carroll and Elsie Clausen

By Jim Schwartz

Carroll Clausen was born in Canby, Oregon, where his family owned a farm. When Carroll was about 10 years old, he was playing with a friend chopping wood. An argument began between the boys about whose turn it was to swing the ax. Carroll put his hand on the wood to be cut so the friend could not chop. The boy threatened to continue chopping and told Carrol to move his hand. The friend thought Carroll would move his hand and Carroll thought his friend would not follow through with his swing. Both children were wrong. All the fingers of Carroll's right hand were chopped off, just above the knuckle. The incident shows the resolve of Carroll and this life-changing impact on his spirit.

A banker in Portland heard about the high school student with missing fingers who was good with numbers and accounting. Carroll was hired by the Portland banker while in high school and continued working at the bank until 1917. When asked if he would be interested in establishing a branch of the Portland bank in Petersburg, Alaska, Carroll was up for the adventure. He left Portland in the fall of 1917 and traveled by train to Seattle and then to Petersburg on the Alaska Steamship Line. Petersburg's population was about 1,000 at the time.

Elsie Roundtree was born in Chehalis, Washington, in 1896. The Roundtree family was involved with logging in the area.

When Elsie was about 8 years old, she fell off a swing in the back yard and severely broke her upper left arm. The young girl was taken to a Seattle hospital where she was the recipient of a brand new medical technique. A six-inch silver rod replaced the middle section of Elsie's upper arm. She spent a couple of years recovering from her accident and surgery. As Elsie grew up, her left arm was always several inches shorter than her right arm.

Elsie Clausen

Elsie's father heard about logging in Alaska from a neighbor. The family moved to Petersburg in March of 1918. They made the trip on a steamship.

On this trip Elsie met Mr. Wheeler of Petersburg, who hired her to work in his drug store. Soon after her arrival, Elsie and Carroll Clausen met and fell in love. She continued to work at the drug store until their wedding the following November.

Carroll and Elsie's first house was near the old hospital. While pregnant with their first child, Elsie became quite the seamstress. Charlotte Marie Clausen was born October 24, 1919.

The Clausen family lived one more year in Petersburg before moving back to Portland for a year.

In the fall of 1921, Carroll decided to try farming with relatives in Saskatchewan, Canada. For Elsie, that winter as the worst time of her life: living in the attic, unfriendly and resentful relatives, bitter cold, and howling winds.

In the spring of 1924, Elsie bought

Carroll Clausen

Carroll and Elsie Clausen cont'd

three train tickets and told Carroll she was going back to Portland with Charlotte and he was welcome to join them. Carroll went with the family. After a short time in Portland, the Clausen family returned to Petersburg in the fall of 1924.

The Clausen family moved into a house on Front Street, a couple of houses past the Elkins. It was only a two-bedroom house, so the following spring they added on a living room and another bedroom upstairs. They loved the view of the Wrangell Narrows and the mainland mountains.

Carroll became the Petersburg Alaska Steamship Company agent. Elsie continued her seamstress work at home.

Life was good for the Clausens. The family pictures show fishing, hunting and camping trips to Castle River, Green Rocks and Thomas Bay. Sandy Beach was a popular spot to spend the summer.

In 1929 Phillip was born. By this time, Carroll was Petersburg city manager. The Depression didn't seem to affect Petersburg much. There were farms to supply much of the food and fish were plentiful. Logging and sawmills were strong and fox farming became a common industry around Petersburg.

Carroll continued being Petersburg's city manager for the next 28 years.

Every year he would take a trip to the hot springs. He and a friend would alternate between Warm Springs Bay, Bell Esland, and Lake Else, south of Prince Rupert, Canada.

Elsie would save her seamstress money and buy cherry furniture. She'd also make travel plans every few years.

Carroll was active in the Elks. Elsie was active in the Hospital Guild. In the later years, both of them were instrumental in starting a museum group.

After retiring from his city manager position, Carroll continued to work part time as a clerk at the Bank of Petersburg.

Elsie was the historian of the Clausen family. She would take the whole month of January and devote her time to making and updating her scrapbooks and photo albums, completing more than 60 of them.

Elsie went on many trips. There were bus tours to different regions of the United States, an Episcopal convention in Hawaii, a Baha'i convention to London, and an extended tour though Europe.

Carroll and Elsie were members of the Episcopal

Elsie, Michelle, and Carroll. Back, Charlotte, Bob, Kay, Mike, Rob.

Church for many years. Elsie became a Baha'i in 1962 and was very active in the Baha'i Community.

The Clausens' daughter, Charlotte, married Bob Schwarz in 1944. After five years away from Petersburg, she and her family returned to Petersburg. They had four sons: Mike, Dennis, Jim and Don.

Carroll and Elsie's son, Phil, returned to Petersburg after serving time in the military. He married Darlene Rosvold. They had two sons, Steve and Terry, and a daughter, Joni.

While still living, Carroll and Elsie had seven grandchildren and six great-grandchildren.

After a battle with cancer, Carroll passed away, in 1973, at the age of 81. Elsie continued volunteering for the Hospital Guild and the museum. She lived at home until 1980, when she passed away sitting on her couch watching the Narrows. She was 84.

Gifford and Agnes Close

By Bruce Westre

Gifford Close (1885-1950) was involved in the logging industry when he met Agnes Haveland (1895-1985) in Washington. They were married on December 12, 1912, and moved to Ketchikan shortly thereafter.

Gifford logged, fished and trapped to support his family. Agnes cooked for the logging crews.

They had three children, Floy Wingren (1913) who currently resides in Lacy, Washington; Gifford Jr. (1917-1965); and Vivian Westre (1920).

In 1930, Gifford went to work for the Forest Service in Petersburg. In 1933, Agnes and Vivian moved to Petersburg to be with Gifford.

Gifford was in charge of the three Cs, unmarried men in need of jobs and the WPA, and married men employment.

Gifford was responsible for construction of the Sandy Beach Recreation Area, the ski jump, the Helm Bay Trail and the Petersburg Creek Trail.

As a family, they enjoyed hunting, fishing, trapping and gardening.

Gifford, Floy and Agnes Close

Vivian attended her freshman and sophomore years of school in Petersburg. After the Depression, Gifford transferred to Wrangell where he worked for U.S Fish and Wildlife Service.

After graduating from high school in 1938, Vivian attended a business college in Seattle. When she completed business school, Vivian went to work for the Reconstruction Finance Corporation, in Seattle, and later transferred to war assets.

After the war, Vivian moved to Fairbanks where she worked payroll for construction of the new airfield.

Vivian returned to Ketchikan where she married Tony Westre in 1947. Tony and Vivian moved to Petersburg where Danny (1951-1966), Sylvia Larson (1953), and Bruce (1956) were born.

Tony fished for a living and Vivian worked at the post office. They later purchased the Sanitary Market. Vivian raised the children and kept the books for the business. She was active in the Cub Scouts and the Emblem Club.

As Petersburg was the starting point for many families, so it is also a place to come home to. Bruce returned to Petersburg in 1979, when he married Wendy Hammer. Bruce and Wendy have two children, James Tyrell (1980) and Krystlyn (1982). Sylvia and Robert Larson returned to Petersburg in 1985, with sons Eric (1980) and Troy (1983). They added Sean to the family in 1988.

With the majority of her family in Petersburg, Vivian decided to move back in 1987. Here she could be closer to her children and grandchildren. Vivian was very active in the Eastern Star chapter until it disbanded in 2002. She lives comfortably at Mountain View Manor, enjoying her family and friends.

Vivian Close Westre

Harry and Minnie Colp

By Douglas B. Colp

Harry D. Colp, the youngest of five children, was born March 25, 1882, at Black Point in St. Margaret's Bay near Halifax, Nova Scotia, Canada.

The family moved to the United States in 1884; first to North Dakota, then to Minnesota, and finally to Allyn, near the head of Case Inlet in Puget Sound, southwest of Seattle, Washington.

Harry came to Wrangell, Alaska in 1898, at the age of 16, on the steamer *Derigo*, to visit his older brother Wallace. He immediately started to work in a sawmill.

In 1899, he spent almost a year on the Iskut, a tributary of the Stikine River, prospecting and trapping.

In 1900 and 1901, he worked in the Wrangell sawmill, carried mail to Kake on a sailboat for Fred Sepek, and prospected in the area.

In 1902, he moved to Petersburg and helped build a cannery, worked in a sawmill, fished and prospected.

Harry had several partners on his many prospecting ventures, including Marlin Kildal, Winn Clother, Bill Shields, Leo Hayder, David Terwilliger and Johnny Sales.

Between 1902 and 1912, Harry corresponded with Minnie Byer, a young woman in Tacoma, Washington, who was taking care of his invalid mother, Mary Ann Colp.

Wilhelmina "Minnie" Byer was born in Silver Bow, Montana, near Butte, on September 7, 1886. Her brother Louis remained there while she, her two sisters, and brother went with her widowed mother, Mary Byer, to Tacoma in 1899. It was here that she met Harry Colp and his mother.

Sometime in October or November of 1912, she wrote Harry and reminded him that they had been corresponding for 10 years. She wrote, "If you want me, come and get me; I'm not waiting longer."

Consequently, Harry found passage on a southbound boat. They were married December 9, 1912.

Their wedding dinner was finalized with popcorn balls, which was to become a tradition for the rest of their lives.

They returned to Petersburg on April 21, 1913, aboard the steamer *Humbolt*. They bought a one-room house on the north edge of town. Their new home

Minnie and Harry Colp with Douglas, Virginia, and Richard

had a stove, a homemade table, and boxes to sit on. It had a bunk bed filled with spruce boughs. Harry's first "Honey-do-job" was to remove the old dried-up boughs and replace them with newly cut ones.

In 1914 and 1915, Harry helped build the first City Dam and helped lay the water main into town. In 1916, he started Silver Fox Farm at Five Mile Creek, north of Petersburg. His partner at the farm was Arnold Schneider. Olaf and Anna Martin were their only neighbors at Five Mile Creek.

Harry and Arnold built all of the buildings on the farm, including the fox pens and fox houses, a warehouse, a fox feed cookhouse, a half-mile of boardwalk, and a floating dock in the creek for his gas

Harry and Minnie Colp cont'd

boat. The fox feed cookhouse had a big 40-gallon, round-bottomed, cast iron pot built within a rock structure. Between two- and four-foot cordwood was used to cook the mulligan composed of fish, beef cracklings, mash, canonical, lard and seal oil. This was a once-a-week job.

The boardwalks were made of two 2-by-12s, side-by-side, framed above the ground. All heavy hauling was accomplished in wheelbarrows on these walks. A tall smokehouse, which could smoke a great many salmon at a time, was also necessary for winter fox feed. Chums and pink salmon were used for fox feed. Silvers, kings, reds and venison were smoked for domestic use.

In 1925, the bottom started to fall out of the fur farm business; so in 1927, Harry gave up the farm and moved back into Petersburg.

In 1928, he went to work for the Alaskan Glacier Sea Food Co., owned by Earl Ohmer. Harry was a skipper on several shrimp boats, including the *Brooklin*, *Kisseno*, *Louise S*, *Charles W*, and the *Charles T*. Harry was fondly known as the "Deacon" among the shrimpers. He retired from shrimping in 1948.

Harry is also remembered for a small book entitled, *The Strangest Story Ever Told*. He wrote the manuscript for the book many years before it was found after his death. His daughter, Virginia, assembled his writings and had the book published. It is a compilation of the strange stories, as told by several prospectors, after they had been into an area in Thomas Bay, known locally as the "Devils Country."

Harry died on June 3, 1950.

Minnie Colp didn't have an easy life on the fox farm with no running water in the house. It was carried in and carried out. The outhouse, which was located a hundred feet away from the house, had the coldest seat in Alaska.

Minnie washed clothes once a week, boiling them in a big copper clothes boiler, and hanging them out on a line to dry, no matter how wet or cold the weather. If the wood box became empty and there was no one around, she would go out to the woodshed, split wood, and carry it into the house herself.

Minnie had an exceptional green thumb and was an avid gardener. Under her supervision, everything grew larger and tasted better. After she and Harry moved back into Petersburg, she couldn't have much of a garden, but she was widely known for her beautiful sweet peas and African violets.

She belonged to the local Hospital Guild and the Charity Box for many years. Minnie had a major stroke on February 29, 1976, and passed away peacefully.

Harry and Minnie raised three children: Douglas, Richard, and Virginia.

Douglas was born in Petersburg on October 25, 1914. From 1916 to 1927, he was raised on the family fox farm, just five miles north of Petersburg at Five Mile Creek.

There was no public school, so his mother taught him, using the Calvert School courses. He began public school in Petersburg, in 1928, and graduated from high school in 1934.

Douglas learned to work early in life on the fox farm. He would help his father fish, feed foxes, clean fox pens, cook fox feed, fall timber, saw and split wood, plant and tend the garden, and take care of the chickens. He'd also hunt deer and trap wolves, marten, and mink — and accompany his father on two-week prospecting trips every summer.

He learned a little geology and how to use a gold pan, to sample hard rock veins, how to set up prospect camps and cook, all of which proved to be very helpful in later years.

Fishing for salmon, halibut and shrimp continued through his high school years. Additionally, he worked in the salmon canneries, on cannery fish packing boats, floating fish traps, at a logging camp, and on a Civilian Conservation Corps' trail-building crew.

In 1935, Douglas left Petersburg to attend the University of Alaska at Fairbanks. He graduated from the University, in 1940, with a bachelor's degree in mining engineering. During his years at the university, Douglas was able to obtain summer work relating to his mining degree.

Except for three years in the Army Air Corps during World War II, Douglas spent his entire life in his chosen field, one of very few mining engineers to have done so.

During his long career in the mineral field, he worked as a mining engineer, mine manager and superintendent, and mining consultant in many parts of Alaska. Douglas taught two-week Mining Extension

Harry and Minnie Colp cont'd

Short Courses. He also taught in the Mining & Petroleum Technology program at the University of Alaska for 10 years.

At the age of 88, Douglas is still involved with two open-pit placer gold mining operations in the Circle area north of Fairbanks.

On February 27, 1943, Douglas married Marcel Silver at the First Presbyterian Church in Fairbanks.

Marcel was born on June 21, 1919 in Seattle, and raised in Bremerton, Washington.

She came to Fairbanks in August 1941, with a girlfriend who had a job with a local dentist. Her new acquaintances persuaded her to apply for a job opening in the Mail & Records Department of the Resident Engineers at the new Ladd Army Air Corps Base, now Fort Wainwright. She was offered a temporary job. The war came along and the temporary job became permanent.

Marcel is still her husband's bride, almost 60 years later. She and Douglas have two sons: Larry D., born October 31, 1946; and Gerald "Jerry" S., born June 2, 1948, in Fairbanks.

They also have two grandchildren, eight step-grandchildren and five step-great-grandchildren.

Harry and Minnie's son Richard was born in Petersburg, on August 24, 1916. He was also raised on the Silver Fox Farm at Five Mile Creek.

Like his brother, his mother taught him using the Calvert School courses. He graduated from Petersburg High School in 1935. He then completed a two-year business course in Tacoma, Washington.

Richard served four years in the U.S. Navy, most of which was in Sitka.

After the war, Richard owned two stores in Petersburg, located on Sing Lee Alley. One was Colp's Cash & Carry Grocery Store. It was the home of "Colp's Regulars." The other was the Furniture Exchange Store, with both new and used furniture. His advertisement read "Not the best, but plenty good."

Richard developed multiple sclerosis around 1946 or '47. His health and physical condition gradually deteriorated until he finally passed away in Seattle, on July 6, 1958.

Douglas and Marcel Colp

Harry and Minnie's daughter, Virginia, was born in Tacoma, Washington, on August 19, 1927, and she arrived in Petersburg six weeks later.

During her high school years, Virginia fished with her father and worked in the salmon canneries.

She graduated from high school in 1945, and then spent a year at a business school in Tacoma, Washington.

Virginia helped her sister-in-law, Marcel, in Fairbanks when her nephews were born. She also worked for about a year at the Air Force Base supply warehouse at Ladd Field, now Fort Wainwright.

In 1950, she was hired as part of the ground crew for Alaska Island Air in Petersburg, which became Alaska Coastal Airlines. She continued with them for a total of 18 years.

She then worked at the Petersburg Motors Service Station for 10 years.

After moving to Fairbanks in 1978, Virginia began expediting for several geological companies that were doing fieldwork for different clients all over Alaska.

The work involved coordinating boats, fixed-wing airplanes, and helicopters with the logistics of supplying fuel, camp gear, food, clothing, and everything needed to search for mineral deposits.

Virginia retired in 1996 and is living in Fairbanks, enjoying her hobbies of traveling, photography, rock hunting, and pursuing her creations of lapidary art.

Bert and Myrtle Cornelius

By Don Nelson

Lorenzo Bert Cornelius came north from Texas, in the early 1920s, to assist his uncle in the operation of the Hogue & Tveten general merchandise store.

His twin sister, Myrtle, was a nurse for Dr. L.P. Dawes. She came south from Juneau, in the mid-1920s, to be with Bert.

The Cornelius Mercantile Company store, on the right, sat across the street from the Wheeler Drug & Jewelry Company store.

Upon the death of S.L. Hogue, in the late 1920s, Bert and Myrtle took over management of the firm.

The large, three-story building was located on the corner of Sing Lee Alley and Main Street, about where Viking Travel is now located. The lower floor on the north side of the building had the grocery business and the south side contained women's apparel. The second story was for housewares, hardware, and toys. The third floor contained living quarters.

The firm also controlled the Citizens Wharf and had a coal business located on the face of the dock. Actual ownership of the dock belonged to various banks through the years, primarily the Bank of Wrangell.

The firm was renamed Cornelius Mercantile Company in September 1932.

Bert was also Petersburg's mortician. His mortuary was located in the back of the building, along the dock approach.

Bert and his wife, Ruth, had three children: Sarah, Berta and Tom, the last born in 1936.

About 1940, the family moved south. Bert remained in Petersburg. Myrtle never married.

Bert and his son opened a war surplus store in the Worth Building, across from the Sons of Norway Hall, in the late 1940s.

Frances Miller began as bookkeeper for Hogue and Tveten, in 1926, and continued on until the mid-1960s, when Cornelius Mercantile closed. Another longtime employee was Elsie (Mrs. Heinie) Dahl. Bill and Harold Ray, who were nephews, came north in the late 1940s to assist in operating the business, as well.

Myrtle was such a kindhearted soul, there's little doubt she probably gave away more clothing to the poor and impoverished than she sold.

Bert was active in Eastern Star and the American Legion.

He had a hunting cabin where the current Rocky Point Lodge is now located, near Papke's Landing. Bert was an avid duck hunter and always had a dog trailing him around town.

Bert died in 1968, and Myrtle died in 1971. Both are buried in the Petersburg Memorial Cemetery.

The Cornelius Mercantile Building was demolished in 1972 to accommodate the widening of Main Street.

Norma Lando and friends

Vernon and Mildred Counter

By Mildred Counter

Although I was born in Seattle, my early years were spent at Bangor, Washington, where I attended a one-room school.

When we moved to Seattle, my father kept the Hood Canal property as a summer home. There we dug clams, picked berries, rowed boats, and paddled our canoes.

My sister, brother, and I were among the first students to attend Alexander Hamilton School, Seattle's first intermediate school. I graduated from Lincoln High School in Seattle.

The year 1930 was not a good year to enter the working world. Job opportunities were almost non-existent during the Great Depression. However, armed with good wishes from friends, I went job hunting on Tuesday. On Thursday, I was called to work at a downtown store.

Two small sisters had joined our family and became models for my photography hobby.

Weekends were spent hiking and camping. One memorable summer hike was from Brinnon across the Olympic Mountains to Lake Quinault, taking the low divide route over and the high divide back.

Alaska was always in my thoughts. A chance visitor for an afternoon of swimming on our beach became a frequent guest. Our mutual interest in Alaska resulted in our plan to marry and go north. But where?

Vernon and I were soon making plans for an extended canoe trip to Alaska for our honeymoon.

There was only one canoe that we considered equal to the trip. It was the Willets canoe, made at Day Island, near Tacoma. It was constructed of cedar, 17 feet long with a 34-inch beam, and contained 7000 nails and screws made of brass and copper. We named our canoe the *Mildred*.

Previous camping trips had taught us which foods to carry. We had purchased a complete set of charts for the trip and planned to go via Yaculta Rapids, in order to avoid the treacherous Ripple Rock in Seymour Narrows.

We started our trip from my parents' home in Bangor, and entered Canada at Sidney, B.C. After the customs agent blinked twice about the size of our boat, he cleared us to proceed to Prince Rupert.

How can I describe the beauty of this trip? The ripples and waves of the water, rocky cliffs along the shore, waterfalls, forests, glaciers and mountains — all became imprinted on our minds.

The mail boat, which brought supplies up the coast every two weeks, limited our access to perishables such as lettuce. Stores did not have pennies. The three-eighths of a cent excise tax on matches infuriated the Canadian people.

Our "old faithful dinner," when there was nothing else to cook, was bacon and eggs, sometimes prepared with seagull eggs. The gull eggs made beautiful apricot-colored pancakes.

As we went farther north and the hillsides became steeper, we found logging camps anchored on rafts. All log scaling was done by the government. Oyster seed could be purchased from the government and attached to heavy ropes dangling from the floats.

One night we stayed in an Indian village, the Kwakiuti village at Blunden Harbor, on the mainland east of Alert Bay. We were treated to tribal dancing, music, and costumes, which were created by Chief Willie Seaweed, one of the foremost mask carvers of the Pacific Coast.

We stayed at the home of the current chief, Joe Seaweed, Chief Willie Seaweed's son. Joe's children smiled shyly at us, as they selected American cowboy records to play for us.

There appeared to be only four people in the village who could converse in English — all the others who came to Joe's house for short visits were smiling, but silent. We were honored by their courtesy.

We then proceeded to Allison Harbor where Vernon helped a logger get his "A" frame section of logs ready for a tug that was steaming along Johnstone Strait.

Our method of travel, without a radio, left us poorly informed. We were only vaguely aware of the unrest in Europe, which had resulted in Germany attacking Poland — and Britain and France declaring war on Germany.

Close to Prince Rupert, we were visited at our campfire by several Canadian gillnetters. We were saddened by their news: Canada had formally declared war on Germany in September 1939.

Our original plan was to continue to Sitka.

Vernon and Mildred Counter cont'd

However, when we reached Ketchikan, we learned that the rushed construction of an airport at Sitka had resulted in a tent city, so crowded that there was no room for us.

We settled down in Ketchikan for the winter. Little did we know that we would have a record 154 inches of rain and winds rivaling the Straits of Magellan williwaws!

We lived at Mountain Point, built a smokehouse, and entered into the Alaskan life. Vernon became a desk clerk at the Ingersoll Hotel and later joined the police force.

A year later, our daughter, Gail, was born. Grandparents in Seattle eagerly awaited a chance to greet their first grandchild, so Gail and I went south for a visit. On our return trip to Ketchikan, we learned of the attack on Pearl Harbor.

A CAA inspector, whom Vernon was acquainted with, advised him that the CAA was recruiting husband and wife teams to man its expanding facilities. This seemed a good way to contribute to the war effort and stay in Alaska. We took and passed the written test, then went to Anchorage to enter a six-month training course. Upon completion, we were assigned to the Petersburg CAA station. Work at Petersburg was interesting and a necessary part of the war effort.

When the war ended and previous CAA personnel became available again, I retired. In 1956, the CAA station in Petersburg was closed. Vernon was offered several excellent transfers, but we loved Petersburg and the people, so we decided to stay.

Vernon had always been fascinated by the fisheries and was fortunate to get a chance to go gillnetting with Erling Strand. When the fishing season ended, the Commissioner's office became vacant and Vernon was offered the position as U.S. Commissioner.

A phone call from Juneau resulted in my becoming Deputy Clerk of the U.S. District Court, a mammoth title for a very small job.

With the advent of statehood, these two federal jobs were discontinued, and Vernon was appointed State Magistrate in Petersburg, later becoming Port Director of Customs, a position he held until his death in 1971.

Our daughter, Gail, had enrolled at the University of Alaska, majoring in home economics. We felt her minor was in home ec and her major was husband hunting. She graduated with honors and married John Stuart Samson, a fellow student at the University. They live in Anchorage.

I began work as a bookkeeper at the Sanitary Market and then at the Petersburg Cold Storage. Dick Brennan recruited me for postal work and I became Postmistress, overseeing the new post office (now the GSA building). I retired in 1981.

When the state took my house to build North Nordic Drive, I saved the eagle trees, but was moved to a new house several miles south of town.

A little gardening, blueberry picking, and annual trips around Alaska have taken up my time. I have two granddaughters, six great-granddaughters, and a great-grandson.

Citizen's Dock

Chris and Nina Dahl

By Clara Dahl Lesher

My maternal grandfather, Anton Anderson, came to America in the late 1890s. The poor economy of Norway motivated him to seek his fortune on the other side of the ocean. His wife, Andrena, with their several small children, chose to remain in the safety of their known world in the Oslo area.

Anton journeyed westward on the American continent, reaching Seattle at the height of the Alaska Gold Rush.

Having no money for ship transportation, he bought an open rowboat and proceeded to row toward the gold fields. Following the coastline of Canada and Alaska, he arrived in Juneau, Alaska, by which time the big gold strikes were over.

Here he settled and sent for his family. In 1901, Andrena gave birth to my mother, Nina, in Douglas. She was their first child to be born in America.

My father, Chris Dahl, was born in Molde, Norway, in 1905. He immigrated to America in 1921, and worked his way across the United States as a farmer, a steel mill worker, and a logger, prior to arriving in Seattle.

He hitched a ride on a longliner, the *Scandia*, arriving in Petersburg in 1925, where he became a deckhand on the *Laddie*, thus beginning his life as an Alaskan tenderman, longliner and seine fisherman. During the off months in Petersburg, he operated his own taxi, an endeavor enriched by being the local bootlegger. He also ran traplines for furs.

He and Nina Anderson were married in 1929. They moved to Blank Island and later to Tebenkof Bay, where they raised blue foxes.

I was born in 1932, in Juneau. Because of my need for proximity to a school, the family bought a mink ranch in West Petersburg in 1936. During this period, Chris also fished, commercially and for mink feed.

Nina worked at PAF during the big salmon year of 1941, as did most of the housewives in Petersburg. As the mink ranch grew, the need for year-round feed did as well, so Chris built a cold storage on site.

With the onset of World War II came the need to feed the armed forces, so along with running the mink ranch, Chris commenced shucking and freezing clams in West Petersburg. The Citizen's Dock in Petersburg became available to him after Earl Ohmer's fire, so the

Chris and Nina Dahl

family moved across the narrows. Crab and shrimp processing were added to the Chris Dahl plant.

In 1945, a partnership with Dean C. Kayler resulted in the Kayler-Dahl Fish Company. The cold storage expanded and a salmon cannery was constructed. After 15 years, Chris became the sole owner. He continued operating the Petersburg plant and also built a salmon cannery in Naknek, Alaska.

In 1969, Whitney-Fidalgo purchased both plants, and Chris retired to become a cattle rancher. Ranching had been his lifelong dream, since first hearing the cowboy song "Red River Valley."

One of Chris' proudest moments was being appointed to represent Alaska on the Saltonstall-Kennedy Fisheries Committee — he, with his eighth-grade Norwegian education, serving with members

Chris and Nina Dahl cont'd

who were schooled at Harvard and Yale.

Chris died in 1975 and Nina died in 1989.

During the 25 years of Kayler-Dahl Fish Co., Inc., the fishing industry in Alaska saw much change and this company was a part of that.

At one time, K-D had fish-buying stations from southern Southeast to Icy Straits. Tenders were sent to Cordova and to the Yukon, fish were flown from Yakutat, fish camps were set up at Egegik, company freighters were used to supply plants and haul product to markets, joint ventures were formed and dissolved.

During this time, every type of seafood and its marketable by-product was processed. At one time, there was even a shrimpmeal plant at the Petersburg site. And who, in the fish business, will ever forget the Japanese technicians and their 10-kilo boxes of salmon roe? Remember how suddenly the roe became valuable when, before, it had all gone down the slop chute?

In the 1950s, the company had a lease on Palmyra Island in the South Pacific with the intention of setting up a processing plant. K-D also handled tuna at the Nawiliwili cannery in Hawaii.

During this time, the vessel *Brothers* from Petersburg, with the Otness boys onboard, was lost at sea while participating in this venture.

So many memories. . .

Carol Enge and Clara Dahl Lesher

As the only child of this family and being a female, I did not carry on the name when I married George Lesher in 1952.

George, born 1927, came from Pennsylvania, but soon became an Alaskan. He loved the hunting and fishing and soon settled into the fishing industry.

After the sale of Kayler-Dahl in 1969, the family bought a mobile home park in Port Orchard, Washington, close to our home in Seattle. George built this up over the ensuing years, continuing to work in the canneries of Southeastern Alaska and Bristol Bay until his death in 1987.

George and I have three children: Lisa, Christopher and Blake. Between them, they have given us three grandchildren.

Although none of us currently live in Alaska, I will always think of Petersburg as home. When I remember my school years, from first through twelfth grade in the same building, walking upstairs to the next higher level — and when I count 33 years in Petersburg, how can I not?

Kayler-Dahl plant and F/V *Baranof*
Alaska State Library
Core: Petersburg-Waterfront-13, PCA 01-1554

Harold and Minnie Dawes

By Rdath Prouty

You could say that Harold F. Dawes came from "pioneer" stock, as the earliest Dawes families lived in Boston when it was yet a colony. In fact, an early Dawes rode with Paul Revere to warn the colonists of the coming of the British.

Several generations later, Harold's grandfather left Maine with his extended family. These pioneers carved a farm out of the forest in Wisconsin Territory.

Harold was born in 1889. It was not surprising that Alaska called to Harold. His eldest brother, Dr. Leonard Dawes, had established his medical practice in Juneau. He encouraged Harold to visit and see what Alaska was all about. After serving in the Army and finishing law school, Harold took his bride, Minnie, to Petersburg.

Minnie Oleston, who was born in 1894, lived on a neighboring farm just a few miles from the Dawes' farm in Wisconsin. Her parents had come to Wisconsin from Norway.

It was 1921 when the young couple arrived in Petersburg. Their first home was an apartment in a building that Harold had purchased. Dr. J. O. Rude had his medical office just down the hall from the Dawes' apartment.

In 1923, a son, Phillip, was born to Harold and Minnie. Six years later, a daughter, Rdath, arrived. The family was complete and they moved to a house next door to the cemetery.

Harold was a U.S. Commissioner and Collector of Customs. He was a member of the draft board during World War II.

He helped establish a Masonic Lodge in Petersburg and, in 1922, was the Master of that lodge. He also was commander of the American Legion Post for a time.

In 1946, Harold was given the job of adjudications officer for the Veterans Administration in Juneau. This meant saying a very fond farewell to the years spent with their many friends in Petersburg.

Harold retired in 1951. He and Minnie moved to Washington State.

Harold died at Edmonds, Washington, in 1970. Minnie died at Edmonds, Washington, in 1973.

Harold Dawes, Carroll Clausen and Justin Lind

Phillip Dawes went to Juneau after graduating from Petersburg High School. There he met Marge Fitzpatrick, from Newberg, Oregon. They married in 1947. After working for the State of Alaska for many years, they retired. In 1999, they left Alaska for a condo in Billings, Montana, where they continue to reside.

Rdath graduated from Juneau High School and went on to attend college. In 1950, she married Fred Prouty in Juneau. They are now retired and living in Port Orchard, Washington. They have four children, nine grandchildren, and two great-grandchildren.

Seated: Hazel Greenaa, Jim Allen, Harold Dawes

Esther Delegard

As told by Esther Delegard

I came to Alaska in 1947, with a co-worker and her small children. They were joining her husband on his trolling boat.

I wanted to see as much of Alaska as I could, and so I had to work to accomplish this. Since I had previous experience in dry cleaning, I walked right into a job at Sitka Cleaners.

Several years later, I received a job offer in Petersburg. I went to work for Hack White and George Nicholson at the Men's Shop on Sing Lee Alley, and I later worked at City Cleaners.

In the late '60s, I married Bob Delegard, and we had two sons, Eric and Bob.

My father's death took me back to Minnesota. While there, I helped a couple get started in the dry cleaning business, but I couldn't take the climate.

I returned to Alaska and went to Fairbanks where my sister and her family lived. The climate was very much like Minnesota's, so when George Nicholson called me to work, I returned to Petersburg.

I later lived in Anchorage a few years and made many trips around the state.

In 1989, I returned to Petersburg and now live at Mountain View Manor. I belong to Pioneers and the Moose Club.

Esther Delegard

Mike and Margaret Durbin

By John and Carol Enge

Margaret McGilton was born in Wrangell, July 27, 1917. By 1920, the family had moved to Petersburg. Summertime found them on Keene Island, raising mink and fox. Margaret recalls rowing around the island while feeding them.

In town, she became an accomplished pianist, sharing her talent with her church and playing at the Sons of Norway dances.

Margaret married Norman Guthrie, from Metlakatla, in 1935. The couple had three children: Norman, Ralph, and Dolly.

Back in Petersburg, Margaret worked in the shrimp and crab canneries.

At one time, she was sent to Cordova to train shrimp pickers.

After the children were grown, she became involved in community affairs. Margaret served as president for both the Emblem Club and the Pioneers, taking an active role in all of their projects. She was a member of St. Catherine's Church and the V.F.W. Auxiliary. She was also a very talented seamstress and rosemaler.

Margaret died September 16, 2003.

Mike Durbin was born in Sacramento, California, on October 25, 1935. He spent much of his youth in logging camps on the northern California coast around Eureka.

He graduated from Sacramento High School in 1953, and he worked in the woods for two years.

He came to Alaska in 1955, and he worked for Ketchikan Pulp Company at Hollis. Mike attended welding school in 1957.

He lived in Ketchikan for three and a half years before being drafted into the Army and spending two years at Fort Lewis in the Port Engineers Department.

After his discharge in 1960, he came to Petersburg. He married Margaret two years later.

He worked in logging camps for Reid Brothers, Don Meurs, J&H Logging, and Joe Pentilla. He not only worked with timber, but operated, repaired, and

Mike and Margaret Durbin in front of a Pioneers of Alaska float, "Pioneers Extend Hands Across the Sea"

maintained all types of equipment. Mike also worked for Mitkof Lumber Company for five years.

In 1973, he opened a business in Skylark City, specializing in design, fabrication and welding. He operated this shop successfully for nine years before selling the business.

In 1987, he built Mike's Welding, where he worked until he retired in 1998.

Mike is a dedicated Pioneer and served several terms on the Utility Board.

He enjoys watching the boats go by in Wrangell Narrows from his home on Wrangell Avenue.

Royal and Clara Duval

By Ruth Dawson

During World War II, Royal Duval first met his brother, George Edward Duval. They had been separated during their infancy and raised by different families. At the time, Royal was working at the Bremerton, Washington, naval shipyard. George talked Royal into a trip to Petersburg to meet his father. While there, Royal fell in love with the community.

As soon as the war ended, my father, Royal, my mother, Clara, my brother, Bob, and I began our move to Petersburg. I believe it was in late 1946.

We boarded the SS *North Sea* for the trip north. My mother and I shared a cabin, while Dad and my brother Bob traveled steerage. Bob told wonderful tales of life aboard the steamship, making me a little envious. Little did I realize then that Mom and I had the better deal.

When we first arrived, we moved in with my grandfather, Charles Oscar Duval, and his wife, Drusie. Their home was on Front Street. The house was rather old. The water bucket and its ladle for drinking water were new and strange to me.

Grandpa's house was rather hidden from the road by masses of raspberry bushes. Those berries were the most delicious ones I had ever tasted. I'm sure my lips and tongue were bright red the whole time we stayed there.

Soon we found a house to live in, located on the lot where Eli Lucas' home is today. At that time, it was a two-room cabin with an unfinished loft. Bob and I slept in the loft, Mom and Dad slept in the living room.

There was no running water in the house, only a cold-water faucet on the back porch. Yes, life was quite different. We learned early to survive on little.

Royal got a job with the Petersburg Light Company and we snuggled into life in Petersburg.

Bath time proved to be exciting one night. We had to heat water, pour it into a tub and bathe in the kitchen. The front door opened from the kitchen onto the road. One night as brother Bob was blissfully immersed in suds, the front door opened and in walked a lady!

"Oh, don't mind me. I've seen men before," she said. Not something easy for a 16-year-old boy to cope with. I think he still blushes in shame when the story is told.

One day, someone gave us some bear meat and Mom boiled it. Unfortunately, it was late in the summer. It was so fishy, we could not eat it! That small cabin reeked of fish for weeks.

Needless to say, we began to look for another place to move into. That winter, we were able to purchase a home at 2½ mile Scow Bay Road. It was a building that had once been a dance hall.

It had a long narrow upstairs and a downstairs consisting of a laundry room and two bedrooms. We kids slept downstairs. Clara and Royal slept in a small room upstairs, while they were fixing up a big bedroom at the end of the hall. Kitchen, living room, and dining room were all one room.

We had a beautiful view of Wrangell Narrows. The snow was deep when we bought the house — white and beautiful. We longed for spring to see what kind of yard and play space we had.

Mom loved flowers of all kinds and was anxious to get her hands in the dirt. What kind of treasures would she find? Imagine the dismay we all felt when the snow melted and we found ourselves surrounded by several feet of beer cans and booze bottles.

However, my parents were hard workers. Little by little, we moved the trash out, and Royal and Clara began the laborious task of making a yard. They carried dirt and sand from various places, used window screens on boxes to sift and blend dirt, and then spread it across the yard. They built a little garden shed, a greenhouse, and a fenced-in chicken pen and yard.

Soon the Duval yard was known for its very beautiful and abundant flowers. People bought fresh eggs from us. The yard had some lovely little wooded spots that were great places to play and have picnics. Many of the younger generation grew up thinking "picnics" and "Duvals'" were synonymous. A trip out the road to the Duvals' meant fun.

Winters were hard in the '40s. We had many, many feet of snow. Our kitchen was on the second floor of the building, yet it was not unusual to look up from dinner and find hungry deer eying us as we ate.

The snow banks were so high we had to tunnel our way out to the road to catch the school bus. The bus was an old station wagon with jump seats. It was large enough for all the children in Scow Bay. (How times have changed. Now there are two big buses to

Royal and Clara Duval cont'd

pick up Scow Bay children.)

We drove a little Crosley, which was fine in the summer. Winter was another story. The snow banks were so high on the sides of the road in town that people couldn't see the Crosley coming. After being rammed at a crossroad, we hoisted a large antenna with a flag on top, so people could see us coming.

Oh, and another thing — Royal was very short. He drove peering through the steering wheel. The comment in town was, "If you see a car coming along the road without a driver, that's Duval."

The deep snows caused a lot of havoc on the power lines. We had many power outages. Because there were no roads out to the hydro plant, Royal would have to don a pair of snowshoes and follow the power lines to the plant at Blind Slough. A blackout on Christmas Day became expected, so we started opening gifts on Christmas Eve, knowing that on Christmas Day, our dad would be gone.

Clara and Royal became active in the Lutheran Church, teaching and filling in for missing pastors. (Royal filled in for almost every church in town.) Clara was active in PLCW. She and Royal both helped build the parish education building. Clara was an organizer and was instrumental in establishing a filing system for Sunday School materials.

Clara and my brother, Bob, joined the fishing community by working in the canneries. I did my part by babysitting, so others could work.

I guess Royal didn't want to be left out of the fun, because the next thing I knew he was working at Kayler-Dahl as a fish cook. Long, long hours and many, many fish. I soon joined the summer cannery crew. Bob had graduated by then and was in the Army.

Since Clara and I didn't drive, after working all day, we would walk the two miles home because Royal had to stay for several more hours. We have good memories of those days.

In later years, Royal and Clara became grandparents to all the kindergarten swimming classes. They were everyone's grandparents. Royal also became a grandparent at the daycare center and was much loved by the children. My parents had a lot of love to give, and they found ways to express it.

After my brother's stint in the Army, he came home for one summer and then left for school. He attended Western Washington in Bellingham.

During his second year, he married Carole Kanouse. They finished college and taught in several locations in Washington. They gave Royal and Clara four grandchildren.

I went to college at Pacific Lutheran University in Tacoma, earning a BA in education. During my last year of college, I met Walter "Bud" Dawson.

The following year, I taught school in Spokane Washington. Our long distance phone bills were so large, we decided it would be cheaper to marry. Bud and I were married June 11, 1958, in the Petersburg Evangelical Lutheran Church.

After five years in the Washington area, we returned to Petersburg, where we have lived ever since.

While my parents were still living, Bud and I had four children.

We both worked in the crab, shrimp and salmon canneries. Bud drove a van for The Trading Union, was a school janitor, and worked at PFI cold storage.

I taught kindergarten for many years in the Petersburg school system. I also taught third grade for one year. I retired in 1987 and Bud retired in 1988.

After teaching a few years at the preschool in the Assembly of God daycare center, Bud and I opened Precious Lambs Preschool in our home. Our last group of preschoolers is in seventh grade at this writing.

We retired from preschool teaching in order to raise a couple of grandchildren.

During his later years, my father, Royal, lived in the long-term care unit of the hospital. Clara was a daily visitor. She not only helped him, but she also assisted other residents with her daily visits.

Royal passed away on November 11, 1985. Clara passed away on May 10, 1988. Although they are no longer with us, while living, they showed us how to live their Christian faith. We want to follow in their footsteps — quite a feat to live up to.

Lars and Meredith Eide

By John and Carol Enge

Lars Eide was born on the family homestead in Stanwood, Washington, on February 1, 1911. He attended high school in Stanwood and went to the University of Washington for one year.

Lars came to Cordova, Alaska, in 1929, to work on a cannery tender. In 1933, he moved to Wrangell, where he worked in construction, logging, and fishing. It was there that he met Meredith Mitchell.

Lars and Meredith Eide

Meredith was born on July 2, 1903, in Wallace, Idaho. Her family moved frequently, and she attended schools in Ely, Nevada, and Missoula, Montana.

At age 19, she entered a nurses training program in Billings, Montana.

In 1937, a public health nurse, whom she had trained with, was recruiting help and asked her to come to Wrangell, Alaska. Meredith was willing to try it and became superintendent of Bishop Rowe Hospital.

In those days, nurses were not allowed to work if they were married. After marrying Lars in 1939, Meredith retired and became a full-time mother and wife.

In 1944, they moved to Petersburg. Lars became owner-manager of the Mitkof Lumber sawmill, located in Scow Bay. This operation was successful for 20 years, employing up to 20 people.

During this time, he built a house across the road from the mill. There he and Meredith raised their family of two sons, Dick and John, and a daughter, Kirsti.

In 1977, Lars sold his interest in the Mitkof sawmill and retired.

Lars has been active in community affairs. He spent three terms as president of the Chamber of Commerce, two terms as president of the Pioneers, one term on the City Council, and has been president of the PTA.

He was on the Salvation Army Board for 20 years. He served as chairman, was involved with fund raising, and assisted with numerous repair projects. Upon his retirement from this board, Lars was given a longtime service award.

Hunting and fishing were special avocations. Lars especially enjoyed trips to the hunter's cabin in Duncan Canal.

Meredith enjoyed knitting and baking homemade bread and pastries. She resided in Petersburg until her death on October 14, 1994, at Harborview Medical Center in Seattle.

Lars Eide, Ken Welde and John Enge

Lester and Mildred Elkins

By Carol Enge

Mildred Apland was born on a wheat farm in North Dakota. She came to Alaska in 1936 to visit a sister in Juneau. She immediately fell in love with both Juneau and the rain. She worked there until she met her future husband, Lester Elkins.

Lester Elkins was born in Kansas City, Kansas, on May 18, 1903. His parents, Lewis and Anna, moved the family to Colorado in 1909. After graduating from high school, Lester attended the University of Denver and was awarded a BS in pharmacy in 1926. He worked in West Virginia, Colorado, California, and Seattle before traveling to Nome, Alaska, where he managed Loman Brothers Drug Store for two years. During his time in Nome, he collected many ivory carvings.

Mildred and Lester Elkins

On his passage south, the ship stopped in Petersburg. Lester debarked and never left. He managed the People's Drug Store for a few years before purchasing it from I. M. Dahl.

It was during one of his trips to Juneau that he met Mildred. They were married in 1939. After their marriage, they purchased the home on North Nordic Drive where they lived for over 50 years.

In the days before the town could lay claim to restaurants, dinner parties were the essence of hospitality. Mildred was always the well-dressed and gracious hostess, entertaining her husband's business associates, as well as their many friends.

Mildred and Lester traveled to most of the major cities of the U.S. and Canada throughout the years, attending his National Board of Pharmacy meetings. They also enjoyed outings in their boat with friends.

Mildred has vivid memories of one trip they took to Blind Slough with Jim and Ann Leekley. She was always a stickler for life jackets and safety equipment, but this morning she decided not to nag, so the equipment was left behind. It was a warm September day when the four left by outboard skiff on the high tide, bound for the Smikum Club in Blind Slough.

As they entered the slough from Wrangell Narrows, the wind was blowing and their boat overturned in a riptide. Since no one could swim and they were heavily clothed, they clung to the side of the boat. As the boat swamped, the anchor fell overboard and the boat was held fast. Someone found a knife and passed it with a warning not to drop it. After cutting the line, they all paddled furiously toward shore while keeping ahold of the boat.

They walked to the cabin. Bordering on hypothermia, they had difficulty getting warm, even after a roaring fire was built. The next day, the men walked to the power plant to obtain help. After that experience, Mildred never set foot on a boat again, unless it was a perfectly calm day.

Lester was very active in the Petersburg community. He served on the city council and as acting magistrate for the city. He chaired Red Cross drives, was a member of the Elks, Eastern Star and the Masonic Lodge, Rotary Club, and the Pioneers of Alaska. He was the Scottish Rite leader in Petersburg for many years. In 1971, he was awarded the highest degree in Scottish Rite, Coronet to the 33rd degree.

Lester was Petersburg's coordinator for Search and Rescue and was a member of the Coast Guard Auxiliary. He was also a member of the Board of Pharmacy for 20 years.

His love of Alaska took him on many adventures. A big game guide for 35 years, he enjoyed trout fishing and moose and duck hunting with his many friends. He was well known for his wildlife and scenic photography.

He spent his last years in the long-term facility at Petersburg Medical Center and died December 17, 1996.

Mildred is a past matron of the Eastern Star, a member of the Lutheran Church and Pioneers of Alaska. She enjoys playing bridge and having company. After the death of her husband, Mildred sold their home and now resides at Mountain View Manor.

Their two daughters, Gail Huffman and Joyce Poore, have given them four grandchildren.

Elstad - Rayner Family

By James Eric Elstad, as told to Janet Elstad

My great grandparents, Frank and Ruie Rayner, came to Petersburg from the Seattle, Washington area early in the century.

Frank was a baker and became a partner in the local bakery. Their children, Ruby and Matt, were raised in Petersburg.

Eventually, Frank traded his interest in the bakery for the fox farm on Sockeye Island. This was a hard life, especially for a woman. There was no electricity. Fresh water came only from the rain and the foxes needed cooked fish every day.

The men did the fishing and the women the cooking and feeding. In the fall, the foxes were killed and their pelts sold through the Seattle Fur Exchange.

The small islands around Petersburg were perfect for this industry because foxes did not like to swim. Many islands in Southeast Alaska are in private ownership today due to the homesteading fox farmers.

However, the fashion designers in Paris convinced women that they looked fat in fox fur, but beautiful in mink. This news resulted in the abandonment of the fox industry and the construction of mink pens much closer to town.

We heard interesting stories of social life on the fox farms in those remote locations. When a new batch of home brew was ready, boats would arrive from the surrounding fox islands and from town. It was party time, for days!

The best story I heard about my great-grandfather, Frank, was the result of his reading an old friend's obituary in the Petersburg Press.

"I used to be sweet on her," Frank admitted to my mother.

"You were always married and you lived on an island, so how could you have a girlfriend?" my mother asked him.

"Well, they had a fox farm on _____ Island. When her husband was gone for the day, she hung a blue apron on the clothesline," said Frank.

My equal opportunity mother replied, "Well Frank, what color apron did Ruie hang on her clothesline when you were gone?"

Granddad sputtered, "Why, she would never do such a thing!"

By Michael Dan Elstad, as told to Janet Elstad

My grandfather, A. O. "Bert" Elstad, came to Petersburg from the Midwest in the 1920s. Bert was a banjo player, who arrived with a band hired to provide dance music three to four nights a week.

There was no undertaker in Petersburg at that time. Good money could be earned in the job of building a coffin, dressing a body in dignified clothes, and providing the burial.

The band made such an arrangement. However, they were a bit squeamish and waited until after the dance and a few drinks before tackling the job.

Emboldened by the alcohol, they took clothes to the warehouse where the body was lying on planks. It's not easy to dress a corpse. Frustrated, Bert lifted the torso of the deceased, trying to bend the arms into the jacket. Suddenly, the body emitted a loud belch.

Everyone tore out of the warehouse. Breathless, they opened another bottle and passed it around a few times. Peeking back in, they finally decided that perhaps it was only some air in the body.

The dressing job finished, they placed the body in the casket made of rough lumber, carried it to a skiff at the harbor, and rowed across the bay to the cemetery. The hole was already prepared, so they placed the casket and covered it with dirt.

Suddenly, someone remembered the head of the casket was supposed to be pointing east. Had they actually placed the head in the right direction? The bottle passed around again and they started digging up the casket.

It was a muddy, slippery job. Nobody noticed when one of the band members slid into the grave and under the casket. They did notice, however, when muffled groans and protests came from the casket.

What next?!?! They were ready for anything, even a body rising from the grave. They watched, fascinated, as the coffin moved and shifted!

Eventually, all was sorted out.

Bert Elstad and John Schoettler started the *Petersburg Press* using a mail order linotype machine, which they had to assemble from scratch. The first edition was August 27, 1926.

Bert married Ruby Rayner, the daughter of Frank and Ruie Rayner. Bert and Ruby had two children, Rodney and Roberta.

Rasmus and Anna Enge

By Marilee Enge Frost and Carol Enge

Six generations of Enges have lived in Petersburg, since Rasmus and Anna first arrived in 1901. Each has been closely involved in the town's growth and progress.

Rasmus Enge was born August 28, 1861, on Tustna, a Norwegian island near the city of Kristiansund. Each year he sailed his schooner, *Socrates*, north to the Lofoten Islands to fish for cod.

After the death of his first wife, Guri, Rasmus married Anna Ervig.

Anna was born in 1860, in Kristiansund, where she later met Rasmus. Together they immigrated to America, leaving Rasmus' two sons, Johan and Martin, with Rasmus' brother Gunnerius, in Norway.

Economic conditions were poor in Norway in the late 19th century. Rasmus and Anna were following the path of other Norwegians who came to America, stopping in the Midwest before moving on to Seattle. It was in Seattle that they met Peter Buschmann, who hired them for his fish processing operation in Alaska.

Rasmus and Anna arrived on Mitkof Island January 9, 1901. They were immediately sent by Buschmann to Sitkoh Bay, along with some other workers, to build a cannery. It was the dead of winter and their boat and barge froze fast in the shallow waters of the bay.

They built a 12-by-14-foot shack to house eight people and endured a harsh winter. When provisions ran out, they were forced to subsist on venison and clams. After Rasmus and Anna returned to Petersburg in the late spring, Rasmus fished herring and halibut for Buschmann, but soon severed relations with him. (*For more about that winter, read the Buschmann story.*)

Anna and Rasmus Enge

Rasmus' sons, Johan and Martin, and his brother Gunnerius, arrived in Petersburg in 1905.

While fishing the following year in a dory off of Point Gardner, Johan drowned. Gunnerius Enge lived in Petersburg for a while, fishing and logging, but after eight or nine years, he returned to Norway.

From 1903 to 1912, Rasmus was involved in a fishing venture, salting salmon and herring from a buying scow on the Stikine River. In 1909, he built an apartment house on Sing Lee Alley and ran a first-floor restaurant. In 1912, Rasmus built a skating rink, which, in 1916, he converted to a movie theater. The Variety Theater operated until the 1930s.

Rasmus and Anna built a large home across the alley from their apartment building in 1927. (It is now Sing Lee Alley Books.) Anna planted apple and cherry trees and cultivated a large garden. She took in boarders, including the many new arrivals from Norway. She was especially fond of children, and cared for many of them when needed. Anna's grandsons have fond memories of overnight visits to her home.

Anna died November 7, 1941. Rasmus died June 22, 1942.

Left to right, Rasmus and Anna's first residence, Enges' Variety Theatre, and the Enge Building.

Martin and Augusta Enge

By Marilee Enge Frost and Carol Enge

Martin Enge, son of Rasmus and Guri Enge, was born October 9, 1888, on the island of Tustna, in Norway. When his father and stepmother, Anna, left Norway for America, he and his brother, Johan, stayed behind with their uncle Gunnerius. Four years later, he brought the boys to Petersburg to join their parents.

Martin and his brother were among the first children to attend school in the PAF cannery bunkhouse. Later, Martin attended Parkland College, now Pacific Lutheran University, in Tacoma, Washington.

Growing up, he fished halibut with his uncle and built a small sailboat, the *Mary*.

On Febuary 7, 1914, Martin married Augusta Rosvold, in Seattle. He also built the purse seiner, *Augusta*, in Seattle that same year. The *Augusta* was one of the most modern and speedy gas boats in the fleet. The couple returned to Petersburg to live.

Martin survived several near-fatal accidents in his lifetime. Shortly before Christmas of 1923, Martin, Knut Thompson, Berger Wasvik, and Hans Lee anchored off Todal Creek, on Kupreanof Island.

While they were in the woods, a northerly wind blew up and their boat broke into pieces. They began the 12-mile trek along the rocky beach back towards town. The cold Taku wind froze their clothes. Hans Lee died. The others continued along the rugged icy beach. (Martin's friends later said his encouragement kept them alive.) They finally reached Harry Colp's place at Five Mile after hiking through the night. Harry said Martin was the toughest man he had ever known.

A shooting accident occurred while deer hunting with his brother-in-law, Ole. Martin survived with a deep scar across his left cheek, which he had for the rest of his life. He continued to hunt until he was 70.

While moored in the Sitka Harbor in 1935, Martin nearly lost his life and his beloved seine boat, when a crewman dropped a cigarette in the engine room of the *Augusta*. The gas engine exploded. Martin grabbed Egil Winther, pushing him through flames to the deck. Both suffered second and third degree burns.

As he neared retirement, Martin gave the *Augusta* to his son Ernest, and he bought a gillnetter called the *Portia*. He continued to fish for salmon, often taking his grandchildren along, until his death on May 13, 1960.

The trail from Norway to Alaska was still a pioneering venture when Augusta Rosvold followed it in 1911. The lives of our pioneers, which have bridged the years, the oceans and this great continent, were formidable. Augusta Rosvold was one of that great band.

Augusta was born April 29, 1892, on the island of Smøla, which neighbors the island of Tustna.

At the age of 19, she joined two brothers in America. In Seattle, she met and married Martin Enge.

Martin and Augusta built two homes and raised three sons, John, Arnold, and Ernest.

Martin and Augusta Enge with John, Ernest and Arnold

Augusta was an elegant lady who helped bring culture to this frontier settlement. Whether dressed casually for boating and picnics, or dressed up for social events, she was always comfortable.

Augusta was active in Eastern Star, Daughters of Norway, and the American Legion Auxiliary. During World War II, she was head of the local Red Cross.

A loving mother, she enjoyed traveling on the family boats or visiting other places in Alaska where she had many friends. Twice during the years, she revisited the Norwegian scenes of her childhood. The first trip was with her son Ernest, in 1922. The second trip was with her husband, in 1949.

Augusta sang in chorales and played the piano. She was well known for her hospitality. She loved to play cards and dance, often bringing friends home for German pancakes in the wee hours of the morning.

Following the death of her son Arnold, in World War II, her health began to fail. Augusta suffered several heart attacks before her death June 1, 1956.

John and Carol Enge

By Marilee Enge Frost and Carol Enge

John Enge was born January 28, 1915, in the Enge apartment building on Sing Lee Alley. His parents, Martin and Augusta, soon built a home on what is now North First Street.

After years of prosperous fishing, the Enges built a beautiful new home next door to the first house, where John has lived almost ever since.

Petersburg was a great place for boys to grow up. John and his two brothers took pleasure in everything it had to offer. Rowing up Petersburg Creek or down the Narrows to Blind Slough, fishing and hunting, and family boat trips to places such as Point Agassiz and Warm Springs Bay gave the boys many happy childhood experiences.

John graduated from high school in 1933. The country was still deep in a depression, so he waited a year for his brother Arnold to graduate, so they could enroll in the University of Washington together.

John alternated between fishing six months for tuition money and attending college for six months. He graduated in 1940 with a degree in fisheries. He first worked for the International Halibut Commission as a researcher. Later, he returned to Petersburg to buy fish at Petersburg Cold Storage.

Shortly after war was declared, December 7, 1941, John enlisted in the Navy. After attending various naval training programs, he was commissioned an ensign in November 1942.

Early in 1944, he was given command of an LST and crossed the Atlantic in a convoy. After arriving in England, the LST proceeded down the Bristol Channel. On August 14, l944, a torpedo, fired by a German submarine, struck the vessel, breaking it in half. The stern sank in four minutes, and 43 of John Enge's men were lost.

He stayed aboard his ship until all the surviving sailors were safely in life rafts. The secret cargo of equipment, which was to be used to sweep for German mines on Normandy beaches, was partly lost. The bow was towed to Falmouth Harbor.

After returning to the States, John was given command of another LST and sent to the Pacific. He served the remainder of the war in those waters, avoiding kamikaze planes bent on suicide paths for his ship. When the war ended, John returned to San Francisco to decommission the vessel. He was discharged in March 1946.

He returned to Petersburg and fished with his father and brother, and cruised the Southeast waters with his friend, Erling Strand. That fall, John met one of the new teachers, Carol Anderson.

Carol and John Enge

Carol was born in Riceville, Iowa, July 31, 1924. She spent her childhood on farms across Iowa. After graduating from high school in 1941, her heart's desire was to attend college and become a teacher. This was in the declining years of the Depression, and money was hard to come by. It wasn't until mid-August, when her dad said, "Let's go down to Indianola to get you registered in college," that Carol knew she would be able to attend.

Her chosen school was Simpson College, a small Methodist school. She enrolled in the two-year Teacher's Training Course, graduating in 1943.

That fall, she began teaching elementary grades

John and Carol Enge cont'd

in a consolidated school near her home. During summer vacations, she worked at the Des Moines, Iowa, ordnance plant and attended summer school at the University of Colorado. In 1945, she traveled to Seattle to work at Boeing Aircraft.

As a Midwest girl, she found the ships traveling in and out of Puget Sound fascinating. Carol was especially intrigued by the ships from Alaska and decided it would be exciting to travel there. After three years of teaching in her home state, she was ready for a change of scenery. She applied to a teachers' agency and soon received a telegram from Les Wingard, in Petersburg, offering her the fourth grade class at $2,400 a year. Compared to her Iowa salary, it seemed a fortune. She immediately wired her acceptance.

Carol traveled by train to Seattle and then to Vancouver, where she boarded the *Princess Louise*. Her 1941 ticket price was about $50. The Canadian ships didn't dock in Petersburg, so she disembarked in Wrangell and chartered a plane to Petersburg.

She arrived on a sunny day and has loved Petersburg from that first moment.

Carol registered at the Mitkof Hotel. Ruth Sandvik, secretary of the school board, soon took Carol under her wing and found her a room at Ole Holm's.

John Enge had only been home from the Navy just a few months, when he sought an introduction to this new teacher at the weekly Sons of Norway dance. Soon Carol and John were going steady and planning to be married. On Christmas Eve day, the first day of Carol's school vacation, they flew to Juneau. They were married that evening at Resurrection Lutheran Church and spent their honeymoon at the Baranof Hotel.

John wanted to fish one last summer with his dad and brother, so Carol returned to her home in Iowa at the end of the school year. Arnold was born in late summer, and John joined them after the fishing season. They spent the winter with her family and then drove to Seattle, where they took the steamship *Baranof* to Wrangell. Martin Enge came to Wrangell to ferry them home and make the acquaintance of his first grandson.

That summer, they moved to Pelican where John was a fish buyer for Elton Engstrom. For the next four years, they experienced life in an isolated village.

Sons John and Steve were born. Carol learned to cope without the amenities of a telephone, transportation, grocery delivery, bakery, or even a much-needed babysitter.

She has always been grateful for the experience because she learned to cook and care for three small children without help.

Those were challenging times, but they had many friends and enjoyed many outdoor adventures — trips to Sunnyside, nagoonberry picking in Phonograph Cove, strawberry picking at Dundas Bay, and wonderful hunting for John.

Carol vividly recalls one hunting trip that occurred on a brisk autumn day. She and John took a boat up Lisianski Strait to Canoe Cove. It was a beautiful day. They climbed to the top of the mountain.

As they sat eating their lunch, John practiced his deer call. Soon a deer came to investigate and John shot it. He cleaned the deer and they started their descent, which was more difficult than climbing unencumbered.

Late in the afternoon, as they were following a trail in the low country, they encountered a brown bear fishing in a nearby creek. John dropped the deer and loaded his gun. Fortunately, the bear went back to fishing and showed no interest. Many years later, Carol heard John tell a friend that in the excitement of the moment, he had ejected the shell from the gun. She had felt safe knowing he would protect her!

In 1952, they returned to Petersburg and bought the family home. John began 25 years of managing Kayler-Dahl Fish Company. He devoted himself to his work and was always on call for the fishermen.

During those years, John was active in many community and fisheries organizations, including the Masons, Elks, American Legion, Pioneers of Alaska, Petersburg School Board, City Charter Commission, Chamber of Commerce, Boy Scouts, Alaska King Crab Marketing Board, Southeast Alaska Regional Aquaculture Association, and the Alaska Fisheries Development Foundation. He also served on the boards of the Bank of Petersburg, the National Bank of Alaska, and Wells Fargo Bank. He lectured on fisheries at the University of Alaska and the Alaska Federation of Natives.

He finished his career with Icicle Seafood, as administrative assistant to the president. In this position, he was in charge of bottom fisheries and

John and Carol Enge cont'd

traveled from Kake to Kotzebue running canneries and various operations. He retired in 1984.

John enjoyed trout fishing and traveling to visit the family in Norway. Visits with his grandchildren continue to be his favorite pastime.

Carol devoted her time to her family and to the Lutheran Church. She taught Sunday School and Bible School for many years and later became a Bethel teacher. She served on the Parish Board, Church Council, and was active in the Petersburg Lutheran Church Women.

She was honored to be elected as a state delegate to the Lutheran National Women's Convention in Washington, D.C. As a state officer, she attended "Women and Children in Poverty" conferences in both Portland and Chicago.

Scouting was also a special interest. Carol was den mother for the Cub Scouts, a Brownie and Girl Scout leader, and served on the Tongass Alaska Girl Scout Council. She also served on the Petersburg Library Board, school board, and was active in the American Legion Auxiliary, Eastern Star and Pioneers.

Two daughters, Marilee and Elisabeth, joined the family in the 1960s. These were happy, golden years, as their family enjoyed the Alaska life. John took the boys hunting and fishing. Depending on the time of year and the weather, everyone ice skated and skied, swam in the cold waters of Blind Slough, and picked lots of berries.

Carol and John's son Arnold went to Lewis and Clark College, in Idaho, before enlisting in the Navy. He served six years during the Vietnam conflict. As a radar technician, he served aboard the aircraft carrier *Enterprise* for two years. Returning home, he pursued his first love, gillnetting in Southeast Alaska. He married Carrie Copony. The couple has two daughters, Kate and Ana. Arnold represents the Southeast Alaska Gillnet Association on the Northern Panel of the U.S.-Canada Salmon Treaty.

John graduated from Oregon State University with a degree in business administration. He worked for the Alaska Commercial Fishing and Agriculture Bank. He married Kathleen Mack. They have five children: Jesse, Alicia, Morgan, Daniel and Elias. They live in Dallas, Oregon.

Steve began his fishing career at age 12. John had bought a little gillnet boat, the *Gypsy*, launching both Steve's and Arnold's fishing careers.

Steve attended Western Washington State College for several years before building the first of many fishing boats.

Carol and John Enge, with Marilee, John Jr., Elisabeth, Arnold and Steve

Through the years, he has fished from San Francisco Bay to Bristol Bay, spending most of his career in Southeast waters. Steve married Kathy Pool, and they have one daughter, Robin. They live in Port Townsend, Wash.

Marilee attended the University of California, Santa Cruz. Her degree in journalism is from San Francisco State University. She worked for the *Anchorage Daily News* for 10 years, and then the *San Jose Mercury News*. She married George Frost. They have two daughters, Marit and Lily. They live in Berkeley, California.

Elisabeth went to Lewis and Clark College in Portland and the University of Washington, graduating with a degree in fisheries. She worked for a number of seafood processing companies, in the Puget Sound area, as a quality assurance coordinator.

Elisabeth is married to Chris Nyssen. They have a son, Sten, and a daughter, Sofie. They live in Edmonds, Washington.

Arnold and Barbara Enge

By John and Carol Enge

Arnold Enge was born September 1, 1916, in Seattle, Washington, the second son of Martin and Augusta Enge.

He graduated from Petersburg High School in 1934 and attended the University of Washington for two quarters.

Arnold fished on his father's boat, the *Augusta*, during the summers of his school years. When the *Augusta* blew up in Sitka in the spring of 1935, he returned home to help his father.

To pursue his dream of flying, Arnold returned to Seattle, took flight training at Boeing Field, and bought a plane. He continued training at Ryan School of Aeronautics in San Diego, California.

Arnold married Barbara Johnson in 1940. That same year, he began flying for Ellis Air Lines out of Ketchikan. In 1942, he enlisted in the Naval Air Corps and was commissioned an ensign at the Naval Air Station in Corpus Christi, Texas. He was then assigned to the 14th Naval District.

While bringing a military plane to Sitka, Arnold crashed on the Mendenhall flats near Juneau. He was killed April 27, 1943.

Arnold and Barbara Enge

Arnold, Martin, Ernest and John Enge

Ernest and Ethel Enge

Adapted from The Good Old Days, *by Ernest Enge*

Ernest Rosvold Enge was born October 3, 1919, the third son of Martin and Augusta Enge. He grew up in the family home on North First Street.

His first memory of fishing was with his friend and neighbor, Stan Johanson. Their favorite pastime was catching minnows in a bucket. The first boat trip he remembers was his dad taking the family to Goddard Hot Springs while making a halibut trip.

When Ernest was 12 years old, he made a fishing trip with Eric Fuglvog. He thought he could hold his own, but after fishing for 10 days on the "outside" for 11,000 pounds of halibut and then having to run to Prince Rupert to sell the catch, Ernest had serious doubts about being a deep-water fisherman.

Bobbie, Martin, Ethel, Signe, Ernest and Bonnie Enge

During high school, he decided to try his luck at fishing "outside" again — this time on the *Augusta*, his father's boat. When the trip was finished and they were on their way home, Osbjorn Odegaard and Ernest were lashing down the sail off Cape Edgecomb, when Osbjorn, not knowing that he and Ernest were pulling on the same line, let go. Ernest went over the rail. Fortunately, one of the crew members in the pilot house happened to look back and saw him go over. It took the whole crew to pull him aboard.

During high school years, he was a star basketball player. They traveled to games in Ketchikan and Wrangell by fishing boat. After a rough trip, they were sometimes too sick to play a good game.

Les Wingard was their coach. Having been a heavyweight boxing champion at Washington State University, his solution to any dispute was to "put on the gloves" and he would referee. They won the Southeastern Basketball Championship in 1938.

Ernest married Ethel Anderson on May 17, 1940, and they built a home on Wrangell Avenue.

With the advent of World War II, he was drafted into the Army. He remembers being a first class private twice, as he was somewhat of a rebel.

After being discharged, Ernest returned to Petersburg to take up fishing again, this time as captain of the *Augusta*. Winter months were spent playing basketball. He was on the gold medal team that won the Southeast championship in 1947.

He was an avid hunter of ducks, geese, deer and moose. He made many hunting trips throughout the years with friends and family members. His usual hunting buddies were Ben Jensen, Ernie Haugen, and his brother John.

Ernest's other hobby was painting, which he had learned in high school from Superintendent George Beck. His many oil paintings are proudly displayed in the homes of friends and family members.

In 1967, he had the *Martina* built at Dakota Creek in Blaine, Washington. He fished this vessel until the early '70s, when he developed multiple sclerosis. It was necessary for him and Ethel to move south to obtain better medical care.

They bought a home in Edmonds, Washington. While confined to a wheelchair, Ernest gardened, wrote five books and many poems about fishing, boats and

Ernest and Ethel Enge cont'd

life in Petersburg.

In 1996, he and Ethel returned to live in Petersburg. They built a new home on Wrangell Avenue near their daughters.

Ernest was a life member of the local V.F.W. and a charter member of Moose Lodge #1092. He died August 6, 2001.

Ethel Marie Enge
By Signe Haltiner

Ethel Marie Anderson was born August 31, 1921, in Seattle, Washington, to Gustave Anderson and Bolette Knudsen. Gustave had emigrated from Sweden and Bolette from Norway. Ethel has two brothers, Alfred and Gustave "Bud."

She first came to Alaska in 1930 with her mother and brothers. They traveled to Sitka on the steamer *Alameda* to meet Gustave, who had been in the Arctic on a polar bear expedition on the schooner *Dorothy*. On the way south, Gustave got off the boat in Ketchikan, obtained a large row boat, and rowed himself to Sitka to meet his family.

In 1933, they left Sitka, hitching a ride on a 28-foot troller back to Seattle.

In 1939, Ethel graduated from Queen Anne High School. She and her mother moved to Petersburg to be with her father and brother Al, who were in Petersburg working on cannery tenders. Ethel found work at Sammy's Café as a waitress.

She met Ernest Enge and they were married.

They built a home on Wrangell Avenue and raised three daughters. Bonnie was born in 1942, Bobbie in 1943, and Signe in 1947.

Throughout the years, she enjoyed many trips on the family boats, traveling around Southeast Alaska and to Seattle. They spent several winters in Santa Barbara, California, and took bus tours to Reno, Nevada, from their home in Edmonds. In 1964, she and her mother traveled to Norway to visit relatives.

Ethel currently lives in the new home they built on Wrangell Avenue. She has six grandchildren and 10 great-grandchildren.

F/V Martina

Inez Engstrom

By Carol Enge

Inez Engstrom was born to Lars and Annie Hanson on July 7, 1913, in the Jorgensen house, which was located where the Alaska Power and Telephone office is today.

Lars was born in Bode, Norway, and came to America in 1911, when he was 41 years old. Annie was born in Hanman, Finland, and also came to America in 1911. Lars and Annie met and married in Astoria, Oregon.

Two of their children, Florence and Hilmar, were born in Astoria. Inez was born in Petersburg.

Florence married Octer Arness and they had two daughters, Arlene and Ann.

Florence died of cancer in 1943. Hilmar mysteriously drowned by the Petersburg dock when he was just 26.

Inez recalls the family living in a one-room shack on Hammer Slough. Her father died in 1933, and her mother later remarried Pete Behrs. They moved to Scow Bay where Annie was an avid gardener and loved sharing her plants with friends.

Inez dropped out of high school during her junior year to work, picking shrimp at Ohmer's cannery.

She was working at the City Café when she met Lennie Engstrom. They were married in 1940 and moved to Wrangell. Lennie was a fish buyer for Engstrom brothers until his death in 1982.

After Lennie's death, Inez moved back to Petersburg and bought a home at 705 Gjoa Street. Like her mother, she was an avid gardener. Inez also loved driving.

As was typical of many of this generation, Inez was an active volunteer in her community. She was the first president of Pioneers Auxiliary in Wrangell and was given a jade gavel in recognition of her work. She actively worked in the Presbyterian Church as a Sunday School teacher and was president of the Ladies Aid. She was secretary of the Emblem Club and later taught a class in leather tooling.

In later years, she loved to crochet and read. As her health began to fail, Inez sold her home and moved to the extended care facility at Petersburg Medical Center, where she resides today.

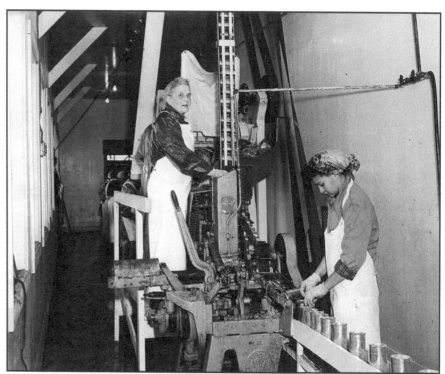

"Canning Line"
The woman on the left is Fern Ludeman. The other woman is unidentified.

Photo courtesy of the Clausen Memorial Museum

Espeseth Family

By Ann Marie Espeseth Oakes

The four Espeseth brothers, Erling, Bert, Carl, and Nels, fished and lived in Petersburg.

Erling and Bert married the Hammerseth sisters, Agnes and Larine. My parents were Erling and Agnes. My siblings were Arnie and Elsie. Bert and Larine's children were Alice and Bernice.

Gus Vallestad, foster brother of Agnes and Larine, also fished and lived in Petersburg.

It was a close-knit family. Bert and Erling co-owned the *Neptune* and the *Bravo*.

As a junior high student, my brother, Arne, installed a washing machine motor in a small skiff. The Coast Guard registered the skiff as *Capt. Arne Espeseth M-S Foo*. Years later, Arne realized his dream of skippering a classic fishing schooner. He found the *Lindy* in a deplorable condition in Crescent City, California. After restoring the vessel, he fished in the Gulf of Alaska.

One of the family's favorite summer trips was walking to Sandy Beach on the three-plank boardwalk across the muskeg. We had a special small brook where we would catch minnows, using a stem of grass around a woodworm as bait.

After the highway was extended, the swimming hole at Fall Creek was popular for Petersburg families. In the winter, when conditions were right, there was ice skating far up the creek.

Another favorite spot was the sand dunes at the mouth of Petersburg Creek. Families also picnicked on Kupreanof at the end of the gravel road at the Indian graveyard behind Sasby's Island.

I remember...

My first hair permanent: Mrs. Ness gave permanents in her home. One couldn't move because the electric cords attached to each curler kept one immobile. My first perm was in 1936.

My first indoor plumbing: We rented the Hallingstad house in 1928, and had indoor plumbing. We also had a grand piano to play.

My first airplane sighting: As a second grader in 1930, I saw three military planes flying over Horn Cliff, heading north along the coast.

The best berry patch: The biggest blueberries and red huckleberries grew on a hillside past Mountain Point. The whole town could have picked their berries in that berry patch.

The cottonwood tree and pink moss rose: The Miller family, at the foot of Lumber Street, had the ancestor of the "Balm-of-Gilead" tree with its sticky and fragrant leaves in spring. They also had the fragrant and lovely moss roses that are still seen in local gardens.

Summer: Walking home on a summer evening from a dance with the mountains creating shadows on the mirror-smooth Narrows. Myriad stars and snow-capped mainland mountains created an unbelievable freshness in the air.

Winter: We loved going out on a winter morning to a cloudless, blue sky. It was so crisp and cold, you were almost blinded by the brilliance of the "millions of diamonds" glittering on the snow.

The Enge theater: Does anyone remember the live musical performance at the Enge theater? Was it about 1928? The program was introduced by Russian princesses.

Reunions: Today we look forward to class reunions, usually four or five classes participating, and lasting several days around the Fourth of July. There are parades, parties hosted by local members for their classes in their homes, salmon barbecues at Sandy Beach, and dinner dances at the Elks Club. This is a great time to return to our hometown.

Shovel ride
Courtesy of the File Family

Bert and Larine Espeseth

By Bernice Stedman, Jill Williams and Rexanne Stafford

Bert Espeseth was born in Tansøy, Norway, in 1891. He came to the United States at the age of 18 to live with his oldest brother, Peter, in Kent, Washington. Bert became a United States citizen in 1929.

On his first trip to Alaska, in 1916, he came looking for the opportunity to go fishing, but there was a fishing strike, so he took a job as a trap watchman. The next year he obtained a fishing chance on the boat *Lincoln*, a three-dory ship skippered by John Linvog.

In 1919, he was on the *Constance* when it was wrecked off Cape Suckling. After spending a few days on the beach, the crew members were picked up and taken to Seward. His next boat was the seven-dory *Scandia* that wrecked on a reef off Montague Island. When the crew went ashore, they found six feet of snow on the ground. They were rescued and taken to Cordova. His next ship was the *New England*, a 12-dory steamer.

In 1923, he married the Larine Hammerseth in Seattle. He had previously met her during a trip to Norway in 1921.

Fishing was not good in those days. Bert made one "hole" trip after another and even had to borrow 50 cents from a friend to get from Seattle to his home in Kent, Washington. He next spent six months working in a sawmill, but the lure of the sea drew him back. He joined the halibut fleet on the *Middleton*, a boat based out of Petersburg.

In 1927, the Espeseths moved to Petersburg for the summer and stayed to build a home and raise their family. They had two daughters, Bernice and Alice.

Bert was a partner in two boats, the *Neptune* and the *Bravo*. After 50 years of fishing, at the age of 76, he retired and was honored by his former shipmates at a surprise party.

Bert was a life member of the Sons of Norway and the Pioneers of Alaska. He passed away in Petersburg in 1969.

Larine and Bert Espeseth

Larine Sigverda Hammerseth was born on the island of Askrova off the coast of Norway, on May 29, 1903. The youngest of 10 children, she had many fond memories of growing up on the Hammerseth farm.

There was always lots of work to do on the farm. Her favorite chore was to card wool for her mother's yarn. Her least favorite was the two-hour rowing trip to Floro, the nearest city on the mainland.

There were 180 people living on Askrova Island and she knew them all. The school she attended was on the Espeseth farm, a one-hour walk over the top of the hill. At the age of 14, she was confirmed into the Lutheran Church and completed her formal education.

She laughingly recalled her last trip to Norway in 1983. At the age of 80, she could not make it over the hill to visit the old school.

Her sister, Agnes, was married to Erling Espeseth. When Larine saw a picture of his brother, Bert, who was living in America, she thought he was very handsome. When Bert returned to Norway, she got to know him and they fell in love. He returned to America and they wrote to each other.

She made the trip to America with Gus Vallestad, Agnes and Erling Espeseth, and the Espeseths' infant daughter, Ann Marie. They joined Bert in Washington. On December 29, 1923, Larine and Bert were married. They made their home in Kent. A daughter, Alice Marie, was born January 24, 1925.

When Bert was fishing in Alaska on the F/V *Middleton*, in January of 1927, he brought Larine and Alice to Alaska to spend the fishing season with him. As they were going through Wrangell Narrows, the mountains and water reminded Larine of Norway and she said, "Oh Bert, I feel like I am coming home."

They stayed at the Sandviks' home until they built their own house in the fall.

Their second daughter, Bernice, was born December 6, 1929, on the sidewalk between their house

Bert and Larine Espeseth cont'd

and the Odegaards' house. Larine said everyone else was much more concerned than she was by the unexpected birth.

Larine worked for many years at Citizen's Laundry and the City Cleaners. She worked at the cannery until she was 70 years old. She then worked cleaning the Sons of Norway until she was 80.

She never owned a car and always walked everywhere she went. The Sons of Norway was an important part of her life. In her younger days, she worked at the dances, dinners, and bazaars. In her later years, she was involved with bingo and seldom missed a Saturday night. She was a trustee of the Lodge and the last of the Daughters of Norway.

Larine was also a member of the Lutheran Church and the Pioneers of Alaska.

She moved to the Sitka Pioneer's Home in November of 1990. She peacefully passed away there on September 2, 1993.

Larine and Bert's granddaughters are Rexanne Stafford, Jill Williams, and Larine MacDonald of Petersburg. Their grandsons are Bert and Karl Stedman of Sitka, and Scott Stafford of Minnesota.

The writing on the bottle reads:
L. PRYER M.D.
DRUGGIST
PETERSBURG, ALASKA

Those Were the Days!

Les Elkins proudly served the community by providing drugs and old-fashioned remedies at People's Drug Store, along with cokes and root beer at a nickel a glass. Les owned the store from 1932 to 1969, when it became Petersburg Rexall Drug.

PETERSBURG
Rexall Drug
"We treat your family as we treat our own."
On Main Street · 772-3265 · www.PetersburgRexall.com

This 1938 photo shows Les Elkins and his clerk, Goldie Severson, at the 10-stool, four-booth soda fountain.

Arvid and Bea Espeseth

By Bea Espeseth

My mother, Agnes Berg, came from Norway at the age of 16. She worked as a housemaid in New York City until she saved enough money to go to North Dakota. There she joined a cousin and both of them trained to be nurses.

My father, Albert Erickson, was born of Swedish parentage in Minnesota. He and his family moved to a homestead near Sheyenne, North Dakota, where Albert met and married Agnes.

I walked two miles to a one-room schoolhouse in a Norwegian community. All religious events took place at the Swedish Lutheran Church.

A north-south road ran by our farm. All Norwegians lived toward the east and all of Swedish descent lived toward the west.

I grew up with two brothers, one older (a tease, of course), and one six years younger, a love who had Down's Syndrome.

As my mother wished (although, by then, she was gone), and with help from my generous and loving father, I graduated from nursing school in 1943. Following two years in the service, I spent the next four years at the University of California, graduating in 1950 with a BS degree in public health nursing, and a certificate in school nursing.

As a small child, I had heard a missionary nurse speak about Alaska. So after working three years for the Santa Barbara County Health Department (where my father had a small, lovely fruit ranch), I moved to the wonderful small fishing and logging town of Petersburg, Alaska, where I worked for the next 25 years.

In 1956, I attended Lenning Varnes' 85th birthday party with Eiler Wikan, who took me to meet more of Petersburg's "older" people. There I met Arvid Espeseth, a very special man with a wonderful family. We were married two weeks later.

Arvid left Norway when it was occupied by the Germans. Until 1956, he worked in the Merchant Marines. That same year, he came to Petersburg to visit his uncles, Bert and Erling, and began his fishing career with them. He later worked with Andy Wikan.

Shortly after we were married, we purchased a lovely old home near the water. Family, friends and neighbors had a great housewarming party for us and presented us with a wall mirror measuring 40 inches by 30 inches. (It now hangs in my apartment.)

In 1958, we traveled to Norway where I visited two of my mother's sisters. More importantly, Arvid was reunited with his mother, two sisters and a brother.

Arvid and I had no children, which saddened us. He would have been a wonderful father.

In 1963, Arvid lost his life in a boating accident.

I kept the home, added an apartment in the basement, and with many friends to help, moved downstairs. I rented out the rest of the house. The last renters, Sylvia and Pete Nilsen and their children, Hannah and Matt, purchased the home in 1989.

My work as public health nurse and school nurse was expanded for 10 years to include twice-monthly trips by plane or ferry to Wrangell. I also made monthly trips to Yakutat for one year. For the last half of my working life, I fortunately had the wonderful and capable assistance of Myrtle White Skaflestad, and later Sigrid Medalen.

Physicians who specialized in chest diseases, orthopedics, and mental health held clinics at the Health Center. However, the major part of my work centered around babies, mothers (especially first-time mothers), pre-schoolers, and school children.

Harold Bergmann was very helpful with the immunization clinics at the school. Whenever I arrived, he would have all the children lined up, which I thought delightful. After a couple of years, this was all done at the Health Center.

I only had a problem with one child (who is now a scientist). I had to catch him and sit on him to carry out his parents' wishes!

All areas of work required monthly reports to the supervisory staff in Juneau. This office had a helpful and supportive staff, who visited Alaska health centers several times a year. Advice by phone was available.

The original Health Center was located in an old Indian school building. When the new city building was being planned, the city council agreed that space for the Health Center should be included. Willmer Oines was most helpful in obtaining their cooperation.

I retired in 1978 and continued to live in Petersburg for another 12 years. I traveled out of Alaska, but Petersburg's 10 feet of annual rain finally sent me to Arizona in 1990.

Nels and Mildred Evens

By John and Carol Enge

Nels Evens was the only child of Martin and Susan (Ebne) Evens. He was born June 20, 1907. His parents had met and married in Alesund, Norway, in 1906.

Martin and his brother, Bert, came to Petersburg as coopers (barrel makers) for the local sawmill. In the early days, barrels were used extensively in salting and shipping salmon to market.

In 1914, Nels and his mother joined Martin in Petersburg, moving into the new home that Martin had built on what is now known as North Nordic Drive.

Nels entered the first grade in 1914. When he was 16, Nels quit school to work at the Petersburg Packing Company cannery.

Nels has many fond memories of growing up in Petersburg. He towed a skiff behind a rowboat to Fredrick Sound, gathering glacier ice for Charlie Mann's ice cream parlor. Nels collected old bottles from the beach to sell to the junk man. He sold newspapers, and because the "Red Light District" girls often paid a dollar for the paper, he would try to be the first boy to sell to them.

By the time Nels had gathered wood and coal, and scrounged for nickels and dimes, there was little time to get into trouble. Along with the other boys, however, he found time to make a baseball field.

He started fishing halibut in 1930 with Louie Martens on the F/V *Star*. He also fished with Andrew Mathisen on the F/V *Lenor*.

Nels remembers one halibut trip they sold in Ketchikan. They were paid only two cents per pound for mediums and one cent per pound for both chickens and large. The skipper, Andrew, gave up his boat share to cover expenses.

In 1937, Nels married Mildred Cornstad in Seattle, Washington.

Nels was engineer for Sverre Johansen on the schooner *Mitkof* for six years. In 1941, he ran the F/V *Galveston* for halibut in the summer and for shark off the California coast in the winter.

In 1942, he purchased a part interest in the *Ira II* from Oscar Nicholson and rigged the boat for fishing halibut and shark.

In 1948, Nels and Mildred sold their home in Seattle and moved north to Petersburg. They bought the Andrew Johnson house on North Nordic Drive.

Nels bought the F/V *Lualda* from Alma Nicholson in 1965. He used this vessel for longlining and tendering until he turned it over to his son, Ray, in 1971. His last work was for Petersburg Fisheries on the company tender, *Viking Queen*. He retired in 1981.

Mildred passed away December 23, 1983. Nels lives at Mountain View Manor.

Grand Marshal Nels Evens and Norman Fredricksen in a Fourth of July parade

The *Ira II*
Courtesy of Ole Nordgren Family

Cliff and Helen Fenn

As told to Kathryn Sneiling

My mother, Anna Kelly, was one of seven children, five girls and two boys. My father, Louis Elkins, was one of eight children, three boys and five girls. Both Anna and Louis grew up in Kansas.

They married in 1901, and they moved to Colorado in 1907. They homesteaded 140 acres of property, three miles from Clifford, Colorado.

I was born in 1913, the sixth child of their eight children. I remember lots of tall grass and buffalo. They built a windmill and little house, putting a well on the corner of the house.

My sister Emily, the third child, was 10 months old when she was bitten by a rattlesnake. Our brother Lester went to the neighbors to get help. My Dad sliced open a chicken and put the dying bird on her arm to pull the venom out. She survived the rattlesnake's bite just fine.

My parents planted lots of cottonwood trees on the property. It was one of the few groves of trees in the area. My dad worked mainly on the Pacific Railroad, but also helped out the neighbors.

My brother Lester also went to work for the neighbors until he completed junior high school.

Later, he worked at the drugstore in Hugo, the county seat, 14 miles away.

We went to town about twice a year, traveling in a horse drawn wagon. It took about three hours each way. We would start early in the morning and return late in the evening.

One of my neighbors said my dad was a coward. When I asked Dad why, he said it was because he was afraid of the dark and whistled all the way home. He would whistle "It's a Long Way to Tipperary."

There was a small schoolhouse, right next to our property, where we went to school. It was called Evening Shades. The four older children graduated from grade school there and then attended the consolidated schools.

Helen Fenn

My three younger siblings went to Clifford School, which also was a one-room schoolhouse.

Lester went on to Denver University and became a pharmacist. Gladys and Emily, my two older sisters, went to Colorado State College in Greeley, Colorado, for two years and received teaching certificates.

I finished my freshman year of high school and then left for Denver, where I worked as a maid and nanny. I had previously met Clifford Fenn in 1931, in Hugo. He visited me in Denver nearly every weekend for the next four years. We married in 1934, in Lamar, Colorado.

My parents, accompanied by my 12-year-old brother Robert, headed for Petersburg in 1936, after giving up farming in Colorado due to the Depression. My brother Lester was already living in Petersburg. Dad and Mother worked at the oyster farm in Beecher's Pass, which my brother Lester owned.

I had other family in Petersburg. My brother Bill — or Willie, as the family called him — worked in the drug store and later worked construction. My younger sister Florence worked in the soda fountain at the drug store.

Cliff and I arrived in May, on the steamboat *Northland*, several months behind my parents. We were delayed because I had been in quarantine with a bout of scarlet fever.

In those days, most all the ships had their orchestras playing through the loud speakers, so the town folks could hear them coming from a long way off. It was usual for the town to come out to meet the ship, and my family was there to meet us.

We moved in with my brother Bill and sister Florence who lived together in the old Mann House, which was behind the hotel. It no longer is standing.

Cliff went to work on a cannery tender and I went to Beecher's Pass with Mom and Dad.

In August, Cliff and I moved into the

Cliff and Helen Fenn cont'd

Hilderbrandt House, which was next to Johnny Sales', who ran a big recreation place complete with roller skate rink. We went there for dances most Saturday nights. It is now the site of the ferry terminal.

I went to work for Myrtle Cornelius at her general merchandise store. Her twin brother, Bert, was the undertaker. The twins inherited the store and building from Mr. Hogue. The store was in the front and the morgue was in the back.

Myrtle was a nurse. She was the first nurse to work in Haines, and she rode a wagon to the native village of Klukwan to deliver babies.

In those days, it seemed that everyone (but me) spoke Norwegian, so I didn't know if they were talking about the weather or talking about the merchandise I was showing them. I worked at the Cornelius store for four years, taking time off in the summer to work in the canneries. I was paid in cash each Saturday night and had to sign a receipt for my $10.

The Great Depression was still on, so there wasn't much money.

I had worked for PAF Cannery, but I moved to Ohmer's cannery.

At the same time, I had applied for a job at the jewelry store. The Loys wanted me to start that day, but I said I needed to finish at the cannery first.

I told Dave Ohmer, my boss at the cannery, that it would be my last day. I didn't know then that when the whistle blew, the cannery would close. So, it turned out to be everyone's last day.

This was 1940. By then, Cliff was working in construction. One of the jobs was tearing up Main Street, which was built on pilings. The tide came in and out, right under the street. All you'd have to do was look down between the boards to see what the tide was doing.

Cliff also was the projector operator for the theater for two or three years. Gross had a theater in town and I don't know what the beef was, but this fellow, Shear, decided he was going to go into competition with Gross and have a better theater.

Shear built a beautiful theater he named the Variety Theater, on Sing Lee Alley. Just past it was the Sons of Norway Hall.

Each show played three nights and I would get to see every one — three times, if I wanted. There were some good movies in those days, and there were always the cartoon and newsreels before the feature.

I began working at the jewelry store on Main Street in 1940. That same year, I was called to serve on the grand jury, which meant going to Juneau. Cliff was a cop, another job he held for a time, and a witness for one of the cases. We lived at Juneau's Baranof Hotel for a month, high on the hog, but the hours serving on the jury were long.

In 1943, Cliff was working for the Forest Service, but he quit in order to join the U.S. Army Transport

Helen's parents, Anna and Louis Elkins, at Beecher's Pass

Service. He was assigned to the tugboat *Sandra Foss*, hauling supplies and men between Seattle and Skagway. Our daughter, Sandra, had just been born. Because Cliff was skipper, he could stop in at Petersburg to see the baby.

He later was moved to the Aleutians for a time and then to Seattle. He stayed with the A.T.S. until the war ended.

While I was in the hospital having Sandra, the Loys offered to sell me the jewelry store for $1,200. Well, we didn't have that kind of money; that was a lot of money back then. They hired me back at $1 an hour.

I took Sandra to the store with me in a wicker pram until she was three months old. By then, she was climbing around and wouldn't stay in the buggy. Dorothy Iverson, who was a nurse's aide, watched Sandra for the next two years.

After the war, Cliff went to work for the Corps of Engineers, dredging Wrangell Narrows.

I joined the Eastern Star in 1937. I went through

Cliff and Helen Fenn cont'd

the chairs and was Matron in 1944. While Matron, I initiated my mother into our chapter. I joined the Emblem Club in 1940. Petersburg's was the first Emblem Club in Alaska. I was number eight on its membership list. By that time, I had Ken, my son, and was too occupied to go through the chairs in two clubs.

Helen Fenn

In 1945, I joined the American Legion Auxiliary under my brother, Robert. My boss, Marie Loy, said we could be delegates to the American Legion Auxiliary Convention in Anchorage. I suggested we include a trip down the Yukon and she agreed. We left the store with the other helper, Cal Ballard, and the two of us made the trip.

We flew to Juneau on an Ellis Airlines Grumman Goose. From Juneau, we took the *Estebeth* to Skagway where we were houseguests at the Kermisies. Next, we took the train from Skagway to Whitehorse. From there, we rode the paddle wheel, steam engine riverboat from Whitehorse to Dawson City. That was as far as the boat went.

We flew back to Whitehorse, changed to another plane for Fairbanks, and took the bus from there to Anchorage. It was a terrific convention.

For the Fourth of July, we went on a picnic by Lake Spenard, which was way out in the country then. It was the first time I had ever seen an airplane pulling people on water skis.

After the convention, I flew to Seward, where my sister Florence lived. Marie came down by bus a couple of days later.

I think we took the *Aleutian* back to Juneau and then the *Alaska* back to Petersburg.

Mother and Dad lived at Beecher's Pass until 1942. They went back to Colorado for a year, because of World War II. When they returned, they lived in West Petersburg.

After Mother had a heart attack, they moved into Lester's float house, which was next to the ferry terminal. Mother had another heart attack and passed on in 1957.

Dad moved into a cabin next to Lester's, and he lived there until he passed away in 1961. Both of my parents are buried in Petersburg.

My brother Lester is also buried in Petersburg.

My brother Robert grew up in Petersburg and joined the U.S. Coast Guard. He married Virginia File. He died in 1966 in Albuquerque, New Mexico, and is buried in the National Cemetery in Santa Fe.

Of all my brothers and sisters, I am the only one left. Except for my sister Gladys, everyone in the Elkins family came to Alaska, either to live or visit, at one time or another.

Our daughter, Sandra, married Ronald Martin. Their son, Chad, married Sue Diedrich. Their son, Shane, married Sandy McCoy. Shane and Sandy have daughters Abby, Rosie and Magge.

Our son, Kenneth, married Denelle Michael. Their son, Kenneth Jr., married Kristine MacHaud. Kenneth and Kristine have a son, Andrew, and two daughters, Julie and Michelle. Michelle married Dave Julian and they have a son, Chase.

Cliff passed away in 1970 and is buried in the Masonic Cemetery in Juneau.

I moved in and out of the Alaska Pioneer's Home in Sitka over the years.

Although I am now settled in at the Home, I take an occasional trip to visit family.

Francisco and Pauline Fernandez

By Jeanette Ness

Francisco "Frank" Villaver Fernandez was born April 2, 1911, in Talisay, Cebu, Philippines. He came to the United States to be with his brother Zoilo, in 1932, traveling steerage on the steamship *Harding*. The vessel left the Philippines, stopped in Japan and Hawaii, and eventually docked at Angel Island, in San Francisco, California, several months later.

Frank worked in Hollywood for a while as a butler for a rich and famous actress. She got him a job as an extra in a couple of movies, including "The Good Earth."

Frank eventually worked seasonally in Alaska with his brother at George Inlet, returning in the off-season to Hollywood to work for MGM Grand. He did this until he was inducted into the Army on July 9, 1942.

Frank served in the South Pacific, fighting in New Guinea and the Philippines, for the duration of the war. While stationed in Luzon, he was assigned to be the houseboy for General Douglas McArthur.

He was discharged February 24, 1946. For his four years of service, he earned $299.96!

After returning to Hollywood, Frank decided to head back to Alaska in late 1947. He lived in Anchorage, working as a baggage handler for Alaska Railroads. He then headed down to Juneau, where he landed a job with Alaska Coastal Airlines. There he met his wife.

Pauline Martin was born May 1, 1926 in Tenakee, Alaska. She originated from X'aakw Hit, the Sockeye House, of the Tak dein taan Clan. Her Tlingit name was Kaash K'aani.

She lived much of her young life in Glacier Bay where she practiced the subsistence way of life. Her family recalls her many stories about berry picking.

Frank worked at Pacific American Fisheries (PAF) and Pauline worked at the Public Cold Storage.

Along with raising their children, Francisco Jr., Jeanette, and Bernard, they became involved in community activities. Pauline was active in the VFW Auxiliary and the American Legion Auxiliary. Both Pauline and Frank became very involved with the local Moose Lodge. Pauline worked for the Election Board and, for many years, was a voter registrar.

Pauline Fernandez

Some of Pauline's fondest memories were those of filleting halibut at the Little Norway Pageant. She did this for many years, impressing the crowd with her skill at fletching the monstrous halibut. She always enjoyed the sometimes-hilarious comments made by the tourists.

Frank and Pauline had many lasting friendships that developed from their employment at the cannery. They were able to travel to the Philippines in 1975, and again in 1979.

Frank died October 11, 1981. Pauline continued working at the cold storage until 1986. She was able to spend time with her grandchildren and shared her stories and wisdom until her passing September 1, 1995.

Both Frank and Pauline were always very generous with their families and friends. Pauline was "Mom" to many members of the community. No one was ever turned away from their door. Frank and Pauline will always be remembered for their quiet sense of humor and the many fine meals they shared with all.

Francisco Fernandez

Claude and Elizabeth File

By Fred File

In July of 1941, Claude and Elizabeth (Murray) File, accompanied by the younger 10 of their 12 children, limped into Petersburg, Alaska, aboard their 30-foot cabin cruiser, the *Walloping Window Blind*.

Claude was born in 1894, in Greenville, Illinois. Elizabeth was born in 1893, in Richmond, Missouri. Their ancestors included Johannes Pieter Pfeil, who immigrated to Philadelphia, in 1741, from Germany; and William Gunnel, who immigrated to Jamestown, Virginia, in 1650, from England.

Both Claude's and Elizabeth's families were farming near Richmond, Missouri, where they married in 1915.

Claude and Elizabeth had 13 children; one later died of diphtheria.

In the mid-1930s, while the family was living in the coal-mining region of Peoria County, Illinois, news of available land in the Matanuska Valley of Alaska came to the destitute farmers in the Midwest. Because he was employed and not destitute, Claude did not qualify for a federal subsidy. Nonetheless, he wanted to homestead in Alaska.

Claude and Elizabeth packed up the family (except for the oldest daughter who was attending college) and, in two automobiles and a utility trailer, headed west in 1938.

The family settled temporarily in the Puyallup Valley of western Washington, where they were employed in farming. Claude studied boat building at the Tacoma City Library and commenced building a 30-foot cabin boat. In June 1941, the family departed from Tacoma for Skagway, Alaska.

Having no previous boating experience, and knowing there were probably some bugs to work out on the boat, Claude was careful, traveling only in

Robert, Fred, Claude Jr., Jacob, Claude, Elizabeth and Amy File

daylight and good weather. The frequent stops made for an interesting and enjoyable trip.

Engine problems occurred about 30 miles south of Petersburg that required a tow into town by a passing fishing vessel.

The family stayed in Petersburg for two years. Everyone found work or attended school. During the spring of 1943, the File family (minus six of the older children, who were committed to military service, marriage or further education) departed Petersburg for the interior of Alaska.

Claude File passed away in 1980. His ashes were scattered in the Gulf of Alaska by his son John File, captain of the tanker *Mobil Meridian*.

Elizabeth File went to her reward in 1994, her ashes interred in her family graveyard at her place of birth in Missouri.

Claude and Elizabeth have two sons, four grandchildren, and nine great-grandchildren currently living in Petersburg.

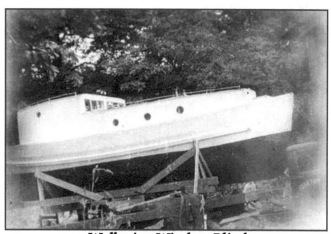

Walloping Window Blind

Knute and Dorothy Fredricksen

By Norman and Lynda Fredricksen

Goodwin Fredricksen was born February 14, 1916, in Langley, Washington, to Fredrick and Gustus Fredricksen. He was the youngest of five children. He had one sister, Mildred, and three brothers, Andy, Alvin, and Walter.

Fredrick and Gustus had come to the United States from Norway. Fredrick was granted citizenship in Minnesota in July 1900.

Goodwin was known as Knute, rather than by his given name.

Knute came to Alaska in 1937. He and his brothers, Andy and Alvin, were lifelong commercial fishermen in the area. In Petersburg he met and married Dorothy Olsen, the daughter of Anna Samuelson Olsen and Christ Olsen.

Dorothy's father, Christ, was born in Norway in 1886. He was the older brother of Jack Olsen of Petersburg. Christ moved to Juneau where he lived until his death in 1967.

Dorothy's mother, Anna, was born in Chicago in 1895. Anna had a son from a previous marriage, Rudolph Adolph Williams, who was born in 1915, in Beaverton, Oregon.

Anna and Christ were divorced. She then married Connie Jacobsen. They lived in the house located south of Petro Marine (formerly Standard Oil), now occupied by Dick Kuwata.

After Connie Jacobsen's death, Anna married Olaf Dahl in 1944. When Olaf had a stroke, they moved to Bellevue, Washington, where they lived until his death in 1957.

Anna moved to Seattle's Ballard neighborhood, where she met her fifth husband, Lloyd Brown. She and Lloyd were married for six years.

Following that divorce, Anna spent many summers back in Petersburg, visiting Dorothy and Knute, her grandsons, and their families.

Dorothy worked as a waitress at the City Café, until she and Knute were married in 1938. After their marriage, Dorothy was a housewife. She kept busy with her three sons, Arnold, Norman and Robert.

Dorothy loved to cook and was known to be a great baker. She had a fondness for Norwegian cookies and always had a tin of cookies on hand whenever family and friends stopped by.

Fish cakes and fish pudding were favorites of the family. A tradition was started when the grandchildren found cans of fish pudding in the toes of their Christmas stockings.

Knute fished with Leonard Martens aboard the *Louie M* and Andy Wikan on the *Pacific Sea*. Walt Hofstad was another skipper he fished with.

Goodwin "Knute" and Dorothy Fredricksen

Knute was well liked and respected by all of his fellow fishermen. Winters often found him working part-time as a police officer, at Mitkof Lumber, or at Standard Oil. He enjoyed carpentry work, hunting and, of course, fishing.

After Knute retired from fishing, he and Dorothy enjoyed traveling to Ballard to spend their winter months. They were married for 60 years.

While in Ballard, Knute passed away in 1998. Dorothy passed away in 2000. Both are laid to rest in the Petersburg Cemetery next to their son Robert.

Knute and Dorothy's son Arnold is married to Sue Randrup. They have four children: Cris, Debra, Cean and Kevin.

Arnold worked at Sanitary Market, White's Shopping Center, Standard Oil, tried his hand at retail in the grocery business, and worked at Petersburg Motors for his brother, Norman, until his retirement. He was a volunteer fireman with the local fire

Knute and Dorothy Fredricksen cont'd

department for 30 years.

Like his folks, Arnold will become a "snowbird," traveling to his new home in Bullhead City, Arizona, during the winters. He has been blessed with seven grandchildren and one great-grandson.

Norman married Lynda Torwick. They have two sons, Kurt and Scott. They purchased Petersburg Motors from Barney White in 1968. As of 2003, they are still running the business.

Their youngest son, Scott, works with them and is next in line to be the "boss." Scott has one daughter, Courtney.

Norman and Lynda's son Kurt and his wife, Debbie, live and work in Ketchikan, Alaska. They have four children: Martina, Shelby, Bryce and Rosie.

Norman was active in the volunteer fire department for 30 years. He served as chief for the last 11 years, until his retirement from the fire department in 1993.

Lynda has been bookkeeper for the family business. In her leisure time, she enjoys the art of rosemaling, quilting, gardening, and, most importantly, being a grandma.

Robert never married. He started working with diesel generators at the City of Petersburg after high school graduation. After further training, he was able to travel and work in Afghanistan, Saudi Arabia, Greenland, Egypt, the Marshall Islands, Johnson Island, and the Antarctic.

Robert returned stateside in 1988 and settled in the Seattle area. He passed away in 1991, at the age of 46, from complications with pneumonia.

Front, from left, Robert, Lynda and Dorothy Fredricksen
Back row, Norman, Arnold and Knute

Petersburg Motors, Inc.
2nd & Haugen Drive

Serving the community since 1945

Automotive Parts & Repair
Gas — Diesel — Wrecker Service

Honda Marine Sales & Service
Honda Power Products

772-3223

Norman & Lynda Fredricksen
Owners & Operators since 1968

Marion and Geraldine Frink

By Carol Enge

Gerry Hildebrand Frink proved that the life of a pioneer in Alaska could be an exciting adventure.

Gregory John "Greg" and Pearl Hildebrand arrived in Petersburg on a houseboat, July 2, 1918, from Olympia, Washington. Accompanying them were their two daughters, Jewel and Geraldine "Gerry."

Greg began work with Bob Allen on the floating machine shop, currently located on the Ocean Beauty dock. Bob Allen's wife was Greg Hildebrand's niece. Gerry attended school in Petersburg before entering high school in Olympia.

In 1921, Greg and Pearl started fox farming on Fair Island in Beecher's Pass. That same year, Gerry married Howard Conn. They had one son, Howard. This marriage ended.

Marion Frink came to Alaska and worked on mail boats out of Ketchikan. Marion and Gerry were married in 1930. Marion had a son, Leslie, by a previous marriage. Marion, Gerry, and their two boys lived on a float house that was positioned about where the present Petersburg ferry terminal is located.

Marion and Gerry started working with her parents on the fox farm and, with a small boat with a 20-foot trawl, began shrimping to provide fox feed and income. Later, Marion bought the *Patsy*, which he used to seine salmon in the late 1940s. He also fished the *Bernice*, a boat built in 1912 for Joe Kildall. Built in Petersburg, it was one of three Kildall boats, each one named for a daughter of John Kildall.

By this time, the fox farm had been abandoned, and the Hildebrand house was moved from Fair Island to Petersburg. Marion and Gerry made their home in this house, located next to the present-day cable television office.

They bought the *Bernice A*, which they ran until they retired. With the *Bernice A*, Marion and Gerry shrimped and packed salmon in the summer.

Gerry was the first woman in the area to run a boat. She was equal to any man in boat handling and dragging for shrimp. She and Marion were a premier shrimp fishing team.

Both of their sons, Leslie Frink and Harold Conn, left Petersburg during World War II to serve in the military. Leslie, however, did not return. He was killed at Guadalcanal. The local Veterans of Foreign Wars' post is named in his honor. Howard married Darlyne Nicholson.

Gerry and Marion Frink with their first mate, Bimbo

Marion passed away about 1980.

Gerry was an active member of the Moose Lodge and served for years as secretary of the Pioneers. She attended many Pioneer conventions where she is still remembered for her love of dancing.

She continued to live in the family home until she entered Petersburg's extended-care facility. Gerry died on January 19, 2002.

Forrest and Christine Fryer

By Don Nelson

Originally from Canada, Forrest and Steve Fryer arrived in Petersburg in the early 1920s.

Both were machinists and were hired by the Petersburg Packing Company.

Forrest ran a cannery machine shop, located at the current location of Hammer and Wikan Hardware.

In 1925, Forrest built his own machine shop on the lower side of Main Street, across from the foot of Dolphin Street. His family lived upstairs in an apartment.

He named the business Fryer Machine Works and it was Petersburg's main machine shop and auto repair service for about 40 years.

Forrest Fryer was a dealer for Standard Oil products, Ford automobiles, and General Motors marine diesel engines. The firm had two Standard gasoline pumps and a Ford dealership showroom on Main Street.

Behind the machine shop, there was a small dock with a hoist and gridiron for boats that was parallel to the old Trading Union float.

Today this location is storage for Petersburg Fisheries.

Forrest and Christine Fryer had five children: Patricia, who married a Concannon and moved to Portland; Beatrice, who married Earl Fosse and moved to Ketchikan; Frances, who was born about 1923; Forrest Jr., who was born in 1930; and Vera, who was born in 1932 and passed away sometime in the late 1950s in California.

Forrest "Mort" Fryer Jr. married, had a family and remained in Petersburg. He was very active in Little League Baseball.

Mort had health complications and developed diabetes at an early age. By the time he died in the early 1980s, he had had both legs amputated.

The baseball complex at the end of Excel Street is named the Mort Fryer Memorial Park.

Christine Fryer was a longtime librarian for Petersburg. Both Forrest and Christine were active in the Eastern Star organization.

Around 1930, Steve Fryer, who had come to Petersburg with his brother Forrest, died of a ruptured appendix at an early age.

Forrest Fryer died in the mid 1960s, and his wife lived to a much-advanced age.

When Fryer Machine went out of business, the big lather drill press and other shop equipment were bought by Petersburg Fisheries and are still in use.

The Fryer Machine Works building was demolished in the 1980s and is now the fenced-in storage lot next to the Glacier Laundromat.

Main Street
Petersburg, Alaska
circa late 1930s

Erik and Marit Fuglvog

By Harold and Lynn Fuglvog

Erik Alfred Fuglvog was born September 21, 1898, in Tustna, Norway, to Johannes and Beret Fuglvog. He was one of nine brothers and sisters and was the last to pass away.

During his early years, he worked on the farm and attended school in Tustna. He was baptized and confirmed in the Gullstein Lutheran Church. He was an excellent hunter and marksman and won several shooting trophies for his rifle skills.

Starting his commercial fishing career in Norway at an early age, Erik fished herring around Iceland on large steamers. He then fished with his own boat off the coast of Norway. In 1918, he served in the Norwegian Army for the mandatory service time of one year.

He immigrated to the United States in 1924. He worked in the Petersburg sawmill for a short time before starting fishing. He fished for a number of years on boats from Petersburg: the *Betty*, the *Middleton* and the older *Mitkof*. During this period, he purchased the Martin Enge house, now owned and occupied by Karen and Shane Drollinger.

Marit Hundhammer was born April 10, 1907, to Hans and Mathea Hundhammer. She was one of seven children. The Hundhammer farm is along the fjord shore on the island of Ertvaagoya in the Tustna commune near Kristiansund, Norway.

As a young woman, she became engaged to her neighbor and sweetheart, Erik Fuglvog. After becoming successful in the commercial fishing industry in Alaska and purchasing his home in Petersburg, Erik asked Marit to join him.

Leaving her family and home in Norway was a very difficult decision for Marit to make, but at age 22, she departed for Alaska.

The journey from Norway to Petersburg was a great adventure for this young lady. Speaking no English, she traveled across the Atlantic and Canada by herself. Marit arrived in Halifax, Nova Scotia, in December of 1929.

Marit was detained there for several days until her American sponsor, John Hammer of Petersburg, could be confirmed by telegraph. As a young boy in Norway, John Hammer had spent several years on the Hundhammer farm.

Erik also contacted the Norwegian consul, informing him that he too would sponsor Marit. It was only then that she was permitted to board the train for her trip across Canada to join her fiancé.

Upon arriving in Prince Rupert, British Columbia, Marit contacted John Hammer. He and Erik took the steamship *Zapora* to Prince Rupert.

Marit Fuglvog and baby Edwin

On December 23, 1929, Marit and Erik were married in Prince Rupert by the Lutheran pastor at the home of the brother of the Norwegian consul. Erik quickly returned to Petersburg to fish, and the young bride remained in Prince Rupert to process her immigration papers.

Years later, Marit mentioned that if she had known beforehand just how difficult her first few years in Petersburg would be, or how homesick she would get, perhaps she would have thought twice about leaving Norway.

In 1930, Erik purchased the F/V *Bravo* and fished it until he had the F/V *Balder* built in 1940, in Petersburg by Lars Westre. Erik rigged the boat for seining, as well as longlining.

A special bunk was built for crewman Gordon Jensen, who was six feet, seven inches tall. Another of

Erik and Marit Fuglvog cont'd

Erik's crewmen was Oscar Wikan, known by some as the Deacon. He fished on the *Balder* for many years.

One day Oscar came to visit Erik at his home. Marit greeted him at the door and called to Erik upstairs, "The Deacon is here to visit." Thinking that it was the minister, Erik greeted Oscar, all dressed up in a suit, tie, and dress shoes. Oscar said that Erik's dressing up for him "was really not necessary."

In 1949, Erik had the experienced Leo Ness skipper the *Balder* for the bumper salmon season. Erik was aboard as a deck hand. During one of the sets, Erik was clearing the cork line when the seine table, which was used in those days, pivoted and threw him overboard. He managed to grab the cork line in the water and held on. Leo saw that Erik was okay, so he continued to complete the set. Once the set was established, Erik was picked up by the seine skiff. He was in good shape with no hypothermia symptoms.

Erik and Marit had two sons: Edwin born in 1931, and Harold born in 1932.

When not taking care of her two boys, Marit enjoyed working in the local salmon cannery during the summer salmon season, and working as a volunteer at the local Charity Box.

She liked to travel. When staying in the Seattle area, she took car trips to interesting places.

Marit had very quick hands and was able to needlepoint and crochet with ease.

Marit and Erik became members of the Petersburg Lutheran Church in December 1935. Marit was an active member of the church, a charter member of the Sons of Norway, and a member of both the Hospital Guild and Pioneers of Alaska.

Marit welcomed the neighborhood children with treats of candy and cookies. She liked to garden and had many interesting plants around her house.

After 55 years as a commercial fisherman, in 1970, Erik retired. His son Edwin skippered the *Balder* for a short time in the late 1960s. This boat was purchased by Walter Hofstad in the early 1970s, and later sold to a Seattle fisherman. The *Balder* is now being used as a crab boat out of Newport, Oregon.

Erik continued fishing by himself on a small scale for a number of years with a seine skiff. It was rigged with a hydraulic reel and conventional halibut longline gear. One day in Frederick Sound near Thomas Bay, he caught a record 406-pound halibut. His grandson, Arne, was along at the time.

Erik was a member of the Pioneers of Alaska and a lifetime member of the Sons of Norway.

Erik Fuglvog

He and Marit made several trips back to Norway over the years. Their first trip was in 1947 with sons Edwin and Harold. Most every year they spent several months visiting in the Seattle area.

Erik passed away March 5, 1986, in Petersburg. He is remembered as an honest and hardworking fisherman.

Marit lived in the Fuglvog family home for 63 years. She was like a grandmother to many of the neighborhood children.

She passed away July 4, 1993. Marit will always be remembered for her friendly smile and great sense of humor.

Erik and Marit's son Edwin married Mildred

Erik and Marit Fuglvog cont'd

Harvey. Their two children, Arne and Karen, live in Petersburg with their families.

Arne is married to Cindy Carr. Their children are Brannon and Cub Finney. Karen is married to Shane Drollinger. They have three children: Kaitlyn, Stuart and Kassidi. Both Arne and Shane skipper fishing boats out of Petersburg, the *Mitkof* and the *Kamilar*.

Son Harold married Lynne O'Hare, who also grew up in Petersburg.

Lynne's parents are Jim and Lucille O'Hare. They managed the Petersburg movie theater in the early 1950s, until Jim passed away.

Lucille later married William "Johnny" Johnson, who worked for the Petersburg Press. In the late 1950s and 1960s, he worked in the clothing department of The Trading Union.

For several years, Lucille worked for the City of Petersburg, with Jim Taylor, until she and Johnny left to live in Issaquah, Washington. Lucille continues to live there, close to daughter Lynne.

Harold Fuglvog spent several years during the summer fishing with his father on the *Balder* and on other commercial fishing boats. Following his two-year military service, Harold continued his education and obtained a BS degree in aeronautical engineering. As an engineer at Boeing and other companies, he worked on the Moon Saturn S IVB program, Mars Lander, and other interesting aerospace programs. He also spent many years conducting test operations on new and developmental airplanes.

Harold and Lynne have three children: Laurie, Heidi and Erik.

Laurie is married to John Mayenburg. They live in Juneau and both work for the State of Alaska.

Heidi married Edward Hines and they have two children, Erik and Julia. Heidi and Edward live in Enumclaw, Washington. Both work for Alaska Airlines.

Erik married Jennell Bona. They live in Duvall, Washington. Erik works for Delta Airlines and Jannell works for Allstate Insurance Company.

Cast of the "Ice Palace," the 1960 film shot on location in Petersburg.
It starred Richard Burton, Robert Ryan, Jim Backus and Carolyn Jones.

Ed and Mildred Fuglvog

By Mildred Fuglvog

Edwin Fuglvog was born in Petersburg, Alaska, January 31, 1931. He is the son of Erik and Marit Fuglvog of Petersburg. He has one brother, Harold, of Issaquah, Washington.

Ed started fishing with his father on the *Balder* when he was 16. He could have started earlier. But because he refused to cook, his brother got the job. Ed thoroughly enjoyed fishing and continued doing it throughout his life.

He completed school in Petersburg and went to Washington State University for one year before going into the Army.

During this time, Ed became interested in amateur radio. Enjoying this hobby immensely, he later got his wife, son, and many others actively involved. His call sign, KL7DYS, is known to many people around the world.

He studied electronics at Oregon Technical Institute for two years, and spent his summers fishing. During this time he met Mildred Harvey of Marysville, Washington. They were married in 1956.

Mildred attended school at Everett Community College and the University of Washington, graduating with a degree in medical technology.

Ed returned to college in Bellingham and became a teacher. Again, summers were spent fishing.

He taught school in Petersburg for five years. After deciding to go into fishing full time, Ed bought the F/V *Symphony*. During his spare time, he taught sea education classes aboard his boat to interested high school students.

Besides raising their two children, Arne and Karen, Mildred worked part time as a medical technologist at Petersburg's hospital.

Ed purchased the F/V *Karen Marie* and, still later, had the F/V *Kamilar* built. Although he fished for all species, Ed most enjoyed longlining for halibut and blackcod. The 2001 blackcod fishery was his 55th season.

Ed always wanted to fly. At age 64, he followed through on a lifelong dream. He took flying lessons and obtained his private pilot license. After purchasing a Cessna 182, he continued to learn as much as possible about flying and soon obtained his seaplane and instrument ratings. Ed and Mildred flew on many trips.

Mildred has always enjoyed sewing, but her favorite hobbies involved the outdoors. She skied, kayaked and biked.

Ed was a member of Petersburg Lutheran Church,

Front, left to right: Cub Finney, Ed Fuglvog, Cassidy Drollinger, Mildred Fuglvog, Stuart Drollinger and Kaitlyn Drollinger. Back: Arne Fuglvog, Cynthia Carr, Brannon Finney, Karen Marie Drollinger and Shane Drollinger.

Sons of Norway Lodge, Pioneers of Alaska, Petersburg Elks Club, and Petersburg Amateur Radio Club. He served on the city council, the Petersburg Lutheran Church Council, the Advisory Panel to the North Pacific Fishery Management Council, the Petersburg Vessel Owners Association, and the Conference Board of the International Pacific Halibut Commission.

Ed died at home, in Petersburg, October 24, 2002.

Ed and Mildred's two children and five grandchildren all reside in Petersburg.

Their daughter, Karen Marie, is married to Shane Drollinger. They have three children: Kaitlyn, Stuart, and Kassidi.

Their son, Ame, is married to Cynthia Carr. Their children are Brannon Finney and Cub Finney.

Andrew and Zella Greinier

By Carol Enge

William Tell Greinier and his wife, Daisy Gray Greinier, followed the migration to the Alaska Territory in the early 1900s.

The Greinier family first came to Burnett Inlet cannery, south of Wrangell, where William had found employment.

They moved to Scow Bay and lived at the site of Warren "Frog" Burrell's current home.

In 1918, their youngest son, Andrew, was born.

Scow Bay was named for a fish fertilizer plant. Andrew worked in this plant, straining oil that was squeezed from the press. He earned $1 a day.

Andrew walked to the one-room school that was located in Mitkof Lumber's present location.

The road to Petersburg was built when Andrew was in the fourth grade. It was a crooked road because the tree stumps weren't pulled out; the road just went around them.

The Greinier family moved to Petersburg after their house burned down. William died soon after due to complications resulting from smoke inhalation during the fire.

Daisy later remarried. Both William and Daisy are buried at Petersburg's cemetery.

Andrew made his first fishing trip for shrimp at age 14. Throughout the years, he fished on halibut boats in the Gulf and shrimped for Clyde Sheldon in the winter.

Zella Drake was born September 20, 1914, in Endicott, Washington. Her mother was a cook, and Zella grew up working in a restaurant.

After high school graduation, Zella enrolled in a business school in Spokane. Following her graduation, she worked for the Air Force in Auburn, Washington.

While her brother, Lee, was serving in the Coast Guard in Petersburg, Zella received word that he was missing. She asked for a 30-day leave to go to Alaska to find out about him. Her request was refused on the grounds that she was needed at her job.

Zella quit and went to Petersburg. She found out that her brother had fallen overboard and got caught in a crab trap.

Zella remained in Petersburg. She worked in the Scow Bay cannery and at the Fur Farm.

She met Andrew Greinier at the Bucket of Blood. They were married in 1948.

Zella joined Andrew fishing. She laughs today about her experiences learning to shrimp. Andrew was a patient skipper and they fished together on the F/V *Bernice A* for 26 years.

Fishing provided an enjoyable lifestyle. It wasn't all work. There was time to anchor up with friends, go beachcombing, clam digging, and to enjoy this beautiful land she calls home.

Zella vividly recalls the 1964 earthquake and its devastating effect on the Thomas Bay shrimp grounds.

It had been their best fishing area; but, since 1964, it never again produced the same quantity of shrimp. She recalled the banks caved in and dirt filled the bay.

Through the years, Zella worked at Winnie's Café, owned by Winnie Gray, Andrew's sister. She also worked for Pat Ridley, preparing tax returns.

Andrew and Zella retired from fishing in 1979. They enjoyed many leisurely years in their home on Haugen Drive. They traveled to Washington State to visit friends and made a trip to Hawaii and Australia.

Andrew died December 19, 1993.

In the years that followed, Zella made trips to Mexico and took cruises on the Columbia and Mississippi rivers. She now resides quietly in her comfortable apartment at Totem Arms.

Swimming at Sandy Beach

Bill and Barbara Greinier

By Carol Enge

William Arthur Greinier Jr. was born in Petersburg on January 18, 1933. He's the third generation Greinier to live in Petersburg.

His grandfather was William Tell Greinier and his father was William Arthur Greinier Sr.

Bill Jr.'s great uncle Bill Dunkelberger was an early shrimp fisherman and was responsible for getting the three Greiner brothers, William Arthur Sr., Ross and Andrew, into shrimping.

Bill worked in his aunt Winnie Gray's restaurant during his teen years washing dishes, clearing tables and anything else that needed to be done. This was good experience for his later career as a chef.

In 1952, he was drafted into the Army and served 21 months at Fort Richardson. He returned home and returned to work for his Aunt Winnie.

Barbara Harris was born on August 31, 1940, in Petersburg, to Hugh and Alice (Anderson) Harris.

As a teenager, Barbara had different jobs. She remembers working at Al's Place, which was an ice cream parlor, for three different owners. She later worked at Winnie Gray's restaurant. It was there she met Bill Greinier.

She and Bill were married September 5, 1959. Their daughter, Cindy, was born in 1960. Their son Joe was born in 1962.

The Greiniers moved to Wrangell in 1964. There Bill worked for Winnie, who had opened up a new restaurant. Their son Andy was born the same year.

The Greiniers returned to Petersburg in 1971, and Bill began fishing. He ran the *Charles W* for many years, beam trawling for shrimp in Southeast Alaskan waters. Bill has many stories to tell about his experiences.

He once received a phone call from a Californian who asked if he and his son could make a trip with Bill on the *Charles W*. The man requested a specific day and Bill agreed.

After the man and his son arrived in Petersburg, they immediately went aboard the *Charles W*. Swinging his leg over the rail, the man shared the sentiment that it was 50 years to the day that he had last stood on the *Charles W*.

This gentleman from California had fished with Bill Dunkelberger, Bill's great uncle, on the *Charles W*.

During one winter, money was short and the man and Bill Dunkelberger lived at Five Mile Creek, living off "out-of-season" ducks. One morning as they were

Beam trawling for shrimp near Petersburg, September 17, 1937
Photo by Sean Linehan courtesy of the National Oceanic and Atmospheric Administration/Department of Commerce

hunting, a Fish and Wildlife agent came out of the woods and arrested them. Because the weather was down to zero and they were out of provisions, they didn't mind spending the next 90 days in jail!

Barbara worked at The Trading Union, Hammer & Wikan, and the drug store. She and Bill catered many festive occasions for friends.

In 2001, Bill retired from fishing and had back surgery. They still live in their Wrangell Avenue home.

By Bill and Barbara's count, six generations of Greiniers have skippered, crewed or cruised on the *Charles W*.

Chris and Petra Gronseth

By Justine Morrell

My father, Kristian Toresen Gronset (known as Chris Gronseth), was born in Kristiansund, Norway, on November 27, 1883.

His two brothers were schoolteachers and later became principals. Dad did not want to be a teacher, so he went to a trade school instead. He was asked to teach at the trade school, but decided instead to come to America.

Dad and two friends arrived in San Francisco three weeks before the 1906 earthquake and fire.

The first floor of their rented house fell into the basement during the quake. They had to climb out of a window to get out. They walked around town, unable to speak English.

Getting hungry, they came across a partially destroyed butcher shop and found a ham to eat. Later, they found their way down to the waterfront.

After some time, still hungry, Dad found a soup kitchen. He told me that when the lady handed him a bowl of soup, he felt like she had saved his life.

Dad found a whaling ship that was heading for the Bering Sea and was taken aboard. He was thankful to leave San Francisco after that terrible disaster.

Returning to the Lower 48, he stayed in Washington and went to Parkland College. There he learned to speak, read and write English.

While Dad was in Washington, he also worked in a logging camp. He was hired as a blacksmith's helper, which became his lifelong trade. There, Dad invented the universal swivel, which turned hoisted logs around, as needed. Sadly, he never took out a patent for it.

After five years in Washington, he took a trip back to Norway, before heading to Alaska. He had a boat built and named it the *Fosna*, after a place in Norway.

Dad arrived in Petersburg in 1912. He joined the Sons of Norway and sang soprano in their choral group.

He went logging for a while in 1913, with Erick Ness. This is where he met my mother, Petra Wanberg.

Mother came from Adesund, Norway, to visit her brother, Joaquim "Jack" Wanberg, who worked at the same logging camp as my father. She later worked in Seattle, while going to night school to learn English.

Mother and Dad were married in Seattle in 1918. Jacob and Esther Johnson stood up for them.

Returning to Petersburg, Dad eventually began his plumbing, blacksmith and tinsmith business. He also made gaff hooks for the stores.

He was a craftsman and made sleds, skis, and a sleigh that is still being used in Petersburg. I remember my mother using it for me.

My mother, Petra, was a homemaker and a great cook. She and Dad always invited bachelor friends for Thanksgiving. One year they also included Bob and Daisy Campbell, who lived on Castle Island. They had the job of tending the buoys and lights in the Narrows.

Chris and Petra Gronseth

I remember being surprised when Mrs. Daisy Campbell walked in wearing an outdated dress. No one had ever seen her in a dress, as she wore knickers all the time.

We had some wonderful trips, fishing and hunting. Mother and I once caught 40 trout at Castle River.

I graduated from Petersburg High School in 1942, and I then attended business college in Seattle.

I also worked at PAF and ran the casing machine. The first year I earned 35¢ per hour.

Two years later, in 1944, I married Mervin Clover. He was stationed at Ketchikan's coast guard base. After the war, we moved to Woodland, California.

We later moved back to Petersburg, where Mervin was manager of the first employment office in town. Five years later we returned to Woodland.

In 1946, Mother died of pernicious anemia. Eventually, Dad lived in California with us. He passed away at age 86, and is buried in Alaska near Mother. Mervin, 49, passed away four days before Dad.

Mervin and I have three children, Jana, Gerri and Murray. We also have five grandchildren and three great-grandchildren. Our son, Murray, died at 23.

I later married Al Morrell, who died in 1994.

Jacob and Gertrude Hallingstad

By John Enge, with Casper Jr. and Jonas Hallingstad

Jacob and Gertrude Hallingstad and their 6-year-old son, Casper, came to the United States from their native Norway in 1906.

They first settled on a farm in Nebraska, but times were tough in the Midwest. Four more children were added to the family at this time: Magna "Maggie," Gertrude, Jake, and Jonas.

A second cousin, Ed Nilson, informed the Hallingstads of the big money to be made in Alaska, so Gertrude held an auction to sell the farm.

Packing up the children and their belongings, they traveled by train to Seattle, where they boarded the S/S *Jefferson*. Adult fare to Petersburg was $18.

Ed Nilson helped Jacob build their first home on Lumber Street; it is still standing today.

Jacob fished halibut out of a dory, and Gertrude ran a restaurant in the Enge building. Jacob's first powerboat was the F/V *Alpha*.

In 1926, they moved to Point Agassiz to homestead. They raised cattle and sold milk in town. Jacob continued to fish, while Gertrude took care of the homestead and raised the children.

They lived there for 15 years before returning to their home in Petersburg.

Jacob and Gertrude's son Casper also became a fisherman. He eventually bought the F/V *Brooklyn* and had a "Jimmy" diesel installed in it at a cost of $400. It was used for 24 seasons.

Casper married Amy Phillips, who was born in Haines and attended Sheldon Jackson School. As a small child, Amy and her family lived in Kake.

Casper and Amy had five children: Casper Jr., Gertrude, Gloria, Jonas and Leonard.

Through the years, Amy was honored for her work in the Alaska Native Sisterhood. She was also active in the Presbyterian Church and Salvation Army. In 1935, on the eve of Prohibition, she marched with the Women's Christian Temperance Union.

Their son, Casper Jr. also became a fisherman and ran the *Brooklyn* after his father retired from fishing. He married Luella Nicholson. They have three children: Carol, Casper "Skip" and Nicole.

Casper and Amy's daughter Gertrude married Myron Lyons. Their children are Myron Jr., Colyn, Jeff, Tom, Byron and Gordon.

Casper and Amy's daughter Gloria married Neil Lyons. Their sons are Jack and Greg.

Casper and Amy's son Jonas, who also is a fisherman, married Sylvia Larson's niece, Kathy Schudlick. They have two children, Jacob and Melanie.

Their third son, Leonard, married and living in Seattle, has four daughters and one son.

Jacob and Gertrude's daughter Maggie married Cliff Roundtree and their son is Melvin Clifford "Sock." Two daughters soon joined the family: Margaret "Sis" and Frances "Babe."

Maggie Roundtree was a stay-at-home mom until her children were out of high school. She then went to work at Earl Ohmer's shrimp cannery, where she worked with shrimp, crab, and salmon for 14 years.

Cliff and Maggie's son Sock married Connie Berg from Ketchikan. They had three children: Clifford Melvin "Fuzz," Julie and Marie.

Sis, who worked for many years at Petersburg Cold Storage, married Elmer Whitethorn, who was an engineer at the cold storage. They had two sons, Elmer Jr. "Butch" and David "Ole."

Jacob and Gertrude's daughter Gertrude married Ole Hemnes. They had two daughters, Mildred "Bobo" and Jacqueline "Snooky." Gertrude, Bobo and Snooky all died of cancer at early ages.

Jacob and Gertrude's son Jake, who owned various fishing boats including the *Green Hornet*, the *Sokol*, the *Ankle Deep* and the *Fram*, married Bessie Thomas. They didn't have any children, but raised Bessie's grandson Larry.

Jacob and Gertrude's son Jonas never married. He was a fisherman and owned the F/V *Iskut*. He died in 1943 of a heart attack.

F/V *Brothers*

Fred and Beulah Haltiner

By Karen Olsen Haltiner

Fredrick Elsworth Haltiner Sr. was born March 28, 1907, in Pleasant Lake, North Dakota, to George and Jessie (Thomas) Haltiner. George and Jesse had two daughters and three sons.

George's parents had emigrated from Switzerland and Bavaria in the mid 1800s. Jessie's father was born in New York and had fought in the Civil War.

Fred's family homesteaded near Aneta, North Dakota. Around 1915, they moved to a homestead in Glentana, Montana, where they raised horses.

In the 1920s, the family moved to Seattle. Fred graduated from Queen Anne High School. He was working at a job delivering laundry when he met his friend's sister, Beulah Dutton.

Beulah Alberta Dutton was born January 23, 1905, in Waterville, Washington, to Franklin and Barbara (Smith) Dutton. They had one son and six daughters.

Franklin Dutton's parents had homesteaded across the country from New York. In 1630, their ancestors came to this country from England with the Winthrop group.

Franklin went to school in DeSmet, South Dakota, with Laura Ingalls Wilder. (One can read about life in South Dakota in Wilder's books "The Little Town on the Prairie" and "The Long Winter.")

Beulah Dutton's family homesteaded in Washington. In 1910, they moved to Naples, Idaho, where they farmed.

In 1916, they purchased a small store. After four years, the store was traded for another store in Kevin, Montana.

Beulah quit high school during her sophomore year and moved to Seattle. She worked winters in a hotel laundry and summers gibbing herring at the Saginaw Bay saltery in Alaska.

Fred and Beulah Haltiner

Fred and Beulah were married in 1928.

A year later, the Depression forced a move north to Southeast Alaska. Fred and Beulah continued to work at Saginaw Bay. Because they wanted to stay in Alaska at the end of the season, they purchased and lived on a 28-foot boat.

For three years, they watched streams for the U.S. Bureau of Fisheries and lived in Kake, Alaska, as cannery watchmen in the winter. For income, they trapped wolves, worth $50 each, and otter.

In 1931, they started fox farming on Hound Island near Kake. It was a hard, but profitable, life. Silver fox were in demand in England, so buyers were eager to buy pelts. Beulah, by herself, would take the skiff into Kake for supplies.

Son Dean was born in Kake in 1932, but died five days later in Petersburg. After that horrible loss, Beulah came to Petersburg to deliver the rest of her children.

Barbara was born in 1936, and Marge in 1939. During these times, Beulah stayed with Elvina Stedman and her family while she was in Petersburg.

Beulah was in the hospital on December 7, 1941, when Pearl Harbor was attacked by the Japanese. She was sent home because the hospital didn't have blackout curtains. Fred Jr. was born on December 11, 1941.

By 1942, World War II prevented the export of furs to England and the market died. Beulah and Fred sold the fox farm and moved to Petersburg to fish.

They lived out the road for a while, but soon moved into town. Fred purchased the F/V *Surf*, which he fished until after World War II. He sold it and bought another seiner, the F/V *Verma*.

Fred and Beulah Haltiner cont'd

Son Bob was born in 1943. Fred and Beulah purchased the home located at 204 Fourth Street, next to the Lutheran Church, in the mid '40s.

Fred was an avid hunter and spent his winters hunting. As president of the Petersburg Vessel Owners Association, he attended fisheries meetings in the winter, fighting to get rid of fish traps.

He also seined in False Pass, gillnetted with Erling Strand on the Stikine River, and was a guide for brown bear hunts with Ralph Young.

Fred and Beulah were active members of the Elks and the Emblem Club. Fred was exalted ruler of the Elks and Beulah was president of the Emblem Club. Fred was a member of the Masonic Lodge and Beulah was a member of Eastern Star.

After Fred died in 1971, Beulah sold the house, moved into a trailer, and anxiously awaited the opening of Mountain View Manor. She was the manor's first resident.

During this time, she enjoyed traveling, visiting extended family, and relaxing on Caribbean cruises.

She died in 1997, at the age of 92.

Fred and Beulah had 10 grandchildren.

Their daughter Barbara graduated from Petersburg High School as valedictorian in 1954. Stories abound about her and Marilyn Myren getting pinched by Fish and Game for illegal beach seining in Petersburg Creek.

She attended the University of Oregon and then Edison Technical School in Seattle. She was an accountant for a firm in Seattle. Barbara died in 1969

Marge Haltiner attended school in Petersburg, but spent her senior year in Seattle where she graduated from Edison Technical School. She was an accomplished pianist.

In 1956, she married her high school sweetheart, Ralph Arden Hall, in Petersburg. He is the son of Ralph and Clara (Pedersen) Hall.

They moved to California, where he was attending Northrup Aviation Institute, and then to St. Louis, Missouri, where Ralph went to work for McDonnell Douglas.

His mother, Clara, sold her Petersburg home and moved to St. Louis to be near Ralph and Marge.

Ralph worked as an astronautics engineer on the *Gemini* space capsule and Marge was able to accompany him to Cape Canaveral for some of the launches. He also traveled the world working on Harpoon missile sites.

Since Ralph was gone so much, Marge was a stay-at-home mom for their five children: Lance, Valerie, Brad, Stuart and Tara.

Marge died in 1997 and Ralph died in 1998.

They had 12 grandchildren.

Valerie Hall Torrence is the only one of their children who came back to live in Petersburg.

Fred Haltiner Jr. has many very good memories of growing up in Petersburg in the '40s and '50s.

Fred Jr. and Karen Haltiner

He would earn money by going to the cold storage and cutting the halibut cheeks out of halibut heads, which were discarded in those days. He would then haul them to homes in town with his wagon, selling them for ten cents a pound.

Fred Jr. also remembers the fishing trips with Pastor Hopp and his sons, hiking up to Petersburg Lake and fishing with homemade poles, and scouting with Scout leaders Bud File and Harold Medalen.

He also began seining with his dad on the *Verma* when he was young.

Basketball and playing tuba for Walt Birkeland in the Viking Band were highlights of Fred Jr.'s Petersburg High School years. After graduating in 1960, he attended the University of Alaska at Fairbanks for one year.

Fred Jr. married Karen Olsen, also of Petersburg, in 1952.

Karen's fond memories of growing up in Petersburg include being in Margaret Hopp's and Toby Oines' junior choir at the Lutheran Church in the early 1950s; going to the Luther League Convention in Missoula, Montana, in 1956; and working in the can

Fred and Beulah Haltiner cont'd

loft at Petersburg Processors cannery from 1958 to 1961.

The can loft operation was not very automated, since cans were assembled individually. During busy hours, especially from six to seven o'clock at night, Pam Martens, Andy Rogers, Doug Holbeck and Karen would be hand-fed fudge by the owners' wives, who encouraged them to speed up, in order to keep up with the workers on the canning line below!

Karen graduated from Petersburg High School in 1958, and from the University of Alaska at Fairbanks in 1962, with a BA in education.

All of Fred and Karen's children were born in Petersburg. Dean was born in 1963, Alan in 1964, and Todd in 1969. They also graduated from Petersburg High School.

Loading seine after a haul
University of Washington Libraries, Special Collections, IND0088

The family lived in the Olsen family home at 007 Fram Street until 1978, when they moved to their new home at 1000 Excel.

In 1967, Fred Jr. purchased the F/V *Siren* and seined salmon and herring and fished crab. He was on the city council for a term in the early '70s and was the first president of the United Fishermen of Alaska, spending time pressing for limited entry.

As the parent of three swimmers from the mid-'70s through 1988, Karen was involved with Viking Swim Club as meet coordinator, president, and the Southeast representative to Alaska Swimming.

She has been a pianist at the Lutheran Sunday School since the '60s and the Sunday School superintendent since the early '80s.

Karen retired in 2000, after working at Berthiel's for 12 years.

Fred and Karen's son Dean has a BBA in finance from Pacific Lutheran University. He lives in Petersburg. Fred sold his boat, the F/V *Siren,* to Dean in 1987, and recently sold Dean the F/V *Island Pride*.

Alan and his wife, Mary, live in the Seattle area. Alan has a PhD in clinical neuropsychology and works at the Swedish Hospital Epilepsy Center.

Todd and his wife, Raina Wikan Haltiner, live in Seattle. He fishes on the *Island Pride*.

Fred Jr. and Karen have three grandchildren.

Fred and Beulah's youngest child, Bob Haltiner, was raised in Petersburg and was in the Petersburg class of '61. He joined the Army and was stationed in Panama during the Vietnam War.

He returned to Petersburg and, in 1968, married Signe Enge Randrup, the daughter of Ernest and Ethel Enge. They raised her daughter, Shelyn, born in 1966, and their daughter, Erin, born in 1975. Their home is on Wrangell Avenue.

In the '60s, Bob logged and worked on the oil pipeline.

Today he fishes crab and salmon, and tenders herring. He owned the F/V *Gjoa*, F/V *Verma*, and a fiberglass boat named the F/V *Gjoa*. His present boat is the F/V *Signe Lynn*.

Shelyn graduated from Petersburg High School in 1984 and is married to Mike Bell. They moved to Idaho in 2001.

Erin went to school in Edmonds and Mukilteo, Washington, when Bob and Signe began spending winters down south, but she graduated from high school in Petersburg in 1993.

Erin fished with Bob until 2001 when she married a seiner, Andy Babich. They own the F/V *Ocean Dream* and live in Gig Harbor.

Bob and Signe have three grandchildren.

John and Marie Hammer

By Bruce Westre

John Hammer, born in Tustna, Norway, immigrated to the United States through Ellis Island in 1909.

His sweetheart was Marie Evenson, who was born in Kristiansund, Norway. John left Marie behind, with the plan to earn enough money for her passage.

As there was no long distance phone service, John and Marie kept in touch by mail. The family has a box of postcards with United States and Norwegian postmarks, bearing testimony to the five and a half years of correspondence.

After leaving Ellis Island, John went to Ballard, Washington, where he lived with the Linvog family.

He worked in a sawmill, where, "If you stopped to eat lunch, you would come back to find your spot taken," he later said.

John also logged in the Everett area.

He was a hard worker, willing to try anything. He shipped out on a whaling ship, stating the conditions were bad.

Eventually, John ended up in Petersburg. He would work during the summer, either crewing on a boat or gillnetting on the Stikine. He'd return to the Seattle area to work for the winter.

In 1914, John returned to Norway to marry Marie. The young couple returned to Petersburg to make their home.

John worked with his friend Andrew Wikan, delivering milk to Petersburg from Point Agazzis. They opened a business called The Dairy.

We all know about John's success as a businessman, and the partnership he shared with Andrew, which lasted until their deaths. Hammer & Wikan, Inc. shares a history with the community of Petersburg — as the town grew, so did the store.

Hammer & Wikan, Inc. celebrated its 80th anniversary in 2001.

Marie worked alongside John.

At times, Marie and Andrew would "hold down the fort" in town, while John gillnetted on the Stikine River in an open skiff.

John would also make trips to Port Alexander to troll for king salmon, making a quarter for each red king he caught.

John and Marie built a home on Lumber Street. They started their family there, bringing Jennie, Agnes, Norman and Art into their lives. The family outgrew the home, so John built another home on Hammer Slough. James, the youngest member of the family, was born there.

John and Marie were active in the Sons and Daughters of Norway and the Lutheran Church.

Many of their friends from Norway had also settled in Petersburg.

John and Marie were real pioneers, taking their lives in Alaska very seriously. They loved the life they had etched out in the community of Petersburg.

Marie and John Hammer

Since 1921

1300 Howkan

Full Service Grocery

- Dairy
- Groceries
- Natural Foods
- Fresh Produce
- USDA Choice Meats
- Fresh Bakery/Deli

(907) 772-4246 (907) 772-2295 (fax)
P.O. Box 249, Petersburg, AK 99833
E-mail: hamwik@alaska.net

Mail and phone orders welcomed
Free dockside pickup and delivery
Courtesy phones on docks

www.hammerandwikan.com

Open Seven Days A Week
Monday- Saturday 7 a.m. to 8 p.m.   Sunday 8 a.m. to 7 p.m.

John Hammer and Andrew Wikan's first store

Hammer & Wikan's second store

Jim and Bev Hammer

By Bruce Westre

James L. Hammer was born on July 12, 1926, in Petersburg, Alaska, the fifth and youngest child of John and Marie Hammer.

Jim grew up in Petersburg, participating in many activities while attending school. He has a lifelong love for all sports and recalls fondly being on the Southeast Alaska Championship Basketball team of 1944.

Following high school graduation, Jim was drafted into the Army.

He spent time at Fort Richardson, Alaska. While there, he contracted tuberculosis, forcing him to spend three and a half years in Army and veterans hospitals, mainly in Walla Walla, Washington.

Jim was in Ketchikan visiting his sister when he met the love of his life, Beverly Olin.

They were married in Ketchikan on November 26, 1949. They then moved to Seattle, where Jim was attending a business college.

With his schooling behind him, the young couple moved back to Petersburg. They settled in, building their home on Lumber Street with the help of family and friends. They continue to live there today.

Jim worked at his father's Hammer & Wikan store while still in high school. He returned to work there following college. After working his way from clerk to produce manager, Jim later became hardware manager.

The years spent working in the store allowed Jim the enjoyment of meeting many new friends, while keeping his old friends active in his life. He served as president of the board of directors of Hammer & Wikan, Inc. for 12 years. Today, he continues to keep an interest in the running of the business.

In later years, Jim purchased a troller, the F/V *Moha*, changing the name to the *Beaver I*. He also purchased a commercial permit, allowing him to do what he loved best — fish! Jim spent 20 years pulling in the big ones, and storing up a whole treasure chest full of memories.

Jim and Bev have five children, all born and raised in Petersburg.

The oldest is Kenneth James, born in 1950, who married Katherine Combs of Grants Pass, Oregon.

Kenneth and Katherine have three children: Carissa B. Recchio, Jacob August and Jens Louis.

Jim and Bev's second child, Christi Ann, born in 1952, married Gene Vincent. They have three children: twins Aaron Daniel and Matthew John, and daughter Tami Jean.

Jim Hammer

Their third child, Robert John, was born in 1954. He married Patrice Motschenbacher of Roseburg, Oregon. They have two sons, Joshua Dean and Chadwick Allen.

Jim and Bev's younger daughter, Wendy Sue, was born in 1959. She married Bruce Westre and they have two children, James Tyrell and Krystlyn Rene.

The youngest child of Jim and Bev is Roger Kevin, born in 1966. He married Kelly Outz and they have one child, Chase Austin.

Jim is a life member of the Sons of Norway and the Disabled American Veterans.

He is active in the Pioneers of Alaska, and has been a member of the Lutheran Church, the Jaycees, the American Legion, and the Elks.

Jim has also served on the city council.

Trygve and Esther Hansen

By Roger K. and Jerrold W. Hansen

Esther Horton was born in Williston, North Dakota, on February 14, 1914, and lived and worked on the family farm. Her father died at an early age. She was raised by her mother, who was of Norwegian decent, in Alexander, North Dakota.

Esther graduated from St. Paul Luther College in 1934, and Concordia College in 1940.

In 1943, she moved to San Francisco, California, and worked in the finance department of the U.S. Merchant Marine Service.

Esther became interested in a teaching position in Petersburg, but her office was reluctant to let her go "...because there was a war going on." She persisted and informed them that she was going anyway.

Upon her arrival in Petersburg, there was some confusion at first with the school administration. The teachers' placement bureau had mixed up hers and her sister's photos. It was straightened out and Esther was assigned to teach music in the high school.

Lloyd Roundtree, one of her former students, remarked, "How she got us boys to sing is beyond me."

While teaching in Petersburg, she roomed with Rae Burke, who later married Bill Stedman.

During the summer of 1944, she took a trip down the Yukon River and worked for the U.S. Army at Ladd Field (now Fort Wainright) in Fairbanks.

While living in Petersburg, Esther often went to the town's social events and produced high school music events.

One story she often told was about a masquerade party where she went as a cowgirl with toy guns. One of the locals said she could have borrowed his real pistols — with bullets!

While coming down the hill in a snowstorm, near where the Elks Lodge now stands, she met Trygve Hansen.

Trygve was born November 17, 1910, in Wrangell, Alaska. His parents were Norwegian immigrants Ole and Jonetta Hansen.

He attended the Episcopal Church school. Shortly afterward, the family moved to Petersburg, living at Hammer Slough, next to the Hammer family. The "Hansen House" is still standing and is the one with the blue roof.

Trygve's father was a commercial fisherman in Petersburg, but during the Great Depression, the family moved away from Petersburg, and lived in Nampa, Idaho; McDowell, California; and Seattle and Kelso, Washington.

While living in McDowell, Trygve learned to play baseball and filled the catcher's position.

While playing at Ballard High School in Seattle, he missed being voted as Seattle's "All High School Catcher" by one vote.

While attending Kelso High School, he played all sports but excelled in baseball at the catchers position. In his senior year, Kelso was undefeated in baseball and upon his graduation, the town of Kelso placed an "advertisement" in the local paper, looking for a catcher with a good throwing arm, good batting average, and good grades.

When Trygve found out that he was going to be the valedictorian, he stayed out of school just to lower his grades so that he wouldn't have to give the commencement speech.

After the baseball team finished the season, one of the townspeople took him for a ride in an airplane. This may have sparked his interest in flying in his later years. After graduation he returned to Petersburg.

While living in Petersburg, Trygve worked for Johnny Sales on the pile-driving barge, building The Trading Union.

One day, he was knocked overboard into Wrangell Narrows with full foul weather gear on. Trygve popped right back up, climbed on the barge, went home, changed his clothes, and went right back to work.

He commercial fished and played baseball in his free time. The only baseball played in Petersburg at that time was the "white kids" against the "Native kids." Because he was the new kid in town, he had to prove himself worthy to play on the "white kids'" team.

To do that, he had to play on the Native team as a pitcher, and it was the only time that summer that the "Native kids" beat the "white kids."

In 1933, Trygve became a Free Mason and joined Petersburg Lodge 262. He was a member of that lodge for 61-plus years.

In 1937, Carl Anderson, part owner of two Alaska Airways Savoia Marchetti airplanes, asked Trygve if

Trygve and Esther Hansen cont'd

he would like to go to New Jersey to help Tony Schwamm rebuild one of them. Since there was no fishing at that time, he decided to go.

While back on the East Coast testing the engines of the plane, the German airship Hindenberg flew over so low they could see the passengers waving. Later in the day, they heard about the explosion and disaster.

While in New Jersey, Trygve started taking flying lessons from Tony.

After crating the airplane and shipping it via the Panama Canal, Trygve and Tony rebuilt it in San Diego. Because all of the instruments were in Italian, they used a hand compass and a road atlas to fly the plane up the West Coast.

After arriving in Petersburg, Trygve still didn't have a pilot's license, so he went to Seattle and took lessons from Lana Kurtzer on Lake Union.

In 1938, he reconnected with Tony Schwamm and Petersburg Air Service was born.

Before joining the Navy as a pilot during World War II, Trygve and other Petersburg residents had to guard certain facilities within the town. With only a .22-caliber rifle, Trygve's responsibility was to guard the fuel tanks at night; every bush looked like a Japanese soldier.

After joining the Navy, he was commissioned as lieutenant junior grade. He was sent to Pensacola, Florida, for naval flight training. While there, a hurricane was approaching and their orders were to fly as far north, as possible, and safely land the planes.

Trygve made certain that his plane was always filled with fuel. "This Alaskan is not going swimming with those squiggly lines (snakes) and moving logs (alligators)!" The hurricane missed Florida.

After his training, Trygve was sent to Kodiak and Dutch Harbor where he flew OS2U observation planes on patrol duty. While at Dutch Harbor, he became squadron commander.

On one of his patrols, he spotted a brown bear on an island and he "buzzed" the bear three times, each time changing the pitch of the prop to make a racket. Finally the bear stopped running, put its head down, and covered its ears with its paws.

Trygve also spent time in Adak and Sitka, Alaska; at the Quillayute Naval Station, in Washington; and in Honolulu, Hawaii.

While at Sitka, when the base was being decommissioned, he took the only fighter plane and flew over to Petersburg, and buzzed the town twice. When asked if the townspeople knew who it was, Trygve replied that they probably figured it out after the second pass.

In 1945, he was discharged from active duty and returned to Petersburg.

Before flying for Petersburg Air Service, Trygve and Andrew Wikan decided to try trapping to earn some money during the winter.

The only animal that the two caught was a beaver. While trying to drown it, they found out that beavers could hold their breath. It was really mad when they pulled it out of the water! They had to kill it by other means. That was the last time Trygve went trapping or hunting.

Aerial view of Petersburg, circa 1930s

He began flying for Petersburg Air Service and Alaska Island Airlines. While flying out of Petersburg, he lived at the Arctic Hotel. (This hotel was the predecessor to the Scandia House.)

One night, upon returning to his room, he smelled smoke in the hallway. Upon further investigation, he found that some Natives had lit a fire on the mattress to stay warm. He promptly doused the flames with a bucket of water from the hallway.

The Natives weren't too happy, as they had all fallen asleep and were rudely awakened by the water. The owner of the hotel was so grateful that he lowered Trygve's monthly rent by $10.

Trygve Hansen and Esther Horton were married on July 15, 1946. More than 125 people signed the guest book at the wedding.

Trygve and Esther Hansen cont'd

Esther would often accompany Trygve on some of his flying trips and he would let her fly the plane, but he said that she just couldn't keep it level.

Another person who flew with him often was the Catholic priest. He liked flying with Trygve because he got to try his hand at flying the plane.

In November 1947, because there was no doctor in town, Esther accompanied Trygve on a flight to Juneau. Their first child, Roger, was born there at St. Anne's Catholic Hospital. Upon returning home with his son and wife, one of the local fishermen remarked, "Stor Viking (Big Viking)."

For approximately two years, the family lived in the Hadland house, directly across from where the Tides Inn Motel office is located today. This was just down the street from his uncle and aunt, Jack and Maren Otness.

The family then moved near the "point" on Wrangell Avenue next to Barney White.

In April of 1949, Trygve and Esther's second son, Jerrold, was born in Petersburg.

The Hansens were told by the Petersburg doctor that because Roger, the oldest son, was developing signs of asthma and had many allergies, they should move to a different climate.

In 1951, the family moved to Grants Pass, Oregon, where Trygve's oldest sister, Olga (nicknamed "Pinkie" for her red hair), lived.

Trygve never flew again, but returned to Alaska and the Petersburg area often to fish with Elmer Martens on the *Lorelei II* and with his brother, William Hansen, on the *Lloyd*. He retired from commercial fishing in 1972.

For 28 years, Esther taught basic math, algebra, geometry, and Latin at Grants Pass High School.

She was a member of Delta Kappa Gamma, the American Association of University Women, and the Order of the Eastern Star Chapter of Petersburg. She was also a charter member of Calvary Lutheran Church of Grants Pass.

Trygve shared several Petersburg stories with his sons, Roger and Jerrold.

One morning, while preparing to a take a fishing party into Canada, Trygve decided to take along a case of oil. This proved fortunate.

While flying into Canada, he noticed the oil pressure in one of the engines had dropped to nearly zero. He quickly landed on a lake and, after examining the engine, he determined that the mechanics had stripped the oil pan drain bolt and the oil leaked out.

He was able to remove the drain bolt and fashioned a wooden plug from a tree branch. He pounded the plug into the bolthole, filled the engine with oil, took off, and headed for Petersburg.

The mechanics had a hard time getting the wooden plug out and were irritated at him for using it. "Hey, anything goes in an emergency."

Another story was about a house near the "point," where the owner had installed a garage door opener. He could never figure out that only on certain days, after leaving the door down in the morning, when he returned later, the door would be in the up position. The mystery was solved one day, when a Canadian ferry ship was passing by, blew its horn, and the door opened up.

Esther passed away on January 1, 1994.

Trygve passed away from complications of a stroke on December 12, 1999, in Grants Pass, Oregon.

Roger graduated from Pacific Lutheran University in Tacoma, in 1970, with a teaching degree; and from Alaska Methodist University in Anchorage, in 1975, with a geology degree. He presently works for the Municipality of Anchorage as a civil designer.

Jerrold received his electrical engineering degree, in 1971, from Oregon State University. Today he works just down the hall from Roger, where he is a project administrator for the Municipality of Anchorage in its Project Management and Engineering Department.

Warehouses on the Narrows

Jacob Hanseth

By Don Nelson

Jacob "Jack" Hanseth arrived in the Petersburg area sometime around the turn of the century. He had emigrated from the Romsdalen area of central Norway, south of Molde.

Jack was a hand logger in the days before chain saws and logging roads. He logged in several locations, including Castle River and Petersburg Creek, hauling logs off the hillsides with a donkey engine on a log float.

Jack was a good friend of the Knutsen Brothers and spent one winter in a cabin at Knutsen's Point. The cabin still stands on Harold Bergmann's property.

His brother, Olaf Hanseth, worked with him in his logging ventures and later in fish trap operations.

Jack Hanseth was the driving force behind the founding and operation of The Trading Union, Inc. in 1920. He not only assisted in getting the business started and helping it through the lean years with financial help, but as the unpaid carpenter and pile driver, he repaired and maintained the store and dock.

Jack was president of The Trading Union from 1920 to 1952.

He and his wife had two daughters, Margaret and June. Margaret was born about 1916 and after graduation married an attorney, Tom Williams. They lived in Seattle where she died in 1987.

June was born about 1922 and married right out of school to a navy man named Pike. They had a daughter named Julie, but the marriage did not last.

She later married a high official in the United Auto Workers union named Cordtz. They lived in high style in the exclusive Detroit suburb of Grosse Point.

The Jack Hanseth family built and lived in the large house currently owned by Fran Westre at 507 South Nordic Drive.

For years Jack had his logging camp, which was on logs, moored on the beach in front of his house. This would now be the entrance to the South Harbor parking lot.

Jack owned and operated two floating salmon traps in the 1930s. One was at the right hand point going into Port Protection and the other was in Warren Channel in south Sumner Straits.

He had a large cabin aft boat, about 65 feet long, named the *Stamsund* that he used to pick up the salmon from the traps and deliver to the cannery. In later years, PAF brailed the fish out of his traps and delivered them to town with their tenders.

In his retirement years, Jack bought a small boat and gillnetted, mostly at Taku and Snettisham.

Jack Hanseth was an expert woodsman and hunter. There weren't many hills and mountains around town that he hadn't brought a deer off of. He was also an avid skier and ice skater.

Jack was a very moral, decent man and a friend to everyone.

As age took its toll, Mr. and Mrs. Hanseth had to give up their active life in Petersburg. In the mid-1950s, they moved to the White Center district in south Seattle.

Jack Hanseth passed away about 1960 and is buried in Seattle.

Brailing a salmon trap

Peter and Anna Hanson

By Ruth Droke

Peter Hanson was born in Norway, in 1865, and died March 22, 1940, in Petersburg, Alaska.

He prospected for gold in Southeast Alaska for the government.

Peter married Anna Spooner and they had several children: John W., Mick, Henry and Katherine.

Anna had a later marriage and was the mother of Margaret and Freeman McGilton. I was told the statue at the Sitka Pioneer's Home was modeled after him. Margaret McGilton Durbin is my aunt.

My dad was John W. Hanson, whom we all called "Pop." He always walked down the street tipping his hat and saying, "Howdo," to people.

He drove the first truck in Petersburg, a Model T. His employer's business was to unload Alaska Steamship and deliver the freight.

Dad worked in the cannery. He also helped dredge the Narrows.

Once when my Dad was hunting and trapping in Thorne Bay, he trapped a wolverine. He had no gun, so he clubbed it. While he was packing it out on a packboard, the wolverine revived and began snarling. Dad managed to get the packboard off, and also ended up with the wolverine.

Hanna Porter sold my parents the property on H Street. On it, Dad and my brothers built the house we grew up in. We called it the Big House. The house is now gone.

Dad was honored, in 1978, with a lifetime pass to the Petersburg Vikings basketball games. He never missed a game.

Dad died November 1, 1978.

My grandmother, Sarah Jackson, was born in Juneau, Alaska. My mother, Selina McCullough, was born in Petersburg.

My grandmother and mother were Tlinget Indians. My mother, along with others, used to canoe from Petersburg to Blind Slough where they would smoke fish.

I remember the many stories she told us about the Tlinget Indians canoeing to Seattle and back.

Hanson-Droke Family

My mother worked at Ohmer's shrimp and crab cannery for many years. She died in January 1982.

My memories of growing up in Petersburg include lots of snow, wooden sidewalks, the Sweet Shop at Heimdahl's Modern Grocery, and the old theater and its Hopalong Cassidy movies.

My husband, Tim Droke, is from California. We lived in Petersburg when we first married and Tim logged for Lloyd Jones. We now reside in Ketchikan, where Tim is a construction engineer.

Our children are: Tim Jr., Sabrina, Leanne and Shanna Lee.

Shanna and Sabrina are both married. Each has two children.

Leanne is going to nursing school and her daughter, Diane, lives in Petersburg.

"Good for 5 in trade"

Hack's
Petersburg, Alaska

Hugh and Alice Harris

By Cathy Harris

Hugh Alexander Harris was born August 19, 1914, in Hamilton, Washington. He arrived in Petersburg the summer of 1921.

He came on a small gas engine boat with his parents, Charles and Stella Harris, two brothers, Rusty and Richard, and two sisters, Edna and Andrea.

Hugh played center on the Petersburg High School boys basketball team during high school. He graduated in 1933, as valedictorian of his class.

Richard and Hugh Harris

From October 1941 to October 1945, during World War II, Hugh was in the Coast Guard stationed in Alaska.

In 1942, Hugh married Alice Stolpe Anderson.

Alice's father had worked for the Canadian Pacific Railroad in Trail, British Columbia. He died in the flu epidemic, as his wife, Agnes, was giving birth to Alice in the next room.

Agnes moved her children, Alice, Clara, and Harold, to Tacoma, Washington, in order to work and raise her family.

Alice came to Alaska to visit her sister, Clara, and her husband, Kurt Nordgren, who ran a fox farm near Petersburg. Their brother, Harold, also came to work on the farm with the Nordgrens.

The fox farm's log cabin was color-coded, disassembled, and relocated to Petersburg. The cabin can still be seen on Wrangell Avenue.

In earlier years, Hugh Harris had been a laborer at Mitkof Marine Ways, a lumberman for Norton Logging at Point Barrie, and could be seen keeping the peace as bartender at Jim Brennan's bar, the Petersburg Bar, and the Moose Club.

He spent many years as a deckhand on the F/V *Lois W* and *Ira II* for his brother-in-law, Kurt Nordgren; on the F/V *Bernice A* with Marion and Gerry Frink; and on the F/V *Charles T* with his brother, Richard, until his retirement.

Alice worked at Petersburg Processors and the Clyde Sheldon Shrimp Cannery. She was active in the Ladies of the Moose.

Hugh and Alice raised four children: Roy, Barbara, Charles and Sharon.

Roy enlisted in the Army and then returned to Petersburg to live.

Barbara married Bill Greinier, skipper of the shrimp boat *Charles W*. They raised three children: Cindy Zimmerman, Joseph, and Andrew.

Charles was born and raised in Petersburg with his brother and sisters. In 1966, he married Catherine McKay and raised one daughter, Carmen Lantiegne.

Carmen's two sons, Tyler and Jesse, are fourth generation Petersburg, Alaskans.

Sharon, their youngest, raised three children, Tammy Fales, Jackie Guthrie and Stewart Eddy.

Their parents, Hugh and Alice, have passed away.

Hugh Harris, Sharon Harris Freeman, and Clara Nordgren Thompson (Hugh's niece)

Henry and Ellen Hasbrouck

By Angie Hasbrouck Hofstad

After serving in the Army Engineers in World War I, Henry Hasbrouck moved to Petersburg from Washington about 1926.

Henry acquired a half interest in a sawmill, which was situated where the Northern Lights Restaurant is now located.

Most of the houses between the south side of Hammer Slough and North Nordic Drive were built on the sawmill's sawdust and slab pile that had been piled on the flats between Hammer Slough and Kolstrand's Creek.

Henry needed loggers, so sent for his brothers, Leon and Jack. Leon stayed in Petersburg, after the mill fell on hard times, and started a fox farm.

While working at the mill, Henry met Ellen Hill, a new teacher. They married and had two daughters, Mary Ellen and Christine.

At that time, a female teacher could not continue if she married, so Ellen became a homemaker.

When the mill failed, Henry turned to carpentry and built houses.

He built a lovely house for his family on what is now Wrangell Avenue. At that time, there were no streets, so he built a plank walk down to the main plank walk on the beach.

This is the house his widow later sold to Red and Margaret Jones.

Henry also built a house in Beecher's Pass for Gregory Hildebrand while Leon was there, caring for the foxes. This house was later moved into town next to the present shipyard, and the Hildebrands' daughter, Geraldine Frink, lived there.

In the winter, Henry trapped for wolves at Petersburg Lake. In 1941, he was reported lost in this same area.

The town clerk notified Leon, who came in from the fox farm to lead a search party for his brother. It was a difficult search in deep snow and no trace was found of him.

Their older brother, Ed, found Henry's body in the spring after the ice breakup, at the lake's outlet. Henry must have gone through the ice while crossing this spot.

Henry's widow, Ellen, was rehired to teach high school English. She taught until her children were ready for college, and then moved to Oregon to teach in a community college.

Years later, her daughter, Christine's, children returned to Petersburg to work. David and Frances earned money to buy a cranberry farm in Grayland, Washington. Their sister, Anne, earned money for college where she majored in genetics.

Cruising

Leon and Sarah Hasbrouck

By Angie Hasbrouck Hofstad

Leon Hasbrouck came to Petersburg, in 1926, to work for his older brother, Henry, who needed workers for his sawmill.

The next year, Leon's wife Sarah "Sie", and their two children, Angie and Leona, came to join him. They lived in a float house in the creek near the slab and sawdust pile, located between Hammmer Slough and the Kohlstrand machine shop.

As the mill was failing, Leon decided to try fur farming. He went to work for the Hildebrands in Beecher's Pass.

Greg Hildebrand kept his foxes in pens and needed someone to fish for fox feed and care for the animals.

Leon and Sie lived in a houseboat on the beach while working there. Sie was proud of the garden she was able to grow and happily sent a photo home of her six-foot tall pea vines. She canned much produce for winter meals.

Just before moving to Beecher's Pass, Sie went south to her mother's for the birth of their son, Theodore Leonard. Sie's mother, Anna Price, was a well-known midwife, and attended all of Sie's children's births.

They later moved across the pass where Hildebrand had more pens, as well as the Maid of Mexico gold mine. Leon was taking part of his wages in fox pups.

About 1930, he had an opportunity to work for Charlie Parks on Coney Island, in Frederick Sound near Dry Straits.

He ran his foxes with Charlie's, loose on the island. He fished for fox feed in Dry Straits and the flats on the north arm of the Stikine River.

There was an island in the mouth of Le Conte Bay that Leon had his eye on for a fox farm. However, it was a "dry island." When the tide went out, you could walk across the mud flats to the mainland, so pens for the foxes would have to be built.

The Forest Service did not consider Camp Island farmland, so Leon got five acres for a homesite and five acres for a wood lot. Because the foxes would be penned, this was enough property.

Leon's brother, Henry, came out to help him build pens and a house for the family. But, first they built a small log cabin to bunk in, while the main house was being built.

They also built a woodshed on the edge of the beach, which was handy for the logs that were brought up from the beach to cut for firewood.

They cooked and heated with wood for many years before converting to oil.

Leon and Sarah "Sie" Hasbrouck

By this time, Leon had a boat of his own to fish for fox feed.

After fall pelting at Coney Island, he took his share of mature foxes to his own pens and moved his family to Camp Island.

They found that the sandy soil on the east point of the island was perfect for a garden. There they raised many potatoes, a variety of vegetables, and berries.

Sie homeschooled the children with the help from Petersburg school teachers, particularly Ellen Hasbrouck. When Leona was ready for high school in the '40s, they moved to town.

Leon had taught himself all the fishing he could, so when the fur market failed, he was ready for a new boat. He had Curly McDonald build him a seiner, the *Wanita*, which he and son Ted fished for salmon, halibut and crab.

For a while, Ted was away from Petersburg in the Army. When he returned, Leon and Ted began fishing once again.

Leon and Ted lost the *Wanita* to an engine fire in

Leon and Sarah Hasbrouck cont'd

Red Bay. The pair then opened a machine shop, Mitkof Sales and Service, on Sing Lee Alley. They ran it for many years before selling to Dave Randrup, who had been their right hand man for years.

Sie busied herself keeping the home fires going, volunteering with the Hospital Guild, and quilting for Lutheran World Relief. She also kept a fine garden.

After retiring, Leon built a RV camper on a large flat bed truck from the machine shop.

Leon and Sie set off on a wanderlust life in 1965, visiting all the relatives in the Lower 48. For a few years, they came back in the spring to fish.

Leon found a small cattle ranch in Idaho that welcomed him back in the fall to help with the roundup. He loved to ride.

He and Sie settled on a lovely homestead in the Idaho hills and gave up their nomadic life. By then, Sie was suffering from Parkinson's disease.

When Leon had a stroke in 1981, Ted, with his wife and two daughters, left Fairbanks and came to their aid.

Leon passed away in 1983. Sie returned to Petersburg in 1984, and stayed with daughter, Angie.

As her Parkinson's became worse, she moved into Petersburg Hospital's long-term care unit. There, Sie was well cared for and she was able to be close to her family and longtime friends.

She died December 4, 1991, just before her 89th birthday. Sie was survived by three children: Angie Hofstad, Leona Nelson, and Ted Hasbrouck Sr. She had 19 grandchildren, 50 great-grandchildren, and three great-great-grandchildren.

Leon and Sie's daughter, Angie, graduated from Petersburg High School in 1943. She attended business school in Olympia, Washington.

After the end of World War II, Angie left her Army job and returned to Petersburg.

Angie Hasbrouck married Oliver Hofstad on October 19, 1946. They live at Scow Bay, close to the place where Oliver was born and raised. (*See Oliver and Angie Hofstad story.*)

Leona Hasbrouck married a navy sailor, Dale Hirt, and had four sons: Dale, Eugene, Mike, and Russell. They later divorced.

While Leona was in school in Seattle, she met and married Ross Nelson. Their three children are Matt, Ross and Joey. Leona and Ross currently live in Clear, a small town south of Fairbanks.

Ted, son of Leon and Sie, was born August 7, 1928, in Malone, Washington. He was brought back to Petersburg soon after his birth.

Ted was well schooled by his father in all the pioneer and boating skills needed for fox farming and fishing. His dad bought him a single-shot .22 rifle and taught him to shoot.

When Ted headed out around Camp Island, he was given only two shells. If he came back with game of some kind, there was cheering.

His formal schooling began at the dining room table with his older sisters, Angie and Leona.

One winter while Angie was at school in Olympia, Ted and Leona had a special friend to keep them company. A small grizzly cub had come across the mud flats with his mother while the tide was out.

Ted Hasbrouck

The next morning, the mother left without her cub. She probably didn't like the constant barking of the foxes in their pens.

The cub could smell the icebox full of flounder feed and demanded some. It took a sharp iron prod to get him out of the box.

Leon and Sarah Hasbrouck cont'd

They named him Poo Bear and he loved to play. When he thought Ted and Leona were taking too long with their lessons, he would peek in the window to urge them to come out.

Eventually he got too big to play with, so Hosea Sarber, the game warden, came to get him.

When Ted was old enough for high school, the family moved to town. He and his dad, and sometimes his mother, gillnetted, trolled, seined, and ran Dungeness crab pots.

After enlisting in the Army, he served in the western Pacific and at Fort Richardson, where he learned about engine repair for the army motor pool.

He met his first wife, Marie Anderson, while at Fort Richardson. After his discharge, they moved to Petersburg. Marie had two children: Mary Ann, who married Darryl Olson, and Billie, who is now deceased.

Ted joined his dad on the *Wanita* and they seined, longlined, and fished for crab.

Ted and Leon opened a gas station and car repair shop, Mitkof Sales & Service. They later sold the shop to Chet Randrup.

Ted and Marie have four children: Glenda, Terry, Theresa and Ted Jr. They later divorced.

Ted met and married Norma Sikel. Ted and Norma have two daughters, Tanya and Tammy.

They experimented with homesteading in Tyonic and Fairbanks.

After Leon's stroke, they moved to Idaho to help

Hasbrouck siblings: Leona Hasbrouck Nelson, Ted Hasbrouck and Angie Hasbrouck Hofstad

Sie on the mini-ranch. After Leon died in 1983, they stayed until Sie was well enough to be moved to Petersburg to stay with Angie.

Ted and Norma moved to the Washington coast, but soon returned to Petersburg where Ted worked at Petersburg Fisheries, Inc. as a mechanic.

Since retirement, Ted works as a handyman and has an extensive clientele who keep him very busy.

He currently has 23 grandchildren and nine great-grandchildren. Seven of his grandchildren call Petersburg home.

Petersburg, as seen from a rooftop

Max and Rose Haube

By Carol Enge

In 1928, Max Haube came from the Philippines to attend school in Seattle. He worked at the Butler Hotel while attending night school.

During this time, Max met a cannery superintendent from Wrangell, Alaska, who asked him to come north to work. Hoping to find better work, he went for one summer, but returned to Seattle.

By this time, the Depression was in full force. Max was unable to find work, so he returned to Manila. Opportunities were no better there and he attempted to return to Seattle.

New immigration laws had been passed with the stipulation that immigrants had to have a letter from an employer, guaranteeing a job. Max wrote his previous employer and was assured a job.

He returned to Seattle and his previous job. Max was soon approached by the same cannery foreman with an offer of work in Petersburg, which he accepted.

After the Petersburg cannery closed at the end of the season, there was no work to be found, so Max went to Juneau. He worked as a cook for a gold mine crew, and returned to Petersburg when the job ended

He was hired by Earl Ohmer of Alaskan Glacier Sea Food to process shrimp during the winter months. During the summer months, he worked at Pacific American Fisheries canning salmon.

Max soon became cannery supervisor in charge of coding, packing, and storing cans.

After several years of supervising salmon processing, Max developed ulcers.

He found work as a logger for a few years, until low prices drove him from the woods.

Max returned to town and did a few odd jobs, before returning to work in the cold storage. He worked another 10 years, grading, sorting, and weighing fish.

Following retirement, Max was asked to attend the 18th Annual Festival of American Folklore in Washington, D.C. His contribution to the festival was a collection of stories describing the fish processing industry in Petersburg.

Max married Rose Johnson from Juneau. They have three children: Anita, Rick and Arnold.

Both Max and Rose are now deceased.

Hammer Slough
Photo courtesy of Seaprints

Ernie and Ruby Haugen

By John Enge

Ernie Haugen was born September 29, 1916, in Silverdale, Washington.

After graduating from a high school in Silverdale in 1933, he attended Pacific Lutheran University for a short while.

Ernie came to Alaska in 1936 with a Petersburg friend, Joe McKechnie. He lived with Joe's family for several years.

After working for the Civilian Conservation Corps and in the local canneries, Ernie got his first fishing chance with Magnus Martens on the *Lorelei*. He fished on several other halibut vessels, including the schooner *Mitkof*, out of Seattle.

Ernie enlisted in the U.S. Navy shortly after the bombing of Pearl Harbor. He served as chief boson mate on the fleet tanker USS *Cuyama* and saw duty all over the Pacific, from Attu to the Solomon Islands.

After he was discharged from the Navy in December 1945, Ernie returned to Petersburg. He fished for a year. In 1946, he bought The Pastime Café from Swede Wasvick.

Ruby Simpson was born June 3, 1920. In 1947, she came to Petersburg to visit her sister, Calla Ballard.

She soon began work at The Pastime Café.

On October 2, 1949, Ruby and Ernie were married. In 1950, they had twin boys, Ed and Larry. Their daughter, Julie, was born five years later.

Ernie operated the café for about 15 years before selling it to the Lattas.

When Hammer and Wikan rebuilt their store in 1961, Ernie went to work for them as a butcher. He continued this work part time until his retirement.

Ernie was very active in both local and state politics. He served on the city council in Petersburg from 1954 to 1963.

During his three terms as mayor, he was instrumental in overseeing the rebuilding of the Crystal Lake Power project and in establishing the Marine Highway.

He was appointed to the State of Alaska Highway Commission and the Southeast Conference.

Ernie was a member of the Petersburg Masonic Lodge, Scottish Rite and Shrine, American Legion, Elks, and was past president of Pioneers.

He enjoyed hunting with John Enge, Ben Jensen,

Ernie and Ruby Haugen

and Martin Enge on the *Augusta* each fall. He was an avid berry picker and enjoyed gardening.

In 1964, he was elected as Republican state representative from the district and served in the legislature for 18 years.

Ernie is credited with helping to get funding to build Petersburg General Hospital. He also pushed for construction of the airport.

He served on the Thomas Bay Power Board and facilitated the funding of the Tyee Power Project, which improved Petersburg's power and light service.

With his help, the state fish hatchery was located on Mitkof Island and many of the roads were paved, such as Main Street, Mitkof Highway to Blind Slough, as well as H Street (which was later named Haugen Drive in his honor).

Ernie died in February 1994, in Seattle.

Ruby enjoyed reading, picnicking, camping, bird watching, playing bridge, and entertaining the dignitaries who came to meet with her husband. She was a member of the Pioneers of Alaska and Sons of Norway. Ruby passed away in April 1995.

Norman and Marjorie Heimdahl

By Don Nelson

Marjorie and Norman Heimdahl lived most of their lives in Petersburg. They were willing to give their time and expertise to many different activities, both behind the scenes and out in front as leaders.

Norman Andrew was born February 2, 1919, and was raised in Petersburg. He was the middle of five children, born to Andrew and Gertrude Heimdahl. His siblings were Mildred, Howard, Vernon, and Albert.

Norm's father, Andrew, came to Petersburg on May 7, 1911. He was engaged in the fishing business until 1914, when he became employed by the Hogue and Tveten store. Between 1921 and 1928, he was manager of The Trading Union.

He bought the Modern Grocery in 1929.

Andrew and his wife, Gertrude, resided in the Tom Hadland house.

Marjorie Mae Zehm was born May 7, 1921, in Odessa, Washington, to Rose and Ernest Zehm. She was the youngest of their four children.

Her brothers, Howard and Walter, and her sister, Dorothy, all lived in Petersburg at one time or another.

In 1929, Rose Zehm died at age 41, when Marjorie was only eight.

During her younger years, different relatives in Washington raised Marge. At the end of her sophomore year, she moved to Petersburg to join her father and work in his bakery. She graduated from Petersburg High School in 1939.

Norman graduated from PHS in 1937. He spent his first four years after graduation fishing, doing odd jobs, traveling, and continuing his education. In 1941, he secured steady employment with the U.S. Army.

Marge spent her first year out of high school furthering her education in Seattle. She married Donald McKecknie in 1941. They had a son, Dennis, and later divorced.

Marge and Norm married February 26, 1944.

Coincidently, Norm's brother, Howard, who was stationed in Missouri, got married on the same day — neither knew of the other's wedding plans.

Brother Albert's birthday is also on that day.

They returned to Petersburg, in 1945, shortly after Norm finished his tour of duty with the Army.

After the war, Norman fished, clerked, and managed the Modern Grocery, which was owned by his father.

He also worked for the Corps of Engineers, dredging Wrangell Narrows; Standard Oil; and put in 20 years with the State of Alaska Employment Services.

Marge worked for the U.S. Commissioners Office with Dale Hirt, the Fish and Wildlife Service, and the Citizen's Steam Laundry, which was owned by Charlotte and Bob Schwartz. She also had about five years working at the U.S. Post Office with Dick Brennan and the crew.

Marge and Norm bought a house in Scow Bay, around 1947, and moved in with their three children: Denny, Roger and Mary.

In 1948, Norm and three of his neighbors, Lee Stear, Fred Seidell, and Bob Henderson, founded the Scow Bay utilities, which was named Scow Bay Water Users Association.

They applied to the U.S. Department of Interior for the permits to build a dam and run a water pipeline across the muskeg to their homes. Permits were granted to lay one mile of pipe and the rights of way were granted to cross Mitkof Highway. For this they paid $10 a year rent.

With help from Seattle's Federal Pipe and Tank Company, they designed and built their dam, and ordered the water pipe and all necessary supplies to complete the project. It had now become a bigger project; other families wanted to be included.

The difficult part was laying the pipe. The ditches were all dug by hand! (Was there any other way, for gosh sakes?)

The first winter was a disaster. They found the ditches had not been dug deep enough, and the water line froze. The next spring they had to re-dig and bury the pipe deeper, again by hand, with #2 shovels, picks and mattocks.

The project was a huge success and was used for many years by the Scow Bay Water Users Association and its members. The dam was the site for many family and neighborhood picnics.

There was always maintenance to be done at the dam, including draining, cleaning out debris, and digging it deeper. It was a great place to gather while the guys were fixing the water system.

Marge and Norm were very involved in the

Norman and Marjorie Heimdahl cont'd

community. Marge directed both community and high school plays, organized pageants and talent shows, and assisted high school cheerleaders and drill teams with their routines.

Norman gained national recognition for his involvement and dedication as a leader in the Boy Scouts. He was instrumental in the development of the Boy Scout camps at both Blind Slough and Harvey's Lake. He even built a cabin on floats, so he could tow it to the different Scout camping sites.

Together, Marge and Norm helped organize July 4th and May 17th celebrations. They especially enjoyed organizing the parades.

Even after they left Petersburg, they continued their enthusiastic Fourth of July celebrations. Many Washington children and adults got to enjoy what Norm and Marge called "A Petersburg-type Fourth."

Another accomplishment they were proud of was the Moose Club. Norm and Marge worked many weekends and nights helping to get the original Moose Club up and running.

In 1960, they opened the Harbor Way Marina and sold boats, motors and supplies. In 1962, they bought the Family Shoe Mart.

In 1967, they decided it was time for Norman's father, Andrew, to retire and close the Modern Grocery. They purchased a home for Andrew and Gertrude in Everett, Washington, where they would be close to their son, Albert.

Norm and Marge closed the store, helped his parents pack up, and moved them south. They also bought his parents' house in town and moved in from Scow Bay.

In 1968, they bought Gurtie's from Gertrude Reeser and renamed it The Fashion Fair. The Fashion Fair occupied the old Modern Grocery site, and their shoe store was right next door. This allowed them to open a passageway between the two businesses — a Petersburg-style shopping mall.

In 1970, the Heimdahls purchased both the building that housed their businesses and the building next door from Ed Hagerman. The building next door housed The Cache, in which they were already partners with Gloria Ohmer and Patti Norheim. Upstairs were rental apartments.

Norman retired from the employment services in 1972. He spent the next chapter in his life trolling the F/V *Orca* and F/V *Marjorie Mae*, maintaining the buildings, and traveling.

Fourth of July parade along Sing Lee Alley, passing the Variety Theatre

In 1980, Marge and Norm closed the doors on their businesses and retired to Kirkland, Washington. In 1984, they sold the buildings to Gloria Ohmer and Patti Norheim.

Marge was a very creative, artistic and giving person. She enjoyed drawing, painting, writing, reading, and writing poetry.

She designed the sets for her many plays, and continually redesigned the look of her stores.

Norman was a tireless worker. He enjoyed helping others with gardening, fishing, and construction projects. There wasn't anything Norm couldn't do, make, or fix, when it came to construction and building maintenance.

Marge kept him busy as her stage manager, building her sets, reconfiguring her stores, and remodeling her houses. He is probably remembered most for digging, by hand of course, a basement under every house they owned.

Marge died July 13, 1993. Norman died August 1, 1996.

Robert and Wilma Henderson

By Robert Henderson

I am Robert E. Henderson, born in Morgantown, West Virginia, on January 15, 1920.

I was educated in Morgantown and received a BS degree from West Virginia University in 1942.

That same year I joined the United States Coast Guard for officers' training. Upon completion I was assigned to duty in Alaska. After serving in the Aleutians, I returned to Ketchikan and later transferred to Petersburg.

I arrived in Petersburg on July 4, 1943, assigned to duty as assistant to the captain of the port at the Petersburg Coast Guard Station. Chief Warrant Officer Iverson was in charge.

The station was located near the end of Bert Cornelius' dock. At the end of the dock was a cannery operated by Earl Ohmer.

A Mr. Porter (I believe that was his name) had invented and built a shrimp-picking machine that was going to revolutionize the shrimp industry.

Shortly after I arrived in Petersburg, Mr. Iverson transferred and I became the commanding officer.

During that year, the *Prince Rupert*, a Canadian passenger ship, struck a rock when it entered Wrangell Narrows from Fredrick Sound. The ship limped into the harbor and tied up at our dock.

This dock handled all Alaska Steam and Northland Transportation ships.

I placed Huey Harris, my chief, in charge of pumping out the ship. We used all our pumps and wired Juneau for help. We worked all night long, just barely managing to keep up with the incoming water.

By morning, a coast guard fireboat arrived and, with their pumps, we were able to get ahead of the water. They also brought a diver, who went down to find the hole and then put a soft patch over it.

It was not long before we had the ship pumped out. But before we could head for our bunks, someone yelled, "FIRE!"

We discovered the cannery was on fire. We cut the lines of the *Prince Rupert* and it anchored out in the harbor.

The fire had had a good start. Even though we had a fireboat and other pumps, the entire cannery was destroyed, along with the mechanical shrimp-picking machine.

We were able to contain the fire to the cannery and the coast guard station was saved.

In September, Les Wingard came down to see if anyone at the station could teach trigonometry to a class of high school boys. I would not have been interested in anything else, but I loved trig. I could not turn it down. I already had a degree so I had no problem getting a five-year teacher's certificate.

My first class included Jim Hammer, Chet Otness,

Citizens Wharf
Photo courtesy of the Clausen Memorial Museum

A. Norheim, Phil Clausen and Jim File. I taught this class during my lunch hour. I really enjoyed the class and, because of it, I later became a teacher.

While at Petersburg, I purchased Leon Hasbrouck's property at Camp Island.

In 1944, I was transferred and reluctantly left Petersburg. But, since I owned property, I had no doubt I would return.

I met Wilma King in Skagway, and we were married on September 15, 1945.

Robert and Wilma Henderson cont'd

Wilma was born on January 15, 1918, near Hampton, Iowa. We set up housekeeping in Seattle where I was then stationed.

I wrote Les Wingard about a math job in the fall. He immediately replied that he not only had a fall opening, but he needed me right away. A teacher had not returned from Christmas vacation. I would finish the year teaching physics and shop.

Wilma and I arrived in early March of 1946. Petersburg was always such a nice clean town. The houses and boats were all painted and well kept. There was the big white schoolhouse on the hill above the town, along with the beautiful Lutheran Church further back.

Housing was very tight, but with the help of Sie Hasbrouck, we found a small cabin between Hasbrouck's house and Mr. Ives', the photographer. Jackie O'Donnell and his family lived on the beach across the road.

The cabin we lived in belonged to a Seattle fisherman, who lived in it in the summer and wanted someone to live in it during the winter. We had to vacate at end of school and move back in the fall.

That was fine, as we wanted to spend the summers out on Camp Island at the mouth of Le Conte Bay.

I obtained a 16-foot seine skiff and a 10-horsepower outboard motor for our transportation to Camp Island. We moved there as soon as school was out and planted a big garden. The Hasbroucks had left a large strawberry bed.

One night an iceberg took my skiff and it sailed down Fredrick Sound. We were stranded. I had been making a trip to town for supplies every other week, but probably no one would miss us until we hadn't shown up back in town in the fall.

One night a young bear came over from the mainland at low tide. I saw his tracks, went back to the house for my rifle and shot the bear on the beach. We skinned him out and hauled the bear meat back in a wheelbarrow.

The Hasbroucks had several ice chests they used to store fox feed, so we filled one with glacier ice and stored our meat there. We also canned the meat we could not eat fresh.

For the next several weeks, we ate bear meat and made strawberry ice cream, using glacier ice to freeze the mix made from canned milk and fresh strawberries. To this day, I cannot even think about eating bear meat.

Looking around the island one day, I discovered a small six-foot skiff overturned up on the beach. It appeared solid, but had lots of space between boards.

I pulled it home, heated up a big pot of tar, and made a tar boat out of the skiff. It floated and did not leak, so I put the outboard on it and flew to town.

We used that skiff the rest of the summer, although I asked Leon Hasbrouck to come out and get us at the end of the season.

We later purchased the Hungerford property at Scow Bay. This allowed us to have a big garden with real soil, raise chickens, and have milk goats. It was a lovely spot right on the beach.

I was so disappointed to learn that they later used rock to fill in that property to make a trailer court.

While in Petersburg we had three children: Richard, Barbara and Anne.

After several years, I transferred to the science department, but still taught the advanced math class. With all the students housed in one building, we were beginning to get a little crowded.

It seemed we had little hope of getting a new building, but Les Wingard and school board president Swede Wasvick had the foresight to spent money on plans for a new high school.

The day arrived when extra federal money was found that needed to be spent right away. They asked for any project with plans already drawn up, and we were the only project on their list with plans. Our new high school was built and we thought we had the best school in the territory.

We did have a wonderful faculty, we had a good student body, and I think our students usually did well when they went on to college. I taught school for almost 40 years. I will say that from the 10 years I taught at Petersburg, more of my PHS students have been successful than those of any other school. This group includes several executive officers of large corporations, engineers, doctors, teachers, fishermen, and even the biggest lobbyist in the State.

I have always been proud of my Petersburg students. Many of them still keep in touch and some even stop by for a visit.

Myhre and Birgitte Hofstad

By Karen Olsen Haltiner

Issac Myhre Hofstad, the youngest son of Morten Petersen Hofstad and Helene Marie Andersen, was born in Heroy, Nordland, Norway, on November 16, 1864. Twenty years later Myhre came to the United States. He came to Southeast Alaska in 1886.

He followed his brother, Edwin, who had come to America in 1881. Edwin was the first customs inspector in Southeast Alaska at Mary's Island.

In 1888, Myhre became deputy collector for U.S. Customs at Sitka, because he was the only applicant who could read and write good English. Ten years later, he was fired from the job when they found out that he wasn't a United States' citizen!

He then joined his brothers, Edwin and Morten Fremann Hofstad, in Wrangell. Edwin was the customs officer and later a U.S. commissioner, and Morten had a store.

During this time, Myhre owned and operated the steam vessel, *King & Wing*, holding unlimited master's papers in coastwise transportation. He was married to Ranghild and had a daughter, Helen. He and Ranghild divorced.

He married Birgitte Hofstad, the daughter of his half brother.

Birgitte Nicoline Hofstad, the daughter of Peder Mortensen and Hanna Albrigtsdatter (Albrigtsen) Hofstad, was born in Bø in Vesteralen, Nordland, Norway, on February 10, 1874. She came to America in 1898.

Birgitte and Myhre settled in Scow Bay in the early 1900s with their two sons: Arthur, born in 1905; and Harold, born in 1906. The family's home was north of the present-day Beachcomber Inn property.

Birgitte's brother, Morten, came to the United States in 1901. He and his wife, Valborg, settled in Scow Bay.

Birgitte's sister, Elise, came to the states in 1904. Two years later, she settled in Wrangell, where her uncle Edwin lived. Elise married Knut Rastad.

In 1915, Myhre and a man named Doyle began the Doyhof Fish Products Company and Myhre became its president. The articles of incorporation said they were "to engage in a general canning business, curing and preparing both salmon and herring for the American market."

The Doyhof store was run by Birgitte. In 1918, Doyhof was classified as a distributing post office and she was put in charge. Mail came from Petersburg on the cold storage company boats, which were not on a regular schedule.

The cannery was sold to the Hume cannery interests in 1918. It became a sawmill in the '20s.

The Hofstads still ran the store and post office through the '30s. Myhre also fished, hunted, operated a transportation service, and prospected and mined for zinc at Chichagof Island.

Myhre died in 1949, and Birgitte died in 1954.

Their sons, Arthur and Harold, were both fishermen. In the 1940s and 1950s, Arthur owned the seiner F/V *Commando*. Harold owned the F/V *Rustler*.

In the 1960s, Harold, along with Erling Thomassen and Andrew Wikan, bought and converted the navy vessel *Iceland* for packing dog salmon from the Aleutian Chain to Seattle.

In their later years they lived in Sitka. Harold died in 1978 and Arthur in 1982.

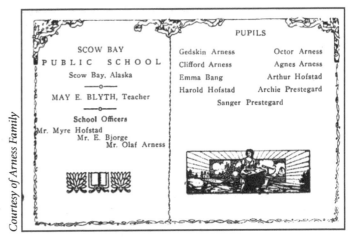

Scow Bay Public School

May E. Blyth, teacher

School officers:
Myre Hofstad, E. Bjorge, Olaf Arness

Pupils:
Gedskin Arness, Clifford Arness, Octor Arness, Agnes Arness, Emma Bang, Harold Hofstad, Arthur Hofstad, Archie Prestegard,
and Sanger Prestegard

Richard and Dorothy Hofstad

By Melinda Hofstad

The first Hofstads in Alaska were two bachelor brothers, Edwin and Issac Myhre Hofstad, who came to Southeast Alaska from Norway in the 1880s. Their enthusiasm for the last frontier began the emigration of an entire family from Hov, Helgeland, Norway, to Alaska.

Their nephew, Richard Hofstad, was born on the island of Heroy in Helgeland, Norway, on March 17, 1883. Unhappy with his prospects of living and working on the family farm, he left Norway at the age of 18 to seek a new life in America.

He traveled aboard the steam powered ship *Oceanus*, arriving at Ellis Island on June 14, 1901. Many years later he told his son, Albert, how thrilling it was for him to see the Statue of Liberty welcoming him to New York Harbor. According to the ship's manifest, Richard arrived in his new homeland with one dollar.

He had a friend, Mr. J. Jacobsen, in Flandreau, South Dakota, who agreed to give him passage to Alaska in exchange for one year's work on his farm.

Richard later shared with his family a story of his traveling by train from New York to South Dakota. He had only four cents left in his pocket.

He was very hungry on the train and a woman came around with a basket full of fruit for sale. There was a strange yellow fruit in the basket, priced at four cents. He purchased this fruit, depleting his entire net worth. It turned out to be a lemon, and for the rest of his life, he never again ate lemons.

Exactly a year to the day after arriving in South Dakota and fulfilling his obligation to Mr. Jacobsen, Richard headed to Wrangell, Alaska.

Richard's uncle, "Gammel" Morten Freeman Hofstad, owned a general store in Wrangell. He and Richard became partners in the store in 1902. By all accounts, this business venture did not end well.

In 1904, Richard moved to Hadley, on Prince of Wales Island, to work as maintenance men in the large copper mine. While in Hadley, Richard met his future wife, Dorothy Smith.

Dorothy Smith was born in Ferndale, Washington, in 1896. Her mother, Maude Aikens, was of English descent. Her father, James Peter Smith, had emigrated from Vejle, Denmark, and was a well noted brick mason in the Bellingham area.

Dorothy had an adventuresome spirit and sought

Dorothy and Richard Hofstad

a teaching job in the Territory of Alaska. In 1917, at age 21, after graduating from Bellingham Normal School (now Western Washington University), she boarded an Alaska Steamship for Hadley, Alaska. Hadley was a remote settlement consisting of a few fishermen and a large copper mine.

A letter written to her mother in Acme, Washington, on August 20, 1917, indicated that her monthly teaching salary was $110, and that she would be teaching six students. Her ship had passed through Wrangell and Dorothy wrote that "Wrangell has 2 autos and 1 horse."

After hearing that Dorothy was living in Hadley, many young, single men found their way to her door. Richard Hofstad's sister, Martine Hofstad Oaksmith (who had also come to Alaska from Norway), lived in Hadley and rented a room to the young teacher.

One thing led to another and a romance ensued. It wasn't long before Dorothy and Richard were married in Seattle at the Dan Drotning home on March 3, 1919.

They later moved to Petersburg and Richard began a fishing career that was to span over 50 years.

They moved to Scow Bay where they proved up a parcel of land, which was a "soldiers rights" land grant

Richard and Dorothy Hofstad cont'd

to Richard's cousin, Ole Husvik. It was located on the beach next to what is now Alaska Marine Lines.

Ole, who as a World War I veteran qualified for a homesteading priority, gave the land to Richard and Dorothy. Soon after, they started to build their home and warehouse, which is today still standing on wooden pilings.

They had three children: Betty in 1919, Richard "Dick" in 1925, and Albert in 1932.

Long winter nights on the homestead were spent listening to AM radio broadcasts straight from Nashville. Richard would play the fiddle accompanied by Dorothy playing the piano and Albert on spoons.

Richard had three boats over his fishing career, the *Helen*, the *Unity*, and the *Tango*, after which the city street Tango is named.

The *Tango* was built in 1915, in Ketchikan, and purchased by Richard in 1928, He seined for salmon and herring and had herring pounds in various sites to provide live bait for the Seattle-based halibut schooner fleet.

In Richard's absence, Dorothy ran the homestead. She gardened, canned, made soap, smoked, and salted fish. She was well known for her huge rhubarb and prolific garden on the beach in Scow Bay.

Dorothy also worked in Petersburg's local canneries, including Oscar Nicholsen's cannery, Scow Bay Cannery, Dean Kayler cannery, PAF, and Ohmer's cannery.

Both Richard and Dorothy were very proud Americans and very strong Democrats.

Dorothy had the distinction of being one of the original organizers of the cannery workers banding together and joining the AFL/CIO. She tended the Union Hall for years and her son, Albert, remembers splitting wood to warm up the hall for cold, winter night union meetings.

Richard fished until his death in 1962, when he collapsed while walking up the ramp from his boat. He had been on his way to visit his daughter for dinner.

He was 79 when he passed from this life.

Dorothy died peacefully in 1987, when she was 90 years old.

They were true Alaska pioneers, remembered with great love and affection.

Richard and Dorothy's daughter, Betty, married Gerald "Bud" Bodding, and they lived their entire adult lives in Ketchikan.

Betty seined many years with her younger brother, Albert, aboard the *Tonka II*, and later worked aboard the Alaska Marine Highway. Bud flew close to 30,000 hours in a Grumman Goose Aircraft for Ellis Airlines, and is affectionately known as "Father Goose."

They had three children: Eric, Jim and Sheila (Hayes). Betty passed away in 1998.

Richard and Dorothy's middle child, Dick, and his wife, Shirley, had one daughter, Laurie.

Dick worked for the Alaska Marine Highway. As the captain of the M/V *Columbia*, he retired after 32 years of service. He and Shirley moved to Cambria, California. Dick passed away in 2003.

Albert, third child of Richard and Dorothy, is married to Melinda Gruening Hofstad, and he has made his lifelong home in Petersburg.

They are commercial fishermen who fish together on their boat, the *Tonka*, for salmon, herring roe on kelp, and halibut.

Albert is keeping the family musical tradition alive by owning every polka CD and tape known to mankind. These recordings are heard blaring off the back deck of his boat wherever he travels.

Albert and his first wife, Karen Hansen Hofstad, have two sons, Larry and Mark.

Karen has lived her entire adult life in Petersburg and has been a business and civic leader in the community, contributing much to the development of the Chamber of Commerce, Southeast Conference, and other volunteer organizations.

Larry's a talented artist and ivory carver living in South Dakota. A gallery owner in Sioux City, he returns annually to fish halibut with his father and brother.

Mark lives in Scow Bay and has followed in the family fishing tradition — he owns the F/V *Norseman* and fishes for salmon, halibut, blackcod, and crab. He and Albert herring pound together in the spring.

During the Little Norway Festival, Mark is known around town as the Viking "Vulgar the Crude."

The Hofstads have had a strong family tradition in the founding and growth of Petersburg throughout the 20th century. As they enter the 21st century, they have high hopes for the community and for the contributions their family will be able to make.

Morten and Valborg Hofstad

By Angie Hasbrouck Hofstad

Morten Hofstad was born, in 1880, to Peder Mortensen and Hanna Albrigtsdatter (Albrigtsen) Hofstad in Gustad, Bø, Norway, in the county of Vesteralen. The Hofstad family had been fishermen for many generations in Norway. Morten's father, Peder, drowned when Morten was just 6 years old.

Morten was the second youngest of eight siblings. He had two sisters, Elise Johanna and Birgitte Nicoline, who both moved to Alaska from Norway.

In 1907, Elise married Knut Rastad from Wrangell. Knut was the captain of a fish packer named the *Baranof*.

In 1925, when they were both in their 50s, Knut and Elise Rastad decided to become chiropractors. They graduated from the Palmer School of Chiropractic in Davenport, Iowa. Elise was a chiropractor in Petersburg for many years and treated many of the local fishermen.

Birgitte married I. Myhre Hofstad, an original resident and cannery owner in Scow Bay. She was also the postmaster for Doyhof, while it existed as a separate post office from Petersburg.

Morten immigrated to the United States through Bergen in November of 1901.

He first lived in Chicago with his oldest brother, Peder Johan Hofstad. He worked for a time in a furniture factory.

He next moved to Wrangell, Alaska, and stayed with his uncle, Edwin Hofstad (born in Norway in 1864). Edwin was the postmaster, customs official, and owned a general store.

Uncle Edwin's home in Wrangell was the starting place for Morten and other family members who moved to Alaska from Norway.

Morten's brother-in-law, Myhre Hofstad, lived in Scow Bay and was partners in the Doyhof Scow Bay Cannery, with a man named Doyer.

Scow Bay was originally called Doyhof after the two surnames of the cannery founders — Doyer and Hofstad. The Doyhof-Scow Bay area was not connected to Petersburg by road until 1920. Once the road was completed, the school at Doyhof was closed and the children attended school in Petersburg.

Myhre Hofstad was also involved in gold prospecting and had many claims around Southeast Alaska in the early 1900s. Morten worked as a laborer in some of these mining camps.

Morten attended Pacific Lutheran College in Tacoma, Washington. He studied the English language and did beautiful calligraphy.

Morten later sent for Valborg Pedersen, his fiancé from Norway.

Morten Hofstad

Valborg was born in 1882 in Litloy, Bø, Norway, in the county of Vesteralen. The Pedersen family had a fish buying business on the island of Litloy.

Valborg had two sisters, Auslaug and Ida, who had also moved to the United States. They lived in Tacoma, Washington. Her half brothers remained in Norway.

Edgar, one of these half brothers, wrote a family history of the Pedersen family, tracing them back to their 1801 immigration to Norway from an area in Prussia that is now part of Poland.

Valborg came to the United States around 1908. She first stayed with her sisters in Tacoma. She and

Morten and Valborg Hofstad cont'd

Morten were married in Tacoma in 1910.

They moved into their newly built house and began their family. It was on waterfront property immediately south of Myhre's house in Scow Bay. Morten also built a warehouse in front of the house.

Morten and Valborg reared five children. The first son, Edmund Peder, was born in 1911. Because there was no doctor or midwife in Scow Bay or Petersburg at that time, Valborg went to Wrangell for his birth. Walter John was born in 1913, Margaret Hanna in 1915, Oliver Andrew in 1917, and Ida Jane in 1925.

Myhre and Doyhof eventually sold the cannery to G.W. Hume. Morten worked at the cannery, first as a foreman, and, in 1913, as winter watchman.

In 1921, Morten was burned in a gasoline fire on board a boat in Ketchikan. He was taken to the hospital with severe burns on both arms and stayed there until he was well enough to come home.

Morten built a gillnetter-sized wooden boat in his warehouse in the early years. It was named the *W&E* for his oldest sons, Walt and Ed. He used it to pack gillnet fish from the skiff fleet on the Stikine River to the G. W. Hume cannery.

The Hume cannery was just north of the Oscar Nicholson's cannery, which later became the Beachcomber Inn.

Later, Morten bought the *Sokol* and used it for many years to pack fish. At a sheriff's sale in Petersburg, he also bought the 64-foot fishing vessel *Galveston* with his eldest son, Ed.

Ed Hofstad ran the *Galveston* and packed fish for Oscar Nicholson's cannery while Morten ran the *Sokol*. Morten used the *Sokol* to pack salmon and also to fish shrimp for Earl Ohmer.

All their lives the Hofstad brothers worked at some fishing enterprise. When they were too young to ship out on a longliner, they used a wooden skiff and rowed across the Narrows to dig clams, which they sold to Mountain Point Cannery.

Their father, Morten, took them on the *Sokol* when he packed fish.

They made many longline trips as teens on the *Star*, with Magnus and Leonard Martens and their father, Louis.

Later in life, they each had their own longline boats. Ed had the *Galveston*, the *Unimak*, and the *Faith II*, all of which were wooden longline boats.

After Ed retired and sold his last boat, he fished with Walt on the *Ira II*.

Walt had the *Argo*, the *Sarah Marie*, the *R&H*, the *Marjorie H*, the *Valeta H*, the *Balder*, and the *Ira II*, which he renamed the *Leeward*.

Oliver owned the *Genedor*, the *Sarah Marie*, and two boats named the *Angelette*.

Longlining was in their blood.

Valborg passed away unexpectedly in 1944, while in Seattle visiting her son, Ed, and his bride, Klara.

Morten died in 1968.

There were many Hofstad relatives who lived and worked around Petersburg and Wrangell in the early part of the 20th century.

The following were cousins of Morten, and brothers and sisters to each other.

Ottar Hofstad was a commercial fisherman who often sold fish in Petersburg.

Richard Hofstad lived in Scow Bay and married Dorothy Smith, a teacher from Hadley, Alaska.

Martine Hofstad Oaksmith first lived in Wrangell. While there she was married to Stanley Oaksmith. She later lived in Hadley and then Ketchikan, where she had a women's apparel store for many years.

Agnes Hofstad Olsen was married to Kris Olsen.

Oliver Hofstad, Margaret Hofstad Jones, Ed Hofstad, Ida Hofstad Severson, and Walt Hofstad

Oliver and Angie Hofstad

By Angie Hasbrouck Hofstad

Oliver Andrew Hofstad, born in 1917, was Morten and Valborg Hofstad's fourth child.

In his early years, he worked with his father buying fish in Port Alexander and other Southeast bays, and he worked for the cannery in Scow Bay where his father was winter watchman.

At age 12, Oliver's first boat was a 24-foot trolling vessel *Fulton*, nicknamed *High Pockets*. He used the boat to take mail between Scow Bay and Petersburg for his Aunt Birgitte, the postmistress in Scow Bay.

When Japan bombed Pearl Harbor, Oliver was fishing shark off the coast of California. He hurried back to Bremerton, Washington, to enlist in the Navy.

Because of his knowledge of boats and the sea, he was assigned to small boat patrol off Southeast Alaskan waters, out of Sitka and Yakatat, skippering a boat belonging to the Molver family of Petersburg. The Navy had commandeered the vessel for patrols.

He later served at the Bremerton naval port.

After his war service ended, Oliver was anxious to get back to Scow Bay and his fishing lifestyle. On the steamer to Petersburg, he met Angie Hasbrouck.

Sarah Angelette Hasbrouck was born in Malone, Washington, September 7, 1925, to Sarah "Sie" and Leon Hasbrouck. "Angie" was 2, and her sister Leona was almost a year old, when they moved to Petersburg.

Her father began working on fox farms and the family moved with him to Grief Island, Woewodski Island, and Coney Island. Her brother, Ted, was born while the family was living on Grief Island.

After Leon had worked on Coney Island a few years, long enough to earn foxes of his own, he moved his family to Camp Island, at the mouth of LeConte Bay.

The sand flats stretched several miles out beyond the island after the tide ran out, leaving the island dry.

There were always icebergs from LeConte Glacier drifting past the island on the outgoing tide. The largest icebergs stayed behind, stuck on the rock reefs in the mouth of the bay. These big gymnasium-sized icebergs would break apart from their own weight when the tide left them high and dry on reefs.

It was always fun when new guests were startled by a large crack and crash. They would jump up and look around saying, "What was that?"

It was very loud when the bergs broke apart. The family was used to it; newcomers were always surprised.

Special tricks were needed to keep a fishing boat moored at the island when the tide was out and the beach exposed. Leon fitted his boat with removable "legs" that kept his boat upright when the tide was out.

More importantly, he tied the boat inside an anchored A-frame float to protect the boat from the icebergs that were always floating past.

One spring thaw a huge piece of flat ice from Le Conte Glacier came out on the tide. It was large enough to lift or drag the anchor, taking the float and boat out to sea in Fredrick Sound, which it did.

Angie's father had to launch the skiff and row after his boat. It was quite a ways from the island before he could get through and around all the ice to rescue his boat and float.

Angie, Leona, Ted, and Sie Hasbrouck, 1940

He then had to wait for the incoming tide to get everything back in place.

When the market for fox furs began to drop, Leon expanded his fishing for fox feed to include crabbing as a means of added income.

The kids learned to dig clams for crab bait. They were paid $1 a sack, each was about three buckets worth.

When Leon gillnetted for salmon on the north arm of the Stikine River, the kids helped with the nets. He built net racks on the beach. When the nets had holes or too much seaweed stuck in the web to fish, the kids mended the nets and cleaned out the seaweed.

They worked not only for their father, but also for their Uncle Ed and sometimes Tom Runstad. They were paid enough to buy school clothes.

Oliver and Angie Hofstad cont'd

Leon and Sie always tried to get the kids to town about every six weeks, staying a week each time. While the town kids were having tests at school, Angie, Leona, and Ted stayed with Aunt Ellen, so the teachers could be sure they were keeping up on their studies.

Aunt Ellen was their Uncle Henry's widow and she taught school in Petersburg for many years.

When Angie was 11, she was sent to Olympia to spend the school year with her father's mother, Hetty Hasbrouck, and his sister, her Aunt Angie.

Angie was peeved because that was the year Poo Bear, a small grizzly cub, came to live on the island and she missed out on the fun.

The family moved to town in 1942. Three high school students were too much for Sie to teach on her own. While homeschooling her children, the local teachers had always been a great help. They welcomed the teens to town.

By then, Leon was commercial fishing full time, as the fox fur market ceased to exist.

Angie graduated from Petersburg High in 1943 and went back to Olympia to go to business school.

She later worked for the Army at Fort Richardson, in Anchorage, and in Georgia.

Oliver Hofstad and Angie Hasbrouck were married on October 19, 1946.

They first lived in Scow Bay and later moved down the road to Skylark. Their third move was further into town where the south boat harbor is today.

Oliver promptly returned to fishing. Soon he had his own boat, the *Genedor*. He seined for salmon and fished halibut and cod.

Later, he bought the *Sarah Marie* from his brother, Walt Hofstad. In 1960, he moved the family to Seattle while building a new boat, the *Angelette*.

After many successful years, Oliver sold the *Angelette* and built a bigger fishing boat, also the *Angelette*, with his sister Ida's son, Mark Severson.

They fished well together until he sold his share to Mark and signed on with the Alaska Department of Fish and Game to skipper the *Steller* in 1980.

Along the way, Oliver and Angie had five children: Andrew Edward, born in 1948; Anna Valborg, born in 1950; Olivia Jane, born in 1952; Ella Christine, born in 1954; and Susan Kayborn, born in 1958.

In 1969, they lost Andy in a tragic accident in Hobart Bay. The boat he was on hit an iceberg and sank.

After retiring from Fish and Game in 1986, Oliver bought a troller named the *Keeper* and took Angie out fishing. After about six years of summer trolling, he retired again and bought a smaller pleasure boat, the *Kristin Ann*, which he uses to fish in the Memorial Day Salmon Derby, and for sport fishing and hunting trips.

Oliver and Angie Hofstad

In 1977, Oliver and Angie moved back to Scow Bay, close to the place Oliver was born and raised.

They currently have 12 grandchildren and six great-grandchildren.

Angie gets many requests for her time to do volunteer work and she is always willing to help out.

She spends many hours working for the Emblem Club, Sons of Norway, World Relief, Hospital Guild, Charity Box, Clausen Memorial Museum, Little Norway Festival, and Pioneers of Alaska.

Angie enjoys her ever-expanding gardens, as well as harvesting the bountiful rain forest edibles.

Together, Oliver and Angie do a lot of cooking, fishing, hunting, and firewood cutting. Like their parents, they live a subsistence lifestyle, but with the help of modern conveniences.

In 2002, for the first time, Oliver and Angie participated in the Southeast Alaska elk hunt. Beautiful cruise, no elk!

Edgar and Caroline Hungerford

By Martha Hungerford Reid

Edgar S. Hungerford, known as "Ted", arrived in Alaska on February 22, 1909, at the age of 24. He is listed in the 1910 census as a resident of Petersburg.

Hungerford is an English family name and also the name of a town in England. Hungerfords joined the large group brought over from England by John Winthrop in 1640, settling in Hartford, Connecticut.

Over the years, various families of Hungerfords slowly migrated inland into what is now New York State. Edgar's father migrated to California from his family home in Watertown, New York, in the 1800s.

Ted was born and raised in the early days of California in the small logging and mining towns, inland from San Francisco along the American River.

He worked as a carpenter in San Francisco after the earthquake, then moved on up the coast to the timber industry near Bellingham, Washington. There he bought a small sailboat, named the *Reliance,* and headed for Alaska, ending up in Petersburg.

Petersburg was very small, with only a plank sidewalk along the shoreline, connecting the cannery, sawmill, and some stores. Boats anchored out in front.

Ted enlarged his boat, installed an engine, and started hauling freight to Kake. He always called Petersburg headquarters, but spent most of his time logging, prospecting for minerals, trapping, and hunting in outlying areas, particularly Rocky Pass.

In 1923, on a visit to Bellingham to see a sister, he met a woman from New York State who changed his life, Caroline Gallup.

They married and had six children: Martha, Marcia, Mary Elizabeth, Caroline Patricia, Edgar and Helen.

In the early years, their floating logging camp was home, as they moved to various Southeast Alaskan logging sites. Eventually, Scow Bay was their address.

Caroline was a registered pharmacist who worked part time at the Petersburg drugstore.

The maternal grandmother, Marcia L. Gallup, came to live with them in later years. She died at home in Scow Bay in 1945.

In the late 1930s, Ted built a small boat called the *Noseeum*. He used it to trap and prospect, and even tried a summer of seining.

It was constructed in a building that previously had been used as the Scow Bay Community Center, and later was a shipyard by Alvin Arness. The last social event at the center, in the fall of 1933, was a potluck dinner with games for the younger folks and a dance.

Scow Bay was a small community about four miles south of Petersburg on Mitkof Island. It had its own post office called Doyhof, which was a combination of the last names of two Scow Bay residents.

Birgitte Hofstad (Mrs. Myhre) was postmistress. She also had a small grocery store with a two-room apartment upstairs that she rented to the schoolteacher.

Access to Petersburg from Scow Bay was originally only by boat, but by the late 1920s a gravel road connected the two communities and Scow Bay children began attending the Petersburg school. The Roundtree family then began its many years of providing the school bus service.

In 1948, the senior Hungerfords moved to Chelan, Washington, where the landscape looked remarkably like the dry hills of the gold country of inland California where Ted was born.

Since most of Ted and Caroline's children were girls, the Hungerford name does not carry on in Petersburg, but you will find descendants among the Reid, Carlson, Ellis, Bell, Morrison, and other family names in the Petersburg telephone book.

Martha married Glenn W. Reid, and they had three children: Jean, Glenn Jr., and Celia, all of them still living in Petersburg.

Marcia married a soldier stationed in Petersburg during World War II named Robert Goss. They spent most of their life in Washington; had three children, George, John, and Jean; and retired to Phoenix, Arizona.

Mary Elizabeth married Alex J. Reid, lived in Petersburg, and then in Ketchikan. Their children are James, Richard, Alex "Sandy", Thomas, Kent, Linda, and Mary Wilma.

Caroline Patricia married James Lafrenz. They lived in Washington State and their children are Timothy, Myrl, Michael and Gary. She died in 1975.

Edgar married Elaine Thompson of Portland, Oregon, and had Julia and Peter. He taught high school art classes until they retired to Tillamook, Oregon.

Helen married Larry Best. They live in Washington State and their children are Carol, David, Laura, Elizabeth, Jett and Steven.

Ole and Liv Husvik

By Erling Husvik

Ole Sjønning Husvik was born May 20, 1890, in Koperdal, Helgeland, Norway.

His father was Peder Salamon Andreason Husvig; his mother, Nikoline Kristine Rolfsen Schonning.

Ole had two brothers and four sisters. His brother Nils and sister Gudrun were the only children in the family to come to the United States.

Liv and Ole Husvik

Ole left Trondheim, Norway, on March 26, 1913, at the age of 23, on the *Royal Edward*, arriving in Boston on April 20. From there he traveled to Everett, Washington, and on to Ketchikan, where he met up with other family members and neighbors from Hov, Lokta and Nesna. Among them were Hofstads, Drotninghaugs and Husviks.

Beginning in 1913, Ole fished and worked in mines and construction in Ketchikan, Wrangell, Scow Bay, and at Hadley on Prince of Wales Island.

He was inducted into the U.S. Army on May 23, 1918, and served in Haines at Fort William H. Seward. He was discharged March 21, 1919.

When asked what he did in the Army, Ole said that he and Charlie Greenaa (a longtime Petersburg resident) shoveled snow.

From 1919 until 1921, Ole was mostly a fisherman. He fished on the *Lenore* with Andrew Mathisen when the boat was new.

In October of 1921, he bought property at 403 Surf Street, where he built a house. It is still occupied by a Husvik, his oldest son Erling.

Ole married Liv Winther on December 24, 1921, in the John Otness home at 105 Dolphin Street in Petersburg. Witnesses were Nils Husvik, Agnes Hofstad and John Otness. John Otness' wife, Ragna, and Agnes were Ole's cousins.

Liv Winther was born July 10, 1894, in Kopordal Donnes, Lokta, Norway.

Liv's father was Jens Jacob Andreas Winther and her mother was Anna Katherine Pedersdatter. She had four sisters and three brothers. Of Liv's siblings, only Egil came to the United States. He settled in Petersburg.

Liv graduated from Teachers Seminary at Tromsø and taught school in Narvik, which is in northern Norway, for five years.

At the age of 26, she traveled to the United States with Agnes Hofstad and her mother, Albine Hofstad, who was Ole's aunt.

They sailed from Kristiania on April 22, 1921, on the steamer *Bergensfjord*, arriving at Ellis Island on May 2nd. From there they traveled on to Petersburg.

Liv's immigration papers state she was coming to Petersburg to "join her friend Ole Husvik."

That summer, Liv and Agnes spent time in Security Bay on Nils Husvik's herring salting scow.

Liv and Ole raised three children, during the '20s, '30s and '40s: Erling, Thor and Sonja.

Liv Husvik with Thor, Sonja and Erling

Ole was a fisherman. In 1927, he and Ole Rosvold bought the boat *Unimak* from John Molver. They fished halibut, blackcod and salmon until 1937, when Karl Hatlen bought Rosvold's share of the vessel.

In the early 1940s, Liv's brother, Egil Winther, bought the *Unimak*.

Afterwards, Ole then fished on many boats in the Petersburg fleet. He also fished for sharks off the Oregon coast and sardines off the California coast,

Ole and Liv Husvik cont'd

where he happened to be on December 7, 1941.

Liv was busy raising a family, but made time to be involved in her community.

She was active in the Daughters of Norway and served as president for five terms. Liv served on the school board and was president of the Parent Teacher Association. She was also active in the Lutheran Church and enjoyed being a member of the church's Ladies Aid.

Liv taught Norwegian at Petersburg High School in the late 1930s. She received a diploma from the King of Norway in recognition for her "Valuable services for Norway during World War II."

Liv died December 7, 1947, in Petersburg, at the age of 53.

In the early 1950s, Ole bought the old Scow Bay schoolhouse, moved it to the lot in front of his house, and converted it into a duplex.

In 1956, Ole, Morten Hofstad and Dan Drotning, who all grew up together, went to Norway to visit their relatives.

Liv Husvik

Ole was actively fishing until the late 1950s. He died March 26, 1961, in Petersburg, at the age of 70.

Erling Winther Husvik, son of Ole and Liv, was born October 26, 1923. He spent his life in Petersburg and, in the late '30s and early '40s, fished with his father.

From January 1942 until March 1946, he served in the U.S. Navy onboard destroyer 533, the USS *Hoel*.

On October 25, 1944, the *Hoel* was sunk in a running sea battle with the Japanese off of Samar Island in the Philippines. Erling and the other survivors spent 48 hours drifting on rafts. On October 26, adrift off of Samar, he turned 21 years old.

Erling was decorated with the Purple Heart for being wounded in the battle.

Upon returning home, Erling fished and worked construction. Among the projects he worked on were the building of the Kahler-Dahl cannery and the Crystal Lake Power Dam.

In the late '40s, he met Maxine Shirley Bredeson from Red Lake Falls, Minnesota.

Maxine's father was Sig Ole Bredeson and her mother was Marie Margrette Tunem.

She was born April 19, 1927, in Thief River Falls, Minnesota. Maxine arrived in Petersburg with her Aunt Edith, Mrs. John Samuelson. She met Erling at a Sons of Norway dance.

On April 9, 1949, Maxine and Erling were married in Ole's house.

During their marriage, three children were born to them: Liv, Heidi and Heather.

Maxine occasionally worked in the cannery and also worked as a teacher's aid for 10 years. She was active in the Petersburg Pioneers, Emblem Club, Petersburg Lutheran Church, and the Hospital Guild.

Maxine enjoyed her sewing circle and playing cards with friends.

In March of 1956, Erling went to work for the U.S. Forest Service. After running the *Maybeso* for five years and then the *Chugach* for another five years, he went to work as a forestry technician. He was promoted to the position of timber sales administrator for the Petersburg Ranger District.

In 1983, Erling retired so he could garden, fish with his sons-in-law, and make road trips with Maxine to the interior of Alaska and Canada.

Maxine died December 31, 2002, in Petersburg.

Erling and Maxine's oldest daughter, Liv Marie Husvik, was born October 17, 1949. Liv married Lynn Ranier Ewing, December 1, 1984, in the Husvik home. (Lynn Ewing was born July 5, 1953, in Sweet Home, Oregon.) Liv and Lynn have a daughter, Sonja Aileen Ewing, born January 5, 1989, in Ketchikan.

Liv married Peter Max Perschon, April 10, 2002, in the Lutheran Church of the Good Shepherd in Billings, Montana. Peter was born on September 14, 1943, in Lobenstein, Thueringia, Germany.

Liv and her sister, Heidi, own a local catering business, Liv & Heidi's Kjokken.

Heidi Signe Husvik was born August 21, 1953. She married Jack Curtis Lyons on October 30, 1982, in the Husvik home. (Jack Lyons was born in

Ole and Liv Husvik cont'd

Petersburg on February 19, 1953.) They have three children, all born in Petersburg.

Britina Liv Lyons was born on February 1, 1984. Drake Erling Lyons was born on April 21, 1986. Jaclyn Mae Lyons was born on May 8, 1990.

Between the catering business and a family fishing business, they stay very busy.

Heather Kay Husvik was born August 3, 1960. She married Dennis James O'Neil on July 9, 1982, in the Husvik home. (Dennis was born on February 17, 1960, in Everett, Washington.)

They have two children, both born in Petersburg. Holli Kay O'Neil was born on November 7, 1982. Megan Laura O'Neil was bornon December 17, 1988.

They are a fishing family and, at times, everyone works together on the F/V *Rogue*.

Thor, Erling and Sonja Husvik

Ole and Liv Husvik's second son, Thor Henry, was born November 3, 1924, in Petersburg.

On February 28, 1957, he married Clara Oakland in Seattle, Washington. (Clara was born in Rock Care, North Dakota, on March 28, 1916.)

Clara had a son, Terry Lewis Dietrich, born August 22, 1945, who was their pride and joy. Terry was killed in a car accident March 28, 1968.

Thor Husvik fished from the Bering Sea to California. He also was a longshoreman on the Seattle waterfront. During World War II he sailed with the Army Transportation Command.

He died July 1, 1980, in Sarles, North Dakota, while visiting Clara's family. Clara died in Seattle, Washington, on October 7, 1991.

Ole and Liv's daughter, Sonya Olive Husvik, was born May 22, 1930, in Petersburg.

Sonya married Charles Stanley Vaughn July 8, 1950, at Ole Husvik's home in Petersburg. (Charles Vaughn was born in Beach, North Dakota, on February 11, 1928.) Their children are Sandra, Ted, and Laurie.

They were long time residents of Sitka and their daughter, Laurie, lives there still. Sonya and Charles now live in Poulsbo, Washington, near Ted and Sandra.

Like their grandmother, Liv, all three of Sonya's children have teaching degrees.

Sonya and Charles' daughter, Sandra Lee Vaughn, was born August 20, 1951, in Portland, Oregon. She married Ronald George Rudy, who was born March 10, 1949, in Port Townsend, Washington. They have a daughter, Sarah Liv Rudy, born November 6, 1993, in Edmonds, Washington.

Sandra and Ron both share a love of Southeast Alaska, Sitka in particular.

Ted Stanley Vaughn, Sonya and Charles's son, was born May 21, 1953, in Sitka. Ted married Deborah Griesbach on August 28, 1993, in Poulsbo, Washington. (Deborah was born October 14, 1955, in Forest Hills, New York.)

She has a daughter, Alicia Danielle, born November 21, 1989, in Bremerton, Washington. Ted adopted Alicia in March of 1995. Both Ted and Deborah teach school.

Sonya and Charles' youngest child, Laurie Eve Vaughn, was born June 10, 1968, in Sitka. She married Duane Edward Seehafer July 6, 1991, in Sitka. (Duane was born August 12, 1962, in Kodiak, Alaska.)

Laurie and Duane have two children, both born in Sitka. Nicole Liv Seehafer was born on August 17, 1994. Erika Louise Seehafer was born on June 29, 1998.

Laurie works at the Sitka School District Office. She used to have a trained search and rescue dog, Jake.

The Husviks have always had busy lives in Petersburg and Sitka, past and present.

"Summers find us fishing, picking berries, gardening, and camping. The winters find us canning and smoking fish, making jelly and baking many traditional Norwegian foods.

"Ole was often heard to say, 'Ya, we have it good in America!'"

Louis and Alex Israelson

By John and Carol Enge

Louis Israelson came to America from Hemnes, Norway. He met his future wife, Alex, in Seattle. She was from Lycksele, Sweden.

After they married, Louie and Alex moved to Petersburg where their three children, Verner, Dorothy and Spencer, were born.

The family moved to a homestead at Point Agassiz in 1924.

Louie commuted to work in Petersburg where he was a well-known and respected carpenter.

Among other things, he built the Lutheran Church, navigation lights in Wrangell Narrows, as well as lighthouses on Lincoln Rock, Five Fingers Island and Sentinel Island. He was also a building inspector for the State of Alaska.

The family remained on the farm at Point Agassiz until moving to Petersburg, so the children could complete their schooling.

Louie passed away in October of 1968. Alex passed away in August of 1988.

In 1941, Louie's son, Verner, and Tony Westre went to Sitka to enlist in the Navy. They were given 90 days grace, so they traveled to Seattle with Eric Fuglvog on the F/V *Balder*, arriving there on December 7, 1941. They immediately reported for duty.

Verner was assigned to a destroyer and later an attack transport in the South Pacific. He was in Tokyo Bay when the armistice was signed in 1945.

Returning home in November 1945 with a carpenter's mate rating, he went to work constructing the Kayler-Dahl fish plant. (This plant is now known as Ocean Beauty Seafoods.)

Verner also helped construct the high school and elementary school buildings, and was employed at Petersburg Cold Storage until moving to Juneau.

Verner met Marnee Philbin at the Petersburg Elks Club. They were married during a blizzard on Valentine's Day at the Wootons' home.

Marnee was born in Seattle and attended school there until she was 9 years old. Her father and two older brothers had come to Alaska to establish a fox farm at Pybus Bay on Admiralty Island.

When their new home was ready, Marnee, her mother and her sister, sailed north on the S/S *Northland* to Petersburg. From Petersburg they took the M/V *Agnes* to Pybus Bay.

Marnee loved the years on the island and being homeschooled by her mother. When her mother suffered a stroke and died, Marnee was sent to stay with an aunt in Seattle.

While in Seattle, she attended beauty school, but she was homesick for Pybus Bay. She returned for a year, but with the onset of World War II, the blue fox market closed, and the family moved to Petersburg.

Marnee first found a job working for Mamie Tveten at the Coffee Counter. She also worked as a beauty operator and waitress.

After Verner and Marnee were married, their first home was a chicken coop they bought from Phil Clausen. They remodeled it into a house, where they lived for 18 years.

In 1968, Verner was offered the position of foreman to construct Bartlett Memorial Hospital in Juneau, so off they went.

For 16 years, while Verner worked for Wick Construction, they moved around Alaska. Upon retiring in 1984, they moved back to Petersburg and built a home at Hungry Point.

Verner enjoys working on his home and doing a little fishing. They have an ever-changing display in their solarium, which both locals and tourists enjoy.

They have two sons, David and Ted.

Louis and Alex Israelson's daughter, Dorothy, married Barney White in August 1936. They have two daughters, Sandra and Susan.

Dorothy passed away July 14, 1974.

Louis and Alex's second son, Spencer, worked as a commercial fisherman before World War II. He joined the Army and served on army support ships in Alaskan waters. He returned to Petersburg after the war.

Spencer met Frances Hegge soon after she settled in Petersburg.

Having grown up in the Seattle area, it wasn't surprising that Fran's first trip was a cruise to Alaska. Onboard the ship she met Dr. and Marie Loy.

The Loys owned a gift shop in Sitka and offered Fran a job. After a year in Sitka, Fran joined Marie Loy on a trip to California.

Marie had purchased Ruth Cisney's beauty shop in Petersburg. After completing beauty school, Fran

Louis and Alex Israelson cont'd

came to work in Marie's shop.

Spencer and Fran were married in 1949.

In 1948, Spencer began working for the Forest Service and was skipper on several Ranger boats, including the *Chugach*. When he was transferred to Cordova, Fran went along to cook and to cruise through Prince William Sound.

They were later transferred to Juneau and Ketchikan before returning to their final port, Petersburg, in 1953.

During the '60s and '70s, Spencer was a forestry technician. His field assignments focused on reforestation and timber stand improvements. He was one of the first forest workers in Southeast Alaska to become concerned about poor natural regeneration on difficult growing sites.

Spencer initiated and became the driving force in developing the B. Frank Heintzleman seedling nursery, located at the former Experimental Fur Farm in Petersburg.

After their return to Petersburg, Fran worked at the Cache for 13 years.

In 1982, Spencer and Fran moved into Spencer's mother's home at Hungry Point, where they enjoy the fantastic view of the mountains, Fredrick Sound, and Devil's Thumb.

Fran is an accomplished portrait and landscape artist, and loves to cook and bake.

Spencer's and Fran's retirement years are spent gardening and traveling around Alaska, the Yukon and British Columbia. They have two daughters, Tekla and Karla, and five grandchildren.

Point Agassiz School, circa mid-1920s
From left, front: Milton Ramstead, Dorothy Israelson (White), Arnold Israelson, Elmer Swanson, Leif Loseth and Raymond Swanson. Middle: Mildred Israelson (Massey), Brita Ask (Bland), Delores Ramstead (Lund), teacher Honey Kelly (Archbold) and Dagney Loseth (Norman). Back: Roy Swanson, Marvin Israelson, Spencer Israelson, Arne Ramstead and Verner Israelson.

Andrew and Anne Israelson

By Norman Israelson

My grandfather, Andrew M. Israelson, was born in Sjona, Helgeland, Norway, May 4, 1874. My grandmother, Anne R. Polinsky Israelson, was born in Glencoe, Minnesota, January 13, 1884.

They married in Little Falls, Minnesota, on February 4, 1908.

I am not sure of their first arrival in Petersburg, but I believe it was around 1910.

I know that my grandfather was a carpenter and he and his brother, Louis, worked on many projects in the area, including some of the first lighthouses.

My grandfather brought his parents, Anton and Maren Israelson, over to Petersburg where they lived until they died. Anton and Maren are both buried in the Petersburg cemetery.

A younger brother, Theodore, died in Petersburg in the early '20s and is also buried there.

My grandparents, Andrew and Anne, lived in Minnesota and in Bellingham, Washington, in the late teens and early '20s.

They returned to Petersburg and soon homesteaded on a dairy farm at Point Agassiz.

Their first housing on the homestead was a small wooden houseboat.

My grandfather built numerous barns, woodsheds, hay sheds, and a milk house. When he did build their house it was the largest one at Point Agassiz, and is now the only one left standing.

Point Agassiz prospered until the late '40s, at

Andrew and Anne Israelson

which time Alaska Steam's frequent schedule to Petersburg made it uneconomical to compete with products from the Lower 48.

There was a school adjacent to our homestead, grades one through eight. My father Arnold, Uncle Marvin and Aunt Mildred all attended the school. The teacher sometimes roomed at our home.

My grandfather was postmaster of Point Agassiz, as well. The old post office sign is in the Clausen Memorial Museum.

My family kept around 25 to 30 dairy cattle and raised several for beef. They also kept up to 200 chickens, and on occasion, a horse or two.

Our herd boss was a cow named "Dolly." My grandfather couldn't bear to put her down, so he barged her to town and gave her to Hjalmer Martinsen.

There was a large garden and it produced all that was needed to fill the root cellar under the house.

I remember well the sad time when my family

Anton and Maren Israelson

Andrew and Anne Israelson cont'd

and the other homesteaders were forced by age and economics to move to town.

Mildred, Arnold and Marvin Israelson

Andrew and Anne, my grandparents, had four children.

Their oldest child was my father, Arnold Joseph Israelson, who was born in Petersburg on July 19, 1914.

Marvin Francis was born January 14, 1916, in Ramsey, Minnesota. Marvin died in Petersburg on March 14, 1994.

Their only daughter, Mildred Lorraine, was born January 8, 1917, in Ramsey, Minnesota. She died August 2, 1978.

The youngest, Ellbert Mansfield, was born November 2, 1918, and died shortly afterwards on November 23, 1918, in Petersburg.

My father, Arnold, spent his early adult years at a variety of jobs. He fished, worked on tugboats, and worked at Petersburg Cold Storage's icehouse. He was a carpenter and a laborer on the Ketchikan Pulp Mill construction. He was also a foreman mechanic for the FAA.

Arnold received his guide license in the early 1940s and he owned and operated the Brown Bear Hunting Lodge on the Alsek River, located 70 miles east of Yakatat.

He married Elizabeth C. Taylor in 1957.

He owned and flew a Super Cub aircraft and also owned and operated the Chevron Distributorship in Yakatat.

Arnold guided until he retired in 1984. He is presently living in Haines, Alaska.

His first wife, Dorothy Noreide, was my mother. They had three children.

I, Norman, was born March 11, 1937, in Petersburg, Alaska.

In my early years, I was a fisherman and trapper in Petersburg. Later, I was a fish buyer and railroad operator in Yakatat.

I served with the U.S. Army in Korea and spent 25 years with Pacific Northern Airlines and Western Airlines. I retired as regional director for Western Airlines and currently live in Sterling, Alaska.

I have two stepdaughters, three granddaughters, and one grandson.

My sister, Sylvia Israelson Geraghty, was born in Petersburg on October 1, 1939.

She was a state worker in Juneau. For many years she operated a store, fuel supply, and fish buying operation at Tokeen.

Her three children are Jim, Michelle and Lisa. She now lives in Wrangell.

My brother, David, was born August 28, 1942.

He served in the U.S. Navy aboard the carrier *Ranger*. He was a draftsman with the Alaska Department of Transportation, and then worked for Chevron as a plant operator in Yakutat.

At the time of his death on January 13, 2002, he ran a sporting goods shop and a gunsmith operation.

David Israelson, Sylvia Israelson Geraghty and Norman Israelson

Andrew and Anne Israelson cont'd

By Annette Olson

Andrew Israelson was born May 4, 1874, in Hemnes, Norway. He came to the United States with his parents, Anton and Maren Israelson, when he was 14 years old.

He later met and married Anne Polinsky on February 4, 1908, in Little Falls, Minnesota. The newlyweds first came to Petersburg in the early 1900s.

His brother, Louie Israelson, had sent for him to come help with the building of Lincoln Rock lighthouse in Clarence Straits. He also helped with the Guard Island lighthouse.

After completing the Lincoln Rock lighthouse, Andrew and Annie stayed in Petersburg until their first son, Arnold, was born on July 19, 1914. Shortly after, they went back to Minnesota where two more children were born: Marvin on January 14, 1916 and Mildred on January 8, 1917.

While the children were still quite young, they came back to Alaska. Andrew did carpentry work and some fishing. One of the homes he helped build was the Hjalmer Martinsen home, now owned by Wildwood Nursery at Papke's Landing.

They left again for a while and went to Ferndale, Washington. They returned and homesteaded at Point Agassiz around 1925.

In April of 1930, Andrew became the one and only postmaster at Point Agassiz. Their home was the post office for the next 13 years. Annie was the assistant postmaster and she continued to draw a very small pension until her death.

Living at Point Agassiz wasn't an easy life. They worked hard. They had a few cows, some chickens, and two workhorses named Dick and Dan. They made their own cottage cheese that they sold in town, along with fresh eggs and other dairy products.

Andrew tried to talk Annie into sewing for people in town. This didn't fly at all! She preferred farm life.

After the Civilian Conservation Corps built the road at Point Agassiz, they salvaged the lumber from the CCC camp and built their big house.

The children attended the red one-room schoolhouse through the eighth grade. The school's second story was living quarters for the teacher. It is the only homestead house still standing and is still used by the family.

In the early 1940s, son Marvin built his parents a cute little house in town where they spent their last years. The house, located at 507 Ira II Street, is still lived in by family.

After moving into their town house, Andrew established a large strawberry patch, selling the berries to the local stores.

Andrew and Annie were both very active in the Lutheran Church. Annie was involved with Ladies Aid.

Sometime in the early 1900s, Andrew and his brothers, Louie and Teddy, sent for their parents, Anton and Maren Israelson. They built them a small house on the property that is at the corner of Wrangell Avenue and Harder Street.

Anton passed away in July of 1920 and Maren passed in January of 1923. Both are buried in the old cemetery across the Narrows.

Andrew and Annie's oldest son, Arnold Israelson, married Dorothy Noreide. They had three children: Norman, Sylvia and David.

Arnold stayed in Petersburg while their children were young. After divorcing, he moved away, ending up in Yakutat where he was a well-known guide for many years. After retiring, he and his wife, Betty, moved to Haines, Alaska.

Marvin never married. He was a fisherman for many years. He was known to be a great shipmate and loved his trapping and outdoors life. Point Agassiz was very important to him.

He also took very good care of his "Ma" and "Pa."

Marvin, along with Carl Thynes Jr., dared to climb the scaffolding and secure the cross on the 80-foot-tall steeple of the Lutheran Church. It was supposed to be 10 feet higher, but Uncle Louie, who built the church, said, "This was high enough!"

Marvin was always so proud of his time in the Army during World War II. He was stationed out on the Aleutian Chain for the most part.

After his retirement at age 62, Marvin bought a 24-foot Fiberform boat named the *Marmot*. He hand trolled until his death on March 14, 1994.

Mildred married Gainhart Samuelson and they had four children together. They later divorced and Mildred married Clarence Massey. They had two children. (*See the Chris and Inga Samuelson story.*)

John and Gina Jensen

By Sue Paulsen

John Jensen, of the hamlet Dal, near Laukvik in the Lofoten Islands of northern Norway, was the first of the family to immigrate to this country. We think he came to the United States in 1903, looked around the farm country of Minnesota, and then went on to Seattle, Washington.

He worked as the engineer of the *Constitution* in the dory fishery of Alaska. His citizenship paper is dated 1906, in Seattle.

Gordon, Erling, John and Ben Jensen

Georgina Knutsen, of Laukvik, married him at her brother's house in Ballard. They then came to Petersburg.

They fished at first, and then established a fox fur farm with Olaf Tenfjord in Tebenkof Bay.

We know their home at Third and Excel was finished in 1918, because John remembered where he was when World War I ended. He was on the roof, shingling, when Knut Thompson came running down the street from the original telegraph office (now the Lutheran manse) shouting, "The war is over!"

John and Gina lost an infant daughter, born in Petersburg. When the next child came, he was born in Vancouver, B. C., where Gina had a sister.

The new baby, Gordon, and his mother came home on the ill-fated voyage of the *Princess Sophia*. John picked them up in Wrangell. The ship then went on to later sink, with all hands, on the return voyage from Skagway.

Two more sons, Bernard and Erling, were born to John and Gina in Petersburg.

The family lived at Tebenkof Bay on the fox farm until the boys were old enough for school. They then moved back to town. The boys learned English in the grade school, which was later known as the American Legion Hall.

John fished his boat, the F/V *Harder*, and worked for the City of Petersburg, keeping board streets in repair and maintaining the water works.

Gina was a prolific needlewoman. She made the banner at the Sons of Norway Hall.

In 1937, Gordon graduated from Petersburg High School and started fishing on the *Teddy J*. He went on to the *Bravo* and *Balder* with the Fuglvogs.

He built his first boat, the *Symphony*, at the Sagstad shipyard in Ballard.

He and Helmi Karjala were married in 1946. Their children are Chris and Sue.

Chris and Sue both reside in Petersburg. Sue is married to Fred Paulsen. They have one son, Gordon.

In 1966, Gordon built the longliner *Westerly* in Blaine, Washington.

He fished for 50 years and spent nearly as many working for effective regulation and conservation of fisheries. Gordon served 20 years on the Alaska Board of Fish and Game.

He once represented both the Petersburg Vessel Owners and the fishermen's union at the International Halibut Commission meetings in Seattle.

Gordon was a founder of Icicle Seafoods, Inc., in 1964, and remains chairman of the board.

Besides being a commercial fisherman, Gordon is also an avid sports fisherman.

John and Gina's son, Bernard E. Jensen, was born on February 29, 1920.

He grew up in Petersburg and graduated from Petersburg High School in 1938, the recipient of the Clifford Mark Fosse Award.

In his early days, Ben spent many enjoyable hours in the woods, hiking and hunting, and taking pictures of his adventures.

He began his lifelong fishing career on the *Vesta* with the Lee family: Harold, Harold Jr., Eldor and

John and Gina Jensen cont'd

Allen. They longlined for halibut.

In 1941, Ben signed up with the U.S. Navy in Sitka, and spent time patrolling the Yasha Island area in Southeast Alaska, with Walt and Oliver Hofstad. He also skippered his own patrol boat, the *Daisy O*, out of Port Armstrong, previously a whaling station.

Ben was transferred to Hawaii for a short time. He finished up his four years of duty in Tokyo, during the occupation following World War II.

He returned to Petersburg and continued to pursue commercial fishing and construction jobs in the off-season.

He worked on several Civilian Conservation Corps projects, including the building of Sandy Beach Road with Ernest Enge and Lloyd Pederson.

Erling, Gordon and Ben Jensen

In February of 1950, he married Doris Bacot of Petersburg. They built a home. As the years went by, they had four sons: John, Stewart, Mark and Tom.

Ben and Doris have five grandchildren. John and his wife, Pam, are the parents of Jeremy and Sam. Mark and Carol Jensen have two boys, Bill and Alan. John and Mark and their families live in Petersburg.

Tom and his wife, Wendy, live in Portland with their son, Mitchell.

Ben and Doris' son, Stewart, was lost at sea in 1971.

Ben fished with his brother Gordon on the *Symphony* and the *Westerly* for halibut in the Gulf of Alaska, and for salmon in Southeast Alaska. He also fished for red and brown king crab in Southeast Alaska on the *Middleton* with Lloyd Pederson and Eldor Lee.

Ben taught the next generation of Jensens the skills and knowledge they needed to make their own careers in fishing.

In his semi-retirement years, Ben ventured out with his own boat, the *High Voltage*, gillnetting for salmon and longlining for halibut, concluding his many hard working and profitable years at sea.

He enjoys the life of a retired fisherman at his home in Petersburg.

The youngest of John and Gina's sons, Erling Jensen, graduated from Petersburg High School in 1941, and has the distinction of having been on that school's longest sports trip in history.

The basketball team took the steamer to Juneau, then on across the Gulf of Alaska to Seward. After arriving in Fairbanks by train, the team came in a close second in state competition. They returned the same long route — a three-week trip in all.

Erling spent his undergraduate years at Washington State University. His military service was spent in and around Anchorage, as a member of the military police.

Erling and Louise Bakko were married in 1951. He received his PhD from Cornell in 1953, and enjoyed a long career in cancer research and microbiology.

In the winter, Erling and Louise live in California and, in the summer, Peterburg.

"Mitkof Marine Ways"
Illustration by Helmi Jensen

Howard and Marie Jensen

By Marlys Jensen

Marie Syverine Wikan Jensen, the eldest child of Andrew and Marit "Margaret" Wikan, was born on July 22, 1913.

Marie Wikan Jensen

Her siblings were Gudolf, who was born April 18, 1915, and died November 18, 1932; Andy, born February 4, 1920, died August 8, 1986; and Bojer, born September 16, 1921, died January 28, 1996.

Marie graduated from Petersburg High School in 1932. When Gudolf became ill with tuberculosis, she postponed her nursing training for one year and cared for him until his death.

Her father and John Hammer started delivering milk from Point Agassiz door to door. Marie reported how she washed the bottles and wasn't paid a penny for her hard work.

Life wasn't always easy for the family. They were all expected to work hard.

Marie told the story of her father going through the garbage at the grocery store to find edible vegetables and fruit for the family.

She also told a story about a velveteen dress that a neighbor had thrown away on the beach. Her mother altered it and Marie wore the dress almost every day to school.

In 1933, she enrolled at the University of Washington for a year and then went on to Swedish Hospital School of Nursing, graduating in 1937.

After graduation, she worked at the hospital in Petersburg until her marriage to Howard Jensen.

During their courtship, they went hunting. Marie shot a grouse in the head with a 30-30 rifle.

They were married on April 2, 1938, at her parents' home. Their first home was at the Experimental Fur Farm south of town.

In 1939, Howard and Marie's son, Richard, was born. He was followed by Darrell, in 1940, and Wayne in 1944.

Howard had a fishing boat built that he named the *Cape Cross*. He commercially fished for 40 to 45 years.

In 1945, the family moved to Lakewood, Washington, living there until 1969. Howard and Marie moved to Lopez Island in the San Juan Islands.

When Howard became ill in 1981, they returned to Lakewood, but kept the home on the island for their family to enjoy.

The family still has the violin that Marie played in a dance band.

She has eight grandchildren and 14 great-grandchildren. She is living at Josephine Sunset Home in Stanwood and suffers from Alzheimer's disease.

Girls with their doll buggies decorated for the Fourth of July
Alaska State Library
Core: Petersburg-Parades-7

Sverre and Alma Johansen

By Stanley Johansen

Sverre Johansen was born in northern Norway in 1887. He immigrated to the United States via Canada, entering at Detroit, Michigan, in 1904. He then headed west to Tacoma, Washington.

Sverre fished on the S/S *Zapora*, where he met and became good friends with Louie Martens. Louie left for Petersburg, Alaska, and Sverre followed in 1910.

Alma Ohlson was born in 1890. She emigrated from Stockholm, Sweden, to the United States, at the age of 12, after her parents had passed on.

She landed at Ellis Island, New York, in 1903, with one dollar in her pocket. A couple befriended and helped her on the ocean crossing.

She then traveled alone by train to her brother's in Tacoma. Alma was working as a domestic in Tacoma when she met Sverre.

Because there wasn't a magistrate in Petersburg, Sverre and Alma were married in Wrangell on November 11, 1911.

After their marriage, they hand trolled for salmon part time at Point Baker, Alaska, fishing from separate rowboats.

Sverre, Stanley, Mildred and Alma Johansen

Sverre and Alma built a home on Petersburg's Second Street. There, their five children were born: Mildred, Carroll (who died during the flu epidemic of 1918), Stanley, Marian and David.

Sverre, Louie Martens and Knut Thompson built the F/V *Dolphin* for halibut fishing. Later, Sverre purchased the F/V *Brothers*. In 1927, he had the schooner F/V *Mitkof* built in Seattle.

Because fishing and marketing had changed, and Sverre was away from home so much, the family moved to Seattle in 1934. They sold their Petersburg home to Knut Thompson in 1936.

Sverre and Alma's son, Stanley, served in the Navy for four and a half years during World War II.

After he was discharged, he went back to fishing, skippering the F/V *Mitkof*.

In 1952, Stanley built the F/V *Alma J* with his father and his brother-in-law, John Lervold.

Stanley fished the F/V *Alma J* until 1982, when he sold the boat and retired.

Stanley married Evelyn Peterson and they raised three children. Stan's son, Dennis, is the only grandson to be a fisherman. He works the Bering Sea and Gulf of Alaska as captain and mate on a factory trawler.

Mildred Johansen and John Lervold married and raised two children.

Marian Johansen married Axel Torget and they have two children.

Mildred, Sverre and Carroll

Sverre Johansen's schooner, the F/V *Mitkof*

Andrew and Laura Johnson

By Harriet Johnson Journey

Andrew Johnson was born May 22, 1888, in Bergen, Norway, to Signa and John Wilhelmson.

While still a teenager, Andrew migrated to the Pacific Northwest.

He worked for a surveying company in Seattle's Greenwood area, and on the Olympic Peninsula near Lake Ozette.

On October 22, 1911, at the age of 25, he received his certificate of naturalization. Andrew then moved to Petersburg, where he worked as a halibut fisherman.

Laura Lambsom Johnson was born and raised in Ellensburg, Washington. As a young woman, she moved to Petersburg to work with a friend from Seattle in the laundry.

Andrew and Laura were married January 5, 1918. To this union, two daughters were born. Mertie Laura was born in 1919. Harriet Signa was born in 1921.

On August 1, 1918, at the age of 30, Andrew was inducted into the U.S. Army in Petersburg.

He served his time in Haines, Alaska, and received his honorable discharge from the Army as a corporal, in February of 1919, at Fort William H. Seward.

In 1919, Andrew and Olaf K. Martin had a 48-foot gas screw fishing boat, the *Sherman*, built in Seattle. Olaf sold his portion of the *Sherman* to Andrew for $2,000 in 1924.

In 1921, Andrew and Laura purchased Lot 1, Block 80, from the town of Petersburg, Territory of Alaska. A home was built.

During the early years in Petersburg, the residents created their own entertainment. Group picnics proved to be a fun summer activity. Any place that could be reached by boat or foot was a spot for a picnic: Sandy Beach, Point Agassiz, or someone's back yard in town.

During winter months, Laura enjoyed participating in community plays, playing bridge, and attending dinner parties. Her interest in music kept her busy singing in small groups and as a soloist. She was the pianist at the Lutheran Church and at other events and occasions.

Laura was also active in the PTA, American Legion Auxiliary, and Eastern Star.

Before she arrived in Petersburg, Laura had worked as a hatter in Seattle, so she enjoyed creating hats and sewing dresses for herself and her daughters.

Andrew fished for halibut. His brother, Willie, fished with him — until Willie decided to purchase a tavern in Petersburg.

Andrew was a conscientious worker. He also devoted a lot of time to the city council, Masons, and Eastern Star.

Friends and neighbors took pleasure in "dropping by" for a chitchat at the Johnsons, so there was always a baked treat to relish with a cup of coffee.

In 1958, they moved to their new home in the Greenwood area of Seattle. Shortly afterwards, Andrew sold the *Sherman*.

Andrew Johnson

Like many other Petersburg families, Andrew and Laura had never owned an automobile in Alaska. But, they were sure glad they had "wheels" once they moved to Seattle. They were grateful to be able to drive to scenic areas, visit friends, shop, and attend Seattle gatherings of the Alaska Pioneers, Ladies of the Golden North, and the White Shrine.

Andrew and Laura celebrated 50 years of marriage in 1968. Andrew passed away December 17, 1973. Laura passed away June 22, 1988.

Mertie Johnson graduated from Petersburg High School in 1938. She attended Whitman College and the University of Washington.

In 1941, she married Edgar Baggen, who had a dental practice in Petersburg. Edgar was also raised in Petersburg. (*See Ed and Ingeborg Baggen story.*)

After their marriage, they moved to Fairbanks, where he practiced until the 1970s.

Mertie and Ed had four children Wendy, Jill, Laurel and Edward.

Andrew and Laura Johnson cont'd

Mertie had lupus and passed away in 1968.

In 1992, Ed passed away from pneumonia related to his Alzheimer's disease.

After her 1940 high school graduation, Harriet attended the University of Washington and Central Washington College of Education. She taught school in Port Townsend, Bellevue, Seattle, and the Panama Canal Zone.

In Panama, Harriet met and married Ewing "Bud" Journey, a third generation "Canalzonite." Bud's grandfather had come from New York to work on the Panama Canal project during its construction days — and stayed!

Harriet and Bud lived in the Republic of Panama for 10 years, while Bud developed the shrimp business. Then, because of the political unrest, they moved to Poulsbo, Washington, in 1963, with their three children, Hayes, Andrew and Molly.

In 1990, Harriet and Bud moved to Port Ludlow, Washington. Bud passed away in July 2001 after a long battle with cancer.

Memories of growing up in Petersburg:

Bicycling to the Scow Bay cannery, rain or shine, to work, piling cans in boxes — for thirty-five cents an hour! Graduating to the PAF cannery in Petersburg as a "slimer,"–for ninety cents an hour!

Camping at Sandy Beach. Getting there by walking on the narrow wooden planks over the muskeg, or going by Dad's fishing boat.

Rowing up Petersburg Creek. And the many times, when we forgot the tide schedule, having to walk the boat out to deeper waters.

Laura, Harriet and Andrew Johnson

Rowing across the Narrows for a picnic with our neighbor, Cecil Anderson, in his boat, the *U and I*, and us in our skiff.

Attending the Sons of Norway dinners and bazaars in its huge building.

Chopping ice off the wooden plank street in front of our house. Sliding down the hill on our sleds.

Attending the big school on the hill that housed all grades, including the high school.

Andrew and Laura, far right, enjoy a "mug-up" with friends.

Joe and Cora Johnson

By Lois Johnson Rhodes

Joseph Ernest Johnson was born December 28, 1903, in Altha, Florida. One of 10 children, Joe grew up on the family farm, helping to raise and sell cotton and peanuts.

At age 17, Joe left Florida to join the U.S. Army. He was stationed at Fort Warren, Wyoming, and served as chief of section in field artillery.

Cora Marie Haug was born November 29, 1908, in Norway, Iowa, the eighth of nine children. Her parents, both Norwegian immigrants, had settled in Iowa, where her father worked as a carpenter.

When Cora was 8 years old, she moved with her mother and three of her siblings to Little Bear, Wyoming, in order to live closer to two of Cora's older, married sisters. Cora's family homesteaded in Little Bear and later ran a boarding house in Cheyenne.

In 1924, Cora met Joe Johnson. They married in 1927. Five years later, the young couple received a fateful visit from Cora's maternal uncle, Jack Nelson, who lived in Petersburg, Alaska.

Jack had emigrated from Norway with his brother, Nels. They originally settled on the eastern shores of the United States, where the two worked as fishermen. They later relocated to Alaska, where Nels joined in the search for Klondike gold, while Jack continued with his fishing out of Petersburg.

After Jack's visit in 1932, Joe was persuaded to come to Petersburg for a visit. In February 1933, Joe made the journey and discovered he liked the area. Upon Joe's return to Wyoming, he and Cora agreed to move to Petersburg.

In September of 1933, Joe, Cora and their infant son, Jim, arrived aboard the steamship, the *Alaska*. They entered into a fox farm partnership with Cora's Uncle Jack.

While Joe readied the house and farm, which were located on Blashke Island, south of Petersburg, Cora and Jim spent the first three weeks in a rented house in town. It rained every day of those three weeks, nearly driving Cora back to Wyoming. With encouragement from her aunt, she decided to stay.

Life on the fox farm proved to be quite an adjustment for Cora. Having been accustomed to electricity, running water, and the luxuries of an oven and a washing machine, Cora had to learn how to adapt. She had to pack in water, cook on a wood stove, and use a washboard.

In May of 1934, Joe and Cora decided to return to Wyoming after a disagreement arose about fish traps being constructed on the island by neighboring fish trap owners. Care of the fur farm was left to Uncle Jack.

Earl Ohmer, a friend and local civic leader, helped resolve the dispute, and the Johnsons returned to Blashke Island in December.

Joe and Cora Johnson with, in front, John and James. Joe is holding baby Lois.

In 1935, Cora gave birth to a son, John, at Uncle Jack's house, which was also built by Skylark Jack. In 1938, a daughter, Lois, was born in a house on Lumber Street that the family rented from Ole Vick. Dr. Joseph Rude delivered both babies.

Shortly after Lois' birth, the family moved to West Petersburg, where Joe worked at the Yukon Fur Farm with Jess Ames.

They remained there until 1940, when Joe purchased Don Milnes' mink farm. He began breeding 25 female mink with six males he had acquired from Jess Ames in exchange for 100 pelts.

Providing feed for the mink was nearly a full-time

Joe and Cora Johnson cont'd

job in itself. Joe built a seine for flounder and sole, and this proved to be a more efficient means of gathering bottomfish for the feed.

Just as the farm began to flourish, Joe learned he might have to serve in World War II. He reduced his stock to all but 12 female and three male mink. Soon after, he was notified he wouldn't be needed after all, and Joe began again from square one.

In 1944, Joe purchased a 26-foot boat, the *Josephine*, to use for supplying feed and the family's transportation across the Narrows to Petersburg.

The *Josephine* also served as a back-up school boat for ushering the Johnson children, and other neighbor children, to school in Petersburg.

That same year, Joe began commercial fishing for halibut, blackcod and salmon. During the next 10 years, he worked as a crewmember aboard the boats *Lois W*, *Gjoa*, *Happy*, *Teddy J*, *Balder* and *Pamela Rae*.

During Joe's fishing season, from May to September, Cora and the children assumed responsibility for running the mink farm. However, by 1954, after Jim and John had left home and mink pelt prices dropped, the business proved too expensive to maintain.

That same year, Joe began working as a skipper aboard a U.S. Fish and Wildlife boat.

In 1956, the family moved into town. Cora started working at Lillian Swanson's dress shop. Cora later worked for Chuck and Olive Fitzgerald as a sales clerk in their store, Chuck's Cash Grocery.

With their three children grown and gone, Cora and Joe moved to Ketchikan in April of 1960, where Joe accepted a job operating another boat for Fish and Wildlife. Cora worked as a cashier at Federal Market, a local grocery store.

Joe's position took them to Kodiak in 1965, and to Juneau from 1968 until 1972.

He operated three vessels for the government, the *Harlequin*, the *Polar Bear*, and the *Sea Bird*. He retired June 30, 1972.

After Joe's retirement, he and Cora returned to their home in Petersburg, but often traveled to visit friends and relatives in California, Washington,

Joe Johnson with fox pelts

Florida, and Wyoming. Both were active members of the Pioneers of Alaska and Eastern Star, in which Cora served as Worthy Matron for four years. Joe also belonged to the Moose Club, the Shriners, and the Masonic Lodge, the latter of which he also served as Master of the Lodge.

Since Joe's death, December 29, 1981, in Sitka, Alaska, Cora has remained in Petersburg, living in the family home that once belonged to Uncle Jack, and where son, John, was born.

In addition to her three children, Jim, John and Lois, Cora has seven grandchildren and eight great-grandchildren.

Arctic Hotel key

James A. Johnson

By James A. Johnson

I was born March 13, 1933, in Cheyenne, Wyoming, to parents Joe and Cora Johnson.

When I was six months old, we moved to a fox farm on Blashke Island, south of Petersburg.

In 1938, we moved to West Petersburg (now known as Kupreanof) to work on the Yukon farm for Jesse Ames. We purchased our own mink farm in 1940.

My father was a commercial fisherman during the summers. My mother, brother John, sister Lois, and I kept the farm going when my father was away.

I started school in 1939. Getting to and from school was somewhat unique. First we had to walk a mile or more to catch the school boat. During the winter months, we had to walk on top of the snow or walk on the beaches; there were no snowplows, or for that matter, cars or trucks.

I was involved in many high school activities. I was yell king for two years, manager of the basketball team for one year, and student body president for two years. I was also a member of the debate team and performed in the senior class play in both my junior and senior years. I was the 1951 recipient of the Clifford Mork Fosse Award.

It was during my junior year that I began my airline career, working weekends and summers for Eldor Lee, who was the Petersburg agent for Alaska Coastal Airlines.

I graduated from high school in May of 1951, and began full-time employment with the airline.

A medical condition kept me out of the military, so I continued working for Alaska Coastal Airlines. I held a variety of positions, including ticket agent, sales agent and station manager. At one time I was a relief agent, traveling from city to city when station managers were on vacation.

I moved throughout the system and it was fun living in different places. Seeing different sides of the business gave me a good understanding of the airline.

While working at the Petersburg office, I met Doris Hollingsworth. We were married on September 19, 1956.

Our daughter, Loxxie, was born February 15, 1961, while we were in Sitka. Our son, Andy, was born September 21, 1965, in Juneau.

On a special note, the doctor who delivered my son was Dr. Joseph Rude. When we asked him if he would be our family physician, he said, "I do not usually take on any new patients, however, I have a vested interest." He delivered both my brother, John, and sister, Lois.

Jim Johnson

On April 1, 1962, Alaska Coastal and Ellis Airlines merged. I was living in Sitka at the time. I was transferred to Juneau to become general sales manager for the new company, Alaska Coastal-Ellis Airlines. The name later reverted back to Alaska Coastal Airlines.

On April 1, 1968, Alaska Coastal Airlines merged with Alaska Airlines. I was named assistant vice president of sales for Southeast Alaska.

In November of 1968, I was transferred to the Seattle corporate office of Alaska Airlines as assistant vice president and general sales manager.

In May of 1972, there was a change in management. Ronald Cosgrave and Bruce Kennedy assumed control of the airline. Former Alaska Coastal

James A. Johnson cont'd

executives, Shell Simmons and Ben Benecke, and former Ellis Airlines executive, Bob Ellis, remained on the board of directors. Ben Benecke became president.

During my years at Alaska Airlines, I held a variety of positions of responsibility:
- 1972 – Vice President Marketing and Sales
- 1974 – Vice President Public Affairs
- 1981 – Senior Vice President Public Affairs
- 1990 – Senior Vice President Alaska Air Group
- 1993 – Upon retirement, Board of Directors bestowed honorary position of Senior Vice President Emeritus

Among the many awards of recognition for community involvement that I cherish most are The William A. Egan Outstanding Alaskan of the Year for 1992 from the Alaska State Chamber of Commerce, and an Honorary Associate of Arts Degree from South Seattle Community College for assisting their Aviation Maintenance Program. The most outstanding recognition was the 1994 naming of the Petersburg James A. Johnson Airport.

I have been blessed to have the opportunities I had during my 42 years in the airline industry. I traveled much of the Lower 48, as well as Europe, Russia, Japan, China, Australia, Bermuda, Jamaica, and the Bahamas. One of the highlights was, in 1992, when the late borough mayor of Ketchikan, Ralph Bartholomew, invited me along with eight Alaskans to travel from Puget Sound to Ketchikan aboard the nuclear submarine, the USS *Alaska*.

This three-day trip, mostly below the surface, was spectacular. We observed the workings of daily activities and participated in a variety of drills as the crew performed their tasks. Upon completion of the trip, we were all given certificates as honorary submariners.

After retirement, Doris and I continued living in our Seattle residence until September of 2000. We sold our home after 32 years and moved to Oro Valley, Arizona, to be with our son, Andy, his wife, and our granddaughter, Makenzi.

We also purchased a home in Overland Park, Kansas, to be close to our daughter, Loxxie, and her family, which includes our our two grandsons Casey and Alec.

I visit Petersburg frequently, as my mother, Cora, and brother, John, and his wife, Dell, live there. My sister, Lois Rhodes, lives in nearby Sitka.

Jim Johnson and Eldor Lee

The following editorial comment appeared in the June 1993 issue of the Alaska Airlines Magazine and is reprinted with the permission of Alaska Airlines and Alaska Airlines Magazine.

"Jim Johnson: 'Mr. Alaska'"
by Raymond J. Vecci, Chairman, President and CEO Alaska Airlines

Jim Johnson is an American original. Storyteller. Philanthropist. Tireless Worker. Supreme optimist. He's one of an increasingly rare breed who has thrived and risen to the top in his field by doing the work and

James A. Johnson cont'd

learning as he progressed. Though Jim never earned a college degree, his efforts and expertise have earned him the respect of his peers throughout the airline industry. His brother likens him to Horatio Alger, a hard-working, intelligent guy who made it on his own.

For 42 years, Jim has helped define Alaska Airlines. He retires next month as senior vice president — a long way from his first job loading bags on floatplanes in his Southeast Alaska home of Petersburg, a community close to his heart.

"He's the epitome of a small-town boy who made good," says longtime friend Margie Johnson of Cordova, Alaska. "And he never forgets his roots. He exemplifies the caring spirit of rural Alaska, where you can depend on people."

She knows. When she broke her back in a car accident in California, the first phone call she received at the hospital was not from a family member, but Jim Johnson.

He has headed up our public affairs efforts for the last 19 years, helping shape airline and business-related public policy and providing a link between the company and the communities we serve.

But his accomplishments go beyond his formal corporate position. Jim's knowledge of the airline industry, along with his big heart, quick smile, willingness to listen, timely humor and strong sense of business responsibility have touched thousands over the years.

Nicholas Nathan, a toddler from Boise, is a good example. When weather precluded a non-profit's group plane from flying him to San Francisco for treatment related to his battle with eye cancer, Jim made sure Nicholas and his mother got a round-trip ride on Alaska Airlines. Similar stories abound and have earned Jim the title, "Mr. Alaska."

Jim's use of company resources to help people only tells part of the story. He generously gives his own time and energy to worthwhile causes. He's served on 21 boards or committees, from community colleges to Junior Achievement. His people skills are illustrated by the millions of dollars he raised for Seattle's Woodland Park Zoo.

In addition, he's been an unofficial ambassador for the state of Alaska, timelessly promoting it as a tourist destination and serving as an insightful, passionate advocate of the state's needs and desires in the corporate arena.

For years, Alaskans looking to do business outside the state enlisted his guidance and introductions. That's one reason why Jim was named "Alaskan of the Year" for 1992, an honor that's particularly notable because he hasn't lived in the state for 25 years.

"He really should have been a politician. No one wins friends and influences people like Jim," says Ralph Munroe, Washington's Secretary of State.

From powerful lawmakers to oil field workers, relating to people of all walks is one of Jim's enduring qualities. He possesses a remarkable ability to make each person he deals with, feel special, because Jim is so genuine in his interest and concern.

Jim was sales manager for Alaska Coastal-Ellis Airlines when that Southeast Alaska carrier was merged with Alaska Airlines in 1968. Charlie Willis, then president of Alaska Airlines, quipped that the price of the acquisition was worth every penny just to get Jim.

He was right, Jim has played a part in many of our greatest achievements: charter service to the Soviet Union at the height of the Cold War, expansion in southward with the dawn of airline industry deregulation, and the launch of scheduled service to the Russian Far East.

Jim played a key role in transitioning the airline from one management team to another in 1972. Two former chairmen of Alaska Airlines, Bruce Kennedy and Ron Cosgrave, credit Jim with giving credibility to the new regime at a time when creditors and customers were ready to give up.

With his genuine concern for people, Jim is the personification of what makes Alaska Airlines special. While his counsel will be just a phone call away, his day-to-day contributions will be missed immensely.

We express our gratitude to Jim for his dedication and service over 42 years, and wish him and his wife, Doris, the best as they begin a new chapter in their lives.

John and Dell Johnson

By John Johnson

I was born December 4, 1935, in Petersburg, Alaska. Shortly after my birth, I moved with my parents, Joe and Cora Johnson, and my brother, Jim, to Blashke Island in lower Snow Pass, south of Petersburg. The family was engaged in fox farming.

In 1938, my sister, Lois, joined the family. With my brother, Jim, needing to enter school, the family moved to West Petersburg, where my father worked for Jess Ames on the Yukon Fur Farm, raising mink.

In 1941, the family purchased their own fur farm from Ben Milnes. Located across from the present ferry terminal, they operated the farm until 1953. My job was catching fish for mink feed and beach seining in Petersburg Creek during the summers.

The years growing up on the mink farm were the most memorable of my life. I was able to run free all over the island, and especially enjoyed fishing and playing up Petersburg Creek. My pioneer parents ensured I had little to worry about, other than behaving myself.

During these early years in West Petersburg, fur farming was on the decline and we were one of the few families with children to help with the chores.

The other two operating ranches were somewhat jealous of us, as children made the daily work easier, or so they thought. We had to catch at least 500 pounds of fresh fish daily before we could go play.

We were mischievous, my siblings and I. Our favorite trick to play on our fellow ranchers was to give the appearance that when we were seining flounder at the mouth of the creek, we were always catching ample fish. This was not always true. To keep up the appearance of a good catch, one of us threw the fish into the boat, the other threw it back into the net. We also loaded the bow with rocks, covered with cleaned flounder. It looked like we always had a load!

But all good things had to come to a close. In 1953, with brother Jim beginning a career with Alaska Airlines, me going off to college, and sister Lois talking about teaching school, it was time to close the business.

I graduated from Petersburg High School in 1953. In 1958, I was a member of the last class to graduate from the University of Alaska (Fairbanks) in the Territory of Alaska.

Commissioned a second lieutenant in the U.S. Army, I served 20 years as a career officer before retiring with the rank of lieutenant colonel in 1979. While in Alaska, I was operations officer for the military humanitarian mission sent to Valdez during the Great Alaskan Earthquake of 1964.

I commanded an infantry company in Korea in 1965, and served in Vietnam between 1967 and 1978. I was a district senior advisor on the outskirts of Hue during one of the most active periods of the war. After a statewide R.O.T.C. assignment at Colorado State University, I returned to Vietnam in 1970 and 1971 as a battalion executive officer with Task Force South, in Phan Thiet, Vietnam. I was next assigned as chief of Plans G-3 for the 101st Airborne Division (AMBL). There, I performed a variety of tasks, including participating in division support for the Vietnamese incursion into Laos from the base in Khe Sahn.

Returning stateside, I was assigned to Team Four, Combat Developments Experimentation Command (CDEC), testing state-of-the-art electronic warfare tactics and equipment (many still in the concept stage), before moving on to serve as secretary to the general staff, CDEC, at Fort Hunter Liggett, California.

In 1977, I returned to Alaska to complete my military service as deputy commander at Fort Greely, Alaska.

Upon retirement, I returned home to Petersburg to manage the employment office for the Alaska Department of Labor for 17 years. My final retirement was in 1995.

I met and married my wife, Dell, in 1961, while serving in the Army at Fairbanks, Alaska.

We raised two sons, Joe and John "Jeff". Both graduated from Petersburg High School. Joe followed my footsteps, serving as a career officer in the U.S. Air Force, while Jeff became a career officer in the maritime service, sailing between Valdez and Puget Sound with various oil companies.

Active in public service and volunteer work, I have served as president of the Rotary Club and vice president of the Chamber of Commerce. I was chairman of the Salvation Army board, Council on Alcoholism, and Petersburg Youth Council. I served two terms on the city council, and one term on the school board and am a lifetime member of the VFW.

Hugh and Eva Jones

By Bruce Jones

Hugh J. Jones was born in Connorville, Oklahoma, on December 24, 1906. He was one of eight brothers and sisters.

Hugh headed west at the age of 16 and worked as a painter for Ford Motor Company in Long Beach, California. He traveled to Juneau, Alaska, in 1929, to live with his cousin.

In Juneau, he met Evangeline Swanson. They were married on December 29, 1930, in Petersburg, and moved there permanently in 1931.

Hugh operated the Reliable Transfer, had a mini-golf range, and worked many years for the City of Petersburg. He later worked for the Bureau of Public Roads and Manson-Osberg Dredging Co.

Hugh was a charter member of the Petersburg Elks Lodge, as well as the Masonic Lodge.

Evangeline was born in Petersburg, Alaska on December 23, 1909, to Carl and Aurora Swanson.

She spent her early years on the family homestead at Point Agassiz.

Because Petersburg didn't have an accredited high school, Eva went to Juneau, where she attended school and took care of the Goldstein family children.

After marrying Hugh, they returned to Petersburg, where she worked for Cornelius Mercantile, Hammer & Wikan, Wasvick & Torwick, and the Sanitary Market. She also did stints on the canning line in the salmon season at both Pacific American Fisheries and Petersburg Fisheries.

In 1956, she and Hugh moved from Petersburg to Seattle, where Eva took care of her ailing mother. She also worked in the South Park dime store and was very active in the senior citizens organization of South Park.

Hugh died in Seward, Alaska, on October 24, 1965.

Eva moved back to Petersburg in 1991, and resided at Totem Arms, Marine View Apartments, and then Mountain View Manor. She was an active member of the Petersburg chapter of Pioneers of Alaska and was a lifetime member of both the Petersburg Emblem Club and the Order of Eastern Star.

Due to failing health, Eva moved to the Dallas Retirement Village, in Dallas, Oregon, where she still resides today.

Hugh and Eva have two children, Marlene "Molly" and Bruce.

Molly was born in 1931. During her school years, she held jobs at the telephone company, Pacific American Fisheries, and Petersburg Fisheries.

She graduated from Petersburg High School, in 1949, and attended Western Washington College of Education, in Bellingham, for one year.

In 1950, she married her high school sweetheart, Carl I. Thynes. Together, they raised four children: Debra, Shelley, Tracey and David.

Molly was very active in the Lutheran Church, directing the children's choir for many years. She also enjoyed gillnetting on the F/V *Molly T* with her husband, and spending time with her children and grandchildren.

Molly succumbed to cancer in 1991.

Bruce was born and raised in Petersburg. During his formative years, he held a paper route for three years. His route was from town to the graveyard. He also washed dishes at both The Pastime Café and Winnie's Café, was a ticket taker at the theater, and drove a delivery truck for Wasvick & Torwick. Bruce also seined with Adolph Mathisen on the F/V *Harmony* for four seasons.

After graduating from Petersburg High School, in 1953, Bruce went to Oregon State College in Corvallis, Oregon and procured a BS degree in business administration. After a two-year army obligation, Bruce was hired by Pan American World Airways and spent two assignments in Africa, as well as in Anchorage, Alaska.

He went on to work for Wein Air Alaska and Kodiak Western Airlines before being hired by the State of Alaska Department of Labor as an employment specialist.

Bruce retired from the state in 1996 and returned to Petersburg.

He married a former Petersburg High School classmate, Marilyn (nee Meeks) in April 1999. Bruce and Marilyn moved to Dallas, Oregon, in 2001, where they currently reside.

Bruce has a son, Mark, who is in the Navy, and three granddaughters.

Bruce was a member of the Petersburg Elks Lodge and Pioneers of Alaska, and just might be remembered for his wry wit and singing abilities.

Wilhelm "Skip" and Marilyn Jordan

By Marilyn Jordan George

Wilhelm "Skip" Jordan was born in Asker, Norway, to Kris and Inga Jordan on May 28, 1913.

He came to the United States from Norway with his parents at the age of 12. They settled in Tacoma, Washington, where Skip's father worked on the waterfront as a longshoreman.

Skip and his sister, Eva, attended school in Tacoma. Skip graduated from South Tacoma High in 1933.

He earned the name "Skip" because he was always leading the others and figuring out things to do. These centered around the waterfront, where he earned his spending money by catching fish and selling them to their neighbors.

Skip was instrumental in starting the Point Defiance Aquarium and was its second aquarist. He collected many of the aquarium's specimens and raised "Dub-dub," the hair seal, on a bottle. The seal lived many years.

During World War II, Skip discovered what a great place Alaska was when he hired on a Prince William Sound herring seiner.

The next year, Skip went to Washington Bay in Southeast Alaska. When he watched a salmon troller catch fish near the Stoffal & Grindahl herring reduction plant, he decided that that was the way to make a living.

He was drafted into the Navy and sent to Iowa State College to study diesel engines. There he met Marilyn Frink. He told her of his dream to go to Alaska and make a living salmon trolling.

After Marilyn's graduation, she took a job in a test kitchen in Illinois.

True to his resolve, once he was discharged, Skip came to Illinois and asked Marilyn, "Is you is, or is you ain't, going to Alaska with me?"

After much soul searching, she said, "Yes." They were married on February 23, 1946.

Skip and Marilyn couldn't find a boat worth the money in the Puget Sound area. His sister, Eva, and her husband, Frank Johnson, lived in Wrangell, Alaska, with their two children, Chris and Ellen.

Frank wrote, "There's a fine 31-foot double-ender for sale here. I think it's just what you're looking for."

The Jordan family, in front, left to right: Barbara, Wilhelm "Skip," Lynda and Marilyn. Back row: Eric and Karen.

Skip and Marilyn sent a down payment and then boarded the *Princess Norah* in Vancouver and headed for Wrangell. They landed there on April 1, 1946.

Mac McKibben, the owner of the fishing boat, took them to the harbor.

Which was their boat? Mac stopped before what they thought was the trimmest small boat in the harbor. The pilothouse consisted of a wheel, a throttle and a compass. It had a horizontal bench and a stool. Under its floor was an engine. This was far different than Marilyn imagined.

Three steps down was the galley. Marilyn suddenly realized a boat is like living in a cube and isn't 31-foot wide. Everything was secondary to the engine, fuel tanks, fish hold and troller pit. Only a six-foot triangle, about the size of a horse stall, remained for her galley and sleeping quarters. She had to remind herself that a boat was, first of all, a means of earning a living.

Wilhelm "Skip" and Marilyn Jordan cont'd

Pointing to a black object the size of a postage stamp, she asked, "What is that?"

"That's the stove."

It was mighty different from the large, thermostatically controlled ovens she was used to using in the test kitchen.

She asked, "Where's the sink?"

Mac replied, "You use a deck bucket."

She pulled Skip's head down, "I don't see a bathroom."

"Ah'll tell ya later. Yas, Mac, we'll take her."

Later, walking down the float back to the boat, Skip asked, "Well, what do ya think of her?"

"Where's the bathroom?"

"Ya use a deck bucket." (Have you ever sat on a deck bucket on a rolling boat?)

Sitting in the galley, Skip looked at Marilyn, "Ya can't wear dot clothes. Here, put on das rain gear."

She looked around and saw no place to change. She just had to do it out in the open.

Skip bought a fishing license and fishing gear.

They were going to run with Skip's brother-in-law, Frank Johnson. Suddenly, with great force, the pilothouse door opened. Frank burst into the cabin.

"There's been a big earthquake in the Aleutians. A tidal wave may be coming. Worse place to be is tied to a float. How fast can you get ready?"

Skip replied, "As soon as Marilyn gets on her shoes."

He forgot to tell Marilyn that they'd be together 24 hours a day. The furthest they could get apart was 15 feet to the troller pit. For the next month, she only visited with men.

Then one day they tied up to the *Pauline*. A girl walked out on deck. The men claimed that the women both exclaimed, "A girl!" and threw their arms around each other.

Dorie Wellesley was Marilyn's first Alaskan girlfriend. They began running with Ed and Dorie. They had a profound effect on the Jordans' fishing life.

Ed said, "I fished by myself for many years before I married Dorie. If she just buys groceries, does the cooking, keeps the boat clean, that is all I expect."

Skip figured that was the way it was done. A year later, he discovered that a lot of women cleaned and iced fish. Seeing that Ed never expected Dorie to clean and ice fish, Skip never asked Marilyn to clean and ice fish either.

The Jordans took out a homesite, five acres, or less, four miles south of Wrangell on the highway. They built a cabin on it and had two children, Eric and Karen, while living there.

They planned for Marilyn to stay ashore. Skip figured out how to make the *Salty* safe for Eric. He put a fish-netting door on Marilyn's bunk and called it "the birdcage." They bought a high chair that folded down into a play table.

Eric could stand up in a fish bin. They made a playpen on top of the locker down below, so that he could crawl around about six feet. When they trolled, the purr of the engine lulled him to sleep. But as soon as they turned it off, he'd be wide-awake and wanting to play.

Skip got a job running the U.S. Fish and Wildlife research vessel *Sablefish* at the end of the 1951 summer. They sold the *Salty* and moved to Ketchikan.

A year later, Skip came running home. "Marilyn, I just found the boat for us."

"I didn't know we were looking for a boat."

"This is it. It has a head, a sink, a big stove. Everything. It is a 45-foot cruiser-troller. Named *Nohusit*. With a boat like this you don't need a house."

The Jordans bought it in September of 1952 and moved aboard in November. They went winter fishing in January.

On March 23, 1953, they had taken fuel at the Standard Oil dock in Ketchikan. Skip was standing on the bow. He told Marilyn to start the gas engine.

She pushed the ignition. With a deafening roar, the boat blew up.

Skip said, "Oh, my God, the children!"

Marilyn has no memory of how she got the 15 feet from the wheel to the galley. Her first recollection is that the galley steps were blown out and she must jump. The high chair had fallen on Karen, and the little girl was crying.

By the time she reached for the high chair, Skip was in the backdoor and grabbing Karen.

"Where is Eric?" she thought.

Just then he cried, "Mama!"

She looked down where the steps had blown out. He was lying on top of the engine. She pulled

Wilhelm "Skip" and Marilyn Jordan cont'd

and pulled. Eric was free. Luckily, his clothes hadn't caught fire. She carried him out on deck in time to see Skip catch the rope that the dock man threw him to pull the boat close enough for all to step off the boat.

Skip was able to save the hull. Eric was burned around his head and hands. The people of Ketchikan started the Jordan Fund for them to rebuild *Nohusit*.

While in Ketchikan, Skip was the motorcycle policeman who led traffic during the building of the tunnel. Marilyn worked at Fishery Products Laboratory.

Once the *Nohusit* was rebuilt, the Jordans went back to salmon trolling.

During the winter of 1954-55, Skip was again a policeman in Ketchikan. Marilyn worked as a chemist at the pulp mill.

After the trolling season, the Jordans moved back to Wrangell. Marilyn became the home economics and physical education teacher at the school. They lived in their cabin on their homesite.

Skip's mother was not well, so they took the *Nohusit* to Tacoma. Their daughter, Barbara, was born there. In the spring, they moved back to Alaska and lived aboard the *Nohusit*. The children always loved life aboard. They had a playpen in the pilothouse that was made into a bed for Barbara.

As they were fishing more out of Petersburg, they moved there in 1959. Lynda was born there in 1960.

In the wintertime, Skip worked under Louis Lehmeyer on a number of building projects such as Lew Williams' and Fred Magill's houses. He also butchered king crabs at Petersburg Fisheries.

In 1965, Skip embarked on a lecturing and charter business. He had signed a national lecture contract using their 16-mm films that he called, "Alaska Fishing Family." He took out two bear hunting groups and two sportfishing groups.

Then Skip became sick. The doctor insisted he fly south for a bone marrow test in July. When he returned home on August 1, the hospital said they would have the results evaluated. The family went fishing in hopes of finding the elusive salmon.

They fished until they brought the children into Petersburg for school. When they hadn't heard from the hospital, the doctor sent a new blood sample south. The Seattle doctor telephoned.

"Jordan has subacute leukemia. Hospitalize him immediately." Skip flew south and lived only 17 days. He died October 4, 1965.

**Bill George
July 2003**

In 1986, upon retirement from salmon trolling with her new husband, Bill George, Marilyn had time to complete her book of her experiences of coming to Alaska. She called it *Following the Alaskan Dream: My Salmon Trolling Adventures in the Last Frontier*. She started with 500 pictures and cut them to 138. She wanted to capture Skip Jordan's life, their life afloat, and the beauty of Alaska. The Library of Congress selected it for their Local Legacy Project.

Shunichi and Hana Kaino

By Nan McNutt

Shunichi Kaino arrived in the United States, in 1912, at the age of 14. He worked with his father at the sawmill in Mukilteo, Washington. His mother made tofu, a soy food product, to sell to the mill workers.

In 1920 he returned to Japan to marry Hana. Upon their return to the United States, they moved to Tacoma, Washington, and later to Eatonville, Washington, where Ted was born in 1924.

The three went north to Petersburg, Alaska, arriving on Christmas Day 1926. Shunichi and Hana started work at Alaskan Glacier Sea Food.

By 1930, Frank was born.

The depression days, of the early 1930s, were hard. The Ohmer cannery had workers split shifts, so all could earn money for bread and milk for their families.

Ted was sent to Japan, in 1935, to live with his grandmother and older sister. (In 1952, he returned to Petersburg with his wife, Shig, and son, Douglas.)

In 1942, the Kaino family was split up and sent to two different Japanese internment camps. Shunichi was sent to Lordsburg, New Mexico. Hana and Frank were sent to Puyallup, Washington. After a few months, Hana and Frank were transferred to Minidoka Internment Camp in southeast Idaho.

Two years later, Shunichi joined the family at Minidoka. Following the war, in 1945, they left for Denver, Colorado, to live with Shunichi's younger brother, Harry, and his wife, Emma.

By 1946, they returned to Petersburg to work at the Alaskan Glacier Sea Food plant, where they were affectionately known as "Papa" and "Mama."

Papa and Mama loved going to the movies. After work they'd rush home, clean up, and quickly eat, so they could get their favorite seats at the theater (upstairs, first row on the right, next to Tsuyo Kuwata).

When Shunichi had any spare time, he was busy weaving special boxes for each of his grandchildren, as well as tobacco and cigarette package containers with designs of shrimp on the cover. These were all made from the unraveled threads of onion sacks.

Hana spent hours crocheting, latch hooking, embroidering, and making artificial flowers.

True to the meaning of her Japanese name, "Flower," Hana was known for her gardening and the beautiful flowers blooming in her yard.

Besides winning at bingo, one of her favorite games, Hana also won raffle prizes. In 1960, Hana won the fire department's Fourth of July grand prize — a car! And in 1962, she won an outboard motor.

Shunichi and Hana Kaino

Papa and Mama were the Grand Marshals of the 1967 Fourth of July parade. However, they might be best remembered for their New Year's Day open house dinners. Every year, Mama cooked for days to prepare traditional Japanese food to entertain all their friends.

Shunichi was superintendent of Ohmer's cannery from 1946 until his death in November of 1978. His loyalty to and love for his work was evident by the long, hard hours he spent at the cannery. His work was his life. Three generations of Kainos worked with three generations of Ohmers.

Ted and Shig worked in the cannery and commercial fished until they retired. Their children also worked there during the summer months. Frank worked one summer on the shrimp boat, *Louise S*.

Mama worked at the cannery until 1980. She died in 1988.

Joe and Fran (Kuwata) Kawashima

By John and Carol Enge

Fran Kuwata was born May 18, 1922, in Petersburg. Her parents were Dick and Tsuyo Kuwata.

Dick and Tsuyo had traveled from their ancestral home in Kumamoto, Japan, to Seattle, Washington, before following the migration to Petersburg. Arriving in 1920, they went to work at Earl Ohmer's Alaskan Glacier Sea Food.

They later ran the Grand Café, which was located where the Ocean Beauty Seafoods bunkhouse is today.

Dick and Tsuyo had three more children: Dick, June, and Susie, all born in Petersburg.

Dick Sr. passed away in 1940, and Tsuyo in 1979.

During her school years, Fran, like her parents, worked at Alaskan Glacier Sea Food.

Joe Kawashima was born in Tacoma, Washington, and first came to Alaska as a gillnetter in Bristol Bay. He arrived in Petersburg in 1941 and met Fran.

They were married September 28, 1941.

Following the declaration of war with Japan, all Japanese families were taken to internment camps. Joe and Fran were first sent to Puyallup, Washington, and then to Tule Lake, California, for the duration.

Their son, Ken, was born while in the camp.

Returning to Petersburg in 1945, they bought a home. Fran continued working in the shrimp, crab, and salmon canneries. In later years, she worked at Ohmer's Greens & Greens delicatessen.

The Kawashima's second son, Gene, was born in 1952.

John Enge, Blake Lesher and Clara Lesher, with Fran and Joe Kawashima

Joe started work at Kayler-Dahl Fish Company as foreman of their shellfish operation. During the salmon season, he was production manager of the salmon egg operation and also in charge of the fish house workers.

Joe was always dependable. During cold weather, he would go to the cannery in the early morning hours to start the boilers. He never took a holiday during the more than 30 years that he worked for Kayler-Dahl and Whitney-Fidalgo. He was always so trustworthy and reliable that management never interfered with his work.

For many years, Joe and Fran held the traditional Japanese open house on New Year's Day for family and friends, serving the many delicacies of their culture.

After retirement, they made occasional trips to Las Vegas. Following several years of poor health, Joe died in February 2002.

Fran and Joe's son, Gene, married Jane French. They have a daughter, Ashley.

Gene follows the tradition of his grandfather, working for Dave Ohmer as production manager of the shellfish operation at Norquest.

Photo courtesy of Clausen Memorial Museum

Dean and Mabel Kayler

By Molly Mowat

Our parents, Dean Kayler and Mabel Otness Kayler, both arrived in Petersburg in 1927. Dad was seeking adventure and Mom was a young schoolteacher.

Although they were raised less than 75 miles from one another in Idaho, they didn't know each other until they met at a dance at the Sons of Norway Hall. They dated for three years and, in December of 1930, they boarded the ship *Victoria* and sailed to Wrangell. They were married and returned to Petersburg the next day. Mom's cousin, Gertie Otness, was their only attendant.

Dad worked at a variety of jobs before they were married. He worked on a government forestry boat lighting buoys in Frederick Sound and Wrangell Narrows. He had also worked for the Bureau of Public Roads.

Mabel and Dean Kayler 1929

After she married Dad, Mom had to stop teaching. Back then, there was a law that teachers couldn't teach if they were married. She had to give up the profession she loved very much.

After marriage, Dad and Mom started Kayler's Milk Delivery. They bought milk from Point Agassiz farmers and delivered it to Petersburg customers. Mom told of washing the bottles in her tiny kitchen sink.

They hired Dave Ohmer and John Robert Otness to distribute the milk products and later supplied Alaska Steamship Company. As business expanded, Lloyd Swanson rented half of his building to them.

During this time, Dad became involved in the seafood industry, starting out with crab, working up to shrimp, and, finally, salmon. His first partner in the crab operation was Jacob Otness. Together they formed the Kayler-Otness Fish Company.

In the winter, Mom and Dad would travel to Washington and Idaho to sell the crab. Because of the Depression, there were no buyers.

This new business was short-lived. One November morning, a fire started in the Petersburg Cold Storage and spread to nearby buildings, including the Kayler-Otness Fish Company.

They often told us how difficult it was to watch their building burn; how Dad had to keep one of the few water hoses on the cold storage because they feared an ammonia leak.

Mom and Dad were destitute. They told us often how grateful they were to Carl "Swanie" and Alice Swanson for supplying their grocery needs, from their store, through that winter. They formed a deep friendship that lasted many, many years.

In 1941, Mom and Dad's situation improved with a banner salmon catch. A ready market was provided by the onset of World War II — they canned for the military. Soon, Dad decided he needed a bigger facility, so he refurbished the old Scow Bay Cannery.

During the canning season, we lived over the old grocery store at Scow Bay. Many days were spent picking berries with Mom for the desserts that were prepared by Magda Lind for the cannery crew in the mess hall. Betty Hofstad was the business secretary.

In 1946, Dad and Chris Dahl became partners and moved the canning operation into Petersburg.

Soon after, our family had to make a final move to Seattle because of Dad's arthritis and worsening heart condition. He was aware he could not continue to function as he had. The decision was made for Chris Dahl to be sole owner, but the business was to retain the Kayler-Dahl name.

In 1969, the cannery was sold to Whitney-Fidalgo Seafoods. It is now owned by Ocean Beauty Seafoods.

In the 1930s, all three of us children, Jeanette, Dean and Molly, were born in the old Petersburg hospital, attended by Dr. Benson and Mina Olson. We three have many warm and wonderful memories of our childhood growing up in Petersburg. The walks along the long boardwalk to Sandy Beach; crab feeds on the beach at Scow Bay; playing "hide and seek" in the evenings on Norway Hill; feeding black bear at Scow Bay; standing at the end of a float trying to lasso and climb onto moving icebergs; our years of knowing and loving our special "Tante" Maren Otness and her husband, Jack; the whole neighborhood going on berry picking expeditions; and, of course, jigging for tom

Dean and Mabel Kayler cont'd

cod through holes on the Kayler-Dahl dock.

After we left Petersburg, we were raised in Seattle. But, because of Dad's poor health, we also spent time in California and Florida.

Jeanette married Gary Rogers and raised two sons in Seattle. They moved to Cooper Landing, Alaska, and lived there more than 20 years before moving back to Washington state. They now reside at Birch Bay. They have three grandchildren: Jamie, Gary Lee and Leslie.

Upon the death of our Dad, Dean took over his small fish-trading firm, Swiftsure Fisheries, and spent his career in this business before selling it in 1981.

Dean and his wife, Leslie, live on San Juan Island, Washington. They have two children, Dean and Heidi, and two grandchildren, Christina and Dean.

Molly married Don Mowat and lived on Bainbridge Island, Washington for 30 years. They raised a son and a daughter, Steve and Kathryn. They currently live in Mt. Vernon, Washington and have four grandchildren: Stephania, Kevin, Ellen and Lauren.

Mabel and Dean Kayler

Fourth of July parade down Main Street

The Kildall Family

By Don Nelson

The Kildall family immigrated to Minnesota from Norway in the late nineteenth century. The father, Michael Kildall, had five sons: Joseph, Peter, John, Simon and Martin.

Two brothers, Joe and Martin, were associated with early Petersburg history, but only Martin Kildall settled and lived in town.

In the latter part of the 1800s, the Kildall family was prominent in the food industry in Minnesota, mainly fish products. The specialty was food products imported from Norway, Sweden, Denmark, England, France and Canada — salt fish, dried fish, cheese, and many varieties of canned goods. Their great specialty (and, in time, the leading trademark of the company) was Genuine Old Style Lutefisk.

Before they came west, early Petersburg settlers Erick Ness, Jacob Johnson and Jacob Hadland used to sell fish, caught on the Great Lakes, to the Kildalls.

By 1894, the Kildall family had reached the west coast. They were involved in salmon traps and supplying salmon to various canneries. The Kildalls also operated the G Street Dock Company in Bellingham, Washington.

One subsidiary of the Kildall Company was the Pacific Coast and Norway Packing Company. It was incorporated for one million dollars and had its headquarters in Minneapolis. J.F. Thurman was president and Joseph Kildall was secretary-treasurer.

Their first venture into the fishing industry in Southeastern Alaska was a floating saltery that they had towed to the vicinity of Blind Slough in Wrangell Narrows. They arrived on August 20, 1899.

They later moved up the Narrows to a spot on Kupreanof Island, six miles south of the future town of Petersburg. The location was known as Tonka. There, they salted herring and salmon. By September 5, 1899, 250 barrels of herring and eight barrels of coho salmon had been salted.

There were two house scows with the operation; one was fitted as a cooper shop and the other as a bunkhouse. There were 26 men employed. They had two 120-fathom seines and two 75-fathom gillnets.

By 1901, they had constructed a wharf and a cannery at this site. The cannery superintendent was Peter G. Kildall.

The cannery building at Tonka measured 40 feet by 170 feet. There were also two bunkhouses, warehouses, and other necessary buildings. The plant operated from 1901 to 1905, when the operation moved to Petersburg.

Tonka was then abandoned. Its buildings and dock stood until a southeast storm demolished them in the 1920s.

The Pacific Coast and Norway Packing Company bought out the Pacific Packing and Navigation company interests in the old Buschmann cannery, held by Northwest Fisheries, in 1906, and moved their operations to that location.

Joe Kildall had three boats built in Petersburg in 1912. They were named after John Kildall's daughters, Eunice, Mildred and Bernice.

The *Eunice* was the flagship of the fleet and continued on in grand style for both the cannery and Oscar Nicholson's Scow Bay Packing Company for many years. She was 64 feet long and had a 50 hp Corliss engine, until a Cooper-Bessemer diesel was installed in 1940. Martin Kildall was the skipper. She was used as a seiner, until 1925, when the 50-foot limit went into effect; then she tended traps.

In 1924, the *Eunice* seined with Olaf Olsen as skipper. After Oscar Nicholson got the boat in 1935, Tony Sather skippered the boat. Alf Abelson also ran it for many years.

She finished out her years in Prince William Sound, until she burned in Cordova about 1960.

The *Mildred* and *Bernice* later saw service with Dean Kayler as cannery tenders. At one time in the early 1950s, Bob Thorstensen (who later founded Icicle Seafoods) ran the *Bernice*. She shrimped for Kayler-Dahl Fish Company with Stubby Dundin as skipper until about 1960. The *Mildred* burned in Wrangell.

Martin Kildall was the only Kildall to live in Petersburg. He married the sister of Sam Gauffin and they had two daughters, Myrtle and Lillian.

They lived in a house on the hill on Front Street that later was the home of the Hugo Stoll family. It was located next to the current home of the Harvey Gilliland family on North Nordic Drive.

Besides skippering the *Eunice*, Martin ran the cannery tender *Kingsmill* for the Petersburg Packing

The Kildall Family cont'd

Company in 1922 and 1923. He also ran the *Jugoslav* in 1920.

Martin Kildall was prominent in early day Petersburg civic and business affairs. He was on the city council in 1912 and 1913. He also served on The Trading Union board of directors and as secretary of the firm in 1922 and 1923.

The Kildall family was truly a prominent force in the Alaska fishing industry at the turn of the century and in the early cannery days in Petersburg.

F/V *Mildred*

Mildred Juanita Kildall Nerland
By Andrew Ronald Nerland

My mother, Mildred Juanita Kildall, was born in Bellingham, Washington, April 21, 1900. Her father, John Kildall, was a fisherman.

It is my understanding that my mother, at the tender age of 3, made a trip to Petersburg with her father in 1903. As such, she was later eligible for membership in the Pioneer Women of Alaska, to which she belonged, and was active in for many years. (Membership required being in Alaska prior to 1908.)

My father, Arthur Leslie Nerland, was born March 11, 1901, in Dawon, Yukon Territory.

My mother and father were married in Seattle on January 16, 1926. In 1930, they, along with my older brother, Jerry, moved to Fairbanks to work for my grandfather, Andrew Nerland.

They came to Fairbanks at the request of my grandfather. He and his wife, Anne, wanted to make a trip back to Norway, which they had left in the late 1890s. They finally made that trip in 1936, the only time they were back in Norway.

The store sold paint, linoleum, glass and some furniture. Over the years, my father changed the store to a furniture and home furnishings store.

My mother worked for years as a gift buyer. She was active in the Girl Scout program, in Fairbanks, and was also an active member of the First Church of Christian Science. She was a PEO and belonged to Eastern Star.

My parents lived in Fairbanks from 1930 to 1988, when they moved to Anchorage. Later they moved to Bellevue, Washington, where they lived in a nursing home.

Mother died in 1992, and Dad in 1993.

My folks had three children. My older brother, Stuart Gerald Nerland, now lives in Anchorage.

My sister, Mildred Lesbeth Milesse, lives in Honduras.

My wife, Delores, and I moved from Fairbanks to Arizona.

Mildred and Arthur now have nine grandchildren and 17 great grandchildren.

Old Buschmann cannery, owned and operated by the Kildall family's Pacific Coast and Norway Packing Company, from 1906 to 1915.

Tom and Lucy Kito

By Carol Enge

Tom Kito was born in Tannowa, Osaka, Japan, on January 11, 1899. In 1914, at 15, Tom and his family immigrated to the United States. The family worked shucking oysters in the Olympia, Washington, area.

In 1917, Tom's parents and two sisters returned to Japan. Tom and his brother, Sam, remained and worked in the timber industry. They made their way to Alaska, working in Ketchikan, Petersburg and Cordova canneries. By 1921, Tom returned to Petersburg.

Lucy and Tom Kito

Lucy Coodey was born August 16, 1909, on Woewodski Island. She was raised by her grandparents. Her grandfather, Charlie Coodey, had a gold mine. They had a large vegetable garden and Charlie hunted to provide the rest of the food. Lucy always reminisced about the stews they had.

Lucy met Tom Kito while working at the Mountain Point cannery. They were married in 1924.

They lived in the Blind Slough area for two years before moving into Petersburg.

Lucy worked in the shrimp, crab and clam canneries. Tom worked for Pacific American Fisheries until his internment at the onset of World War II.

In December of 1941, all Japanese were taken from their homes and lodged in the Petersburg jail for three weeks before being shipped to Annette Island en route to Fort Richardson. Carroll Clausen, the magistrate at the time, came to take Tom to the jail. He was a good friend and was very apologetic about the task he was given.

Lucy chose to stay in Petersburg with the children, Richard, June, Anne and Jeanette.

Tom's relocation took him to Fort Lewis, Washington; Phoenix, Arizona; San Antonio, Texas; and finally to Lordsburg, New Mexico, where he was detained as a prisoner of war.

Tom was later transferred to Idaho's Minidoka Internment Camp. He worked outside the camp at the Anderson Ranch Dam project.

In his free time, Tom carved a miniature fishing boat complete with operable parts.

At the end of the war, Tom returned to Petersburg. Tom was hired by Knut Thompson at Petersburg Cold Storage. He worked there until his retirement in 1965.

Despite his internment experience, Tom was glad he had immigrated and had remained in the United States. He was a proud and responsible citizen.

For years, Tom and Lucy shared a Japanese New Year's Day open house with family and friends.

Tom died on March 27, 1997, at the age of 98.

Tom and Lucy's son, Richard, was born on February 9, 1931. He graduated from Petersburg High School, in 1949, as valedictorian.

He served in the U.S. Marine Corps, 1952 to 1954.

Returning to Petersburg, Dick was a fisherman and a cold storage worker. He became a pioneer in the harvesting, processing, and marketing of herring roe on kelp and sac roe.

Dick and his wife, Violet, had sons Richard Jr., Thomas, Tyrone and Therman. Violet passed away. Dick later married Leilani Bean in 1975.

Dick served as a councilman and mayor of Petersburg, and served on the boards of SeaAlaska Corporation and Alaska United Drilling. He was a loyal member of the Alaska Native Brotherhood, Tlinget & Haida Central Council, and was president of the Indian Association. He was also commander of the American Legion and VFW.

He owned Kito's Kave from 1967 until his death on November 14, 1987.

June Kito married Ben Berkley. They have one daughter, Roseanne Kito Anderson. June died of cancer in 1948.

Anne and husband Therman Lewis returned to Petersburg. They had two daughters, Patty and Cathy.

After graduating from high school, Jeanette moved to Seattle to attend beauty school. She met and married Ted Yomada.

Sig and Jensine Klabo

By Carol Enge

Sig and Jensine Klabo were among the early Norwegian settlers of Petersburg.

Sig was a halibut fisherman. At one time, he owned the F/V *Thelma M*.

Coming in from one trip, the *Thelma M* sank off Portage Bay. The crew barely had enough time to get off in the skiff before the boat went under.

At an earlier time, Sig was on a boat as they rounded South America's Cape Horn, bucking a gale as they pulled into Argentina.

Sig would always say, "Don't I know, wasn't I there?" They called him "Captain I," as he always knew a better way to do things.

Sig Klabo

Sig also fished with Oscar Sandvik on the *Don Q*.

Once he lost his footing and took a header over the rail. One of the PAF tenders was right behind the *Don Q*, towing a scow alongside.

Sig went right between the scow and the tender, but the skipper heard him yell, looked back, and spotted him. They turned around and picked him up.

The *Don Q* went on its way. It was over an hour before they missed Sig.

Sig and Jensine did not have children.

Jensine was very active in the social life of this frontier community. She was an officer in the Sons of Norway when it was first formed, and active in the Lutheran Ladies Aide.

Upon retirement, Sig and Jensine moved to Ballard, Washington, where they purchased a home.

Jensine Klabo

The Lando Family

By Sig Mathisen

The Lando family came from Landøy, near Vaerøy, one of the southernmost Lofoten Islands in northern Norway. The family had a long history of fishing in the Lofoten Islands, with family ties in the Bergen area to the south.

Kristoffer Hanssen Lando was born in Bergen on September 1, 1881, one of eight children of Hans Knutsen and Nikoline Knutsdtr.

He served time in the Norwegian Army. He was married in 1905. His wife died in 1908.

In 1909, he left for the United States, following his brothers, Soren and Thomas, and other relatives, who were already pursuing the fisheries in the Pacific Northwest.

He returned in 1916. In 1918, he married Bertine Marie Andreasdtr Haugsbo.

In 1920, they left Norway on the steamer *Bergensfjord* with 1-year-old daughter Nellie Amanda. They came to Petersburg where his brother and sister-in-law, Thomas and Jenny (Loken) Lando, and their son, Robert, had moved in 1915.

Kristoffer "Chris" purchased a house, in 1921, from Olaf Hanseth. Chris and Bertine's daughter, Klara Berget, was born October 16, 1921. Their son, Chris, was born September 10, 1923, three months after his father died of tuberculosis.

Bertine also became ill. In the spring of 1925, she left with her young family for medical treatment in the south. She died in California in December of 1925. She was 41.

For the next eight years, until September of 1934, the three children lived at the California Girls and Boys Aid Society Home and Orphanage.

By then, there was no fear of the children having the dreaded tuberculosis disease. Their uncle, Thomas, now had enough money to bring them back to Petersburg. The children joined Tom and Jenny's two children, Robert and Norma, at their house on the corner of what is now Fifth and Excel.

Thomas Lando was a partner for many years, in the fishing vessel *Odin*, with Anton Noreide and Louis Severson. His expertise was in herring seining, and he also ran the vessel salmon seining. The halibut boats purchased bait from their herring pounds at Noyes Island and Seymour Canal.

Nellie Lando Hyvari, Chris Lando and Klara Lando Mathisen

Ledgers and ship logs, recording the transactions of many of the old time Petersburg fishermen, remain in the archives of the Lando family.

Thomas had to retire because of his arthritis and pain from an early injury. As a young immigrant in New York, he was one of the few survivors of a tragic bridge collapse. Found in the tangled mass of bodies, Thomas was badly broken up.

The Lando family was very active in the Petersburg Lutheran Church and the Sons and Daughters of Norway.

Thomas and Jenny's two children both married and eventually moved south.

Norma married Karl Omdahl, a pilot. They had two children, Carl and Judy. They had the Rasmus Enge house on Sing Lee Alley, which is now the bookstore.

Robert married Inez Erdahl. They moved south in 1961.

Nellie, daughter of Chris and Bertine, married Sulo Hyvari. They moved to Seattle where Sulo worked as an electrician. They had five children: Sharon, Shirley, Susan, Sonja and Sulo.

Chris and Bertine's middle child, Klara, married Aril Mathisen. They continued to live in Petersburg where Aril fished. They had four children: Aril Jr., Sigurd, Lenore and Wayne. (*See Mathisen stories.*)

Chris and Bertine's son, Chris, graduated from Petersburg High School, and attended Washington State College for a time before joining the Navy during World War II.

Chris was stationed far out on the Aleutian Chain, serving as a signalman for the duration of his stay. This extended time of detailed communications may have

The Lando Family cont'd

been the cornerstone that shaped his later years as unofficial historian of Petersburg.

After leaving the Navy, Chris lived in Seattle for a while. He married Effie Otte and they had a son, Mark Bellamy; but the marriage didn't last long.

He came back to Petersburg and fished on local vessels before taking over the garbage collection business in town.

He later married Shirley Wellbourne. They lived together in Petersburg until Chris died January 7, 2001.

Chris was an avid recorder of audio, visual, and written media, documenting the history of Petersburg. He owned the first wire recorder in town and recorded with a vengeance. He next had a 16mm movie camera and captured life in our fishing town on color film.

After tackling and mastering his Macintosh computer, Chris chronicled family histories and town history. He was an invaluable source for people researching Petersburg.

Chris built his archive of information mainly from old Petersburg newspapers, along with information gathered in the local coffee shop.

He and Palmer Pederson spent a lot of time sitting on the stools at the coffee shop counter in their later years. Sometimes they would have slightly different recollections of "who did what" in the early days of Petersburg, Alaska.

Some of their friends (Leo Ness, Jim Hammer, John Enge, Earl Walker, Ken Welde, Marvin Kvernvik, Duke Miller, Eldor Lee, and Nels Evens) would be there, too, enjoying morning coffee, and sometimes refereeing these lively discussions. The correct interpretation of the story would eventually emerge. Having obtained the answers Chris was looking for, he would head home to write it all down.

Chris Lando

I enjoyed these special times in the coffee shop as much as any of the older generation, and willingly soaked up the lectures on history like an eager student.

My Uncle Chris treated it like a job or mission. He arrived precisely at 9:30 a.m. After having his morning coffee, he would type and edit, adding the significant information he had heard that day to his growing Petersburg chronicles. He would then return to the shop at 3 p.m. for the gathering of the afternoon coffee crowd.

Sometimes the afternoon session lasted until 5 p.m., or later, with a brief intermission to retrieve the mail. There was a little different crowd in the afternoon. It was a little less history and more social. Chris would see his brother-in-law, Leif Mathisen, and his wife, Ruth, at the coffee shop. Often his sister, Klara, would come there to visit with him.

Chris always planned to write a book someday, but it was obvious to me he would never be done with his research. Instead, he gave this information away to others who were writing, editing old film, and documenting Petersburg's history.

It is likely that if you read or study Petersburg's history, my Uncle Chris most likely had a hand in collecting and making that information available.

Chris Lando, in the rear, talking with the next generation's historian, Heidi Lee, and Ken Welde, in the coffee shop on Main Street. After many decades and under several different names, the coffee shop is no longer in business. It is now the cookhouse for Norquest Seafoods.

Harold and Magnhild Lee

By Robin Lee-Smith and Heidi Lee

Harold Marius Lie was born in Arnes, Harstad, Norway. Harstad is north of the Arctic Circle and life there was not easy.

Harold's mother, Amalia Stoltenburg, the daughter of a prominent doctor in southern Norway, created a stir when she fell in love with Peder Lie, a peddler who came to town to sell boat supplies. When they married, Peder settled down to start a ship's chandlery.

Eventually, they moved north and bought a farm at the water's edge outside of Harstad. There they raised their family.

The men fished from wooden dories and the family enjoyed the dairy products and produce from the farm.

Harold Lee Sr.

When Harold was 18 years old, the price for cod was very low. He decided to leave Norway and start a new life in America. He took passage on a ship to Halifax, Nova Scotia, and eventually arrived in New York City.

Coming into America, immigration officials decided his last name would be better understood if changed from "Lie" to "Lee."

Like many immigrants, Harold endured hardship and hunger as he worked his way across the country. Hearing of the gold rush and lured by stories of fortunes being made in Alaska, he planned to travel north to the Klondike via the Stikine River.

While still in Seattle, he visited friends from Norway, the Kildahls (Kildall), who ran a saltery near the small settlement of Petersburg. They offered him a job running their fish house.

He came north by steamship in 1902, and lived with the Kildahls for two years. The saltery was located on Wrangell Narrows on the north side of the entrance to Blind Slough. He never made it to the Klondike.

When he was 22, Harold spent the winter as watchman at the saltery. One day, he retrieved an old dugout canoe that had drifted ashore with the tide. He repaired the canoe with hopes of paddling it to Wrangell, a town he had only heard about.

That fall, paddling with the tide, he headed north up the Narrows, past Petersburg, entered Frederick Sound, and followed the Mitkof shore toward Dry Strait. The first night he camped at Ideal Cove.

The next morning, the weather worsened as he continued his journey. There was no chance to reach Wrangell and no turning back. Late in the afternoon, he was glad to see smoke in the distance. The smoke came from a Tlingit fishing camp at what is now known as Ohmer Creek.

The Tlingits shared their food with him and let him sleep in a smokehouse. Bears prowled around all night, enticed by the smell of fish.

Neither Harold nor his hosts spoke much English, but his new friends were able to tell him they would show him an easy way to get back to Wrangell Narrows. They helped drag his dugout up a little side creek to a series of beaver dams.

On his own then, and following their directions, Harold thought it was a wondrous thing to travel peacefully through the island following a waterway, which until then had been known only to generations of the land's original inhabitants.

Harold moved to Petersburg, bought land on Hammer Slough, and built a "bachelor cabin."

Fishing the waters of Southeast before the advent of power motors, Harold was known for his seamanship and skill with sails.

He and his friend, Atomic Ole, built a big skiff, named it the *Wolverine*, and bought one of the first seven-horsepower engines in town.

Harold and Magnhild Lee cont'd

Harold also built his first fishing boat, the *Rival*, on Hammer Slough. He used the *Rival* to gillnet on the Stikine River and longline in Frederick Sound. He built one of the first gillnet reels around — a huge and heavy thing.

In 1915, Harold married Magnhild Husby, who had come to Petersburg to work in her sister, Asbjorg's, restaurant.

One stormy night while he and Magnhild were fishing near the mouth of the Stikine, the net and reel were torn loose and carried away in the storm. It was a devastating loss.

Harold and Magnhild began their family. Son Allen came first, then Eldor, Harold Jr. and Ruth. When Eldor was born, the family moved from Hammer Slough to a house a few blocks above Main Street.

About 1930, Harold made a deal with a Texan, desperate to return to Texas, who wanted to unload his schooner, the *Vesta*. The *Vesta* was a traditional schooner built for sea travel and longlining. She was 56 feet long with an aft wheelhouse, a wood stove, and dory on the stern. She was painted light gray with a white stripe. Harold traded the *Rival* and $1,500 for the *Vesta*.

During the 1930s, until they had collected enough money, the family all contributed their shares (earnings) toward the purchase of a Cummins engine. Harold skippered the *Vesta* longlining for halibut and blackcod, seining and packing salmon.

The *Vesta* was a great source of pride for the family and, one by one, as they grew up, the boys joined him working on the boat.

Active in the growing community of Petersburg, Harold was a member of, and helped build, the Sons of Norway Hall. He was also a member of the Moose Lodge. Being a vessel owner and observing the local custom, he always wore a shirt and tie, hat and topcoat.

Harold still hoped to find gold and carried a prospector's hammer with him while hunting and exploring. In his free time between fishing, overhauling gear, and making nets, he enjoyed making things with wood and spending time with the family at their Sandy Beach cabin.

The family had also purchased a farm in East Stanwood, Washington; as years went by, Magnhild and Harold spent time there as well as in Petersburg.

Harold enjoyed his family and loved to tease his grandchildren. A favorite trick was to run his tongue around inside his cheek, as he told a horrified grandchild he was eating a fish eye. He loved sweets and put sugar in and on everything, saying he "couldn't take the chance" it would not be sweet enough.

Harold retired from commercial fishing when he was 72. He was known for his intelligence, physical strength, sense of humor, and fair play. He was a fine and gentle man with a sweet smile and peaceful countenance.

Magnhild Husby Lee

On a hill overlooking the beautiful Tingvoll Fjord, lay the Husby family farm, Oppigaren, or Upper Farm. It was here, near Tingvoll, Gyl, Norway, in 1892, that Magnhild Husby was born to her parents, Randi and Erik Husby. Ultimately, there would be eight children in the family

Randi and Erik turned the farm into an agricultural school to teach new farming methods. They also developed an agricultural school in neighboring Kristiansund.

As a child, Magnhild loved being outdoors, helping with the farm chores and taking the long hike to the upper mountain meadows, where the farm animals would graze in the summer. The family had a cabin high in the meadows and Magnhild loved being there, looking out over the fjord, and running and playing in the heather.

In 1906, Randi and Erik make the difficult decision to move the family to Portland, Oregon, where they would join Randi's sister and her family. Magnhild, then 14, had a hard time saying good-bye to Norway. Like the rest of the family, she did not speak a word of English.

Her father, Erik, started a nursery in Portland.

Magnhild began public school in the first grade because she didn't know English. It was very humiliating for the teenager, but as a result, she learned a huge lesson about accepting people who are different. She knew what it felt like to be on the "outside." As she learned the new language, she acted as translator for her father in his business dealings for the nursery.

The children all pitched in towards the family income. Magnhild worked as a maid during the week, seeing her family only on weekends.

Harold and Magnhild Lee cont'd

She was excited, at 18, when her parents decided to send her to Petersburg, Alaska, to work with her older sister, Asbjorg, who was partner in a restaurant located in the Enge building in Sing Lee Alley.

Her trip north on a steamer culminated on a clear, cold winter day, as the ship wound its way up Wrangell Narrows. She was rowed ashore and escorted down the boardwalk to her sister's house by a crewman. Little did she know at the time that her future husband, Harold Lee, was in the group of bachelors on the dock watching her arrival.

Magnhild Husby Lee

As a young unmarried woman in Petersburg, Magnhild lived with her sister and worked at the restaurant, as well as cooking for several logging camps in the area.

She became known for her energetic ways and joined a women's basketball team. Her philosophy was, "Why walk when you can run?"

During this time, Magnhild met Harold Lee. He became a good friend and watched out for her. They were married two years later.

"*Married at Ballard, Washington on January 2, 1915, Mr. Harold Lee and Miss Magnhild Husby. Mr. & Mrs. Lee arrived on the* Jefferson *last Saturday evening, and will make their home in Petersburg. Mr. Lee, who is owner and captain of the gasboat,* Rival, *has resided here for a number of years. Miss Magnhild Husby-Lee, spent some time in this city a couple years since with her sister, Mrs. John Molver. The young people have the hearty wishes of a host of friends for a happy and prosperous life.*" (*Petersburg Weekly Report*, January 16, 1915)

Magnhild and Harold began their married life in Harold's "bachelor cabin" on Hammer Slough. They worked together on the *Rival*, gillnetting by hand, around the mouth of the Stikine River. When their first child, Allan, was born in 1918, Magnhild stayed home to care for the family. Then came Eldor in 1920, Harold Jr. in 1922, and Ruth in 1924.

The couple purchased a home on Third Street, where they lived for many years and enjoyed being neighbors with the Jensens, Thompsons and Sathers. The kitchen had a nook where the family enjoyed many a mug-up with homemade bread, coffee, and good times next to the big oil stove.

Magnhild enjoyed walking on the double plank boardwalk out to their cabin at Sandy Beach. She and the children spent summers at the cabin and all the children learned to swim at Sandy Beach. Harold Jr. remembered the "golden sand dunes they ran on," before the sand was used to build the road to town.

The "Lee kids" were an active bunch. There are many stories of summer solstice bonfires, hiking the mountains and muskegs in the area, wonderful times up Petersburg Creek, building and defending the "Hill Gang fort," and ice-skating on the muskeg ponds.

Magnhild was always relieved when the kids were home safe and sound. She often had a feeling when they would arrive and would have a hot meal ready.

For an entire summer, during the Depression, the family lived on their boat, the *Vesta*. They took basic staples out with them and lived on wild game, seafood, and berries. The family remembers that summer fondly.

As her children grew, Magnhild became more involved in community life. Because of her honesty, intelligence, and open ways of dealing with people and issues, in 1930, she was elected as the first woman on Petersburg's city council. She had felt the city council was secretive about its decision-making, and she

Harold and Magnhild Lee cont'd

worked hard to make politics public. She was also instrumental in the vision for Petersburg's future power supply.

Magnhild served many years on the school board, the library board and the election board. She worked with Tlingit and other community leaders to integrate the schools into one system. It didn't make sense to her to have the children separated or to have the expense of running two schools.

During that time, people questioned how a woman could be a good mother and also be so involved in town business, but Magnhild knew that her husband and family stood behind her. In her mind, family always came first and her family knew that.

When the kids were in high school, the family spent some winters on the farm they had purchased in East Stanwood, Washington.

Magnhild was always very proud of her children and encouraged them to further their education.

She enjoyed her reading club and felt women could benefit from joining the speaking club, Toast Mistresses. All her life she was an avid reader and loved discussions of any kind, on any topic.

In their later years, Magnhild and Harold spent time at both their Washington farm and their home in Petersburg.

Their son, Allen, died in an accident at age 22. Eldor and Harold Jr. lived and raised families in Petersburg. Ruth moved away after high school to make her home down south.

From her roots in Norway to her life in Alaska, Magnhild Husby Lee made a difference to the people, and communities, in whom she invested her life. She knew that we keep learning all our lives and that it was important to ask questions. She was willing to take a public stand for things she believed in.

During the more than 60 years she lived in Petersburg, nearly everyone who resided there came to know her. They learned of her passion for honesty and of her vigorous opposition to injustice at all levels of society.

**Longlining aboard the *Union Jack*
May 1913**
*University of Washington Libraries,
Special Collections, Cobb 3692*

Eldor and Pauline Lee

By Polly, Robin, Eric and Anne Lee

Eldor Lee was born of Norwegian immigrants, Magnhild and Harold Lee, in the small house, or "bachelor shack," that Harold had built on the shore of Hammer Slough. He joined an older brother, Allen.

The family moved to the old parsonage near the Lutheran Church, then to another house nearby. Another brother, Harold Jr., and a sister, Ruth, had already joined the family.

The house was always full of young people, singing around the piano and planning adventures. Eldor was full of fun and a natural leader.

Growing up in the freedom of Alaska and exploring the country around him influenced Eldor his entire life. From his earliest years, he hunted and fished the streams, muskegs, and mountains surrounding Petersburg.

Some of his greatest joys were being outdoors and exploring new country, climbing mountains, or following a creek just to see where it went.

In his earlier years, Eldor and his boyhood friends caught the tide and rowed up Petersburg Creek, down Wrangell Narrows to hunting and fishing spots, and to Blind Slough for camping trips. In winter they would ski and skate on the frozen muskeg.

One fine day, when he was about 67, on a hike up to Petersburg Lake, he looked like a youth, while trout fishing in Petersburg Creek with his pant legs rolled up, wading in his sneakers to get to the "hot spots."

During Eldor's high school years, the family lived part time on their farm in Stanwood, Washington. Eldor was a very good athlete and played basketball for Petersburg, Stanwood, and Mt. Vernon, Washington. He was a key player when Petersburg High School won the 1938 Southeast Championship.

After high school, he continued playing basketball at Washington State University, and for Petersburg in the Gold Medal Tournaments in Juneau.

He never lost his love of the game, and Eldor enjoyed visiting with old teammates and opponents wherever he went. In later years, he told stories of playing basketball in the Sons of Norway before the gym was built.

When World War II began, Eldor joined the U.S. Coast Guard. He skippered a 72-foot patrol boat throughout northern Southeast Alaska. He was sent to the South Pacific aboard the patrol frigate, USS *Glendale*. After a very hard tour of duty, he returned, profoundly saddened by his war experiences.

He was decorated for his service from 1942 to 1945. Shipmates remember him as a fair and honorable person who stood up for his shipmates.

While in the South Pacific, Eldor and his sister Ruth's friend, Pauline "Polly" Martin, began a letter writing friendship, which bloomed into love.

Eldor Lee

In 1946, they were married. He had returned from the service and she had graduated from nursing school. They established their home in Petersburg and raised three children: Robin, Eric and Anne.

When the children were young, Eldor and Polly enjoyed taking the family across the muskeg, walking on the frozen snow on clear, cold nights to town, where they would have hot chocolate with Magnhild and

Eldor and Pauline Lee cont'd

Harold, Eldor's parents.

Eldor worked at several jobs in Petersburg, including postmaster, terminal manager for Alaska Coastal Airlines, and as the first terminal manager in Petersburg for the Alaska Marine Highway System. He was on the city council and worked briefly as city clerk.

It was not in his nature to work indoors and he always returned to fishing. He loved coming home with tales of adventure, comradeship and danger, such as exchanging cigarettes with Japanese or Russian fishermen out in the Gulf of Alaska.

During the transition to statehood, Eldor served as a delegate to the Alaska Constitutional Convention where he was instrumental in drafting language to ban fish traps. These huge traps, mostly owned by wealthy out-of-state interests, corralled the returning salmon by the thousands.

As a commercial fisherman, Eldor felt it was a high priority at the convention to make sure that traps would be outlawed when Alaska became a state. Largely as a result of his perseverance, language drafted into the constitution banned the traps, resulting in great and positive changes for the salmon industry throughout coastal Alaska.

Eldor held the strong belief that the fish in the ocean were, and should always be, a public resource. He never reconciled this belief with the State of Alaska's Limited Entry and I.F.Q. (Individual Fishing Quotas) systems of fishery management that came later.

In the late 1950s, Eldor joined his lifelong friend, Lloyd Pederson, in the exploration of king crab fishing in southeast waters. Working from Lloyd's boat the F/V *Middleton*, they prospected for and found king crab. The price was low, but they caught lots of crab.

Other boats soon followed suit, and the Southeast king crab industry was born.

Eldor bought the F/V *Silver Crest* in 1973 and fished for halibut and salmon.

All three of his adult children worked with him on the boat at various times. For several years, until he retired in 1999 at age 79, Eldor ran the *Silver Crest* with Eric as crewman.

Throughout their life together, Eldor and Polly made many trips throughout the United States and Europe. Sometimes they would take the *Silver Crest* out for pleasure cruises, exploring island and bays in the area around Petersburg.

After building their dream home overlooking Frederick Sound, Eldor was happy there, working in the yard, and having family and friends visit.

He shared his great love of the outdoors with Polly, their children, and grandchildren, Andrea and Tyler. He loved telling stories of his youth, such as searching under the board streets for coins (collecting was best in front of the bars), and taking the coins to the store for treats. There were no pennies to find because Petersburg did not use pennies at that time.

Eldor passed away, in 2002, at the age of 81. For two days following his death, flags at state buildings throughout the state were lowered to half-staff in his honor, in recognition of his service to Alaska.

Throughout his life Eldor was known for standing up for what he believed, his work ethic, and his wonderful sense of humor.

Pauline "Polly" Lee

Pauline Sarah Martin was born in a log cabin in the Missouri "breaks" of Eastern Montana. Her parents and her father's family had "proved up" on adjoining homesteads on the Missouri River. They were ranchers who raised cattle, horses, and wheat.

When Polly was 3 years old, her family moved to Sumner, Washington, to be near her mother's family.

In school she was active in Scouts, choir, orchestra, and sports; she was editor of the high school school newspaper. Polly graduated from high school in 1940, and from Tacoma Beauty School the following year. She attended Pacific Lutheran College, which became practically deserted when World War II broke out.

After attending Knapp's Business College in Tacoma, Polly went to Anchorage to work for the U.S. Army Corps of Engineers. There, in 1941, she married Walter Tadlock, a lieutenant in the air force. After only three months, he disappeared while on a non-combat flight over Prince William Sound.

Polly attended Tacoma General Hospital School of Nursing. Two of her classmates were Alice Espeseth and Ruth Lee of Petersburg, Alaska. The three young women developed a lasting friendship.

Ruth suggested that Polly might write to her brother Eldor, who was in the Coast Guard in the South Pacific. They corresponded until Eldor returned from the service during her senior year of nurse's training.

Eldor and Pauline Lee cont'd

In February 1945, Polly and Eldor were married in Sumner, Washington. In September of that year, Polly graduated and went north to join her husband.

Pauline "Polly" Lee

On a moonlit evening in September of 1945, Polly Lee carefully negotiated the gangway from the steamship to the dock, as her new husband, Eldor, and father-in-law, Harold Lee Sr., waited below to greet her. Not realizing that the tide would be very low when she arrived, Polly had dressed carefully for her arrival, wearing a stylish narrow skirt and high-heeled pumps making her descent very difficult. Polly had arrived in Petersburg, where she and Eldor would make a home.

Their first home was the "old Lee home," three blocks up from downtown.

Polly remembers the Petersburg "customs" at that time. One could give the telephone operator special messages to pass on as needed. People could shop at the local stores, charge the purchase, and pay at the end of the month. Or, one could call up a grocery order and it would be delivered. The delivery person would put ice cream in the freezer if no one was at home!

She learned all the things that could be ordered from Sears Roebuck and Montgomery Ward catalogs. If a steamship strike lasted a long time, she learned how to make variations on carrot and cabbage salad.

Those first years were filled with hiking, hunting, and fishing trips; working at the hospital; and having their first child, daughter Robin.

Polly loved taking Robin in a box tied to a sled for walks on the frozen snow. She loved skiing in the winter and swimming at Falls Creek in the summer.

On the summer muskeg, she learned of interesting plants, frogs, and insects. Fall brought the bright colors of the mosses and grasses. There were large hoar frost crystals and more snow than today.

Three years later, son Eric was born. The family built a home on Wrangell Avenue where they lived for 25 years. Daughter Anne joined the family in 1961.

Polly continued to work at the hospital and doctor's offices, as well as being involved in community work. She was a member of C.I.C. (Civic Improvement Council), which worked for city clean up, for better garbage disposal, rat control, lighting along the bulkhead above the harbor, and beautification projects around town. She was one of the founders of the Petersburg Arts Council.

Polly developed a lifelong interest in studying and making art; she traveled to study the art, history and cultures of other countries. Governor Egan appointed her to the Alaska State Council of the Arts in 1980. She served for 12 years, helping to develop arts programs and arts awareness across the state.

As Polly became more committed to her art, she put together a complete studio and gallery at her home. For 30 years she made ceramic art, participated in statewide exhibits, and held her own show once a year, featuring small sculptures and functional pottery.

She was awarded several commissions by the Alaska State for Art Commission for large ceramic wall murals for public buildings. Her work is also installed at ARCO, in Anchorage, and the municipal building in Petersburg.

In the early 1990s, she turned her focus to painting and creating three-dimensional work that made a social or political statement. During this time she began the study and teaching of Tai Chi.

Harold "Hi" Lee

By Roxy Lee

Harold "Hi" M. Lee Jr. was born March 19, 1922, to Harold and Magnhild Lee, early Norwegian immigrants. He joined brothers Allen and Eldor, and two years later Ruth joined the family. They lived on Third Street in the former Lutheran Church parsonage.

During school years, Harold worked at the theater for free shows. He knew every cowboy movie made, acting out the stories with his buddies Tommy Thompson, George Nicholson, Erling Jensen and Pete Thynes. They called themselves the "Hill Gang."

Harold started fishing at an early age with his father and brothers on the family boat F/V *Vesta*. In high school Harold was yell king, played basketball, and bought a piano, teaching himself to play after taking some private lessons.

Harold "Hi" Lee Jr.

His family spent time in Stanwood, Washington, near Magnhild's family, so Harold attended East Stanwood High for several years.

His brother, Allen, was tragically killed in an airplane accident in 1942. That summer Eldor and Harold ran the family boat for the grieving family.

Harold joined the U.S. Coast Guard in 1942, going to Ketchikan for his training. He was one of the lucky ones, staying in Southeast Alaska and running a 50-foot coast guard cutter on supply detail, from Gustavus to lighthouses and locations all over the Inside Passage.

After his discharge in 1946, he enrolled at the University of Washington and later at Seattle School of Photography on the G.I. Bill. After photography school, he used his talent filming weddings, social clubs, families, and doing portrait work.

On January 18, 1953, Harold married Roxanne Swenson in Bayport, Minnesota. He often told the story of Roxy's Minnesota friends questioning "this guy from Alaska, taking away one of theirs, and then to top that, he was a halibut fisherman!"

They made their home in Petersburg, first in the Lee family home, and later purchasing a home on Second Street from Alma Nicholson Wallen.

Harold was a great family man, taking the kids hunting, fishing and berry picking. The family also enjoyed their cabin at Blind Slough.

Harold spent 18 years with Alaska Coastal Airlines, eventually as Alaska Airlines station manager. He also worked for both the State of Alaska Employment Service and Icicle Seafoods.

Through the years he fished on the boats *Vesta*, *Teddy J*, *Middleton*, *Cheyenne*, *Pearl F*, *Harmony*, *Symphony*, *Verma*, *Decade*, and lastly on the *Marathon*, skippered by son-in-law Sig Mathisen.

Active in his community, Harold was president of the Chamber of Commerce and a member of the Centennial Committee, Sons of Norway and Elks. He helped establish the museum, taking care of the "Fisk" for years. He was on the Little Norway Festival Committee for years and skippered the *Valhalla* for the Vikings. He was recipient of the Norwegian-American Award. He was on the school board and the Clausen Memorial Museum board, the latter for 12 years.

Harold retired in 1985. He then helped out at Lee's Clothing, providing wonderful support for Roxy and her staff. His warmth, humor and quick wit brought a smile to all who knew him.

He also helped build their new

Roxy Lee

home on Wrangell Narrows, where he enjoyed the beautiful view of the water, boats, and mountains.

Harold died of multiple myeloma cancer on September 5, 1997, surrounded by his loving family.

In 2001, the Clausen Memorial Museum honored Harold posthumously with a month-long show of his work "Through The Lens of Harold Lee."

Roxane Swenson Lee

By Roxy Lee

In June 1947, after graduating from Stillwater High School in Minnesota, I boarded a westbound train in St. Paul. My destination was Petersburg, Alaska! My Aunt Lillian L. Swanson surprised me with a graduation present: two suitcases and one ticket to visit her in Alaska. I arrived in Petersburg aboard the SS *Alaska* and was off on a glorious adventure that would last a lifetime.

In the summers I worked in Petersburg, and would travel back to the University of Minnesota, where I received my degree in retailing.

In the summer of 1952, I met Harold "Hi" Lee, a young and handsome Norwegian fisherman, born and raised in Petersburg. We were married in Minnesota in 1953 and returned here to make our home.

Hi and I raised three children: David, Heidi and Cynthia. We lived on Second Street for 28 years before building our home, in 1986, two and a half miles south of town on Wrangell Narrows.

While the children were growing, I volunteered with the Scout troops, Alaska Music Trails, Lutheran Church and Little Norway Committee. In 1978, I was appointed to the Alaska Women's Commission. I served until 1983, helping women assure their rights in the workplace and at home.

In 1969, with my family's help, I decided to follow my dream and establish Lee's Clothing in downtown Petersburg. Hi and the kids stained the shelves, priced the merchandise, and hauled the freight. In September, we opened in the Swanson Building, across from the present location.

We moved across the street in 1985 to a larger space, built 88 years ago by my Uncle C.E. Swanson. This September (2004) will mark our 35th anniversary.

David lives in Corvallis, Oregon, and Cynthia and Heidi manage Lee's. Although I stay active in the store and Petersburg civic affairs, Palm Springs beckons me in the winter. By spring, I'm home starting the garden and enjoying my grandchildren, Allan and Maya, and my home on the water.

"Good Merchandise and Good Service"

Lee's Clothing INCORPORATED

Established by Harold & Roxy Lee in 1969

Our family store has been outfitting customers with clothing, shoes and outdoor gear for 34 years.

Owned and operated by Roxy Lee
Cynthia Lee Mathisen, manager
Heidi Lee, assistant manager

P.O. Box 747
212 Nordic Drive
Petersburg, Alaska
907-772-4229
Fax: 907-772-3542
S.E. AK: 800-478-7702

We are proud to carry on the tradition begun by Uncle Swanie and Aunt Lillian.

C.E. Swanson Merchandise
Established, in 1926, by Alice and C.E. Swanson. Uncle Swanie's store carried groceries, hardware, outboards, and trading furs. C.E. Swanson Merchandise was located in the modern day site of Lee's Clothing.

The Lillian Shop
Established by Lillian Swanson, sister of C.E. Swanson. From 1938 to 1955, the shop carried the latest in women's apparel, shoes, foundations, millinery, and children's wear. The site is now occupied by Wells Fargo Bank.

James and Anne Leekley

By Janet Leekley Eddy

James Leekley was born at Ocean Park, Washington, in 1911.

The model fur farm he set up, while a student at Oregon State University, attracted the attention of the federal government. So, instead of going to Alaska as he had hoped, he became a biologist on an experimental fur farm in New York.

Robin, Jim, Jeri Anne, Anne and Janet Leekley

Jim married Anne Peterson from Oregon. Their first child, Janet, was born in New York, October 13, 1939. Soon after, Jim was offered the job of biologist-in-charge of the Petersburg Experimental Fur Farm, on Wrangell Narrows, nine miles south of Petersburg.

Moving to the "wilds" of Alaska was a very big deal. Friends and family feared for their safety! Jim left Anne and the baby in Oregon with relatives while he traveled north and got settled in Petersburg. In Seattle, a local pickpocket relieved him of all but 65 cents and his steamer ticket. The ticket included meals, so he continued to Petersburg.

Jim's first stop upon arriving was a visit to C.E. Swanson, a local grocer, who loaned him survival money until his first paycheck.

The following month, Anne, her sister Margaret Peterson, and baby Janet boarded an Alaska steamship bound for Petersburg. They had a unique, "coming to Alaska" experience!

Ships were slower in those days and, upon arrival in Ketchikan, the passengers were anxious to walk around and have their first look at Alaska. The sleeping baby was left in the charge of a stewardess and off they went with no worries. After all, the ship was not due to sail until evening.

Anne soon became nervous about being away from the baby, so they returned to the ship. The dock was empty — no ship! The two women were horror-stricken. Anne cried. Marge screamed.

The police arrived and, upon hearing the problem, laughed and assured the women that the vessel had only moved to the oil dock. They offered to take them to the ship. There were a few raised eyebrows when the good missionary ladies saw two crying women emerge from a large black police car and rush up the ship's gang plank.

Jim and Anne had two more children. Robert James was born April 4, 1942. Jeri Anne was born January 6, 1946.

The school bus only came out the road across from Mountain Point, so Jim or Anne had to drive the children part way from the fur farm every day.

Although Anne had attended normal school and was a qualified teacher, life at the fur farm was far from normal. Along with the work of raising a family in an isolated area, in the era of wringer washers and clotheslines, she also did the farm's secretarial work.

Like most Alaskans, their life was part subsistence. They had a huge garden, wild game to hunt and

James and Anne Leekley cont'd

process, crab traps to pull, and fish to can. There was a cool room in the basement for root vegetables and another room for cases of canned goods.

Imagine life before "search and rescue" or medevac flights!

Jim and Anne, along with Les and Mildred Elkins, once swamped a skiff in Blind Slough during a sudden storm. Heavy wet clothes almost pulled them under. They reached shore and faced hypothermia! Drowning, getting lost, accidents — just part of life in Petersburg, Alaska.

Ordinary activities often became major challenges. The road was dusty in the summer and icy in the winter. Some sections were very, very muddy!

Every spring, the giant mud hole between town and the oil docks stopped traffic. Kids, going to and from school, had to walk across mud to get on the bus.

It was a scary night when Jim had to carry his sick son across the mud to a car that would take them to the hospital for Robin's emergency appendectomy.

The electric line came in from Blind Slough. It ran partially along the beach, making the frequently needed repairs difficult. However, electricity or not, the animals needed to be fed.

The phone existed only because the fur farm was on the town side of Papke's Landing. During World War II, the military wanted Papke to be the "lookout" for foreign invaders at the end of the Narrows. After the war, the personnel at the fur farm kept up the phone line, strung on trees into town.

In those days, everybody had to know how to do everything!

Fish processing often involved the whole town. When the canneries were overflowing, a call went out, babysitters were located, and all able-bodied adults went to work. Jim, Anne, and everyone else at the fur farm might put in a shift at the Scow Bay Cannery after the farm work was finished.

During slow times, the canneries were generous about running home-canned fish through their retorts for cooking and the final sealing.

The fur farm's original mandate from the Department of Agriculture and the University of Alaska was to improve the fur quality of foxes, mink, and marten via food and breeding. The availability of fish and fish by-products from the canneries was an important part of the Petersburg location.

Some winters Jim went up into the Arctic and the Aleutians, bringing back wild animals to breed with

Old Mitkof Highway

domestic varieties, always trying to improve the color and texture of the fur. This information was made available to private fur farmers across the country.

There were some important experiments done at this farm. The sonic boom test was to determine if pregnant mink were affected by such noise. One of the first experiments to be done with eagles and DDT was carried out at the Petersburg station.

Orphaned wildlife such as deer, mountain goats, and wolves were raised on the farm. And yes, the wolves were kept separate from the deer!

The University of Alaska honored Jim for his accomplishments in the fur industry and other experimental projects. The Petersburg Experimental Fur Farm was closed down in 1972. The time when furs were both the warmest of clothing and a major fashion statement had past.

Paul and Florence LeRoy

By Florence LeRoy

Paul LeRoy was born in Spooner, Wisconsin, in 1917, to Paul and Myrtle LeRoy. He came to Alaska in 1945 from Carnation, Washington, to work as a logger in Wrangell and Craig.

Florence Bell was born in Detroit, Michigan, in 1920, to Roy and Harriet Bell, a World War I veteran and his English bride. Although her father was American, he served in the Canadian Armed Forces.

In 1921, the family moved to Saskatchewan, Canada, where Florence's father was awarded land as recompense for his war services.

Florence graduated from Saskatchewan City Hospital as a registered nurse in 1944.

Paul and Florence met in Vancouver, British Columbia, where she was working as a nurse, supervising the maternity ward.

They married in June of 1947 in Lashburn, Saskatchewan, where Florence's parents were still residing. A honeymoon trip brought them to Craig, Alaska, where they lived for the next 13 years.

Both Paul and Florence worked at the Libby, McNeil & Libby cannery until the cannery buildings burned down in 1957.

Their two daughters, Linda and Deborah, were born in Klawock, Alaska, at the Presbyterian Missionary Clinic.

In 1960, the family moved from Craig to

Margaret Durbin, Florence LeRoy, Ruby Martens and Ken Welde

Petersburg, so the girls could have the advantage of a larger school system and Florence could resume her nursing career.

Florence joined the nursing staff at Petersburg General Hospital. After a few months, she assumed the role of administrator. She held this job until retiring in 1982.

Paul worked for Pacific American Fisheries in Petersburg until he hung up his diesel mechanic's hat and started his own business, which he called Viking Plumbing and Heating.

Paul and Florence were blessed with seven grandchildren. Linda's sons are Derek, Troy, Kristoffer and Kevin Thynes. Debbie's daughters are Carina, Talya and Melissa Bartlett.

Paul, who passed away in 1991, was a member of the Moose Lodge, Elks Lodge, Masons, Shriners and Pioneers of Alaska.

Florence is active in the Women of the Moose, Emblem Club, Pioneers of Alaska, Order of Eastern Star, Alaska State Hospital Association, and Association of Western Hospitals.

She is a past president of the Emblem Club, was the Grand Igloo trustee of the Pioneers for three years, and is a past Worthy Matron of the Order of the Eastern Star.

Paul LeRoy, Swede Wasvick, Stan Reid and Gordon Jensen

Justin and Magda Lind

By Gerald Lind

My father, Justin N. Lind, was born in Minneapolis, Minnesota, shortly after his parents, Petrus and Biata (Swanson) Johannson, arrived in the United States from Sweden. While in Minnesota, they changed their family name to Lind. There were so many Johnsons, Johannsons, and Hansons in the area they had a difficult time getting their mail and documents.

They soon moved to Mukilteo in the Everett, Washington, area. My father had to ride a school boat to and from the Everett schools. By the time he graduated from the eighth grade, he had skipped three grades.

He quit school, over his father's loud objections, and got a job at the railroad maintenance shop in Everett. He became a journeyman mechanic at a very young age.

Dad played a lot of baseball in the evenings and on Sundays. He even played in the Pacific Coast League for the Seattle Indians, the city's first professional baseball team.

He got a job as mechanic and ambulance driver for Gereid's Mortuary in Everett. He received his mortician's license after studying mortuary science. He also studied electricity and radio.

My mother, Magda E. Johansson, was born and raised in Skellefteo, Sweden. While she was studying to become a history teacher, her mother died. Her father sent money for her to come to the United States in August of 1920.

She found work in Everett, Washington, as a cook and maid for the Ruckers, who were millionaires. The family's two young girls taught my mother to understand and speak English like an American.

My mother and father met at a Vasa (a Swedish-American fraternal organization) social event in Everett and married about a year later, on June 23, 1923.

I was born on June 25, 1925, in an apartment over Gereid's Mortuary.

In 1929, Lloyd Swanson, my dad's first cousin, asked my father to come to Alaska to build a building and install a new telephone system for Petersburg. In April of 1930, after a nice trip north on the M/V *Northland*, we arrived in Petersburg. Over the following years, that ship became our favorite for traveling between Petersburg and Seattle.

Lloyd, my father and their uncle, who was a carpenter, built the first half of the Swanson building and installed a newer and better telephone system. Dad and Lloyd gradually added two apartments upstairs. Lloyd kept busy running phone lines and putting up telephone poles.

Magda, Gerald and Justin Lind

My father used half the main floor of the Swanson building as a shop for building windows, doors, and beautifully lined caskets. He kept everyone's radio working, helped build the Petersburg Cold Storage, and did a lot of electrical work around town.

As the hard '30s progressed, Dad worked as the first, and only, licensed mortician in the territory. For many years, before and after World War II, he was chief of police.

Dad built and operated two complete salmon canneries, one for Ray Wood and another, Petersburg Processors, for Ray Wood and Eilert Holbeck.

In those years, he was in charge of installing and operating three bowling alleys in the Elks Club basement. He and Lloyd Swanson installed the pipe organ in the Lutheran Church.

He spent the rest of his life helping others, and

Justin and Magda Lind cont'd

Ethel Lind

died on July 8, 1974.

In her first years in Petersburg, my mother worked for Gussie York at Citizen's Steam Laundry, and also sold cookies and Swedish delicacies.

Her cooking ability soon brought her many catering jobs for organizations, large dinners, and weddings. She was also chief cook and steward at the Scow Bay cannery for several years.

Mom was very active in the Lutheran Church and Emblem Club.

Sometime in 1959 or the early '60s, Mom and Dad received the honor of being chosen as Grand Marshals for the Fourth of July. As such, they rode in the old Model A fire truck at the head of the parade. On the front of the truck was a large banner proclaiming, "Mom Marries Them," and on the back of the truck was another large banner that read, "Dad Buries Them." (This old fire truck is still being used today for the Fourth of July parade.)

Mom passed away on August 26, 1964.

I had my fifth birthday after we arrived in Petersburg, so I had to wait until 1931 to start school at age six. Our class was very large right from the start, and ended up as the largest class to graduate from Petersburg High School until sometime in the '80s.

We were a feisty bunch of kids. We even went on strike in the fifth grade. We didn't do anything except antagonize our new teacher, and we wound up being expelled. Of course, our parents got us reinstated.

I grew up in Petersburg hunting, fishing, rowing, playing basketball, pool, ping pong, horseshoes, and generally getting in and out of trouble. I graduated in 1943, third in our large class of 26. Within just a few months, all of the boys in our class were serving our country in World War II.

After the war, I met a beautiful girl, Ethel Jean Lampman, of Snohomish, Washington. A year later we were married, right here in Petersburg.

Our first years of marriage were spent working in the summers and going to college in the winters. In those first years, we had a daughter, built a small house, and lost a son.

After 16 years of commercial fishing in the summers and working for the City of Petersburg and the hospital during the winters, we took advantage of our schooling by purchasing a fairly large store.

Being in business and president of organizations like the Chamber of Commerce, the P.T.A., the Rotary Club, the Fourth of July Celebration Committee, and serving on two state boards, was a really wonderful time in our lives.

In l971, we sold the larger store and had a 36-foot fiberglass commercial fishing boat built. We began 22 of the best years of our marriage — fishing and traveling all of Southeast Alaska.

Ethel and I had 50 years together before she died of cancer in 1997, a month before her 70th birthday.

It's now 2003 and I'm still active in charitable organizations, right here in Petersburg, and I love it.

Gerald Lind

Ed and Sibyl Locken

By Carol Enge and Donald Nelson

Among the early pioneers who founded Petersburg, perhaps few were as diligent in their endeavors as Ed and Sibyl Locken.

Ed Locken was born in Gudbransdal, Norway, on November 16, 1896. He left Norway in 1907, first for Albert Lea, Minnesota, before moving to North Dakota where his brother lived. He worked for the Northern Pacific Railroad in Montana for a short time and next worked in Seattle sawmills. In 1912, he moved to Petersburg with Knut Steberg and worked in a cannery.

Ed enlisted in the U.S. Army, in 1917, and was stationed at Camp Lewis, Washington. Upon his discharge, he was employed as a bookkeeper at a sawmill in Eagle Gorge, Washington, where he met and married the owner's daughter, Sibyl DeSpain.

Sibyl was born in Willow Springs, Arkansas, on July 11, 1899. As a young woman, the family moved to Tacoma, Washington, where her father had a sawmill. She attended the University of Washington before marrying Ed and coming to Peterburg with him in 1919.

Ed Locken

Ed managed the Buschmann-Thorpe sawmill until the mill went broke. He then found a job as an assistant cashier at the Bank of Petersburg. In 1940, Ed became manager, director, and part owner of the bank.

Loan-making decisions were based on his best judgment and the mood he was in. After most of the bank directors had retired and moved south, Ed felt the need for a counsel of local businessmen.

In the late '50s he asked Knut Stenslid to sell some of his stock to John Enge and Art Hammer. They became directors and remain as such today.

Both of the Lockens were charter members of the Masonic Lodge and Eastern Star. Ed helped to form the American Legion Post, which is named for him.

Ed was mayor of Petersburg. He served on the city council many times. A staunch Republican, he was elected to the Alaska Territorial Legislature, in 1950. He served six years.

Ed and Sibyl were childless, but they were surrogate parents to many youths who remained friends through their lifetime.

Sibyl wrote letters to many local servicemen all throughout World War II.

Sibyl Locken

As a pioneer Alaskan, Sibyl embraced her civic duties during the five decades she lived here. She was instrumental in establishing the Episcopal Church, which she attended and actively supported. She organized the public library and served as president until her retirement. As a charter member of Eastern Star and American Legion Auxiliary, she chaired both organizations and worked diligently on their many projects. She was a life member of the Salvation Army Board.

Ed was an outdoorsman. He enjoyed duck hunting and trout fishing, often taking his young friends along. He was founder of the Smikum Club, located at Blind Slough. This was a hunting cabin for a select group and could only be reached by boat.

Ed was also a philanthropist and humanitarian. He served on the Salvation Army Board and was a life member of the Sons of Norway. He was a member of the Chamber of Commerce, Rotary Club, and Norway Chamber of Commerce in Seattle.

Ed died May 9, 1967, following a stroke.

Sibyl moved to Seattle in 1971 to receive needed medical care. She returned only once, in 1972, when the Eastern Star honored her on the 50th anniversary of her membership.

She passed away January 15, 1976, in Seattle.

The extent of Ed's and Sibyl's benevolence on behalf of this community will never be known.

The Next Stage®

We've been a part of the local scenery since 1912.

Wells Fargo's history in Petersburg dates back to 1912 when the Bank of Petersburg first opened its doors to serve the people of Petersburg. The bank merged with National Bank of Alaska in 1972. And today we are still serving the financial needs of Petersburg's residents and businesses as Wells Fargo Bank Alaska. So, you might say we've grown up together! Thanks for all your support over the years.

*Yesterday: Staff at the Bank of Petersburg, circa 1950.
James Wheeler, Norma Tenfjord, Fred Nelson,
Randi Peterson, Ed Locken, Carroll Clausen*

Today: Staff at Wells Fargo Bank Alaska in Petersburg.

©2003 Wells Fargo Bank Alaska, N.A. All rights reserved. wellsfargo.com Member FDIC.

Jack and Mary Alice Longworth

By Alice Longworth

My first year of teaching was in 1938 in Portland, Oregon, my hometown. I taught one year at Sellwood Grade School and another at Chapman Grade School.

My field of work was in intermediate grades and physical education. At Chapman, I was surprised to learn I had lunchroom duty for the full school year, which had been the duty of the last hired teacher.

I was really looking around for something more exciting. In the summer of 1940, I attended summer school at the University of Oregon in Eugene. There I met a member of my graduating class from Western Oregon University. She mentioned to me that the superintendent of Petersburg schools, George Beck, was on campus interviewing teachers, and she gave me his telephone number.

Petersburg, Alaska, sounded very, very interesting to me. I called Superintendent Beck immediately. He wished to see me in two hours. I knew I would still be in class at that time, so I sent my twin sister. (He never let me forget that.) I wanted to be sure not to miss him. I arrived a little late.

The open positions were just what I was most interested and experienced in, fourth grade and physical education. He also mentioned physical education for high school girls. He sent me a contract as soon as he returned to Petersburg. Later, I was pleased to learn that the high school girls' class, scheduled for three times a week, from 7 to 8 p.m., included teaching basketball skills.

On August 19, 1940, I departed from Seattle on the SS *Yukon*, a combination freighter/passenger ship. My mother and father drove me to Seattle's Pier 42 to see me off. My mother looked at the *Yukon*'s black rusted hull and said, "Alice, you'll never make it."

I chose a stateroom on the top deck. I found I had to go outside, in the rain on the open deck, to reach the dining room and social hall.

A 10-year-old boy from Petersburg, Lee Carlson, was assigned to my stateroom. The purser explained that the room steward would watch for him, so I wouldn't have to babysit.

After five days of docking at small canneries and loading canned salmon cargo, the *Yukon* arrived in Petersburg. We tied up to a crowded dock behind The Trading Union store. A group of townspeople were standing on the dock to meet those who were returning from trips and to look over the new teachers.

On the voyage, I had already met several who would be teaching with me. The *Yukon*, the last boat to arrive in August, was called the "Teachers Boat." When we had passed Scow Bay, four miles from town, one teacher called out, "There's your school, Alice." I saw a building badly needing paint by a small dock. (Later it became a cookhouse at a logging camp.) The teachers were all laughing because I believed them.

Superintendent George Beck greeted us and gave the new teachers a list of places where we could rent a room during the school year. He stated, "All of these homes are near the school and you can easily walk to school from these locations." These were rooms in the homes of townspeople, who rented to fishermen and cannery workers during the fishing season. After the season, the fishermen returned to Norway and the cannery workers returned south.

After a night in the town's hotel, the next morning I took my list and stopped at a large house on the top of E Street hill. This home belonged to the Berger

Mary Alice Longworth

Jack and Mary Alice Longworth cont'd

Wasvicks. Their children were grown and had moved out except for the youngest daughter, who worked in town. Mrs. Wasvick said she had one bedroom left. Then she asked me, "Are you Norwegian?" She was smiling as she asked, thank goodness! I explained that I was Welsh, English, and plain American. My last name was Foster.

Mrs. Wasvick was very cordial, and I lived there my first school year, 1940-1941.

Superintendent Beck taught chemistry, French and art. Many of our local citizens learned to oil paint with Beck as their teacher. Pete Thynes and Ernest Enge produced beautiful paintings while in high school.

Petersburg was a town of 1600 people. It's located on Mitkof Island, which is about 25 miles long and 16½ miles wide. Fishing and cannery work provided the main employment for local citizens. State and local government, schools, and the hospital, along with supporting businesses, were the work of the town.

There were two movie theaters and a dance every Saturday night where the ladies had free admission. Downtown were two bars, one drugstore and soda fountain, two meat markets, and four grocery stores. Businesses supporting docks and fishing interests were often connected to the canneries. There were two beauty shops and one barber. Several churches were represented. Most active were the Lutheran, Presbyterian and Catholic churches.

Two card rooms were connected to the bars and restaurants. Four canneries for salmon and shellfish were operating. Halibut were frozen at the Cold Storage. Plank streets were the roads traveled by people, bicycles, delivery trucks, and a few passenger cars.

There were many activities for the active population. Social organizations, clubs, and lodges were available. A ski hill was located two miles from town across the frozen muskeg. There was an active ski club, which had a ski jump on the hill and a cabin where some groups stayed overnight.

On Saturdays, the ski club served hot chocolate, baked beans, and coffee. Ski club members were all ages, from the age of 4, to old-timers over 80. At over 70 years of age, Andrew Wikan was still an expert on the jump. I remember a group of us helping him look for his glasses that he had lost on one of his jumps.

A majority of Petersburg Norwegians were excellent in winter sports. Most of them had become U.S. citizens. Sometimes ski clubs in Juneau would invite Petersburg skiers to participate in their ski race events in Juneau, and we would invite them to come to Petersburg.

This was an interesting and active town. We had the seashore where we waded in the water; very few swam. Icebergs floated by all summer and were often grounded on the beaches.

Fall Creek provided good ice-skating in the winter and excellent sport fishing in summer. Small boating was popular on good weather days and weekends.

Petersburg had one picnic beach near town, about two miles away. It was open to the public and had real sand on the beach. A sandy beach was a treat because so many of the island beaches are rocky.

Evidence of old Indian activities was found at Sandy Beach. Pilings from native fish traps were almost rotted away and appeared at minus tides. Also, there were petroglyphs on some of the rocks. I asked some local Indians about them, and they said, "Oh, those were carved by the old ones."

The first year I was in Petersburg, a shrimp boat captain, Bill Greinier, invited the new teachers to a day of shrimping. Of course, we were anxious to go. Shrimp boats leave the dock at dawn in the summer — that was 2:30 a.m. Daybreak comes early in Alaska.

There were four teachers on this trip. On the boat *Charles T*, we arrived at the shrimping grounds after an hour-and-a-half run. The trawl was swung around to the stern of the boat to be towed for catching shrimp.

When the bag had filled, Captain Bill swung the net to the side of the boat. Having only one crewman to help him, he passed out rubber gloves to the guests. Little did we know we would be part of the crew! We were allowed to sort out the debris the net had picked up, as the boxes on deck were filled with the catch. We found seaweed, odd shells, octopus, small crabs, minnows, mud, and various other sea life.

Finally, after throwing back everything but the shrimp, the boxes were hosed with fresh seawater and stacked on the deck ready for the run to town.

It was time to eat. Guests usually brought something for lunch and the boat furnished lots of coffee. The crewman heated up their food and we all sat down to eat. I noticed the captain enjoyed the

Jack and Mary Alice Longworth cont'd

dessert we had brought. The boat returned to dock about 2:30 p.m. It had been a long day, but a very interesting one.

In July 1942, I married a U.S. Fish and Wildlife enforcement officer, John E. Longworth.

Jack Longworth

War had been declared with Japan and Germany. Japan had invaded the Aleutian Islands in the far western section of Alaska.

My husband enlisted in the U.S. Coast Guard, as had many Alaskans. He was stationed in Petersburg for three years, and later in Skagway, Alaska.

Halibut boats in outside waters sighted Japanese submarines surfacing in the waters where they were fishing, although they didn't pay much attention to each other.

Everyone in town helped with the war effort. Men, who were too old to enlist, and high school boys, who were too young, joined the local Home Guard and patrolled the streets, docks, and neighborhoods during the blackouts. No lights could be showing at nighttime. Tarpaper covered the windows of homes; even the school windows were covered.

Also, both the town and our public school had air raid drills. The sirens sounded continually for at least five minutes, as the children marched out.

The school was three stories high and the tallest building in town. It included all the lower grades, as well as the high school. My class called the drills, extra recesses. While outside, we played games; some went across the street and climbed trees.

Women knitted long wool stockings and sweaters for the soldiers. My husband was quartered at the coast guard station at the harbor.

A lookout station was built on top of the school's gymnasium building and volunteers took turns manning it. They were to report the approach of planes. On the wall inside, there was a chart with silhouettes of planes and a phone to call the Coast Guard.

I was a volunteer at 6 a.m. Because I was teaching, that was the only time I had available. My partner at this time in the morning was Ruth Sandvik. Both of us wondered, "If this is blackout time, why aren't the navigation lights in the Narrows turned off?" They pointed straight as an arrow toward Petersburg.

During this year, we heard a radio announcer in Seattle announced that Sitka had been bombed. Checking this out, I learned that the Aleutian Island of Kiska had been bombed; it's more than 1,200 miles away. The radio announcer had made a mistake, stating Sitka for Kiska.

After the war, my husband, Jack, worked in construction with Arne Tronas and as a fisherman with Fred Haltiner Sr. He also was a warehouseman for Icicle Seafoods. He enjoyed establishing Alaska's state government and served in the House of Representatives for three terms, 1961 to 1967. He was also a member of the Petersburg City Council for several terms.

Jack died in 1985.

We raised four children, three girls and a boy, all of who left the state to attend college.

Anna Susan, the oldest, married Nick Martinsen, a Petersburg classmate. He works for Varian, Inc., a California electronics firm. They have lived in Pleasanton, California, for many years. Their plans are to retire to Washington State, near their daughter, Norine Foster.

Bonnie Kay, my second daughter, was a state librarian in Denver, Colorado. She married Patrick Dolan, a college professor of American literature.

Son John Richard lives in Petersburg. A retired teacher, he owns Petersburg Cyclery, a bicycle shop. He is married to the town's veterinarian, Dr. Jane Egger.

My youngest, Mary Lou Longenbaugh, lives in Tumwater, Washington. Her husband, Patrick, from Sitka, works for the Washington Department of Fish and Wildlife.

I have lived in Petersburg for 62 years and I wouldn't want to live anywhere else.

I now have family to visit when I take trips, but I have learned that my children and grandchildren like to visit Petersburg best.

Art and Ethelyn Lopez

By Carol Enge

Art Lopez came to California from his native Cali, Columbia, in 1948, to visit other Cali emigrants. He found work as a gardener in San Francisco. Moving north, he worked in irrigation for sugar beet farms near Walla Walla, Washington.

It was here that he met Ethelyn Martin, formerly of Kake, Alaska. She was a kitchen worker for the Washington Pea Growers Association.

They were married on June 15, 1950. The following year, when they were expecting their first child, Ethelyn insisted that the baby be born in Alaska.

Art and Ethelyn moved to Kake, staying there for two years. Art learned the ways of subsistence living. Ethelyn's brothers taught him how to hunt, fish and trap. For a short time, he worked on the Thompson floating crab cannery.

By 1954, Art and Ethelyn had moved to Petersburg. At first, they stayed with Ethelyn's sister, Doris Nannauck. It was during this time that Ethelyn learned to can the venison, fish, and berries that would be the staple food of the family throughout the years.

During this time, Art worked at Ohmer's cannery, cooking crab for $28 a week. Ethelyn also worked in the cannery, during the summer, to supplement her family's income.

John Robert Otness gave Art was given his first halibut fishing opportunity.

Later, he fished with Nels Evens on the *Lualda*, with Ernest Enge on the *Augusta*, and with Ed Fuglvog on the *Karen Marie* and the *Kamilar*.

He was involved in numerous building projects around town. His daughter, Ceceila, remembers her dad and Chris Christensen working on the Clausen Memorial Museum.

Art and Ethelyn have seven children: Michael, Cecelia, Chris, Christina, Carmen, Marty and Lorenzo.

Art passed away in June of 2000.

Ethelyn worked in the elementary school for 20 years as a teacher's aide. She was very instrumental in introducing the Tlingit culture into the classroom and teaching the children her native language.

F/V *Augusta* unloading at Petersburg Cold Storage

John and Dora Loseth

By Leonard Ingle

John Loseth was born in Kristiansund, Norway, on February 29, 1884. He emigrated from Norway in 1907, through England to Quebec (in Canada), and then on to Chicago, Illinois, on the Grand Trunk Railroad. After arriving in Seattle, Washington, he traveled by boat to Petersburg.

John and Dora Loseth

Dora Loseth was born in Tingvoll, Norway, on November 17, 1889. Dora left Norway in May of 1912, and went to England, where she sailed from Liverpool on the ship *Franconia*. After landing in Boston, she took a six-day train trip to Seattle. She worked in Seattle for about a year, arriving in Petersburg in 1914.

John and Dora were married on March 9, 1914. They were the first couple married in Petersburg's Lutheran Church.

Their son, Leif, was born in Petersburg on December 19, 1914. Their other children were all born on the farm at Point Agassiz: Dagney on August 24, 1919; Della on February 2, 1923; James "Jimmy" on August 17, 1924; and David on May 17, 1933.

The kids attended the Point Agassiz schoolhouse, about three miles from the homestead. They had to cross Muddy River to get to school. In the winter when Muddy River was frozen, they walked across; the rest of the time they took a boat across the river.

During Leif's first year of school, he lived with the Swanson's on the north side of the river.

The Loseths homesteaded by Brown Cove about 1915. Their main industry was milk cows. They also raised fox, which didn't work out. They grew hay and kept chickens, ducks, geese, and, at one time, a horse. They received the horse in trade for a tractor.

John's first boat was the *Comrad*. He used it to haul ice from Le Conte, fish halibut, run to Hazy Islands for seagull eggs, prospect, and haul milk to Petersburg from homestead farms on the mainland. He later owned a boat called the *Ramona*.

John loved to prospect. He had claims from Icy Cove to Taku Harbor.

The Loseths moved back to Petersburg, about 1939, when David started school. By then, the Point Agassiz school had closed due to a lack of students.

They rented a house on Lumber Street. In 1941, they bought the house on Birch Street.

Leif, David, and Jimmy all got into fishing, and Della and Dagney both married fisherman.

The first two generations of Loseths have all passed away, but there are lots of descendants still living in Petersburg. The homestead is still in the family.

F/V *Comrad* in 1912

Frank and Laura Luhr

By Beulah Reid Luhr

Frank Alexander Luhr was born to John and Edith (Clukies) Luhr on McNeil Island, Washington, April 18, 1906. John Luhr had immigrated to the United States from Bremerhaven, Germany, in 1880. Edith Luhr, whose parents were British, arrived in 1894 from the island of St. Kitts in the British West Indies.

Frank Luhr and Laura Annie Bollen, daughter of Frank and Annie (Ulsh) Bollen from McNeil Island, Washington, were married September 12, 1929.

Frank Norman was born June 8, 1931; Donald Hugh on April 6, 1933.

Frank worked as a guard at the federal prison on McNeil Island, where they made their home — until 1936, when the government asked the civilians to leave. They bought a home on Sales Road, in South Tacoma by McChord Air Force Base.

Frank continued working as a prison guard and ran the shore boat between Steilacoom and McNeil Island for 17 years. During World War II, Laura worked at Fort Lewis.

During the summer of 1944, Frank took a leave from McNeil Island and traveled to Petersburg to fish with his father-in-law, Frank Bollen, aboard the *AB&G*. Fishing was good that year and Frank was hooked.

He came home and sold the Sales Road house. They moved to his brother Bill's home, at Luhr Beach on the Nisqually flats, until they could travel to Alaska.

The Luhrs arrived in Petersburg aboard the steamer *North Sea* in 1946. They lived with Laura's parents, until they bought a home from Lloyd Pederson on the corner of South Nordic Drive and Baronof Street.

Frank bought the troller *Alpha* from Casper Hallingstad Sr. and fished it for six years. Son Don fished with his parents, while son Frankie went with Grandpa Bollen aboard the *AB&G*. The boats tied up together in harbor at night and Laura cooked for them.

They did not have fathometers, radar, stabilizers, GPS, or radios during those years, nor did they have limited entry, quotas, or treaties with Canada. You were allowed to keep what you caught, if you were man enough to deal with the weather, rough seas, and fog.

Frank Luhr and Frank Bollen both fished the outside waters of Cross Sound, Icy Point, and Yakobi Island, selling fish to buyers in Deer Harbor, Green Top and Dixon Harbor. They made regular trips to Pelican and spent several Fourths of July in town. Don remembers the baseball games on the mud flats and being driven off when the tide came in.

Frank and Laura had the *Laura Ann* built and it was ready to sail for the fishing grounds in June of 1952. This boat had a diesel engine and many more amenities than the *Alpha*. They continued to fish, albeit in the waters around Petersburg, until they sold the *Laura Ann* in 1968 due to Frank's failing health. The *Laura Ann* has been renamed the *Miss Laura* and still fishes the Sitka area.

Frank passed away in Seattle, Washington, from a thrombosis, on June 20, 1970.

Laura worked at the Family Shoe Mart and Fashion Fair, until she married Herb Stewart on November 26, 1972. (Herb fished the troller *Illahee* during his early days.)

They built a home in Scow Bay and lived there until 1988, when it was sold to John and Sheri Eide. The Stewarts moved to an apartment at the Totem Arms. Laura died of pancreatic cancer on March 22, 1989. Herb died of heart failure, while vacationing in Port Angeles on April 29, 1991.

Frankie quit school in his senior year to join the marines. He served in Korea. He met and married Virginia Johnson in 1955, and acquired two daughters, as well. Frankie and Ginny had two sons. Richard Frank was born in 1957. Robert Alan arrived in 1959.

They lived in Juneau for a while and then moved to Port Angeles, Washington, where Frankie owned and operated a machine shop.

Frankie and Ginny divorced and both remarried. Frankie married Donna Hill and they were nomads, following dredge work up and down the West Coast before settling in Washougal, Washington.

Frankie died of lung cancer on September 8, 1988. His wife, Donna, died from lung cancer a few years later. His son, Rob, has also died.

Don, graduated from Petersburg High School in May of 1951. He fished a 28-foot troller that summer and tagged along with his parents on the *Alpha*. That fall, he resumed seeing Beulah Reid. They were married in 1952. That was the end of his commercial fishing for the next 20 years.

Don and Beulah Luhr

By Beulah Reid Luhr

Don Luhr, son of Frank and Laura (Bollen) Luhr, married Beulah Reid, daughter of Robert and Vena (Ward) Reid, on May 31, 1952, at the Reid home in Scow Bay.

Captain Lloyd of the Salvation Army officiated. Beulah's brother, Sonny, was best man, and Patty (Wasvick) Parr Simpson was maid of honor. The reception was held at the Moose Club.

Their first home was a second floor apartment in the Enge building on Indian Street (now known as Sing Lee Alley). Daughter Donna Lee joined them on February 22, 1953.

The apartment had a very old and noisy Fairbanks Morse refrigerator and most of the rooms were closed off in the winter to conserve heat. Don worked for Cliff Roundtree's transfer service and brought home $257 a month.

Don logged with Bob Reid the summer and fall of 1953. Beulah was a bull cook for Martha Reid, when Reid Brothers logged at Petersburg Creek.

That fall they moved to the Hoogendorn Apartments and lived on the second floor next to Art and Francis Peterson.

The winter of 1953-1954 was very cold. When the wind blew out of Petersburg Creek, it would cause the curtains to stand out from the windows. The old heating system was so inadequate; they would go to bed with Donna in the middle to keep warm.

February of 1954 found the family moving to Kalispell, Montana. This move was short-lived. Don returned in June. Beulah, Donna, and infant son Robert Wayne, who was born on June 26, returned in July. While in Montana, word was received of the death of Bob Reid, Beulah's father.

Don had rented the Ben Baker home on South Nordic Drive for his family to live in. They remained there until the spring of 1956, when they moved to the Sam Hansen house on the corner of South Nordic and Union Street. Michael Todd joined the family on August 22, 1956; Joyce Ann on April 23, 1959.

The Luhrs eventually purchased the Hansen house and lived there for 30 years.

Through the years, Don worked for the City of Petersburg, J & H Logging, Barite Mining, and Ellis Machine. In 1978, he purchased the *Mrs. Mac* from Al McKibben and went trolling.

Beulah worked for Norm and Marge Heimdahl at the Family Shoe Mart. She became partners with the Heimdahls and the Dusty Rhodens, when the Fashion Fair was purchased from Gertie Reeser. She retired in 1979 to fish with Don.

Beulah served a stint on the city council, the hospital board, and has been on the advisory board of the Salvation Army for many years. She was active in Alaska Crippled Children's Association, served three terms as Emblem Club president, and was president of the Alaska State Association of Emblem Clubs.

Don has been active in the Elks and is a Past Exalted Ruler.

After surviving a heart attack in May 1982, Don decided he needed a boat requiring less upkeep than the *Mrs. Mac*. He purchased a Snowball hull, in 1983, and completed the *Carefree*, with the help of Pete Thynes, in time for the 1984 fishing season.

In the meantime, Beulah went to work at Hammer & Wikan to subsidize the fishing income and make the purchase of their home at 188 Mitkof Highway possible.

Life was much more relaxed when the Luhr kids were growing up. Television did not dominate their lives and organized sports, other than Little League, were not on the scene. The kids belonged to Boy Scouts and Girl Scouts, Little League, Rainbows, attended Sunday School, and participated in school activities.

The family went boating, camping, and spent a lot of time swimming at Blind Slough. Petersburg Creek was another favorite spot during the summer.

Don was an avid duck hunter. He went on a yearly hunt with friends, using the Roundtree cabin in Beecher's Pass. Don and Beulah hand trolled for several years before Don became serious about fishing and became a power troller, which he is to this day.

Don and Beulah's daughter, Donna, graduated in 1971. She attended the University of Alaska for the fall term, moved to Juneau and then to Anchorage, where she met and married Alyn Dunaway. They have a son, Gregory, and a daughter, Sandra, and live in Wasilla, Alaska.

Robert graduated in 1972. He married Nancy Opsal, daughter of Nels and Ilene (Olsen) Opsal, in

Don and Beulah Luhr cont'd

November of 1972. They have two sons, Jason and Shawn, who were raised in Petersburg, graduated from Petersburg High School, and continue to make their homes here. Jason married Stacy Peterson in February of 1995. Robert and Nancy divorced early in their marriage; Nancy moved to Wrangell.

Robert's son, Kyle Skinner, born September of 1985, also lives in Petersburg.

Robert married Colei Stockton, daughter of Mel and Sherry Stockton, in 1995. They had two children: Trystin, in April 1996; and Leighnei, in October 1999.

Michael graduated in 1974 and attended Bates Welding School in Tacoma. He returned to Petersburg to work and start his own business, working out of Ellis Machine Shop.

In 1981, he purchased the business from Dave Ellis and renamed it Piston and Rudder Service. The scow that houses the machine shop is on the historic register. The Allen family brought it here in the 1920s.

Michael married Kathy Williams. They have one son, Justin, who graduated from Petersburg High School. They divorced. Michael later married Barbara Richmond. They have one daughter, Bradee, and two children from Barb's previous marriage, Sabrina and John Richmond. Sabrina and John both graduated from Petersburg High School.

Joyce Ann graduated in 1977 and attended Highline Community College to become an airline agent. She worked for Cascade Airways in Idaho and Washington until 1985. She married Rob Cummings.

Rob was enamored of Alaska, so they make their home here. Rob works for Alaska Airlines. Joyce has worked for First Bank since July of 1985. They have three children: Skyler, born in 1986; Jessica, born in 1987; and Chad, born in 1991.

Wheeler Building construction, 1930s

Peder and Anna Lund

By Diane Forde

Peder Peterson Lund was born in Gjovik, Norway, December 20, 1886, the youngest of six children. He came to America, when he was 17 years old, to join his two sisters, who had married Wisconsin dairy farmers. While there, Peder learned the lumber trade and became a championship skier.

In 1903, Peder arrived in the Pacific Northwest. There, he worked in lumber mills. He met Anna Haegeland, who was born January 7, 1888, an immigrant from Mosby, Norway. They were married in Seattle on March 26, 1910.

Soon after Peder and Anna were married, they traveled to Alaska to work for the Knutson Brothers Sawmill in West Petersburg, joining other Scandinavian immigrants who became the core of Petersburg's building and fishing community.

In 1914, Peder Lund and Pete Slugen built the Lund family home on Lumber Street. Twenty years later, Arne Trones rebuilt it.

Peder and Anna were charter members of the Sons and Daughters of Norway. In 1912, they helped to build the Sons of Norway Lodge.

In the early 1940s, Peder joined Olaf, Eiler and Andrew Wikan; Frank Wykoff; Heine Dahl and others in building the original ski cabin and ski jump. He also taught many how to jump.

After working for Knutson Brothers, Peder worked for the Sons of Norway store in Sing Lee Alley. When the store burned December 8, 1919, he clerked for The Trading Union store where he remained for 35 years. After he retired from The Trading Union, he owned and operated a gas-powered gillnetter.

Peder and Anna divorced in the mid '40s. In 1955, she married Osbjorn Odegaard.

Peder died of a heart ailment January 6, 1959.

Anna was a homemaker and mother, worked long hours at PAF cannery, and in later years, was a chambermaid at the Mitkof Hotel. She loved cooking, flowers, making root beer and "homebrew," and keeping a beautiful home. One of her favorite things to do was to bring home French donuts for the family from Parr's Bakery.

Anna died January 10, 1962.

Lund family, front row, from left, Roy, Peder, Anna and Helen. Back row, Philip, Sigrud, Gudrun and Arne.

During these early years, two of Peder's brothers also arrived in Petersburg and contributed to building the town. Paul was an industrious businessman and was instrumental in developing Citizen's Steam Laundry. He served on the city council and was the instigator of building the Petersburg Cemetery.

Ironically, Paul was one of the first people buried there, after he drowned in a hunting accident in November of 1928.

Ole, the other brother, was a carpenter. He helped construct many of the local homes, including the George Reynolds home on Excel Street. Ole died at the Sitka Pioneers Home in 1950.

All six children of Peder and Anna were born in Petersburg. Helen, Roy and Arne remained. Arne bought the family home. Philip, Sigrid and Gudrun moved to Washington State. Gudrun and her husband, Lester Nygren, now reside in Abbotsford, B.C., Canada.

George and Mary Lyons

By Heidi Lyons

George Lyons was born in Minnesota, of Scotch and Irish ancestry. He left home at an early age; little is known of his early family life.

Mary Wagner, who was of German heritage, was also born in Minnesota. Mary and George met in Grand Rapids and were married in 1916.

They soon started a family. Courtney was born January 8, 1917. Myron was born November 24, 1918. Myrtes was born October 14, 1920. Burton was born September 17, 1922. Neil was born April 30, 1925.

In 1927, the family moved to a logging camp on Hood Canal in Washington State where George worked. Their son, Jack, was born in Everett.

While in Washington, George met Ralph and Frank Wooten and became interested in fishing in Alaska. In 1930, after buying a boat called the *Capella*, George and Mary packed up and headed north.

Five weeks later, they landed in Petersburg. They set up their home at about 2 ½ miles south. With the help of Petersburg locals, they soon had a home built.

After converting the *Capella* into a fishing boat, George went trolling.

As with many people in Petersburg, winters were hard. George did anything he could to keep his family going. He trapped, worked for the WPA, dug ditches for the city, and took whatever work that came along.

Anna Marie was their first child born in Petersburg, on September 4, 1930. Bill arrived on December 11, 1933. A few years later, on November 18, 1939, Dave came along, He was the last child born to George and Mary.

In 1939, the family moved to Pybus Bay to farm foxes. In those days, just about every island near Petersburg had a fox farm on it. George continued to fish while fox farming, feeding the foxes the fish he could not sell.

During this time, the kids helped raise the foxes. They kept them fed by handlining for scrap fish, cooking their feed, and then distributing the feed all around the island, since the foxes ran free.

When World War II started, several of the young Lyons men went off to war. Courtney went into the Army. He was in the African offensive and eventually ended up in Germany. Myron was also in the Army, starting off in the Pribilof Islands. He then went on to India. Burton was in the 82nd Airborne and fought in Germany. Neil was also in the Army, serving at Fort Richardson, in Anchorage, until the end of the war.

The family left Pybus, so the younger children could return to school — and because the fur business had dropped off. George had many jobs during his life, including being a stream watchman for Fish and Wildlife. For many years, he was sling tender for the Alaska Steamship Company.

Mary had a very busy life taking care of her children. She was a very devoted mother and was known around town for all the wonderful crafts she made. She is especially remembered for her sock monkeys. Many people also remember her Mina bird that would sit in the window and whistle at all who walked by.

George and Mary Lyons

As the children grew up, they went many different ways. After the war, Courtney worked for the Puget Sound Dredge Company for many years, helping dredge Wrangell Narrows. He eventually started his own machine shop. In 1998, Courtney passed away at the age of 81. He and his wife, Mary, never had children.

Myron fished halibut and trolled, but also worked construction on many projects in and around Petersburg, including the White Alice Station in Duncan, and the road extension past Blind Slough

George and Mary Lyons cont'd

(with Green Construction).

Both Myron and his wife, Gertrude Hallingstad Lyons, have passed away. Myron was 78. They left a family of five boys: Myron, Colyn, Jeff, Byron, Tom and Gordon.

Myrtes Lyons went on to school, and then returned home for a short time. She met and married Harvey Wyborny, and then moved to Ventura, California. Myrtes worked for the California court system for years, as a court stenographer. Myrtes and Harvey have four girls.

Burton became a fisherman when he returned home after the war. He fished with many different people. He then got his own boat and trolled, until he retired to Mexico.

Burton was known around town for having raised a baby seal. It would follow the boys around, as they rowed their skiff all over the Narrows. They built a home for the seal by damming a creek next to their house. In 1999, Burton died in Mexico at the age of 77. Burton and his wife, Anna, had no children.

Neil also entered the fishing business after his military career. Neil decided he wanted to stay closer to home. He went to work for Petersburg Cold Storage, which involved him with many fisheries. The Cold Storage was bought by PFI, and Neil worked there for many years until he retired.

Neil married Gloria Hallingstad and they have two children, Jack and Greg.

Anna Marie graduated from Petersburg High School. She then moved to Seattle, where she met and married Don KirVan. They are in the landscaping business and traveled all over the world for their business. Anna Marie and Don have no children.

Anna and her husband built their house on the Hood Canal property, where her parents, George and Mary, lived in the 1920s.

Jack joined the military after the war. When he returned home, he went into fishing. He was lost in a boating accident in 1953.

After his military service, Bill trolled for a while. He also worked as a mechanic for Barney White at a local auto shop. He then went to work for the City Light Department caring for the big diesels at the power plant. Bill and his wife, Ann Arness Lyons, have three children together: Debbie, Barbie and Jim.

Dave was also in the military. He ended up in Puerto Rico. He is a well-known troller, who owns a boat named the *Kraken*. He now lives in Sitka, so he can be closer to his fishing grounds. Dave also fishes for halibut and blackcod.

Dave and his wife, Deborah, do not have children.

Both George and Mary Lyons lived to be in their 80s. A large number of their offspring still live in Petersburg, with many grandchildren and great-grandchildren.

Camping

Gordon and Georgia MacDonald

By Jean MacDonald Morton

Gordon and Georgia met and married in South Bend, Oregon. Their son, Lewis, was born there. Gordon was working with his older brothers, building warehouses and sheds. They constructed a building on the Columbia River, near their home in Skamokawa, which stood for over 90 years.

Gordon first came to Alaska in 1910 with his brothers George, Allan, Louis and Neal. In Ketchikan and Wrangell, they were involved in the timber logging and lumber mill industry. Neal stayed in Wrangell and became a fox farmer.

Gordon and Georgia lived at the logging camp in a float house, until they came to Petersburg. They had four more children, born at home: Gordon Jr. in 1920, Donald in 1922, Neal in 1925, and Jean in 1929.

In Lewis' senior year, he was a member of the 1929 Petersburg High basketball team that won the Alaska State Championship. He married schoolteacher Adelia Hanson and they had a daughter, Carol Jean.

Lewis worked for the Alaska Department of Fish and Game for many years. He lived in Juneau, where he owned the Harbor Market Juneau and worked on the Alaska ferry *Wickersham*. He married Mary, from Douglas. They had daughter Amie. Lewis died in 1974.

Gordon Jr. graduated from Petersburg High School in 1939. He then went to work in the logging camp with his dad. After his father's death, Gordon joined the Army. When World War II was over, he made his home in Juneau, working heavy construction.

He married Annette Shanks and had three sons and a daughter. Daughter Janet graduated from Petersburg High School in 1968, the same year Gordon died in Wrangell. His children still live in Juneau.

Donald graduated from Petersburg High in 1941. His interests were in engineering and mining. He joined the Army Air Corps, during the war, and married Joanne Pruski, from Chicago, Illinois. They had daughter Bonnie, and a son, Doug. They divorced.

Gordon MacDonald, 1909

Don later married Penny Quarnberg of Juneau. They lived in Vancouver, Washington, and had two sons. They later divorced.

Don spent most of his time in the Pelican area, involved in mining and engineering. He now resides in Anchorage. His children reside in the Lower 48.

Neal was a fisherman all his life except for a brief interval when he was a taxicab owner/operator in Petersburg with Jim Miller. Neal went into fishing full time, spending the winters in Seattle, where he met Jan Knight. Neal and Jan were married in Petersburg.

Jan had a son, Terry, and daughters Sherrell and Cathie from a previous union.

Neal and Jan lived in Petersburg, eventually building their home at Hungry Point. They had two sons, Clifford and Jimmie. They divorced. Neal married Judy Johnson from Juneau.

Neal worked and crewed on several fishing vessels before owning his own; the last and best being the *Little Lady*. Neal passed away in Seattle after suffering a stroke in Petersburg in 1994. His son, Clifford, and stepson, Terry, still live in Petersburg with their families.

Georgia Jones MacDonald, 1909

Frederick and Enid Magill

By Enid Magill

Frederick Haynes Magill's parents came from Canada to homestead in Dayton, Washington.

When the gold rush started in Nome, Fred's father, Frederick Hamilton Magill, and an uncle spent a year in the far north. They didn't make a fortune, so Frederick Hamilton returned to Washington.

Fred's father returned to Alaska after obtaining a job as an engineer on a vessel going to Wrangell, Alaska. He then moved up to own the schooner *Peerless*, which was the mail boat to many mining camps and fox farms in Southeast Alaska.

Sarah Haynes came to Alaska and taught at Indian schools throughout Southeast Alaska, including Kake, Hoonah and Juneau. The school in Juneau stood where the governor's mansion now stands.

Frederick Hamilton married Sarah Haynes in Juneau, about 1910. Sarah was about 37; Fred about 36.

After Frederick Hamilton and Sarah were married, they moved to the Windham Bay mining camp. They also lived at Fox Island.

Their son, Fred Haynes Magill, was born June 14, 1914; daughter Helen was born in 1916. (Helen Magill Smith still resides in Juneau.)

In 1936, Sarah again had a job with the Native Service and taught in Petersburg at the Indian school. It stood where the Petersburg's museum now stands. Following this, Sarah retired for a short time, only to go back to teaching at Petersburg's white school during World War II. She died about 1953. Frederick Hamilton died in Seattle in the late 1960s.

In 1944, Enid Swanson came to Petersburg to work at the hospital. Ruth Wetterborg Sandvik was sent to meet the steamer and welcome Enid. Mary Hungerford Reid interviewed Enid for a school job.

Fred and Enid were soon married. Their daughter, Pat, was born April 16, 1946. Son Frederick Swanson was born January 25, 1948.

Pat and Rick were 6 and 4 years old when they began gillnetting with their parents on the Taku River and other areas. After their children were raised, Fred and Enid fished for shrimp for many winters.

In the summers, Fred fished for halibut and seined salmon. He built several fishing vessels during the off-season. One was the F/V *Elizabeth*, which was the first vessel built by an Alaskan Native. When Fred was 68, he finally got his "new" boat, F/V *Confidence*.

Fred and his long-time friend, Dale Brouilliard, dug a couple of 1,000-foot long ditches and built a trailer park called Fort Magill. Fred was also a lifelong prospector who enjoyed his nickname, "Hardrock."

Fred and Enid's son, Rick, bought a new gillnet boat and announced to his mother that she could go gillnetting with him.

"The only thing you need to know is how to change oil," Rick declared. There was more to it than that, of course. But, as captain, Enid didn't lose any deckhands overboard, and they caught lots of fish.

Fred Haynes Magill died November 15, 1990. Enid continues to live in Petersburg. Their son, Rick, lives in Seattle area, and is active in the Alaska commercial fishing industry. Their daughter, Pat Magill Stevens, is a realtor in Juneau.

Fred and Enid have seven grandchildren and three great-grandchildren. Many of them are Alaskans. Two great-granddaughters visit Petersburg each summer. Their great-grandson, Tyler, recently became wrestling champion of Alaska's age 12 division.

Pat, Fred, Enid and Rick Magill

Lon and Camille Marifern

By Camille Marifern

I was born and raised in Petersburg. Our banner in the 2002 Fourth of July parade said it all: "Five generations of Martens, fishing and fun!"

My mother, Thelma Martens, was born and raised in Petersburg. While attending beauty school in Seattle, Thelma met and married my father, Roy Torwick.

They spent several years in Port Alexander, before moving to Petersburg where they raised three children, Roy Jr., Camille and Lynda.

Dad was involved in fish, either catching it or buying it, on the docks in Pelican and Kodiak for Booth Fisheries. When Dad retired, he returned to Petersburg and lived in our apartment until shortly before his death in 1989.

Mother preceded him in 1978. Roy Jr., "Little Roy", died of heart failure in 1996 at the age of 61.

Lon Marifern was born and raised in the Seattle area and came to Alaska in 1954.

He and I met in Pelican, Alaska, that same year. Lon had just been discharged from the U.S. Coast Guard, honorably, I might add.

I was on my way to college at Western Washington in Bellingham that September; as it turned out, so was Lon. We had a great year.

Pastor Stubb married us at the Chapel of Flowers in Bellevue, Washington, on November 25, 1955. I had the date engraved on the inside of Lon's ring — just as a reminder.

We spent summers in Pelican working, and winters in Seattle, where I worked at Littler's Clothing store. Lon took up flying at both Kurtzer's and Kenmore Air Harbor.

After three years of traveling back and forth, we felt it was time to stay put. We were expecting our first child. Pat arrived June 2, 1958.

Lon had his first airplane, a Super Cruiser, rebuilt at Kenmore Air Harbor. Once the plane was all set, Lon took off for Petersburg and started Lon's Flying Service. Pat and I followed shortly.

Our other two children were born in Petersburg: Bruce, in 1960; and Julie, in 1964.

Through the years, Lon was involved in many businesses. There was Lon's Flying Service and Towne Trailer Park. We built and operated the Viking Theatre for 10 years before selling it. Lon and I, along with Jim and Donna Martinsen, built the Marine View Apartments, which we're still operating today.

After 10 years with Lon's Flying Service, Lon sold the business and flew for the Alaska Department of Fish and Game. What was to be for a short time, turned into 20-plus years. Only once in those two decades did he not receive the contract. Lon retired once and was called back for one more season.

Camille and Lon Marifern

He loved flying and it was hard when he sold his last plane. A year later, I asked how it was, and he said, "Camille, it's like you selling your sewing machine."

I was very quiet and said, "Okay."

We don't talk about that any more. There are seasons for everything, and the flying had ended.

We owned the F/V *Camlon*, a 30-foot Tollycraft, for several years. We gillnetted with it for one season, our first and only summer gillnetting. We put all our gear onboard and gave it our best.

Leaving the float in Petersburg for the first trip, I informed Lon he couldn't yell or swear at me or I'd get off the boat. He didn't and I stayed the season.

I remember when we caught the net in the wheel, and Lon wanted to call a boat to tow us in.

I said, "No, just cut."

Hanging over the stern of the boat, Lon cut out what he could, saying, "Don't drop me!"

I replied, "Don't worry."

Lon said, "What do you mean don't worry? I'm

Lon and Camille Marifern cont'd

the one with my head almost in the water and you've got my feet!"

With the remaining web wrapped around the shaft, we limped into town and got a diver to cut out the rest. Good thing we were only on Frederick Sound.

That summer we fished from Tree Point to Lynn Canal, a real experience to be sure.

At one point I asked why we weren't fishing with the other boats, and Lon's comment was, "Because most people don't jump up and down and yell 'Yippee!' when they haul in their fish."

For two greenhorns gillnetting, we actually had a good season.

We bought an apple orchard in Yakima, Washington, and worked the orchard for five years. When my father had a stroke, we returned to Petersburg.

Two of our children, Pat and Bruce, still reside in Petersburg.

Pat and her husband, Mark Weaver, have two children: a daughter, Morgan, who is a freshman; and son Jay, who is in seventh grade.

Bruce and his wife, Barbara, have a son, David, a fifth grader; and a daughter, Samantha, a second grader.

Julie and her husband, Craig Erickson, have two sons: Taylor, a sixth grader; and Jordan, who is 3 years old.

For these three families, we are truly blessed.

Lon retired and we headed south for some sunshine. In 1991, we purchased a doublewide mobile home in a gated community, just outside Desert Hot Springs, California, and have lived there ever since. Winters in Desert Hot Springs, summers in Petersburg.

The desert heat seems to agree with us, although it has taken a few years for us to dry out. Who knows what the future holds? But, it's bound to be exciting!

Front row, left to right: Morgan and Jay Weaver, Taylor Erickson, David and Samantha Marifern. Back row: Mark and Pat Weaver; Craig, Julie and baby Jordan Erickson; Bruce and Barbara Marifern.

Old sawmill

Courtesy of Clausen Memorial Museum

Loui and Ragnhild Martens

By Polly Koeneman

Ludvig Mortenson was born in Mosjoen, Norway, August 17, 1875, where he fished in the Lofoten Islands and built boats. He moved to Tacoma, Washington, around 1900, and got a job fishing halibut in 1901.

When he received his citizenship papers, he changed his name to Loui Martens.

In 1908, he met Ragnhild Tjomsland, who was the sister of Knut Thompson.

Ragnhild was born in Kristiansund, Norway. When she was 19, she came to Tacoma to spend a year with her uncle.

She got a job as a cook at Pacific Lutheran College and met Loui shortly after. They were married and soon began a family. In 1910, their son, Magnus, was born in Tacoma.

In 1911, the family of three moved to Petersburg, where Loui fished halibut.

In 1914, he built a small house on the beach (the current Max Worhatch home).

Daughter Thelma and sons Leonard and Elmer eventually joined the family. With the arrival of each new child, Loui added another room to the house.

In 1938, at the age of 52, Ragnhild died of streptococcus infection from a raspberry sticker. Loui died on December 25, 1941.

Loui and Ragnhild's oldest son, Magnus Albin Martens, was born January 10, 1910, in Tacoma. He became a good fisherman, first with the small troller F/V *Seal*, then the halibut boat F/V *Lorelei*, and later with his combination boat, the F/V *Pamela Rae*.

He met Ruby Phyllis Welde. They were married in 1938.

Ruby was born on a farm in Milaca, Minnesota, in 1915, to Peder and Ragna Welde. She has a brother, Ken Welde, and a sister Evelyn Welde Wasvick.

Ruby had visited Petersburg twice, before permanently moving here at the age of 19. She was very active in the Lutheran Church. Magnus and Ruby had two girls, Pam and Polly.

Magnus was a very able carpenter who built both his home, at 709 Wrangell Avenue, and his daughter Polly's home at 917 Sandy Beach. He also helped build the old Petersburg Hospital and the Lutheran Church Education Building.

Magnus fished until 1983, when he was killed in a fishing accident while salmon seining onboard the F/V *Pamela Rae*. Ruby still resides in the house that Magnus built in 1942.

Magnus and Ruby Martens' daughter, Pam, was born in Petersburg on April 15, 1942. After graduating from Petersburg High School, she attended college for two years at Washington State University.

Pam met Robert Magnus Thorstenson when he was superintendent of Pacific American Fisheries (PAF) in Petersburg. They married in January 1963. They moved to Bellingham and had their first child, who they named Robert Magnus Thorstenson, Jr.

When PAF sold off its canneries, Pam and Bob sold all of their possessions and started Petersburg Fisheries, Inc.

They arrived in Petersburg via Grumman Goose on April 10, 1965. Bobby was 18 months old. Pam was four months pregnant with Tani Rae.

Bob's intention was to move his family directly into the cannery

Ragnhild Martens

Loui Martens

Loui and Ragnhild Martens cont'd

superintendent's house. Built in 1900, the house had never had winter residents. It was bitterly cold and the house felt like a morgue. Pam's mother, Ruby, took one look at the place and took Pam and Bobby home with her. Ruby and Pam scoured the superintendent's house for a week before it was habitable.

Petersburg Fisheries grew into Icicle Seafoods. The business needed a better location to conduct its business, so company headquarters moved to Seattle. Pam and Bob moved their family to Seattle in 1978, and they still reside there.

Bob and Pam's son, Robert Magnus Thorstenson Jr., was born in Bellingham, Washington, on November 15, 1963. He graduated from the University of Puget Sound with a major in finance and accounting.

Bobby began fishing with his grandfather, Magnus, at the age of 14. He has been captain of the *Pamela Rae* since age 19, following the tragic accident that claimed the life of his grandfather.

Bobby married Gina Wuflestad in 1988. They have four children: Sylvi Elise, born in 1992; Magnus Karl Vivang, born in 1995; Ingrid, born in 1996; and Gunnar, born in 1999.

Bob and Pam's daughter, Tani Rae, was born in Petersburg on September 30, 1965. Tani graduated with honors from Seattle University with a bachelor's degree in education. She taught fourth grade in Ketchikan, Alaska, where she met Leif Stenfjord. They married in 1991.

In 2001, they moved to Petersburg. They have three children: Thor, born in 1992; Annika born in 1995; and Anders, born in 1999. Leif and Tani own Petersburg Properties. Tani coaches high school swimming and enjoys running marathons.

Bob and Pam's youngest child, Peder Helgi Thorstenson, was born in Petersburg on May 25, 1969. Peder graduated from Eastern Washington University with a degree in finance and accounting. He fishes salmon in Bristol Bay on his boat the F/V *Corvus*. He also fishes halibut, blackcod, and salmon in Southeastern Alaska on his boat F/V *Viking Spirit*.

Peder married Kathleen Travers in 1998. They have three children: Connor Patrick Loui, Margaret Ruby, and Elizabeth Grace.

Magnus and Ruby Martens second daughter, Polly Anna, was born in Petersburg on November 27, 1949. She graduated from Petersburg High School and attended a business college in Seattle.

Polly and Tim Koeneman met while working together at PFI in the summer of 1970. They were married the next December.

Tim left graduate school at Oregon State University to take a job with the Alaska Department of Fish and Game (ADF&G) in Ketchikan.

Ragnhild and Loui with daughter Thelma and sons, from left, Elmer, Leonard, and Magnus.

The Koeneman family moved back to Petersburg when Tim transferred to ADF&G's Petersburg office in 1974. Polly's father, Magnus, and her Uncle Ken Welde helped them build their house at 917 Sandy Beach Road.

Polly worked in several retail shops in town. She also worked for the Petersburg School District for 13 years, as the high school secretary.

Polly's hobby of passion is rosemaling. She has taken a number of classes, including three tours to

Loui and Ragnhild Martens cont'd

Norway and two trips to the Vesterheim Museum in Iowa to study the art. Polly likes to rosemal gifts for her family.

She is also active in the Lutheran Church, reading group, and Muskeg Maleriers, a painting group.

In 2000, Tim retired after 26 years with ADF&G. He remains an active member of the Alaska Army National Guard. He was selected for battalion command, in 2001, and promoted to lieutenant colonel. Polly and Tim have three children: Megan Welde Lovejoy, Tiffany Lisbet, and James Peder.

Tim and Polly's daughter, Megan, was born in Corvallis, Oregon, on December 8, 1973, when her father was in graduate school. She graduated from Petersburg High School, in 1991, and attended Gonzaga University.

Megan moved back to Juneau, Alaska, and worked at Costco, before getting a job at the ADF&G Mark, Tag, and Age Laboratory. Megan met Brandon Lovejoy. They were married in Juneau in 2002. They have one daughter, Makenna Rayne.

Tim and Polly's second daughter, Tiffany Lisbet, was born in Petersburg on February 25, 1975, her father's birthday.

Tiffany graduated from Petersburg High School, in 1993, and attended the University of Arizona.

Tiffany came back to Petersburg briefly, doing quality control work for Icicle Seafoods. She then moved to Seattle and worked at Nordstrom's downtown store. In 2002, Tiffany moved across country to Hartford, Connecticut, where she manages the women's sportswear department for Nordstrom.

Tim and Polly's son, James Peder, was born in Petersburg on November 9, 1979.

At the age of 14, he began salmon seining on the *Pamela Rae* with his cousin Bobby, and did so for many years. He also gillnetted for salmon in Bristol Bay and Southeast Alaska.

Jamie graduated from Petersburg High School, in 1998, and attended Embry-Riddle Aeronautical University in Prescott, Arizona. He now lives in Juneau and works at the restaurant, The Hanger.

Magnus Martens and Ruby Welde's wedding. From left: Belle Wasvick, Ruby, Magnus and Leonard Martens

Leonard and Emily Martens

By Carol Enge

Leonard Martens was born on October 6, 1913, to Loui and Ragnhild. His was the first recorded birth in the incorporated City of Petersburg.

He grew up in the family home on what is now North Nordic Drive, and was a member of the "Point Gang." He fished with his father on the *Star* and later worked in the cannery.

A bout with rheumatic fever caused him to lose his hair and he was thereafter known as "Baldy."

Emily Martens

After marrying Emily Linvog, he had the boat *Loui M* built. He spent his life fishing halibut and blackcod. He built their home on North Nordic Drive.

Leonard died in 1982.

Emily was born to Olga and John Linvog in 1917. Olga and Augusta Enge had traveled from their native Norway together and remained lifelong friends. Emily had grown up with the Enge boys, so it was inevitable that she should explore the Alaska she had heard so much about.

Life dealt her a few sad blows. Their son, Loui, tragically drowned in 1950. Then, in 1954, she lost a baby girl.

Her surviving son, Colin, lives in Petersburg. A fisherman like his father and grandfather, he fishes for salmon, halibut, blackcod and crab. Colin has a son, Brian, with his first wife, Jenny. Now married to Cheri Morrison, he has second son, Colin Jr.

Emily and Leonard Martens

Emily was a longtime employee of the Bank of Petersburg and National Bank of Alaska. She was an active member of the Emblem Club, Eastern Star, and the Toastmistress Club.

She is remembered for her hospitality and as a gourmet cook. After the death of her husband, her health failed.

Emily currently resides at Bethany at Silver Lake in Everett, Washington.

Ski cabin

Robert and Margaret Martin

By Margaret Martin

I was born July 26, 1920, in Caledonia, Minnesota, the ninth child of August and Augusta Meyer.

Caledonia is a farming community of thrifty German immigrants.

After graduating from Upper Iowa University, I taught English and social studies in Iowa schools.

In the fall of 1944, I traveled by train on the "Milwaukee Road" (Chicago, Milwaukee, St. Paul and Pacific Railroad), from La Crosse, Wisconsin, to Seattle, Washington. The trip took three days and two nights.

In Seattle, I boarded the *North Sea* for Petersburg and found, among the passengers, Esther Evans, Rae Burke Stedman and Esther Horton Hansen. All of them would join me as first-year teachers in the Petersburg school.

I taught for four years. In September of 1947, I married Robert "Tink" Martin. At the end of the school year, I was informed that it was the policy of the school board not to hire married female teachers and to consider my position vacant for the coming year.

Thereafter, I concentrated on raising sons. Bob was born in 1948, and Terry in 1949.

We left Petersburg for Seattle, in 1957, because of Tink's association with the J.A. Troxell Construction Company, which was headquartered in that city. We have lived in many places because of the nature of Tink's work, including a 13-year residency in Fairbanks. Tink worked on the Trans-Alaska Pipeline and built islands for exploratory oil drilling on the Beaufort Sea and Prudhoe Bay.

We left Alaska in 1986 and retired to the Chehalis/Centralia area of Washington State.

We remember fondly camping at Five Mile and hiking to Colp's Lake, walking the boardwalk to Sandy Beach, dancing at the Sons of Norway Hall, and going to cowboy movies on weekends at the Coliseum. We could see passenger ships gliding down the Narrows from the front window of our home in "Skylark City," and the map of North America superimposed on the side of Petersburg Mountain after the first snowfall. We also remember walking on the lawns from Chris Wick's home to the Rosevold's corner, when spring breakup made the road impassable for cars or foot traffic. Most of all, we remember the fine friendships made during our years spent in "Little Norway."

Tink and Meg with Terry and Bobby

By Robert "Tink" Martin

I was born August 10, 1922, in Glenoma, Washington, the sixth child of Robert and Elva Martin. I attended the University of Washington.

In 1942, I traveled to Alaska, stopping in Juneau to visit my two sisters and families. I was offered a job at Alaska Coastal Airlines. There I met Petersburg's Bill Stedman and Walt Ludtke from Eureka, California.

In 1944, I joined the Navy and served for two years in a carrier aircraft service unit. After my discharge in 1946, Walt and I returned to Alaska on Gordon Jensen's boat, the *Symphony*.

We went to Petersburg to see Bill Stedman, and decided to stay, even though our jobs at Alaska Coastal were waiting for us.

In Petersburg, I worked at Fryer Machine Works. Bill, Walt and I purchased and operated Red Top Taxi. I worked at Union Oil, for Joe Lundberg Construction Company on the water dam and ACS building, for J.A. Troxell on the Blind Slough hydroelectric project, and for Empire Construction Company on the city sewer and water project.

I was a member of the Petersburg City Council, appointed to fill a vacancy, and then elected to a term.

Martinsen's Dairy

By Marjorie File

Many of our citizens can claim hardy Norwegian fishermen as their ancestors, dating back to the turn of the last century. If you were to strike up a conversation with one of our long-term residents, they would confirm that the efforts and tenacity of one particular fisherman's family provide the story of a memorable long-lived dairy — Martinsen's Dairy of Petersburg.

Nicholai Martinsen and his wife, Jeanette "Nette" (nee Petersen), traveled from the Lofoten Islands, Norway, in 1901. They lived temporarily in Duluth, Minnesota, before settling at the northwest corner of Mitkof Island. As was the custom among the early settlers, Nicholai traveled to Petersburg alone to prepare the way for Nette, who arrived in 1907. They purchased a small home on Front Street. It was eventually remodeled to accommodate a growing family. The home would fondly become known as the dairy house.

My grandpa, Nic, became an American citizen on December 5, 1905. Locating his citizenship certificate among other personal documents in the old black floor safe was a joyous occasion, since very little family history was set down in writing. I pondered over the spelling of Grandpa's name on his certificate — Necalai Marthieneesen.

Nic gillnetted from a skiff on the Stikine River during those early years, and possibly fished up until his illness in the late 1920s. Nic would always bring in 12 king salmon, whether the fishing was good or bad. He also captained the boat *Mars*, a small halibut schooner. The duration is unknown, but I did find one mention of a fish delivery in a *Petersburg Weekly Report* that was dated September 25, 1915.

Jeanette Martinsen

On January 6, 1908, Nic and Nette's first child, Selma, was born. Clara joined the family on January 13, 1910. Their son, Hjalmer, was born on January 26, 1912.

With small children in the family, Nic and Nette sought a source of fresh milk. I came across a record of Grandma buying her first cows in the *Weekly Report* dated March 15, 1918. "...*Alfred Swanson* (brother to Carl A. Swanson) *last week sold to Mrs. Martinsen his place in the north end of town, together with personal property, the latter including 2 milch cows...*"

In the summer of 1918, Carl A. Swanson and family moved from Scow Bay to Point Agassiz, taking with them a young cow they purchased from Nette for $10. Through the years, he built up his stock. Before moving south, in 1943, Swanson sold the entire lot to Martinsen's Dairy.

Grandma was excited to have her own milk cows. Her children now had fresh milk, and soon the supply would overflow to the neighborhood. My mother has a memory of her bringing gifts of cream to friends and neighbors. More cows joined the first, which raises the question ...who had the bull?

Grandma's cows were grazed and milked on Kupreanof Island at Sasby's Point. It was a short row straight over to the island from the dairy house. A familiar sight from town side was Nette sitting on her stool, milking her cow at the beach. After the morning and evening milking, the

Nicholai Martinsen

✤ 189 ✤

Martinsen's Dairy cont'd

cans were placed in a cooling tank and delivered to customers in the morning. Dressed in a long black cotton dress, white apron and scarf, Nette's appearance was reminiscent of faraway Norway, as she pushed her two-wheeled cart, bearing milk can and dipper, along wooden plank streets. It all began with bringing surplus milk to neighbors with children and to the hospital. Grandma always insisted they had priority. Although a business had not been intentional, Grandma had begun a local dairy.

When Nette and the children spent the night at Sasby's, they slept in the larger of the two original houses, which is habitable today. The summer that Dad and Mom (Hjalmer Martinsen and Marjorie Michaelson) were courting, the upstairs room facing the bay was pointed out as "his room."

A very small dilapidated barn, also housing an old Edison generator, was still standing behind this house in the 1970s. My thought was that Grandpa Nic had built it for Grandma's cows.

My grandmother was a kind, no nonsense, determined woman. These traits served her well in both establishing the dairy and with the numerous challenges many of the early pioneer women faced. One challenge was met head-on when, in August 1919, town authorities were reprimanded for gangs of vicious dogs roaming the streets. Fights developed into "battles royal," and, as far as she was concerned, no citizen was safe outside of their home. As the dogs were chasing her calves, biting some severely, the marshal was admonished to "cope" with the problem.

Near the latter part of the 1920s, Grandpa Nic was suffering from what might have been undiagnosed arteriosclerosis. At age 16, Dad took on a man-size share of the dairy, assisted by his hard-working mother and sisters. Grandpa passed away August 28, 1931, at age 55. I was surprised to discover in his obituary that Grandpa had a brother, Marcus, in Norway, and a sister, Ellen Christenson, in Minnesota.

In addition to grazing, grass was cut for the cows at Point Agassiz and up Petersburg Creek. This labor-intensive job of keeping the herd in grass gave way to shipping hay and grain from Washington State via steamship. Two silos that had been erected to store the grass were dismantled and sold to John Wallace at Farragut Bay. During those years of buying hay, I recall only one bad shipment. "Only fit for bedding," Dad said, and promptly shipped it back.

Although Dad had grazing rights, on November 20, 1953, six years before statehood, the Department of the Interior's Bureau of Land Management deeded a parcel of grazing land to him at Petersburg Creek. Known to locals as the "Creek" or "Crick," it is a little "Eden" hide-away for those desiring peace and solitude. This was so for my dad. After the evening milking, he would grab his tackle box and fly rod, and head across the grass flats for Hoagy's Hole. Sometimes we could head him off and he would bat balls to us. By early summer, the herd would have devoured every bit of grass in the vicinity of the barn. When the sun baked the mud, it made a nice hard surface to play ball. (Watch out for those cow patties though!)

Martinsen cows returning from their summer "vacation" up Petersburg Creek.

My dad was a very capable carpenter, who, I am certain, learned the trade working along side his father. His skills served him well at a young age and all through the dairy years. He built a long, flat-bottomed river punt that enabled him to make the run up and down the creek channel, even at low tide. Navigating the channel over the sand flats was a must for him, when the schedule was tight because of the tides.

The summer dairy schedule was orchestrated by the tide book. After milking, the cans were kept chilled overnight by piping the frigid waters from the backside of Petersburg Mountain directly into a cooling tank. The tank, located in the front side room of the barn, was an attraction to the younger children. They loved

Martinsen's Dairy cont'd

scooping up, in a tin can, the minnows that had swam through the pipe.

In the morning, Dad made his daily commute with the five-gallon milk cans to the dairy house. He bottled the milk, loaded the cases into the truck, and began his delivery runs. Customers knew Hjalmer was on the way when the "clinking" bottles could be heard in the neighborhood. Occasionally, my mom would have to finish delivering the milk, as he had to rush back to the Creek because of the tide.

Dad's first delivery truck was a Model T. All of his new trucks were outfitted with a wooden roof over the bed. Neighborhood kids, kids from town, and then the Martinsen kids, were always ready to make "four-bits" or a dollar. Standing on the running board, hands gripping the wooden roof supports, they'd run bottles of milk up to customers' porches. A frequent scene during the cold winters was forgotten bottles on porches with caps perched in the air atop frozen cream.

During the summer of 1937, my mother, Marjorie Lorine Michaelson, traveled from the Lakewood area of south Tacoma, Washington. She visited her dad's brother, Ed, and his wife, Alice, at their home on north Wrangell Avenue. Also living in Petersburg was uncle Clifford Michaelson, wife Alice and young son Clifford. Tragically, Clifford drowned in May 1935, while working on Blind Slough.

Lorine's paternal grandfather, Henry Michaelson, with his parents and siblings, immigrated to America from Valdres, Norway, in 1878. They settled in Pierce County, Wisconsin. Henry's wife, Elizabeth Kammen, was born in Northfield, Minnesota, the daughter of Norwegian immigrants. In the late 1890s, Henry and Elizabeth moved from Amery, Wisconsin, becoming early pioneers of McNeil Island, Washington, before a final move to Tacoma.

Lorine's maternal great-grandfather emigrated from Ireland; her great-grandmother from France. Their children, Frank Waldron and Ella Mae (Maxwell), were born and married in Illinois. Lorine's mother, Marjorie, the youngest of many siblings, was born in Norton, Kansas. The family's final move was to the Lakewood area of Tacoma.

It was bound to happen that Mom and Dad met, as Nette and Alice were friends. Hjalmer and Lorine married November 29, 1937, in Tacoma.

Two weeks prior to the wedding, Dad was scouting out hay dealers around Mount Vernon, Prosser, and Walla Walla. After the honeymoon, they moved into the dairy house with Nette. In 1942, they purchased the Pederson house out at the "Point."

Nette passed away September 10, 1945. The Point house was sold to Doyle Cisney in early January 1946. Hjalmer and Lorine moved back to the dairy house. By then, their three older children, Marjorie, Jim and Nick, had been born.

In 1941, the old small barn on Hungry Point was burned down to make room for a larger building. The new barn was constructed on the same site. The up-to-date barn was well planned out. It required a substantial amount of concrete for the flooring, gutters and feeding troughs. Each cow had her personal stall complete with stanchion and nose-operated drinking fountain. Our hayloft had a beautiful wood floor. Many dances were hosted there while the cows "vacationed" up the creek.

During her junior and senior years, Colleen Mortensen Nicholson said the kids held several barn dances. When she called Dad requesting the use of the barn, his response was, "You know the rules." She was amazed at the trust he had in them. Word got out, someone was delegated to bring a windup phonograph, and the dance was on.

Martinsen's Dairy grew to the height of its operation, as the town of Petersburg continued to grow with its fisheries-based economy. Although the herd was predominately Holstein, a breed noted for producing large quantities of low-fat milk, my dad always kept a Jersey for cream. For a few years, he also had an Ayrshire cow, a hardy breed originating in Scotland. Dad had ordered several Herefords from Seattle, and she came in the lot.

The herd was tested for disease by the territorial veterinary, which always found the cows well maintained. I remember a cupboard in the barn stashed with various remedies, a veterinary manual, plus the cows' breeding records. There was no local veterinary, so phone contact was necessary for advice. If a cow needed medical attention, the local physician would make a barn call.

Norman Wilson worked at the dairy the longest, staying with us through the 1940s. Memories of

Martinsen's Dairy cont'd

Norman include his run-ins with one territorial bull up the Creek. It did not like fishermen, or people in general, disturbing its domain. I don't know who was the most stressed, but the bull, under an onslaught of verbal abuse, would finally be secured in the barn. This same bull kept Clara Hall and her son, Arden, up a tree at Hoagy's Hole most of one day, until one of the dairymen showed up. Needless to say, Clara and Arden were furious. To top it off, while they were held prisoners in the tree, their lunch was on the ground, carefully guarded by the bull.

In the fall and winter of 1946, a prolonged longshoremen's strike, in Seattle, came on the heels of World War II. This created a crisis situation in Southeastern Alaska, always dependant on food deliveries from "down south." Meat was especially scarce, so triplet calves born in May in the barnyard, and raised by employee Buddy Mortensen, were "sacrificed" sometime that winter.

My dad, who was milking 22 cows, had a major problem in late September of the same year. Efforts to get 240 tons of hay and 10 tons of feed unloaded from the *Northern Voyager* at the dock failed. Cement, coal, and other freight for Ketchikan would have to be unloaded to obtain access to the Petersburg cargo. Finally, in late November, the vessel *Commonwealth*, called at Petersburg with 70 bales of hay from Prince Rupert to tide the dairy over until the dispute ended.

At the dairy house, the milk room fronted the roadside. On their way to and from town, folks liked to stop by and chat with Dad while he bottled milk. Andrew Gjerde was a regular, and bringing news from town he often tagged his stories with, "Now don't take my word for it." Andy was high-spirited and he always livened up my dad's day.

Every evening, cases upon cases of stacked bottles were waiting for one of my two brothers (or a neighbor) and me to wash. Enveloped in clouds of steam and the clean scent of chlorine, we labored over two deep galvanized sinks. Occasionally, a bottle with a hairline crack would break on the spinning, electrically driven, bottle brush — and that was scary. I was always a little on edge: I just knew that in one of those cases there was a cracked bottle. If you panicked and left the broken bottle flopping on the brush too long, the shaft would bend or, worse, break. From then on it was all manual, plus the dread of confronting Dad with yet another broken brush.

Spring officially came to Petersburg in May, when a scow-load of mooing cows left their barn in town for the grass flats of Petersburg Creek. From all over town, kids came to watch the show of cows — and especially the bull — loading onto the scow. Dad managed the smaller scow with his skiff at first. When the herd increased, so did the scow size and several boats lending a hand might be necessary. Maneuvering the scow around and into the mouth of the Creek was difficult when the current was running strong. Dad was always very appreciative when my husband, Fred, was available to assist with his seine boat, the *Jerry O*.

It was the third and last load of cows headed for the creek barn one spring that became the final trip of dad's "six-cow scow." Just outside the government dock, the bull got frisky and a cow jumped overboard. The scow ran right over the top of her. A few moments later, the outboard kicked up as she surfaced from behind the skiff. Meanwhile, the bull stomped a hole in the scow and it began to sink. Dad quickly beached it on the sand flats above what is now Bergmann's property. As the cows unloaded, they discovered the run-over cow already ashore, waiting for them; off they went, continuing their journey over the flats up to the barn. Poor Daisy, a typical Holstein, her low-slung bag was vulnerable as she stepped over a log and trod on one of her own teats, ripping it off. What a trip!

The cattle favored the tender grass on the flats, and often would keep grazing while the tide rose, stranding them on tiny islands. They would fuss and bellow, waiting until the very last minute before plunging into the water. It was odd to be moving along in a skiff and suddenly come upon half-bodied cows, standing upon submerged islands.

Almost daily the herd meandered far up the Creek, often as far as two miles from the barn, to the Clay Banks. The "girls" really got a workout. The cows became conditioned to the sound of Dad's outboard returning from town; the lead cow would start the herd back to the barn. Not only the cows, but also about half of the town were conditioned to Dad's routine.

Dad had one of the first outboards in Petersburg, a loud 14 hp Elto. Later he moved up to a 22 hp Elto, eventually purchasing an Evinrude. They all had a very

Martinsen's Dairy cont'd

distinct sound (mostly loud) and could be heard from a great distance. Upon reaching the barn, Dad always whistled. A few of the pokier gals would be spurred on, knowing a shovelful of grain would be waiting.

When a pregnant cow didn't come home for a couple of days, Dad sent my two young brothers to retrieve her. She had calved at the Clay Banks and the bull stayed with her. The bull was very testy about Jim shouldering the calf and leading the cow back to the barn. Jim had to fire a warning shot to get the bull to back off. On the return trip, Jim asked Nick to pack the rifle, but he refused, so Jim thumped on him, and Nick took off for the barn to tell Dad. When Jim showed up with the calf AND the gun, Dad gave him "the boot" — and Mom chewed Dad out!

During the summer months, a string of friends joined us at the Creek. My creek buddies were Camille Torwick Marifern and Lois Johnson Rhodes. A tent was pitched to handle the influx. At night the tent would be wall-to-wall sleeping bags filled with happy but tuckered out kids, and one dog.

Ours days were taken up exploring in the skiff, hiking, and trying to reach Hoagy's Hole to fish or swim without the bull noticing. Invariably one of us would step in a cow patty and let out a shriek — so much for sneaking around the bull!

After Dad began using electric compressed air milkers, we knew when the generator quit we had to crawl out of our cozy sleeping bags and get ready to leave. When the last cow had been lovingly slapped on the rump, as she headed out the barn door, we loaded the boat for town. Just maybe, Mom would have "skinny hotcakes" (otherwise known as Swedish pancakes) waiting for us at the dairy house.

When the milk boat was anchored farther from the barn because of the tide, it was much harder on the men who carried the five-gallon cans of milk. Two cans, weighing about 80 pounds full, were carried on shoulder yokes. Often we manned the oars to reach deeper water in the channel before Dad could use the motor. I can still see him sitting in the back peeling an orange, directing our route.

By 1966, because of his illness, my hard-working father considered quitting the business. Although my mother worked very hard to keep the dairy going, it was impossible without experienced help. My brother Jim was milking and bringing the cans to the dairy room. Mom bottled the milk, which required lifting the heavy cans, and she also delivered. She was a strong, hard-working woman, but with two young girls at home, a sick husband, and holding down a part-time job, she could not keep up the pace.

Hjalmer Martinsen

So, the cows were butchered and the meat sold. This was a very difficult time for my father. Can you picture a man having to put his animals down, almost family members, which had faithfully provided a livelihood for him and his loved ones for so many years? Dad didn't assist in the butchering, but about every 15 minutes he would slowly drive by.

In October 1969, Dad moved to the Pioneer Home in Sitka, where he passed away March 9, 1970, at the age of 58. It saddens me that I was too self-involved and not more supportive of my father. I'm just now fully appreciating his many talents and capabilities.

Thanks for the memories and heritage Dad! Wish I could hear you coming around the bend of the Creek again, heading home.

Hjalmer and Lorine's children are Marjorie (File), Jim, Nicholai "Nick," Lorraine (Heikkila), Jean (McCay), and Carol (Louthan). Direct descendants of Nicholai and Nette, now living in Petersburg, include three grandchildren, Marjorie, Jim and Jean; seven great-grandchildren; and 20 great-great-grandchildren.

Petersburg Masonic Lodge

History of Petersburg Lodge No. 262, Free & Accepted Masons
Now Petersburg Lodge No. 23

So far as is known, the first get-together of Petersburg Masons, as such, was a welcoming party for Brother Lorenzo B. Cornelius and his bride on November 11, 1921. Only Masons and their ladies were present.

This party inspired the thought of some sort of Masonic intercourse or activities, and on the initiative of Brothers Cornelius and Nelson, the local Masons were contacted one by one relative to organizing a Masonic Club.

The proposal was favorably accepted and matters took shape during the winter months until things finally crystallized into a formal meeting on April 8, 1922, which was called for the specific purpose of organizing a Masonic Club with the idea of preparing for the ultimate organization of a Masonic Lodge in Petersburg.

A total of 12 Master Masons were present, viz:

D.B. Cornelius	R.C. Mathis
Frederick Nelson	R.N. Rogers
Ed Locken	H.F. Dawes
K.L. Steberg	A.C. Huss
T.S. Elsmore	H.J. Grub
T.J. McBride	Nels Nelson

The meeting was held at the home of Brother Mathis (dentist). Brother Dawes was elected temporary chairman and Brother Fred Nelson temporary secretary.

Petersburg Masonic Lodge's first 10 Masters

Front, from left: Frank Havens (insert), Ed Locken, Joseph McKecknie, Harold Dawes and Forrest Fryer.
Back: K.L. Steberg, Fred Nelson, Erling Johansen, Sam Gauffin and Tom Elsemore.

Petersburg Masonic Lodge cont'd

The following were elected as officers of the Club:

Harold F. Dawes, President
Ed Locken, Vice-President
Frederick Nelson, Secretary-Treasurer

It was decided to meet twice each month for rehearsing degree work, and additional once-a-month for a social evening with the ladies. The initiation fee was fixed at $10, and the monthly dues at 50 cents. A committee was appointed to draft by-laws for the Club. After the meeting a luncheon was had with the ladies.

The next meeting of the Masonic Club was held on April 21, 1922, at the home of Brother and Mrs. K.L. Steberg. Two new members were present: Ed Walvick and W.F. Coulson.

The proposed by-laws were read and thoroughly discussed, and finally adopted as amended. The Secretary was authorized to "expend monies out of the Club's funds for the relief of distressed worthy Masons and/or their families".

At a meeting on May 5th it was decided to use the upstairs of the Sons of Norway Hall as a meeting place, at a rate of rental of $3 each meeting.

At the June 2nd meeting there were three new members present, namely: Howard Owens (5/19), J.L. MacKechnie (6/2), and L.A. Woodward (6/2). At this meeting the Club selected candidates for the various offices of the lodge-to-be, in order that they may study and learn their parts.

Brother MacKechnie, being the only one who had held a minor elective office in his home lodge in Washington, was chosen to be Worshipful Master. Those elected for offices were:

J.L. MacKechnie	Worshipful Master
Ed Locken	Senior Warden
Thos.S. Elsemore	Junior Warden
Harold F. Dawes	Senior Deacon
L.B. Cornelius	Junior Deacon
Frederick Nelson	Secretary

Club meetings continued and rehearsing was carried on religiously through 1923, until late in the year when it was decided to ask the Grand Lodge for dispensation to work in the degrees. A petition with 16 signatures was sent to the Grand Master, asking for the dispensation. The signers were:

J.L. MacKechnie	T.J. McBride
Ed Locken	William Fels
Thos.S. Elsmore	Raymond C. Mathis
Frederick Nelson	Howard Owens
Harold F. Dawes	John Hansen
P.F. Harley	*Frank Barnes
L.B. Cornelius	*Leonard Campbell
Harry J. Grub	Robert N. Rogers

of Wrangell

(*Historical note: By 1974, Campbell and Nelson were the only survivors.*)

The petition was granted, and the Institution of Petersburg Lodge U.D. was conducted on January 11, 1924, by Most Worshipful Brother Maurice S. Whittier, Grand Custodian, who was accompanied from Juneau by Brother Nelson who was then a resident of Juneau (from March 1923 to May 1925).

It is to be noted that the first petition for the degrees was received at this meeting of Institution, being that of Clarence D. Lawrence of the U.S. Army Signal Corps., employed at the local Cable Office.

Andrew and Tora Mathisen

By Sig Mathisen

The patriarch of the Mathisen family in Petersburg was Andreas (Andrew) Meyer Mathisen. He was born in 1882 at Fauskevag, just south of Harstad on the island of Hinnoya in northern Norway.

This is very beautiful country. The geography and climate is similar to ours even though it is north of the Arctic Circle at latitude 68°40". The beach area at Grasholmen is sandy and is a treasured spot for locals and tourists in the summer.

Andrew was the first of 10 children born to Mathias and Leonora Jensen. Two died shortly after birth.

Andrew was not only a respected fisherman, but was also well known as an expert marksman. He served in the Norwegian Army.

In 1906, he married Anne Theodora (Tora) Ursin, who was from the well-to-do and prominent Ursin family of Trondenes.

Anne Theodora (Tora) Mathisen

In 1907, they bought a farm and boat harbor that had previously been in the Ursin family. It was at Leikvika, a few miles south of Faustevag. Three children were born there: Annea in 1907, Laurits (Adolph) in 1909, and Anna in 1910.

Andrew got the urge to go to the northwestern area of the United States where his younger brother, Martin Walstrand, had immigrated. Martin had sent information of the great economic potential. Huge virgin fish resources were to be found there.

Andrew left the family and relatives to go and find out for himself. He arrived in Seattle, Washington, in 1910. With his brother, he shipped out for the halibut fishery on the dory steamers *Weiding Brothers* and *Chicago*.

Once, while hanging over the side of a halibut steamer in a dory to avoid getting smashed, Andrew dropped into the sea. A fast-thinking fisherman, Jens Olsen, (who later had the *Sylvia*) quickly cut loose in his dory and pulled him to safety.

Andrew also worked on a whaler out of Kodiak.

Andrew moved to Petersburg in 1911. Here he also became a well-respected fisherman and began running vessels — first, the *Thelma* for his brother Martin, and then, the *Lovera* for Erik Ness.

In 1913, Andrew's younger brother, Marian Sigurd, arrived in British Columbia to work in a ditch digging project near Vancouver. Later he worked a summer at a cannery in Lynn Canal before coming to Petersburg.

All the brothers were very strong, but one story of Sigurd stands out. While he was working at one of the camps, a big Irish bully egged Sigurd on to fight with him. As the bully lunged, Sigurd grabbed him in a bear hug, squeezed him unconscious, and dropped him on the floor. He wasn't bothered much after that.

Another younger brother, Hjalmer Valen, also went to British Columbia and remained there. Andrew's three sisters and his youngest brother, Magnus, stayed in Norway.

(Magnus celebrated his 107th birthday in March of 2002. I met him, in 1999, at Kveldsol, an old folks home in Sorvik. He told me, "My brothers were tough…but I was the toughest!" Because he lived well into his 108th year, he was. Magnus passed away in October of 2003.)

Andreas (Andrew) Mathisen

Over the years, careers of the extended family revolved around the fishing industry. Andrew's brother, Marian Sigurd Mathisen, had a boat for a time, fishing halibut and, during one period, shark. He also had a fox farm at Sunset Island, and later was partners with Porter Apple at Roberts Island, in Port Houghton, about 40 miles north of Petersburg.

Andrew and Tora Mathisen cont'd

Marian Sigurd worked as a trap watchman for some time. He was married for a short while to a woman named Mae, but mostly lived as a bachelor. They had no children. He had a place at Castle Island, but mainly lived at his small house on North Nordic on the Narrows.

Andrew's wife, Tora, and the three children, Annea, Adolph and Anna, arrived in Petersburg mid-August of 1916. They lived for a year at a new residence built by Erik Ness adjoining his home property. (This is where Eagle's Roost Park is now located.)

During this winter, Andrew went south to build a new fishing vessel of his own and to also go through the citizenship process.

His new vessel, the *Lenor*, arrived in Petersburg in May of 1917.

In October of 1917, Andrew and Tora bought the Ursin home from Tora's relatives. It was a beautiful site on Wrangell Narrows, now North Nordic Drive, where they lived the rest of their lives.

In 1918, a son Leif was born. In 1920, son Arild (Aril) arrived. When Bernice was born, that make six children in all. Three were born in Norway and three in the new country.

The children all attended school in Petersburg. Aril was the valedictorian of the Class of 1939. Most of the children were married in the Mathisen house and lived in Petersburg.

As a side note, I should say that, during World War II, Andrew was placed in charge of the fleet in Petersburg. He also developed contingency plans in case of bombing or invasion.

Andrew and Tora's oldest child, Annea, (born April 27, 1907) was 9 years old when the family immigrated to the United States. Nea attended school in Petersburg until high school. The Mathisen family grew with the births of Leif, Aril and Bernice, and it became necessary for Nea to quit school to help out at the family home.

Later Nea worked at the Home Café (a restaurant located above the present Lille Hammer) as night cook with Tora Norheim. In the late 1920s and early '30s, she and sister Anna operated the Bluebird Café. Nea was the cook and Anna the waitress. Nea's warm personality and contagious laughter brought many of the local bachelors to the Bluebird for all their meals.

Nea married Duke Miller on October 14, 1933. They raised two daughters: Mary Ann, born December 26, 1934; and Sylvia, born November 29, 1936. Duke and Nea bought the house at First and Dolphin streets in 1936 from Petersburg Packing Company. It remained the family home until after Nea's death.

Duke Miller grew up in Petersburg in one of the town's first families. He ran cannery tenders and, like his brother-in-law, Marvin Kvernvik, kept on the boats until late in life.

Aril "Audie" Mathisen and Klara Lando
August 29, 1941, the day before they wed.

During World War II, Nea worked as a volunteer nurse's aide at Petersburg Hospital. She was diagnosed with Parkinson's disease in 1947. This progressive disease handicapped her for the last 12 years of her life. Nea died in 1959 at the age of 52.

Nea is remembered for her wonderful cooking, especially during the holidays when she and her sister Anna spent days making fattigmand and lefse together. The Mathisen family made a type of lefse, called Krina

Andrew and Tora Mathisen cont'd

lefse, which isn't made by anyone in Petersburg today.

The flour dough was rolled out and baked on top of the oil stove, then topped with an egg, flour and cream mixture and baked inside the oven. When soaked out, it was buttered and spread with cinnamon and sugar. Two sides were placed together, sandwich style, and cut into pie-shaped wedges. This was a favorite of the Mathisen family and always on the table during holiday gatherings.

**Mathisen Family photo
Front porch of their family home, 1943**

Adolph married Francis "Bunny" Roundtree. Their son was Andrew, known as Andy.

Adolph followed in his father's footsteps in the fishing industry with boats *Ankle Deep*, *Pearl F*, and, finally, *Harmony*. He was also in the shipyard business with Mitkof Marine Ways.

After Andrew died, Adolph and Bunny inherited the Mathisen home and property. More weddings took place there as the next generation came up. It continued to be the family gathering place for Christmases, until the family became so large it couldn't accommodate us all.

It was a place politicians socialized because Adolph and Bunny were political, as well as exquisite hosts. The table would be set with all the traditional delicacies — pickled herring, smoked salmon, lox — and, also likely, the traditional "old fashioned." Like his father, Andrew, Adolph was always a gentleman.

Bunny and her sister-in-law, Anna, got together after the kids were grown and started a gift shop in town. They thought of the obvious "Bunnanna" for a name, but settled on "Star." It was a fine venture, until Anna became terminally ill with cancer.

Anna married Marvin Kvernvik. They had a son, Jerry, and two girls, Janet and Kathryn. Marvin Kvernvik, who was from Ruston, Washington, first came up to work with fish traps at the local cannery. Through the years, he fished, ran cannery tenders, and did construction at the cannery. He was also involved in the longshoring and freight business, Special Processors, with his brother-in-law, Conner.

Marvin Kvernvik recalled his fishing time with his father-in law, Andrew, and how Andrew wouldn't let him go to the roller. "Too many leevers." Marvin laughed about this with me years later, over coffee down at the Homestead Café, because he had been running a lot of equipment with a lot of "leevers" for quite some time at the cannery. He couldn't argue with "the old man," though, and left that task alone while on the *Lenor*.

Anna was the last of the three sisters to pass away. It left a sad void in the family. The women of a family are always the cohesive force that binds the people together. As much as everyone has worked to maintain our family ties, we miss that bond.

Bernice married Conner Kinnear and they had three girls: Carol, Miriam and Sandra. When the girls were still quite young, Bernice and Conner both drowned in a boating accident.

Leif Mathisen married later in life to Ruth Nellis, who had a son, Mark. Leif was also a fisherman. He had his own boat for a short time, the *Green Hornet*. Mostly Leif fished on the family's boats and others in the fleet. He was well known as a good, clean cook.

He was in the U.S. Navy during World War II. After retiring from fishing, he worked several years as night watchman at the cannery.

Andrew and Tora's son, Aril "Audie" Thormod, spent a couple of boyhood summers helping his Uncle Sig at the fox farm at Roberts Island, but mostly fished with his father.

Audie and Klara Berget Lando were married at the Mathisen home, in Petersburg, on August 29, 1941.

They had four children: Aril Jr., born November 23, 1942; Sigurd Raymond, born August 14, 1946; Lenore Bernice, born April 21, 1952; Wayne Thomas, born January 22, 1959.

Audie served in the U.S. Army during the war.

Andrew and Tora Mathisen cont'd

He then fished on the *Lenor* with his father until Andrew retired. After fishing the *Lenor* for several years, he sold it to his son, Sigurd. He then bought the *Miss Norma* and finally the *Symphony*, which he passed on to his youngest son, Wayne. Audie was one of the original stockholders of Icicle Seafoods.

Aril Jr. married Anne Brevig. They have two children, Tiffany and Jon. Sigurd is married to Cynthia Lee, who runs Lee's Clothing, her mother's store in Petersburg. Sigurd runs the vessel *Marathon*. Their son is Allan. Lenore fishes with her brother, Wayne, and manages the Beachcomber Inn for her brother, Sig. Wayne runs the vessel *Symphony* and is married to Franci Loiacono Wickam. They have two children, Lindsey Wickam and Andrew.

The family home our father built on Wrangell Avenue is next to the house Bernice and Conner built. There was a trail between the houses going down to Andrew and Tora's, our grandparents. It was a well-used trail.

Grandpa Andrew had a wonderful garden that received many visits from the kids, although we never went inside the net fence. Well…sometimes. The strawberries and the raspberries were indescribable.

Adolph and Bunny's home was further north on Wrangell Avenue, above Uncle Sig's house.

It was a great place to grow up and we did have a feeling "of place," for this was where the family put down new roots in a new land. The roots took hold and the family tree has flourished.

Sigurd, Andrew, Aril and baby Lenore (1952)

We grew up on and in the water — rowing, fishing, playing, hunting, and eventually taking to the waters in the commercial fisheries.

At this time Aril, Sigurd, Lenore and Wayne all make livings from the sea. Lenore is also a bookkeeper and manager. Aril once had a publishing business in Washington. But, by and large, the old fishing blood of past generations runs warm in our veins.

Duke Miller recently passed away, so there is now only one member of that first generation of our family alive today. Uncle Leif is 85 and lives with his wife, Ruth. They still have a small house at Hungry Point on North Nordic, but at present are living at Marvin Kvernvik's family house on Second Street, to be close to the hospital for Ruth.

Leif keeps tabs with some of our Norwegian relatives, and now we are corresponding regularly by e-mail with Norway. Our ties are being rebuilt because of the ease of this new technology. It was especially incredible to be able to receive photos of Great (in some cases great great) Uncle Magnus Walstrand's 107th birthday on March 1, 2002, the same day as the party! This ability to send real-time news and photos back and forth will bring us all closer in the future.

Bunny and Adolph Mathisen

Adolph and Frances Mathisen

By Carol Enge, from an interview with Andy Mathisen

Adolph Mathisen was born to Andrew and Tora Mathisen in Harstad, Norway, on July 18, 1908. He came to Petersburg, in 1918, with his mother and sisters, Anna and Annea.

The family lived in a house where Eagles Roost Park is currently located. The next year his parents bought a house on North Nordic Drive, where members of the family still live. Many weddings and Christmas observances were held there.

Adolph engaged in the fishing industry at an early age. He was skipper of the F/V *Ankle Deep*, F/V *Pearl F*, and F/V *Harmony*, longlining for halibut and seining for salmon.

Frances "Bunny" Roundtree was born June 19, 1907, in Tacoma, Washington. Her mother came from Denmark and worked for the Roundtree family in Centralia, Washington.

When her mother died, the Guy Roundtree family adopted Bunny. She came to Petersburg with the Roundtree family in 1918.

During her school years, Bunny was employed at a Chinese restaurant in Sing Lee Alley.

She completed her high school education at Lincoln High School in Seattle.

Returning to Petersburg, Bunny married Adolph Mathisen in January of 1929. They had one son, who they named Andrew.

The Mathisens lived in their home on Wrangell Avenue before inheriting the family home on North Nordic Drive.

Bunny embarked on a lifetime of community service. She worked diligently with the Red Cross during World War II. As a member of the Hospital Guild, she rallied volunteer workers for the building of the new hospital.

She served as president of the Emblem Club and was a member of the Chamber of Commerce and the Petersburg Democratic Committee.

With her sister-in-law, Anna Kvernvik, Bunny purchased a gift shop from Izzy Roundtree, which they named The Star. They ran the store for many years, until Anna developed cancer and they decided to retire.

Adolph served on the International Pacific Halibut Commission and was a member of the Fishermen's Fund board, which administered benefits to injured fishermen. He was an active member of the Elks and Rotary clubs and was a driving force behind the building of the new hospital. He also served as chairman of the hospital board.

Bunny, Andy and Adolph Mathisen

Bunny and Adolph were always gracious hosts at the many social events held in their home. For many years, Bunny hosted a luncheon for out-of-town dignitaries attending the Little Norway Festival.

She and Adolph were recipients of the 1973 Norwegian-American Award.

Bunny made many trips stateside to visit friends. She also took her granddaughters on a trip to Russia and to visit the family in Norway.

Following his retirement, Adolph was known for his superb smoked salmon. He continued with a lifelong interest in fisheries and was always willing to share his knowledge with young people just starting in the industry.

Adolph died August 24, 1980, following a heart attack. Always the host, he requested that his memorial service be conducted at home with his many friends and family attending.

Bunny passed away January 6, 1988, at the long-term care facility of Petersburg General Hospital.

Andrew Mathisen

By David Boeri

"I arrived in the Petersburg Hospital on October 13, 1929. One would have thought a Bush was president. The economy was in shambles. And you couldn't borrow a dime." — Andy Mathisen

The first line of his prospective — and friends hope, distant — obituary will probably note that Andy Mathisen was a fishing guide. He was the first of his kind in Southeast Alaska to introduce fly fishermen to salmon and salt water.

He was also an innkeeper of some renown and built the first modern motel in Petersburg.

As a boat designer and builder, Andy, with his friend Tom Greer, produced the first welded-aluminum self-bailing skiffs in 1982. Later models would feature a down-turned chine, which is now an industry standard.

If the obit writer covers his bases, he will also note that Mathisen had been an insurance salesman, a software promoter and multi-striped entrepreneur. Of course, since this is Petersburg, the youthful Mathisen seined, trolled, longlined, owned, and operated boats of his own and others.

With a little legwork among the still living, the obit writer will dig up some quotes that testify to Andy Mathisen's productive efforts in two fields of endeavor: the first, promoting tourism; the second, as Mathisen himself might say, protecting wilderness and rivers from ourselves — and others more motivated by profits than good sense.

Serving on the Chamber of Commerce, Little Norway Festival, the local Fish and Game Advisory Board, World Championship King Salmon Derby, Alaska State Tourism Advisory Board, the Federal/State Land Use Planning Commission, and the Pacific Marine Fisheries Commission — Mathisen was a member and a player; a doer, when others didn't.

As for fighting environmental battles, Mathisen has been unbowed, unapologetic and unrelenting. He takes no prisoners. One victory he shared in — saving Petersburg Creek — may be his biggest contribution of all.

Somewhere toward the end, in the way of most obits, he will be noted as the father of three incredible daughters and the grandfather of six — most of them Alaskans, all of them good citizens.

Missing from his obituary will likely be his calling hours. Gone, too, will be the color, the flesh and blood, the vinegar, mischief, fun, friends, and attitude that are Andy Mathisen.

Andy Mathisen

I met Mathisen, his motel, Petersburg, and Alaska, all in the same day. I think it was in the mid-'70s. All but the motel left a lasting impression. He was on his own hook by then, a single dad in the prime of career number three; a motel owner, commercial salmon smoker, and a sports fishing guide, dapperly dressed in Orvis fashion with a rakish Stetson adorned by a tied fly.

In a town of slimy baseball-capped fishermen splattered with gurry, blood and scales, Mathisen stood out in more ways than one. Brooms in the mast didn't measure his success. There was no sweat on his brow and he gave the impression he was on easy street. What pressures there were to putting guests in his rooms, a fly on the water, and a fish in his customer's creel, he didn't let on — all the more, one suspects, to create that air of confidence and imminent success so vital

Andrew Mathisen cont'd

to customer and clients alike.

He had a fundamentally different view of fish than the town he lived in. In a society of the hook, net, and purse men who loved catching fish, Mathisen actually enjoyed fish for being themselves. He had scales and gurry, boats and boatloads of fish behind him. That gave him standing, even though he didn't have to keep the fish he caught anymore. But when he caught them and kept them, he treated them like the gourmet food they were — a rather obvious point often ignored, he thought, by commercial fishermen and processors who did everything but.

In a town of Norwegians and Lutherans, who valued sweat-on-your-brow hard work and frowned on ostentation, Mathisen's leisurely looking pursuit was a novel kind of work. His nonconformity was apparent. So, too, were his devil-may-care attitude — and his congenital contempt for the greed, hypocrisy, and lack of imagination he said contaminated the commercial procuring and purveying of fish. Having already succeeded in fishing and insurance, often being one, he didn't suffer fools gladly.

Needless to say, these traits contributed to a certain bad-boy reputation, which had the effect of bringing out more mischief. Like Groucho Marx, he lived by the adage, "I'd never join a country club that would think of having me as a member."

He loved all wildlife and wilderness, fine food, women, homegrown strawberries, new potatoes, and a pipe, with a sensitivity that suggested Mediterranean genes obtained by a long-ago Viking raider. Fun loving, free-spirited and flouting convention, he played pied piper to a collection of greenies, newcomers, and young men and women, who all collected around him and his house thinking, "This guy pushing 50 is the cat's meow."

Andy Mathisen

Now that he and I are so much older, I think of the many lessons I learned and the maxims he passed on. "Liars going first generally get the worst of it," and "Not to let schooling interfere with one's education, so you better top it up, Davey."

But, you couldn't make this up. I swear.

Writing on photo: On the Great Glacier, Stikine River near Wrangell, Alaska June 21, 1914, J.E. Worden

Tourists on the glacier
June 21, 1914
Photo by J.E. Worden
Alaska State Library
Core: Stikine River-3

Alexander and Anna McGilton

By Ralph Guthrie

Grandma Anna McGilton was born in Wrangell. Her maiden name was Spooner. She had two sisters and a brother. My mother didn't have any history of the sisters, but the brother was named Jim Hanson.

Anna was taught, like Tillie Paul, a more modern way of marriage. I believe, in the 1880s, at age 13, she was to be betrothed to an older Native man, but she chose to marry a Norwegian named Peter Hanson.

Henry, Richard, John, Albert, Katherine, and Bessie were born of this marriage. Peter and my grandmother moved to Skagway during the gold rush years. She worked as a cleaning lady for a hotel and Peter was a customs agent for a while.

Peter became enamored with the gold rush and went to Dawson. While he was gone, a landslide at Dawson killed a number of miners, and Grandma thought he had perished in this slide.

A year or so later, Peter came back to Skagway where they had a tearful reunion.

Peter was now a miner. They went to Juneau where he worked up a stake, so he could prospect. Grandma worked as a cleaning lady there. When she had free time, she would paddle in a native canoe over to the Taku village to visit with her brother, Jim.

Once a storm came up and she was almost lost, with all of her children. She managed to make the beach. After that, though, Peter wouldn't let her paddle to Taku again.

Grandma told me that she worked at both the Taku Harbor and the Gambier Bay canneries. She also cooked at Heddy Camp mine on Woewodski Island, while Peter was prospecting or working for a stake. They eventually moved back to Wrangell where Peter prospected for a while. Then he was off again to a major goldfield. Peter was gone for seven years without sending even a note to my grandmother. Times were hard for her, trying to raise so many children by herself.

She eventually met Alexander McGilton, who was a crab fisherman and a troller. He had left an Ohio potato farm and started fishing crab out of Everett, Washington, before moving to Wrangell. There he met Anna Hanson.

He and Anna moved to Grief Island and started a fur farm. Fred, Freeman and my mother, Margaret, were their children.

Alexander, my grandfather, loved to farm. He raised anything that would grow in the soil of Duncan Canal and Mitkof Island. My grandparents eventually moved to what is now known as Papke's Landing.

Gramps started fishing again, much to my grandmother's dismay. During the Depression, he fished and sold his catch door-to-door. He also cut firewood for the businesses of Petersburg.

The Bank of Petersburg had possession of a small sawmill that Charley West had built. The bank offered my grandfather a chance to buy it; he took the chance and purchased it.

This old mill had a beautiful view and a nice garden that Gramps and Gram kept up. For us children, it was a wonderful place to play.

Gramps fished crab and pioneered much new fishing ground. He seined and halibut fished. My brother, Victor, started learning the trade from him. When I was young, Gram would help Gramps work on the seine.

For many years, he fished the *Chum*, a boat that he built. He also had a small Bristol Bay hull, called the *Duncan*, that he used awhile for crab.

Alexander and Anna McGilton cont'd

By Carol Enge, as told by Margaret McGilton Durbin

Alexander McGilton was born in southeast Ohio of Scotch-Irish ancestry. In his early days, he was in the Army and was serving on guard duty in San Francisco during the earthquake. He moved to the Puget Sound area, where he was a woodcutter. He then moved north to Alaska.

By 1915, he was in Wrangell, Alaska, where he worked in the sawmill, fished, and trapped. He met and married Anna Spooner.

Anna is well remembered for the beautiful Indian moccasins she made. In those early days, many settlers were transient, moving to find work.

Alex and Annie had two children, Fred and Margaret.

Fred was born in 1914. He was a boat builder and an outdoorsman all his life, trapping, fishing and hunting. He was a commercial troller with his boats the F/V *Rainbow* and F/V *Peggy*. In 1950, he married Willie Brooks.

Willie Brooks had come to Alaska in 1938 with a husband and two daughters, Jean and Doris. In the early '40s, Willie cooked on a Stikine riverboat that hauled heavy supplies to Telegraph Creek for an airport project. The war in 1941 brought blackouts to rural Alaskan communities and orders to leave. By that time, Willie was divorced. She took her daughters to Seattle where she worked at Boeing Aircraft.

Willie always thought of Alaska as home. As soon as the war over, she returned. This time she came to Petersburg, where she met Fred McGilton. She said he was the sweetest, most wonderful man in the world.

Together they had many moose hunting trips. She remembers shooting two bull moose at Half Moon Slough without getting out of sight of the wanigan.

She was crushed when Fred died the day before Thanksgiving 1963. He had gone out on the F/V *Peggy* to drop anchors for his father's boat at Blind Slough. He had apparently trapped a wolf and had packed it halfway down the beach.

Searchers later found the wolf, but not Fred's body. The skiff from the *Peggy* was spotted circling by someone aboard the state ferry *Malaspina*. Despite a long search, Fred's body was never found.

Willie had been a professional seamstress and continued to sew for family and friends. She was an avid berry picker and knew all the best nagoonberry patches. Willie died on Christmas Day 1992.

Unidentified family

Louis and Marie Miller

By Don Nelson

Lars Ivar Myklebust was born in Valldal, Norway, in Storfjorden, on June 9, 1861. He immigrated to the United States when he was 18 years old, settling in Minneapolis, Minnesota. He changed his name to Louis Miller.

Louis moved to Seattle right after the city's Great Fire of 1889.

Marie Sunde arrived in Seattle in 1889 from Norway, along with her four older brothers. She was 15 years old. Marie was born in Sandefjord in southern Norway, on January 9, 1874. Her father was an Antarctic whaler.

The Sunde brothers quickly established themselves in Seattle as leading civic and business leaders.

They established the waterfront firm of Sunde & D'Evers, a fishing supply store that catered mostly to the halibut fleet. Carl Sunde was the manager, Ingward was grocery manager, and Hans was in charge of the sail-making department.

Julius Sunde was a founder and operator of Seattle's Norwegian-language newspaper, *Washington Posten*. He later moved to Petersburg and at one time operated a card room on Main Street.

Carl Sunde was also a founder and leader of the Seattle Singers Association, which traveled extensively putting on concerts.

Louis Miller and Marie Sunde were married May 11, 1894. Three children were born in Seattle, however, one died from food poisoning at age two.

In the spring of 1898, Louis Miller headed for the Klondike to find gold, but was unsuccessful.

After his Klondike experiences, he signed up with Peter Buschmann, who was active in establishing fish plants in Southeast Alaska.

In the spring of 1900, Louis was sent to Taku Harbor, where Buschmann had a salmon mild cure station, to work as a carpenter. Next he was given the job of building a salmon hatchery in Basket Bay on Chichagof Island.

The summer of 1901 found Louis Miller at Buschmann's cannery in Petersburg, building seine skiffs. Upon returning to Seattle that winter, it was decided that the family would move to Petersburg.

On May 19, 1902, they left Seattle on the steamer *Dolphin*, along with the Pete Norberg family. At the time, their son Dick was 7, and daughter Edna was 3.

Marie and Louis Miller

Louis built a cabin on the site of the current Tides Inn, at the corner of First and Dolphin.

At that time, the Rasmus Enges were living across the Narrows, so they didn't see them too often. In fine weather, on Sundays they would row across and visit with them.

Also that spring, the Peter Jorgensons arrived in town. They had just been married.

In the summer of 1902, there were five white families in Petersburg: the Enges, the Norbergs, the Millers, the Jorgensons and the Per Ness family.

After the 1902 canning season, when most of the crew were headed back to Puget Sound, Louis Miller was offered a job constructing a store building for the cannery. It was decided the family would remain in Petersburg that winter.

This building was used as the cannery company store until The Trading Union was formed in 1920. The store was then sold to The Trading Union by the Petersburg Packing Company. The building still stands at the corner of Dolphin and Main Street. It is owned and used by Dr. D.A. Coon.

Louis and Marie Miller cont'd

That winter the only residents in town were the Miller family, Mr. and Mrs. MacFarland and their 1-year-old daughter, Mr. and Mrs. Per Ness and 1-year-old son Leif, and Dr. and Mrs. Watkins and their 3-year-old boy.

The Jorgensons lived across the Narrows. The Enges and Norberg families had moved to Seattle for the winter.

Marie Miller was caring for young Leif Ness when his brother, Bjarne, was born on New Year's Day morning 1903. Attended by Dr. Watkins, Bjarne was the first white child born in Petersburg.

Early in 1903, word was received the cannery would not operate that year. The Miller family moved to Juneau. In Juneau, Louis and Marie had two more children: Louis "Duke" in 1903 and Frances in 1906.

With the cannery again starting up in 1906, Louis returned to Petersburg. In April of 1907, the rest of the family followed.

That year, Louis constructed a small house on the south side of Hammer Slough to live in until the family home could be built. This house, at 12 Hammer Slough Street, is still the home of Louis and Marie's youngest daughter, Frances.

During these early years in Petersburg, Marie Miller was a leader in the social life of town. She was always on the program for skits and plays at the Fishermen's Home. She had a wonderful memory and could recite one poem after another.

Marie was very popular and loved to dance. She never missed a Saturday night at the Sons of Norway Hall. She also loved music and would often wind up the great big Victrola and play her favorite records.

Between 1907 and 1912, Louis Miller built seven company houses for cannery personnel. These were at 200 Second Street, 202 Second Street, 302 Second Street, 103 Excel Street, 105 Excel Street, 107 Excel Street, and the house on the northeast corner of Dolphin and First streets. Most of these houses are still standing and in use.

Also during this time, he built a large two-story home on the corner of what is now Excel and First streets. Built for Pete Jorgenson, Louis charged $400. The telephone company now occupies this site.

In 1908, he built the three-story residence of Charles Smith, which the city later purchased for use as a hospital.

Another structure that went up in this period, by the hands of Louis Miller, was the Native school, located where the Clausen Memorial Museum is now, at Second and Fram streets.

Other structures put up by Louis were Cal Barkdall's Petersburg Hotel, on the southeast corner of First and Dolphin, and the city's first powerhouse in Hogue Alley on Hammer Slough. He was also in charge of a crew that started construction of the Sons of Norway Hall.

When the Petersburg Fire Department was organized in November of 1910, G.H. Peterson was appointed as first fire chief, After a few days he decided against serving. Louis, another organizer of the department, was appointed. Louis is credited with being Petersburg's first fire chief.

Louis had a floating boathouse in the slough that he used to haul boats in for repairs. Louis and his son Dick were also involved with beach seining.

In the summer of 1910, they, along with Pete Lee and 7-year-old Duke, caught 150,000 humpies in the bight across from Hoagie's Hole in Petersburg Creek.

In Louis' twilight years, his life was devoted to visiting and reliving the old days with his many pioneer friends. Much time was spent walking to town and attending movies with his ever-increasing flock of grandchildren.

He was kept busy building rowboats and gas boats for the kids, and much time was spent up Petersburg Creek at the family cabin.

Marie adapted well from the refined young lady of city life on Seattle's Queen Anne Hill to a struggling wife and mother in the primitive environment of early Petersburg. Finally, in her later years, she enjoyed a comfortable and satisfying life in her home.

Louis Miller died on March 7, 1955. He was nearly 94 years old. Marie followed him on March 19, 1957, at the age 83.

Richard and Verne Miller

By Don Nelson

Richard Ingmar Miller was born on November 28, 1894 to Norwegian immigrants, Louis and Marie Miller, at their home on Seattle's Dexter Avenue. His father was a fireman with the Seattle Fire Department at the time. His mother was a member of the pioneer Sunde family of Queen Anne Hill.

Dick arrived in Petersburg in May of 1902, with his parents and younger sister, Edna. His father was now a carpenter for Peter Buschmann.

At the end of the 1903 canning season, the family moved to Juneau where Dick attended four years of grade school.

When Dick was 12 years old, the family, which now included a brother and another sister, moved back to Petersburg. Dick and his sister Edna attended school at the cannery mess hall for one year. They next attended school at the telegraph office, which was at what is now Fourth and Excel streets. In 1909, the family sent Dick to Seattle for further schooling. He returned to Petersburg in 1910.

In the summer of 1910, Dick and his father caught 150,000 humpies in Petersburg Creek. They received one half of a cent for each fish.

Since Louis Miller was a carpenter and erecting houses at a furious rate, much of young Dick's time was spent assisting his father. One of the structures the two built was the Petersburg Hotel for Cal Barkdall. It was located on the southeastern corner of First and Dolphin streets.

The next year, Dick went to Security Bay with old Bill Stafford aboard the *Annie*. They hand trolled for king salmon, which they split and salted in tierces on board the boat. In the spring of 1912, they moved their operation to Affleck Canal in Sumner Strait on the *Gina*. Later they proceeded to Forrester Island on the west coast, where Dick hand trolled for red kings, for a 25 cents each.

For the next five years, he beached seined and gillnetted on the Stikine River. In 1918, he went into the U.S. Army at Chilkoot Barracks in Haines. He contracted the flu there and spent the rest of his army service at Fort Lewis in Washington.

Upon Dick's return to Petersburg in 1919, he and his father rebuilt the combination boat *Thora*. Dick fished her as a purse seiner and beam trawler for shrimp. In 1925, he ran the *Louise S* for Earl Ohmer, while his younger brother, Duke, took over the *Thora*. Also in 1925, Dick ran the *Laddie* as a salmon tender for the Petersburg Packing Company.

He left the fishing industry in 1926, when he was appointed wharfinger for The Trading Union's dock. He was also the agent for Northland Transportation Company. Dick ran the dock for 40 years.

In May of 1945, he entered into a partnership with his brother, Duke, to form the Public Dock Company. They leased the northern half of the dock and warehouse from The Trading Union.

Dick and Duke also served as agents for the Railway Express Agency, Pacific Fruit and Produce Company, and they had the beer and Coca Cola distributorship for Juneau Cold Storage Company. They also sold lumber products and propane gas from the Public Dock.

With the 1949 demise of the Northland Transportation Company, the Public Dock became agent for the Alaska Steamship Company. (The Alaska Steamship Company was bought out by Foss Tug and Barge in the late 1960s. The company is now known as Alaska Marine Lines.)

During his long tenure with Northland Transportation and the Alaska Steamship Company, Dick Miller was well known up and down the coast and in maritime circles.

In 1937, Dick married Verne Hannah in Petersburg.

Verne was born July 20, 1902, in Ketchikan. Her father, John Hannah, had followed the mining camps in the old West in the latter part of the 19th century. He ended up in Ketchikan and became a mariner.

Verne lost her father when she was a young girl. Her mother, Clara Hannah, had been born in London, England. She immigrated first to California and then to Sitka, where she was employed as a domestic. As a young girl, Verne and her mother lived in Treadwell (Douglas), Juneau, Tenakee, Katalla and Hyder.

Verne first arrived in Petersburg in 1934, teaching school with teachers Impi Aalto and Ann Eide (who married Knut Thompson).

Her mother, Clara Hannah, was the Petersburg city librarian in the late 1930s and 1940s.

Richard and Verne Miller cont'd

Dick was an avid outdoorsman. He enjoyed trout fishing and deer and duck hunting. He had an 18-foot round-bottom skiff with a 9.8 hp Johnson outboard that he used on trout fishing trips to the Salt Chuck, Castle River, and up the Stikine River. His companion was usually Sam Gauffin.

Dick had climbed just about every hill and mountain in the Petersburg area, usually returning with a buck on his back. In later years, he owned *Drake III*, a small yacht that was used for many family outings. For several years, he also had the school boat contract for West Petersburg.

Dick was such a kind-hearted and generous individual. He never drank or smoked, except in his later years, when he usually had a pipe stuck in his mouth. He was a true gentleman.

During the 1950s and 1960s, Dick served as president and secretary for the Petersburg Cold Storage Company. He was a member of the American Legion, the Pioneers of Alaska, the Sons of Norway, and the Masonic Lodge.

If he felt sorry for someone, many a delinquent freight bill was forgiven or a travel ticket on a steamer subsidized. He was often pulled from the comfort of his home or interrupted by a call to help someone unload items from their boats with the dock winch.

In 1938, Dick built a home on what is now Balder Street, across from the school. Here he and Verne raised their two children. Richard Kent was born in 1941. Mary Carolyn "Bonnie" arrived in 1943. Dick also built a small house next door for Verne's mother.

By 1965, Dick had had enough of serving the public and being under pressure from his transportation and freight duties, and he retired. At that time, he turned the dock over to Duke.

In 1966, Dick and Verne Miller left Petersburg to reside in Gig Harbor, Washington, where they stayed until the fall of 1982. At that time, they moved into the Martha and Mary Nursing Home in Poulsbo.

Verne died in 1985 and Dick lingered until July 31, 1990. He was 96. Both are interred in Gig Harbor.

Kent currently lives in Ketchikan, where he has a civic consulting firm. Bonnie died in Anchorage in 1972. Dick and Verne had five grandchildren.

Public Dock, 1946

Louis "Duke" and Annea Miller

By Sylvia Ewing

Louis C. "Duke" Miller was born in Juneau on August 27, 1903, to Norwegian immigrant parents Louis and Marie Miller.

His parents first arrived in Petersburg in May of 1902. Duke's father was a carpenter, who had worked for Peter Buschmann helping build the Petersburg Packing Company. The family returned to Petersburg from Juneau in 1907.

Duke got his nickname after performing in an eighth grade school play. His character was a duke in England and a classmate began calling him by that name. Since that time, he was known as "Duke."

After only one year in high school, he quit to go to work. He gillnetted with his brother, Dick, on the Stikine, and also did some seining and shrimping.

In 1924, he took the job of engineer for the town's diesel generator plant. He had the night shift, and control of the town's three streetlights.

After the movie was over at the local movie theater, and after checking to see if any steamships were at the dock, he would blink the lights three times. The hospital then had a half hour to let him know if they needed power, before he turned the generators completely off for the rest of the night.

In 1925, he was hired as engineer of the *Marion*, a tender for the Petersburg Packing Company. Eventually he became the skipper for many Pacific American Fisheries boats, including the *Marian*, the *Orient*, the *Karluk*, and the *Virginia E*.

In 1945, he joined his brother, Dick, and operated the Public Dock, which they leased from The Trading Union. Duke and Dick were agents for the Northland Transportation Company and the Alaska Steamship Company.

Duke later became manager of the terminal at Scow Bay after Foss Tug and Barge took over for Alaska Steamship. He retired from Foss in 1972.

Duke married Annea Mathisen in 1933.

"Nee" was the daughter of another pioneer Petersburg family, Andrew and Anne Theodora Mathisen, who emigrated from Norway. At age 9, Nee arrived in Petersburg in 1916 from Harstad, Norway.

Duke and Nee Miller had two daughters, Mary Ann and Sylvia.

In 1959, Mary Ann married Jack Noble in California. They had three children: Karen, Pam and Steven, and six grandchildren. In 1971, Sylvia married Frank Ewing in Petersburg. She has a stepson, Lynn, and granddaughter, Sonja.

Following Annea's death, Duke married Effie Myers in 1959. Duke and Effie lived in Petersburg until 1972. They moved to Washington State because of Effie's health.

After Effie's death in 1988, Duke returned to Petersburg. He lived at Mountain View Manor and, later, Petersburg Medical Center's extended care facility.

Duke was an active member of the local Elks Lodge and was an Exalted Ruler. For many years, he was a member of the Pioneers of Alaska and the Petersburg Volunteer Fire Department.

Duke Miller died November 30, 2003.

Louis "Duke" Miller

Mjorud Family

Adapted from Herb Mjorud's Your Authority to Believe

John Mjorud came to the United States from his native Norway. Hearing about San Francisco and its gold, he went there to seek his fortune.

His adventurous spirit led him to board a steamer bound for Kodiak, Alaska. There he found his place as a commercial fisherman. While in Kodiak, he panned enough gold to make a wedding ring for Magna Melhy, the girl he left behind.

John returned to Norway. He and Magna married, but the thrill of his adventures in America called him back.

Determined to be an Alaskan fisherman, he contracted to have a 36-foot salmon troller built. To cut costs, he helped in the construction. Naming the troller *Magna*, he brought his family aboard and they set out for Alaska, taking eight days to reach Ketchikan.

By this time, there were four children: Hedvik, Herb, Sarah and Jane.

The Mjorud family eventually came to Petersburg in March of 1916, having heard that it was a good place to raise children. Most of the people were recent Norwegian immigrants, and John thought Magna would be happy there.

Coming into the docks, they were met by Anna Enge. She asked if they had a place to stay. Hearing a negative answer, Anna invited them to her home on Sing Lee Alley.

Herb was 10 when his father first took him on his fishing boat. He learned to be a deckhand and cook. During the school year, he was active in sports. His senior year of high school, he was a member of the 1929 basketball team that won the All-Alaska Championship. Other members of the team were Joe Kahklen, Louie McDonald, Leo Ness, Harold Runstad and Swede Wasvik.

Herb attended the University of Washington in Seattle and was a member of the rowing team for four years. He was captain when his team won the 1933 National Championship. Each summer brought him back into commercial fishing, which made him financially independent.

It was while fishing out at Port Alexander that he met and married Gundhild Anderson.

Gundhild had come from Norway at the age of 15, one of eight children. She had all the Norwegian graces of hospitality and homemaking.

Gundhild and Herb had two sons. Together they enjoyed outdoor activities, such as hiking, mountain climbing and picnics.

After their marriage, Gundhild continued to work as a clerk.

Herb fished during the summers and enrolled in the University of Washington law school. He purchased a half-interest in a large troller, the *Ellie IV*. This paid his way through law school and provided funds while he established himself as an attorney. He graduated in 1938 with honors.

1929 Alaska State Basketball Champions, from left: Frank Gordon, Joseph Kahklen, Harold Runstad, Herb Mjorud (captain), Aubrey Shaquanie, Arnold Wasvick and Lewis McDonald.

Shortly after completing law school, Herb's sister Jane converted him to Christianity. In order to better understand the Bible, Herb attended the Lutheran Bible Institute.

He and Gundhild became active in the Phinney Ridge Lutheran Church. Wanting to study for the ministry, they moved to St. Paul, Minnesota where Herb entered Luther Theological Seminary.

One of Herb's early ministries was Central Lutheran Church in Anchorage, Alaska. The church called him to be an evangelist, but after a difference in interpreting the Bible, he formed the Mjorud Evangelic Association.

Herb passed away in Minneapolis, Minnesota.

John and Asbjorg Molver

By Laurence and Twila Molver

Asbjorg Husby was born October 2, 1881, in Kristensund, Norway. She came to America (Portland, Oregon) in about 1908, via Montreal, Canada. She worked as a domestic for a Portland area doctor.

In 1910, she left Portland and came to Petersburg to work in a restaurant located in the Cornelius Building, owned by a friend of her mother's, a Mrs. DeRosa. A fire gutted the building later that year. The restaurant was moved to a new building built in Sing Lee Alley, across from the Enge residence.

The building had two floors with the restaurant on the first floor. Asbjorg was the cook, and her younger sister, Magnhild, was the baker. They lived in an apartment on the second floor. At this time, Asbjorg bought the restaurant from Mrs. DeRosa.

Johan Lauritzen (John Molver) was born May 25, 1880, in Langevag, Aalesund, Norway.

He went to night school in New York after arriving in the United States. He then joined the U.S. Army Transport Service and served in the Spanish-American War on the SS *McPherson*.

A lad of 18, he had enlisted using his given name, Johan Lauritzen.

After he was mustered out of the service, he changed his name from Johan Lauritzen to John Molver.

He arrived in Nome, Alaska, in the late 1890s, as ship's carpenter on the *City of Seattle* steamer. He became winch operator on the vessel, unloading freight from the boat to the barge, which could traverse the mud flats.

John Molver

After leaving Nome, John moved south to Petersburg, and settled down in 1904. In 1910, he built the boat *Olga*, with the help of his younger brother, Maurius. The boat was named after their sister, who still lived in Norway. Maurius left Petersburg, but returned in 1913, aboard his newly acquired 70-foot schooner, the *Seymour*.

On January 31, 1912, Asbjorg Husby and John Molver were married in Wrangell, because Petersburg had no magistrate at that time.

Asbjorg had gone to Wrangell on the steamer, and John was to follow in the *Olga*. On the way through Dry Strait, the *Olga* got stuck on a sandbar.

Since John was alone on the boat, he had no choice but to get off the boat, lift it off the bar with sheer strength, and shove it back into the water.

Asbjorg Molver

The boat immediately started moving because the motor was still in gear and running. He had left the gear engaged to help get the boat off the bar.

John held on and was dragged through the water behind the boat, wondering if he was going to get to the wedding after all. He managed to drag himself along the side of the boat, grab a fender, and climb back on board.

After the wedding, they returned to Petersburg on the *Olga*, taking the route through Wrangell Narrows, well away from Dry Strait.

John and Asbjorg began married life in a little house near the Lester Elkins' home. They later bought the Swenson house next to Hjalmer Martinsen's house.

Their first child, Robert, was born in 1913. When he was 2 years old, John and Asbjorg returned to Norway to visit family and to introduce Robert. While in Norway, the European war situation became much more dangerous, and John felt that they shouldn't attempt the return to Petersburg.

While in Norway, daughter Randi (pronounced "Rondi") was born in January of 1917. After the war, the family returned to America. Before returning, John sold some of his family farm property in Norway to pay passage and for getting their lives back together

John and Asbjorg Molver cont'd

after the war years. That money bought a new house upon their return to Petersburg, as well as a workboat, the *Unimak*.

Their third child, Laurence, was born December of 1923 in Petersburg. Their oldest child, Robert, died in February 1924, during surgery in Seattle.

The *Unimak* was sold in 1927. The proceeds were applied as down payment on the *Excel*, a larger and newer boat, which John rigged for longlining halibut.

Throughout World War II, the U.S. Navy took the boat from John Molver, paying him only $10 per day. The *Excel* was used as a patrol boat between Cape Ommaney and Yakutat. John had to sell the *Excel* after the war, because the money from the Navy did not cover the amount due on the contract.

John sold some more of his Norway farm property and, in 1948, bought the *Baltic*, in partnership with son Laurence. The boat was fished in partnership for a year. After John retired, Laurence continued to fish the *Baltic* for eight more years.

John Molver passed away in 1957, following complications after surgery.

This photo was taken in about 1927 from the top floor of the Petersburg school. The entire student body, and their teachers cleaned up the grounds in front of the school to create a functional play area. Construction of the school had been completed in 1923. Four years later, the grounds still had leftover building materials lying around, as well as slash remains from clearing the property.

Laurence and Twila Molver

By Laurence and Twila Molver

Laurence Robert Molver was born in Petersburg, on December 21, 1923, the third child of John and Asbjorg Molver.

Laurence was a Boy Scout. In high school, he was the editor of the school yearbook, the *Flood Tide*. He was the valedictorian of his graduating class and, for a time, was manager of the basketball team, the Petersburg Vikings.

In his sophomore year, Laurence and Erling Jensen were walking on the Hammer Slough bridge, when Erling pointed out a young boy in a skiff. The boy had dropped his oar. As he stretched out to retrieve it, he fell out of his boat. The boy was struggling to keep afloat. Laurence went into the water and rescued him. He never learned his name.

During his high school years, Laurence fished with his father, learning all the fishing tricks and skills from the best of the older Norwegian fishermen.

In September of 1943, Laurence joined the U.S. Merchant Marine in Prince Rupert. He sailed in Alaska for one and one half years, as first mate on the *Junaluska* and the *Commonwealth*, bringing supplies to those working on the Alaska Highway.

Beginning in February of 1946, at the age of 22, he sailed around the world as quartermaster on the oil tanker SS *Carlsbad*. His one and a half years of travel took him from the Suez Canal to the Persian Gulf (Bahrain Island), to Ceylon, Singapore, and through the Panama Canal.

Laurence has many interesting stories of his sailing experiences and adventures. He could navigate by the stars. His navigation skills were well recognized by his shipmates throughout his maritime career.

In 1950, Laurence met Twila Jean Ball, who was visiting her aunt, Helen Fenn, in Petersburg.

Twila was born on October 28, 1927, to Dave and Emily (Elkins) Ball, in Dolores, Colorado. She first came to Petersburg with her parents in 1940, at the age of 12. She spent three months visiting her grandparents, Lewis and Anna Elkins, who were living at Beecher's Pass in Wrangell Narrows. She also visited the families of her uncle, Lester Elkins, and her aunt, Helen (Elkins) Fenn.

In 1950, Twila returned to Petersburg to stay with her Aunt Helen. She worked that first summer in the telephone office, operating a 1902 model switchboard.

Helen took Twila to the Elks Club that summer. While she was playing a slot machine, Laurence introduced himself and asked her to dance.

They were married the following January, in 1951, at the home of Cliff and Helen.

Laurence and Twila first lived in a small home in Skylark City, an area south of downtown Petersburg. They contracted with Ralph Susort to build them a house next to the home of Laurence's parents.

Laurence owned the halibut boat *Baltic*. He and his father ran it together for the first year. Laurence skippered it with a crew of five after that. Twila cooked on the *Baltic* for the first two years of their marriage, while they packed salmon for local canneries.

They had two daughters: Lauren Jean, born March of 1953, and Maura Rae, born March of 1956.

Twila then stayed home and cared for the children, while Laurence fished. She enjoyed visiting with the other women in the neighborhood, befriending young mothers and the elderly alike. There was lots clam digging and berry picking to be done, as well as trips to the local swimming holes in the summer and skating in the winter.

Her house became the home to a menagerie of animals. Over the years, their pets included many cats, a dog, rabbits, a rat, mice, chameleons, turtles, budgies, wild birds, and hogs. And, if her children had had their way, there would have been a horse and a monkey!

Laurence sold the *Baltic* in 1957, but he continued to fish on other boats until 1963. He then went to work on the new Alaska State Ferry, the *Matanuska*, as an able-bodied seaman. After Laurence began this job, Twila would greet people at the ferry terminal, frequently taking them on impromptu tours of the town, including the local canneries. Her friendliness was recognized, and she was awarded the title, "One Woman Chamber of Commerce."

In 1968, the family moved to Ketchikan to accommodate the requirements of the ferry's weekly change of crew schedule, but they have maintained their close friendships with many Petersburg residents.

Laurence retired from the ferry system in 1986. He remembers his fishing and sailing days well, and he enjoys sharing the stories of those days.

George "Bud" and Alice Mortensen

By Colleen Mortensen Nicholson

His name was George Stringham Mortensen, but he was known to all as "Bud." He and his family lived in Petersburg since 1944. Bud's temporal life came to a close in 1964, but his 20 years in Alaska gave him adventure and pleasure that he often expressed to his family with wonder and gratitude.

His working life was spent mostly indoors as cook and owner of different restaurants for many years in southwest Montana. During the depression years, this was a very difficult business to be in, yielding long hours and short return. The only thing it had going for it was that his family was always fed and clothed.

In 1940, the threat of war loomed and defense work began in earnest. This caused Bud to move with his wife, Alice, and children — Colleen, Buddy and Ruthie — to the West Coast, finally settling in Bremerton, Washington.

Bud came to Petersburg in the spring of 1943 to work for Pacific American Fisheries. Arriving in April, his job was to cook for the crew on, first, the pile driver and, then, the rigging scow, as they set up the fish traps operated by that cannery. After the season opened, he was cook on the tender *Redoma*. As a man who had started life in southern Idaho and southwestern Montana, he soon realized that life on the water was just what he had been searching for.

This change in his life came about in an unusual way. It definitely surprised his family. On a March day of that year, Bud had business in Seattle and decided to wander around the docks and floats of Lake Washington. He met a man who had time to chat. In the course of the conversation, he learned that a cook could find work in the fishing industry. The stranger gave him instructions for applying and encouraged him to "do it now." That man was Oscar Nicholson.

He returned to Bremerton and announced to his family that he had a job in Petersburg and would be leaving in a few weeks. Returning in the fall, he decreed that the next year they would all go and make that town their home. So began the migration of the Mortensen family to Petersburg.

May 24, 1944, was a rainy, gray day when the Mortensen family stepped off the *North Sea* to become residents of Alaska's Little Norway. Frances Robinson, Alice's sister-in-law, accompanied Alice and children. Alice's brother, Jerry Robinson, also worked for PAF.

Alice Gayle Robinson Mortensen was born in Lima, Montana, and her first 18 years were spent there. Her courtship with Bud began when he came to Lima to cook at the Roundhouse for the Great Northern Railway. This was where the train engines were turned around for return trips, either east or west.

After their marriage, Alice's life followed the process of moving to Alaska. She liked living in Petersburg from the very beginning. She found it to be a wonderful place to raise the family, especially in contrast to the congestion and the overcrowding of life in Bremerton.

During the first few years, Bud worked in restaurants and meat markets in the winter, and cooked on various boats during the fishing season.

Alice worked as part-time cook at The Pastime Café the first summer. By fall, she had full-time employment at the Lillian Shop. This store was a treasure trove to our small town. It provided the clothing needs of women, children and home seamstresses, as well as offering a fine assortment of linens for the home. Working there was pleasant for Alice; it was a sure way to make the acquaintance of local residents.

For two years in the early '50s, Bud and Ernie Haugen were partners in The Pastime Café, where both cooked. But the call of fishing wasn't finished with Bud.

By 1953, he was on the Akwe River, living in a tent, catching salmon in gillnets, operating skiffs, and delivering the catch to a cannery scow in Dry Bay. All supplies came from Yakutat, a small town located north of the camp.

At first, the fish were brought to Kayler-Dahl cannery in Petersburg, but later the Yakutat cannery became their buyer.

Bud's summers began in April and ended in October, when he returned to Petersburg and the social life he loved.

He was always available to work at local stores in the meat departments or in one of the restaurants. He was active in the Elks and Masons and especially enjoyed preparing chili or clam chowder for a crowd.

On the Akwe River, his adventures included hunting moose and protecting his gillnets from brown

George "Bud" and Alice Mortensen cont'd

bears. Bud and his brother Clint had a dream of how to augment their fishing season activities when things were slow.

They set up a sawmill, using a chainsaw arrangement, and logged the evergreens that grew around the site of their camp. By cutting enough lumber over a span of three years and by staying late in the fall, they built a large two-story cabin.

When an oil exploration crew left many bags of unused cement, they made forms and poured blocks to build a very large fireplace for the cabin. It was the start of their fall hunting parties and encounters with wildlife, which sparked the stories told and retold during winter visits with friends and family.

Bud's skill at meat cutting was a real asset when they extended their building efforts to include a large meat house. His former restaurant experience gave him the expertise to build a walk-in freezer powered by a gas generator.

The game taken by guests could now be cut up, boned, wrapped and frozen. This saved space and transportation costs for their clients. It also meant that the meat taken away was often restricted to steaks, because trophy heads were the real prizes. As a result, there were roasts and stew meat to spare, brought back to Petersburg and generously shared with family, neighbors and friends all over town.

Bud and Clint smoked all the king salmon they caught and canned the results. Wild strawberries were abundant on the sandy beaches around their camp. Gallons were picked each summer; the jam was canned for winter use at home. Their fall homecoming was eagerly awaited by many for the shared bounty their summer adventures produced.

When the Akwe River camp was established, Alice began her summer job as camp cook. She was hostess to the many people who came to stay — or to just stop by in their small planes on the way to other destinations. Her summers began in early June and didn't end until late September.

Life at camp was busy, but pleasant. A gas generator provided electricity for lights and washing clothes and a good well provided potable water. There was a large wood-burning cook stove that provided heat and the means for cooking for a large group.

Many local friends made fall hunting trips to the Akwe camp for assured game and good fellowship. While it wasn't Petersburg, it always had a Petersburg flavor. Local folks knew the camp on the Akwe well enough that it could be included in Petersburg's story. It was definitely an extension of life here.

Winter was the time to enjoy community life in Petersburg with family and friends. Alice's summers changed in 1963, when she decided it was time to stay in town. She found work at The Trading Union and continued to work there for 11 years.

During that time, she gained support from the store management to start a women's department. At the time, there was only one small retail store.

Alice started first with lingerie, and dresses and sweaters from the Jantzen line, and then added Catalina. It was very well received. In later years, the section expanded to a much larger part of the store. It was significant to local shoppers.

In retirement, Alice remained active in the women's activities in the Lutheran Church. Her apartment was the favorite stopping place for all her family and friends.

Through friendships made during her summers on the Akwe River, she was adopted into the Raven clan of the Tlingit Indians. Those friendships continued all her life.

Alice was on the committee for the funding, design, and construction of Mountain View Manor. She was on the board of the Senior Nutrition Program for several years.

Alice died in her sleep on February 2, 1989. She had been seemingly healthy and active right up to the end. That was just the way she would have planned it.

Unidentified gentlemen

Frederick and Edna Nelson

By Don Nelson

Petersburg had already evolved from a seasonal cannery settlement into a modern Alaskan city when Fred Nelson arrived on December 16, 1919. He had been lured north by his friend Ed Locken and the offer of a job with local businessman K.L. Steberg.

Fred immediately became involved in the many ventures of Steberg, which included real estate, insurance, the Pacific Steamship and Wells Fargo agencies, and the Standard Oil Company. He was also city clerk for a year.

This began 36 years of dedication to the development and growth of Petersburg. Fred was so proud of his new home that he dived in with both feet, helping promote and advance the town.

Frederick Nelson was born on May 5, 1893, to Nils and Marie Berg Nilsen, in Tromsø, Norway. His father was a shoemaker. As the oldest son in the family, he was in line to take over the family business. This was the custom in the old country, but Fred decided to leave home, immigrating to America at the age of 17.

Fred got a job piling lumber at a sawmill near Redding, California, making $1.25 for a ten-hour day. He remained at this job until he had enough money to take the train to Portland, Oregon, where he had an uncle.

Along with working at odd jobs, Fred took a business course at the YMCA. Upon his graduation in May of 1915, he began employment with the Union Pacific Railroad.

Fred then spent a year in France with the 31st Army Engineer Regiment in World War I.

He returned to Portland, in July of 1919, and worked as an office manager in a small sawmill. When Locken got a job at the Olaf Arness sawmill, he wrote Fred that Petersburg seemed to be an ideal place to put down his roots and start a career.

After working for K.L. Steberg for three years, Fred was temporarily assigned to Standard Oil in Juneau. In late 1924, Nelson returned to Petersburg to become manager of the local Standard Oil station. He now had a wife, Edna Marie (nee Miller). He managed the station for 30 years and was followed by Willie Rodenburg, Joe Kelly and Oscar Jones.

In addition to managing Standard Oil, Fred Nelson became active in other business and civic endeavors in the Petersburg of the 1920s.

Fred and Edna Nelson

He started the American Legion organization in 1920, and helped found the Masonic Lodge shortly after. Nelson was also active in the Eastern Star, Rotary Club, and Chamber of Commerce, in which he served several terms as president. In the 1920s, he also spent time on both the school and hospital boards.

Fred didn't enter local politics because of a Standard Oil policy. He was a common sight along Main Street, always dressed in a suit, necktie and Stetson hat, holding a cigarette in his fingers. He was usually whistling the latest tune.

In 1920, Fred helped organize The Trading Union. He served as a director and secretary in 1921 and 1922. In 1926, when it became apparent a facility to process, freeze and store fish products was needed in order to maintain a halibut fleet in Petersburg, several civic leaders started the Petersburg Cold Storage Company. Fred helped organize the corporation. He was on the board of directors and was secretary from the beginning until 1951.

In 1922, he became a director in the Bank of Petersburg and served as vice-president for 25 years.

Frederick and Edna Nelson cont'd

In July of 1950, Fred became president of the bank and held that position until the National Bank of Alaska acquired the Bank of Petersburg in 1972.

Fred Nelson retired from Standard Oil and the bank in 1955. Even though he moved to the warmer and drier climate of Southern California, he always kept abreast of the activities in Petersburg, retaining his pride and affection for the town.

Fred died December 19, 1987.

Edna Marie Miller was born October 24, 1898, to Norwegian immigrants, Louis and Marie Miller.

She was born in a house on the corner of Blanchard Street and Western Avenue in downtown Seattle. Her father was away at the Klondike gold rush when she arrived. Edna joined an older brother, Dick.

The family left Seattle on the steamer *Dolphin* on May 17, 1902, and four days later arrived in the small village of Petersburg. Dick and Edna, along with three younger children, were the only white kids in Petersburg in the winter of 1902-03.

In 1903, the family moved to Juneau. In April of 1907, when Edna was 8 years old, they returned to Petersburg. She attended the first school in Petersburg, held in the cannery mess hall.

As a young girl in Petersburg, her friends were Grace Linscott, whose father was manager of the Pacific Coast and Norway Packing Company sawmill; Helen Smith, whose father was manager of Harvey's Olympic Mine on Woewodski Island; Blanche O'Dell, who later married Dan Sutphen; and Luttie Pautske, whose dad was the local barber.

In 1914, at the age of 15, Edna had her first paying job — janitor and assistant to the teacher, Miss Carhart. Her first chore of the day was to start the fires in the three coal stoves. Then, she had to shovel snow before the kids arrived. From 9 a.m. to 3 p.m., she corrected papers.

After school, she took out the stove ashes and swept the floors, carried up the coal buckets for the next day, and split kindling. Edna also cleaned the blackboards and erasers, and scrubbed the "he and she two-seater," along with providing a fresh Sears Roebuck catalog for the outhouse. On Saturdays she scrubbed the floors of the school.

In September of 1915, she received her teacher's certificate from the governor's office. Required under a new territorial law, Edna qualified because of her time as a teacher's assistant.

In 1917, Edna attended Western Washington College in Bellingham and, by 1919, was ready to teach. From September 1919 to May 1922, she taught first grade in the school that was located on Third and Dolphin streets.

Some of her pupils during those years were Leo Ness, John Enge, Harold and John Holten, Leonard and Thelma Martens, Edgar Baggen, Lewis MacDonald, Gudolph Wikan, John and Oak Otness, and Mildred and Alma Cornstad.

Fred Nelson had met Edna when he first arrived in town. They were married July 14, 1924, in Juneau. Three sons were born to them: Frederick Louis "Bud" in 1925, Donald Richard in 1931, and Robert Marion in 1936. (*See Don Nelson story.*)

Bud graduated from high school in 1943 and received an appointment to the U.S. Naval Academy in Annapolis. He made the Navy his career, retiring in 1974 with the rank of captain.

Except for an occasional visit, he never returned to Petersburg. Bud died in 2000.

After graduating from Petersburg High School in 1954, Bob attended Oregon State University. After serving four years in the U.S. Army, he returned to Alaska and worked in Juneau and Anchorage. Bob was finance director for the City of Anchorage.

In 1998, Bob returned to Petersburg, where he lives six months every year. In the winter months, he lives in Palm Desert, California.

Edna maintained her household at the Standard Oil home. She managed many a big dinner and hospitality for people visiting and conducting business in Petersburg.

When she was a teenager, Edna joined the Daughters of Norway. She was a founder of the local Eastern Star organization and a charter member of the American Legion Auxiliary for 70 years, until she passed away.

In 1957, after Fred's retirement from Standard Oil, Edna and Fred moved to the San Diego area where she lived until his death. In 1988, she returned to Petersburg where she stayed with her son, Don and his wife.

Edna died on March 28, 1992.

Donald and Betty Nelson

By Don Nelson

Donald Richard Nelson was born in Petersburg on April 19, 1931, to Fred and Edna Nelson. He was delivered by Dr. Joseph O. Rude at the Petersburg General Hospital.

Don's father was manager of the local Standard Oil plant, so he grew up in the Standard house, located three quarters of a mile, south of town.

His grandparents, Louis and Marie Miller, were among the earliest settlers in Petersburg.

Don's house had great access to the beach, boating, and the wide-open spaces of muskeg and woods. All of this was taken advantage of by Don and his pals "out the road."

Many summer days were spent at the family cabin up Petersburg Creek, usually with a boyhood pal.

Bud, Don, mother Edna and Bob, 1937

As a young boy during World War II, he lived, like everyone else in Petersburg, a life focused on the war. With contingents of army MPs and the U.S. Coast Guard guarding the oil stations and docks, many friendly relationships were made with the troops. As a boy of 10, Don helped man the airplane spotter facility on the gymnasium roof, looking for aircraft activity.

Along with chums Leif Wikan and Palmer Odegaard, Don combed the beaches and empty warehouses for scrap rubber to be used in the war effort. They found upwards of 600 pounds, for which they received one cent per pound.

Don was baptized into the Petersburg Lutheran Church and, in 1945, was confirmed under Reverend Thomas Knudson. He attended Petersburg public schools after a great start with the remarkable first grade teacher, Impi Aalto. Don sailed thru grade school with average grades.

He was assistant manager for the Vikings basketball team in 1947 and manager in 1949. In those days, travel to other towns for games was done on fishing boats. The team's boat was the flagship of the fleet, the *Symphony*, with Gordon Jensen as skipper.

Don's first job was sweeping and cleaning the 550-seat Coliseum Theater for Dave and Caroline Westerberg. In 1943, he started working for his uncle Dick Miller at the Public Dock.

At that time, the Public Dock was agent for Northland Transportation Company, Railway Express Agency, and Pacific Fruit and Produce Company. After school and on Saturdays, Don toiled for 25¢ an hour, sweeping the warehouse, checking freight, and collecting bills from the merchants along Main Street.

In May and June of 1948, Don, his parents, and his brother Bob traveled by train for a "See the USA" tour to the East Coast. After witnessing brother Bud's graduation from the U.S. Naval Academy at Annapolis, they bought a car and drove back west.

At age 17, he started work in the summers for fish buyer Knut Thompson, for $1.60 per hour. This was the beginning of his career in the seafood industry. In July and August of 1949 and 1950, he was deckhand on the fish tender *Hazel H* with Charlie Anderson. They packed salmon for the Libby, McNeil & Libby cannery in Craig.

In the winter of 1949-1950, Don attended trade schools to learn the refrigeration trade. For a while, he did service work in town. From October 1955 to April 1957, he worked for Leonard's Refrigeration Company in San Diego.

A draft was in effect during the Korean War. In January of 1952, Don traveled to Fort Richardson,

Edna, Bud, Bob, Don and Fred Nelson, 1948

Donald and Betty Nelson

along with half a dozen other Petersburg boys, for induction into the service.

After three months in U.S. Marine Corps' boot camp, he spent 15 months with the 12th Marines, 3rd Marine Division in Camp Pendleton, north of San Diego. In August of 1953, the 3rd Division was shipped to Japan, relieving the 1st Division.

Don never saw action in Korea. After five months at Camp McNair, on the slopes of Mount Fuji, he was rotated back to the states for discharge. He left the marines in Kodiak in January of 1954.

In May of 1957, Don started working at the Petersburg Cold Storage. Here he spent his working career, becoming foreman in 1961 and manager of the cold storage in 1976.

These were the glory days of the Petersburg fishing industry, when Tom Thompson became manager of the cold storage and, in 1964, with the birth of Petersburg Fisheries by Bob Thorstenson.

Don and Betty Nelson

Thanks to the efforts of the outstanding fishermen of Petersburg's fleet, and the efforts of other processors, fish started pouring into town. Product, along with lucrative fish prices, resulted in prosperous times.

By 1981, when giant Icicle Seafoods had grown out of the original Petersburg Fisheries headquarters, decision-making for the company moved to Seattle. At this time, the cold storage manager's job was eliminated. Don started a new career on the company tender, *Kupreanof*. He spent 12 years as deck hand and engineer until he retired in 1993.

On November 23, 1961, Don married Betty Tennison in Juneau.

Betty Irene Conine (Tennison Nelson) was born in Olympia, Washington, on July 12, 1925, to John and Ida Conine, who had come to Olympia from Colorado in 1921.

Betty has two sisters and one brother. Mr. Conine worked mostly in the plywood mill in Olympia. Betty attended the Olympia public schools, but matrimony took priority at age 17, when she married Link Tennison. Link was in the Navy during World War II.

The couple had four children: Dale in 1943, Karen in 1944, Clyde in 1947, and Michael in 1948.

Betty and her family came to Petersburg in April of 1950. Her sister, Lois Kummert, and her family had preceded her. The Tennisons arrived in Wrangell on the SS *Denali* and brought to Petersburg by Fred Magill on the *Elizabeth*.

Living day by day and raising a family in the 1950s was a struggle, especially after a poor fishing season. The family lived in several homes before settling at Sandy Beach.

Betty worked in the Kayler-Dahl cannery and slimed salmon at the K-D cold storage before moving to the Petersburg Cold Storage in 1959. She was on the original halibut fletching crew for four years.

After their 1961 marriage, Don and Betty lived on the third floor of the Hoogendorn Apartments, located on the corner of Lumber Street and South Nordic Drive. The rent was $30 a month.

In 1965, they bought a small house at 1100 Front Street, which is now North Nordic Drive. After eight years, they moved into a larger home near the ball field at 202 North Tenth Street, where they live today.

Betty had resumed housewife duties, raising two more youngsters. When the kids were a little older, however, she returned to work in the PFI crab plant. Later, she was employed in the lunch kitchen at the school. Betty was also active in the Women of the Moose and the VFW Auxiliary.

Their first child, Carol Ann, was born in 1963. Three years later, John Frederick came along. Both attended and graduated from the Petersburg schools. Carol and John were both members of the Viking Swim Team for a number of years. John also spent four years in Little League.

Carol graduated from Oregon State University in 1987. She now lives in Juneau and has a family of two boys and a girl. John took up computer drafting and works for the engineering department of the City of Juneau. He is married and has three girls.

Betty and Don now enjoy visiting their six grandchildren in Juneau and absorbing California sunshine in their San Diego winter home.

Erick and Agnes Ness

By Leo Ness

Erick Nesje was born on the family farm in Nesjestrand, Norway, in 1877, to parents Peder and Ingebord Nesje. Five children were born to this family. The eldest, Lars, inherited the family farm, as was customary in Norway.

Work being scarce at home, at the age of 17 Erick immigrated to the United States. He temporarily settled in Bayfield, Wisconsin, in 1894. Erick worked on farms, in a copper mine, and also fished on Lake Superior. In the early 1900s, Erick became a U.S. citizen and changed his last name to Ness.

Agnes and Erick Ness with, from left, Carl, Leo and Ragna

In the spring of 1906, Erick came to Alaska, settling in Petersburg, which became his permanent home. At first he worked and fished for the local cannery. He obtained land and built a cabin on the hill north of the present Icicle cannery. It became known as Ness Point.

In 1908, Erick started logging at Muddy River. Using a steam donkey for power, this developed into a prosperous business. Many places north and south of Petersburg were logged. By 1918, the difficulty Erick had in obtaining material caused the shutdown of the logging operation.

In the winter of 1909, Erick married Agnes Anderson. They built a large permanent home on the land where the cabin used to be. Three children were born to this marriage: Ragna, Leo and Carl.

After logging ended, Erick started fish buying and processing. He also began a local insurance company. He owned three different boats, each connected to various businesses. They were the *Ragna*, the *Lovera*, and the *Harder*.

In the early years, Erick was very active in the civic affairs of Petersburg. He served on the city council as mayor, and served on committees for the water dam, the first hospital, city floats, the Public Cold Storage, and Blind Slough Power. He was also very active in Sons of Norway Lodge, especially with the building of the lodge hall and the store, which became the present The Trading Union.

After several years of suffering from cancer, Agnes Ness died in 1925.

In later years, after the children had grown and left home, Erick married Anne Fosse. He kept up the insurance business and had several rental units. They had beautiful lawns and gardens at the old home on Ness Point. The home site is now Eagle's Roost Park.

In 1954 at the age of 77, Erick Ness died. He was a true Alaska pioneer.

All three of the Ness children were born in Petersburg, at the home at Ness Point, and graduated from Petersburg schools. Before the children started school, however, the family spent a lot of time in logging camps.

Summer vacations were busy times picking berries, fishing trout and camping at Sandy Beach. As the boys grew older, they spent a lot of time hunting. In high school, all three played basketball and took part in school plays.

Erick and Agnes' daughter, Ragna, was born in 1911. On her birthday, January 31, 1925, her mother, Agnes, passed away, after a long illness with cancer.

Erick and Agnes Ness cont'd

After high school, Ragna married and moved to Seattle, where she and her husband, Pedar Magnus Ness, made their permanent home. They have one daughter, four grandchildren and two great-grandchildren. Ragna passed away August 7, 2003.

Carl went to the California School of Fine Arts in California. After serving in the U.S. Merchant Marine during World War II, he moved to New Mexico. He was a design draftsman for Dynaelctron Corporation at White Sands, New Mexico. Carl was a well-known artist in the Southwest. He and his wife, Frances Marie, have three children and four grandchildren. Carl died June 15, 2003.

Leo Ness was born in 1912 and has always made Petersburg his home.

He started seining and fish packing during high school vacations and later started longlining.

Leo enlisted in the Navy in 1942 and was honorably discharged in September of 1945.

While in the service, Leo met and married his wife, Ruth. They returned to Petersburg, built a home on Gauffin Street, and Leo resumed fishing. He owned the seine boat *Libby 8* for many years.

Leo started fishing at the age of 15 and retired at the age of 75. His hobbies are gardening, hunting, picking berries, reading and visiting old friends. He is a charter member of the Pioneers of Alaska, life member of BPOE, and belongs to the VFW and American Legion.

Leo and Ruth have two sons, Steve and Jonathan. Steve and his wife, Joyce, live in Seattle, where Steve is the head finance officer for the Veterans Affairs office. They have two children.

Jonathan and his wife, Jeanette, have three children and remain in Petersburg. Jonathan is Petersburg's postmaster.

Erick Ness

Neil and Margaret Newlun

By Neil Douglas Newlun

Newly married in Reno, on October 3, 1970, Margaret and I got off the M/V *Taku* in the wee hours of June 26, 1971. We had five children and a pet turtle crammed into two vehicles, brimming with personal effects. There were Margaret's children by a previous marriage, twins Todd and Tonya, and my children, Neil Jr., Melodie and Gail.

I was a U.S. Forest Service engineer and had transferred from Grants Pass, Oregon, to Petersburg.

To me, I felt that I had died and gone to heaven; I was back home on Alaskan soil. However, as we traveled the narrow street where Kito's Kave and The Star used to be in downtown Petersburg, Margaret later told me that she was thinking, "My God, what has he gotten me into?"

That first winter we huddled around the floor furnace at night, trying to keep warm, and shoveled snow during the day. It was April and there was still over eight feet of snow in the yard of our house, across the street from the Lutheran Church.

I was born March 1942, in Cottage Grove, Oregon. I had an older brother, Bruce. We lived "out in the sticks," about 20 miles south of town, and went to a two-room schoolhouse in Curtin, Oregon.

My father was a logger, trapper and a miner, with an option to log and buy 460 acres of second growth timber. I can remember going out with him, watching him fall the huge Douglas fir trees. He had his own D7 Cat and logging truck.

One summer day in 1949, my father came home with a brand-new 1949 Ford sedan and said, "We are leaving." Little was taken from the house — my parents' mattress and a change of clothes for us boys — and we were gone within four hours.

We went south, where we lived at my grandfather's place in a surplus army tent, near Oroville, California. We were there for several months before moving back north to Drain, Oregon, where I finished the third grade.

In late June of 1950, after a long bus trip to Seattle, my mother, brother and I boarded a Pacific Northern Airlines Constellation, bound for Ketchikan. We were the only kids on the flight and were treated like royalty. We got to go up into the cockpit and talk to the pilots.

I can remember looking out of the window and seeing the vast clear cuts on Vancouver Island. It was quite a shock landing on the water at Ketchikan in a Grumman Goose.

Ketchikan was a boomtown at that time, due to the logging and the building of the pulp mill. Housing was non-existent. We lived in the Marine Hotel until November, when we finally found an apartment.

My mother worked in Barron's Café, where we also took our meals. Although it was against the rules to cook in the hotel, we sometimes prepared meals on an overturned iron because we were so tired of restaurant food.

I went to school in Ketchikan, through high school. In the summer I fished or worked on a produce boat and, in winter, I worked for Race Avenue Drug Store. The boats I worked on were the *Ussona*, *Irene V.*, *Billy & I*, *Christian* and *Urania*.

I married Carole Rose Jones in July of 1960. Carole's father was Waldemar Jones, a well-known basketball player back in his day, as was his son Wally Jr. Her mother was Flora McNeil of the James and Jennie McNeil family of Klawock.

After a poor seining season in October 1960, I got a job with the U.S. Forest Service and remained with the government for nearly 30 years.

This marriage never worked out. I was single for five years before meeting the love of my life, Margaret Valeta Stulce, in Grants Pass, Oregon, in 1970.

Margaret was born in St. Louis, Missouri, in August 1947. We don't know much about her lineage, only that her Miller cousins rode with Jesse James.

Margaret and I have 10 grandchildren, of whom only Tonya is married into Petersburg lineage.

Tonya married Michael Roy Jones (deceased), son of Red and Margaret (Hofstad) Jones. Their son is Evan Michael. Her second husband is Joshua Miller, son of James and April (Otness) Miller. Their children are Travis James and Justin Joshua. This branch of Millers claim to be related to Jesse James also.

In 1978, I got back into fishing on a part-time basis, hand trolling on the F/V *Cape Fanshaw*.

In 1996, I switched to power trolling and bought the F/V *Cape Decision*.

Margaret works at the school and her hobbies are collecting dolls and making shaker cards. My hobbies are collecting Alaskan trade tokens and genealogy.

George and Gusta Nicholson

By Doug Welde

In 1875, George Mattias Nicholson was born in Fosnavåg, Sunnmøre, Norway. He came to the United States in 1900 and went to Menomonie, Wisconsin.

He worked at several jobs, including longshoring.

He moved to Duluth, Wisconsin, where he met Gusta Webenstad in 1915.

Gusta was born in Kristiansund, Norway, on January 31, 1885. She emigrated in the early 1900s.

George and Gusta married in 1915. They came to Petersburg on their honeymoon. They were visiting the Tom Lando family and decided to stay.

George built a house next to the Landos, by the Lutheran Church. (Now Ken Welde's home.)

George worked as a fisherman and was a policeman for a while; most of the time he worked as a slingman at the Public Dock.

They had three children, Evelyn, George and Erling.

Besides raising the family, Gusta did a lot of baking for folks around town. One of the cakes she baked was for Magnus Martens and Ruby Welde's wedding. When Ken Welde picked up the cake for his sister's wedding, he impressed Gusta. She told her daughter, Evelyn, "What a fine young man he seemed to be." If she only knew!

Gusta passed away after losing a fight with cancer on April 12, 1939.

George was active in the Lutheran Church and the Sons of Norway. He passed away in 1963, while a resident at the Pioneers Home in Sitka.

Evelyn Nicholson was born in Wrangell on January 6, 1917. Gusta had traveled to Wrangell for Evelyn's birth because there was no doctor in Petersburg at the time.

Her first week of grade school was dreadful. She was embarrassed to attend; kicked and screamed the whole way. In school, you spoke English. Evelyn didn't know how; her folks and neighbors all spoke Norsk!

Evelyn graduated from Petersburg High School in 1935. She then attended Pacific Lutheran College in Washington for one year. When her mother became ill, she returned home to help her father take care of her younger brothers.

She married Kenneth Welde on September 6, 1941. Their son, Douglas, was born in 1944.

Over the years, Evelyn worked as a waitress at Sammy's Café, a telephone operator, on the slime lines in the canneries, and as a nurses' aid in the hospital.

She was active in the Lutheran Church. She loved to sing in the choir and was often the soloist. She was also the organist for several years.

Evelyn died October 20, 1983.

George and Gusta's son, George Arnold Nicholson, was born in Petersburg on July 1, 1920. As a child he was bedridden with rheumatic fever.

In 1938, he graduated from Petersburg High School. Because of the effects of his childhood illness, he was unable to play basketball. However, he was manager for the 1939 State Champion Petersburg Vikings under Coach Wingard.

George Jr. and Erling, in front. Gusta, George and Evelyn.

When World War II started, George enlisted in the Army. He was given the rank of warrant officer and became the skipper of a crash boat in the 11th Army Air Corps in the western Aleutian Islands at Dutch Harbor.

After the war, George met Eva Jane Guthry from Waco, Texas. They married.

George fished halibut for several seasons. Then, he bought the dry cleaners from U.V. "Hack" White, running the business until he sold it to Roald Norheim in 1960. He and Eva moved to Sitka and started a dry cleaning business there.

George loved to sport fish and spent a lot of time up the Salt Chuck and Castle River in Duncan Canal. George and Eva took their young nephew Douglas with them quite often.

George passed away in Sitka on September 12, 1963. Eva moved back to Texas, where she passed away in 1977.

(See the Erling and Colleen Nicholson story.)

Erling and Colleen Nicholson

By Colleen Nicholson

Erling William Nicholson was born in Petersburg on May 26, 1924. He was the youngest of three children. He attended all 12 years of school in Petersburg, and liked saying that the class of 1942 had the distinction of being the only class to have graduated four "Erlings": Erling Husvik, Erling Jensen, Erling Nicholson, and Erling Thynes.

After graduation, Erling Nicholson enlisted in the Army before he was drafted. In later years, he liked to tell us that Petersburg had a very efficient draft board. He would say the number of men drafted from this small town was out of proportion to the population.

Erling was sent to Annette Island for induction and from there was assigned to the Army Air Corps' Air Sea Rescue division. He lived his three years in the service on one of the boats that monitored the waters around the Aleutian Islands. Names like Amchitka, Yakutat, Cold Bay, Seward and Adak were some of the places remembered by the "crash boat" guys when they got together to reminisce.

His discharge in February of 1946 allowed him to return to his favorite place, Petersburg. During the first months at home, he worked for Tony Schwamm with Petersburg Air Service. A heavy snow had caused the newest plane of the company to sink nose-down into the water. It had been secured to the float because the wingspan was too long for hangar housing. Extra help was needed to raise it and repair the damage done by its saltwater immersion.

While working there, he met Colleen Mortensen, an office worker. There began a friendship that became courtship and, finally, a 55-year marriage that ended only when Erling died on December 16, 2002.

In the spring of 1946, a longshoremen's strike lasted three months, putting a strain on all supplies in local stores. It was especially felt by the public, as food products — especially fresh vegetables, meat and dairy products — were unavailable.

In late May of that year, the strike was settled. The first steamship with supplies was due on June 1. The stores were overwhelmed by the need to unload freight and restock shelves, as well as serve the public.

Help was needed beyond the regular store employees. Erling was asked to come help for a few days, in whatever job was assigned. He spent the first three days on the run — moving cases of supplies, delivering orders to homes all over town, and helping wherever needed.

That "few days" of employment extended into 42 years of full-time work. After filling in with the hardware department for a few weeks, he was asked to stay on as a permanent clerk. He worked with such "hardware experts" as Ernie Sarff, Dan Sutphen and Heinie Dahl. He said his education in the hardware business was like a college course. He loved it.

During these years at The Trading Union, he served as temporary general manager, as well as hardware manager. He was manager of hardware for at least 27 years. Housewares were included in that department until about 1973.

Erling served on the city council, the school board, and was on the utility board for many years. While part of the utility board, he was assigned to Thomas Bay Authority and was able to visit the Bradfield Canal site on several occasions.

All of these experiences gave him great satisfaction. He loved his hometown and was proud to serve in appreciation of all he received here.

When his employment with The Trading Union ended in January of 1988, he worked two more years at Christensen's Lumber and Home Center, a wonderful way to end his career in retail sales. His retirement party was a source of joy and appreciation to be remembered by so many.

In addition to his civic involvements, Erling was an active man in Petersburg Lutheran Church, taking his spiritual gifts seriously. He taught Sunday School, served on church council, and was probably, at the time of his retirement, the only person to have sung in the church choir for 45 years. He had a lovely tenor voice and loved to sing.

Erling died December 16, 2002, after a 15-year struggle with Alzheimer's disease.

Although Colleen Jeanette Mortensen was a reluctant transplant from Bremerton to Petersburg in 1944, that all changed when school started.

Bremerton schools were vastly overcrowded due to World War II, and classes were attended in shifts. In contrast, Petersburg High School was blessed with small classes, fine teachers, relaxed atmosphere, and

Erling and Colleen Nicholson cont'd

interesting social events. The Mortensen kids entered into these activities with enthusiasm.

Colleen's first work experience was as a waitress at The Pastime Café, her first summer in Petersburg. Her other jobs — working in the cannery, short stints at the telephone office and Wasvick and Torwick store — ended when she went to work at Petersburg Air Service. "Time Flies, Why Don't You?"

That work was challenging, exciting, and a wonderful way to gain a variety of new experiences. Besides performing office work, scheduling passengers, and record keeping, many new opportunities came in various forms.

The fur trapping industry was reopened and trappers brought their pelts of beaver, marten, mink and ermine to the hangar at various times of day. She was taught to measure the pelts, follow the chart of value, and record the transaction, paying them from money kept in a cigar box.

There were times when a new propeller or new plane was to be tested, and she was included in the trip. On one occasion, she accompanied her boss, Tony Schwamm, on a fur-buying trip to outlying camps. It was probably the best job a girl could have.

In addition to those advantages, when the veterans of World War II began to return in the late fall and early winter of 1945-46, the hangar became a place to visit. They caught up on hometown news while waiting for jobs and the fishing season to begin.

It was at the hanger that Erling Nicholson happened by, and there began a relationship that lasted through 2002.

After their marriage in 1947, Colleen was a homemaker and stay-at-home mother. She and Erling raised three daughters: Gayle, Kim and Natalie.

In 1967, an opening with the food stamp program for the State of Alaska became available. Colleen took this job. In the beginning, she could work out of her home. Soon the job was moved to the city clerk's office and, while working there, Colleen accepted a job with the city. Her work for the city in the clerk's office continued until her retirement in 1983.

The most satisfying of all her work outside home came from her affiliation with the Lutheran Church. Here she was nurtured in the Christian faith and had opportunity to use her gifts as Sunday School teacher, choir member, occasional council member, and with the variety of activities in the Women of the Church.

Gayle Nicholson Trivette lives with her husband and sons in Juneau. Kim Nicholson Jacobs and her family live in Culbertson, Montana. Natalie Nicholson lives in Redmond, Washington.

The Nicholsons enjoyed their four grandsons' visits. The two grandsons from Montana spent several summers with them, and the two from Juneau came at various times through the year.

Colleen's brother, James "Buddy" Wyatt Mortensen, graduated from Petersburg High School in 1948. He served in the Air Force during the Korean War and later became a family practice doctor. He began his medical practice in Ketchikan in 1964.

In 1977, Buddy moved his family to Bellevue, Washington, where he joined the practice of Dr. David McIntyre, an ophthalmologist.

James came to Petersburg as a visiting ophthalmologist from 1985 to 1997. He is now retired and lives in Bend, Oregon.

Petersburg Lutheran Church

Oscar and Alma Nicholson (Wallen)

By Darlyne Conn

Oscar Skaanes was born in Levanger, Norway, on July 14, 1879. He was the only child of Nickolai and Pauline Skaanes.

In 1897 at the age of 18, Oscar went to sea on a Norwegian sailing ship and became an able-bodied seaman. He jumped ship in San Francisco in 1902, and signed up with Alaska Packers to go to Wrangell, Alaska. He worked with his cousin Olaf Olson, also employed by Alaska Packers.

They heard that a Norwegian had started a salmon cannery in Petersburg, so off they went to seek employment with a fellow countryman. They fished salmon and halibut from skiffs that they rowed to the fishing grounds, chopping ice off icebergs to preserve the fish. Eventually both men owned and operated powerboats.

When Oscar took out United States citizenship papers in 1906, he changed his name from Skaanes to Nicholson, in honor of his father Nickolai.

In 1907, he started the first theater in Petersburg. He sold it to C.E. Swanson in 1916. He married May Friday, a Wrangell Indian woman. She died in February of 1919.

In 1919, Oscar became superintendent of Petersburg Packing Company, which later became Pacific American Fisheries.

Because of the Depression, PAF did not operate in 1932. In order to provide the townspeople employment, Oscar resigned from PAF and leased the bankrupt Scow Bay Cannery by paying off the creditors. He called his new property Scow Bay Packing Company, which he operated from 1934 through 1940.

From 1941 until his death, he had a custom-canning agreement with PAF. He leased the cannery to various canners, including Dean Kayler, Rogers & Oaksmith, and Libby, McNeil & Libby.

Oscar had four fish traps that supplied the cannery with salmon. One trap was at Port Protection, two at Point Baker, and one at Warren Channel. He also had four tenders, the *Eunice*, the *Jugoslav*, the *Laddie* and the *Ira II*.

Oscar died May 29, 1948, in Petersburg.

Oscar Nicholson

Alma Cornstad was born in 1910, in Everett, Washington, to Peter and Caroline Cornstad. In 1914, the family moved to Douglas, Alaska, where Peter obtained the winter watchman's job at a gold mine.

In the spring of 1915, the family moved to Petersburg, where two of Caroline's brothers lived.

In 1927, Alma was the valedictorian of the first class to graduate from Petersburg High School after it received its accreditation.

(Alma's daughter Luella was the first of the second generation to graduate from Petersburg High School. Her grandson, Stuart Conn, was the first of the third generation to graduate, and her great-grandson Joshua Conn was the first of the fourth generation to graduate.)

Alma married Oscar Nicholson in 1928. They had two daughters, Luella and Darlyne. They made their home in Seattle in the winters and in Petersburg in the summers. After Oscar's death, Alma continued the custom-canning arrangement with PAF until fish traps were abolished with the advent of statehood. Eventually, the cannery collapsed into Wrangell Narrows during a high windstorm.

Alma married Bjarne Wallen in 1950.

In 1958, Alma and her friend, Bernadine Trones, spearheaded the "Little Norway Festival." It has become an annual event every spring, bringing many visitors to Petersburg. In 1971, Alma and Bernadine received the Norwegian-American award from the Little Norway Festival Committee for "Making a Dream Become a Reality."

Alma also talked Solveig Simonsen, a local Norwegian woman, into designing a bunad that would be Petersburg's own. Solveig's design is a beautiful royal

Oscar and Alma Nicholson (Wallen) cont'd

blue dress embroidered with Alaskan wild flowers.

Today the leikarring dancers all wear the Petersburg bunad when they dance at the annual Little Norway Festival and when cruise ships are in town.

Alma created and embroidered eight of the dancers' bunads. Many other Petersburg girls and women can be seen wearing the Petersburg bunad as well.

In 1959, Alma and Bjarne decided to transform the Scow Bay cannery mess hall into a restaurant and cocktail lounge. They named it the Beachcomber Inn. It prospered as *the* place to go for an evening of dining and dancing.

Alma and Bjarne decided to retire in 1975. They moved to her home in Seattle, which she had been leasing to the Japanese consul since Oscar's death in 1948. Big city life soon lost its luster. In 1980, they sold the Seattle home and moved back to Petersburg.

Alma died on July 2, 1985. Bjarne soon followed her, passing away in 1988.

Oscar and Alma's descendents have remained in Petersburg's fishing industry. Their daughters, Luella and Darlyne, married local fishermen.

Luella married Casper "Cap" Hallingstad, who owned the F/V *Raven* and skippered the F/V *Brooklyn*. She worked for 13 years in the fish houses of PAF and Petersburg Cold Storage.

Darlyne married Howard Conn, owner of the F/V *Rosco I* and the F/V *Vicki Rae*. She was bookkeeper for Kayler-Dahl Fish Company and Petersburg Cold Storage. Darlyne was also office manager for Petersburg Fisheries, Inc. Darlyne and Howard's children are Stuart Conn, Vicki Curtiss and Toni Rogers.

Stuart fished for many years with his father before purchasing the F/V *Stephanie Ann*. He later leased a local seine boat for the summer season.

Vicki is married to Troy Curtiss, who has the F/V *Coral Sea*. She has worked for the Petersburg Fisheries division of Icicle Seafoods Inc. as a bookkeeper since 1971, and as office manager since 1994.

Toni is married to Dennis Rogers, who had the F/V *Vicki Rae*, but now owns the charter yacht M/V *Alaska Adventurer*. Toni was employed as a receptionist for Petersburg Fisheries.

Oscar and Alma's grandson, Casper "Skip" Hollingstad, and great-grandsons, Joshua Conn and Trevor Rogers, are currently employed on Petersburg fishing boats.

Alma Nicholson Wallen

Alma and Mildred Cornstad with John and Arnold Enge

Kurt and Clara Nordgren

By Ole N. and Kandi Nordgren

Kurt C. Nordgren was born February 11, 1912, in Tacoma, Washington.

He came to Petersburg in 1929 and spent the first winter with Ole Johnson in his trapper's cabin at Jap Creek. When they came to town, they walked the boardwalk from Sandy Beach.

Later, Kurt had fox farms at Pt. Barrie and Level Island. In 1941, the cabin he built at Level Island was taken apart, towed to town, and became the living room of his new home. The house is still stands at 1002 Wrangell Avenue. Today it is the home of Karen and Don Cornelius.

In 1938, Kurt married Clara Stolpe in Tacoma, Washington. Clara's brother Harold Stolpe was Kurt's partner on the fox farm. They worked together until they all moved to Petersburg.

Kurt then became a fisherman. He first ran the F/V *Gordon D*, later bought the F/V *Lois W*, and then the F/V *Ira II*. He was also a shipwright at Petersburg Shipwrights.

Kurt and Clara had three children: Clara, Ole N. and Carl.

Daughter Clara married Jim Thompson. They lived in Wrangell and had one son, Mathew. Ole married Kandi Campbell in 1964, and they have two children, Vicki and Ole D. Carl lives in Georgetown, Texas, and is not married.

Clara died in 1975 and Kurt in 1982.

Sons of Norway
Fedrelandet #23

Anton and Sophie Noreide

By Marjorie and Willmer Oines

Anton Noreide was born in Forda, Norway. He left Norway at the age of 16 on a sailing ship, where he worked as a cabin boy. The ship sailed around Cape Horn and arrived in San Francisco after he turned 18.

In San Francisco, he was hired by a railroad company to build rails to Mexico. The rail crews were determined by nationality (Italians, Japanese, Norwegians, etc.). It was said the crews buried someone everyday, and families in the old country often never heard from their loved ones again.

Anton moved to Seattle where there was a large Scandinavian community. While attending one of the Norwegian Club meetings, he met Sophie Severson, whom he eventually married.

At 17, Sophie embarked on a sailing ship, leaving her house and home on a large rock in the North Sea at Myrvog. Interestingly, both she and Anton had been baptized in the same Lutheran church in Askvold, a halfway point between their two towns.

She entered the United States through Boston and went directly to a farm outside of Chicago. The owner of the farm was a widower who paid her fare from Norway. She was to care for his children and cook. Unfortunately, she was badly treated by the widower.

She wrote to her brother Louis Severson, who was in Seattle, and asked him to help. He contacted the Chicago police who located Sophie and put her on a train to Seattle. She worked in a Seattle laundry for about 10 years.

She married Anton when she was 28 years old. Their first baby died at birth. In 1916, their second child, Dorothy, was born in Seattle.

Anton had traveled to Petersburg and was fishing for halibut. Sophie and the baby soon joined him.

Sylvia "Toby" was born December 10, 1916, in Petersburg. The Noreides' son, Arnold, was also born in Petersburg.

Anton co-owned the *Odin* with Tom Lando and Louis Severson. Fishing was his livelihood and he enjoyed it. He also liked hunting and fishing.

Sophie loved gardening. She had potatoes, raspberries, carrots, strawberries and currant bushes. The berries are still producing in the yard of their home, which Grant and Lila Trask currently own.

She was an excellent cook and enjoyed knitting and tatting. When she sat down, her hands were always busy. She was a physically strong woman who loved to sing. Granddaughter Marjorie Oines remembers singing Norwegian songs with her.

Sophie and Anton Noreide

Sophie worked for Dave Ohmer Sr. picking shrimp. Marjorie remembers stopping by to visit her grandmother's work station and being astonished that she could not see her grandmother's fingers, as they moved so fast picking shrimp. Ohmer is remembered as saying Sophie was one of the better pickers. (He purchased Sophie's and Anton's grave plots in the Petersburg cemetery.)

Both Anton and Sophie visited their homes in Norway years later.

The King of Norway recognized Anton's brother Olai for outstanding contributions through his ownership and editing of the Forda newspaper.

On his deathbed in the Petersburg hospital, Anton asked his son-in-law Willmer if it was hard for him to watch his own father die. Even in death, his mind was active, questioning and interested.

Anton Noreide died in 1968.

Anton and Sophie Noreide cont'd

Sophie loved her home and found it hard to be in the long-term care facility of the hospital, just a block from her home. She often walked to the east door and looked out at her house.

Sophie Noreide died in 1997.

Anton and Sophie's daughter Dorothy was called the "Belle of the Ball," in high school, while daughter Sylvia was the "Belle of the Basketball Court."

At that time, there was a basketball program for girls. In a game against Ketchikan, Sylvia scored 26 points. That was the highest individual score for girls until Bridget Dahl broke the record in 1982 by scoring 27 points in a game.

Sylvia received an athletic scholarship to Linfield College in Oregon, which she attended for one year. She then transferred to Seattle Pacific College (now Seattle Pacific University) and graduated with a degree in Christian Education.

She used this education by serving as a piano teacher to some 50 pupils, including Sandra White Edgars, Jeri Ann Leekley, Amelia Kito, Kim Nicholson

Noreide Home

Jacobs, and Sue Jensen Paulson.

In 1940, Sylvia married Willmer Oines in Seattle. They lived there for two years, before moving to Ferndale, Washington, for two years. Their twins, Gary and Marjorie, were born in Ferndale. Their third child, Tom, was born in 1950.

Sylvia worked as a file clerk with the Forest Service for about 18 years. She took the job to pay her daughter's way through nurse's training. When that goal was met, she continued because she enjoyed the job and was good at it.

Sylvia taught Sunday School for 35 years and was the Petersburg Lutheran Church pianist and organist for many years.

She loves the out-of-doors and shared that enjoyment with Marjorie and Tom. There is a tree on the face of Petersburg Mountain that she has watched grow. She looks at it daily, when there is no mist or cloud to obscure it, and says, "I remember when that tree was so small."

Gary took after his grandfather Anton and enjoys history, reading and politics.

Sylvia took her children on picnics as often as possible. Sandy Beach and the boardwalk were her special haunts. She often rowed up Petersburg Creek. She continues to love that activity and often goes to Sandy Beach and Blind Rapids to sit in the sun.

Dorothy married Arnold Israelson. They had three children: Sylvianne, Norman and David. Dorothy later married Mel Brady.

Anton and Sophie's son, Arnold, served in the Navy during World War II.

He returned home to become a fisherman. He later moved to Ballard, where he and his wife, Ruth, raised three children. Arnold died in 2001.

Anton and Sophie with grandbabies Gary and Marjorie Oines

Jorgen and Tora Norheim

By Jeanne Norheim

Jorgen Norheim was born in Bulandet, Norway, July 22, 1897. His father's name was Edward J. Norheim and his mother's name was Anne Johanne Norheim.

His father, Edward, was born February 21, 1864 and died June 5, 1945. His mother, Anne, was born October 25, 1866 and died in 1944.

Jorgen served in the Norwegian Army and fished in the North Sea (now Norwegian Sea). As a young man, he and other young men from Bulandet went to the rescue of a large Greek freighter, breaking up in the heavy seas of the North Sea. In open dories, they saved all the crew except the engineer. King Haaken of Norway summoned them to Oslo and each received a medal for bravery on the high seas.

Tora Tviberg was born in Tolpinrud, Honefoss, Norway, on February 25, 1902, one of nine children born to Andreas and Marie Tviberg.

She went to grade school and was confirmed into the Lutheran church. Tora then went to work for relatives in the western part of Norway. While traveling on the train, she met a soldier who was flirting with her. They were soon married. Tora was 20 and Jorgen was 24.

Later, they left Bulandet and made their home in Honefoss, where Jorgen began and completed a master painter apprenticeship.

Louis Severson Sr. wrote them and encouraged them to come to Petersburg. Louis and Jorgen had been neighbors and friends in Norway. Louis painted a beautiful picture of Petersburg, so they came.

They knew no English words, except "ham and eggs." So, on the ship and train, you know what they ate? They didn't much like ham and eggs after that.

They had two sons, both born in Petersburg: Arvid, on June 17, 1928; and Roald, October 30, 1929.

Jorgen fished and painted many houses and buildings here. Tora worked in the local canneries until she was 75 years old.

Jorgen died May 9, 1969. Tora died in 1994.

Tora, Roald and Jorgen Norheim. Arvid is standing.

Jorgen and Tora's son Arvid went to Petersburg High School. He was a fisherman, skipper of the F/V *Unimak*. He married Patty Ohmer and they have three children, Susan, Sally and Kraig.

Susan married Rocky Flint from Juneau. They have two children, Casey and Karyn. Sally married Al Dwyer from Boston Massachusetts. They worked for the State of Alaska and moved back to build their dream home on Sandy Beach Rd.

Kraig was a fisherman and is now a state surveyor, in Juneau.

Jorgen and Tora's son Roald married Jeannie Wasvick. They have two sons, Michael and Ladd. The boys both graduated from Petersburg High School and were star basketball players.

Mike is a 747 pilot for Northwest Airlines. He married Jan Manzoni. They have three children: Chad, age 22; Mia, 19; and Anna, 13. They live in Gig Harbor, Washington.

Ladd married Brenda Strickland and they have two children: Taylor, age 15; and Ariel, 13. Ladd has been a fisherman since age 11, when Baldy Martens took him seining. He owns the F/V *Frigidland*. Ladd, Brenda and their children attended school here. Brenda has her own business, The Framer's Loft, located in Sing Lee Alley.

Roald and Jeannie still live in Petersburg. Jeannie is a graduate of Good Samaritan Hospital School of Nursing and was hospital superintendent in the late '50s. Together they owned and operated the City Cleaners and opened the first flower shop in town, Flower-Rama. After 18 years, they built Norheim Building Supply (now Christensen's Lumber).

Jeannie went to work for the U.S. Forest Service in 1981 and retired after 17 years. Roald sold the building and he retired, as well.

They are both still active with their community and family — and live for the "good times" at Grief Island in Duncan Canal, their home away from home since 1961.

Kristian and Agnes Odegaard

By Clara Dobrasz and Rhoda Gilbert

Kristian Odegaard was born on the island of Tusna, near Kristiansund, Norway, January 15, 1901, the third of seven children. The family fished, farmed, and built boats.

In 1922, he hopped on a ship and went off to join his older sister, who had already immigrated to America and was living in Seattle, Washington.

While on the ship, Kristian became smitten with a city gal named Agnes Wold, from Trondheim. The oldest of nine children, she was on her way to Fargo, North Dakota, where an uncle lived.

When he got to Seattle, Kristian started writing to Agnes with hopes that she would join him in Seattle. This didn't take too much convincing — Agnes was not happy on the farm in North Dakota.

When she finally arrived in Seattle, Agnes did a little housekeeping, found a friend to share a room with, and got a job as a waitress.

Kristian was working in a logging camp around the Arlington area and had only Sundays off. He would hitch rides and walk to Seattle to visit Agnes.

During the summers of 1924 and 1925, "Chris" — as he was now called, having conformed to the "new American way" — and his younger brother, John, went to Petersburg to pitch fish for Pacific American Fisheries (PAF).

Chris loved Petersburg, which was very much like his old homeland. He only had to convince his city gal, Agnes, to marry him and make their home in Alaska. They were married in Seattle in October 1925.

In the spring of 1926, Chris and Agnes moved to Petersburg. He started fishing with Hans Anderson aboard the *Betty*.

In 1927, they started building their house. The following year, Clara, their first child, was born. Their second child, Palmer, was born in 1931. Another son, Gordon, surprised them in 1939.

Chris continued to fish and took on many other jobs during the winter months. During the Depression, he worked for the Civil Conservation Corp during the winter and as a night policeman. He also worked as a caulker for McDonald's shipyard every winter until the shipyard was torn down.

Chris began to build his first boat, the *Thor*, in the 1940s, but was taken seriously ill and had to go to Seattle for a lengthy stay in the hospital. The *Thor*, much to his disappointment, was completed without his supervision while he was gone.

Agnes and Chris Odegaard

Chris had a twinkle in his eye and looked at the world with humor.

He told of the time when as a night policeman, while wrestling a drunk Indian woman into a cell, the cell door accidentally shut, locking him up with his dangerous prisoner. The keys lay out of reach on the desk, so he had to sit there until his relief, Ellery Carlson, showed up in the morning.

To our knowledge, that is the only time Chris ever spent the night with another woman.

Agnes spent her time taking care of her family, working in the cannery, and doing some fishing with Chris. She knitted and crocheted beautifully. After many a loaf went flying into the creek, she became a great bread maker.

Agnes died in 1982 and Chris died in 1990.

Their son Palmer still lives in Petersburg.

Clara and Gordon have made their homes in Washington State.

Jack and Vera O'Donnell

By Nancy O'Donnell White

In 1936, shortly after her high school graduation, Vera Waist left her hometown of Waldport, Oregon, to travel to Petersburg with her maternal uncle, Ernest Buker. There she shook crab in the cannery, worked as a waitress, and held a variety of other jobs until she married Jack O'Donnell in 1938.

Over the course of the next six years, three daughters were born: Hazel in 1938, Nancy in 1941, and Diane in 1944.

During those years, Jack worked as a fisherman, primarily as a seiner. Vera was a stay-at-home mom.

Early in their marriage, Jack and Vera lived across the Narrows from Petersburg on Kupreanof Island.

I remember Mom telling us that she had to carry buckets of water each day from the creek to wash Hazel's diapers.

Later the family moved to Petersburg and resided in Skylark City, in a small house that had been brought from Ketchikan on a log raft. It was directly across the street from the current O'Donnell home.

I remember vividly an earthquake we experienced in that little house. It was 1949. Each evening before bed, Mom would read to us three girls. Since we were a fidgety bunch, she admonished us regularly to hold still. On this occasion, she warned us a few times and we obediently held very still, on threat of being sent to bed with no story. However, the bed continued to move. As Mom admonished us for the last time, we all pled innocent.

I remember looking at my sisters as the bed rolled and heaved. We were all screaming, "Earthquake!" at the same time. Fortunately there were no injuries, but I still get queasy thinking about how the bed literally felt like Jell-O, quivering and heaving.

Mom was wonderfully caring and patient with us. We had a succession of canine and feline friends, and Mom was equally caring and patient with them.

The O'Donnells left Petersburg in 1949 to live in Port Angeles, Washington. We resided in Port Angeles for five years. While there, Jack commissioned the construction of the *Alaska Maid*.

Diane and I attended Monroe Elementary School. Hazel attended Roosevelt Middle School and Port Angeles Senior High.

We came back to Petersburg for the summer of 1953 and stayed in our same little house.

I remember playing the card game Nertz with Hazel and Frankie and Homer Sarber. The Sarbers had an excellent collection of Classic Comics. I recall my first exposure to classic literature — *The Hunchback of Notre Dame* and *The Three Musketeers* — in the form of comics.

We arrived in Ketchikan by boat, the *Alaska Maid*, in December 1954, with all our possessions strapped aboard, including the Willys Jeep tied down on deck. We cut quite a figure crossing the Strait of Juan de Fuca, Dixon Entrance, Georgia Strait and Queen Charlotte Sound with a car on board, not to mention a cat and dog.

On our way north, we encountered a winter storm and anchored in Swanson Bay off the Canadian Coast. Since the locals were extremely isolated in these out-of-the-way bays, they typically relished an opportunity to speak to anyone new.

One of the locals rowed out to visit us and regaled us with poetry and stories, usually attributed to William Shakespeare, but claimed by our raconteur as his work. Admittedly, we were not particularly worldly, but even *we* could recognize Shakespeare!

When we returned to Petersburg in October 1955, we resided on the *Alaska Maid* for nearly a month before Walt Hofstad generously offered his house near the power plant. We stayed there until Dad and his friend Mark Petit could build our house out in Skylark City.

I remember attending Luther League on Wednesday nights at the Lutheran Church. Furthermore, I remember attending Lutheran confirmation classes, taught by Willmer Oines, with my best friend Marilyn Smith. Willmer was a patient and humorous instructor and wonderfully spirit-filled.

During the winter of 1956, there was a hard freeze that froze Fall Creek and Blind Slough. The O'Donnell girls bought ice skates and joined friends for their first skating experience. I have never forgotten skating, for what seemed like miles, on the ice at Blind Slough.

In 1956, Jack and Vera bought property in Port Alexander, an Alaskan village on Baranof Island.

Port Alexander was very nearly a ghost town. Its population of eight year-round residents swelled to

Jack and Vera O'Donnell cont'd

50 in the summer.

There the O'Donnells ran a grocery store, an oil dock, and a fish-buying scow for the next four summers. Jack and Vera transported the salmon to Petersburg, typically every two to three days.

Vera, Nancy, Jack and Diane O'Donnell

From 1956 to 1958, the O'Donnell family fished bait herring for the halibut fishermen from Petersburg and Kake. Each spring, as soon as school was out in May, the entire family, including all pets — dog, cat and parakeet — would board the *Alaska Maid* and depart for Saginaw Bay and Sunshine Cove.

Each morning at about 4 a.m., Dad would get up, start the engine, and go up onto the flying bridge to begin looking for schools of herring. As soon as he saw a likely school, he would stomp on the roof — our cue to pour out of the foc'sle, onto the deck, and prepare to make a set.

There was no power-block on the *Alaska Maid*, so the whole family got plenty of exercise strapping the herring seine aboard. We kept the herring alive in a herring pot in Sunshine Cove.

Every day we got to witness a convocation of bald eagles in the trees that surrounded the cove. The eagles would entertain us by diving into the water of the herring pot to snatch a single herring, and then retreat to a tree to enjoy their catch.

It was a real privilege to grow up in such a pristine and inexpressibly beautiful spot as Alaska.

Hazel graduated from Petersburg High School in 1957, I graduated in 1959, and Diane in 1963.

Bathing Beauties
Courtesy of the Stenslid Family

Earl Nicholas Ohmer

By Judy and Susan Ohmer

Earl Nicholas Ohmer made his way west from Dayton, Ohio, then north from Seattle, arriving in Petersburg in 1914. His Alaska-bound map was the words of a new friend, Mr. DeArmond, "Keep the land on your right."

With these directions, Earl made his way slowly into the Territory of Alaska, following the entire coastline without a chart. Arriving in the developing Norwegian fishing village of Petersburg, he pioneered the shrimping industry in Southeastern Alaska.

Earl began to experiment with the catching and processing of shrimp aboard the *Osprey*. By 1916, he and his brother-in-law Karl, who was based in Seattle, were in business.

They added boats to their fleet over the years, boats of character and colorful history. One of their first was the *Kiseno*, a boat that took its name from their initials: Karl I. Sifferman and Earl N. Ohmer.

There was the *Charles W.*, a schooner they noticed when a crowd had gathered on a Seattle dock for a marshal's sale. Realizing that the bidders were deliberately keeping the price of the boat low — and this was a sad and wrong thing for the widow, who had little else — Earl and Karl went to opposite sides of the crowd and began bidding the price higher. When they realized they were bidding against themselves, they bought the boat and dubbed it the *Charles W.*, after Karl's grandfather.

Soon after, they purchased another boat, naming it the *Charles T.*, after Earl's grandfather.

They painted the boats gray with red trim, a tradition that stood throughout the history of the shrimping business in Petersburg.

Earl had the ready appearance of a pioneer scouting new territory. He ran his business in the same manner, expanding from shrimping into salmon, halibut and butter clams, and fur farming and gold mining. At one point, he had 12 cannery boats in the shrimping fleet and a second processing plant in Cordova.

Generations of many Petersburg families have worked along side the Ohmers in the shrimping business. Most notably are the Kainos, the Greiniers, and the Kawashimas.

Earl was dubbed the "Shrimp King of Alaska." His cannery, Alaskan Glacier Sea Food Company, with its label "Frigid Zone," set the gold standard for quality, handpicked shrimp across the country.

He took great pride in his product, the crew who produced it, and the nomenclature on his window and stationery: "Earl Ohmer and Sons." Family, community, and legacy were important to him.

Earl was adventurous, industrious, and hospitable. He was a one-man chamber of commerce, employment office, museum curator, and 24-hour loan officer. He served on the city council and was elected mayor. He was chairman of the Alaska Game Commission and was sought out as Territorial Governor — and, in the words of his granddaughter Katelyn "Penny" Ohmer, he got involved in "any other thing he could get into for the good of the city, his neighbors and friends."

He was accepted and respected outside the town he called home. The Martins of Kake, Tlingits of the Eagle clan, adopted Earl. His Native name was "Tatuten," meaning, "Still Waters Run Deep." National and territorial politicians, stateside businessmen and industrialists, and movie stars also welcomed him. To all, he answered the telephone, "Ohmer talkin'."

He was easily recognized, sporting a winsome smile, a twinkle in his eye, and blue smoke that he blew from his pipe. While a description of Earl may sound like one of Santa Claus, he looked like a cowboy clad in riding breeches, leather leggings and a 10-gallon hat. His sealskin vest was open, showing his gold watch chain and gold nugget; various ivory-handled jack knives dangling from his belt.

Earl and the big fish, a 126-pound salmon

His cowboy appearance was real. Prior to venturing to Alaska, Earl graduated from St. Boniface

Earl Nicholas Ohmer cont'd

University in Canada. He had planned on being one of the Royal Mounted Police. He was disqualified for being too short, but spent five years breaking horses for the men who rode.

Earl then packed up, headed west, and settled into ranching in Eastern Oregon. He roped and wrangled for many years, serving as deputy sheriff along the way. But then, people began building fences — and cowboys don't like fences. It was then that Earl set out for new territory in Alaska.

In 1943, a fire destroyed his cannery at Citizen's Dock. Earl rebuilt, determined to provide jobs for the many workers who relied on him. By all counts, he should have been a rich man. But he added things up differently than most, and people came before profits.

Earl believed it was more important to extend a loan or provide a job (even if he had more workers than were needed to get the job done) than to see his profits soar. He knew the dignity that work affords.

Earl came from a long line of entrepreneurial, hardworking businessmen. When Earl first departed Dayton, Ohio, he left behind a family tradition in manufacturing and invention (Ohmer cash registers, taxi meters, trolley car fare boxes, and lawn mowing machines). He also left a family history of horticulture — from wheat farming in Argyle, Minnesota, to the developing and propagation of the Nick Ohmer strawberry. His family home (1350 Creighton Avenue, in Dayton) is on the National List of Historic Houses.

He loved the Territory of Alaska and knew he was home. He would often sit on the porch in the evening, smoking his pipe and commenting, "It's 60 degrees, best temperature in the world, by golly. We're living in God's country."

Earl Ohmer totem

A signed Earl Ohmer photo

Earl Ohmer married Loyla Von Oston in 1918. They raised four children: Bob, Dave, Jim and Patti.

When Earl passed on in 1955, his son Dave assumed the leadership and presidency of Alaskan Glacier Sea Food Company. Dave left his father's office untouched, even to the last ashes in Earl's pipe.

In 1983, this office, a landmark on Main Street, was repositioned at the Clausen Memorial Museum. This decision came with an unknown blessing — in 1985, the cannery burned to the ground again, taking with it all historical memorabilia and family treasures.

Earl's collection ranged from Native totems and carved fishing hooks to machine wax recordings, from pocket watches to pipes, from a gun collection to baleen carvings, from furs and flying fish wings to glass balls. His office wall was a community bulletin board, completely covered with pictures of friends and visitors, cartoons, and certificates.

Earl's artifacts, and the spirit he created around him, can be experienced at the museum, or you can glimpse it in talking with family members who carry on some of his traditions.

Loyla Ohmer

By Judy and Susan Ohmer

Loyla Von Oston was one of the first children in Petersburg, arriving in 1903 with her father, Captain Von Oston, when she was only 3 years old. They sailed to Alaska when the town of Petersburg was not much older than she was.

Her father purchased a house and the two of them returned to Tacoma to get the rest of the family.

When Loyla, her little sister Edna, and parents, Henriette and Carl Von Osten, settled in Petersburg, the Norwegian language was commonly heard on the streets. Loyla's mother was of Norwegian heritage and her father German/Prussian, so there was a comfort in calling the developing Scandinavian town home.

As young girls, Loyla and Edna enjoyed their dollhouse furniture, setting it up in different ways and telling stories of life. They also treasured their Noah's ark with the carved wooden animals.

As they grew, they learned the homemaking and handicraft skills necessary for a self-sustaining life-style: sewing, knitting, cooking, baking, preserving, laundry, cleaning, and gathering the harvest of the various berries and clams that were so plentiful in Petersburg.

Loyla married Earl Nicholas Ohmer in 1918. They reared four children: Bob, Dave, Jim and Patti.

In addition to her own family, Loyla also cooked for the cannery mechanic, and the assistant mechanic, plus his wife and baby, who lived with the Ohmers for several years. The child was born in the front bedroom because someone in the hospital had measles, and they were trying to avoid exposure to the disease.

Dinner was served and grace was said at 5:30 each evening. Those who were not seated at that point got to clear the table, wash and dry the dishes, and clean up the kitchen.

The women made clothes for all the children.

In the summertime, Loyla and the children headed for "Bum's Retreat" at Green Rocks, across from Papke's Landing. They left for the cabin the day after school got out and didn't come back until the day before school started, except for a trip to town for the Fourth of July parade and celebration.

They packed water from the creek and recycled it through dishes and baths until it was finally used on the garden. They referred to the outhouse at "Bum's Retreat" as "Bum's Relief."

Earl would join them every weekend aboard the *Jim*, bringing guests and fresh foods from town.

In keeping with their family tradition, he would prepare salmon Indian-style, as it was called, with the side of fish standing up before the fire on a stick.

In both the spring and fall, picnicking at Sandy Beach was popular. They pulled a wagon over the boardwalk and enjoyed the changing colors of the muskeg at the different times of year.

Berry picking was often a part of the adventure, depending on the season. Blueberries, huckleberries, salmonberries, and cranberries were profuse. At Sandy Beach there were clams to dig — and nobody could fry pink-necked clams better than Loyla, crispy on the outside and succulent inside.

At Christmastime, Loyla organized the children to fill over 100 decorated boxes with candy and nuts to give to the cannery workers. Colorful ribbon candy was a favorite. Another holiday treat was pitting dates, filling them with walnuts, and rolling them in powdered sugar. Loyla baked walnut bread that was especially good as toast. And she made melt-in-your-mouth Berliner Kranse, using her favorite recipe:

Loyla's Berliner Kranse

8 egg yolks (4 hard and 4 raw)
1 pound butter
1 teaspoon vanilla
½ teaspoon baking powder
2 cups powdered sugar
6 cups flour

Press sugar and hard-boiled yolks together. Add raw yolks and mix well. Work in butter and flour. Chill overnight. Pinch off a small portion and roll the size of little finger. Shape into small ring and lap end over each other, pinching together. Dip in beaten egg whites and then into granulated sugar. Bake at 400 degrees until light brown.

Loyla had many interests. She enjoyed gardening, especially for an early spring bloom of daffodils and

Loyla Ohmer cont'd

narcissi. And she loved to pick cranberries in the fall. She grew rhubarb to supply the many requests for her famous Rhubarb Cream Pie with Mile High Meringue.

She was an avid bridge player, meeting every Friday in a different friend's home. She was also enthusiastic about solitaire, playing many varieties, among them "free cell." She was an animated member of the community theatrical productions that were presented at the Sons of Norway. She liked the stage and the entertainment it provided for the town.

Loyla was active in Eastern Star and in the Women of the Moose. She collected ceramic Siamese cats, displaying them on a mirrored shelf in her living room.

She was busy with many handiworks. She wove afghans on a loom and crocheted the squares together. She knit mittens, caps, and sweaters, and braided rugs from wool strips she'd made from old shirts and pants.

When she wasn't busy with family and community activities, Loyla loved to travel. She visited California, Canada, Bryce Canyon, Chicago and Washington, D.C. She even traveled further north into the interior of Alaska. She also visited her father in New York. He had retired to Long Island to make sails. Loyla would return with gifts he had made for her children — tents and saddlebags for their bikes, complete with snaps. In later years, she visited extended family in Norway.

After Earl Ohmer's death in 1955, Loyla married Eiler Wikan. They lived in a cottage at the end of what was called "Lutheran Hill," with a field of daffodils in the front yard. After church on Sundays, they would make Swedish pancakes for the grandchildren. In the winter, they made potato balls for dinner, carrying on the Norwegian tradition they both loved. They also had a cookie drawer, the special place for the store-bought treats that the grandchildren loved to raid. And she still made Berliner Kranse.

Alaskan Glacier Sea Food advertisements from a bygone era.

(See Dave Ohmer's page for another ad.)

David Paul Ohmer

By Judy and Susan Ohmer

Dave Ohmer was one of the first generation of children born in Petersburg. He was reared there as the town was developing into a noted seafood producing area of Southeastern Alaska.

He had the typical freedoms of boys of the wilderness and was almost expected to be packing a fishing pole, a basketball, or a .22 rifle.

Childhood summers included time at Green Rocks — rowing skiffs, picking berries, jigging fish and chopping wood. As a teen, he would entertain tourists by diving from Citizen's Dock and swimming across Wrangell Narrows. Winters meant ice skating and sledding parties.

And basketball was king. In 1938, the Petersburg Vikings won the Southeast Alaska basketball championship. Dave and fellow high school seniors, Ernest Enge and Eldor Lee, gloried in that distinction for the rest of their lives.

Dave quested after gold, sunken treasure, truth, and the meaning of life. He believed people should, "always leave a place better than they found it," and that "a man's only as good as his word." He was a seeker and a giver. He understood the struggle of the underdog, and he lived by a code that sometimes only he understood.

Dave was color blind, except for red. While he accommodated to this by forever buying red pickup trucks, Dave wanted to fly, and his colorblindness restricted him. One of his greatest life disappointments was that he couldn't serve his country in the U.S. Air Force because of his eyes. Given that, he never thought he'd done enough in World War II, although he served in the U.S. Merchant Marine.

In 1945, his father called him home to work beside him. Dave always regretted not being able to complete college, but would not have considered refusing his father. Dave and Earl worked alongside each other for 10 years.

In 1955 following his father's death, Dave became president and CEO of Alaskan Glacier Sea Food.

During the 24 years of his leadership, he consolidated ownership and control of the company, still listed as "Earl Ohmer and Sons." This period was marked by a growing interest and fierce competition for Alaska's seafood by large outside companies.

Dave addressed the challenges of the seafood industry by pioneering other non-developed fisheries that he believed offered opportunity.

He was a major impetus behind the harvesting of naturally produced herring roe on kelp. He explored the possibility of sea cucumber production. He was one of the first producers of Bairdi crab, making a commercially viable product from something that was considered a pest and routinely destroyed.

Dave led Alaskan Glacier Sea Food through its most difficult period.

Dave Ohmer and his shrimp totes

Dave's office was the pocket of his Pendleton shirt, where he recorded loans and advances on one of many envelopes stuffed there. He did have a desk at the cannery on Main Street and continued his father's tradition of collecting memorabilia. Much of Dave's treasure came from sunken ships and far-flung friends. A bulletin board covered his entire wall, displaying pictures and cartoons.

His standard dress was wool plaid shirts and white cords, later replaced with khaki pants when he couldn't get the cords. Dressing up meant adding a string tie with an 1882 silver dollar cinch. Children liked to encourage him to do cartwheels, because coins fell out of his pockets — Petersburg's version of a piñata.

Dave is remembered for his lyrical radio calls with the cannery boats, every morning at 10 a.m. and every afternoon at 4 p.m. "KWY 73 Petersburg" checked in like clockwork with "WD 8415 the *Charles W.*" and the rest of the fleet. In his whiskey baritone voice, he

David Paul Ohmer cont'd

answered the phone, "Dave talkin'." Women were always "darlin'," if they were younger than he was and "mom," if they were older.

Dave had a sentimental side that preserved tradition and honored those who'd gone before him. He regularly visited with the town's old-timers, having coffee and sharing stories. He brought them home to dinner; Atomic Ole, Corbit Ship, Gainhart Samuelson, Ralph Young, and others became part of the family. Dave made sure the pioneers were properly buried and had headstones commemorating their lives.

He stood on principle. He gave many decades of service to the Petersburg Volunteer Fire Department. Dave quit when a decision was made to let a house burn down because the owner didn't pay taxes to support the department. (The house was out of the city limits.) Dave believed in helping neighbors throughout the community.

The hardest thing he ever had to do was to carry the news to the Japanese families, who worked alongside him at the cannery, that they would have to be part of internment during World War II. He held their jobs, fought for their return, and helped them resettle their lives.

Dave served for many years on the hospital board, the Salvation Army board, and was a member of both the Elks and the Moose clubs. He was grateful to be the Grand Marshal in one of the Fourth of July parades. He was honored to be adopted into the Raven clan of the Tlingits; his Native name meant "The End."

He married Gloria Lucille Anderson on May 6, 1951, in Juneau — with a 35-cent dime store ring with a pink stone and glass "diamonds" for Gloria's finger. The real ring from Seattle's Frederick & Nelson hadn't shown up.

Maxine and Quentin DeBoer were to stand up for them, except Quentin couldn't get there because of foul weather, so a man off the street stood in.

Gloria and Dave's wedding took place at 1 a.m. to accommodate the three-day waiting period and allow Dave to be back in Petersburg later that morning to buy halibut. The line, "and with this precious token," still brings a burst of laughter.

The Ohmers' dining room table welcomed everyone — from the Catholic priests who passed through the mission town to Coastal and Ellis pilots laid over due to weather, from children whose parents were ill to salesmen who stopped by, from fishermen who were down on their luck to guests who were touring the Great State of Alaska. There was always room for one more. And when the food supply was

Dave Ohmer's wall of friends

low, there was always an "Ohmer Special," which was an open-faced fried egg sandwich with mayonnaise, lettuce, and tomato.

Dave celebrated 60 birthdays, usually with chocolate cake and chocolate frosting. But he enjoyed it most after it had been in the freezer for months, at which time he'd pour canned milk over the top.

Dave Ohmer died in 1979. He and Gloria had raised five children: Judy, David, Becky, Katelyn "Penny," and Susan.

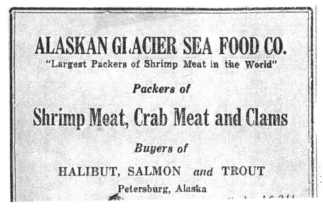

Torn from history...an Alaskan Glacier Sea Food advertisement from many years ago.

(See Loyla Ohmer's page for more ads.)

Gloria Lucille Ohmer

By Judy and Susan Ohmer

Gloria Lucille Anderson arrived in Petersburg on April 28, 1949, aboard an Alaska steamship for a two-week visit with friends. By the time she was to return to Everett, Washington, 14 days later, she had already decided that "this was her spot," and she'd taken a job. She said, "I loved Alaska. It offered opportunity — and the exhilaration of possibility. It was a land of extremes and of characters. I felt as if I were coming home for the first time."

Born in Chicago on November 24, 1925, Gloria started kindergarten in Everett, Washington, as the Great Depression began. It was, she said, a time of incredible struggle, heartache, of sadness, loss and hunger. But somewhere in a child's view of life, she learned to look for the good around her. This viewpoint sustained her through many challenges for the rest of her life.

Both her parents worked. She came home from school to an empty house, built a fire, started dinner, and watched over her little brother. She dreamed of a home filled with laughter and warmth, with someone to greet her and be interested in her day. This colored her life and propelled her into many adventures, among them the trip to Alaska.

Opportunity on the "Last Frontier" presented itself immediately. Gloria wasn't familiar with the work she was first asked to do, but said, "I could probably do that." These became her words to live by as she went from opportunity to opportunity.

Her first job was as cook at a remote construction site where the city was installing new transformers at the hydroelectric plant. She bought the only cookbook she could find, purchased eight months of groceries, and flew to Blind Slough. She cooked from April through November, learning to bake bread and feed a hungry crew.

After six months at the camp with *Joy of Cooking* as her Bible, Gloria returned to Petersburg. She accepted other work, from clerking at Electro Service, to stretching mink skins and doing autopsies at a fur farm, to working in the post office. "I continued to be inspired by the rugged frontier and the chance to carve out a life of my own making."

One morning, while she was putting in a window display at Don Pettigrew's service store, there was a tap on the window. She turned around to find a man making a face at her. Dave Ohmer later came in to apologize; he'd thought she was someone else.

They began a friendship that deepened. Their dates included dancing at the old Elks Club, digging clams, playing cards with the DeBoers and Pettigrews, and hunting. Of the family stories about their hunting trips, her children believed that she had once climbed into the cavity of a moose to stay warm. To set the story straight, she later claimed that she had only used ducks for mittens.

Gloria Lucille Ohmer, 1948

After her marriage, Gloria said that she chose to "focus on raising our five children, keeping books for the cannery, and doing charitable and community service work." She noted that Petersburg didn't have social services such as orphanages and foster homes, alcohol treatment programs, meals-on-wheels, humane societies, or domestic violence shelters. "People needed to help people."

Gloria considered herself a "behind-the-scenes worker," who supported others to a healthier, happier life. She was also a leader, an initiator of ideas, and a woman of big heart. "Our home was always open and was usually very full." Indeed, her children were accustomed to stepping over sleeping bodies in the living room on many mornings.

Gloria and Fran Lund headed up the Alter Society's December bake sale, the primary fundraiser for St. Catherine's Catholic Church, which was a mission church at the time. Their baking began in October. Lefse, fattigman, krumkaka, sunkaka,

Gloria Lucille Ohmer cont'd

hjortatak, Berliner kranse and rosettes were among the many Norwegian specialties that filled the huge tins and vats in their kitchens. They also pickled herring, and baked Swedish limpa and stollen for the popular event.

Her hands have always been busy. The Norwegian baby sweaters she knitted were legendary. Her first quilt won the top prize at the Alaska State Fair. She embroidered, beaded, arranged flowers, wove baskets, and created a colorful garden. She also liked to pound down walls, build cabinets, and turn wooden bowls.

While many children think their moms can heal "boo-boos" with a kiss, Gloria's kids were witness to near miraculous healing — hamster resuscitations and goldfish revivals occurred with regularity, with solemn funerals being attended when the pet was beyond even her ability to cure.

Any creature — human, furred or finned — who crossed the threshold of Gloria's home and stayed for more than 15 minutes was, literally, family. Even when she didn't have a child on the court, Gloria was the unofficial keeper of statistics at the high school basketball games. She enjoyed reading poetry, novels and cookbooks. She has always been busy bringing in and putting up the harvest — cranberries, clams, rhubarb and other Alaskan bounty.

Hospitality was basically Gloria's middle name. She is highly regarded for her cooking talents, from Alaskan seafood to international menus, as well as family favorites. A birthday treat was a dinner of your choice, where she was known for such selections as teriyaki chicken, halibut cheeks, buttermilk biscuits, and split pea soup.

She was a magician in making-do, innovating, and stretching things to go around — with a head of cabbage and a pound of hamburger, her "poor man's sukiyaki," she could feed a dozen people.

Gloria was musical, but when asked about it she said that she just "played for my own amusement." She began in grade school with treble cleft instruments: E flat alto horn, trombone, and C soprano sax.

In high school, she played bassoon in concert and glockenspiel in marching band. It was during her solo in *Grand Canyon Suite* that she learned it didn't work to chew gum and play a reed instrument.

As an adult, she played ukulele, harp, piano, organ and banjo. She became the organist at St. Catherine's Catholic Church, by what she called accident. She currently stars on bass washtub in Petersburg's Norwegian kitchen band, the Lefse Marching Band.

Front row: Marian Anderson, Susan, Becky and Penny. Back: Judy, Dave, Dave Jr., Gloria Ohmer

Helping people explore the "Last Frontier" was, and still is, an important Ohmer family value.

Gloria and Dave's five children (Judy, Dave Jr., Becky, Katelyn "Penny," and Susan) chose careers that promote the well-being of their community.

Today, Gloria owns Petersburg's Tides Inn Motel. She and her sister-in-law, Patti Norheim, had previously owned a store in Petersburg for 16 years.

When an opportunity to become a partner in the Tides Inn Motel, with Karen and Albert "Albie" Hofstad, surfaced a few years back, Gloria jumped at the chance.

After a year and a half, Gloria purchased the remaining interest from the Hofstads and has expanded the facility to accommodate growth from the small cruise ship industry, especially from the Cruise West vessel, *Sheltered Seas*.

Her current husband, Don Koenigs, was a busy contractor in the region for most of his life. He took his turn at community service in Petersburg, serving as mayor and city manager.

A May 2002 *Alaskan Southeaster* magazine article said Gloria was "typical of the rugged individuals who helped build Southeast from territorial days. Her success is a shining example of what a person can accomplish with desire and hard work."

Willmer and Sylvia Oines

By Willmer Oines

I was born near Ferndale, Washington, July 12, 1918. Sports have been a major interest throughout my life. I played baseball and basketball throughout my grade school and high school years, and I seldom miss a basketball game in Petersburg.

I attended the University of Washington architectural school for two years. I was able to use this training in later years, as I was the architect who drew the plans for the Lutheran Church Parish Education Building, as well as for many homes in the Petersburg area.

While attending the university, I met Sylvia "Toby" Noreide at the Lutheran church we were both attending. We were married in 1940.

Sylvia "Toby" and Willmer Oines

In June 1946, we moved to Sylvia's hometown, Petersburg. I bought two lots on North Third Street. There was a schoolhouse that I tore down on the lot. I used the lumber to build our present home.

The first summer I went to Nellie Juan, located outside of Cordova, and worked in a fish cannery. Then I worked two years for Kayler-Dahl as a carpenter and shop machinist.

In the middle of the canning season, Pete Johannsen asked if I wanted to work for Union Oil. Ole Lien had just retired and they needed someone right away. After finishing the salmon season, I began working there. I worked for Union Oil until my retirement in 1985.

I served on the city council from 1949 to 1958 and was involved in numerous construction projects. The city needed additional electrical power. R.W. Beck was contracted to design and build a larger dam, new pipeline and powerhouse. I recall that Ed Locken, Bank of Petersburg manager, thought the $1,000,000 cost was more than the city could handle. It turned out to be the best investment the city ever made. Being on the Power and Light Committee, I was responsible for seeing that the project was on schedule.

I was appointed by the mayor to serve as council representative on the hospital board. In 1956, a new hospital was built with federal funds and volunteer help from the community.

My last project while on the council involved planning the Tyee Project. This project provides electricity for Petersburg and Wrangell, giving us inexpensive power for as long as the rain falls. It includes an intertie with Ketchikan and will eventually include all of Southeast Alaska.

In 1959, I was elected to the school board and served until 1984. I enjoyed being involved with the kids and especially with the athletic department. I attended every basketball game and was honored with a life pass to the games.

During my 25 years on the school board, many projects were completed: a new grade school, swimming pool, gymnasium, and preliminary plans were started for a new high school and auditorium.

Throughout the years, I was interested in Christian work. As a member of the Lutheran Church, I was superintendent of the Sunday School and a beloved Sunday School teacher. I served on the church council for many years and was always available to help with church maintenance.

After I retired, Sylvia and I enjoyed traveling to Seattle, Hawaii, Palm Springs and Sitka, visiting family and friends. One memorable trip took us up the coast of Norway. At the family homes of relatives, we shared stories of the traumas they experienced during the Nazi occupation.

We now have six grandsons and we continue to live in the house I built in 1947.

Chris and Agnes Olsen

By Karen Olsen Haltiner

Kristian (Chris) Olsen was born in Vistdal, Romsdal, Norway, on April 1, 1884. His parents were Ole Olsen Oren, a shoemaker and farmer, and Anne Pedersdatter Lange. They raised a family of two girls and six boys. Chris and his sister Karen were the only ones who emigrated.

Chris left home for America on March 21, 1906, and landed in Halifax, Nova Scotia. He proceeded across country to Fir, Washington, where he logged and worked on farms. The day his train passed through Minneapolis his sister Karen was married, but he didn't know it.

He helped fall a giant fir tree that was displayed during the Alaska-Yukon Exhibition on the University of Washington campus. He then came through Petersburg in 1907 on his way to Katalla, near Cordova, to work on Guggenheim-Morgan's railroad. In those days, wages were 40 cents an hour. Some men deserted when offered one dollar an hour to work with a competing company that was fighting for the right-of-way; only one railroad could go through the narrow pass.

Chris also worked in construction at a mine in Juneau for a year. Returning to Petersburg in 1912, he logged for Erick Ness and the Todal brothers' company at Big Creek on Kupreanof Island. He worked there until 1917, when he started fishing.

He recalled the big set (estimated at 300,000 pinks) at Chaik Bay in a seine that was actually three seine nets tied together. They brailed fish for several days until big tides came and the fish escaped. However, they saved 90,000 from the set! Several summers he ran seine boats for PAF, but did not like being a skipper.

In 1926, Chris married Kirsten Pileberg and had a house built at 208 Fourth Street (later owned by Sid Wright). They had two children. Raymond was born in 1927 and Irene was born in 1928.

After they divorced in the early 1930s, Chris married Agnes Hofstad.

Agnes and Chris Olsen

Kirsten and the children moved to Juneau. Chris had sold the Fourth Street house for $4,000.

Ray and Irene spent summers in Petersburg with Chris and Agnes. They also spent time with their cousins in the Egil Winther and Haakon Berg families. Their stories (Pileberg, Olsen and Cashen) can be read in *Gastineau Channel Memories*.

Agnes Rebecca Hofstad was born to Albert Emanuel Hofstad and Albine Johanna Husvik on September 10, 1896, at Hov, Kopardal, Helgeland, Norway. There were three girls and four boys in the Hofstad family.

They lived next door to the Peder Husvik and Jens Winther farms. Uncles Myhre, Edwin and Morten Hofstad had come to Sitka and Wrangell in Southeast Alaska in the 1880s, seeking better fortune. They fished, prospected, and worked as customs agents. Siblings Martine, Richard, Ottar and Hardy followed them to Southeast Alaska in the early 1900s.

In 1916, Agnes came to Hadley and Petersburg to be with her sister, Martine Oaksmith's, family. Martine's husband, Stanley, was a carpenter and worked at the copper mining smelter in Hadley on Prince of Wales Island. They had four young children.

Agnes told of trying to learn English by going to the store with a grocery list; she ended up with onions instead of oranges by mispronouncing the word! She also worked as a waitress and in the cannery.

Agnes returned to Norway in 1919, when her father was ill. After his death, she brought her mother, Albine, and her good friend Liv Winther to Petersburg. They entered at Ellis Island on May 2, 1921.

Agnes and Albine lived on the first floor of the Chris Wick house on South Nordic Drive. Ole Husvik and Ragna Otness were Agnes' cousins.

In 1925, she graduated from Wilson Modern Business College in Seattle. She came back to Petersburg to work as the bookkeeper at The Trading

Chris and Agnes Olsen cont'd

Union. She worked there until 1933. She then worked at the Cold Storage until the late 30s.

Agnes and Chris Olsen were married Dec 16, 1933, at the Ole Husvik home. They had to wait until her mother was away in Ketchikan, visiting Martine's family. Albine didn't want Agnes to marry a divorced man! They purchased the Sam Gauffin home at 007 Fram Street. In 1947 and 1948, they tore it down and built a larger home.

In 1940, their daughter Karen Olsen was born in Seattle. Agnes had a Cesarean at age 45!

Agnes was active in the Lutheran Church and, during World War II, in the Red Cross. She also was the bookkeeper at the hospital from 1955 to 1957. She held many offices in the Daughters of Norway and was treasurer at the time of her death in 1957.

Chris fished halibut on various boats (*Augusta, Sherman, Edgecombe*) throughout the '20s and '30s.

The fall of 1941, he fished sardines in California with his brother-in-law, Hardy Hofstad, aboard the *American Eagle*. After Pearl Harbor, they had to run up the coast without lights and ran aground off of Oregon. They lost the boat, but everyone was saved.

Around 1943, the crew of the *Edgecombe* (Chris, Olaf Wikan, and Eiler Wikan) quit and shipped out on Per Sather's *Zarembo*, fishing for many years.

Chris retired from fishing in 1954 when he was 70. He returned to fishing in 1957 for Andy Wikan on the *Curlew*. One trip, his legs swelled up and they had to cut his boots off and run him to town! In 1961, at 77, he retired a second time.

After his retirement, he spent his winters in Seattle with Ray and summers in Petersburg with Karen. He died in July of 1972 at the age of 88, in Petersburg.

Chris took great pride in doing things well. He was noted as being one of the fastest baiters and hook ganchers in town. He also iced all of the halibut on the boats except for the *Curlew*'s.

Chris' son, Ray Olsen, went to Petersburg High School from 1941 to 1943. He joined the U.S. Merchant Marine for a year after World War II. He was in the Army at Fort Richardson during the Korean War.

In 1951, he married Alice Thornborrow, who was from California. He began fishing again and returned to Petersburg in 1953 to work at Standard Oil. Alice taught everyone in the Sewing Club how to make tacos — a newfangled food in Petersburg!

By the time they moved to Seattle in 1959, Alice and Ray had four children: Christine, Eric, Dave and Jim. Two more children, Gary and Kathy, were born in Ballard. Ray drove oil trucks for many years and crewed in the summers on boats. He purchased the *Leviathan* in 1969, and later the *St. John II*, longlining in Alaska until he retired in 1992.

Baby Karen, Ray, Chris and Irene Olsen

Five of Ray's kids began fishing with him. Christine was the first full-time halibut fisherwoman in Area 3 and Area 4. She paid for college and has a Master of Fine Arts from the University of Washington. Ray's four sons all own longliners: Eric owns the *Lorelei II*; Dave, the *Augustine*; and Jim and Gary, the *St John II*. Ray and Alice have 12 grandchildren.

In 1948, Chris' daughter Irene married Frank Cashen in Juneau. They raised a family of eight. Kirsten, Phil, Becky, Dan, Nick, Rob, Ray and Joe all graduated from Juneau-Douglas High School.

Irene began to work part time (two months, every two years) in territorial days, as a secretary in the House of Representatives. She retired in 1990, after having been Chief Clerk for many years. Sons Phil and Rob became fishermen. The rest have state jobs. After working as a secretary in different offices for many years, Kirsten Cashen Waid, Irene's daughter, became Senate Secretary in 2003.

Irene and Frank have 15 grandchildren and 3 great-grandchildren.

(*See Haltiner story for more on Karen Olsen.*)

Jack Olsen

Adapted from a story by Richard Bayne

One of the toughest men ever to set a longline on the storm-tossed waters of Southeast Alaska, or pelt a fox on its blustery islands, may be Jack Olsen.

He was born in the little town of Hammesbaget, in the land of the Vikings, on April 24, 1889. Olsen remembers that, at the age of 15, he was already making his own living, working underground in a Norwegian iron and copper mine. He might have spent his life in the mines had he not found a letter from his brother awaiting him, when he returned home for Christmas after three years away. His older brother, who had gone to America years before, wrote that a steamship ticket awaited him in Trondheim. "Come to America, as soon as possible."

He sailed from England to New York on an old freighter that had been converted to a passenger ship. The trip took 60 days. He crossed the United States without a meal because "somebody swiped my wallet pocket while I was asleep." Arriving in Portland, knowing no English, he sang a Swedish mining song. Three longshoremen understood him. After explaining his dilemma, they took him to a nearby boarding house and fed him.

The first summer in Astoria, Oregon, he fished with his brother on the river, worked in a machine shop and a door factory, and did some logging at various times. In later summers, he made trips to Alaska aboard the old windjammers that sailed to Bristol Bay to fish salmon.

"The first job I had in Petersburg was longshoring for 50 cents an hour. And boy, we sure had to work for them, no fooling. And so, that was the beginning of my 'get rich in Alaska.' Then I went fishing on the cannery boats and, boy-o-boy, that fishing was a tough life. We sat in the dory from early morning all winter."

When he wasn't fishing, Olsen built houses, installed furnaces, worked on a pile driver, was a loft man and bartender, and followed many other pursuits.

During the years of working on boats in Alaska and in his other trades, Olsen had his share of close calls — but luck was always with him. One time, he was on the deck of the *Augusta*, which was laying at the Sitka oil dock, while Martin Enge filled the gas tank in the foc'sle. Suddenly, an explosion blew the boat open and threw Olsen 10 feet into the air. He landed unconscious on his belly on the dock, with his head lying over the water and his feet over the dock. "I lost most of my hearing, but got out of it just the same."

Another time, Olsen's trolling boat blew up at the dock in Petersburg, as his partner tried to light the oil stove. The explosion destroyed the boat and broke a window in a house two blocks from Main Street. Fumes from the leaking oil and gas in the bilge caused the explosion.

One adventure that remains strongly etched in his mind happened as the outcome of his occasional work pelting foxes. Jack had joined Stanton Price and Andy Anderson on one cold and fateful day, Christmas Day 1938.

"We had gone to Sunset Island, near the entrance to Windham Bay in Stephens Passage. We were on the north side of the 900-acre island, setting traps to select those foxes they would pelt and those they would turn loose for breeding stock," Olsen recalled.

While the temperature hovered around zero, a fierce Taku wind of 50-60 mph pushed the chill factor lower.

The wind whistled from the north through the trees and piled breakers

Jack and Rose Marie Olsen

against the rocks below the bluffs. Because of the wind, they had gone across the island on foot rather than risk going around in an open skiff. Olsen was going full speed ahead to make it out of the wind and not paying attention to the two behind him. Both Price and Olsen pushed through the brush to avoid an ice covered cliff, but Anderson didn't "vant to go through the brush," so he followed the edge that was steep and icy. Anderson slipped and plunged down the steep ice onto rocks 35 feet below.

Price ran to get the boat about a mile across the island, abandoning his snowshoes. Olsen doubled back past the cliff before he could find a way down the bluff to the water. Then he scrambled over the rocks, just out of reach of the crashing surf, towards the injured man. He was stopped short by a projection of rocky land where the swell constantly broke over the rocks. Not knowing how deep the water was, he hesitated. Then Anderson regained consciousness and let out a terrible yell.

Olsen remembers, "I just forgot myself. I yumped in, but couldn't move fast enough to make it around the projection in time. The next swell come and hit me in the butt and heaved me up on the rocks. Before I could get up, the swells took me out again." Olsen should have drowned, but before he had gone out too far, he was stopped by a rock that he grabbed until the swell passed by.

"When the swell got off there, I got on my feet in a helluva hurry before the next swell come and got through to Andy, who was laying on a rock slab about 40 feet from the water. His leg was broken and his jaw was cut up so you could see his teeth loose in his mouth, and his face vas all battered up. Aw, it was terrible." In wet freezing clothes, Olsen stood by, "I talked to him and told him, don't bother to move."

It was a long wait for Price, some 35 or 40 minutes, although once across the island, he'd managed to start the kicker right away, but it was still a yeoman's task to work the small 16-foot skiff around the mile square island through the bucking swells and frigid waters.

Olsen said, "The wind was blowing something fierce for a rowboat, and nobody should have been out in it, but I worked my way around the other side and Anderson was still alive. Right away, I could see we were going to have problems with the 10-foot sea that was running there. I couldn't keep the boat from slamming up against the rocks. It began breaking up and water was squirting in the seams."

But how could Olsen, at five-feet-six-inches, and weighing just 150 pounds, carry the injured 240-pound man the 40 feet to the waiting skiff by himself? Somehow he did, although Olsen wondered where he got the strength.

"The luck was that we landed on a shelf that was almost the height of a table. I could stand straight and take him in my arms. So I told him, 'Now you got a good arm, throw that over my neck and hang on.' By yimminity, if I didn't pack him for 40 feet down to the skiff dat day."

With the boat slamming against the rocks, Olsen had to go back into the water to position Andy — broken, in shock, and bleeding — where Price could help bring him aboard. Olsen climbed aboard, helped by yanks and pulls by Price. He, too, was black and blue and bruised from his bout with the breakers. Numb and practically immobilized from enduring the cold in frozen clothes, once again he was soaked in the surf. As his clothing soaked a second time, the fabric broke and tore with each movement of his limbs. Soon, "it was broken to pieces."

Price maneuvered the skiff around to the other side of the island and into the calm water where Anderson had a cabin. Olsen began to warm some, as he ran back and forth between the cabin and the skiff, carrying clothes and a sleeping bag to cover Andy. "The more I worked, the warmer I got, and my clothes dried little by little."

Anderson's wife, Hazel, went into hysterics when they arrived. She feared riding the small boat in such violent weather, but Olsen and Price finally managed to get her aboard for the eight-mile trip to Entrance Island, where Anderson's 40-foot gas boat was anchored in the cove.

It took an hour and a half to make the run. Price remembers it was a hairy trip. Because of the break in the seam and the heaving water, "the boat leaked, as fast as I could bail it out, and I just barely kept it under control with one hand bailing and the other steering the motor. Andy was laying there and he couldn't stop the bleeding, and I was pretner out of my mind from the cold. In the open skiff, the cold and wind was most unbearable, and if the single motor had stalled, we vould have had no chance to survive.

"I was froze stiff just riding in the boat," Price recalls. "I had no coat, just a life jacket, and I had a helluva time keeping that boat before the wind and waves. Andy couldn't make a sound and Jack was shaking. The mystery is, a man does these things on the spur of the moment. He trusted me to go around the island and get the boat before he'd drown."

Under the circumstances, they never expected

Jack Olsen cont'd

Anderson to survive to Entrance Island, he was so broken up, but he did. Once into the cove, a man named Otto, together with his wife, pitched in to chop a door from a cabin, strap Anderson to it, and help carry him from the skiff to the cabin of the larger boat.

"We worked together to get Andy fixed up," Olsen said. With Andy aboard the gas boat, Price headed back to Sunset Island despite the merciless seas.

Though numb with cold, Olsen climbed down into the engine room to adjust the governor to autospeed. It would take eight hours to make Petersburg, the nearest hospital or doctor. As they took off, Otto's wife lighted the oil heater near where Andy lay bundled up on the makeshift stretcher.

On the way to Petersburg, about 50 miles south of Entrance Island, "we run into a helluva blizzard, and I had to stick my head out the window to see ahead." But when he'd gone down into the engine room for a few moments, Olsen had found a bottle of moonshine that he swears helped him warm up and saved his life. It was during prohibition, "… and I took that fifth of moonshine with me to the pilothouse and I was munching on that all the time, and at ten o'clock that night there vas nothing left in the bottle, and that was what kept me alive without freezing to death."

But nothing could save Andy Anderson. "You gotta be tough and stay with us," his friends urged, but Andy answered, "Nay, I'm not tough anymore."

Anderson died in the hospital in Petersburg, soon after the amputation of his mangled arm and leg.

In 1948, Olsen was married for the first time "to the best, most vunderful woman that ever lived." Her name was Rose Marie. They were married 27 years, until her passing.

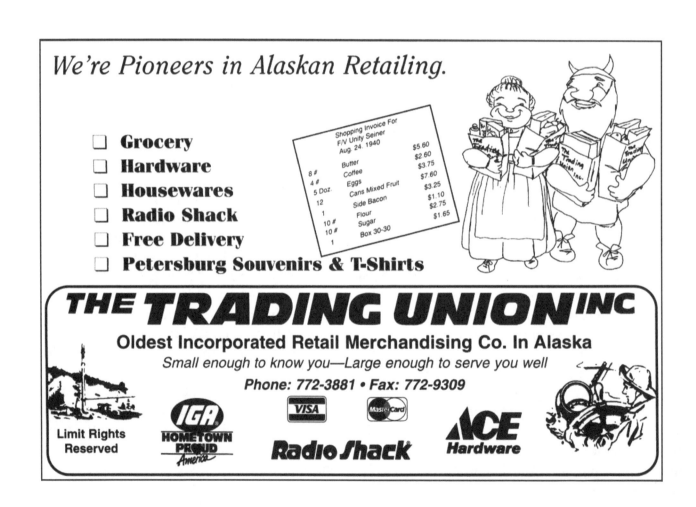

Melvin, Ilene and Irene Olsen

Interview with Ilene Olsen Opsal and Melvin Olsen

Martin Olsen was born in Norway. When he immigrated to America, he headed for Minnesota where he worked in the fields. He served in the U.S. Army during World War I and received U.S. citizenship when he was discharged.

Martin met Guda Andoya, who had also emigrated from Norway. After they were married, they moved to Portland, Oregon.

Their three children, Melvin and twins Ilene and Irene, were born in Portland. Martin came to Petersburg to fish and then returned to Portland to bring his family here.

Petersburg Public Schools have never been as exciting as when the Olsen twins attended. They kept everyone on their toes. Irene and Ilene, identical twins, had fun sitting in for each other because the teachers couldn't tell them apart. They had wrestling matches with the boys and even got beat up by a teacher. Rules were definitely different back in those days.

Ilene worked at Marie Idem's Sweet Shop. Both girls worked as waitresses at Hack White's Recreation, where they had a union representative totally confused. Ilene was working the morning shift when he ate breakfast. When he returned for dinner, Irene was working. He thought the two girls were the same person, so he was going to charge Hack with working a waitress too many hours.

Melvin fished on the F/V *Ankle Deep* and F/V *Egil*, worked at the sawmill, and retired from Petersburg Fisheries' cold storage in 1991.

Melvin met Lynn Evans, who had come from Colorado to visit a friend. They were married April 28, 1954, and had five children: Laine, Scott, Brad, Nika and Lori. Melvin still resides in Petersburg.

Lynn was a good mother and companion, as well as an avid gardener. Through the years, Lynn worked at Just for Kids and Petersburg Cold Storage.

Lynn passed away January 8, 2002, and willed her body to science.

Ilene Olsen married Nels Opsal in 1953.

Nels Opsal was born May 11, 1915, in Vinje, Norway, to Ole and Marit Opsal.

At the age of 19, he immigrated to America and started fishing out of Seattle. After two years, Nels came to Petersburg to join his father and brother Halvor. He fished with Lloyd Pederson and later bought the gillnetter F/V *Moppet*.

Ilene worked at the post office for 23 years, until she found it necessary to retire after breaking a vertebra. She enjoyed fishing with Nels. He died on July 16, 1985. Ilene died November 10, 2003. Their daughter, Nancy, lives in Wrangell, Alaska.

Irene Olsen married Hack White. She, too, has passed away.

**Winter & Pond postcard of the *Northwestern* stranded in Wrangell Narrows
June 1, 1919**
*Howard and Mabel Jonish Collection,
Archives and Manuscripts Department,
Consortium Library, University of Alaska Anchorage*

John and Ragna Otness

By Norman Otness

John J. Otness arrived in the United States in 1912 at the age of 22. He was born and raised in Otness at Valsoyfjord, Norway.

He spent his first winter in this country in Idaho, working as a logger to earn sufficient money to follow his brother, Jacob, to Alaska.

Ragna Husvick was born in what is now Richmond, B.C., Canada, of Norwegian immigrant parents. She traveled to Alaska to visit a brother.

John and Ragna Otness were married in Petersburg in 1915.

John had originally operated the power company and subsequently purchased the F/V *Teddy J*, in partnership with Charlie Anderson. (Anderson later sold his interest to John and operated the *Hazel H*.)

John and Ragna had five sons: Arthur, Ralph, John Robert, Stanley and Norman, all of whom fished commercially in Alaska and elsewhere on the Pacific. All were graduates of Petersburg High School.

John Otness was a fine musician, a violinist who enjoyed entertaining friends in duets with Ragna, who played piano. In the silent movie era, Ragna occasionally played in theaters during the films.

In 1950, John Otness died following a stroke he had while on the halibut grounds. Ragna died in 1977.

Arthur Otness was a full-time fisherman. He served in the U.S. Army during World War II, achieving rank of master sergeant.

He first fished halibut in Petersburg with his father, then out of Seattle on the schooner *Celtic* and, ultimately, on his boat, the *Brothers*.

Arthur was lost in a severe storm off Hawaii while fishing tuna in 1954. He was married and the father of two sons.

Ralph Otness fished for many years, originally with his father and eventually out of Seattle on boats such as the *Pioneer*, the *Celtic*, and the *Susan* (with Elmer Martens), and on the *Lualda*, owned by the Nicholson family of Petersburg.

Ralph served in the Army Transport Service (ATS) during World War II, delivering military supplies and fuel in the Aleutians. Ralph is married, the father of a son and daughter and several grandchildren.

John Robert Otness was also a full-time fisherman. During WWII, he skippered large tugboats for the ATS, all along the north Pacific. Following his father's death, John R. operated the *Teddy J*.

John R. was lost at sea in 1962, on a return trip to Petersburg from Seattle. He was married and the father of six children.

Stanley Otness also fished halibut with his father, and later John R., on the *Teddy J*. He also fished on the *Lualda*, the *Brothers*, and the *Iceland*, in addition to gillnetting in Southeastern.

Stan served on towboats and freighters in the South Pacific during WWII. He also served in the Army during the Korean war.

Retired from Chevron Oil, Stan is married with two daughters and two grandchildren.

Norman Otness fished out of Petersburg during the 1950s. He served in the U.S. Army, graduated from the University of Washington, and retired after a long career at Boeing in Seattle. He is married and has one son, one daughter and two grandchildren.

About 1940, John R. and Stan had an interesting experience working for Carl Vevelstad on his nickel/copper claim on Yakobi Island. Several young men from Petersburg, teenagers, worked hauling supplies and drilling for blasters throughout the summer. Chet Otness, Arnold Noreide, Erling Husvick, Chris Lando and Phil Greenau were some of them.

John R. was eventually called to testify at a legal proceeding in Juneau, which resulted in the Guggenheim organization jumping the claim.

Stan recalls Mr. Vevelstad's motto for the boys, "Eat a lot, sleep a lot, work a lot."

On the subject of the Otness family in Petersburg, it should be remembered that Jacob Otness, brother of John, also came to America in 1912.

Jacob managed the Petersburg Cold Storage for many years and was an early mayor of Petersburg.

He and his wife, Maren, had three sons: twins Oak and John, and Chester.

All are deceased.

Sons of Norway coat check tags

Oscar and Rikka Otness

By June Vick and Roy Otness

Oscar Larsen Otness was born to Tora Annette Oldsddatter Otness, on October 18, 1902, in Valsoyfjord, Aure, Romsdal, Norway. He grew up and began commercial fishing in that area.

There he met and married Inga Fredrikka Nilsen Klinge. Inga was born May 3, 1900, in Smøla, Nordmore, Edby, Norway. A daughter, Odlaug, was born October 3, 1922, in Smøla.

In search of a better life for his wife and child, Oscar decided to immigrate to America and join his older brothers, Jacob, John and Arne, who were commercial fishing and living in Petersburg, Alaska.

On March 26, 1923, he landed in Newfoundland, Canada, and took the train across Canada to Prince Rupert. In Prince Rupert, he met brother John, who was there selling fish from the F/V *Teddy J*. Oscar came to Petersburg with his brother and fished, until he had earned enough money to send for his family.

Rikka and Odlaug came to America through Ellis Island, on September 15, 1923. They crossed the country by train to Seattle, and continued to Petersburg by steamer. Oscar and Rikka settled into their new home in Petersburg, where Oscar continued to fish and Rikka became the homemaker.

Besides fishing on the *Teddy J*, Oscar also fished on the *Excel*, the *Westward* and the *Urania*. He later bought his own boat, the *Marion*.

Fishing in those days was very different than it is today. There was no cold storage when he first started. Fishermen first had to go out and drag in icebergs from the glacier and bring them to a scow in Scow Bay where the ice was ground up. They then fished for bait, usually herring, and then baited their gear. Finally, they traveled out to the grounds to start their fishing trip. After they had a load, they could either sell to the scow, or run their fish to Prince Rupert for a better price.

The social life in Petersburg was centered around the Sons of Norway Hall, where many dances and bazaars were held. Since Oscar played the accordion, he was often called upon to play for the dances with his brother, John, who played the fiddle, and John's wife, Ragna, who played piano.

Odlaug was eventually joined by five more brothers and sisters: Margaret, Nels, twins Roy and Ralph, and June. All of the Otness children graduated from Petersburg High School.

After graduation, Odlaug went to Seattle and attended beauty school. She returned to Petersburg and opened her own shop. She soon married Bob Swartz, a member of the U.S. Coast Guard stationed in Petersburg during World Was II. After the war, they moved to his home in Kansas. They farmed and raised cattle, and they soon began raising their seven children.

Margaret also married a fellow in the Coast Guard, Jim Miller. He started a taxi service with Sock Roundtree. While on a hunting trip, Jim drowned with Bernice and Conner Kinnear. They had two daughters, and she was pregnant with their third when he died.

Two years later, Margaret married another coast guardsman, Clyde "Tex" Barnard. They had two more children. Margaret now lives in Groton, Connecticut.

Nels married a local girl, Dorothy Sutphen, while serving in the U.S. Army. Nels began fishing with his father on the *Marion* at a very early age. He continued to fish commercially, and has owned several of his own boats, the *Gjoa*, the *Seanna* and the *Dorothy Jean*. Nels and Dorothy raised five children.

Ralph began fishing with his father and brothers on the *Marion* and continued in the fishing business all his life. He married Virginia Soderlund and moved to Seattle. They had three children. Sadly, Ralph died of leukemia on June 18, 1991.

Ray also began fishing with his father and brothers on the *Marion*. He continued to fish on many boats. He served two years in the U.S. Army. When he returned to Petersburg, he married Arlene Williams, a new nurse in town. They have two children.

After another year fishing, prices for fish were so poor that he decided to go to school. He attended Western Washington University, and graduated with a degree in education. He returned to Petersburg and taught sixth grade for 27 years, fishing in the summer.

June married Gordon Vick from Ketchikan. Gordon was in the commercial fishing business all his life. For many years, he ran a tender for Icicle Seafoods. June and Gordon had two sons. June worked in many retail businesses in Petersburg. Gordon died in 2001.

Oscar and Rikka were dearly loved by all of their children and grandchildren. Rikka died in 1982 and Oscar died in 1987.

Herman Papke

By Frieda Menish

Herman Papke was born on September 28, 1873, in Alsace-Lorraine. After a stay in Australia, he came to Alaska on a geodetic survey.

In 1902, he moved to his homestead of 40 acres and built a log cabin. The cabin was dug into the ground, making it necessary to stoop to get in the door. His cabin was like the nest of a sorcerer. Garlic hung everywhere and a bit of rosemary was tied with an old piece of seine twine. His chopping block was covered with scraps of meat and fat.

He became one of the most beloved old-timers of Petersburg, and certainly one of the most notorious. He was a man of constant charm and intelligent wit. He loved the outdoors, Southeast Alaska, and the freedom and beauty he found here.

Herman Papke

He wrote in his diary from the day he began his homestead until his death in 1964. He recorded the weather, temperature, direction of wind, birds and animals he sighted, flowers blooming, vegetables and fruits. Legend has it that he is responsible for spreading those beautiful purple lupine flowers all over the island.

Papke was one of the most advanced gardeners of his time. The apple trees along his beachfront produced juicy yellow apples. His cabbage and cauliflower were as large as the wooden orange crates that he used to protect them from giant slugs. He continually worked to improve his varieties by grafting various plants and trees.

His haven was full of just about everything that would grow in the wet climate of Southeast Alaska. To alleviate the problem of his plants drowning, he hand dug a two-foot-wide draining trench around the garden and home site. He also put up a fence to protect his garden from the deer that roamed the area. Between harvesting his garden and fishing, he ate well.

He shared his garden produce, plants and flowers with his many visitors. Birds were his favorites. They were his companions and friends. Hummingbirds fluttered around his head and swallows were always welcome in his home.

Papke had a telephone. When he sighted a steamship or barge coming through the Narrows, he would turn the crank of his phone and relay the message to the steamship office in town, enabling them to have longshoremen on hand to unload the ship.

In 1935, a Territory of Alaska work party built the 14-mile road to Papke's Landing and a large dock. People could now drive out to "the end of the road" to visit him. When his log cabin burned down, due to the accumulated soot in the chimney, townspeople got together to build him another cabin.

There are many tales told of his eccentricities. It took a brave person to accept a cup of Papke's coffee. His pot was always on the stove and he continually added grounds and water. The heavy white porcelain mugs were darker than the brew he served in them, but it didn't deter his hospitality.

The small cabin the townspeople built for Papke is still there. The apple trees are still out there in a row along the beach, although crippled limbs are weighed down with moss and age. All the strawberries and raspberries you can eat are still growing in his garden.

But the beloved hermit, Old Papke, is gone. His prostrate trouble turned to cancer. His own doctor, he knew this was the end. Taken to the hospital, he refused to submit to an operation unless his friend, Ralph Hall, was with him. Papke did not survive the operation.

Gordon and Polly Parr

By Mary Jane Larsen

Gordon and Polly Parr observed their 70th wedding anniversary at the Lutheran Church Holy Cross House. The overflowing crowd of family and friends all knew that this marriage is a beautiful love story and an inspiration to many.

Gordon was born in Granite Falls, Washington. His family moved to Port Angeles in 1924. Gordon was active in football, baseball and basketball. In high school, he was president of both the senior class and the student body. After graduation, he was encouraged to report for induction in the San Francisco Seals, a pro baseball team. Within a week, he realized he had left his heart in Port Angeles and he returned.

Gordon and Polly Parr

Pauline Godeleman's family moved to Port Angeles in 1926. Polly was in the eighth grade and soon attracted to this handsome classmate with the dark, wavy hair. They became close friends, but it wasn't until their senior year that their relationship became serious. On Christmas Day, they climbed Mt. Angeles and made a commitment. They married June 25, 1932.

These were depression years and both felt lucky to have jobs. Polly was working at a tearoom and Gordon was employed at a fiberboard plant. In 1941, they were attracted to Alaska and moved to Anchorage. Gordon worked for the North Pole Bakery Co. and the Anchorage Baking Co. With a shortage of housing, they lived in a wooden frame army tent that summer.

When word of Pearl Harbor reached Anchorage, there was a request for volunteers to go to radio school to aid the war effort. They immediately volunteered. In radio school, they learned how to collect weather information and disseminate it to U.S. and Russian airmen using Morse Code. Vern and Mildred Counter were also attending the school. They became friends.

The Civil Aviation Authority assigned them to the airport in Fairbanks. Temperatures were 30 degrees below zero, housing was inadequate, but they soon decided that working opposite shifts and passing in the dark Alaskan night was no way for a family to live. Two children, Ron and Patty, had joined their family.

Spring found them on their way to Port Angeles. Passing through Wrangell Narrows, Devil's Thumb and Petersburg Mountain offered a spectacular sight. The Parrs were soon planning a move to Petersburg. Mildred Counter wrote that there was a bakery for sale. They eagerly moved in time for Ron and Patty to enter school and purchased the bakery from Knud Stenslid. Gordon soon realized he loved the bakery business.

Although they worked long hours, there was time for community involvement: city council, garden club, Elks and Emblem Clubs, as well as their own interests. Gordon loved fishing with Vern Counter and son Ron. For Polly, it was sewing, pottery, and working with oil paints, watercolors, glass, copper and other mediums. She loved playing bridge and the organ.

They had another daughter, Mary Jane. Upon Mary Jane's graduation from high school, they purchased a Roll-Along camper and toured the United States for a year. When they returned, they built their current home on Sandy Beach Road.

In 1976, Gordon closed the doors to the bakery and fished with Magnus Martens on the *Pamela Rae*. Gordon and Polly have made many more trips through the U.S., Alaska and Canada. They are currently on their fourth motor home, but feel the time has come to spend more time in their home and garden.

Polly loves flowers and has always had a large vegetable garden. Recently Gordon was sighted in the garden. When asked what he was doing, he replied, "Just trying to find one more thing to make Polly happy." Life doesn't get any better than that.

Their son, Ron, married Patty Wasvik and they have one son, Hunt. Patty married Al Dowd and they have three daughters. Mary Jane is married to Doug Larsen and they have three daughters and a son.

Charlie and Anna Pautzke

By Matt Holmes

Charlie Pautzke was 42 years old when he showed up in Petersburg in 1915. It's not clear how long he'd been "up north" seeking fortune when he hit town, but he left behind an active life in Auburn, Washington. With over 20 years in Auburn, Charlie had a wife and four children, had been on the city council, and had led a busy life within a large civic and social circle. But for some reason now lost to time, Charlie was able to convince his wife Anna, a sensible woman of strong conviction and strong faith, to let him go north.

Charlie loved to hunt and fish, and most of all, he loved having a good time with the boys, which is probably why he set himself up as a town barber, shortly after arriving in Petersburg. Barbering ran in the family, and so did hunting and having a good time. He quickly joined the Arctic Brotherhood and received acclaim for shooting more ducks than anyone else on hunting trips.

In 1916, Charlie brought his oldest boy, William, to town. Bill, age 14, made friends with Erling Strand, Carvil White, Carroll Clausen and Art Peterson, among others. Bill seemed to have the time of his life hunting, fishing and horsing around. Besides cutting wood and slinging fish, he worked as the night watchman at the power plant.

At the end of summer, 1917, the rest of Charlie's family arrived. Anna had been reading the Petersburg newspaper regularly, which revealed what a good time the outgoing Charlie was having. Along with Anna came Luttie, 18; Karl "Collie", 14; and Clarence, 10.

Charlie's business was doing well and he had a partner. The family spent the next five years living the life of the town. Anna became active in the Moose Club's "Mooseheart Legion." Charlie was a high vote-getter for terms on the city council and school board, and he was also active in the Moose Club.

Bill played basketball and baseball against Kake and organized a number of social events for the Moose. Collie and Clarence were regularly on the honor roll at school. Collie was a charter member of a new Boy Scout troop in 1918. In 1920, Clarence had his appendix taken out at Petersburg Hospital. Luttie, as outgoing as her father, became one of the most popular young girls in town.

Shortly after arriving, Luttie took first prize at the Firemen's Masquerade Ball. She, like Bill, was working and having fun. Within a year she was the Postmaster, with friends that included Mary Allen and Elsie Roundtree. In 1921, she became engaged to a man from Ellensburg, Washington. Preparing to leave town, Luttie had a week's worth of parties and showers. The week culminated with a large event at the Arctic Brotherhood Hall, where Mayor Ed Locken made a speech and presented her with parting gifts.

The Pautzkes returned to Auburn in 1921. Anna had sent Collie to Bellingham a year earlier to continue high school, because Petersburg's school only went to tenth grade. It's not really clear why they left Petersburg, but family lore has it that Charlie sent his savings south to a trusted banker friend in Auburn, who apparently absconded with all the money. Luckily, Anna had maintained the family home in Auburn, even after the family came north.

Charlie died in 1932 at age 59. Anna died in 1969 at the age of 93.

Bill Pautzke became a patrolman for the State of Washington and was killed in the line of duty in 1930.

Clarence, a noted fisheries biologist in Washington State, became the state's first assistant commissioner of the Alaska Department of Fish and Game after statehood. In 1961, President Kennedy appointed him U. S. Fish and Wildlife Service commissioner. He later served as assistant secretary of the interior department. He died in 1971.

Collie Pautzke was variously a chemist, naturopathic doctor, researcher, tinkerer and inventor. He died in 1985.

Luttie was a wife, mother and family caretaker, and worked as a bookkeeper. She died in 1972.

While Bill Pautzke lived in Petersburg, he owned a box camera that he used to photograph his friends and scenes of life in town. He filled two photograph albums, which came to Collie's daughter, Karlene.

Collie's grandson, Matt Holmes, grew up looking at these scenes of old Petersburg. He moved to town in 1984, where he settled and had his family.

(Many thanks to Chris Lando, who researched the Petersburg newspaper and compiled references to the Pautzke family. M.H.)

Lloyd and Betty Pederson

Adapted from an interview by Julianne Curry

Hjelmer and Annie Pederson came from Norway to Minneapolis, Minnesota, and then to Bellingham, Washington, where Pacific American Fisheries employed Hjelmer.

Their son, Lloyd, was born January 29, 1921. Nine months later, Hjelmer moved the family to Petersburg to pursue a longlining career in the "Last Great Frontier." He bought the F/V *North Pole*.

Palmer was born in 1922. Once he reached kindergarten, the family started moving back and forth between Bellingham and Petersburg, in between fishing seasons.

Lloyd, 7, was returning to Petersburg with his mother and brothers on the M/V *Aleutian*, when the steamer ran aground in Seymour Narrows. Annie ran into Lloyd's room to awaken him. He must have been a little cranky because he said, "Next time the boat runs aground, don't awaken me."

They were lowered into a lifeboat and later lifted back onboard the *Aleutian*, where they waited two days to be transferred to a passing liner. Lloyd recalls that on the *Aleutian*'s next journey, it sank in Kodiak.

When asked about life during the Depression, Lloyd recalled it was just a way of life. As kids, they didn't really understand their parents were struggling. No one else had any money either.

Hammer & Wikan and The Trading Union allowed credit accounts where you charged all you needed throughout the winter. When the fishing season ended, you would pay your bills, and then start all over again.

During the Depression, the community supported one another. Boats would take turns going longlining and would come back with halibut for anyone who wanted it. If there were no halibut, cod would suffice.

The family lived in the house on North Nordic Drive (where Ron and Patti Simpson now live). Walking to school each day, Palmer would kill grouse in the heavily wooded areas. Later in the 1930s, the huge trees were logged and used to build homes.

Lloyd remembers rowing up Petersburg Creek every day with his brothers and friends. He recalls the 25¢ movies they went to every weekend. By 1935, he started fishing with his father during the summers. His childhood was virtually over.

At school, all grades were in the same building. In the winter when it snowed, the students would shovel off the roof and sidewalks. If something broke, members of the shop class (located above the old gym) would fix it. At one o'clock on Friday, the whole school assembled in the auditorium for singing and other festivities. The superintendent would play the piano. After school, they would clear out the desks and have a dance.

1938 Southeast Champions

The high school basketball team was a story in itself. Coach Les Wingard led them to winning 24 out of 25 games, two years in a row. This was before the towns were split into regions as they are now. The teams they played included Wrangell, Wrangell Institute, Metlakatla, Ketchikan, Juneau and Sitka's Sheldon Jackson.

All the traveling was done on local longliners, except when Coach Wingard's brother was in town. He was head of Department of Fish and Wildlife, and they would time it so the department's huge cruiser would pass through Petersburg to the team's next destination. When the team won the Southeast championship in 1939, they were unable to go to the territory championship games for lack of money.

When war was declared in 1941, Lloyd realized he was to be drafted into the Army. He quickly enlisted in the U.S. Coast Guard. He was sent to Ketchikan, but his superior needed someone who knew the waters

Lloyd and Betty Pederson cont'd

around Petersburg, so he was sent back home. His job was to maintain the buoys in the Narrows. They were kerosene-lit and needed frequent tending.

There was one trip, during his four years with the Coast Guard, that Lloyd will always remember. On the cruiser *Baltimore*, they were told to rig it up for handicap access, but they were not told the reason for it. The commander told the crew to proceed to Auke Bay, near Juneau. There they were told Franklin D. Roosevelt, President of the United States, was returning from Yalta and wanted to get in a little fishing before he returned home.

Escorting President Roosevelt were two destroyers, one of which Lloyd was on. Onboard with him were Admiral William D. Leahy, the president's personal physician; Vice Admiral Ross McIntire; and the president's dog, "Falla."

Lloyd did not get the pleasure of watching Roosevelt catch his one and only codfish.

Lloyd returned to fishing after the war. In 1948, he purchased the F/V *Middleton* from longtime fisherman Gus Isaacson. Lloyd fished happily on his boat for several years until his father came to him with an idea. Throughout all of their years longlining, they would bring up crabs with spikes from the bottom. People knew so little about them. When Lloyd was little, his father would tell him not to touch them because they were poisonous.

Fish and Wildlife had told the Pedersons no crab existed this far south. Ignoring that "fact," they began prospecting for the crab in 1953. They also experimented with stainless steel pots. After four years, Fish and Wildlife established a king crab season.

The king crab industry was soon followed by brown crab. Brown crab were much more agile than king crab, so Lloyd experimented with fiberglass pots. Instantly, the pots were coming up full. Tanner crab was discovered soon after.

Next, Lloyd tried his hand at seining. It was difficult to find a market, because all the salmon traps were owned and operated by companies and private businesses. When Alaska was granted statehood in 1959, the fish traps were voted out. This helped to shape an industry. The price of pink salmon shot up to 55¢ a pound.

In 1993, Lloyd bought a white Rambler station wagon. He would later adorn it with buoys, flowers, a moose rack, posters and bumper stickers. The car is much photographed by tourists and always in the Wonderfulness Parade. It is famous enough to have its parking tickets paid for by the Petersburg Chamber of Commerce.

After 40 years of loving care, Lloyd sold the *Middleton* to Seattle's Kurt Hanson. He then had a fiberglass gillnetter built. He named his new boat the F/V *Betty Jane*.

Betty Pederson feeding the deer.

Betty Rogers Pederson was born on December 3, 1919. She was the daughter of Carl and Hanna Elizabeth Rogers. Because there was no doctor in Petersburg in 1919, Elizabeth Rogers had returned to her family home in Evanston, Illinois, to give birth to Betty, their first child.

Betty graduated from Petersburg High School and attended Seattle's Griffin-Murphy Business School. Betty worked for many years as a bookkeeper in The Trading Union office.

Lloyd and Betty were married in March 1942. They soon had children: Janice was born in 1943, Roger in 1945, and Jean in 1948.

Betty is a member of the Emblem Club and Women of the Moose. She loves to feed the many deer that gather in her yard.

Their daughter, Janice Mikkelsen, lives on Whidby Island. Roger lives in Seattle when he isn't working on a Crowley Maritime tugboat. Jean Curry resides in Petersburg.

Lloyd and Betty currently fish and also travel in their motor home.

Arthur and Frances Peterson

By Don Nelson

Frances Miller Peterson is truly a pioneer of Petersburg. She arrived in town in April of 1907 as a 6-month-old baby. Frances moved into the house her father built that summer, 12 Hammer Slough Street.

Margaret Frances Miller was born in Juneau on October 30, 1906, to Louis and Marie Miller.

Louis was a teamster, who hauled freight to the Perseverance Mine on Gold Creek.

In 1903, they had moved to Juneau from Petersburg. When the cannery in Petersburg started up again in 1906, Louis moved back. In 1907, the family followed. This included Frances, her sister Edna, and her brothers, Dick and Louis "Duke."

Frances entered the first grade in 1912, in a school located on the southwest corner of Third and Dolphin streets. Some classmates and friends in the early years were Magna Hallingstad, Bertha Lero, Reidar Thomassen, Dick Brennan, Agnes Vick, Marie Hadland, Helen Lund, Mungie Larsen, Medvig Mjorud and Nels Evens.

In those early days, when a student finished the required amount of education, the commissioner of education in Juneau issued diplomas. In 1924, Frances and Berit Johnson were the first two students to receive graduation diplomas in Petersburg.

After graduation, Frances attended Seattle's Peterson Business College for one year. She returned to Petersburg, where she was a bookkeeper at Earl Ohmer's Alaskan Glacier Sea Food Company. She remained at Ohmer's for 18 years. She struck up a close bond and friendship with the many shrimp pickers and workers, whose families, in many cases, had multiple generations working for Ohmer.

As Ohmer's receptionist, she met many of the celebrities and dignitaries who used to visit Ohmer regularly, including Bill Boeing, president of Boeing Aircraft Company; Max Fleishmann, Fleishmann Yeast; Lawrence Rockefeller; and composer Irving Berlin.

Arthur and Frances Peterson

Frances was also a longtime bookkeeper for the Hogue & Tveten store and, later, Cornelius Mercantile Company. Here she became acquainted with the many new arrivals to Petersburg and the local fox farmers, whom Myrtle and Bert Cornelius were known to take under their wing.

A long friendship with Art Peterson, the local fishing fleet machinist, ultimately resulted in their marriage on October 25, 1943, in Wrangell.

Arthur L. Peterson was born in Escanaba, Michigan, on March 10, 1900, to Norwegian immigrants Peter "Trixie" and Ingeborg Peterson. At an early age, Art moved to Everett, Washington, with his older brother, Roy, and his parents. Art went to school there through the fifth grade.

In 1912, at age 12, Art moved to Petersburg with his father. His mother and brother Roy remained in Everett. His father was a fisherman and was away from town much of the time, so Art stayed with Rasmus and Anna Enge, whom he considered second parents. Art's father, Trixie, gillnetted on a boat of the same name on the Stikine River, before becoming a partner with Rasmus Enge in a fox farm on Graves Island.

Art started gillnetting on the Stikine at that time with tutors Lars "Seagull" Hansen and Ole Rosvold.

In 1920, Art started crewing on Petersburg Packing Company cannery tenders. He learned his machinist trade as an engineer. He later became the cannery port engineer. Art also ran the cannery yacht, *June*, for cannery superintendent Oscar Nicholson. At that time, before marine radios, this fast boat was used to communicate with the many outlying fish traps.

In the late 1920s, Art spent the winters in charge of Charlie Mann's card room and pool hall, where he learned to play a mean game of pool. In the early 1930s, he started working for Fryer Machine Works, which was located on the waterside of Main Street at the foot

Arthur and Frances Peterson cont'd

of Dolphin Street.

In the late 1930s, Art moved over to the floating machine shop owned by Bob Allen (presently the Piston & Rudder, owned and operated by Mike Luhr). Art bought this shop in 1943 and operated it for 22 years. Frances did the accounting.

At first, Art and Frances lived in the Hoogendorn Apartments, across the street from the Miller home.

Art and Roy's father, Trixie Peterson, died in 1938. Roy brought their mother, Ingeborg, to Petersburg about 1946. Ingeborg died in 1949. Roy, who was a gillnetter on the Stikine, died shortly after.

Besides caring for Art's mother in her last days, Frances was busy caring for her own parents. Marie Miller died in 1957 and Louis Miller died in 1955.

Francis and Art moved into the old Miller family home in 1959. Their time was spent renovating the house and maintaining a beautiful yard and garden.

Art spent many long hours servicing the "Great White Fleet" of Petersburg. He was always modest in his work charges. While comparable businesses were charging seven or eight dollars an hour, his hourly charge was three dollars. His customers were the elite of the fleet and very few accounts turned delinquent.

Art sold the shop in 1965. He then went back to his apprentice place of employment, the PFI cannery machine shop. He was in seventh heaven standing behind a lathe in a pair of dirty coveralls. Here he enjoyed life until he retired at age 80.

Art was not only was a master mechanic, but an expert at every thing he did, from fixing up the old house, to gardening, to boat building. He built a 22-foot speedboat with the finest mahogany woods — stained dark and varnished — truly a masterpiece. It was powered with a Ford V-8 engine and was the fastest boat in town. Art was consistently a winner at the local Fourth of July races.

Art and Frances had no children of their own, but both loved kids and were very close to their nieces and nephews, who spent much time at the Miller home on Hammer Slough.

Frances was a charter member of the local Eastern Star chapter. Art and Frances had a host of close friends, including Swede and Evelyn Wasvick, Hugh and Eva Jones, Arnold and Emmy Lindstrom, Chet and Charlotte Steear, and Dave and Caroline Westerberg. They kept very active with parties, gatherings and outdoor activities.

Many a weekend was spent cruising Wrangell Narrows and Duncan Canal, going on picnics. Art was a great fisherman and duck hunter, and spent much time each fall with his friends in the hunter's cabin at the Salt Chuck in Duncan, in which he was the principal owner.

Art's legs finally gave out and he was confined in his home until he broke his hip in 1990. He spent his last days in Petersburg's long-term facility and passed away on March 13, 1993, at age 93.

Frances, age 97, still lives at the family home that her father built in 1907.

"The Great White Fleet"

Ruth Lee Powels

By Ruth Lee Powels

I was born on February 17, 1924, at the Petersburg General Hospital to parents Harold and Magnhild Lee. I was the only daughter with three older brothers. What could be more wonderful?! I was known in the town as "Sis Lee." I am still called Sis by some of my old friends and it warms my heart.

Petersburg was a great place to spend my childhood. As a member of the "Hill Gang," we had the "little woods" as a playground to spend our days. We built forts, had bonfires to bake potatoes, and we ran and played to our hearts' content.

In the winter, we ice skated in the muskeg and skied the Dam Mountain hillside. In the summer, while camping in our family beach cabin at Sandy Beach, we learned to swim.

Life was beautiful in the small town of Petersburg. Our days were filled with happiness. But it was a sad day, in June of 1940, when my oldest brother, Allan, was killed in an accident while in Juneau. We all grieved, but we were very aware of the kindness shown from all of our wonderful friends.

My high school days were filled with many activities, including working with the newspaper. I especially enjoyed working with Mina Olsen at the Petersburg General Hospital during my senior year.

After graduating from Petersburg High, I spent a year in a pre-nursing program at the University of Washington in Seattle. My best friend, Alice Espeseth, and I then spent three years as cadet nurses at Tacoma General Hospital. We graduated from TGH as registered nurses in 1946.

Soon after graduation, I married David Powels, who was home from four years in the U.S. Navy.

I worked at the hospital at Washington State College, while David finished earning his civil engineering degree.

Together we raised three children: Jimmy, Davey and Pamela. We lived in many different states, as well as in Germany and Canada. Our children grew up and became an airline pilot, a general contractor and a schoolteacher.

Our favorite family vacations were to Petersburg to visit family and friends. It was great for our children to experience the town of Petersburg. It is something we always will cherish and love to remember.

On September 17, 2002, our son David died tragically after an accidental fall on a fishing trip. He now rests in peace in the Petersburg Memorial Cemetery with his grandparents and other relatives and friends. He will be truly missed by all who knew and loved him.

David and I have been married for 56 years. We have had an interesting and exciting life. We now reside in San Ramon, California.

Daughters of Norway

Edmund and Louise Preuschoff

By Edmund G. Preuschoff

In 1909, Edmund Paul Preuschoff arrived in Alaska, in search of better opportunities than existed in Oregon at that time. Born in Nebraska in 1884, he was the oldest of six children.

His German immigrant parents moved from Nebraska to Oregon when Ed was a small boy. He completed the sixth grade in a Catholic elementary school in Oregon. He then had to quit school and go to work to help support the family.

His first work in Alaska was in the Treadwell gold mine, south of Douglas. Due to rumors that the mine was in danger of collapsing, Ed left that job and went to Petersburg. He had saved enough money to be able to bring his two younger brothers, Frank and Hans, north to work with him.

In Petersburg, the three brothers formed the Preuschoff Brothers Logging Company. From 1911 to 1920, the company was very successful. The *Petersburg Weekly Report* of June 11, 1920, called them "…the most successful loggers of Southeastern Alaska."

They logged at Beecher's Pass, Ideal Cove, and Red Bay on Prince of Wales Island, providing red cedar logs for boat building, and spruce and hemlock logs for lumber and piling. The piling they provided certainly assisted in Petersburg's early growth, as they provided logs for re-piling all of the Petersburg Packing Company building and wharf, as well as logs for the Alaska Fish and Cold Storage plant at Scow Bay. Jack Hadland and his tug, the *White Bear*, towed the log rafts to the mill and other destinations.

While commercial fishing was the mainstay of the economy of Petersburg, the fur business in Southeast Alaska became a large but short-lived industry in the 1920s and 1930s. The trapping of mink, marten, otter, beaver, and other fur-bearers involved many people and families.

Raising foxes on isolated islands provided work and a very good living for some hard-working families. Fox fur coats, jackets, shawls, and muffs were in style with women in the Lower 48. With some blue fox skins selling for up to $120-$125 each (in 1920s' dollars), it is easy to understand why the fox farming business grew rapidly.

About 1921, the three brothers sold their logging equipment and went into business raising blue foxes for skins and for breeding stock to sell to other fox ranchers. Soon they were doing well. In fact, so well that Hans partnered with Bob Allen and established a ranch on Entrance Island at Hobart Bay.

Edmund Preuschoff

(By 1940, the fox farming business had begun a steep decline. Women's fashions dictated mink for beautiful fur coats, stoles and jackets.)

In the early days, the Preuschoff brothers felt that two of their sisters in Oregon should be brought to Alaska. Marie and Frances came north and were soon married. Marie became Mrs. Jim Allen and Frances became Mrs. Jake Hallingstad.

In 1926, Edmund Preuschoff married Louise Seitzer, a German immigrant girl he met in Oregon City on one of his trips south to visit his family, relatives and friends. He and Louise were married in the Earl Ohmer home in Petersburg.

Her wedding present was a full-length otter coat made of skins that Edmund had trapped in his spare time. The coat was made to order by the W.W. Weaver

Edmund and Louise Preuschoff cont'd

Co. of Reading, Michigan.

Of the five young Preuschoffs who came to Petersburg from Oregon City, only Ed, the oldest brother, had any children. Edmund G. was born in 1929 and Katherine Marie was born in 1932. Eventually Edmund and Louise had to consider either homeschooling their children or moving to town.

Edmund sold his share in the fox operation on Lung Island to Frank and moved to Mitkof Island. He built a new home and a small mink ranch near the highway, about six miles south of Petersburg. The new mink operation was not successful due to lack of capital, low fur prices and Ed's worsening health.

Meanwhile, Frank Preuschoff continued on Lung Island until his death in 1940. Brother Hans had earlier given up his operation on Entrance Island and was employed at the city electricity generating plant at Blind Slough. Later, he was employed in summers by the U.S. Forest Service as trail boss. He continued in this until his death in 1947.

Edmund passed away in the summer of 1941.

His children, Ed and Kay, graduated from Petersburg High School in 1947 and 1949, respectively. For several summers, Ed worked for his Uncle Hans, who was a trail boss for the USFS. In 1947, Ed went south to attend Washington State University, returning in the summer of '48 to work for the Forest Service, this time as trail boss.

After her husband's death, Louise worked for Cornelius Mercantile Co. and later became secretary to school superintendents George V. Beck and Lester Wingard. She married Lars Westre in 1948. In 1949, she and Lars retired to Seattle.

Kay went south with her mother and Lars. She attended WSU until 1953, when she was killed in an auto accident three weeks prior to her college graduation.

Ed returned to WSU and completed his studies before and after the Korean War. He earned both BA and MA degrees and has done graduate study at other institutions.

Louise passed away in 1962. Lars Westre passed away in 1964.

Now retired, Ed lives in Othello, Washington, with his wife Julia. He returns to Petersburg on occasion to visit friends. He has been a teacher, elementary school principal and high school principal in several school districts in Washington.

Like his father and uncles before him, he enjoys hunting and trout fishing and has pursued these hobbies throughout the Northwest. Ed and Julia have three grown children, two girls and a boy — all with college degrees, all married with growing families.

Louise Preuschoff

What Ed learned in Petersburg as a young man from his Uncle Hans Preuschoff, from Bill Chipperfield and Knox Marshall, and the other good men of the Forest Service has "stood him in good stead" throughout his life.

Petersburg Main Street
Photo courtesy of Clausen Memorial Museum

Edward and Ida Ramstead

By Diane Forde

Edward Ramstead was born in Sedan, Minnesota, on July 14, 1886. Ida Strandberg was born in Strandquist, Minnesota, on May 14, 1897. Edward's parents were from Norway and Ida's were from Sweden. Edward and Ida were married in Strandquist on December 6, 1916.

Ida and Edward lived and worked in Minnesota and North Dakota as newlyweds.

Their son Milton was born in Dodge, North Dakota, on September 7, 1917. Their next four children were born in Minnesota: Arne on September 23, 1919; Dolores, February 20, 1921; Glenn, November 17, 1922; and James, November 6, 1923.

Edward was a master carpenter. He was working on the lodge at Glacier National Park in Montana when brother-in-law Carl Swanson asked Edward to bring his wife and their five children to Alaska. The Territory of Alaska would build a schoolhouse at Point Agassiz and furnish a teacher if there were seven pupils in residence there.

On March 15, 1925, the family left friends and family and headed to Seattle by train, then via the steamboat *Admiral Rogers*, and arrived in Petersburg on March 28. The trip to Point Agassiz, eight miles across Frederick Sound, was by gas boat.

The family settled in with Carl and Aurora Swanson (Ida's sister) until their home on the new homestead could be built. In order to get lumber and supplies, Edward found carpentry work in Petersburg during the week. He worked on the family home on weekends.

By September 1925, the house was livable. Their daughter Marie was born September 26, and the school was ready. (The schoolhouse is still standing at Point Agassiz today after being moved to Thomas Bay in the '50s, and back to Point Agassiz in the '80s.) Daisy Oja was hired as the first teacher; enrollment was a little over the required number.

The Ramstead Family, from the left: James, Milton, Arne, Edward Sr., John, Ida, Edward Jr., Dolores, Marie, and Glenn.

The Ramsteads spent several years improving the dairy herd, the land, and purchasing a 30-foot boat to be used to transport the family. Edward continued to work in the building trade. Products from the family farm were exchanged for their groceries and fuel for the boat.

Ida worked the farm, cooked, baked, sewed clothing, and spun the wool. She churned butter from sweet cream and sold the butter in half-pound printed molds to many customers in Petersburg. With her husband, Edward, she created a healthy lifestyle for their brood, without electricity or indoor plumbing.

Other families at Point Agassiz at the time were the Andrew Asks, the John Loseths, the Louis Israelsons, the Andrew Israelsons, the Carl Swansons, the Jacob Hallingstads, the Ole Olsons, the John Steears and bachelor Robert Oscar Parks.

Edward and Ida Ramstead cont'd

On April 8, 1930, son, Edward Jr. was born to the Ramsteads. On March 23, 1934, their eighth child, John Alden, was born. Eldest daughter Dolores went to high school in Petersburg, in 1933, and worked for her room and board. Her senior year, 1938, she kept house for her two brothers, James and Glenn, so they could also attend school in town.

In the fall of 1938, Marie and Edward Jr. joined their siblings in Petersburg as the Point Agassiz School had closed.

In 1939, the war broke out in Germany. The Ramstead family, except for Dolores, left for Nordland, Washington, on September 3, via an Alaska Steamship vessel. Shortly thereafter, the four oldest boys went into the service. James and Glenn joined the Navy; Milton and Arne, the Coast Guard.

After leaving Alaska, Ed and Ida lived in Nordland. They then moved to Seattle's Beacon Hill, where they lived for 27 years, before moving to Edmonds, Washington.

Edward died April 20, 1979. Ida followed him on May 11, 1981.

Milton married Kathryn Hiller in 1942. Their children are Mike, Linda Jansen, Carolyn Hatcher and Roger. Milton died May 26, 1986.

Arne married Rita Dixon in 1945. Their children are Richard and JoAnn.

Dolores married Arne Lund in 1940. Their children are Dennis and Diane Forde.

Glenn married Shirley Hegira. Their daughter is Kathy Muir. Glenn's second wife is Setsuko, and their children are Gunnar and Crystal.

James married Beverly Coleman in 1947. Their children: Patricia Smaaladen, Susan, James Jr. and Julie.

Marie married Paul Zobrist in 1947.

Edward married Joyce White in 1951. Their children are John, Jay, Mark, Todd and Lisa. DeBenedetto. He later married Kayjo and their child is Cindy DeBonis.

John married Ruth Matland in 1961.

Unidentified group

Elise Hofstad Rastad

By Ida Hofstad Severson and Marie Winther

Dr. Elise Rastad, as she preferred to be called, was one of the few old-timers at the Pioneer's Home in Sitka to reach the great age of 100 years.

Elise Hofstad was born September 24, 1870, in Norway. Not much can be traced from her early life, except her home was in Kvalo, Bronoi, Norway.

Later in life, she traveled farther north in that country and lived in Bodø and Vatso.

Elise immigrated to the United States in 1903 with her mother — who, according to the daughter, lived to be 104 years of age. They went to Chicago where her brother Peder Hofstad owned and operated a photography shop.

She started working as a nurse's aid in a hospital. There she became concerned about the diets of sick people and health problems, to which she later dedicated so many years of her life.

In 1906, she moved to Wrangell where her uncle Edwin Hofstad, a customs officer, resided. In fact, he was one of the first customs officers in Alaska. She met her future husband, Knut Rastad, captain of the fish packer *Baranof*. They were married in 1907 and made their home in Wrangell until 1921, when he retired from his business.

They had both passed 50 by then, but enrolled together in the Palmer School of Chiropractic in Davenport, Iowa, and graduated in 1925.

The next 15 years they practiced in Rock Hill, South Carolina. They were long remembered there for their services, skills and, above all, their compassion for the sufferings of their fellow men. Money was scarce in those depression years. Payment often consisted of farm products, as well as chickens and pigs. Nobody was turned away from their door. Many received treatments at home if they were unable to come to their offices.

Knut Rastad passed away in 1942. Elise returned to Alaska and lived in Scow Bay with her sister and brother-in-law, Birgitte and Myhre Hofstad. She also continued her chiropractic practice there. She moved into Petersburg after her sister and brother-in-law had passed away, continuing her practice in a small house in Skylark City. She retired and moved to Sitka's Pioneers Home when she was 86 years old.

Much of her longevity she attributed to fasting, exercise and fresh air. She cautioned her patients, "Eat little." Often she would comment, "Jesus fasted 40 days, why shouldn't we? " Rain or shine, she took long daily walks. When offered rides on these excursions she would quip, "Why ride, as long as I can walk?"

Siblings Morten Hofstad and Elise Rastad

The above story was written in September 1970 for Elise Rastad's 100th birthday. It was a tribute to her longevity and an offering of congratulations on this very rare occasion. Her niece, Ida Hofstad Severson, and family friend Marie Winther closed their tribute by writing, in Norwegian, "En lys og fredelig lifsaften, Mrs. Rastad."

Elise's story was published in the *Petersburg Press* on September 16, 1970. The *Sitka Sentinel* newspaper also congratulated her on her 100th birthday, mentioning that she had continued giving treatments to patients with aching backs and necks after moving into the Pioneers Home. Her strong, efficient hands had long ago earned her the reputation of being very effective. She gave advice to all that good nutrition, good exercise and good posture are all very important for long life.

Dr. Elise Hofstad Rastad died in 1971. She was 101 years old.

Reid Brothers

By Martha Hungerford Reid

The Reid family's American history began in Scotland on a farm near the city of Aberdeen. In the early 1900s, Alexander P. Reid and six of his brothers and sisters began immigrating to the United States.

They settled mostly in Montana and in western Canada. By 1905, Alex had found work in Kalispell, Montana. He took his meals at a boarding house. There he met Wilma Thompson, granddaughter of the owner of the establishment. Wilma's English ancestors dated back to the early 1600s on the East Coast, near Boston.

Alex married Wilma in 1905.

In 1909, the Reids filed on a homestead near Chester, Montana.

They built a homestead cabin and began wresting a living from the unbroken sod of the western prairie. Nine children were born to them.

At the height of the Depression, work was hard to find for many, including the younger Reid generation.

Two young men, who were friends of the Reid brothers, had traveled to Petersburg, Alaska. They found good jobs at Martinsen's Dairy and came home with silver dollars in their pocket. Hearing of this, John and Gordon Reid left Montana and came to Petersburg in 1937. They worked at Olaf Arness' sawmill. In 1938, they bought the boat *Neptune* from Bert and Erling Espeseth to try fishing.

In 1939, Glenn joined them as soon as he graduated from high school. The brothers did some logging in Duncan Canal for the Arness sawmill. Stanley and Alex Reid moved to Petersburg, in 1940, and Stan worked at the sawmill with Glenn.

Alex graduated from Petersburg High School in 1941, while working part-time at Fryer Machine Shop.

In the meantime, older brother Robert Reid and his family also joined the group. He worked at Fryer's helping to keep the engines of the Petersburg fishing boats in repair.

Since the majority of their family was in Petersburg, Alexander and Wilma Reid left the farm in Montana and came to Petersburg by steamship from Seattle in 1940.

The elder Reids started a chicken ranch in Scow

Glen, Gordon, John, Alex, Robert and Stanley Reid

Bay and sold fresh eggs and fresh chicken. These were immensely popular items and a real novelty in Petersburg. There was very little fresh food at the time. Fruit and vegetables came in a can, and frozen food was not available. There was plenty of fish, venison, and clams, of course.

The big family was soon separated. World War II interrupted. By 1942, all except Robert were serving in various branches of the armed services for the duration of the war.

Alexander and Wilma Reid stayed on in Petersburg during the war. They returned to Montana shortly after peace was declared and after all their sons had come safely home.

Robert, Gordon, Glenn, Stanley and Alex remained in Petersburg after the war. John settled in the Seattle area.

Robert and Vena Reid

By Beulah Reid Luhr

Robert T. Reid was born to Alex P. and Wilma (Thompson) Reid on September 19, 1908, in Sun River Bench, Cascade County, Montana.

He married Vena Ward in July of 1932, in Chester, Montana. She was born June 19, 1915, the daughter of Lester and Laura (Martell) Ward.

Bob joined his brothers, John, Gordon and Glenn, in Petersburg in 1939. Times were hard in Montana and work was available in Petersburg. Bob was able to get employment with Fryer's Machine Shop, where he worked for many years as a mechanic and machinist. Bob also logged with his brothers and on his own.

Upon finding work and housing, he sent for Vena and children, Robert "Sonny," Beulah and Les. They traveled by train to Seattle, where they boarded the steamer *North Sea*.

Their first home on Scow Bay Loop Road was quite small. It had a living room, bedroom and kitchen. Yep, you guessed it, no indoor plumbing!

We used the outhouse during the day; we kids used the chamber pot at night. We were too chicken to make the walk to the facilities in the dark. Bathing was done in a tin washtub in the kitchen next to the stove. What great fun we thought it was, but what a chore for Mom!

Mom used a wringer washing machine. Clothes were hung on an outside line or draped around the house to dry.

Our play areas were the street, a huge stump pile, the beach, and the wonderful woods where the Ted Morrisons and Stan Reids now have their homes.

Gordon Wallace "Kelly" was born October 18, 1940, and brought home to the little house. We were pretty crowded and soon moved to the Benjamin house (now the Herff home). This was a three-story house with enough bedrooms for all of us. Indoor plumbing was a real treat, but Mom still had a wringer washing machine in the basement with a large area to dry clothes.

Mom and Dad set about filling the house up: Claudia arrived on July 24, 1942 and Lawrence Dale "2-Bits" on December 22, 1944.

This old house was generally filled to the brim with family, friends and neighbors. Dad was a great collector of stray animals and people; many were brought to our home over the years.

In 1950, the family purchased the home of Lee and Ruth Steear. It was across the road from where we had first lived on Scow Bay Loop Road.

Sonny (born February 8, 1933, in Chester, Montana) graduated from Petersburg High School in 1951. Beulah (born in Chester on October 12, 1934) graduated from PHS in 1952. She married Don Luhr on May 31, 1952. *(See Don and Beulah Luhr story)*

Bob and Vena separated that year. Vena took the three youngest kids and moved back to Montana.

Leslie (born January 20, 1936, Chester, Montana) continued to live with Dad, and graduated from PHS in 1954. Leslie was working with Dad when Dad was killed in a logging accident in June of 1954.

In 1954, Sonny Reid married Marjorie Rhodes, daughter of Jim and Elsie Rhodes. They have one son, Scott. They lived in Juneau for many years, where Sonny was an airplane mechanic and pilot. Marjorie and Sonny divorced. Both have remarried.

Sonny married Dorothy Hall of Craig in 1981. They summer in Juneau and winter in Yuma, Arizona.

Les Reid married Janet Kvernvik, daughter of Marvin and Anna Kvernvik, in June 1961. Les logged for Reid Brothers for many years. He is now a fisherman, who resides in Juneau. He and Janet have three children: Brian, Marva Ann and Denise.

Kelly Reid married Jennie Purdue in December 1964. They made their home in Juneau for many years, along with children Ruth Ann and Roger. They retired to Prescott Valley, Arizona.

Claudia went to school in California. She married Leroy Allen in 1958, and had four children: Karen, Ken, Keith and Kurt. In 1962, Claudia divorced Leroy and moved back to Petersburg. She married Jerry Kvernvik, son of Marvin and Anna Kvernvik. They have one daughter, Kursteen. Claudia presently lives in Juneau, works on the Alaska Marine Highway System, and is married to Brian Russell.

Robert and Vena Reid's youngest child, Lawrence Dale, graduated from PHS in 1963. He married Roberta Snow, his high school sweetheart. They had one son, Don, and two daughters, Margo and Kim. Dale and Bobbi divorced in the 1970s. Both remarried. Dale, wife Jani, and stepson Steven reside in Juneau.

John and Bernice Reid

By Martha Hungerford Reid

Born in 1914, John Reid arrived in Petersburg from Montana, in 1937, with his brother Gordon. They came from Seattle by steamship traveling steerage. Together they worked at fishing, logging, and at the Arness sawmill.

In 1938, they bought the fishing boat *Neptune* from Bert and Erling Espeseth.

When World War II started, John was one of the first young men of Petersburg to be drafted into the Army. Most of his wartime was spent in Alaska on the Pribilof Islands in the Bering Sea, the very last outpost of America's defense line.

They were frozen in all winter and got their Christmas mail and supplies in the spring. There were no cell phones in those days to check in with the rest of the world.

After the war ended, John married Bernice Benjamin, granddaughter of Olaf and Constance Arness. Four children were born to them: Duane, John, Debra and Margaret.

They bought a house on Palatine Avenue in the Greenwood district of Seattle, where they lived the rest of their lives. John entered the construction trade, working as a carpenter building houses in Seattle.

In 1957, he came to Petersburg and built a house in Scow Bay for his brother Glenn. John also constructed several brick fireplaces for various residents of Petersburg.

John died in 1985 and Bernice in 1991. Both of them died of cancer.

Gordon and Connie Reid

By Constance Reid Dibble

Born in 1916, Gordon Reid came to Petersburg from Chester, Montana, in 1937, with his older brother John. It was during the Depression and they were looking for work.

They did find work on fishing boats, beach logging, and at the Arness sawmill at Scow Bay, which later became Lars Eide's mill. John and Gordon bought the fishing boat *Neptune* from Bert and Erling Espeseth in 1938.

When World War II started, Gordon joined the U.S. Coast Guard and John went into the U.S. Army. After the war, Gordon came back to Petersburg and continued fishing and working in the sawmill.

Gordon married Connie Collier, whom he had met in Seattle. They lived in Petersburg and had three sons: Mark, Darby and Michael.

Gordon started working on the construction of the road extension from Blind Slough to the end of the road.

During the time Gordon fished, he worked on Norman Tate's boat, the *Surf*, Red Olson's *Discovery*, Leon Hasbrouck's *Wanita*, and Fred Magill's *Elizabeth*. He also fished herring with Jack O'Donnell.

Gordon really enjoyed his hunting trips in the fall, bringing home the winter supply of deer, goat and moose. Connie was busy with Cub Scouts and Presbyterian Church work, and she was an Avon Lady for several years.

In 1965, Gordon went to Sitka to work on the airport construction project. The family followed. They lived in Sitka for nine years. In 1974, Gordon, Connie and Michael moved to Juneau.

Gordon finally retired from construction and went to work for the National Marine Fisheries Service. Connie worked for the U.S. Coast Guard.

In 1986, Gordon was diagnosed with cancer. After receiving treatment for several years, he retired from NMFS. The family moved to the Snohomish area in 1989. Gordon died in 1994.

Sons Mark and Darby still live in Sitka and work in construction. Darby married Shannon Burnett in 1980. They had two children, Kirby and Kayla. Kirby was fatally injured in a boating accident in 1998.

Connie married Arthur Dibble, in 1998, and lives in the Snohomish area of Washington State.

Glenn and Martha Reid

By Martha Hungerford Reid

Glenn Wesley Reid was born on the Fourth of July in 1920, in Colville, Washington, where the family lived for a few years. Soon they returned to the family farm near the small town of Chester, Montana.

Glenn, with brothers Stanley and Alex, attended a one-room prairie schoolhouse that was two and a half miles from their farm. The Reids' long legs served them well. They made good time back and forth every day. When it came time for high school, they lived with a sister in Chester, or sometimes boarded out with other families in town doing chores in payment.

Glenn's claim to fame in Chester came one night when he was driving his father's 1935 Plymouth sedan around town. It was full of teenage friends, eager to joyride. The car slid on the ice as he was rounding a corner, and ended up on top of a fire hydrant, breaking it off at the base. Water gushed through the car. The doors flew open as teenagers scattered to the winds, leaving Glenn alone. Soon the water tower in town was drained and everyone in Chester was out of water. He was not popular with the townspeople or his father.

After graduation from Chester High in 1939, Glenn came to Alaska to join his older brothers. He worked at the Arness sawmill and he and his brothers did some beach logging in Duncan Canal. After the wide-open spaces of Montana, the closeness of the landscape in Southeast Alaska was startling, but he liked it. The huge trees they cut down and yarded to the water's edge were quite a challenge.

One of Glenn's first jobs at the sawmill was when Olaf Arness showed him a big pile of sawdust and asked him how much he'd contract to move it from under the saw and over to the regular sawdust pile. Glenn looked at the pile, thought he could probably do it in three days, and said $18.

After removing the top layer of sawdust from beneath the saw, he discovered, hidden underneath, strip after strip, and layer after layer of cedar tree bark. He had to chop it all out with an axe. When he was finished days later, Olaf gave him his pay, saying in his heavily Norwegian-accented English, "Here is $20. You sure as hell earned it!"

Several of the Reid men lived in a rather dilapidated house on the sawmill property. Mrs. Arness charged them $6 per month for the house. After they had paid the rent, Olaf approached Gordon and said, "Here is your money back for the house. It's not worth a damn thing. But don't tell the old lady."

One of the first things Glenn did after a year of paychecks was buy a small piece of waterfront property from Fred Patton, about two and three quarters mile south of Petersburg. (It is now owned by Allen and

Martha and Glenn Reid, 1945

Beth Richards.) Glenn also bought a small three-room house on a log float from Mr. Patton's son-in-law, Mr. Starkenburg. The house was pulled up onto the land, the log float dismantled, and the logs sold to the mill.

He negotiated with Olaf Arness to buy some of the Arness waterfront homestead, number 38. This sale finalized after Glenn return from the Army in 1946.

During World War II, Glenn did most of his army service in the Aleutian Islands running a power barge, transporting supplies between islands. Later he was transferred to the military police and served his last six months at Nyssa, Oregon, guarding German SS soldiers at a prisoner-of-war camp.

Transferred from the Aleutians to the Lower 48,

Glenn and Martha Reid cont'd

in 1945 Glenn married Martha Louise Hungerford.

Martha had spent her entire life in the Petersburg area. She first lived with her parents and siblings in her father's logging camp, and later at their family home in Scow Bay. Martha graduated from Petersburg High School. During the war years, she lived and worked in Bellingham, Washington.

Glenn and Martha had three children: Jean, born in 1946; Glenn Jr., born in 1948; and Celia, in 1951.

The Glenn Reids joined with the Alex Reid family and started a logging operation in May of 1946. Their first logging "show" was on Kupreanof Island near Skiff Island. They had built a house on skids that could be moved about. It had a large kitchen/dining room area, two bedrooms for the expanding two families, and a ladder to the attic for the crew.

It was almost impossible to buy equipment so soon after the war. Manufacturers that had turned to producing essential items for the military had not had time to retool. They managed to buy a small Caterpillar tractor, but it had no attachments or canopy. Dean Kayler had loaned the Reids $5,000 and they also had their saved military pay and separation bonuses.

On May 26, 1946, all their possessions, including eight-month-old baby Jimmy, were loaded aboard a log float and towed to the south end of Rocky Pass by Sheldon's boat, the *Collette*.

Power saws were not yet invented, so cross cut saws were employed. After all his experience with an axe at the sawmill, Glenn still managed to cut through his heavy leather boots and sever one of his toes, a couple of weeks into the logging project. (Power saws first came out the next year. Enormously heavy, they required two men to operate them, one on each end.)

The men had gone to Juneau and came home with a large black wood-burning army surplus cook stove, with a huge top surface and an enormous oven. After a while it was converted to oil; it served valiantly for many years in the cookhouse kitchen. A big sheet of plyboard, varnished with legs attached, served as the cookhouse table. Luckily, a gasoline-powered washing machine became available in Wrangell and was added to the floathouse.

The only way to get to Petersburg from Skiff Island was a 16-foot outboard skiff. No radio available. No airplane service. Point Baker, across Sumner Strait, was the nearest connection to civilization. That summer, on a calm early August day, Glenn and Martha took the skiff 50 miles to Petersburg. Martha stayed until Jean was born two weeks later.

The Reids logged at numerous locations in Southeast Alaska's Tongass National Forest. This included a long stay at Thomas Bay, where they constructed many of the roads now happily used by moose and deer hunters in the fall. Over time, they had acquired a great deal of equipment, buildings, boats, and a large crew. In 1968, after more than 20 years and the births of capable sons willing to be loggers, the logging outfit divided in two.

Alex and his family moved to Ketchikan and logged in that area. Glenn started the first crushed rock and ready-mixed cement plant in Petersburg.

For some time, they had observed the two pulp mills in Southeast Alaska (Ketchikan Pulp and Sitka's Alaska Lumber and Pulp) acquiring small logging outfits in the Tongass National Forest. One after another, their logger friends "went broke," until the only independently-owned firms were the Reids'.

The Reids were also on the borderline. Due to government regulations, no logs could be exported to the Lower 48. They had to be processed in Alaska. Therefore, logging firms were forced to sell their logs to the two pulp mills for this processing.

It was alleged that the two pulp mills conspired to keep log prices so low that eventually all other firms would fail; only the mill-owned logging camps could survive. With accounting, depreciation schedules and income tax, it worked out that it was much cheaper for the mills to own the logging sales. The mills had their huge allotments of timber from the U.S. Forest Service, but they wanted the private sales as well. Since they, as mills, could not bid on them, they needed their fronts — the small defunct camps — to acquire them.

In 1973, both Glenn and Alex independently sued both Ketchikan Pulp and Alaska Lumber and Pulp, accusing them of antitrust price-fixing. In 1984, after 10 years of litigation in the federal court in Seattle, an appeal to the U.S. Ninth Circuit Court, and the Supreme Court's refusal to consider the final appeal, the Reids prevailed. They felt they had done this in the name of the over 100 small logging businesses no longer in existence in Alaska.

Stan and Elda Reid

By Beverley, John and Stanley Reid

Stanley D. Reid came to Petersburg on September 5, 1940. He was born in Colville, Washington, on January 25, 1922. The family returned to Chester, Montana, when he was 6 years old. He attended Chester schools and graduated in May 1940.

He came to Petersburg where his brothers, John, Gordon and Glenn, were working at the Arness sawmill. In Montana, Stanley had been working from daylight to dark for one dollar a day. Besides joining his brothers at the sawmill, he also fished a couple years with Mr. Hungerford.

Elda and Stan Reid

During World War II, Stanley was a sailor in the U.S. Army Air Corps, serving on a 104-foot crash boat, which was similar to a PT boat. These boats operated with a crew of 12 to 16 and had medics on board. They were built particularly for rescuing pilots, but more often they picked up guys who had some kind of accident — perhaps a broken arm or leg, or appendicitis — and took them where they could get medical attention. Civilians from distant outposts were also rescued and taken in, when necessary. There was no radar on the boats at that time. Dead reckoning was used to set the course.

After he came home from the war, Stanley fished with Norman Tate. In 1949, he started as a machinist at North Pacific Cannery in Scow Bay. Lloyd Swanson was his boss. In 1951, Oaksmith and Rogers took over the cannery and he worked for them for three years.

At that time, he bought a cabin from Cliff Roundtree that was on the beach by his folks' place. He still uses that building for a boathouse.

As the years went by, Stanley worked as a cannery machinist at Hydaburg, Klawock, and then at Pacific American Fisheries in Petersburg. In 1985, Stanley retired from Icicle Seafoods, as the cannery was known at that time.

Elda Filax was born in Broadacres, Saskatchewan, Canada, where she attended Morton School. She moved to Winnipeg to finish high school and go to nursing school. Elda received a letter from Evangeline Tate, requesting she come to Petersburg after her graduation from nurse's training. Elda worked her way across Canada for the next six years, going where the wages were better. In 1947, Dr Benson sent her an offer of a job at the Petersburg Hospital.

She met Stanley at the Tates'. Stanley and Elda were married on June 5, 1948. They lived at Stanley's folks until they located out the road at Three Mile.

At the hospital, Elda worked mainly night shift, as well as giving anesthetics. While nursing on the prairie, she had been taught how to give anesthetics. One couldn't always wait for a doctor to travel 100 miles for surgery.

She worked 25 years at Petersburg Hospital.

She and Stanley have lived in Scow Bay 54 years. Their three children are Stanley Donald, John Edward and Beverly Jean.

Stanley Donald was born July 1949. He married Carol Stromdahl in 1967. They live in Adna, Washington, where he works for Cummings Northwest in nearby Chehalis. Their three children are Wendy, Heather and Steven.

John Edward was born March 1951 in Wrangell. He married Patty Pollock in 1970. They presently live in Mukilteo, Washington, where they own a store. They have two children, Sherry and Justen.

Beverley Jean was born April 1952 in Petersburg. She married Brian Coleman in 1969. They live in Randle, Washington, where he is a contract timber faller. They have four children: Roxanne, Tonya, Jett and Dannille Kay.

Dorsey "Dusty" and Ruth Rhoden

By Ruth Rhoden

Dorsey Lee "Dusty" Rhoden was born in Jacksonville, Florida, in 1929. His father was a bus driver and his mother a homemaker. He has an older brother and sister. He spent his childhood running barefoot through fields, chasing rabbits with a big stick. In high school he excelled in swimming and diving.

In 1947, his brother decided they should both join the U.S. Coast Guard. The recruiting officer promised them that they could serve their three-year enlistment in Florida. Six weeks later, Dusty was in Ketchikan. Shortly afterwards, he was sent to Petersburg, where he stayed until his discharge in 1950.

Ruth Gayle Mortensen was born in Chateau, Montana, in 1933. She joined older sister Colleen and older brother James. Her father, George "Bud," and mother, Alice, were both commercial cooks.

In 1940, the Mortensen family moved to Bremerton, Washington. In 1944, they moved to Petersburg, where Ruthie's father worked for Pacific American Fisheries, cooking on cannery tenders and rigging scows.

Her mother worked for a time at The Lillian Shop, a women's clothing store was owned by Roxy Lee's aunt, Lillian Swanson. It was located in half of the building where Wells Fargo Bank is now located. The other half of the building was the post office.

When the family arrived in Petersburg, the population was less than 1,500. Everyone knew immediately that they were the "new people" and were very friendly.

In 1944, there was no landfill in the harbors. All of the buildings on the beach side were built on pilings. Many of the streets off Main Street were made of wood planks. The rest were gravel and could get very muddy during the spring thaw. The main road only went to Papke's Landing. At that time it was called "the end of the road." At the opposite end was Sandy Beach.

When Dusty came to Petersburg in 1947, Ruthie saw him and their fates were sealed. They spent a good deal of time at the town's favorite "parking" spots. One was the cemetery hill, and the other was the old garbage dump on Sandy Beach Road.

The dump was located about where Anne Leekley's house is now. It consisted of a dock built out over the water. The garbage truck simply backed out to the end and dumped the garbage into Frederick Sound. Claude Roundtree owned the garbage business and was helped by sons Lyle and Lloyd. The garbage just floated in and out with the tide.

Dusty lived on the 52-foot coast guard boat. On Mondays, he and the other two coastguardsmen took the boat out Wrangell Narrows and filled the navigation lights with kerosene. On Thursdays, they went out again to make sure the lights were still working. It was rough duty.

Ruthie worked at various times at the Sweet Shop, The Pastime Café, the Recreation Café, and finally, at Parr's Bakery — her favorite job of all.

Ruthie and Dusty Rhoden

In 1950, Dusty and Ruthie were married and left for Jacksonville to start their life together. Five months later, Alaska called. They were soon back in Petersburg.

Dusty fished shrimp and seined with Clyde Sheldon for a couple of years. He then worked for Cliff Roundtree at Reliable Transfer. He moonlighted as a bartender at the Harbor Bar, owned at that time by Ted Reynolds. He did this for 15 years.

He was famous for arm wrestling. Only one person ever beat him — Jerry Hestad, a local friend and cousin to Ilene Opsal.

Ruthie got a job at the Telephone Exchange, the local telephone company owned by Lillian and Lloyd Swanson. This was a very fun place to work and it provided jobs to many teens over the years. The switchboard consisted of only 150 numbers. Consequently, many people were on party lines. For example, everyone who lived in Scow Bay was on the

Dorsey "Dusty" and Ruth Rhoden cont'd

same party line — about 15 to 20 families. Because there was a lot of "listening in," you had to be careful what you said.

When there was a fire, the call came in to the operator who activated a siren, then told the firemen where to go. It was a very busy time because everybody else called in, too, to find out where the fire was.

There was no police station. If the policeman was needed, the operator would turn on a special light on a telephone pole. Crime was not rampant.

Herman Papke had a phone. He would call in to report a freighter or passenger ship passing his place on the way to town, so the longshoremen would be ready. (Papke was a very popular character. When Ruthie was initiated into high school, she had to get his signature on an egg.)

In 1953, their daughter, Darcy, was born. About that time, Dusty went to work for the city in the public works department. In those days, the city did many things for the people of Petersburg. If you had a sewer problem or frozen pipes, you just called the city and they would come and fix it for you. If there was a charge, it wasn't much.

In 1955, Ruthie and Dusty bought Jim and Elsie Rhodes' house on the corner of Third and Fram streets. Ruthie's parents and sister lived only a block away.

Son Cole was born in 1958.

In 1968, Dusty and Ruthie went into partnership with Don and Beulah Luhr and Marge and Norman Heimdahl. They operated the Family Shoe Mart and Fashion Fair until 1979, when the businesses were sold. Ruthie then went to work as bookkeeper for Alaska Island Air. She worked there for six years.

After 30 years, Dusty retired from his job at the city in 1984. At the time of his retirement, he was superintendent of the public works department and fire chief. Dusty retired just in time to help build their new home on Wrangell Narrows in Scow Bay.

The Rhoden children, Darcy and Cole, both live in Petersburg.

Darcy and her husband, Rod Judy, own and operate Pacific Wing, an air taxi service. Their daughter, Stacy, is a librarian in Honolulu.

Their son, Matthew, works for them as a mechanic. Matt is married to a great girl, Donel, who is a budding photographer.

Cole is a pilot and flies for Pacific Wing. His wife, Charlie, works for Alaska Airlines. His son, Scott, is in college. His daughter, Holly, is a senior in high school.

At this writing, Dusty keeps busy fishing, gardening and gathering firewood.

Ruthie is a hothouse plant and enjoys reading, knitting and watching Dusty garden. They both feel blessed that they live close to their children, grandchildren, and sister Colleen Nicholson. They are also both glad that someone invented lutefisk.

Sunday School angels
About 1919

Carl and Elizabeth Rogers

Adapted from an interview by Julianne Curry

Carl Ferdinand Rogers was born February 17, 1882, in Sweden. He came to America when he was a young man and worked as a chef in restaurants in Tacoma and Seattle.

On March 16, 1917, he arrived in Petersburg to take over management of the Wester Hotel and Baltimore Grill.

While running the Baltimore Grill, Carl was shot by his partner. X-ray photos disclosed a small flat piece of the bullet lodged near his brain. He was taken to Seattle and operated on at Providence Hospital.

Hanna Elizabeth Johnson was born in North Ljunga, Sweden, on October 26, 1887. She had three older brothers. Elizabeth's father immigrated to America and settled in Evanston, Illinois, before sending for the family.

Rather than leave with her family, Hanna decided to stay in Sweden with an aunt and uncle who owned a fur business.

Two years later she joined her family. It was there she met her first husband, Albert Rogers. Hanna and Albert were married April 12, 1912.

Tragedy struck the young couple in California on July 17, 1916. While on a picnic, Albert dove into a shallow lake and broke his neck. He died a short time later.

Albert's brother, Carl Rogers, lived in Petersburg. After Albert died, Carl wrote Elizabeth and asked if she would like to come to Alaska and work in his restaurant. She soon found herself embarking on another adventure.

Elizabeth and Carl were married February 19, 1919. They had two daughters, June (White) and Betty (Pederson). (*See Lloyd and Betty Pederson story.*)

The family spent three summers in Port Alexander, where Carl and Elizabeth ran a restaurant. Returning to Petersburg, they built a log cabin on a Wrangell Avenue. (Ray Olsen now owns it.)

After years at the hotel, they bought a little place called the Sandwich Shop, where the Moose Club is now located. They sold pies, bread and sandwiches. Elizabeth would pack the bread and pies she had baked at home and walk to the store.

Like most people, they were having trouble making ends meet during the Depression. But the family was never hungry. Betty and June would often go to the beach and dig clams. A small garden provided potatoes and carrots, and there was never a shortage of fish and venison.

Petersburg Boardwalk
Alaska State Library, Skinner Foundation Collection, PCA 44-1-9

As they grew older, Carl had a stroke that left his speech impaired. On December 23, 1958, he had a fatal heart attack. He was 76 years old.

In 1978, Elizabeth died of natural causes at the Pioneer Home in Sitka. She was 90 years old.

Ole and Ellen Rosvold

By Mickie Rosvold

Ole Bergam Rosvold was born on the island of Smøla in Norway, in 1887. He first came to Petersburg, in 1909, at age 22.

He was engaged in commercial fishing. Early records report him as captain of the vessel *Seagull*, fishing halibut in the area. His sister, Augusta Rosvold, was also an early resident. In 1914, she married Martin Enge, son of one of the original settlers, Rasmus Enge.

In the spring of 1914, Ole's fiancée, Emelie Askeland, came from Seattle to stay with the Martin Enges. Emelie was from Haugesund, Norway. She had joined her brothers and sisters in Seattle. (Emelie's niece, Tora, who married Pete Thynes, came from Norway a generation later. Her children and grandchildren are still living in Petersburg.)

Emelie and Ole were married in July 1914. Emelie, 21, died in childbirth in June 1915. She and her infant daughter are buried in the old cemetery on Kupreanof Island across the Narrows.

After a few years, Ole returned to Norway. He later married Elen (Ellen) Anvik.

In September 1922, Ole, Ellen, and two-year-old daughter Borghild immigrated to the United States, arriving on the *Bergensfjord*. Mrs. Martin Enge and her youngest son, Ernest, were on the ship with them.

Ole and Ellen's son, Arthur, was born in 1923. Daughter Darline was born in 1930. All three children graduated from Petersburg High School.

The Rosvolds moved into their new home in 1924. The house, on what is now 403 South Nordic Drive, remains in the family.

Ole continued to fish. In 1927, he and Ole Husvik bought the *Unimak* from John Molver. They fished blackcod, halibut and salmon until 1937. At that time, Ole went to work as a foreman in the cold storage, leaving fishing to spend more time with his family.

Ole, Ellen, and daughter Borghild became U.S. citizens in 1938.

Ellen and Ole Rosvold

Ole died in 1950; Ellen in 1969. They were both active in the Sons and Daughters of Norway and in the Lutheran Church. Ellen was known for her beautiful yard and bountiful garden.

Their daughter Borghild married Mike Brasted of Seattle. Borghild and Mike's daughter, Annette, and son Gary were born there. Borghild was widowed. After the children were grown, she returned to Petersburg. She was employed as bookkeeper at The Trading Union. She died in Petersburg in 1983.

Art's wife came from New York as a teacher. He and Mickie raised their three children, Eric, Korey and Ellyn Marie, in the community. All graduated from Petersburg High School. Eric has three children and makes his home in Petersburg.

Ole and Ellen Rosvold cont'd

Borghild, Arthur and Darline Rosvold

Art and Mickie moved permanently to their part-time home in central Washington in 2002. Their daughter Ellyn and her husband and two children moved to the same area in 1994. In 2000, Korey and his wife moved from Seattle to join the family "east of the mountains."

Ole and Ellen Rosvold's daughter Darline married Phillip Clausen, who is the son of Carroll and Elsie Clausen. Their children, Steven, Terry and Joni, were raised in Petersburg.

Steven and his family are currently living in Seward, Alaska. Terry and his family are in Seattle. Joni, who had five children born in Petersburg, passed away in 2001. Darline died in February 2002.

Many of Ole and Ellen's descendents and their families have been involved in the fishing and maritime industries. All maintain close ties to the community.

Augusta Enge with son Arnold
Ole and Ellen Rosvold with daughter Borghild

Borghild and her mother, Ellen Rosvold, on porch of the house the Rosvold family was renting from Nels Berg. Art Rosvold was born in this house.

Guy Roundtree

By Connie Roundtree

Guy Turner Roundtree was born in the Boistfort Valley of Lewis County, Washington, on October 30, 1872. Originally from Kentucky, the Roundtrees were early settlers in the Pe Ell area in Lewis County. Signing on as hunters, these pioneering Roundtrees had joined a wagon train and headed west from Knox County, Illinois. Guy's father, John, had three sons, Fred, Guy and Otis, and one daughter, Lena.

Guy Roundtree

While growing up in the Boistfort Valley, Guy's first jobs were connected to farming, logging and surveying. He was an assistant surveyor for his Uncle Hiram Roundtree, who was researching mining claims. Guy was proud of the fact that with only six years of formal schooling, he was considered a trusted assistant, helping to survey claims in the Wildwood area.

Guy married Frances Hogue, a neighbor. They had one daughter, Elsie (Clausen); two sons, Claude Lyle and Clifford; and one adopted daughter, Frances "Bunny" (Mathisen).

Guy came to Alaska in 1918. He sent for his family and they lived in a house on North Nordic Drive, just over the hill from the old Main Street.

Guy took jobs with logging outfits. He helped log a steep hillside at the south end of the Narrows on Mitkof Island. He also had fishing jobs and a liquor store, known as Guy's Place.

After a divorce from his first wife, Frances, Guy married Lucy Onee. Lucy was born in Port Protection, grew up in Kake, and had two sons, Louie Minard and Philip Darrow. Lucy and Guy had three girls, Lucille, Mabel and Agnes.

Lucille Kasbohn, who has six boys and one girl, lives in Wisconsin. Mabel Erickson has two daughters: Betty lives in Juneau and Barbara Kellie, in Petersburg. Agnes Bohannon lives in Ketchikan. She and Harvey "Bo" Bohannon have two girls, Michelle Killian and Sandra Harvey.

Guy and Lucy Roundtree lived in Ketchikan for years. Guy was in demand as a crewman on fishing boats because of his skills as a boat cook. Good meals were important to the men. They worked long, backbreaking hours, pulling nets by hand, unloading fish, and "icing up" without the modern equipment of today.

Guy lived to be 93 years old. He passed away in Ketchikan on April 11, 1965.

During World War II, the U.S. Coast Guard controlled access to the Petersburg waterfront and port area. Identification photos were needed by fishermen, cannery workers, businessmen and others to access the waterfront through gates on the docks. The water approaches to the boat harbor were also guarded by the Coast Guard.

Guy Roundtree's photo, to the left, is one of those World War II identification photos.

The photographer for many of these 1942 identification photos was Mary Allen, the daughter of John and Minnie Allen.

Many of the photos may be viewed at the Clausen Memorial Museum.

Claude and Isabella Roundtree

By D.J. Roundtree

Claude Lyle Roundtree was born August 24, 1900, in the Boistfort Valley in Lewis County, Washington, to Guy and Frances Roundtree.

The Roundtrees were farmers. Their children were Elsie (Clausen), Clifford, Claude, and adopted daughter Frances "Bunny" (Mathisen).

Besides farm work, Claude worked in the woods. He remembered working a full month, just to pay for a pair of boots.

Guy brought his family to Petersburg in 1918. Petersburg became the permanent home for all four children. Claude worked for Hogue & Tveten as a delivery driver. In 1919, with brother Cliff, he joined the Army and drove army trucks in Georgia.

In 1921, Claude married Mrs. Emma McQee, a sister of George Strom. The couple left the island and lived in the Seattle area. The marriage was short-lived.

Claude returned to Petersburg and worked as a Trading Union butcher with Henry Adsero. He was also a bartender at the Elks Club on Main Street.

Claude married Isabella Mary Robison, daughter of Petersburg Cold Storage engineer Dick Robison.

The couple lived up Hammer's Hill (Lumber Street) and also in a house on the corner of Fifth and Fram streets.

Two sons were born: Claude Lyle Jr. in 1928, and Lloyd Richard in 1931.

Claude was a volunteer at the Petersburg Fire Station, becoming senior fireman after 28 years of service. In the early days, he would try to get to the fire hall first so that he could be the driver.

Claude was a natural mechanic. He could invent, or make, a necessary part if he couldn't buy or find it. His tool shop in the later Roundtree house on South Nordic Drive was famous.

For recreation, Claude and his wife, Izzy, used a large punt named the *Izzy* to go to either of two small cabins. One was at Five Mile on the north end of Kupreanof Island. The other cabin was near the Smikum Club at Blind Slough, on Mitkof Island.

The Roundtrees took both boys and their dog everywhere they went. Friends often took their own boats and joined them.

Claude was an experienced outdoorsman. An avid duck hunter, he shared his hunting skills with his two boys.

Claude joined the City of Petersburg Sanitation Department as a driver. He soon bought his own truck, and took a contract with the city. Both boys were helpers in the family operation.

Claude and Izzy bought the log cabin at Beecher's Pass in 1956. It had been built in 1927, with logs from Thomas Bay, and needed repairs. Claude had all the right skills and the Roundtrees turned the cabin into a showplace.

Cargo was hauled to Beecher's Pass aboard the 22-foot cabin cruiser, *Stukie*. Supplies were loaded at Papke's Landing, where Hermann Papke frequently came down to talk to Claude on the dock.

Many summers were spent at the cabin with family and friends. The cabin is still owned by the Roundtree family.

On May 15, 1964, Claude died from a sudden heart attack while anchoring the *Stukie* at Beecher's Pass. Claude was survived by his wife, Izzy, sons Lyle and Lloyd, their spouses, and six grandchildren.

Isabella "Izzy" Mary Robison was born in Tacoma Washington, on August 17, 1911, to Mary Etta (Miller) Robison and Herbert Richard Robison.

The Robison family had four children: Agnes, Herbert Jr., Izzy and Loretta. While living in Seattle, the children entered school. Dick was a fireman learning refrigeration in his spare time.

In 1918, Dick got a job as chief engineer for the Seward Cold Storage plant in Seward, Alaska. The family joined him. While there, Mary Etta took in sewing for the Seward ladies.

When Dick transferred to Scow Bay, as an engineer on the *Glory of the Seas* (a processing ship anchored by the dock), his family returned to Seattle. Izzy attended Ballard High.

In 1926, Dick moved the family back to Alaska. He had taken a job as the engineer at the new Petersburg Cold Storage.

Dick arranged to have a local moving company meet the steamship with a truck and workers to move the family's trunks to a rented house up Lumber Street. The two young men who worked for the moving company were brothers Claude and Cliff Roundtree. The men were wearing suits because there was a dance

Claude and Isabella Roundtree cont'd

that night. Izzy and Loretta were quite impressed with their welcome to Petersburg.

The Robison family's home number two was the Knutson house on the corner of South Nordic Drive and Skylark Street.

Claude and Izzy were married on July 4, 1927, by Magistrate Carroll Clausen, Claude's brother-in-law. Frances and Art Peterson were witnesses. The wedding party went out boating for the rest of the day.

Claude and Izzy Roundtree

The Roundtrees started housekeeping in a little house behind Cap and Amy Hallingstad's home on Lumber Street. Their windows looked down on Hammer Slough.

Claude worked as a driver with the Reliable Transfer Company, a butcher at The Trading Union, and a bartender at the Elks Club.

Their first child, Claude Lyle Jr., was born April 30, 1928. Lloyd Richard was born in 1931.

Izzy and Claude played an active role in the town's social life. They danced at Johnny Sales' dancehall and the Elks and Moose Clubs.

Izzy was as keen about the outdoors as Claude. They took the boys outboarding in a big punt, called the *Izzy*, to Duncan Canal, Beecher's Pass, Harvey's Lake, and to Five Mile, which was located on Kupreanof Island.

In 1956, Claude and Izzy bought a log cabin in Beecher's Pass from the Brennan and Wingard families. The "Brenwyn" had been built in 1927 for Bob Allen. Since the cabin needed much repair, Claude enlisted the ideas and workmanship of Cliff and Maggie Roundtree, sons Lyle and Lloyd, Pete Thynes, and their young families.

The Beecher's Pass cabin has been a showplace for many years, with much use by family and friends, as well as by stranded boaters.

Izzy had many jobs in Petersburg. Her cannery work started when she was hired by Viv Prince to come to work on the slime line at PAF. She much preferred working on the "filler" or, best of all, "the air hoist." She added humor to the boredom and fatigue of the long summertime hours.

Other jobs were at Slicker's Café, Citizen's Steam Laundry, The Star and The Cache.

After Claude died in 1964, Izzy moved to Sitka to take a job as a distributor for a wholesale grocery and liquor company.

She met and married John Dahlke, a retired master mechanic. John had worked on various construction jobs in the interior of Alaska.

Izzy played bridge and was an active Emblem Club member, becoming district deputy and past president. A stylish dresser, Izzy was also an excellent housekeeper and a superb cook. Her apricot brandy was a local favorite.

Claude and the boys were the focus of her life. She welcomed both daughters-in-law: Dorothy Jane "D.J." Henderson married Lyle in 1952. Irene "Ikie" Wasvick married Lloyd in 1954.

After John's death, Izzy returned to Petersburg. She lived in the Totem Arms Apartments, Mountain View Manor, and the hospital's long-term care facility, where she would make the nurses laugh.

She died peacefully on August 13, 1999.

Lyle and D.J. Roundtree

By D.J. Roundtree

Claude Lyle Roundtree Jr. was born in Petersburg on April 30, 1928, in a doctor's office located upstairs over the Alaska Communications System (ACS) / US Army 1st Signal Corps office. The ACS building was on Main Street next to Brennan's Bar (located near the present corner of Main and Gjoa Streets). Lyle was the first child of Isabella Mary Robison Roundtree and Claude Lyle Roundtree.

The Roundtrees lived in a small house up Lumber Street, behind Amy and Casper Hallingstad's home. The windows overlooked Hammer Slough. Claude was a Trading Union butcher and driver, as well as an Elks Club bartender.

A second child, Lloyd Richard, was born in 1931.

Lyle and Lloyd, along with the Thyne, Ohmer, Holten, Lando, Stutphen and Swanson kids, were part of the "Hill Gang." The kids were glad that they lived on "The Hill," not "Out the Point" or "Out the Road." By this time, their house was on the corner of Fifth and Fram streets.

Both boys learned to drive a truck by the age of 12. They worked hard with Claude, after he started his own business contracting with the City of Petersburg Sanitation Department.

The boys were taught the "ways of the woods" by their father, who was an excellent hunter. He also showed them the best ways to field dress game and have respect for the bounty they harvested.

Besides hunting, fishing and camping with his family, Lyle loved outboard engines. Sponsored by local merchant Hack White, Lyle took part in, and often won, hydroplane races throughout Southeast. He understood and respected the boat's limitations, while driving his skiff to every bay, bight, slough, creek and river in the area. Lyle's tales of his boating adventures were truly treasured by his friends.

In the 1940s, an attack of rheumatic fever endangered his life. The local physician, Dr. Benson, had heard of penicillin, a new drug being used by the Navy in the Anchorage area. Somehow, the doctor had penicillin airmailed to him. After several injections, Lyle began to get well.

The damage to his heart kept Lyle out of military service. He did, however, serve as a seaman on the U.S. Coast Geodetic Survey vessel, the *Baker*. The *Baker* was surveying the ocean bottom from Cook Inlet to Nome.

Local jobs included Hack's Cleaners, a taxi company driver, Sanitary Market driver, and Trading Union butcher, as well as a PAF cannery worker.

Airplanes always fascinated Lyle. In 1956, he took a position with Alaska Coastal Airlines. (It later became Alaska Airlines.) This began a career as an airline agent that spanned some 30 years.

D.J. and Lyle Roundtree

In 1952, Lyle married a Californian who had come to Petersburg to teach the third grade.

Dorothy Jane "D.J." Henderson came from a pioneer family in northern California. Her mother was Fannie Jane Whitaker Henderson. Her father was Jesse Fear Henderson.

Lyle and D.J. married in Vallejo, California.

They lived in the Wheeler Apartments above Heimdahl's Market on Main Street. Lyle worked for the City of Petersburg Public Works Department.

An unexpected heart attack sent Lyle to Vallejo College to take business classes. When they returned, the Roundtrees moved to the present-day ferry terminal area, where they lived in two small rental houses before building their own family home at 1109 South Nordic Drive.

Three children were born to the Roundtrees: Dana Jane in 1953, Patrick Lyle in 1956, and Dean Arthur in 1964.

In 1956, the family began going to the newly purchased Roundtree cabin in Beecher's Pass. For many years, fellow airline employees, relatives, and

Lyle and D.J. Roundtree cont'd

childhood friends enjoyed the warmth of the fireplaces and the many conversations that took place around them. The cabin is still an integral part of the Roundtree lifestyle.

Lyle met an untimely death near Buoy 31A in Wrangell Narrows on May 22, 1991. An unusual wave swamped and overturned the skiff in which D.J. and Lyle were returning to town in from Beecher's Pass.

Lyle and D.J.'s daughter, Dana, married Rick Douville. They have three daughters, Kellie, Marie and Cori.

Patrick married Tanya Deffenbaugh. Their three sons are Kyle, Jesse and Patrick Oliver.

Dean married Kathleen Fisher. Their two daughters are Alexia and Ariel.

Lyle Roundtree

Writing on photo:
Workmen PC&NP Co. sawmill
Petersburg, Alaska
W. H. Case
*Alaska State Library,
Core: Petersburg-People-2,
PCA 01-1550*

Lloyd and Irene Roundtree

By Irene Roundtree

A pioneer in Southeast aviation, Lloyd Richard Roundtree was born June 20, 1931, in Petersburg, the second son of Claude and Isabella "Izzy" Roundtree.

He attended Petersburg schools and had a typical childhood, including Cub Scouts, Boy Scouts, basketball, skiing and camping. At age 16, he shrimped with Ross Greinier on the now famous *Charles W*. He also fished on several other boats and worked both with and for his father, running the Petersburg Sanitation Department.

As a teenager, he got his first taste of flying by working with the local flying service. Instead of payment, he was taught to fly. He earned his private license in 1949. Slim Walters, Quentin DeBoer and David "Brownie" Brown were his instructors. Captain Brown was a teacher, mentor and lifelong friend. Flying eventually became Lloyd's life's work and love.

He enjoyed hunting and fishing and admired many aircraft. His gun collection was envied by all.

Lloyd flew his Cessna 185 out of Petersburg for a year or so, for Alaska Coastal Airlines. He was known for his meticulous care of equipment and his passengers. He carried this excellent reputation throughout his entire career.

In 1955, he married a local girl, Irene Wasvick. They had three children: Dane, Shannon and Stacey.

Grumman Goose

When first married, Lloyd worked for the construction company, Stock & Grove, building the road from Papke's Landing to Blind Slough. He then worked for The Trading Union and the City of Petersburg, where he was great with heavy equipment. He knew where every shutoff valve was located throughout the town.

In 1965, he went to work for Lon's Flying Service; in 1967, he purchased the company. Lloyd and Lon Marifern were the first two pilots to spot herring and other fish by plane for fishermen. They were also the first company in Southeast Alaska to purchase a DeHavilland Beaver for commercial use.

For the next 26 years, he and Irene ran the company, which they renamed Alaska Island Air, Inc. Lloyd flew all over Southeast Alaska and also flew aircraft south for major maintenance. He purchased a Grumman Goose and this plane was to become his special joy. Each night before returning to the airport hanger, his "baby" received a bath in freshwater at Petersburg Lake.

Business prospered during the logging years. His fleet of aircraft included three Cessna 180s, a Cessna 185 amphibian, a DeHavilland Beaver, and the Grumman Goose. The company had a scheduled mail run, subcontracted by Alaska Airlines, and passenger service to Kake and small communities on the west coast. He was known as one of the Super Bush Pilots in Alaska and the Lower 48.

He inspired many young men to enter the aviation field. More than 50 pilots went through his doors and on to other airlines, corporate and charter jobs. Some retired from flying to meet other challenges. Lloyd stressed safety and meticulous maintenance. Wanting his pilots to learn this lesson well, safety was preached to all employees, all the time.

He was very mechanically inclined and could build and fix anything. Kenmore Air Harbor was the

Lloyd Roundtree fueling his plane.

Lloyd and Irene Roundtree cont'd

main supplier and overhauler. In the early days, he flew engines, repair parts, refrigerators, people, ball teams, fishermen, government employees, medics, campers, boaters, you name it — if it fit by size and weight into one of the airplanes — Alaska Island Air flew it!

The company earned many safety awards and accolades. Lloyd was one of the founders of the Alaska Air Carriers Association, which is still in high gear today. Much was accomplished by uniting Alaska's air carriers and charter companies. Lloyd was vice-president and on the board for several years. The group had authors, astronauts, and many dignitaries as speakers at their conventions. It was both educational and interesting.

Lloyd and his son, Dane

Lloyd and Irene's son, Dane, also became a pilot. Lloyd had already taught him to fly, so at the age of 16, he obtained his student certificate in Petersburg. He attended Spartan Aviation School in Tulsa, Oklahoma, and acquired his seaplane ratings at Kenmore Air in Seattle. Dane is now a businessman in town and has two children, Jennifer and Casey.

Daughter Shannon and her husband, Al Peeler, are a fishing family. They have seven children: Jessica, Justin, Nathan, McKenzie, Max, Zach and Emma. Stacey and her husband, Ken Madsen, are also in the fishing industry. They have Jacob and Rebecca.

Shannon and Stacey are both great stay-at-home mothers. The girls are very active in school and church activities, and the men have their own boats to take care of. All three families reside in Petersburg.

In 1980, Lloyd retired from flying. He then purchased his second love, a 49 Grand Banks yacht,

Lloyd aboard the *Copesetic*

the *Copesetic*. The Roundtree cabin in Beecher's Pass was a favorite anchorage.

For 16 years, Lloyd and Irene cruised the waters and bays of Southeast Alaska. Their special friends, Bob and Ruth Munro of Kenmore Air, accompanied them on the *Copesetic* on their travels. Sport fishing, sport crabbing, grandkids and the boat took up most of their time. A wonderful time was had by all.

Lloyd passed away May of 1996, after being medivaced to Seattle. Alaska Airlines flew him low over Wrangell Narrows to his final resting place at home.

He was a true pioneer and a born and bred Alaskan. He was a member of the Pioneers of Alaska, Elks and Moose Lodges, Volunteer Fire Department and Lutheran Church.

Lloyd was also a Korean War veteran, spending his service years in and around Anchorage. He was a lifetime history and aviation buff.

He lived his life to the fullest and the typical "Lloyd look" included small Eric cigars and sunglasses. The seaplane float was named "The Lloyd Roundtree Seaplane Facility" in his memory.

He was a good husband, father, grandfather and a great friend. His phenomenal memory and storytelling will be, and has been, missed by all who knew him. He is gone, but not forgotten.

Copesetic

Melvin "Sock" and Connie Roundtree

By Connie Roundtree

Melvin "Sock" Roundtree was born on April 5, 1921, in Petersburg, Alaska, to Clifford and Magna Roundtree. Sock received all his schooling in Petersburg. While he was still in high school, he owned and drove an International wood-sided station wagon as a school bus. After high school, he joined the U.S. Merchant Marine. When World War II started, he joined the U.S. Coast Guard and was stationed in Ketchikan for four years. Sock held the rank of coxswain and operated a 38-foot picketboat, hauling servicemen, mail and supplies between Ketchikan and Annette Island, where there was a large army base.

It was while Sock was in Ketchikan that he met me, Connie Berg. I had borrowed a beat-up Model T truck and was trying to teach myself to drive. I hadn't quite mastered the shifting of gears properly, so I ground and jerked my way to a stop at the coast guard base checkpoint, south of town. Sock happened to be on duty at the checkpoint that day. He decided I needed driving lessons and tracked me down in Wacker City, eight miles north of Ketchikan.

Connie and Sock

Sock and Connie

I was born in Ketchikan, Alaska, to Arne and Julia Berg, on September 9, 1926. I was raised in Wacker City, an area now called Ward Cove. As children, my brother, sister, and I trolled for salmon, speared crabs, beach combed, picked wild berries and wildflowers, skated and swam in the lakes, and hiked the deer trails.

My mother and I also worked at Brindle's Ward Cove Packing Company — lots of fish, long hours, and it was fun! I attended Wacker School where my mother taught. She taught all eight grades, from 1925 to 1938. The last few years of grade school I attended school in Ketchikan, graduating from Ketchikan High School in May 1944.

Sock and I were married in my parents' home on June 21, 1944. After the war ended, Sock and I headed for Petersburg with our baby son, Clifford, who was born February 27, 1945. He was immediately named "Fuzz" because of his downy snow-white hair.

Rentals were virtually non-existent in Petersburg, but Sock's grandparents owned two rentals. One was called "Hitler House" and the other "The Shack." Maggie, my mother-in-law, and I painted the one-bedroom "Shack" and made it pretty. There was barely room for little Cliff's crib at the foot of our bed.

Sock's father, Cliff, drove the station wagon school bus while Sock was in the service. He was happy to turn the school bus job back over to Sock when he returned after the war. Sock really enjoyed the kids. He always treated them to an ice cream cone at the end of the school year. On my birthday, any kids who

Melvin "Sock" and Connie Roundtree cont'd

had their parents' consent could ride to Blind Slough at the end of the bus route, where we'd roast hotdogs.

On July 11, 1946, daughter Julie was born. It was time for a bigger home! Sock's Uncle Jake sold us a 50-by-100-foot piece of land and Sock began building a house, using only a shovel, handsaw and hammer. This would be our "temporary" home, to be used as a bus garage later.

We moved into our dream garage just in time to welcome baby daughter Marie, born January 29, 1948.

When the Wasvick & Torwick grocery store closed, Sock contracted to haul mail from Alaska Coastal's floatplanes to the post office between school bus runs. In the summer, Sock drove dump trucks on construction jobs.

We lived in Wrangell when Sock worked for Berg Construction and in Sitka when the airfield was built on Japonski Island.

In 1966, Sock bought the Reliable Transfer business from his parents. Most all incoming and outgoing freight, including canned salmon, was handled by Reliable Transfer. He was also the agent for Alaska West and Lynden Transport.

For Sock and me, being able to work with the people of Petersburg, who envisioned a swimming pool in our town, was a tremendous experience.

Kids of all ages were really something — they went to work raising money for a pool. They had dances at the Moose Club and American Legion halls, held bazaars at the Sons of Norway, had a barn dance at Martinsen's Dairy, and a dunking booth on the Fourth of July.

Because it was a community effort, I hesitate to name anyone, but one donation stands out. Petersburg Fisheries wrote a donation check on the back of a king crab shell. The bank accepted it! The shell now resides at Clausen Memorial Museum.

Superintendent Don Schultz and the school board discovered tobacco tax money, which could only be used for new school construction. The city chipped in funds, the kids donated the $25,000 they had raised, and the swimming pool became a reality.

Our son Fuzz was first married to Laurel Tate of Petersburg. They have twins, Guy and Katrina. Fuzz's second wife was Lynn Stromdahl. She had five children, Rick, Darrel, Tim, Alta and Lisa. Lynn passed away from cancer in 1992.

Our daughter Julie married Jerome Dahl. They have two children, Bridget and Jerome Jr.

Daughter Marie married Larry Colman. Their children are Ronda, Copper, Barry, Crystal and Jesse.

Sock passed away in Petersburg on November 2, 1972. I found I couldn't walk the familiar paths without Sock ... so I left "for a while."

I am still here at Puget Island and Rochester, Washington, near my son, Cliff, and his family, and my daughter Marie and her family.

Julie, Magna Roundtree (Sock's mother), Connie, Sock, Julia Berg (Connie's mother), Cliff and Marie

Dr. Joseph and Amy Rude

By Audrey Rude Gilbert

It has always seemed very "right" to me that my first memories are of being on a train headed west from Minnesota to Seattle, en route to Ketchikan, Alaska. Dad was to be associated in a medical practice with a doctor already established in that Southeast Alaska town.

After his discharge from the U.S. Army following World War I, my father, Joseph O. Rude, finished his medical studies and was eager to pursue his career.

He met Amy Brekke while attending Bible School. They were married the very day Dad enrolled in medical school at the University of Minnesota. No G.I. Bill in those days!

Eight years later, with three children and a baby on the way, they arrived in Ketchikan, where brother Jim was born.

Jim, Audrey, J. Donald, Lorraine, Amy and Joseph

According to what Mother told me, there was a young doctor in Petersburg who approached Dad with the idea of exchanging locations. The young unmarried doctor was in search of more social life than Petersburg provided. With the blessings of Dad's employer, the change was made.

I have always believed that our move to Petersburg was arranged through divine guidance. Petersburg is a small town founded by Norwegian immigrants interested in establishing businesses in fishing and lumber. Both Mom and Dad were of Norwegian parents, who had left their homeland to locate in the farming heartlands of Minnesota and neighboring states. Both spoke the language, they were of the Lutheran faith, and the hospital was supported by the Lutheran Church.

Mom and Dad quickly assimilated into the working and social life of Petersburg. Activities at church, school, and fraternal organizations, such as the American Legion, were of primary interest. Hiking, sport fishing, and hunting provided other ways to spend leisure time.

Before we departed Petersburg, the new Lutheran Church was built up the hill. I well remember when the gymnasium was built. Visible from our kitchen window, we could see the crews of men hurrying to complete this much-anticipated structure. It was the scene of future sports activities and such formal events as the junior prom. The second floor included a manual arts training department.

I will forever appreciate the time volunteered by townspeople — Laura Johnson with the first Girl Scout troop, Tom and Grace Windsor with the Boy and Girl Scouts, and Bunny Mathisen with the 4-H Club. The skating rink behind the Catholic Church was dug by townspeople, as were swimming holes out the road, and the ball field that was built past Sutphens' house.

I remember the excitement when a real carnival and fair came to town with a merry-go-round and Ferris wheel, and the Saturday matinee at Enge's theater or the Coliseum Theater. At the Sunday night movie, if your name was drawn, you could win money. Dad once won $87. There was also the occasional talent show. Colleen MacDonald and I sang some Shirley Temple song, and lost out to the more talented tap dancer Justine Gronseth. I remember when each of us Rude kids got a dollar in paper money, which was a novelty, as silver dollars were more common to us.

Petersburg was a town where everybody knew my name. It was a town where the language of the native Indians could be heard on the street, mingled with languages of Japan, China, the Philippines and Scandinavia.

The holidays were always special, and still are. May 17th looms large in the spring, now a full-blown, nationally known celebration. The celebration was smaller, but no less important, in the old days. I

Dr. Joseph and Amy Rude cont'd

remember Mom telling me about a midnight picnic, when a wreck of a small boat was set afire and pushed out to sea.

The Fourth of July was a time for a new dress and perhaps a "waffle weave" jacket or coat. All kinds of races occupied the earlier hours of the day. I remember a fierce tug-of-war conducted on the remaining floor of a torn down building on Main Street. This was a day for root beer floats. The older kids set up their stands and sold homemade root beer — the stronger the better. A parade for the kids took place on Main Street. I once won $5 for the best decorated doll buggy. My brothers, Don and Jim, won both first prize and grand prize, for dressing like old miners with provisions and being pulled by our little dog, Terry. One year Dad towed Dorothy Young on a surfboard 'round and 'round the harbor...quite a sight.

Halloween was celebrated with the usual trick-or-treat. Sometimes there was a costume party in the gym. Thanksgiving dinner often featured a roast venison or goose instead of turkey.

There were two bazaars a year: one organized by the women of the Lutheran Church, one by members of the Daughters of Norway. Wonderful dinners were served upstairs in the Sons of Norway Hall, while the lower level was reserved for the various bake, gift, and craft tables, and the ever-present "Fish Pond."

Preparations for Christmas started early. The harbinger of the season was the arrival of the Montgomery Ward and Sears Roebuck catalogs. We girls often stood around the post office desk, thumbing through the pages, marking them for further scrutiny, consulting with one another as to the prettiest this or that. One steamship company provided a Santa Claus for the local children. Notified ahead of time, the younger school children were escorted by teachers and older students down to the dock. We each received a small stocking filled with hard candies and a Christmas orange. We ate the orange segment by segment — it was a real treat. This was the only Santa I knew of who traveled by ship and came from the south!

A Christmas Sunday School program was performed for proud parents each year with bathrobed "kings" and "angels" wearing the white junior choir half-robes and a "halo" of silver rope tied around their heads. The youngest children sang their sweet rendition of "Away In A Manger," and the baby Jesus lay in a manger — the first Christmas, celebrated ever after. The Norwegian Christmas custom of visiting home to home, store to store, and eating one's way around town was also fun. If there was ever a Christmas without snow, I don't remember it.

Winter provided wonderful activities. Of course, the early settlers built a ski jump. I have a wonderful picture of Dad soaring through the air much like Ernie the Eagle, the British entry to the Winter Olympics a few years ago.

Skating on the pond near our home, or at Falls Creek, was always fun. The beauty of the snow-covered hills and mountains is unforgettable. Finally the snow would melt and the contest would begin: How long would it take for the snow to melt on Petersburg Mountain? Sometimes it hung on until July.

I regret missing my teen years in Petersburg. I never climbed Petersburg Mountain, or worked in the cannery, or even hiked to the water dam. Perhaps it's not too late!

I can only say I had a wonderful childhood in Petersburg and feel lucky to be able to visit regularly, just last May, in fact. Petersburg, the home of my childhood, the home of my heart.

I graduated from Juneau High School in May 1944. In August, I left to attend college in Minnesota.

I became engaged to Richard Gilbert, a G.I. from Maryland, who had been stationed in Juneau.

While I spent a few days in Seattle, Dick was in the military police at Portland Army Air Base. I managed to get on his duty train and got off with him.

We were married in Missoula, Montana. We lived in Portland until his discharge in March 1946, and then returned to Maryland, his home state.

Six years later, Dick received his law degree. He was in private practice and was named to the Maryland Court of Special Appeals 20 years later.

I have lived in Annapolis for 29 years.

Dr. Joseph and Amy Rude cont'd

By Donald Rude

All four of my grandparents were born in Norway. On the maternal Brekke side, they came from Viki Sogn; on the paternal Glorud side, from Mysen in Ostfold. Great-grandfather Glorud shortened the name to Rude. He farmed in Minnesota, as did his son, my grandfather, who was a boy when they arrived in 1872. My mother's parents came as Lutheran missionaries in about 1893.

My grandparents were married in 1894 in Nebraska, but lived many places thereafter.

My father, Joseph, was born on a farm near Gary, Minnesota, April 13, 1895. My mother, Amy Brekke, was born at Grafton, North Dakota, July 5, 1901. They met while they were both in a boarding high school. Joseph's education was delayed by farm work and military service during World War I. They were married September 21, 1921, after he finished high school and started at the university. He graduated from medical school in March 1929 and immediately left for Ketchikan, Alaska, with his pregnant wife and three children.

Their first home in Ketchikan was in a house on pilings on the outside of the street that was also on pilings. At high tide, they were 50 feet offshore. Not a very good introduction for a girl from the Midwest. On one occasion, we three kids managed to hoist a big block of wood over the fence in back and amid shrieking and yelling, dropped it into the water. Naturally, mother thought it was one of us kids. Soon after that we moved to a house onshore.

After three months in Ketchikan, and with a new son, Dad heard about an opening in Petersburg and traveled there on a herring seiner, either the *Phoenix* or the *Odin*, to investigate. He liked what he saw and we moved.

At first we rented the Evans' house on Third Street next to Ole Holm, but then bought the Knut Thompson house on Third Street, where our neighbors were the John Jensens and the Harold Lees. Other nearby neighbors were the Bill Steadmans, Ole Ekrems, Lany McKecknies, George Nicholsons, Carl Thynes, Dan Sutphen, Claude Roundtree, Bill Halts, Tom Lando, Egil Winther, Earl Ohmer, Robert Allen, Tom Elsinore, Olaf Waswick, Arnold Waswick, Anton

Jim, Don, Audrey, Amy, Lorraine and Joseph Rude

Noreide, Ed Thorson, Jacob Otness, John Otness, Carl Harlin, Harry Loy, Chris Gronseth, Louis Vick, Jack Wanberg, Ivor Holm, Jim Allen, Knut Stenslid, the Grebstads, Israelsons, Justin Lind, and the Bergs. The Lutheran Church and parsonage were just across the street. The John Maakestads occupied the parsonage at that time. Of course, the U.S. Marshal, the jail and the hospital were just down the street.

It was a close-knit neighborhood — one extended family. We considered ourselves the Hill Gang, at least among the youngsters. There were three other groups, the Point Gang, the Town Gang and the Out the Road Gang. There was some rivalry between the gangs, but nothing serious.

Although both our father and mother spoke fluent Norse, none of us kids picked it up and most of our friends spoke English, even at home. Our parents used Norse to talk about adult-only affairs. Our life centered around the school, the church, and our home. Dad quickly became involved with hospital, church

Dr. Joseph and Amy Rude cont'd

and the Commercial Club. He was elected to the school board, but otherwise was not involved in the local politics. There were no service clubs at that time, but there were the Masons.

Dad had evening hours on some days, and since we could hear him start his car downtown, we knew when to turn off our lights. Sometimes, he would bring ice cream from the drug store, which had to be eaten right away because we had no refrigerator.

There were two movie theaters, The Variety, owned by Rasmus Enge, and the Coliseum, owned by Mr. Gross in Juneau, with different managers. However, most entertainment was in homes. Ours was periodically the scene of pinochle games with the neighboring parents. The Sons of Norway was often the site for dances and bazaars. There were some radio sets, and Dad had one of the few private motor vehicles.

Streets were plank, and repairs were made with lumber carried on two-wheeled carts. Main Street was still a plank street, but soon was filled. However, the tide still came up under the buildings on the shore side. Because the side streets were plank, it was possible to use sleds and even skates on the streets when conditions were right. There was also a dike and a pool, where the grade school is now, that was used for skating. When the road was completed to Falls Creek, there were many skating parties there.

For a time, there was roller-skating at Johnny Sales' dance hall, near the present ferry landing. Of course, roller-skating was possible on the plank streets.

Many people had cabins at Sandy Beach, which was reached by boat or a plank walkway over the muskeg. This was the place for all school picnics and many church and private picnics. Sometimes there were outings to Harvey's Lake or Point Agassiz, or a rowboat excursion up Petersburg Creek. There were few pleasure boats, but Dad soon got a skiff and later a round-bottomed boat with a one-cylinder inboard engine. He later had a very unreliable outboard.

In 1935, he bought an 18-foot Chris-Craft that was shipped out from Michigan. With this boat, he ran races against Art Peterson's runabout every Fourth of July. He also pulled Dorothy Young on a type of surfboard. Dorothy did not hold onto anything, but balanced on the board as it was pulled around a circuit. She got lots of cold dunkings that way.

Dad was an ardent fisherman. In May and June, we often went out early, bringing home several nice king salmon that we caught before he had to go to work. He was also an enthusiastic hunter and brought back many moose from the Stikine River. One time, he ran the boat almost to Telegraph Creek.

In the fall of 1940, he was invited to Juneau to interview with Dr. Lemuel Dawes. He accepted when asked to join Dawes' Juneau practice. That seemed like the end of the world for us kids, but it was a great opportunity for Dad. He still, however, considered Petersburg his true Alaska home.

In 1988, after 47 years in Juneau, he returned to Petersburg for the 75th anniversary of the Lutheran Church. The following morning, he had a stroke that disabled him. He never returned to Juneau, but spent the next three years in the Pioneers' Home in Sitka, where he died in January 1992.

My mother, Amy, was active in the church and the school, and with other interests throughout her life in Petersburg and Juneau.

In 1970, she began to show early signs of Alzheimer's disease and slowly became disabled, having to enter a nursing home in 1980. She passed away in March of 1988.

Lorraine, their older daughter, returned to Petersburg as a teacher in 1944. She married Thomas Thompson. They raised five children: Harold, Mark, Amy Jo, Gretchen and Tommy.

Donald, the older son, kept returning to Petersburg to work at the cold storage and to fish on various boats, until finishing his education as a surgeon. That work took him to East Africa and other countries, as well as Washington, New Mexico, and Alaska. He married Olive Ann Olson, a nurse from North Dakota. They have a son and a daughter.

It is of interest that a search of the records shows that one of Olive's great-aunts married one of Donald's great-grandfathers in 1802. Olive died in 1999, shortly after a month-long trip to Norway.

Audrey, the younger daughter, married a GI who had been stationed in Juneau. He became an attorney and judge in Maryland. They have two sons.

Jim, the younger son, became a navy flyer and then a TWA pilot. He lives in Massachusetts and has a son and a daughter.

Harold Runstad

By Betty Runstad

Hans Runstad and Jennie Farstad came to this country in their late teens. They both had grown up on the island of Lepsoy, out of Alesund, north and west of Bergen, Norway. This island is not large, and is divided in the middle by a mountain. (We would call it a hill.) On the south side lived the Farstads, Jennie's family. On the north side lived the Ronstads, Hans' family. Hans and Jennie were married in Everett, Washington, and traveled to Petersburg, where they raised their family.

Harold was born in 1911, Irene in 1913, Mildred in 1915, Norma in 1916, and Maurice in 1919. Jennie raised her family with one goal in mind — they would all receive college educations, no matter how long it took. "You will go out and get an education and a profession." They all did so.

Harold was the first son of Hans and Jennie, born April 7, 1911.

Harold Runstad

Harold was a basketball player in high school and a member of the 1929 Championship team. In those early days, they went to games by boat, a three-day trip that, if all the stories I heard are true, were great trips with dancing the whole way. Herb Mjorud, his good friend, told wonderful stories of those trips.

Harold was a wonderful dancer. As one of our friends said, "Wow, could that man DANCE!"

He was a superb, caring, and very bright man. Harold went to the University of Washington at the start of the worst financial depression this country has ever known. It took him six years to graduate.

Harold would go to the university for two quarters, then return to Petersburg to prepare the nets and boats for the fishing season. His fishing partner was Erling Strand. From the stories I heard, they were a frightful team, guarding their fishing spots by getting there first. He would fish spring and summer, making enough money to help the family and would return to the university to pursue his degree.

Harold received a degree in civil engineering in June of 1936. He went north to fish one last summer.

We were married October 10, 1936, and he started working at Boeing that same month. He was the 225th engineer hired in 1936. He had an outstanding career, both in airplanes and space. His work was classified top secret from 1940 until he retired, and I know very little about his titles.

When Harold retired, we traveled to Norway. We went by air from London to Bergen, to Aalesund, then by ferry to Lepsoy. We took the mail boat over the top of Norway, stopping in 38 fjords. That is indeed a magnificent country.

Many Runstads and Farstads are still living in Norway and, while we were visiting, they gathered the family together. (Several of them have visited here in Seattle and Everett.) The family is delightful.

We do not speak Norwegian, which is very sad for us. They had an interpreter for us to converse. In the olden days in Petersburg, the elders were learning English from their children and not speaking Norwegian with them.

Harold and I have a son, H. Jon Runstad Jr., and a daughter, Jill Runstad Hally. Both reside in the Seattle, Washington area.

Hal died in November 1994, and I continue to live in the Seattle area.

Johnny Sales

By Jack O'Donnell

Johnny Sales was a fine old gentleman from South Carolina who spent a good share of his later life in Petersburg. He loved the taste of whiskey and moonshine and would pour himself half a glass from a demijohn he always kept handy under the sink.

He was a frustrated farmer, displaced in Alaska. He had a few pigs rooting around on the hillside whenever it was clear of snow. People always chuckled at his efforts to create a farm, but he had the last laugh. The pigs eventually cleaned away the forest of tree stumps that discouraged others from buying the land.

Over the years he built several shacks in Petersburg. However, what decided him to build a dance hall and soft drink parlor way out on the outskirts of town was a mystery, for there were probably only a dozen cars in town, at most. Prohibition of liquor was in effect, so there was no possibility of earning a profit selling liquor. Besides, he always offered his guests a free drink, so apparently had no plans for a speak-easy.

He spent years struggling alone to get his dance hall constructed. When finally completed it was barely adequate to stop the rain from dripping in. He had an outhouse for women at one end of the hall, and another for men at the other end. The men's toilet was merely a large opening in the floor with a low bulkhead to prevent anyone from walking right in and dropping through to the beach 20, or more, feet below. It created a dizzying effect for anyone unfortunate enough to really have to go. When the tide was high, the distance down was not as far, of course, but then there was always the danger of drowning. Most men familiar with his toilet facilities used to slip out the back door exit and relieve themselves on the dance hall wall.

There was very little profit for Johnny, as half the customers entered through the back door to avoid the admission fee. I think Johnny really didn't care, as he was more interested in having company and enjoyed visiting with everyone. He invited his special friends back to his living quarters in the rear, where he always poured everyone a free drink of his moonshine.

His main source of income was a pile driver, which was constructed on a scow with a log A-frame to accommodate the hammer, which weighed perhaps 300 pounds. A piling was hoisted up to the maximum height of the A-frame, perhaps 40 feet, then sharpened on the bottom end with an axe to allow it to drive downward into the mud flats. This piling would then be lowered until the end touched bottom, which usually was 10 feet, or less. This was to make certain the piling, when driven as deeply as possible, would still have at least 10 feet remaining above water at high tide.

Each time the hammer was hoisted to its maximum height on the A-frame track, the front end of the scow would dip deeper into the water, as the one-cylinder engine labored to pull the hammer. Then, when the hammer was released to drop and hit the top of the piling, the engine would run freely, "Putt-putt-putt," and the front of the scow would leap upward creating a rocking horse effect.

If a piling was driven four feet down into the mud, Johnny considered that sufficient. Far too often, the lifting pressure of the tidewater at extreme high tide, plus the slight bump from a boat making a poor landing, was enough to have some of Johnny's driven pilings leap out of the mud, unless they had been fastened securely to another structure.

Johnny always seemed to take it all pleasantly and, if necessary, would return and redrive the same piling. He owned the only pile driver available. People who needed repairs done, or a new dock constructed, couldn't get too sarcastic about his pile driving, or they might wait years for him to return again.

He never married while in Petersburg. If he did enjoy a love life with a woman in town, he was discreet.

Once his pigs cleared enough ground for Johnny to plant a vegetable garden, he fenced-off that area and had truckloads of shrimp shells unloaded. Spread all over the ground, the stench of decaying shells was so nauseating passersby nearly choked. Cars rolled up windows and floored the throttle to escape, as quickly as possible. The unfortunate pedestrians had to stagger on past without drawing a breath as long as possible.

His garden flourished each season, and the neighborhood continued to endure the stench, partly because he was such a pleasant man, and partly because he always gave away most of his crop to anyone who stopped to visit.

(Story from Alaska Panhandle Tales or Funny Things Happened Up North, *1996, Frontier Publishing.)*

Chris and Inga Samuelson

By Annette Olson

My grandfather, Chris Samuelson, was born in Norway in 1878. He married Inga Pellaberg. They had one son, Gainhart, who was born December 23, 1912, in Aalsund, Norway.

They came to the United States when my father, Gain, was only 2 years old, and lived in Portland, Oregon, before coming to Alaska.

My grandfather was a fisherman. He longlined and trolled on his boat, the F/V *Raider*.

Before coming to America, he was a painter by trade. His boat was perhaps a little "punky" in spots, but the *Raider* always sparkled like a yacht.

His favorite saying was, "A good coat of paint covers a multitude of miseries."

One of my memories of my grandfather was that he always had mothballs in his coat pockets. He was also very neat, always going around with a whiskbroom. I remember how the furniture in his Portland home was always polished.

We loved to go visit our grandfather on his boat. He had a table that folded down and he gave us vanilla wafer cookies. Such a treat — store-bought cookies!

My grandfather took the last passenger steamship from Petersburg to Seattle and he never came back. He had a two-story home in Portland, Oregon, to which he retired.

My grandmother, Inga Pellaberg Samuelson, was a sister to Karl Hatlen.

She helped as a midwife. One of the babies she helped into the world was Dave Ohmer Sr., at the Hatlen home.

This house was once the Weston Hotel. The Hatlens purchased the building and property. They rebuilt a house on the same spot, in 1937, and moved in when it wasn't quite finished. Family still lives in this home located at 306 North First Street.

My father, Gainhart Samuelson, had several jobs. He was part owner in a transfer business with Red Jones and he drove a truck for the City of Petersburg.

He married Mildred Lorraine Israelson on November 18, 1935.

My mother, Mildred, was born January 8, 1917, the daughter of Andrew and Anne Israelson.

For their honeymoon, my parents hiked in from Brown's Cove to Crystal Creek — quite a hike! They stayed in a little trapper's log cabin built by Mildred's brothers and Gain. The walls still stood in the 1990s.

They had four children together: Darlene was born May 20, 1937; Annette, born October 17, 1944; Gainhart Jr. "Bud", born February 13, 1947; and Janice, born November 29, 1951.

Chris and Inga Samuelson with young Gainhart

When my parents first married, my father and his brothers-in-law built a log house close to Muddy River on land loaned from the Loseths.

His plan was for Mom to homeschool the children and live there forever. However, when Darlene was old enough for first grade, Mom put her foot down and public school it was.

After my grandfather retired, my father ran the F/V *Raider* until she fell apart; he didn't have his

Chris and Inga Samuelson cont'd

father's painting skills.

My father was part of all the different fisheries at one time or another, either by himself or with others.

Dave Ohmer Sr. hired him for several summers to prospect for Dungeness crab for the Ohmer cannery fishermen, from Duncan Canal to Sitka, Alaska, running the F/V *Charles T.* My brother, Bud, would go along.

Gain was a great storyteller and quite a prankster. He loved playing a good joke on his friends.

![Mildred, Darlene and Gainhart Samuelson]

Mildred, Darlene and Gainhart Samuelson

A true Alaskan, he loved the great outdoors — fishing, hunting, and trapping.

He spent his last years in Portage Bay and Farragut Bay, where he had some cattle. In June 1966, he drowned in Portage Bay.

My parents had divorced years earlier, and my mother Mildred married Clarence "Jack" Massey on August 13, 1953.

Clarence Massey was born September 3, 1924, in Lebanon, Missouri.

He served in the U.S. Navy during World War II aboard the USS *Lansdowne*. This destroyer was nicknamed the "Lucky L" because it made it through the war without any damage.

It was also the ship that transported the dignitaries from Japan to the USS *Missouri* for the signing of the Japanese surrender.

At the time he married my mother, Jack owned and operated the Red Top Taxi. At one time, he was a partner in the business with Guy Winslow.

He spent a lot of time managing the Moose Lodge. For several years he worked in the post office.

In the late 1960s, he began working for the Alaska Marine Highway, assigned to the *Malaspina*.

Jack died in a tragic car accident in 1974, while the ferry was in dry dock in Seattle, Washington.

They had two children: Bette, born August 14, 1954; and Andrew, born July 18, 1957.

With six children, Mildred was quite busy. She did, however, work for several years at The Pastime Café, until the fall of 1956.

She was such a good storyteller. My sister Darlene had a stuffed panda bear named "Pudda." Mom would change her voice to a throaty sound and talk "Pudda" for us. She was great fun!

Mom said she had always wanted to be an English teacher. And could she ever bake! To this day, we've never found a cinnamon roll that compares to hers.

Mom's greatest love was her family. She passed away on August 2, 1978.

Mildred and Jack Massey

Nils and Malla Sandvik

By Mildred Sandvik Lewis

Nils Sandvik was born in Sandvik, Norway, near Aure. He immigrated to America at the age of 18, coming through New York City. He traveled by train across the United States, stopping in Montana to work in a sawmill. Fellow Norwegians were also aboard the train, going to the West Coast.

Since their knowledge of English was limited and not wanting to show their ignorance, at each mealtime they would order the same thing.

Nils reached Portland, Oregon. There he met Malla Øie, a girl from Hardanger, Norway, who had traveled to the U.S. with her brother, Sivert. Their older sister, Anna, and her husband had immigrated earlier and had a dairy farm near Portland, Oregon. Malla was working in Portland when she met Nils.

Nils and Malla were married in 1912. They built a home in Portland. Oscar Sigurd, their first child, was born in September 1914. Twin girls, Freda and Mary, were born in August 1917. Mary died during the 1919 flu epidemic.

In 1917, when the U.S. entered World War I, Nils tried to enlist in the Army, but they wouldn't take him because he had three children.

Nils fished in Alaska for years before the family decided to move to Petersburg in 1920. An old-timer from Petersburg, Jack Mattson, helped them unload their luggage into a small boat, as there were no docks for the steamers to tie up to.

In 1925, another daughter, Mildred, was born. That was the year of the big snow. People had to board up windows on the first floor of their homes to protect the windows from being broken by the snow.

Nils and Malla learned English from their children and friends. Norwegian was not spoken in their home in order to become familiar with the English language. However, a few Norwegian words were used in their daily life such as "skopp" (cupboard), "bnev" (knife), and "skammel" (stool).

Growing up in Petersburg in during the Depression was unique, as it was a close community. Fishing was good, but prices were low. At times a boat had a "hole trip," meaning the skipper and crew did not make enough to pay expenses.

Money was scarce. Children ice-skated with Borden milk cans attached to their shoes until they could afford ice skates. Scooters were made from wooden apple boxes and roller skates. Most homes burned wood and coal, and not many had central heating. Coal was imported and delivered by Hogue & Tveten. Wood was plentiful, but you had to cut your own, and the sawmill also sold slabwood.

Everyone knew everyone else and, nine times out of ten, would lend a hand when needed. You could leave your skiff with the oars in it and no one would touch it. Folks didn't lock their doors unless they were leaving town for a while. If a woman was seen wearing a hat, she was either going to church or a funeral.

To give directions, you would say, "Up the street two houses past John's house." There were no house numbers or named streets. The streets were constructed of heavy wooden planks nailed to stringers with spikes. They were two or three feet off the muskeg. There were very few automobiles in town. Citizen's Steam Laundry, The Trading Union, and a few other businesses owned Model T trucks.

I cannot think of a cleaner or nicer place to grow up in than Petersburg, nor nicer people.

Malla Sandvik was loved by many Petersburg children and was called Grandma Sandvik by them. She passed away in January 1963 at the home of her daughter Mildred.

Nils entered the Pioneer Home, in Sitka, at the age of 80. When Mildred went to see him and told

Nils and Malla Sandvik cont'd

him halibut was selling for $1 a pound, he said, "What am I doing sitting here. I should be looking for a fishing chance." He passed away at the age of 94.

Nils had fished all his life on boats, such as F/V *Don Q*, F/V *Lena*, and F/V *Alice B*. His nickname was "Steinbeat."

Nels and Malla's son, Oscar, passed away in 1969 at the age of 55.

Their daughter Freda married Irvin Jepson and they live in Honolulu, Hawaii.

Their daughter, Mildred, has lived in Petersburg all her life. She married Tom Lewis. Tom was born in Foster, Oregon. He worked as a logger for 30 years in Oregon and Alaska. After marrying Mildred, Tom went to work as an oiler on the Alaska State ferry *Malaspina*.

Tom and Mildred both enjoy sport fishing and moose hunting. Mildred shot her first moose up the north arm of the Stikine River while hunting with her husband and Fred McGilton.

One morning about 7 a.m., Mildred was climbing a tree to look for moose. She saw a cow and bull moose in the meadow below her. She fired at the bull, which just stood there. The cow circled around the bull for a while and finally stomped off into the woods.

Mildred, Oscar and Malla Sandvik

Mildred came down from the tree to inspect her kill. Heading into the wind as she walked toward her moose, she heard a moaning sound and turned to see the cow behind her. She ran back to her tree, scrambled up, and waited three hours for the men to return.

The men pulled the moose to a beaver pond and then down to the river, using a winch connected to a chain saw. To their knowledge, this was the first time such a device had been used.

After 20 years, Tom retired from the Alaska State ferry system as a junior engineer. Mildred and Tom have traveled to Tok, Alaska, for many years, fishing for grayling trout and moose hunting. Tom belongs to Dousers of America, Masons, and Pioneers of Alaska. They have four sons, Robert, Steven, Theodore and Thomas.

Gronseth Cabin at Sandy Beach
Courtesy of Justine Morrell

Oscar and Ruth Sandvik

By Ruth Sandvik

In the fall of 1941, Ruth Wetterborg was hired by the Petersburg School Board to teach seventh and eighth grade English and history. The former teacher, Raymond Otis Warfield, had quit in August, leaving Superintendent George Beck in a bind. Alice Longworth had introduced Mr. Beck to Ruth at summer school at the University of Oregon.

A newspaper article, written by then Oregon State Senator Richard Neuberger, stated that when Ruth Wetterborg arrived in Petersburg on the SS *North Sea*, she stepped into the brawny arms of Oscar Sandvik. It wasn't that simple. This is what really happened: Alice and Ruth invited "Grandma Sandvik," her daughter, Mildred, and her son, Oscar, to dinner. Later, after Oscar and Ruth were married, Ruth commented about the dinner with him, "You didn't talk very much." Oscar replied, "I didn't have a chance," evidence of his quiet sense of humor.

Young couples in those days had few social activities: dinner with family and friends, dancing at the Sons of Norway, ice skating at Fall Creek in the winter, and swimming at Fall Creek in the summer. Oscar and Ruth indulged in each of these activities at least once before they were married.

In February 1943, on a Thursday noon, Oscar gave Ruth a diamond engagement ring. The students noticed right away and gave Oscar and Ruth an engagement party that very Friday evening, complete with food and congratulations. On May 25, 1943, Oscar and Ruth were married at the home of Malla Sandvik by the Reverend Thomas Knudsen, the Lutheran minister. The newlyweds rented an apartment in the home of Ann Ness; later the duplex where Dale and Leslie Bosworth now live. In 1944, Oscar and Ruth purchased the Bob and Helen Allen home at Second and Fram streets, where Ruth still lives.

Good friends made life in Petersburg enjoyable. Gordon Jensen and Oscar built a warehouse together, south of town by Enge's rock. They also built the Sandviks' garage. The Jack Longworths and the Sandviks played bridge for 10 years. Jack kept score and the men won 60 percent of the time. Jack always succeeded in bidding Ruth up higher than she should have bid.

Neil Alexander was born in 1945, Mark Severin in 1948, and Diane Ruth in 1956. The boys learned to hunt and they fished halibut with their dad, earning college money on the F/V *Munroe*. All three children graduated from college. Neil saw service in Vietnam.

Oscar and Ruth Sandvik

Raising the family in Southeast Alaska, the Sandviks ate plenty of venison and seafood. Before home freezers, everyone rented a box at the Petersburg Cold Storage to store their harvest.

In the spring of 1946, when Neil was 1½ years old, Oscar, Ruth and Neil took passage to Seattle on the SS *North Sea* to buy a replacement vessel for the F/V *Don Q*. The steamer hit a reef in Milbank Sound at 9:43 in the evening. Women and children were lifted over the side to lifeboats and taken to Bella Bella. Later,

Oscar and Ruth Sandvik cont'd

the passengers were transported to Vancouver, B.C., by steamer, then to Seattle by train.

About every three years, the F/V *Munroe* needed shipyard attention in Seattle. Ruth, who didn't know the difference between a troller and a seiner, had an opportunity to learn and enjoy life on the sea the eight or nine times when the family traveled to Seattle.

One exciting event on the Inside Passage occurred in 1958, when the steering chain broke while transiting the Ripple Rock area of Seymour Narrows. Oscar maneuvered the *Munroe* into a harbor north of the heaviest current. Mark squirmed into the lazarette to place the chain back on the starboard pulley. Later, the Canadians, tunneling beneath it with a charge, blew up Ripple Rock. At the time, it was the largest non-nuclear explosion ever.

In 1964, Superintendent Jack Hayward hired Ruth to be the first full-time Petersburg High School librarian, if she would return to college for additional training. Later, in 1971, she was able to earn her Master of Library Science degree. The high school students later gave Ruth the title of "Purple Librarian."

Having studied with Lloyd Reynolds in Oregon, Ruth taught calligraphy to whomever was interested. For 10 years, she has been a member of the local Tai Chi group. She is also an avid walker and has climbed Petersburg Mountain many times, the last when she was 80. She continues to walk the 4.5-mile loop route.

Ruth has always been an enthusiastic gardener. As a newcomer in 1945, she shocked the neighbors by working in her garden on her knees wearing shorts, sometimes on Sundays. She began by creating a lawn using Scott's lawn seed. Mainly a flower gardener, Ruth later studied and became a Master Gardener.

Oscar, Diane, Mark, Neil and Ruth Sandvik

The Sandvik children couldn't have grown up in a better town. The outdoors, exemplified by Petersburg Creek, was right next door. Up the creek by Martinsen's barn lay Hoagy's Hole, a great trout spot. Next was Miller, a coho hole and the gateway to the Clay and Sand Banks, where the wily steelhead lay.

School classes had yearly expeditions to Fall Creek and Crystal Lake, the source of water for the Blind Slough Power Plant. Kids could climb straight up the pipeline or zigzag through the woods to reach the lake. Other activities included swimming at Blind Slough, hikes, climbing Petersburg Mountain, basketball games, Fourth of July parades, and visiting Ethel and Harold Bergmann on Kupreanof.

Oscar Sandvik was a hard-working longline man, fishing halibut and blackcod. His nickname, "all-night Oscar," was given to him by Hugh and Richard Harris, when they fished all night after waking up late one morning. He occasionally fished tuna off the West Coast and tried salmon trolling, only to admit he liked halibut fishing best. In 1966, on the last trip he fished with the *Munroe*, he had sons Neil and Mark as his only crewmen.

Oscar and Ruth Sandvik cont'd

Oscar belonged to the Petersburg Chapter of the Pioneers of Alaska, Lodge 26, Free and Accepted Masons, BPOE #1615, the Petersburg Vessel Owners, and the Deep Sea Fishermen's Union.

Oscar died August 8, 1969, at the age of 54. He seemed too young to depart this earth. It is coincidental that he passed away a few weeks after the vessel he owned for more than 30 years, the F/V *Munroe*, sank outside Port Houghton in a tragic accident.

Petersburg has always given Ruth opportunities. The FM radio station, KFSK, along with National Public Radio, began locally in 1977. Ruth and her longtime friend, Alice Longworth, began as disc jockeys in 1978 when they substituted for Sandy Slack, noted Petersburg restaurateur and "founder" of KFSK. Alice and Ruth played big band music of the '40s and '50s and are at it still.

Organizations? Petersburg, Alaska, thrives on organizations. The first was the Garden Club, which evolved into the Civic Improvement Council. When Ruth began attending city council meetings, she was the only woman who had done so except for Magnhild Lee, a city council member in the '30s. The CIC was given the job of listing derelict shacks and automobiles about town and solving the rat menace. Ruth was on the board of directors of the Petersburg Public Library, the Arts Council, Narrows Broadcasting (KFSK), Clausen Memorial Museum, Mountain View Manor Food Service, and St. Andrew's Church. Ruth is or has been a member of the Sons of Norway, Order of the Eastern Star, and the Pioneers of Alaska.

It is said one should retire in a college town to enjoy lectures and entertainment. Thanks to Syd and Vara Wright, Petersburg has filled the bill for Ruth and her family. Each year the high school gave a Shakespeare play and a senior play, the most memorable of which was *Charlie Brown*. And each year the townspeople produced a Broadway musical. Never to be forgotten were the musical performances sponsored by Alaska Music Trails and later Petersburg Performing Arts.

Ruth's dream of European travel came true in 1972. Helmi Jensen and Ruth's daughter, Diane, accompanied her on a 46-day trip to Scandinavia and Europe via Pan American Airlines. Ruth has since traveled extensively all over the world with friends: Alaska with Mildred Counter, South Seas with Sharla Coon, Mexico with Fern Hayward, India and Africa with old friends from Portland, to Hawaii with the Mark Sandviks, and Greece and Turkey with Fern Hayward and Harold Bergmann.

Today, Neil works for Crowley Marine Services. Mark works for Icicle Seafoods. Diane is a freelance writer and editor. All of them work in the Seattle, Washington area.

These are just some of the highlights of one family's life in Petersburg.

Whether one disparages the endless rain or revels in the sporadic sunshine, one thing is clear — every day in Southeast Alaska is unique.

"Betsy Ross" rides with friends on a post-World War II Fourth of July parade float.
From left: Ruth Sandvik, Alice Longworth, Augusta Enge and Jesse Andersen.

John Sasby

By Dick Brennan

John Sasby was a real solid chunk of early Petersburg — about five foot three vertical by five, four-and-a-half wide, not fat. Flapping boots on tree-trunk legs and flailing arms; a big, woolly, grey sweater on a bear; a broad ferocious face, violent in a bush of whiskers, beetling brows and Katzenjammer moustache; borne along with the truculent roll of a bloodthirsty Turk — the whole darn thing bellowing like the Great Bull of Baal. Rather terrifying until one glimpsed the bright shine of twinkling blue eyes, unmistakably humorous, kindly and generous.

Usually, when in from Stikine River gillnetting, he was roaring drunk and fuming snoose, but he never staggered; he just rocked and rolled along rather more smoothly than when sober. BOOMPH! Ham fist on the bar; "SKAAL PAA GOMLA NORGE; WOOMPH." The mudsills rocked in the muskeg, but, by golly, no shingles came off the roof when Sasby was on this side of the Narrows. Money was confetti.

He was really quite humorous if one could understand his peculiar mixture of Norsk, English and Sasby — which, along toward his end in the '30s, only a few who had known him many years could.

I recall his grand fraternal reunion. Seems he was of a well-to-do family of consequential position, always writing, insisting and using consular influences to get him to spurn this savage wilderness, return to Norway and take-up his proper status in the society of civilized human beings. Finally, after nigh 30 years, a brother was sent to fetch him. He arrived here while Sasby was out on the Stikine. A pleasant dude-dressed fellow, obviously of some learning, culture and means. All awaited the joyful brotherly meeting after those many long years. Would they fall into each other's arms, slap backs, shed tears, paint the town red and take a bath in Aquavit?

At last, Sasby came in. The brother was told, and he waited there in front of the Dory Bar watching him come stump-stumping along down the whole length of the plank Main Street, swinging a bucket of "hooligan" (eulachon).

Finally coming abreast, the brother with shining eyes said softly, "Hello-o-w, John." Sasby glared ferociously up under bushy brows, "UHH, you here too now, huh."… and stump-stumped on along toward the Guilt Edge Saloon. (Jim Brennan had accidentally got a couple boxes of gilt-edged glasses and decided to go fancy, name and all. This didn't last.)

(At this writing, in 2002, the old Sasby Property on Sasby's Island is owned by Richard and Sharon Sprague.)

Sasby's Island

Photo by Marilee Enge

Per and Louise Sather

By Patty Sather Thomassen

Per Kruger Sather was born to Ola and Oline Sather on October 28, 1900, in Valsoybotn, Norway. His father was a doctor and traveled to New York, Minnesota, and Seattle to study.

Per's older brother left to go to Minnesota to farm. Per, Ola, Smehaug and Ingebrigt left Norway in 1923. After a stopover in Benson, Minnesota, to visit their brother, they went to Silvanna, Washington, for a logging job. Deciding logging wasn't for them, they came to Alaska, arriving March 15, 1924.

They bought the F/V *Gjoa*, which they fished until 1927. They took the boat to Seattle and Per went back to Norway to see about a farm. Deciding that it wasn't what he wanted, he returned to Seattle and had the F/V *Zarembo* built. While they were working on their boat, Mr. Amundsen, the Arctic explorer, asked Per if he would build his mast and boom. Per did.

He fished Southeast Alaska with good crews. Olaf Wikan fished with him for 33 years. Others on his crews were: Chris Olsen, Leif Thorsen, Harold Medalen, John DeBoer, Swede Wasvick and Eiler Wikan.

In 1937, a good friend, Lars Stokke, brought his sister Louise from Wrangell. They had grown up in the same area in Norway, went to the same church and school, but hadn't met until she came down to the Petersburg harbor to meet him.

They were married on August 6, 1937, and had four children: Oline, Anna, Patricia and Per Jr. They lived in the house now owned by Tom Abbott.

Louise died in 1958. Per continued to raise Patty and Per Jr.

He fished with a good crew until 1964, when he sold the boat to John DeBoer, whom he thought of as a son. He fished with John until 1969, when he decided the ocean was too much for him.

He then bought the F/V *Sea Fly* from Bud Schoonover and trolled for salmon around Southeast Alaska until 1974. His grandson Ky Thomassen went with him. When his health started to fail him, he sold the F/V *Sea Fly* to Ted Kaino.

Louise and Per were very active in Eastern Star, serving as Worthy Matron and Worthy Patron. Per was also an active Mason and a Master of the Lodge. He was well known for his exceptional ability to memorize the lodge work. Per passed away in July 1979.

Oline married Hunt Gruening in 1963. They have children: Kimberly Louise (McNickles), Peter Sather, and Tiffany Oline (Williams). Anna married Dale Decker in 1964. They have Kirsten Marie (Bowers), Kirk, and Karen Louise (Doubek). Patty married Palmer Thomassen in 1962. They have Ky Michael, Sabra Oline (Johnson), Palmer Jr., Raean Manell (King). Per Jr. married Lynda Basher in 1978.

Per Sather

Louise Sather

Bob and Charlotte Schwartz

By Jim Schwartz

Charlotte Schwartz was born Charlotte Marie Clausen in 1919, in Petersburg, Alaska. Her parents were Carroll and Elsie Clausen. They had been married just the year before. Carroll, who had come from Portland, Oregon, managed the local bank. Elsie, who had moved up from Chehalis, Washington, was a seamstress working at home. They lived in a house west of the hospital.

The Clausens moved to Portland for a year and also lived in Canada for a while. By the fall of 1924, they had returned to Petersburg and bought a house on Front Street, two houses north of the Elkins' place.

Charlotte was 10 when her brother, Phillip, was born. Phil was a fun addition to their home and Charlotte was the perfect age to babysit. She recalled those childhood days fondly — lots of picnics, beach walks, clam digging, playing in the woods, good friends, camping, boat rides, and hiking to Sandy Beach to swim and stay over.

Charlotte felt that the Depression really didn't affect Petersburg much. There seemed to be enough work for people. The Civilian Conservation Corps (CCC) built trails in the Petersburg area that people used and appreciated.

There were two movie theaters in town and a roller skating rink. Even high school was an enjoyable time. Charlotte was Prom Queen her senior year in high school. She always said that she and her friends had climbed almost every mountain you could see from Petersburg. She chuckled when she told the story of beating Claire Strand, the new teacher, in a race across the Wrangell Narrows. Charlotte was rowing and Claire had an outboard motor. Charlotte spoke of going to Papke's Landing often and spending time camping down the Narrows, at Green Rocks, Blind Slough, Duncan Canal, Harvey's Lake and Castle River.

After high school, Charlotte went to business school in Seattle for a year. She came back to Alaska and got a job in Juneau working for the territorial legislature as a secretary. In 1940, she met and married a "charming" man named Hilding Hegland in Juneau.

Hilding lost his job in Juneau and they moved to Sitka. Charlotte gave birth to Michael in 1941. Hilding lost his job again because of gambling problems. Charlotte left Hilding and returned to Petersburg. She divorced Hilding in the winter of 1941.

She worked at the drug store and on the fur farm at 9 Mile in Petersburg.

Charlotte was in Petersburg when Pearl Harbor was bombed. She remembered the town blackouts, the fear of attack, and the absence of the young men who had gone off to war.

Charlotte was offered a job in Juneau to work for the territorial government. She took the job, but had to leave Mike with Gramma and Grampa Clausen until she got settled.

Charlotte Clausen Schwartz

Charlotte was in Juneau just a few months when she met a man whom she had served sodas in Petersburg, Bob Schwartz. Bob had been working near Sitka and was transferred to Juneau to manage a parts business. They went out on a date and were married by a ship's captain two weeks later. She wrote her mother, "Mom, I have met a man who has melted my heart. He wants to take care of me."

Bob was drafted by the U.S. Army and was given orders to report for basic training in California. Within weeks, Charlotte and Bob traveled to Petersburg to pick up Mike and head to Seattle on the steamship. The family took the train to California. When Bob was sent overseas to the Philippines, Charlotte went back to

Bob and Charlotte Schwartz cont'd

Seattle where she had girlfriends in the same situation; their husbands had gone to war. Charlotte, then pregnant, was able to live with a family that needed full-time childcare. Dennis was born in 1945.

When Bob returned from the war in 1946, his cousin in Los Angeles offered him a job. The family moved to Whittier and built a house. By 1950, Bob and Charlotte had decided that Southern California was not for them, despite the possibility of a lucrative future with a family-owned business. They moved back to Petersburg and went into partnership with Charlotte's brother, Phil, and his wife, Darline. The two families bought a chicken farm at Twin Creeks. The men took care of the chicken-raising business and the women started a weekend "Chicken Dinner Out" restaurant venture.

After two years, it became obvious that the business could not sustain two families. Bob and Charlotte purchased the Citizen's Steam Laundry. They would spend the next 27 years making a living in the laundry business. Right in the middle of all these changes, Jim was born in 1952.

The family lived above the laundry that was attached to the present-day NAPA store, across from the Wells Fargo Bank. Bob started work about 5:30 a.m. and quit about 8 p.m., seven days a week. Charlotte worked in the laundry, as Bob's partner, and did the books. The boys were there to help out with delivering and picking up laundry for the whole town. In those days, few people owned washers and dryers.

Bob became a volunteer fireman in 1952 and stayed with it for 25 years. He was involved with the PTA, the Boy Scouts, Alaska Health Planning Board, the Petersburg Utility Board, the Moose Club and Alaska Native Brotherhood, among others.

Charlotte was active in establishing an Alcohol Recovery Council, the museum board, Alaska Native Sisterhood, among others.

It seems like significant changes happened around a birth in the family. The fourth boy, Donald, was born in 1959. Just about that same time Charlotte discovered the Baha'i Faith. After studying it for a year, she decided to become a Baha'i. Bob became a Baha'i about a year later. They became active in the growing Baha'i community of Petersburg. In 1963, Charlotte and her mother, Elsie, traveled to the first election of the international leadership assembly in London, England. This was one of the highlights of her life.

In 1968, Bob was granted permission for a pilgrimage to the International Baha'i Center in Haifa, Israel. Bob planned the trip of a lifetime. After his pilgrimage, he traveled for two months, visiting Baha'is around the world.

Charlotte was elected to represent Alaska at a Baha'i election in the Holy Land two weeks after Bob was there. She joined Bob in Thailand and they traveled together the rest of the way around the world.

Bob Schwartz

In 1970, a fire broke out in the living quarters of the laundry. Bob and Charlotte found themselves literally with just the clothes on their backs. The town of Petersburg rallied and donated clothing for the Schwartzs. The whole family worked together and got the business back working within 24 hours. Bob and Charlotte and the kids moved in with son Mike and his wife, Kay, for two months. They then bought a

Bob and Charlotte Schwartz cont'd

trailer and lived in the Town Trailer Court for a short time, finally moving to Magill's Trailer Court.

Bob and Charlotte sold the laundry in 1979. They were ready to retire — sort of. They both had been driving the school bus for their son Mike for several years. They continued driving for another five years. Bob and Charlotte moved into Elsie Clausen's house after she passed away in 1980. They saved their money, bought a motor home and started traveling. They traveled for vacations and they traveled for the Baha'i Faith. These were truly "Golden Years" for them.

Their sons were now living lives of their own. Mike and Kay were living in Petersburg, and their three children had returned to Petersburg to live. Mike and Kay were both entrepreneurs and semiretired.

Dennis and his Italian wife, Pat, were living in Redmond, Washington, with their three boys. Dennis was following up his PhD in chemistry. Pat was an occupational therapist.

Jim and his Japanese wife, Leslie, were living in Petersburg, as well. Their two children were off to college. Jim was teaching elementary school. Leslie was a physical therapist at the hospital.

Don and his Chinese wife, Lih, were living in Boise, Idaho, with their two boys. Don was teaching middle school and Lih was an office manager. Adding up the whole family, Bob and Charlotte had 10 grandchildren and nine great-grandchildren.

Bob and Charlotte started slowing down when they turned 80. They didn't get out as much, but cards became their passion. Bob and Charlotte played cribbage daily and kept running scores monthly. They also played bridge weekly with high stakes of nickels. People stopped by their house daily to chat and have coffee or tea. Charlotte stopped smoking because of her emphysema. She struggled a bit, but Bob took good care of her. Both of them were so excited to celebrate the year 2000 — the Millennium.

In the spring of 2000, Bob became sick with cancer and passed away in July at the age of 83.

Charlotte rallied physically and began driving again. She continued to play cribbage, host coffee time, and play bridge. In January 2001, six months after Bob, she passed away. She was 81.

Pacific Coast and Norway Packing Company cannery September 9, 1907

Photo by John N. Cobb
University of Washington Libraries, Special Collections Division, Cobb 2507

Louis and Ragna Severson

By Greg Severson

Louis Christopher Severson was born in 1882 to Sivert Olsen in Sunnfjord on Værøy-Landoy, Norway, an island near Florø in the county of Sogn og Fjordane.

He immigrated to the United States through Ellis Island, New York, in 1905, having traveled steerage class on a ship of the Bergen Line.

The name he gave at immigration time was Lyder Christopher Sivertsen Vaeroy-Landoy. The officials streamlined it to Louis Christopher Severson.

Louis stayed the first year or two with an older brother in Duluth, Minnesota. He fished in Alaska in the summers. During citizenship classes sponsored by the Lutheran church in Seattle, he met Ragna Midthun.

Ragna was born in 1888 to Nils and Guri Midthun in Voss, Norway, in the county of Hordaland. Her family farm was across the lake from the town of Voss.

Ragna was the youngest of nine children. Most of her siblings immigrated to the United States. Her older brother Ole was a prospector in the Gold Rush of 1898 in the Klondike. Her oldest sister, Martha, stayed in Norway and inherited the ancestral farm of the Midthun family. (This farm is still held by Midthun family relatives today.)

Ragna immigrated to the United States through Ellis Island, New York, in 1907. She also sailed in steerage class on a ship of the Bergen Line. She worked as a domestic in households in New York City and Chicago, eventually moving to Seattle, where two older sisters, Anna and Bertha, already lived.

In 1913, Louis and Ragna were married in the Immanuel Lutheran Church, in downtown Seattle at Second and Virginia streets. Around 1915, they moved to Petersburg to live permanently. There they bought a house and had four children: Herman was born in 1922, Louis G. in 1925, Gertrude (Gallagher) in 1928, and a child who died at birth.

Louis bought a fishing boat, the F/V *Odin*. The *Odin* was a 48-foot wooden boat. Its primary fishery was herring, but he also seined for salmon. The *Odin* was one of the boats used to haul gravel from Thomas Bay to Petersburg in the 1930s. The gravel was used for aggregate to lay the concrete foundation for the Lutheran Church at Fifth and Excel streets.

Louis fished every summer and earned enough to sponsor his sister Sophie and her husband, Anton Noreide, to come to the United States. He also sponsored a cousin, Thomas Lando, from the same area of Norway. Louis, Anton and Tom fished together on the *Odin* for many years.

The *Odin* had a gasoline engine. In 1958, the vessel blew up in Petersburg's harbor. Louis did not survive the accident.

After Louis' death, Ragna moved into a newly built apartment in her son Louis' house. She lived there for nine years, knitting, crocheting and baking.

Ragna took long walks around Petersburg every day. She moved to the Pioneer's Home, in Sitka, and lived out her twilight years, continuing to take long walks almost every day of her life.

Ragna passed away in 1975.

**Seated, Gertrude, Ragna and Louis.
Standing, Herman and Louis.**

Louis and Ida Severson

By Louis George Severson

Louis George Severson was born in Petersburg on February 4, 1925, to Louis C. and Ragna Severson. He had an older brother, Herman. A younger sister, Gertrude, was born three years later.

His childhood was spent with neighbors from the Westre, Lund, Wikan, Molver and Hammer families who lived close by. There was the Point Gang, the Hill Gang and the Road Gang for the kids of the 1930s. As members of the Road Gang, Larry Westre, Roy Lund, Jim Hammer, Laurence Molver and Louis were close in age and spent their long summer days in skiffs, along the board streets and under them, and up on the muskegs.

Louis attended school in Petersburg and was immediately drafted into the military upon high school graduation in 1943. He first went to Juneau for boot camp and then Adak Island. Next he went to Georgia for paratrooper training. After VE day he ended up in the Philippines, in the World War II Pacific Theater.

He returned to Petersburg after the war and fished salmon, herring, halibut and blackcod during the summers. In the winters, he attended Griffin-Murphy Business College in Seattle for a semester or two. He fished on the *Bravo*, *Munroe*, *Teddy J.*, *Pamela Rae*, *Symphony*, *R & H*, *Phoenix*, *Odin* and many other vessels during the post-war period.

In 1949 he proposed to Ida Hofstad. They were married in Seattle at Ballard First Lutheran Church, on October 29, 1949. They moved back to Petersburg to make their home and raise a family.

Ida Jane Severson was born in Scow Bay on May 4, 1925, to Morten and Valborg Hofstad. She had three older brothers and one older sister. Brothers Edmund, Walter and Oliver were all vessel owners and commercial fishermen. Sister Margaret was married to J.W. "Red" Jones when Ida was 12 years old.

Living in Scow Bay, Ida had young friends and schoolmates among the Hungerford sisters. They came over at times to play on Morten's well-groomed lawn at the home that he had built. He often cautioned the youngsters, "Don't wear out the grass," when he wanted them to stop playing before the wet lawn became muddy. In high school, her friends were Alice Espeseth, Bobo Hemnes and Mildred Sandvik.

Ida attended grade school and high school in

Louis, Mark, Nancy and Ida. Greg is standing.

Petersburg and graduated in 1943. She then moved to Seattle and attended Peterson Business College for two years. Afterwards, she worked for the U.S. Fish & Wildlife Service and spent six months in Juneau and six months in Seattle each year.

Ida was a real Alaskan woman. She was always up for camping, sport fishing, hiking or boating — come rain or shine. She was an excellent cook and very handy with sewing and knitting. An avid reader, berry picker, and gardener, she played pinochle and bridge with the best of them.

Ida and Louis had many wonderful years raising their three kids — Greg, Mark and Nancy — among their many friends, neighbors and relatives. They loved to travel, making trips to Norway, Hawaii, Mexico, New Zealand, the East Coast and the Panama Canal. And for 30 years, every March, they would be in Palm Springs.

Ida died of cancer August 25, 2001.

John and Maria Silva

By Lewie Silva

John Silva Sr. was born June 24, 1885, in Salamanca Mexico. He moved to Laredo, Texas, at 15 years of age. He worked in Texas, Kansas and California before coming to Alaska in 1916, aboard a sailing ship.

He went back to Mexico briefly and brought back his future wife, Maria. They were married in Petersburg and had four children: TheoDula, now deceased; John Jr.; Tony; and Lewis, who still resides in Petersburg. John and Maria have eight grandchildren and two great-grandchildren.

John worked briefly at the sawmill in Wrangell, and then moved to Petersburg to work at the local sawmill. John chose Petersburg to live because of its beautiful mountains, streams, waterways, the great hunting and fishing, and for opportunities of work.

He started working for Dave Ohmer Sr. at Alaskan Glacier Sea Food and for the local cannery and cold storage, PAF. He worked at these two canneries for 38 years. Maria also worked for the local canneries for over 25 years.

They built their home on Sing Lee Alley Bridge and lived there for many years until their retirement. The Silva home was located next to the Sons of Norway Hall and has since been torn down.

Because of their length of residency here and love of this town, in 1980 they were both chosen as Grand Marshals for the local Fourth of July parade. John was also recognized on his 97th birthday as being the oldest man in Petersburg at that time.

John passed away in 1982 and Maria in 1985.

John and Marie Silva

Photo by Dr. R.C. Smith

Ben and Margit Smith

By Ted and Lynn Smith

Ben T. Smith met Margit Theodorsen in Craig, Alaska, in 1934. "B.T.," as he was called, had moved to Craig to fish with his brother.

Born in Andrews County, Texas, Ben moved through New Mexico, Arizona and California, finally settling in Alaska. Here everything he loved was abundant — fishing and hunting, wild unsettled areas, and friendly people — just the things for Ben.

Margit Theodorsen was born in, and attended school in, Stanwood, Washington. After graduating from high school, she attended Tacoma's Pacific Lutheran College, studying for a degree in teaching.

Her first offer of a teaching position was a town in Alaska called Craig. An adventure in a three-room school was just what she was looking for.

After her first year in Craig, she moved back to her folks' home in Stanwood for the summer. She had met a young man in Craig, but wasn't sure she wanted to live in Alaska. After most of the summer had passed, she was offered her position in Craig again, which she accepted...and the rest is history.

Ben and Margit were married April 30, 1936, and spent their honeymoon on a 36-foot troller.

Their first child, Ted, was born April 5, 1937. In 1942, they moved to Ketchikan where their second child, Jim, was born on June 21, 1942.

They lived in Ketchikan with time for roaming Southeastern Alaska and working at various jobs.

Third child Marilyn was born June 14, 1945.

At this time, Ben was a partner in an airline, Ketchikan Air Service, while also working for Ellis Airlines. He also worked on construction jobs and for

Martinsen's Dairy truck
Photo courtesy of the Martinsens

Margit and Ben Smith

a sawmill.

In 1949, Ben accepted a $50 a month raise from Union Oil and moved to Petersburg to manage the Union Oil plant. Both he and Margit fell in love with the community and decided Petersburg would become their permanent home.

In October 1950, their fourth child, Tom, was born. He was the apple of everyone's eye and destined to be raised in Petersburg.

Union Oil grew as the town grew. Ben purchased the business. He prospered as the company prospered. When he retired, his son Ted took over.

Margit began teaching in Petersburg in 1952 and worked for about 30 years.

Ben passed away July 18, 1991. Margit died March 13, 1999. They are buried side-by-side in Petersburg Memorial Cemetery, where they continue to be a part of the community they both loved.

They had eight grandchildren, three great-grandchildren, and a host of friends.

Jim and Alice Stafford

By Rexanne Stafford

Jimmie Rex Stafford was born in Springfield, Missouri. He first came to Alaska when he was 17 and in the U.S. Coast Guard. He quickly became friends with the locals. When he got out of the service in 1946, he came back to Petersburg to make it his home.

Jim worked in the summers for the U.S. Forest Service as a deckhand and a cook aboard the *Ranger 8*. The skipper was George Reynolds. In those days, there were only four people in the entire Forest Service. He spent his winters playing in the Seattle area with friends from Petersburg. In 1947, he started fishing with Bert Espeseth on the F/V *Bravo*.

Jim Stafford

He married Alice Marie Espeseth in 1950.

Alice was born in Kent, Washington, in 1925. She had moved to Petersburg with her parents, Bert and Larine Espeseth, when she was 2 years old.

Bert had originally come over from Norway when he was 19. When he went back to Norway some years later, he brought back Larine Hammerseth as his wife. They had both grown up on Askrova, a tiny island off the coast of Norway, near Florø.

Bert was fishing in Alaska during the summer and they anticipated making Washington their home. However, Larine made a trip north with tiny Alice, a bed and a woodstove to spend the summer in Petersburg while Bert fished. As they were coming up Wrangell Narrows, she said, "Oh Bert, I feel like I am coming home!" So that summer they built a house and made Petersburg their home.

Alice only spoke Norwegian until she started school. She was an active, spirited girl and very well liked. She was Prom Queen in her senior year and went on to become a nurse. After returning from nurses training, she started dating Jim Stafford.

When Jim went to ask Bert for her hand in marriage, Bert was sitting in his chair, reading a paper. Jim asked if he could marry Alice. Without lowering the paper, Bert said, "No time for jokes!" That must have meant "yes" because they were married in February of 1950.

Rexanne was born in 1951, Jill in 1953, and Scott in 1956.

Alice worked many years as a nurse. Jim spent most of his adult life in the fishing industry.

After Alice passed away in 1985, Jim moved to Arizona. He comes home every year to visit his family.

Rexanne Stafford still resides in Petersburg. In Juneau, she has daughter Gina and two grandchildren, Jordan and Dylan. In Colorado, she has stepchildren Sean and Deanna, and grandchildren Shelby and Brandon. Her husband, Jack Hicks, passed away.

Alice Stafford

Jill Williams and her husband, Rick, also live in Petersburg. They have four children. Jenna is married to Eric Evens. They live in Petersburg have two children, Kirk and Julie. Ian is in college. Alice Marie lives in Petersburg. Jacklyn Olsen lives in Washington.

Scott Stafford is a doctor in Minnesota. His wife, Jackie, is also a doctor. They have a son, Eric. Scott and Eric come home to Petersburg every summer to visit and fish.

Sons of Norway
Fedrelandet #23

The founders of Petersburg's Sons of Norway were Americans in the truest sense. Brave and free, they left their homeland and traveled across an ocean and a continent to the wilds of Alaska in their quest for a better life.

From the moment they first entered Wrangell Narrows, their lives were forever changed. While they would always be true to the land of their birth, they had, at last, found a home here in Petersburg.

1920

1990

The 1898 founding of Petersburg, by Norwegians, resulted in a lifestyle centered around the customs and traditions of Norway.

When locals decided to build a hall, they raised the money for construction by selling shares for $5 a piece.

Using lumber from the local mill, construction began on September 24, 1912. Countless man-hours and sheer determination allowed the volunteers to dedicate the new lodge on Christmas Day 1912.

Charles and Hester Stedman

By William K. Stedman

Charles Frederick Stedman was born in Washington Territory on December 7, 1872, to Reuben Benjamin Stedman and Elizabeth Lewis Stedman. He is often referred to as the "Spokane Cowboy." His death certificate says he was born in Spokane, lending credence to Spokane being the place of his birth. The death certificate of his youngest son, Kenneth, reports that Charles was born in Wenatchee.

In 1880, Charles and his parents were living in Jackson County, Oregon. By 1882, Charles and his family are in Yakima County, Washington.

It has been told that Charles drove either horses or cattle up from Texas through California. There he met 16-year-old Hester Virginia Gagnon, a resident of Grass Valley and his wife to be. After he married her, around 1897, they spent their honeymoon on horseback, returning to his home in Washington. Since his older brother Will had horses and a drayage in Republic, it is possible the horses were for Will.

In 1900, Charles and his new family are in Chelan County, Washington. Charles and Hettie have a son, William. Elizabeth, Charles' mother, is with them.

There is a set of four photographs taken in Seattle, sometime in 1901. The first photo is William Reuben Stedman, age one and a half. The second photo is of Charles Fredrick and Hester "Hettie" Virginia Stedman. The third photo is of William, Charles' brother, with wife Clara Stedman. The final photo is the only known photograph of Elizabeth Lewis Stedman. These were probably the last photos taken before Charles and his family headed for Alaska, and most likely taken just before they shipped out.

Charles apparently had "Gold Fever." They took a boat up to Skagway around 1901-02. When he realized the streets were not paved with gold, they came south to Juneau, and later Wrangell.

Their second son, Kenneth, was born in Juneau on January 25, 1903.

By September of 1907, Charles and his family are in Wrangell. By 1909, Charles, Hettie, William and Kenneth are living in Petersburg.

In 1912, Charles moved the family out to Kake, where he worked as a machinist in the salmon cannery owned by P.E. Harris. Charles received his patent for his homestead on the west side of Kupreanof Island in July of 1922. They had a fox ranch on Horse Shoe Island on the north end of Rocky Pass, in partnership with a man named Sinclair. They remained there until the market for fox furs died.

While there, Charles acted as a hunting guide in the Rocky Pass area. One of his clients was an author by the name of Stewart Edwin White. There is a photograph of Charles with a hunting party — complete with tent, stove, guns and gear — in the possession of his great grandson, Bruce Stedman.

Charles was also a shipwright, building a number of boats. A half hull for calculations still exists, as well as photographs of two of his boats.

In 1932, after Charles' health began to fail, they returned to Petersburg and lived with their son Bill, later taking a house about a mile and a half south of town for themselves. In 1934, they moved to the Del Paso Heights area of Sacramento, California. On February 17, 1937, Charles died of acute edema of the lungs, following surgery at Sacramento County Hospital. Charles was buried in the city cemetery on the 23rd of February.

Gillnet boat

William and Elvina Stedman

By William K. Stedman

William Reuben Stedman was born December 7, 1899, in Chesaw, Washington, located in the northeastern corner of Okanogan County, to Charles Fredrick Stedman and Hester Virginia Gagnon. His birth certificate says midwife Clara Stedman delivered him. Clara was the wife of Will, Charles' older brother.

They headed for Alaska. In 1903, Kenneth was born in Juneau. By 1907, they are living in Wrangell.

While in Wrangell, young Bill, better known as Willie, took a job selling the *Saturday Evening Post*. In one of the issues, there is a picture of Willie in coveralls and a stocking cap with a *Saturday Evening Post* bag over his shoulder. The accompanying article states: *"Alaska. Many an Alaskan household has been made much brighter during the long winter evenings by the enterprise of this hustling little business man — Willie Stedman, of Wrangell, Alaska. And being a JOURNAL boy in Alaska in the wintertime isn't quite the same as being a JOURNAL boy in the states. Young Stedman has had to face the blinding snow and cutting wind of the Northland to serve his customers, but he has not once 'stayed home' nor disappointed them."*

The Stedmans moved to Petersburg in August of 1909. They stayed until April of 1912, when they took a homestead just outside of Kake, a Tlingit Indian village about 40 miles from Petersburg, on the west side of Kupreanof Island. There they had a fox farm.

In 1915, Bill left Kake, where he had been logging with Ted Hungerford. He moved back to Petersburg to attend school. He stayed in school for a year and a half, until he began driving truck for Hogue & Tveten.

In January of 1920, he purchased Lot #2, Block 15 from the Seattle Trust Company, for the sum of $100. With the help of his father, he built the house he later raised his family in. The large beams that support the house were hand hewn from logs. Since Charles was a shipwright, the house was built tight as a ship. The house is warm and tight and has been owned and occupied by Stedmans to this present day.

In 1922, Bill met Agnes Elvina Bratseth, the new schoolteacher at the Doyhof school.

Agnes was born October 8, 1902, in the small farming community of Dwight, North Dakota, to a family of Norwegian immigrants. She was the eleventh and last child born to Angram Bratseth and Ingrid Ellen Nordhus. Delivered by Mrs. Carlson, a local midwife, Agnes was raised by her older sister, Anna.

When she was 2, Elvina's father died. He was laid out on a couch in the living room of the big ramshackle house on the Dwight farm. When her sisters brought Elvina into the room, she walked up to her father, touched him, and said, "Papa sleep."

When Elvina was 5, the family moved into Wahpeton to a house right next to Aunty Gottleman's. They had rented out the farm for a part of the crop, but the farmer wasn't much of a farmer and the yield was poor. Her mother washed and ironed to earn additional money.

After her mother died, Elvina walked to school. After school she stayed with the Sleepers, but she said she hated to go there after awhile because, "Grandpa Sleeper always beat me at checkers. I never won."

Anna got three rooms over the Johnson's house. She and her sisters, Myrtle and Elvina, shared them until Myrtle graduated from high school. The house had no electricity, but it did have a heater and cold running water, something that not many houses had in those days.

After Myrtle graduated, Anna and Elvina moved in with Aunty Gottleman, into a large upstairs bedroom in her home on 6th Street.

Elvina attended school in Wahpeton. She was a member of the Girls' Glee Club and the Wauhinkapa Camp Fire Girls. She enjoyed success as an actress in local American Legion plays, both before and after her graduation in 1920.

She next attended Fargo Agriculture College. From there she went out into the country to teach in a one-room, eight-grade school. At the end of the school year, she went to Wrangell, Alaska, to spend the summer with her sister, Inga Carlson. While there, she was offered a teaching position in a small one-room schoolhouse located in Doyhof, just 35 miles north on Wrangell Narrows. (Doyhof was located just south of Petersburg in the area now known as Scow Bay. The cannery community is no longer in existence.)

Elvina met Bill Stedman while teaching that year. After only six weeks, they were married on December 3, 1922. R.L. Clifton performed the wedding ceremony. Witnesses were Ragnhild Larsen and Arthur D. Larsen.

William and Elvina Stedman cont'd

At the time of their marriage, Elvina was making $150 a month and Bill was making $125 a month.

Soon after, Bill quit his job and went halibut fishing with Ole Johnson. He made more money in 10 days than he had made the entire previous month. In late September of 1923, Bill and Ted Hungerford purchased the logging outfit of T.J. McBride, Ole Lein and Lars Housnes.

Son William Kenneth was born September 27, 1923. Delivered by Dr. A.B. Jones, he was the first child born in Petersburg's new hospital. Two months later, they went logging out in Rocky Pass. The trip was made with the boat *Reliance* pulling the steam donkey and a wanigan, where Elvina and a young girl, Lillian Anderson, were keeping house. Elvina and Lillian were relaxing when Bill burst into the wanigan and asked if everyone was all right. It seems the wanigan had broken loose from the towline and had been drifting. The girls weren't even aware there had been any problem until Bill came in.

They landed the wanigan and steam donkey on the beach at high tide and waited until the tide went out so they could off-load the steam donkey and get to logging. When they awoke at low tide, the wanigan's stern was over the edge of a drop-off. They had to quickly move all the gear forward to stop the wanigan from sliding over the edge. When the tide came back in, they moved to a safer location.

They logged until the Fourth of July 1924. When they returned to Petersburg, they found the inside of their house had been damaged by fire. The schoolteacher, who had been renting their house, filled the stove with soft coal; it had exploded. Their neighbor Ted Johnson spotted the fire and called the fire department.

Bill and Elvina lived in a house near the cable office until the house was rebuilt. Bill worked at the power plant at night and repaired the house during the day.

On October 9, 1925, their first daughter, Marian Louise, was born; a nine-pound baby. She was followed by Virginia Ann. Elvina had quit teaching, but kept her hand in it by becoming a school board member.

Bill had an orchestra, the Red Devils, that played the local dances at the Sons of Norway Hall and at Johnny Sales'. Bill played trumpet, Norm Rustad played sax, Bob Lando played drums, and Mary Allen played piano. Two Indian gentlemen, named Ben and Bill Bailey, also played sax. They practiced at the Stedman house, where the kids would sit on the steps and listen until they were made to go to bed.

When Bill and Elvina's children had graduated from high school and were out on their own, they saw three of Bill's brother Kenneth's children through high school. Kenneth, Charles "Bunkie," and Richard "Dick" grew to view Elvina as their second mother.

Bill and his brother Ken owned and ran Stedman's Gift Shop. They had it for three years before selling it to the Schulters in 1928. Bill then began working for Standard Oil where he worked for 20 years.

During World War II, Alaska was within a war zone, so there were U.S. Coast Guard and Army Signal Corps stations in Petersburg. Many young sailors and soldiers found a "home away from home" at the Stedman house and came to think of Elvina as their second mom. A sampler on the wall in the front entry of the home summed it up with these words: "Dear house, you're really very small, just big enough for love, that's all."

If you arrived at dinnertime, her invitation was, "Stay to dinner. I'll throw another spud in the pot." Very rarely was there just the Stedman family of five at the dinner table.

Bill was transferred to the Ballad area of Seattle, where he worked until he retired. By then, his multiple sclerosis had become so advanced it was difficult for him to work. They returned to Petersburg where Elvina went to work at the Lillian Shop.

Two years later, they purchased the restaurant called the Recreation, better known as the "Rec." Elvina kept the business going, nursing Bill in an apartment over the restaurant. She'd run up and down the stairs as many times a day as necessary.

In 1947, Bill was baptized at the same time as his oldest grandson, Bruce. Elvina had wanted Bill to be baptized ever since she had found out from Hettie, Bill's mother, that "the boys" had never been baptized. Rae, their daughter-in-law, suggested, "Since Bill was to be baptized, then why don't we have Bruce baptized at the same time?"

They lived over the restaurant for five years before MS finally took its toll. Bill passed away on November

William and Elvina Stedman cont'd

19, 1952. He was buried in the Petersburg Cemetery, overlooking Wrangell Narrows.

After Bill died, Elvina moved to the Lower 48 and began work as a housemother at the University of Oregon. While there, she decided to continue with her own education. She earned a teaching certificate in 1958 at Monmouth, Oregon.

Elvina's first job teaching in almost 30 years was at St. Helens, Oregon. After two years, she responded to an ad for teachers to go overseas to teach the children of United States' service personnel.

Her first assignment was Iceland. She found that the name, Iceland, is the coldest thing about the place. Her first school was a Quonset hut at the U.S. Air Force base at Keflavic. In addition to the regular American children, she also taught the children of American servicemen and Icelandic mothers. The children spoke both languages fluently. Elvina was able to travel on air force planes on her vacations; she flew to Norway and saw family members that first year.

The following year, she was assigned to the air force base at Ankara, Turkey. Instead of a Quonset hut, this school was on the second floor of a new apartment building. Each grade occupied an apartment and hers, the fourth, had a view of this historic city and the capital buildings.

This time, Elvina did not have to rely on the air force to travel. She was able to visit Istanbul and Gareme on weekends. On her holidays, she toured the Holy Land, went on a boat trip on the Jordan River, and traveled to as many of the European countries as she could.

She returned to the United States and taught at Columbia Heights Elementary School in Longview, Washington, for eight years. While in Longview, she learned to drive. She spent many years afterwards traveling by car and bus with Beulah Owsley, her friend and roommate from Petersburg. She joined what she called "old folks' clubs," but she had to join groups with members younger than she was because, "All the groups my age just want to sit around and complain about their aches and pains and they never go anywhere or do anything. I want to go, go, go."

At age 65, Elvina was told she had to retire from teaching, but that didn't stop her. She stopped teaching in the public school system and went to work in a private school, Carrols Elementary. She taught there until she retired.

She continued to travel and remained active in community and church affairs until a stroke slowed her down. She was a member of Trinity Lutheran Church, the Monticello Hospital Auxiliary, and numerous other groups. She had to leave her little apartment and take up residence in a retirement home, although she didn't spend much time there. She always had visitors that took her to see and do.

She died of pneumonia on December 18, 1988, in Battle Ground, Washington, at the Meadow Glade Manor nursing home. Her ashes were buried alongside her husband, Bill, in the cemetery at Petersburg, Alaska.

Photo courtesy of the Stenslid Family

Ragna Stenslid in her bunad

William Kenneth Stedman

By William K. Stedman

William K. Stedman was born on September 27, 1923, in Petersburg, Alaska. His parents were William Reuben and Elvina Stedman. He was the first baby born in the new hospital located above the U.S. Army Signal Corp office, where the U.S. Forest Service building on Nordic Drive is now located.

Bill attended grade school and graduated from Petersburg High School. During high school days, he worked for Tony Schwamm at Petersburg Air Service. While working for Tony, he took flying lessons and soloed after graduation in 1941. In the evenings, he was a projectionist at the Coliseum Theater.

In the spring of 1942, Bill went to work for Morrison-Knutsen, a construction company that had a contract to build the airport at Northway, Alaska. One of the airports constructed during World War II, the Northway airfield was used to receive men and equipment being flown to Alaska and for staging planes being flown to Russia on lend-lease.

In 1943, Bill worked in Juneau for Alaska Coastal Airlines. By fall, he and two of his co-workers decided to go to San Francisco and join the aviation arm of the U.S. Navy. His two friends were accepted, but Bill was rejected because of a perforated eardrum.

Returning to Seattle, he found that Tony Schwamm was getting out of the Navy on a medical and wanted to return to Petersburg to restart Petersburg Air Service. After finding another Waco airplane, he and Bill flew it to Petersburg.

In the fall of 1944, Bill met new schoolteacher Rae C. Burke. They were married in the fall of 1945. Their son Bruce was born in December of 1947. Son David was born in May of 1949.

In September 1949, Bill and his family moved to Los Angeles, so Bill could attend Northrop Aeronautical Institute.

In December 1950, they moved to Juneau, where Bill accepted employment with Alaska Coastal Airlines. Bill was transferred to Petersburg in July 1951.

Bill still lives in the original Stedman house, built in 1916. Rae went back to work, teaching until she died in December 1980.

Bill flew for Alaska Coastal Airlines in Petersburg until 1969. Afterwards, he flew for Alaska Island Air for 18 years. In 1981, he married Carol Nelson.

Gertrude Stenslid and her daring friends make use of some skunk cabbage leaves at Green Rocks, in the 1930s.

Photo courtesy of the Stenslid Family

Knud and Ragna Stenslid

By John and Tim Carter

Knud Stenslid was born in 1882 in Mulda, Norway. At age 13, he came to America. He arrived at Ellis Island, New York, in 1895. Some of his brothers had preceded him to America.

He went to St. Louis, where he became a baker's apprentice. After some years, he went to Winner, South Dakota, to join members of his family.

Knud wasn't in South Dakota long before he traveled to Seattle, Washington.

Ragna Lang was born in Vistdal, Norway. She also came to America through Ellis Island. She arrived in Seattle with at least one of her sisters, about the same time as Knud.

Knud and Ragna met in Seattle at the Sons of Norway Lodge in Ballard. They married in Seattle and traveled together to Petersburg. It's unclear when they first arrived in Petersburg, but it is believed to be around 1913.

In Petersburg, Knud began working at the bakery next to the Arctic Hotel. He was also an early investor in the Bank of Petersburg.

Knud and Ragna returned to Norway, where Ragna became pregnant. It is uncertain whether their original intention was to return to Petersburg, or whether the decision to return was made while in Norway, but they did return.

In 1916, Knud and Ragna arrived in Petersburg for the second time. They bought and ran the bakery. They also bought a house and moved it to the lot next door to the bakery.

Knud and Ragna's daughter, Gertrude, was born on March 15, 1917.

Knud later sold the bakery and bought the Arctic Hotel, which he ran for many years.

Their son, Rangvald, was born in 1922. When he was a teenager, he bought a small fishing boat named the *Snort*.

Gertrude graduated from Petersburg High School in 1935. She went to Seattle to attend the University of Washington.

Rangvald graduated from PHS in 1940 and also went to the University of Washington.

When World War II broke out, Rangvald enlisted in the U.S. Navy and became a navy pilot. He was killed while training in 1943. The death of Rangvald was tragic for Knud and Ragna.

In 1945, their 3-year-old grandson, John, came to live with them to help take their minds off of the loss of their son. John lived at his grandparents' home until 1947.

Knud and Ragna Stenslid

John remembers helping his grandfather at the Arctic Hotel, the old raised wooden streets of Petersburg, the old Indian woman who lived a block away from the Stenslids, and the Fourth of July celebration where everyone had a Norwegian flag in one hand and the U.S. flag in the other.

In 1947, Knud and Ragna's daughter, Gertrude, settled in Seattle with her family.

In 1950 or 1951, Knud and Ragna sold the Arctic Hotel and retired to Seattle, living only a few blocks from their daughter and grandsons.

Ragna died in 1955 from a stroke. Knud died in 1965 of natural causes.

Harold and Pat Stolpe

By Carol Enge

Harold Axel Stolpe was born March 25, 1914, in Nelson, British Columbia. After the death of his father, Harold moved to Tacoma, Washington, with his mother and sisters.

He was lured to Alaska at age 16, by his friend Kurt Nordgren. The pair embarked on a fox farming adventure on Skiff, Level, Meadow and Barrie Islands. When prices in the fur market declined, the family moved to Petersburg.

Their log home was dismantled and floated to town, where it was rebuilt on Wrangell Avenue. While working at the Arness sawmill in Scow Bay, Harold cut lumber to build a home for himself and his mother on Sandy Beach Road.

During his lifetime in Petersburg, Harold worked on a fox farm, was a fisherman, and the head sawyer at the Arness sawmill. He ferried workmen across Wrangell Narrows to the Hansen mill on the M/V *Scout*, longshored at the Public Dock, worked at the Scow Bay cannery, and was the only telephone serviceman in town for many years.

He installed some of the original cable for television in Petersburg and Wrangell and did line work in Kodiak and Seward. His last job was at Petersburg Fisheries, Inc. as boilerman, retort cook, and crab cooker, as well as doing needed odd jobs.

Patricia Anne Cox was born August 31, 1922, in Seattle where she grew up. After graduating from Queen Anne High School, she met and married Bud Anderson. They had five children: Knut, Erik, Paul, Patty and Mark. They moved to Petersburg in 1953. She soon got a job working the telephone switchboard.

While working there, she met her future husband, Harold Stolpe. After her divorce, she and Harold were married and moved into his home. They have two sons, James and Klas.

Pat's humor and dedication to her work have led her to many jobs, including waitressing at The Pastime Café, cooking at the Beachcomber Inn, working at the Cache, and bookkeeping for Hammer & Wikan and Lee's Clothing.

She also worked at the U.S. Forest Service doing budget and finance, and dispatching work crews. Her forte, however, was radio dispatcher for Petersburg Air Taxi, Afton's Flying Service and Viking Airways. There wasn't a job she didn't enjoy.

She is a member of Women of the Moose, Pioneers of Alaska and the Episcopal Church.

After retirement, Harold enjoyed visits from his grandchildren and building a cabin down Petersburg Narrows, where the family had many wonderful times. Harold passed away in April 1993.

Pat continues to live in the house that Harold built for himself and his mother on Sandy Beach Road near Hungry Point. Pat loves people and they love her.

Pat and Harold Stolpe

Erling and Claire Strand

By John and Carol Enge

Peter and Laura Sommers were among the earliest Norwegian immigrants in Petersburg. They arrived in 1900 and built a home on Nordic Drive. Peter had the F/V *Eleda* built in Seattle and used it for both salmon fishing and longlining. Returning to Norway to visit family, Laura invited Peter's young nephew, Erling Strand, to join them in Alaska.

It was January of 1912 when Erling left Torvik, Norway, to come to Petersburg with his Aunt Laura.

Erling and his friends played in skiffs, often building a shaft and wheel to steer. He started fishing with his Uncle Peter on the *Eleda* when he was 12. In those early years, they fished out of a rowboat. He said when the Stikine River wind was blowing, outboard engines were not dependable. When Peter died, Erling took over the *Eleda*. He attended Pacific Lutheran Academy, graduated from the University of Washington in 1928, and was a member of the Chi Phi fraternity.

Claire Harris was born in Spokane, Washington, on May 29, 1915. She had been valedictorian of her class and planned to attend Stanford University. However, because of the Depression, money was scarce. She attended Eastern Washington College, graduating with a degree in elementary education. She taught in rural Washington for two years before seeking adventure in the far north.

She traveled to Petersburg on the SS *Alaska* in 1937, and she stayed at the Arctic Hotel with other single teachers. She paid $20 a month rent at the hotel and $30 a month at a boarding house that included two meals a day. Claire's salary was $1,400 a year. For three years she taught fourth grade and high school girls' physical education. She always planned to go to the wild parts of Alaska, but instead she met Erling Strand. They were married in 1940. Because married teachers weren't allowed to teach, she started a family and fished with Erling.

Erling was active in the Democratic Party and served on the state Democratic Central Committee for many years. After statehood, Governor Egan named Erling one of the first members of the Alaska Board of Fish and Game.

Fishing was his life. John Enge and Herb Mjorud spent many summers fishing with him on the Stikine River, earning money to go to a university. The family enjoyed many recreational trips on the boat to Warm Springs Bay and cruising around Southeast Alaska, as well as skiing, ice skating, and swimming in the cold waters at Sandy Beach and Blind Slough. Erling was a great storyteller and willingly shared his many experiences. He passed away October 4, 1986.

After their children — Erling John, Nancy, Floyd and Laura — grew up, Claire returned to teaching for the next 25 years. She was active in local and state Democratic politics, and served on both the State Pharmacy Board and Professional Teaching Practices Commission. Claire was a member of the Sons of Norway, Pioneers of Alaska, Emblem Club, many teaching organizations, and was president of the Associated Teachers of Petersburg. Clair passed away July 4, 2000, after a lengthy illness.

John Enge, Erling and Claire Strand, and Vera Sommers

Leif and Alta Stromdahl

By Mary and Jim Stromdahl

Hans and Lena Stromdahl came to the United States in the early 1900s to make money to take back to Norway. The plan was to use this money for electricity on the Stromdahl farm. They were able to accomplish this, but decided to stay in Petersburg.

Their son Leif was born in 1918 in Seattle, but grew up in Petersburg. Leif started fishing with his father on the Stikine River when he was 9 years old. His father became ill when Leif was a young boy. He died when Leif was about 14. Leif continued in the fishing industry.

After Pearl Harbor was bombed, Leif joined the U.S. Navy and became a chief petty officer. He met Alta Meagher in Seattle. They were married in 1944.

After the war, Leif and Alta, with their two children Jim and Lynn, moved back to Petersburg. Over the next 10 years, three more children were born: Carol, Donna and Marie.

In 1948, Leif had the fishing boat *Astrid* built in Seattle. He fished it for 20 years. In 1968, he sold the *Astrid* to Bill Phillips. His next boat was the *Coral*, and he seined with this boat until his retirement in 1984.

Leif and Alta Stromdahl

Leif passed away in 1997.

At present, Alta lives with her daughter Carol Reid in Chehalis, Washington. Leif and Alta had 17 grandchildren and 15 great-grandchildren.

F/V *Astrid*

Carl and Aurora Swanson

By Debbie Johnson

Carl Alfred Swanson was born October 28, 1881, to Nels Peter and Caroline Swanson, three miles from Walnut Grove, Minnesota. He was the second of 10 children, three of whom died in infancy.

Carl started teaching when he was 17 years old. He walked 20 miles to take an oral exam from the county superintendent of schools and was granted a one-year's certificate to teach. His first assignment as a teacher was at a school four miles from his home; he was paid $26 a month.

Aurora and Carl Swanson

At the age of 23, he was hired to teach in Marshall County. He paid board and room to the Strandberg family. This is where he first met Aurora Strandberg.

Aurora was born in 1886 in Lyksele, Sweden. Her parents moved to Strandquist, Minnesota, when she was between 2 and 3 years of age.

Carl said that she was very beautiful and had a wonderful, fun personality. When he asked her to marry him in 1906, she thought they were too young at the time.

In 1908, Carl was offered a teaching job in the Philippines; there was also an opening in Puerto Rico. While he was deliberating between the two positions, he was offered a job with the Bureau of Education in Alaska. He accepted and received free transportation to Kasaan, Alaska, and a salary of $80 per month.

Teachers had to report to the first Teachers Convention, in August of 1908, in Juneau. There was a banquet at the Governor's Mansion and 10 days of discussion. Judge Gunnison, Governor Hoggart, and a doctor from Washington D.C. delivered addresses.

In February 1909, Aurora wrote Carl a friendly letter. When he wrote back and asked her to marry him, she accepted and set sail for Alaska, departing on the SS *Cottage City* March 17. They were married in Ketchikan on March 19, 1909, by Judge Stackpole. They then took the mail boat 35 miles out to Kasaan Bay.

Their first child, Evangeline Aurora, was born in Petersburg on December 23, 1909. Aurora was attended by a medical missionary who had spent seven years in China. Elmer was born July 5, 1911. Brother Raymond joined the family on October 29, 1913.

Carl taught in Native schools for a total of six years — four years on Prince of Wales Island in Kasaan and Shakan, and two years in Petersburg. When Carl was offered the superintendent position for Southeast Alaska in 1912, he declined.

Carl served on the very first Petersburg City Council, and in 1910, they organized the first Volunteer Fire Department. He was the town clerk and city magistrate in 1913 and earned $50 a month. He resigned after several months, as it didn't pay enough to support his growing family. He was also a trustee in the Arctic Brotherhood organization.

This same year, they went to considerable expense establishing a store operated by the Petersburg Co-operative Association. The fishing had been very poor that year, so it didn't get off the ground.

In 1913, Carl also found himself involved in politics. He ran for territorial senator when the Territory of Alaska was organized. He said he "put up a good race, but lost out."

Carl and Aurora Swanson cont'd

After losing the election and with the failure of the Co-op store, they decided to move back to Minnesota. Selling everything they had, they left in November on the SS *Humboldt*. They arrived in Minnesota just before Thanksgiving. They were gone for two years. During that time, Alaska was calling them home.

Things were worse monetarily for them in Minnesota. They returned to Petersburg with three chairs, two beds, a range, and $40 in their pockets! Carl rented a house for his family at $10 a month, charged a tenant $5 for a room, and looked for a job. He began working for Jacobsen, who had a contract to rebuild the vessel *Mars*. He worked from March to July at 40 cents an hour. He continued on with Jacobsen, rebuilding another fishing vessel for Rasmus Enge. In the fall of 1916, he was asked by Mr. Arness, who owned the mill at Scow Bay, to take over the Scow Bay school at $110 a month.

In May of 1917, all of Carl's family, except one sister, moved up to Petersburg from Minnesota. This included his parents, Nels Peter and Caroline Swanson; brothers John, Alfred and Ernest; and sisters Anna and Emma. Hulda, the married sister, remained in Waukegan, Illinois. One month later, Nels Peter passed away. He is buried across the Narrows, on the island of Kupreanof, at the old Petersburg graveyard.

In the summer of 1918, Carl decided to resign from teaching school at Scow Bay to try salmon trolling. Aurora suggested they put up a tent at Point Agassiz. They sold their house in town, towed lumber to Point Agassiz, and built a cabin. Salmon fishing turned out to be "slim pickins," so he sold the boat and turned toward their way of life growing up in Minnesota — dairy farming.

Carl took the steamer to Seattle to buy cows, a horse and machinery. Buying a wagon, plow, rake, one horse, mower, a cream separator, milk bottles, and pails at Sears Roebuck, he signed a contract with an agent for the seven cows and the horse to be shipped up on the next available ship. He returned to Petersburg; the horse and cows arrived two weeks later — and were just let loose to roam around town. Carl's boat was out of commission, so he had rowed the eight miles to town from Point Agassiz in a canoe. Towards evening of that day, Carl's brother Alfred helped him get the animals aboard a scow and over to Point Agassiz. Jack Hadland towed them across. In Carl's own words the story goes, "Jack Hadland had been up towing logs all the night before and so, as they approached Agassiz, Jack gave the scow a good push and went to sleep! We were drifting toward shore, but a strong headwind blew up and we started to drift out again. I ran forward to throw out the anchor, but it caught on my coat and I went to the bottom in 10 feet of water! I got hold of the line and climbed up. We then dumped the first cow overboard, but instead of swimming ashore, she headed out into the Sound. I jumped into the canoe and securing her to the boat, towed her ashore. When she started for the scow again, I had to tie her to a rock. We agreed to see if the horse would go ashore. He did not want to jump into the water, but we finally pushed him in. He was soon trotting up to the green grass and the remaining cows took the hint. We dragged the canoe above the high tide mark and got up to the house for supper at 11 p.m. A long day, as I had started for town at 4 a.m. Aside from cramps in the neck from exhaustion, I felt well enough to go down to look at the scow before sunup. It was still high and dry on a sandbar and Jack was still sleeping. I chased the cows up to the barn and went in for breakfast. My sister Emma came out to help, as Aurora was in town helping cousin Alex."

Aurora gave birth to their son Roy on Alaska Day, October 18, 1918, under Dr. Anna Brown's care. Inez and her twin, Wilfred, were born in 1922 at Point Agassiz. Wilfred died at birth. Carl found a twin tree and buried Wilfred there, marking the grave with a cross and a little white fence. The fence is gone, but the tree is still there. Gloria was born in 1926.

Aurora was a hard worker, fun, and very supportive of her husband. She was a very good guitar player. Whenever there were festive occasions and music was needed, she would perform. She knew many hymns and would sing and play the guitar in the evenings with the family.

Aurora was also very active in community activities. She ran for school director along with husband Carl, John Thornadsater, and Mrs. E.P. Refling in March of 1913. John Thornadsater won 42 votes, and Aurora was close behind with 30! She was elected secretary of the Women's Christian Temperance

Carl and Aurora Swanson cont'd

Union, which held its first meeting in July of 1913. In 1918, she became president of the local chapter.

Aurora was very involved, on a daily basis, in her community in times of national crisis. During the First World War, there was food conservation in all communities across the United States, including those in Alaska. During the first week of January 1918, delegates from various local organizations met at the Arctic Brotherhood hall and organized the Petersburg Food Conservation Committee. Aurora was appointed to take charge of the food conservation work at Scow Bay. This involved securing signatures from homes pledging to observe "wheatless" and "meatless" days and to take up other food supply conservation issues that the National Food Administration would suggest.

During the dairy years, they kept the farm going at Point Agassiz. When Inez was in sixth grade, they rented the house next to the cemetery (Charlie Christensen's present homesite). Roy and Inez delivered milk in town, and Inez went to school. Aurora and little Gloria went back and forth from Point Agassiz to Petersburg. They would go to Point Agassiz on the weekends. Carl would stay at Point Agassiz during the week, bringing the milk into town every other day. Aurora kept up both homes until 1943, when Carl and Aurora sold the cows to Hjalmer Martinsen, Nette Martinsen's son.

Carl built and helped build many homes in Petersburg, including the Knut and Dorothy Fredricksen home on south Nordic, the Les Elkins home, the little blue house next to the Phil Clausen home, and Susan and Jeff Erickson's home.

Carl and Aurora eventually moved to Seattle where they made their permanent home. In the South Park neighborhood, Carl invested in a number of houses to remodel for their children's inheritances.

After having lived in Seattle and elsewhere with husband Hugh Jones for many years, their oldest child, Evangeline Jones, returned to Petersburg in 1993. In March of 2000, she moved to Oregon with her son, Bruce H. Jones, and his wife, Marilyn. Evangeline passed away November 13, 2003, in Dallas, Oregon.

Inez is the only child of Carl and Aurora still living. She and her husband, Russell Van Buren, live in Washington State. Their son, Clayton, and his family, and their daughter, Diane, also live in Washington.

Carl and Aurora Swanson

Although Carl and Aurora no longer have any grandchildren living in Petersburg, there are many great-grandchildren and great-great-grandchildren who call Petersburg home. The great-grandchildren include Debra (Thynes) Johnson, Shelley (Thynes) Reid, Tracey (Thynes) Reid, and David Thynes. Great-great-grandchildren include Joshua Reid, Sonja (Johnson) Campos, Trisha (Reid) Highland, Erin (Johnson) Compton, Gabriel Johnson, Bosjun Reid, Tyler Reid, and Joshua Thynes.

Carl passed away in Seattle in August 1957. Aurora passed away in Seattle in July 1965. Both are buried there. What wonderful Godly pioneer folks they were. Their memory will live long in the hearts of their remaining daughter, their grandchildren, great grandchildren, and great-great grandchildren.

Lillian L. Swanson

By Roxy Lee

Lillian L. Swanson was born in Apple River, Wisconsin. She was one of seven children of Ida and John Swanson, Swedish immigrants. Ida ran a boarding house in St. Peter, Minnesota, after her husband died at an early age. The family later moved to Portland, Oregon, where Lillian grew up.

After high school, Lillian took secretarial training. Moving to Petersburg, she became a clerk and secretary to James H. Wheeler, a family friend. Her brother and sister-in-law, Carl E. and Alice Swanson, were already residing here.

In 1938, she established the Lillian Shop, a women's and children's apparel store. It was located on Main Street on part of the present site of Wells Fargo. She operated this business until 1956.

Due to a heart condition, she died at Petersburg General Hospital in June of 1957. She was buried in the family plot in Portland, Oregon.

Lillian was very active in community affairs. She was a longtime secretary of the Chamber of Commerce, and was the Petersburg Business and Professional Women's first president.

She had a beautiful singing voice and performed at public functions.

Lillian brought her niece, Roxane Swenson Lee, to town, helped with her college education, and instilled in her good business ethics. Roxanne later established her own store in 1969.

Many remember Lillian with her smile, red hair, friendly ways, and black high heels, making her way down Petersburg's Main Street.

Aunt Lillian takes Roxy on her first buying trip to Seattle.

Wally and Colleen Swanson

By Colleen Swanson

When Colleen McDonald and Lewellyn Swanson married on September 21, 1947, they brought to their union a mix of Scandinavian and Scottish heritage.

Colleen's mother, Andrea Aaberge, was born March 15, 1898, at Terry, South Dakota. Ann's Norwegian immigrant parents were Sophia Medgaard of Smoglie and Jorgen Anderssen of Sogn. Jorgen was prospecting for gold at the time.

Colleen's father was Lauchlin Randolph "Mac" McDonald. He was born on April 22, 1886, in Lawson, Missouri. His family emigrated from Knoydart, Scotland, to Canada during the Highland Clearances.

Ann Aaberge and Mac McDonald met in Bellingham, Washington. Ann was attending a teachers' college and Mac was employed building boats at the Holland-McDonald Yard. They later settled in North Bend, Oregon, where Mac trolled for salmon on the *Ann*, as well as doing boat work. Their daughter, Colleen Mae, was born there on July 28, 1926.

Wally and Colleen Swanson

In 1933, they packed their belongings, and with old friend Ray Brixner, set off for Juneau in the 42-foot double-ender troller. One victim of the journey was Ann's collection of *National Geographic* magazines stored in the fishhold. It did not survive the doses of salt water.

Mac found work in Petersburg in Carl Andersen's shipyard. After the Andersen yard was destroyed by fire, Mac and a group of local fishermen, and others, incorporated as Mitkof Marine Ways, Inc.

Colleen recalled, "Childhood in Petersburg was very pleasant. We biked or walked to Sandy Beach over the three-plank muskeg trail. It seemed so very long, but when one turned the corner and could see the water, what a thrill it was. I learned to swim as a Girl Scout, with lessons given in the Narrows by Dorothy Young."

Mac died in 1953.

Ann worked for years as the Petersburg High School secretary. Ann died in 1991.

Lewellyn "Wally" Swanson's mother, Lillian Holm, was born February 26, 1904, in Danvers, Minnesota, to Nels and Ellen Holm, Norwegian immigrants from Eldholm. The family moved to Snohomish, Washington, where they farmed.

Wally's father, Lloyd Theodore

Wally and Colleen Swanson with their children Carol Ann, John, Tom and Rob

Wally and Colleen Swanson cont'd

Swanson, was born February 29, 1904, in Minneapolis, Minnesota, to Gustaf and Hilma Swanson, immigrants from Sweden and Finland. Gus was a journeyman machinist and tool and die maker. He also worked for the Great Northern Railroad.

Lloyd and Lillian were married February 17, 1924.

Wally Swanson was born on March 22, 1928, in Everett, Washington.

Lillian's brother, Chester Holm, had previously settled in Petersburg with the telephone business. He died in a Blind Slough hunting accident. Lloyd came up to settle the estate and soon sent for Lillian and Wally. Lillian and Lloyd's second son Norris Oliver was born in Petersburg March 24, 1933.

In addition to the telephone business, Lloyd worked as an electrician and cannery foreman, as well as cold storage engineer.

Lloyd died in 1970 and Lillian died in 2001.

Colleen and Wally were married September 21, 1947, at the Petersburg Lutheran Church. They were the first couple to be married in the new church sanctuary. Until then, services had been held in the church basement, as the upstairs was unfinished. It took a great deal of labor to carry the theater-type seating upstairs and build a temporary backdrop for the altar, but the stained glass windows made the unfinished room very lovely. One complication was that the pipe organist was in the basement where the console was located, while the soloist was upstairs "doing her thing."

Wally started working in canneries in 1942. In 1951, he was an engineer at Kayler-Dahl Cold Storage. In December 1965, he started at Petersburg Fisheries, Inc. He retired in 1990.

Wally enjoyed the pleasures of Mitkof Island, deer hunting, basketball and public service. He was a member of the fire department resuscitation squad (an EMT group taught by Dr. Russell Smith) and served on the city council for four years.

Colleen worked in the telephone office and canneries, gardened and sewed.

She was hired in 1960 by the Petersburg School District as the first elementary school secretary-bookkeeper. She retired in 1982. She participated in the Lutheran Church music program as choir director and organist.

Four children were born of this union: Robert Lee, Thomas Lloyd, Carol Ann (McCabe) and John Randolph. There are nine grandchildren, and three great-grandchildren.

Photo courtesy of the Clausen Memorial Museum

Norris and Mary Anne Swanson

By Norris Swanson

My mother's brother, Chester Holm, arrived in Petersburg sometime after World War I. He was lost in a boating accident in Blind Slough. At the time, he owned the Petersburg Telephone office, which he had started with Dan Sutphen.

After my uncle's death, my father, Lloyd Swanson, traveled to Petersburg to handle his estate for my grandparents. He liked Petersburg so much that he purchased the company and moved his wife Lillian and 1-year-old son, Lewellyn "Wally," to Petersburg. This was in 1929.

Norris, Lillian and Wally Swanson

Since there were several Swanson families in Petersburg at the time, my father was known as "Telephone Swanson."

My father was also an electrician, builder, and foreman for Dean Kayler's salmon cannery and worked in the cannery business for many years.

The building on Main Street that he built to house the telephone office included an electrical business and rentals for apartments and businesses. This became a family business run by my father, my mother, my brother and me.

My father, Lloyd, passed away in June of 1970 at the age of 66.

My mother, Lillian, passed away in July of 2001 at the age of 97.

I, Norris, was born in Petersburg, at the Petersburg General Hospital, on March 24, 1933.

I grew up in Petersburg, finished high school, and went to electronics school for two years at Oregon Technical Institute in Klamath Falls, Oregon.

I was drafted into the U.S. Army in June of 1954 and honorably discharged in June of 1956. A radar mechanic in the service, I worked on radar that controlled four 120-millimeter antiaircraft guns. This experience, along with my schooling, qualified me for a position in the CAA (which later evolved into the FAA), as an electronics technician in the communications section.

I retired in 1989 after more than 34 years of government service. I was in real estate for several years after that.

On March 29, 1969, I married Mary Anne Roth. She had a daughter, Leslie Ann, so I became father to a very lovely 9-year-old. We adopted our son, Gregg, in December 1970.

Leslie Ann married Donald Smith in 1981 and we now have two grandsons, Nicholas and Nathan.

Gregg is single and a computer technician for MultiCare Health System in Tacoma, Washington.

After my wife retired in 2000, we built a new home on our property in Shelton, Washington, where we thoroughly enjoy the retirement life.

Norman and Vange Tate

By Evangeline J. Tate

My grandparents, Gurine and Helge Egland and Peter and Johanna Aubramen, were all born in Norway. Peter and Johanna changed their last name to Johnson when they immigrated to the United States in about 1899. They all settled in Iowa. Later, my grandmother Egland (née Larson) lived in South Dakota.

My mother, Lizzie Emma Johnson, was born in 1884. She grew up in Nordness, Iowa, where her father, Peter, had a general merchandise store that included the local post office.

My father, Hans Egland, was born in 1883. In 1899, at the age of 16, my father came to America aboard the SS *Belgenland*, landing at Ellis Island. My parents were married in 1908 and came to Canada in approximately 1910. Hans was the Canadian Pacific Railway (CPR) agent in the small town of Midale, Saskatchewan (population about 200). It was located on the Soo Line between Minneapolis, Minnesota, and Moose Jaw, Saskatchewan.

My mother was active in the Lutheran church, where she played the organ; and in the Homemakers' Club, for which she wrote the club song. My parents conducted a Lutheran Sunday School in our home for 16 years until a Lutheran church was built in Midale.

Dad was the secretary-treasurer of the school district and of our church. He instigated the building of a creamery — a place for the local farmers to bring their cream.

My parents, Hans and Lizzie Egland, had eight children — seven daughters and one son. I, Evangeline "Vange" Jeanette Egland, was their fourth child, born March 3, 1916. I attended Midale Elementary and completed twelfth grade in 1933. I took nurses training at Winnipeg General Hospital, receiving R.N. status at the University of Manitoba, graduating in 1938. Afterwards, I worked briefly at the Winnipeg General Hospital, and then worked at Worrall Hospital in Rochester, Minnesota, for seven months.

In 1940, I followed my sister, Jo Barnreiter, who had come to Petersburg as a missionary nurse in 1936. We both worked in the original hospital that was owned and operated by the Petersburg Lutheran Church at that time.

Norman Tate and I were married in 1942.

Norman's father, Nollie Tate, was born in 1882 in Waco, Texas. Nollie came to Alaska as a young man, intending to mine. This did not work out for him, so he and a cousin built and operated a salmon cannery at Union Bay, between Wrangell and Ketchikan.

Norman's mother, Flora Amelia Radloff, was born in 1890 in Ballard, Washington. She grew up in the Seattle/Tacoma area. Nollie met Flora in Tacoma and brought her to Alaska, where they were married at the Wrangell Episcopal Church in 1912. Legislator Frank Barnes was their best man.

Flora and Nollie's three children, Richard, Virginia and Norman, were all born in Wrangell. Norman was born on July 11, 1916. Flora and the children moved to Petersburg in 1922, following Nollie's death due to diabetes, just one year before insulin came into use.

Flora was a gourmet cook. She ran several boarding houses before becoming the cook at the Petersburg Hospital, where she worked for 25 years.

After Norman and I married, we purchased an old cannery warehouse from Fred and Gertrude Paten that was located on the beach at Scow Bay. Norman converted it into a home and there we raised three daughters: Beth Hagerman, Holly Trotter and Laurel Tate. In 1973, we built a new "round" house on the same location.

Norman was a commercial fisherman until about 1972. He ran the F/V *Surf* from 1946 to 1966. He also had several other boats over the years. He had built a bulkhead on the beach, where he moored his scow and had a gravel business for several years. In the 1990s, he logged spruce and red cedar logs and milled lumber with a chainsaw mill. He went into the long-term care facility in 1998 and died there on August 14, 1999.

In 1943, I taught a class of nurse's aides. In 1944, I taught home nursing to 77 women. I was active in the Episcopal Church for 30 years.

In 1981, I, along with Martha Reid and Lorraine Thompson, named the Petersburg streets after former Petersburg fishing boats. I also published a book of my poetry in 1989. I lost a leg in 1999 due to diabetes, but I still live in my Scow Bay home.

Our three daughters have given us six grandchildren and six great-grandchildren.

(Vange Tate passed away March 5, 2003.)

Jim and Billie Taylor

By Billie Taylor

James G. Taylor was born in Blaine, Washington, in 1912. Jim's dad ran a grocery store and Jim went through school there. After high school, he worked at a Standard Oil gas station, and next worked for Metropolitan Life.

He married Billie E. Walken, who was born in 1916 in Bellingham, Washington. Her parents were from Germany and had settled in Alger, Washington, were they had a small mill and logging business.

Jim and Billie Taylor

Jim and Billie had daughter Lynda in 1945.

After enlisting in the U.S. Army, Jim was sent to Petersburg. He worked for the Communications System. He made friends in Petersburg, the first being Swede Wasvik, but he missed his family who remained in Bellingham. When Lynda was eight months old, she and Billie arrived in Petersburg on a steamer.

While serving in the Army, Jim was sent to Big Delta, Alaska. Once the war was over, Jim and Billie decided to stay in Petersburg.

Jim worked as city clerk for 22 years and also as magistrate. He was a key figure with the Bank of Petersburg, and spent 12 years as a board member for the National Bank of Alaska, which is now Wells Fargo. Jim also worked as a longshoreman for extra income. He was one of the few businessmen in town, as most men fished or logged. He had breakfast at The Pastime Café for about 50 years; for a good many of those years, he had the same counter stool. It was his routine and a way of keeping up on important news in town.

Being a businessman, Jim served on local boards and was active in Rotary and other civic organizations. He loved his hunting and fishing and had many experiences with longtime Petersburg friends Swede Wasvik and Henry Freel. Jim and Swede fished on Swede's boat in the early days. Later on, they used Jim's boat, the *Taylor Maid*, which Jim and Henry Freel built and launched in Hammer Slough.

Jim and Billie lived in the old PFI house, kitty-corner from the old hospital. Their daughter, Tammie, arrived on the scene in 1955.

Tammie has fond memories of living in the neighborhood. Chris Gronseth lived across the street. She spent many hours watching Chris make gaff hooks in this garage where he had his blacksmith shop. While he hammered out the molten metal to a rhythmic "bang, bang ba, bang," she would chatter her head off, while following him from station to station as he made his magic tools.

Billie remembers the plank streets in early Petersburg and the large amounts of snow in the early years. She was a homemaker and enjoyed cooking and caring for their home on Front Street that they built on the old Duvall Property. Billie liked entertaining their friends and was known for her duck dinners.

Billie and Jim spent 50 years in Petersburg until Jim's stroke in 1995. He was to spend the last of his years in a nursing home in Oregon.

Lynda Floor is married to Bruce, who sneaks in an annual fishing trip to Petersburg in between "filling teeth." Her grown sons, Jim Johnson and Tom Johnson, reside in Oregon near Lynda. Billie and Jim have one great-grandson and one great-granddaughter.

Tammie Briggs lives in Poulsbo, Washington, with her two daughters, Ashley and Taylor.

Billie now resides in Poulsbo, close to Tammie.

Haakon and Eleanor Thomassen

By Patty Thomassen

Haakon Thomassen was born to Ivar and Charlotte Peterson Thomassen on November 14, 1904, in Bodø Norway. In 1911, at the age of 7, he came to America with his two younger brothers, Erling and Ray. His three older sisters, Anna, Hannah and Inga, were already here.

In 1914, the family moved from Poulsbo, Washington, to Petersburg, to help Ivar gillnet the north arm of the Stikine River. They lived in a warehouse in Scow Bay that they had bought from Albie Hofstad's father, Richard. Haakon fished for years with his father and then by himself.

In 1939, Haakon married Eleanor G. Stoll. They had four boys: Ted, Palmer, Steven and Fred. Haakon ran the *Pafco 7*, the *Libby 14*, the *Middleton*, and the *Lancing*. He also fished on the *Don Q*. In 1957, Haakon became the third owner of the *Baltic*. Besides Eleanor and his sons, over the years his crew included Pete Rayton, Pete Thynes, Leif Thorsen, Fred File and Tom Stewart. They fished up around Dutch Harbor, Sand Point, Squaw Harbor, King Cove and Perryville.

Haakon's health began to fail. In 1971, he sold the *Baltic* to son Steven. Haakon fished with Steven for a few years, and then got off the boat for good. Haakon died November 24, 1978.

The F/V *Baltic*

Photo courtesy of Clausen Memorial Museum

Knut and Ann Thompson

By Carol Enge

Knut Thompson and his second wife, Ann, were pillars of strength in the young community of Petersburg. Whether it was serving numerous terms as mayor, helping to form The Trading Union, or raising money to build the Lutheran Church, Knut was very civic minded.

Ann's kindness and understanding of people, organizational ability, and volunteer work made her a leader in many organizations: the Lutheran Church, Eastern Star, Daughters and Sons of Norway, Alaska Pioneers, Hospital Guild, and the Charity Box, which she helped found. Ann is lovingly remembered for her daily visits to the long-term care patients to read to them in both English and Norwegian.

Knut was born near Mandal, in southern Norway, in 1909. He was the eldest of son of a Norwegian farmer. He could have taken over the family farm when his father died, but he didn't like farming. He first worked in Tacoma piling sacks of wheat in a warehouse. He did this for two years, earning 25 cents an hour, until he had enough money to build a needed barn on the family farm in Norway.

Knut Thompson and Earl Ohmer

Knut returned to Norway to help build the barn and then came back to Alaska. Knut lived in Petersburg with his sister, Ragnhild Martens, and her husband, Louis, while fishing with Louis on the *Star*.

Knut and his first wife, Froydis, had three children: June, Ruth and Tom. The family lived in West Petersburg until Froydis died in 1932. Knut bought Sverre Johansen's house on North First Street. He became a commissioned fish buyer at Petersburg Cold Storage and over the next 40 years handled transactions for millions of pounds of halibut.

Knut's second wife was Anna Eide, who was born in Stanwood, Washington, on February 22, 1899. She was one of nine children.

June and Ruth stand behind Tom, Ann and Knut

Anna attended parochial school and high school, and then continued her education at the State Normal School (now Western Washington University) in Bellingham. She taught school in Plummer, Idaho, and Wrangell before coming to Petersburg to teach fifth grade in 1935. That was the same year she met and married Knut.

Throughout the years they traveled extensively on business and pleasure trips, including one trip to Knut's former home in Norway. Ann's hobbies included oil painting, needlework, sewing, quilting and playing bridge.

Knut died in 1971. Ann passed away peacefully in her home in Petersburg on July 10, 2000, at the age of 101.

Tom and Lorraine Thompson

By Lorraine Rude Thompson

Recently, I realized five decades of my life had been spent in Petersburg, and many good memories were centered around that town. I realized also what a great place it was to grow up in, and a wonderful place to raise a family.

Our journey had begun in Minneapolis, early in 1929, soon after Dad had finished his internship at the University of Minnesota. The Rude family arrived in Petersburg from Ketchikan early in the summer of 1929. Our father had been associated with Dr. Ellis there, but an opportunity came up for him to set up a medical practice in Petersburg. So, after only a few months we were on the road (or water) again. In Ketchikan, our brother Jim had been born and joined me, age 6, Don, age 4 ½, and Audrey, age 3.

We seemed to fit into Petersburg quite easily — perhaps because Mom and Dad could speak Norwegian and we were Lutherans!

Tom Thompson

Looking back to school days, I recall so many great teachers. I had Mabel Otness, Chris Christensen, Virginia Peters, Verda Grindrod, Tom Winsor, Al Boyer, John Honn, Bob Summers, Ellen Hasbrouck, and our superintendents, George Beck and Les Wingard.

Dorothy Wingard took us under her wing and taught the boys and girls how to dance — beyond the call of duty on her part, and so much fun at the high school parties.

Of course, I recall the summers as sunny everyday! A walk across the boardwalk to Sandy Beach for a picnic and swimming was always fun. Many families had nice cabins there; they often reached the area by boat. When the road was lengthened, the chance to swim at Falls Creek was an option. It was also a popular place for all of us to go ice-skating in the winter months.

As kids, we often spent time with families who lived on Fox Island. At that time, those places seemed so very remote — no plane service! Dad had ordered a boat from the Midwest. That opened up a lot of new territory for camping and hiking, and we visited great places like Point Agassiz, Petersburg Creek, Harvey's Lake, Le Conte Bay, Duncan Canal and, of course, the entire length of Wrangell Narrows.

In 1940, I graduated from Petersburg High School with a record class of 24 students (seven of us were female). In the fall, I was on my way to Minnesota to attend St. Olaf College.

Early in 1941, the rest of my family moved to Juneau. I was afraid I'd never see Petersburg again. I was wrong. Mr. Wingard needed a teacher and told me to come back or he'd never speak to me again. (World War II created a shortage of teachers and I think he was desperate.)

Anyway, I was happy to sign a contract in Petersburg, as I had become engaged to Tommy Thompson. By now, he was in the crash boat branch of the Army Air Corps and stationed in the Aleutians. He had graduated from Petersburg High School in 1941 and attended Washington State University until he joined the U.S. Army.

It was interesting to teach in the school I had attended as a student for 11 years. I felt at home and there was a great group of teachers on the staff. Esther

Tom and Lorraine Thompson cont'd

Lindenmeyer, D'Annette Snyder and I rented a house together. Others who had signed contracts, when I did, were Rae Stedman, Esther Hansen, Esther Evans and Noca Wikan. We did have such good times playing pinochle, attending dances at Sons of Norway, and hiking and boating.

In August of 1945, the war was over and Tom had "leave." We married in Juneau on September 10. Tom's parents and sisters came from Petersburg. Harold Lee was to be best man, but his ship was out at sea, so he missed the wedding. Our friends, Katy and Joe Alexander, were our attendants.

Tom was discharged in the spring of 1946 and went to work at the Petersburg Cold Storage for his dad. We had an apartment over Zehm's Bakery (now People's Drug Store) and I became a homemaker instead of a teacher.

In the fall of 1947, we spent about six months in Beaverton, Oregon, living with June and Robert Naze, Tom's sister and brother-in-law. Tom had decided to go to school in Portland. He took classes in accounting and business procedures.

On our return to Petersburg, we decided to build a home on property at Second and C streets. It meant a lot of clearing, but, at that time, the fish business was quiet during the winter months.

In 1950, we moved into our new home, along with our newborn son, Harold Knut. Two years later, Mark Edward was born in Juneau. Grandpa Dr. Rude wanted to deliver a grandchild, so we obliged. Mark was followed by sister Amy Jo in 1954. She was named for her maternal grandparents, Amy and Joe Rude.

Four years later, on the day of the Yakutat Earthquake, Grechen Kay was born. The hospital was "quaking," but we thought it was just a truck going by!

It wasn't until 1963 that number five child, Thomas L., joined us. That was the last human addition, but we did adopt dogs, cats, goldfish and turtles.

Besides the fish business, our life centered around the schools and church. Tom had become manager of the cold storage; eventually, the cold storage plant and Petersburg Fisheries merged to become Icicle Seafoods. Tom was named vice-president, although I felt he was the "trouble shooter" for all three plants because he was away so often.

One by one, the kids went off to jobs or to college.

In 1980, Tom decided to buy the Sitka plant that Icicle owned. It was Tom's dream to have a small seafood business involving the whole family and this was that project. All of the family worked at Sitka Sound Seafood at one time or another — even I served as receptionist at the front desk, where I met many fine fishing families from the community.

We left Petersburg expecting to eventually return. I may do so when, and if, my kids and grandkids leave Sitka. Until then, I'll keep visiting my oldest and best friends in "my home town."

Having friends you've known since childhood is one of the best things about small town life.

Tom and I traveled with many of the "old gang" — up the Alcan, down the Mississippi, through the Panama Canal, to Europe, Australia and New Zealand.

We were always happy to have lived for 50 years in beautiful Petersburg, Alaska.

In November of 1997, Tom died of heart failure while working on his pleasure boat, the *K.D.B.*

Grechen, Harold, Amy Jo, Tom L., Lorraine and Mark Thompson

Ed and Ingeborg Thorsen

By Trygve Thorsen

My father's name was Edward Thorsen. He was born in 1904 at Veidholmen, Norway, on the island of Smøla, near Kristiansund. His parents were Theodor and Anna Nordseth.

Ingeborg and Ed Thorsen

Ed was a fisherman in Veidholmen. He owned a boat and fished for sye, a kind of rockfish.

My mother, Ingeborg, was born in 1906. Her parents were John and Trina Hals. Trina passed away when my mother was 8 years old.

Grandpa John was a shoemaker in Norway and also a chief cook on big ships. He went to America and got a chance to fish in Seattle. He fished most of his life in Alaska.

Ed came to America to fish herring in Alaska with Iver Norseth (Holms) in 1924. Arriving in America, he changed his last name from Nordseth to Teodorsen, and later to Thorsen.

In 1929, he went back to Norway and married my mother at the Hopen church. They took the steamship from Kristiansund to Halifax, Canada, and then boarded a train to Prince Rupert. While on the train, my mother asked my dad for an apple and he brought her a banana.

My dad had two boats in Alaska, the *Emerald* and the *Spencer II*. He fished halibut, blackcod and salmon, until he retired in 1971. My mother was a housewife and worked in the local cannery. She was a very good cook. They had four children: Trygve, Alvil, Elsie and Ruth. All were raised in Petersburg.

My father passed away in 1984 and my mother in 1986.

I was born in 1929 and have lived in Petersburg all of my life. When I got out of school, I went fishing with my dad for about three years, and then the draft came up. I was in the U.S. Army from 1951 to 1953 and was a corporal when I got out. Then, I went back to fishing with my dad and spent a year at the Edison Technical School, learning welding, drafting, plumbing and wiring.

When I returned to Petersburg, I married Lee Bennett. Our children are Linnea, Wendy, Melissa and Derek. I took over my dad's boat, the *Spencer II*, and fished it for a few years. I also worked at Alaskan Glacier Sea Food and fished with other skippers: Ray Evens on the *Lualda*, Ed Fuglvog on the *Symphony*, and later on the *Westerly* with Chris Jensen.

The last few years I have tendered on the *Southeast* and the *Kamilar*. I have fished for more than 50 years and currently hand troll on my new boat, the *Linnea*. I also cook on the *Tyler Two* for Scott Newman on his bear guiding trips.

Lee and I have 10 grandchildren and two great-grandchildren.

Trygve Thorsen

Bob and Pam Thorstenson

By Bob and Pam Thorstenson

Our 12 years of living in Petersburg and the start-up of Petersburg Fisheries, Inc. were the happiest years of our lives.

Bob and Pam Thorstenson

We sold all of our possessions, including Bob's beef herd and Pam's car and furniture, in order to start the company. We were determined to move to Alaska, become Alaskans, and shovel snow with our neighbors.

We loaded our few personal belongings onto the *Chichagof* — mostly wedding presents that had come south from Alaska the year before on Pam's father's halibut boat — said goodbye to our neighbors, and headed for Petersburg to a new and risky venture.

We arrived in Petersburg, via Grumman Goose, on April 10, 1965, with Bobby, age 18 months. Pam was four months pregnant with Tani Rae. We had planned to move directly into the cannery superintendent's house.

This house had been built in 1900, but never had had winter residents. It was still bitterly cold and the house felt like a morgue. Pam's mother, Ruby Martens, took one look at the place and took Pam and Bobby home with her. Ruby and Pam scoured the house for a week before we finally moved in.

The kitchen was a peculiar setup with no outside windows, no storage, and appliances that must have been 50 years old.

There was no central heat, only electric heaters on the walls. You had to stand directly in front of them to feel any warmth.

The ceilings were 12 feet high and the windows were turn-of-the-century — looking out of them was like looking through the bottom of a bottle.

In spite of all this antiquity, Pam prevailed. She entertained family and friends, visiting cannery men, and even hosted our bankers for lunch one day.

In the fall, when the company was fighting for its very existence, Pam came out to the cannery and worked casing salmon cans and pulling salmon eggs.

Ruby cooked for us, but became so disgusted with the old and broken electric stove that she called The Trading Union and had a new stove delivered. She said, "If the company can't afford a decent stove, I'll pay for it myself!"

Although these were difficult times, we were both busy and challenged and living life to its fullest.

Beach seining, about 1937

PETERSBURG FISHERIES
a Division of Icicle Seafoods, Inc.

Circa 1930 photo courtesy of Clausen Memorial Museum

In January 1965, the Pan American Fisheries plant in Petersburg, Alaska was bought and reestablished as Petersburg Fisheries, Inc. That purchase marked the beginning of what is now Icicle Seafoods, Inc.

The Petersburg plant is well diversified. It operates year round, processing several varieties of seafood. The plant provides approximately 500 jobs each salmon season, as well as about 80 full-time year-round jobs. In addition to the processing jobs, Petersburg Fisheries provides a market for local and out-of-state fishermen to sell their product.

Petersburg Fisheries today

Icicle Seafoods has become one of the largest seafood processors in Alaska. It is also one of the largest seafood exporters, but we have not forgotten our commitment to our employees, fishermen, customers, stockholders — and to the production of the finest Alaska seafood available.

Since 1965, Petersburg Fisheries has been a cornerstone of its community.

Carl and Gudrun Thynes

By Marie Ellen Michl

Both Carl and Gudrun Thynes were born in Sykkylven, Norway; Carl on September 2, 1887, and Gudrun on December 13, 1893. Carl was the oldest of six children and Gudrun was the oldest of 11. They attended the same school and, for a time, were taught by Gudrun's father, Carl Tandstad, who also directed several choirs and an orchestra in Sykkylven.

Times were difficult in the early 1900s, so Carl and his brother, Ole, decided to come to America to see if things were better here. They went to Albion, California, where they found work in a sawmill. Unfortunately, Carl was involved in an accident at the mill that resulted in the loss of a leg. He returned to Sykkylven and went to work as a carpenter, house painter, and a builder of beautiful furniture, some of which is still being used by family in Norway.

Carl and Gudrun were married on November 19, 1920, and began raising a family. Peter was the first-born. Erling arrived two years later.

Carl still had a desire to live in America. He went first and sent for Gudrun and the boys after he had established a home for them. Carl's brother, Ole, and Gudrun's brother, Elias, were in Alaska. Since Ole was sponsoring Carl, this is where Carl had to go.

After his 1926 arrival in Petersburg, he decided it was the place to stay. He worked as a carpenter and house painter. He lived with Ole and Elias in a little shack located where Ken Welde's garage now stands. Carl bought the adjoining property and, with the help of Ole and Elias, began building a house for his family.

Even though the house wasn't finished, he sent for his family. After their arrival in Halifax, Nova Scotia, they traveled by train to Prince Rupert, where Carl was waiting for them. They went on to Petersburg by boat, arriving in Petersburg in August of 1929.

One year after their arrival, a third son, Carl, was born. Kenneth followed two years later. Three years after that, another baby was on the way. Gudrun refused to go to the hospital to have what she was sure was another boy, so she had this baby at home. Dr. Rude was called and he delivered a healthy baby girl, Gladys. Four years later, daughter Marie Ellen arrived.

With six children to support, it became increasingly difficult to make ends meet. When a job as school custodian became available, Carl took the job. He worked for the Petersburg schools for 25 years before retiring. He took great pride in keeping the school buildings clean, neat and comfortably heated. Carl was like and respected by students and faculty.

Carl was an avid hunter. Even though he had only one leg, he hiked up mountains and across muskegs in pursuit of deer. He enjoyed many hunting trips with his sons and friends. Of course, Gudrun always had a hot meal ready when they arrived home. Carl was a very talented artist. One of his paintings is on display at the Seaman's Mission Hall in Sykkylven. His rosemaling was beautiful and beyond compare, as was his intricate woodcarving. He was also in great demand to paint names on the local fishing boats.

Gudrun was very active in the Lutheran Church. She sang in the choir, taught Sunday School, and belonged to Ladies Aid. She enjoyed playing the guitar and would often join Marie Winther and Pastor Knutson for an afternoon of singing and playing old songs and hymns from Norway. Gudrun was an accomplished seamstress. She made many of her clothes, as well as those of her children. She made many beautiful children's bunads, some of which are still in circulation in Petersburg.

Gudrun was well known for her baking abilities and always had a good supply of her famous sour cream cookies on hand. Her krumkake were extra special because she added a secret ingredient that she was reluctant to reveal to anyone outside the family. She was a good friend and neighbor and became known as "Grandma Thynes" to many.

Peter, Erling and Carl stayed in Petersburg. Peter and his wife, Tora, raised four boys. Erling and his wife, Jeanne, had four boys and live in the house Carl built. Son Carl and wife Molly (both deceased) had three girls and one boy. Kenneth and wife Dorothy raised two boys in Ketchikan. Gladys and husband Harley raised two daughters and a son in Seattle, where Marie Ellen and husband Wally raised two boys and a girl.

Carl Thynes passed away in 1975 at the age of 88. Gudrun passed away in 1982, at 89. Their legacy was a wealth of love and closeness in the Thynes family that continues today. They were two very special people, who were very proud of, loved, and thoroughly enjoyed all of their many descendants.

Pete and Tora Thynes

By John and Carol Enge

Among the Norwegian immigrants who helped build our town were Pete and Tora Thynes.

Pete was born in Sykkyllven, Norway, on March 4, 1922. He emigrated with his mother and brother when he was 7. They traveled on the *Havangerfjord* to Halifax, Nova Scotia. His father, who had come to America earlier, met their train in Prince Rupert. After coming to Petersburg, they lived in the house his father, Carl Thynes, had built on Excel Street.

Starting school was hard for Pete because he only spoke Norwegian. His first and second grade teachers, Gertie Otness and Mabel Otness Kayler, helped him learn English. In the third grade, the boys on the playground taught him "bad" English words and told him to ask the teacher to interpret. The teacher punished him for using the words. This was the only time his father went to school to reprimand a teacher.

Pete fished on many boats. The *Teddy J.* was one of the first. With World War II, he joined the Air Corps and was sent to Cold Bay on a crash boat with the l0th Emergency Rescue Boat Squadron. Later, he was stationed in Adak and Anchitka. On one trip to Seattle to pick up a boat, they traveled through Petersburg in the middle of the night, stopping so Pete could visit. His mother awakened and felt Pete was coming. She got up, made a pot of coffee, and was putting out a plate of cookies just as he walked in the door.

Following his discharge, he returned to Petersburg and, with Ernie Haugen, bought The Pastime Café. He was only there 11 months, long enough to meet his future wife, Tora.

Tora Kommedal was born on a little farm in Stavanger, Norway, on April 8, 1925. She came to America in 1947 to visit relatives in New York and San Francisco. Her aunt posted $10,000 to sponsor her, as was required for immigrants. She attended Edison Vocational School to learn English.

The family decided Tora should come to Petersburg to visit her cousin, Emily Martens, and work in the cannery. She arrived in June and was soon hired as a waitress in The Pastime Café. It was difficult for her to take orders with her limited English, but her employers both spoke Norwegian.

Pete and Tora were married October 18, 1947, and rented an apartment over the Coliseum Theater for $35 a month.

Pete returned to fishing and joined Fred Haltiner on the *Verma*. He later took a job with the Bureau of Public Works. He worked for the Bureau for 20 years. After statehood, his salary was cut by $1,000. With a growing family, he couldn't afford to stay on.

He returned to fishing, buying a share in the *Arne* with Fred Hendrickson. Selling the boat in 1974, Pete had a new troller/sailboat built in Port Townsend, the *Tora*. He and Tora fished it until retirement in 1998.

Tora and Pete Thynes

They began building their home on South Mitkof Highway in 1950, helped by many friends.

Pete and Tora raised four sons: Chuck (married Stephanie), Ted (married Cynthia Ewing), Steve (married Linda LeRoy), and Peter.

Tora had all the graces of homemaking and hospitality. Besides raising her children, she had time for her many friends, knitting Norwegian sweaters, sewing and playing bridge.

Tora fished until the tragic death at sea of their son Ted, his wife, Cindy, and their grandson Ryan, 2. After that, she was reluctant to go, but eventually overcame her fear and fished with Pete for 20 years.

They are both members of the Sons of Norway and Pioneers. Tora has been active in the Lutheran Church, serving as chairman of the Ruth Circle, making quilts for World Relief. She is a past president of Pioneers Auxiliary 10.

Pete passed away February of 2003.

Carl and Molly Thynes

By Shelly Reid

Carl and Molly were that special couple who seemed like they had been together forever. In fact, they had been childhood sweethearts!

Marlene Aurora Jones was born in Petersburg on September 25, 1931, to Hugh and Evangeline Jones. Molly was older than her brother, Bruce. Both of the Jones children were raised and schooled in Petersburg.

As Molly grew into a young lady, she had her eye on a young man who lived up the hill. As a teenager, Molly worked at the soda fountain at Les Elkins' drugstore and as a switch-board operator for the local phone company, which she enjoyed very much.

Carl Idar Thynes was born in Petersburg on November 28, 1930, to Carl and Gudrun Thynes. Carl was the first child to be born in the United States. Two older brothers, Pete and Erling, had been born in Norway. Younger brother Ken and two younger sisters, Gladys and Marie Ellen, were born in Petersburg.

Carl grew up working hard to help his folks make ends meet for their large family. He hunted to help put meat on the table and, during the summers, he went halibut fishing and salmon seining. Throughout high school, he enjoyed a variety of sports and activities; varsity basketball was his favorite.

Molly had had a crush on Carl, as early as people can remember. When she was still in elementary school, she would tell Carl's brother, Erling, that she was going to marry his brother someday. Molly and Carl were a couple throughout their high school years. They graduated from Petersburg High in May of 1949.

That fall, they headed south to college. Carl wanted to become a school teacher and went to Washington State in Pullman. Molly headed to Western Washington in Bellingham. They went back home to Petersburg to work the next summer. That fall they decided to get married.

At the tender ages of 19 and 18, Carl and Molly were married on September 17, 1950. They chose Juneau as their honeymoon destination. Shortly afterward, the newlyweds headed back to school at Western, where Carl pursued a degree in elementary education. The following summer they returned to Petersburg, so Carl could earn money fishing. They went back to Western for the fall of 1951, but after that quarter, Carl was drafted into the U.S. Army.

Carl was sent to Elmendorf Air Force Base in Anchorage. He and Molly were lucky to be stationed with lots of friends around them — Roy Otness, Casper Hallingstad, Lloyd Roundtree, Jim Rhodes and Harold Fuglvog — to name some of them. Many fun stories were remembered and told through the years!

That summer their first daughter arrived. Debra Lynn was born in Anchorage on June 11, 1952. When Carl was discharged late in the winter of 1953, he took

Molly and Carl Thynes

his young family back to Petersburg, so he could fish that spring and summer. On May 26, 1954, their second daughter, Shelley Rae, was born in Petersburg.

The Thynes family was back in Bellingham for fall quarter at Western. Soon, their third daughter, Tracey Aurora, was born on May 24, 1955. What a crew!

Carl graduated from Western Washington with a degree in elementary education and began his 20-year career with the Petersburg Public School District. He taught in sixth and seventh grade classes for 13 years.

Carl was always willing to go the extra mile to help people. When his buddy, Lloyd Roundtree, needed

Carl and Molly Thynes cont'd

him, Carl tutored him in math almost every night for months, so Lloyd could pass his pilot's license test. Lloyd later built a very successful air charter business.

During the summer of 1962, Carl was granted a math/science scholarship to attend the University of Utah in Salt Lake City. The family packed the old Buick Special and drove from Prince Rupert to Seattle, then on down to Utah for the summer. The family had a really great time and enjoyed all the sunshine!

The year 1967 was a special one for Carl. On July 6, 1967, David Carl was born! After being teased all those years about being the only "Thynes boy" who had all girls, he finally had his son. The following year, Carl received the news that he had been granted a sabbatical leave for the 1968-69 school year to attend the University of North Dakota in Grand Forks.

Molly, Carl, and the four kids packed a dozen suitcases and a wooden playpen, took the ferry to Prince Rupert, and caught the B.C. passenger train across Canada to Winnipeg, where they rented a car and headed south to North Dakota. That year Carl had a monumental workload and, in the spring, had a dreadful case of appendicitis. After having his appendix removed, he ended up with a horrific staph infection.

Carl earned his master's degree in Grand Forks and returned to Petersburg, already hired as the high school principal. After seven years at that job, Carl retired with a full 20 years under his belt.

On summer breaks, Carl was off from his school responsibilities. He and the girls would gillnet with the *Elding*. When David was big enough to go on the boat, Molly and David became Carl's crew.

During their retirement years, Carl and Molly spent summers gillnetting. They had been fishing the *Elding* since the '60s. Before Carl actually retired, they decided to build a "retirement" gillnetter in 1973.

When the *Molly T* was finished, the fiberglass Tollycraft was launched in Anacortes, Washington. They cruised north along with the Schultz's boat, the *Misty*, and the Marifern's boat, the *Camlon*. Molly was very artistic and loved to decorate with flower arrangements — even on the boat.

Molly and Carl enjoyed their grandchildren. When the kids got to be elementary school age, they would walk the trail to grandma and grandpa's house for lunch on Fridays. In the fall, Carl couldn't wait until Halloween. He loved it when the kids would dress up and come over to trick-or-treat.

Christmas was always their favorite holiday, though. Thanksgiving weekend was the weekend to get the tree. Then Carl would break out the Christmas music and Molly would start baking! After all the holidays, when winter started to feel like it was hanging on too long, they could run off to Reno and gamble with a few rolls of quarters. Retirement was fun!

The summer of 1987, however, brought tragic news. Molly was diagnosed with ovarian cancer and began a long and difficult battle to get well. She fought this horrible disease for three years with Carl by her side every step of the way. On January 18, 1990, Molly passed away at her mother's home in Seattle.

Carl tried to carry on and fished by himself the following summer. That fall, he noticed he wasn't feeling well. He was diagnosed with liver cancer right after Thanksgiving and passed away at Virginia Mason in Seattle on December 15, 1990.

Molly and Carl left a legacy of giving and helping others. Molly didn't have a professional career — her life was raising her children, being involved in the Lutheran Church, volunteering to lead the Junior Choir, and arranging altar flowers for Sunday's service.

She was active in the PTA, loved to bake, and gave home perms to friends and neighbors. She also went trolling for king salmon. Molly taught her daughters the art of cooking and housecleaning!

Besides being a full-time teacher and administrator, Carl was on the church council, taught Sunday School, and spent many years on the hospital board, working hard to get raises for the nurses. Carl and Molly sang in the senior choir at church, with their highlight being the singing of Handel's *Messiah*.

When their kids were small, the family spent lots of time in the hand-built wooden punt Carl had built upstairs in the old gym. They enjoyed fishing and going up Petersburg Creek to Don Nelson's cabin. Later, when the kids were bigger, they loved the family time they spent at Pearl Island. Camping, fishing, woodcutting — it was all an adventure for this family.

It seems like Carl and Molly were always a couple — one name could hardly be said without the other. They were together in almost everything they did for as long as anyone can remember!

Roy and Thelma Torwick

By Lynda Fredricksen

Roy Edward Torwick was born June 20, 1907, in Seattle, Washington, to Randi and Johaan Torvick. He had one older brother, John Alvin, who was born in 1905. His father's name was Americanized to John and the last name was changed to Torwick. There was a family in the area with the same last name and to avoid confusion, the "v" was changed to a "w."

Roy and his brother, Al, spent a large part of their childhood in Yakatat, since their father was involved in the building of the first cannery there. He was known as "Yakatat John." The cannery was later sold to Libbeys.

Thelma Sophia Martens was born January 17, 1912, in Petersburg, to Ragnhild Camilla Tjomsland and Ludvig Mortenson. Like the Torwicks, her father's name was Americanized to Loui Martens. Ragnhild was a sister to Knut Thompson, so her family name changed in this country, as well.

Thelma was one of four children and the only girl. Her brothers were Magnus, Leonard and Elmer. Thelma spent her childhood in Petersburg. After graduation, she traveled to Seattle to attend beauty school and learn the profession of being a hairdresser. It was while she was in Seattle that she met Roy. They were married in December 26, 1931, and began their life together in Port Alexander, Alaska.

Roy started out as a fisherman and remained in the fishing industry all his life. For a few years, Roy and Swede Wasvick were partners in a store they named Wasvick & Torwick. In the early 1950s, Roy was offered a job as fish buyer for Booth Fisheries in the little fishing village of Pelican. This was the start of a different career in the fishing industry, lasting until his retirement.

Winters were spent in Petersburg and Seattle; each summer, Pelican was home. In 1966, he traveled to Kodiak to work as the superintendent of Alaska Ice & Storage. In 1975, Roy retired and moved back to Petersburg to be near family. He passed away February of 1989.

Thelma and Roy were divorced in 1965. Thelma moved to Sitka. She met and married Arne Dorum, a friend from many years before. Thelma had a stroke in 1977 and was brought back home to Petersburg to be with family. She passed away in 1978.

The first of Roy and Thelma's three children was Roy Jr., born in Petersburg on August 25, 1934. His sister Camille followed on December 9, 1936. Lynda was born on June 26, 1945.

Thelma and Roy Towick

Roy Jr. followed in his father's footsteps and took up fishing at the age of 12, when he hand trolled with Art Theburg on the *Deep Sea*. Over the years, he fished commercially for halibut, blackcod, salmon and crab. He fished with each of his uncles and several others in Petersburg and owned his own boat for a time. Roy Jr. met and married Phyllis Peterson from Wrangell in 1959. They had two sons, Mark and Gregg, while living in Petersburg. They moved to Sitka in 1968 and relocated to Sterling in 1975. Roy Jr. worked for Samson Tug & Barge while in Sitka and then for Crowley Maritime up north. He was medically retired with a heart condition in 1993 and passed away in 1996, while on vacation in Las Vegas. He was brought home to Alaska and laid to rest.

Phyllis was the Postmaster of the Soldotna post office for many years. She has retired and lives in Sterling, as do son Mark and his family. Son Gregg and family reside in San Diego.

Camille married Lon Marifern, whom she met

Roy and Thelma Torwick cont'd

her first year in college. Lon was a flying enthusiast. Soon after moving to Petersburg with their infant daughter, Pat, he started a business called Lon's Flying Service. He was involved in many other business ventures through the years. Two more children joined Pat: Bruce and Julie.

Roy, Camille, Roy Jr., Phyllis and Lynda Torwick

Camille was the bookkeeper for all the various business ventures and worked at the cannery for a few summers. She always has a project on hand, usually knitting and a couple of quilt tops.

Lon has retired and they spend the winter months in Desert Hot Springs, California, where they enjoy the warm weather and golf.

Lynda married Norman Fredricksen in October of 1963. Norman was working for The Trading Union at the time. A couple of years later, he went to work for Barney White at Petersburg Motors. In 1968, Norman and Lynda purchased the business. In 1984, a lot was acquired on Haugen and Second streets, where a new garage was built.

In September of 1966, son Kurt was born. Brother Scott joined the family in June 1969.

The family spent summer weekends "out the road" at Banana Point or Green's Camp in their camper. Norman often remarks that he should have brought along a phone, so he could sit and watch it not ring. How times have changed; now we carry a phone with us wherever we go.

Son Kurt married Debbie Hamilton of Ketchikan. After graduation from the University of Alaska, they settled down in Ketchikan by way of Anchorage and Bethel. They have four children: Martina, Shelby, Brice and Rosie. Both Kurt and Debbie work in the field of psychology.

Scott married Rachel Newport and they have one daughter, Courtney. They have since divorced and Scott is working at the garage with his father.

Norman is looking forward to retirement and the time to do all those things that have been put on hold.

Warmer weather in the winter months is a definite attraction!

Lynda takes care of the bookwork for the business. Through the years, she has been actively involved in the local rosemaling group, which continues to meet and do projects for the various businesses in town.

She has been a member of the Emblem Club and served a year as club president. Lynda was a part of the group that formed the State Association of Emblem Clubs in 1990 and served as state president in 2001-2002. These days, Lynda is enjoying being a grandmother, quilting, beading, gardening and doing decorative painting.

Unidentified bathing cuties enjoy a day at Sandy Beach

Chris and Mamie Tveten

By Margaret Tveten Nilson

My father, Chris Tveten, was born in Norway in 1874. He came to Petersburg where his friend Jacob Hadland was working. John Thomasetter, my father's cousin, also came to Petersburg and was a bookkeeper for Buschmann.

Chris married Mamie Hadland, Tom Hadland's oldest daughter. He soon became a partner with Mr. S.L. Hogue, forming the mercantile firm of Hogue & Tveten. He was also an agent for the Alaska Steamship Company and a coal dealer.

Chris was Petersburg's first city treasurer and, in 1912, served as the city's third mayor. He died in 1940.

Mamie Hadland was born in Bayfield, Wisconsin, the eldest of 11 children. The Hadland family came to Petersburg in 1905.

Mamie and Chris had four children: Paul, Arthur, Ruth and Margaret.

Paul attended the University of Washington for several years. He then went to Fairbanks, Alaska, and married Ruth Chapman. Paul and Ruth have four adopted children.

Arthur attended a printing school in California. He married Sigrud Lund, but later was divorced.

Ruth attended nursing school and received her degree in nursing. She married Fred Arnat.

Margaret attended Linfield College for one year before going to business school. She married Melvin Nilson and they adopted a son, Craig, before having three more children, Kurt, Marsha and Ann.

Warren G. Harding was the first sitting United States president to visit Alaska. Sailing with him on the army transport ship *Henderson* was future President Herbert Hoover, who was at the time secretary of commerce.

In Vancouver, B.C., Harding became the first U.S. president to give a speech in Canada. He then traveled south to San Francisco, California, where he died in his hotel room on August 2, 1923.

Wrangell was amongst the ports Harding stopped in, while visiting the Alaska Territory to dedicate the Alaska Railroad in July 1923. Many Petersburg residents traveled to Wrangell to see President Harding.

Gus and Perla Vallestad

By Carol Enge

Gunvald Reider Johanssen Vallestad was born on January 2, 1905, in Tansøy, Norway. At age 11, he went to live with Larine Espeseth's family, the Ander Hammerseths of Tansøy. He remained with them until he was 18 years of age.

In 1923, Gus immigrated to the United States along with Larine Hammerseth and Erling and Agnes Espeseth. They were met in New York by Lars Hammerseth, who then obtained work for Gus on a sailing ship between Brooklyn and England. After sailing for three years, he came to Petersburg as a crewmember on the *Dredger*, which did the first dredging in Wrangell Narrows.

Gus returned to Petersburg two years later, 1928, and lived with Larine and Bert Espeseth until 1938. He married Perla Jappeson of Norway and bought a house on what is now North First Street, where he lived the rest of his life.

Gus worked as a halibut fisherman on various Petersburg vessels. He was a well-liked crewmember and earned a good reputation as a cook, having an exceptionally clean galley. He retired in his 70s.

Gus enjoyed the outdoors and spent much time through the years skiing, skating, hunting, and sport fishing. He loved children and was extremely patient with the neighborhood kids who played basketball and sometimes broke a window.

Gus was a charter member of the Moose Lodge of Petersburg and continued his membership throughout his life. He was well liked for his sharp wit, dry humor, friendliness, and unfailing courtesy.

Gus and Perla Vallestad

The neighbors fondly remember the times he would have too many at the Harbor Bar and would totter up the walk, chatting to the dandelions.

Gus died April 9, 1986, at the age of 81.

Fishermen

Berger and Petra Wasvick

By Irene Roundtree

Berger Vassvika was born in Vassvik, Norway, in the village of Vassvika, in 1884. On coming to America he changed his name to Wasvick.

In 1905, after entering through Ellis Island, New York, Berger took the train cross country to Ballard in Seattle, Washington.

Petra Pedersen, Berger's wife to be, was born in Nesna, Norway, in 1887.

She had worked as a maid for King Haakon, saving her money so she could come to America.

In 1906, at age 19, she was aboard the *Mauritania*, on its maiden voyage. It was the sister ship to the *Lusitania*. After arriving in New York, she took the train to Seattle, where she was met by her cousin, Kia Shey. While in Seattle, she did housework.

Berger was fishing on boats around Puget Sound and in Alaska, which would come to Seattle to sell fish. He met Petra and they married in 1908.

Their son, Arnold, was born in 1910, followed by three daughters: Julia in 1912, Belle in 1914, and Clara in 1921. They lived in Ballard and later moved to Silverdale and lived on their farm.

Berger was still going to Alaska to fish, but at the urging of Knut Thompson he sold the farm and moved the family to Petersburg in 1924. He continued to fish and was well known for being one of the best cooks in the fleet.

For several years, he and Petra owned and operated The Pastime Café. It was a place for enjoying great food and visiting with friends.

Berger and Petra Wasvick

Television was brand new to him. When visiting his daughter Clara in Oregon, he loved sitting in her rocking chair watching his favorite — Laurel and Hardy movies.

At age 75, he retired from his last cooking job aboard the F/V *Unimak*.

Berger passed away in 1958 and Petra in 1962, in Portland, where they had retired.

Berger and Petra Wasvick

Arnold "Swede" and Evelyn Wasvick

By Irene Roundtree

Arnold "Swede" Wasvick, at age 14, moved with his family to Petersburg from Seattle, Washington.

He went to Petersburg schools and was a star basketball player. He was a member of the first Viking team to win the first All-Alaska basketball tournament in Fairbanks in 1929. In the final game, they beat Fairbanks by a score of twelve to five.

Swede and Evelyn Wasvick

In 1929, he met Evelyn Welde at a dance at Johnny Sales' Roller Rink. They were always a beautiful couple on the dance floor, and their favorite was the Swedish Waltz. He could also do a mean Charleston.

They were married that year and through the years were blessed with five wonderful daughters: Arliss, Jeannie, Irene, Patti and Lynn.

Arnold fished as a young man and was an avid hunter and sportsman throughout his life. He fished on a variety of boats and was known, like his father, as a great chef. In later years, he was well known for making large batches of lutefisk, which were prized by family and friends.

Evelyn and Swede bought The Pastime Café and operated it for many years. Evelyn did most of the cooking at home and Swede carried it all down to the café in his panel truck.

During lunch breaks and after school, the five girls would carry pies, cakes and salads down to their father. In the evenings, the girls peeled buckets of potatoes for the next day's French fries.

After the kitchen and card room were added, cooking was done at the café. The daughters were happy about that!

The card room was a very popular place. Many a phone call was answered, with the caller asking, "Is my husband there? Dinner is ready!" They later sold the café and went into the grocery and hardware business with Roy Torwick Sr.

Evelyn and Swede were always into cooking. Their next venture was going to work for Meurs Logging Company. They worked there for 20 years before they retired. Evelyn had the distinction of being the first "lady logger" to receive retirement benefits in the state of Alaska.

They had a busy life with five daughters and were active in the Lutheran Church, the school, and the city, where Swede was mayor for several terms.

He refereed ball games and was president of the school board. He was a Past Master of Petersburg Masonic Lodge #262 and held the highest honor achievable in the Scottish Rite, a 33rd degree. He also attained the Chair of Grand President of the Pioneers of Alaska.

As a volunteer fireman for many years, when the alarm went off, Swede would say, "Where's my pants,

Swede and Evelyn Wasvick

boots, jacket and hat?" And the five girls would all run, grab his clothes, throw them at him, and out the door he'd go!

The completion of Mountain View Manor was a result of his determination and his love of seeing a job

Arnold "Swede" and Evelyn Wasvick cont'd

well done. He personally flew 20 to 30 times to Juneau and Anchorage to fight for the many dollars to build it. He would take no skimping and deleting of its design. He did it, too! The Manor and the park behind it were later dedicated to him in his memory.

Evelyn was his inspiration and stood by him in all he did. They left their home on the street named "Five Daughters' Hill" in the early '80s and moved to their newly built dream house on Wrangell Avenue. Many wonderful get-togethers, holiday gatherings and quilting sessions were held there. Friends, children and grandchildren enjoyed the home where Gram and Gramp lived.

In 1992 after a brief illness, Swede passed away at the age of 82. Evelyn passed away at home on February 28, 1998, at the age of 89.

They left a large legacy to their remaining family that will continue through the years.

All five daughters married hometown boys. Arliss and Sam Thomas' three children are Kerri, Kirk and Kelly. Arliss passed away in 1994. Her children reside in Alaska and Montana.

Jeannie and Roald Norheim have two sons, Mike

Evelyn and Swede Wasvick

and Ladd. Mike is a Northwest Airlines pilot and lives with his family in Gig Harbor, Washington. Ladd is a Petersburg fisherman and owns the F/V *Frigidland*. He and his family make Petersburg their home.

Irene married Lloyd Roundtree. They owned and operated the flying service Alaska Island Air for many years. They have three children: Dane, Shannon and Stacey. Dane became a pilot and is now a businessman in town. Daughters Shannon Peeler and Stacey Madsen, whose husbands are fisherman, are homemakers. They also all reside in Petersburg.

Patti married Ron Parr and their son is Hunt. Ron is now deceased. Hunt has been a fisherman for 25 years and crews on one of Petersburg's highliner boats. Later, Patti took in a foster child, Debi. Patti is now retired and married to Ronald Simpson.

Lynn married Ted Smith. They had two children, Renee and Rory. Rory is now deceased. They added to the family with adopted son Billy and foster child Marci. Lynn was a homemaker, while Ted operated and owned Alaska Fuel Service. He has since retired and is again the mayor of Petersburg, continuing to be very active in community affairs.

Evelyn Wasvick with Irene, Jeannie, Lynn, Patti and Arliss

Peder and Ragna Welde

By Doug Welde

Grampa Peder Welde was from Byudalen, which is farm country in northern Norway. He was born in 1877, the third of eight children of Carl and Pirnille Welde. The children were Indiana, Svenn, Peder, Ole, Alex, Sara, Olger and Otto.

Alex and Otto were the only siblings to come to the United States besides Peder, who went to Minnesota and settled in Minneapolis. He was a carpenter by trade and work was plentiful. There he met Ragna Ness, who he later married.

Ragna and Peder Welde

Grama Ragna was from Molde, on the coast in central Norway. She was born in 1880, the youngest of five children of Peder and Ingeborg Nesje (Ness). The children were Lars, Anna, Karen, Erick and Ragna.

When Ragna came to the United States, she first went to Bayfield, Wisconsin. She then moved to Minneapolis, where she met and later married Peder Welde on September 11, 1907.

Ragna and Peder lived in Minneapolis where Peder did quite well as a carpenter. The first two of their three children were born there — Evelyn on June 13, 1908; and Kenneth on December 7, 1910.

They moved to the Mille Lacs Lake area of Minnesota, where they bought 80 acres of farmland. This would be a healthier way to raise a family. Their third child, Ruby, was born on July 8, 1915.

Evelyn was the first of the Weldes to come to Petersburg. She arrived in the spring of 1925 to help her mother's brother, Erick Ness, take care of his ill wife, Agnes, and their children, Carl, Ragna and Leo.

Evelyn later met and married Arnold "Swede" Wasvik. *(See Wasvik story.)*

The rest of the Welde family made their first trip to Petersburg in 1928. The Great Depression was in full swing. Life was very difficult on the farm and there was work to be had in Petersburg, Alaska! They drove across the country along the Yellowstone Trail from Minnesota to Seattle in the family car, and lived in a tent along the way.

After several trips back and forth between the farm and Petersburg, Peder finally sold the farm in 1938, and the family settled in Petersburg. Peder built a home next to his brother-in-law, Erick Ness. Those properties are now the location of Eagle's Roost Park, overlooking the Narrows on PFI Hill.

Peder was a carpenter and helped build many historic homes and buildings in Petersburg, including Petersburg's first hospital. He was a very gentle man and, as he worked, he always hummed and whistled.

He and Ragna were both active in the Lutheran Church and the Sons and Daughters of Norway.

Peder Welde died in 1954 and Ragna Ness died in 1976. They left a legacy of their children, grandchildren, and many great-grandchildren.

Their daughter Ruby made several trips between the farm in Minnesota and Petersburg with the family. She became a permanent resident of Petersburg in 1938. She later met and married Magnus Martens. *(See Loui and Ragnhild Martens story.)*

Ken Welde made his first trip to Petersburg in the spring of 1928 with his parents and younger sister, Ruby, to visit relatives and work. That first summer he worked in his Uncle Erick's herring saltery on the old inner bay cannery site in Washington Bay.

The next summer he worked on a fox farm in

Peder and Ragna Welde cont'd

Tebenkof Bay for Olof Tenjford. After his first five days there, Olof left him alone in charge for a week and a half. That was an experience he will never forget!

In the fall, Ken returned to Minnesota to attend Agricultural College in St. Paul. By spring of 1930, he could no longer afford college. He went to live with his Uncle Alex on his farm near the Welde farm, which was rented out. About then, the renter skipped out. Ken ran the family farm until his family returned.

Ragna and Peder Welde

Ken returned to Petersburg in 1934 to help his uncle Otto, as a carpenter. He worked at several jobs for the next few years. In 1938, while working for Hugh Jones at Reliable Transfer, he and friend Arne Lund became partners and bought out Jones. They later added oil delivery to their business. Their office was in the front corner of The Pastime Café.

By 1941, there were three delivery businesses in town. Because business was slow, they dissolved their partnership. Arne bought Ken out and kept the oil delivery business. It was known as Dependable Oil.

Ken went to work for the City of Petersburg Public Works in 1947. When Jack DeZorto quit in 1949, Ken became superintendent of Public Works, a title he held until he retired in 1972.

Ken joined the Volunteer Fire Department in 1937, after the Public Dock burned. It was on the site of what is now the PFI cold storage. He became fire chief in 1954 and retired from the department in 1972.

Ken met Evelyn Nicholson in 1938. They were married on September 6, 1941. They had one son, Douglas Kenneth, who was born on January 28, 1944.

Doug graduated from Petersburg High School in 1963. He worked for Petersburg Processors cannery in early summer, finishing the season with Uncle Mungy (Magnus Martens) on the *Pamela Rae*. He seined on the *Pamela Rae* through 1964.

Doug went to Western School of Heavy Equipment in Weiser, Idaho, that fall with his best friend, Don Jones. Both received their draft physical notice before Christmas and joined the air force.

Doug was a heavy equipment operator in the U.S. Air Force Civil Engineers and spent 1965 in Massachusetts, at Westover AFB; 1966 in Phan Rang, Vietnam; and 1967-68 in Kansas, at Forbes AFB.

In Kansas, he met Naomi Elaine McDaniel, born on October 20, 1945, the fourth of six children to Harvey and Muriel McDaniel in Paxico, Kansas. She graduated high school in 1963. She was working as a Southwestern Bell long distance operator in Topeka, when she met Doug. They married July 2, 1967.

After Doug's discharge in November 1968, they moved to Petersburg. Doug worked at The Trading Union that winter and fished crab and seined with Fred Haltiner on the *Siren* until the middle of 1970. He then went to work for Bob Kaer at the City of Petersburg Power and Light Department. He was on the picket line when the lights went out in 1973.

He went seining again with Fred. In late 1974, he was hired on as an equipment operator at the city's Public Works Department, working for Dusty Rhoden.

Doug joined the Petersburg Volunteer Fire Department in early 1969. He became an EMT in 1979. He made assistant chief in 1985. After years as a paid firefighter, the fire marshal retired in mid-2002.

Doug is still a volunteer EMT and assistant chief. He is a member of the Lutheran Church, Petersburg Rod & Gun Club, Rotary, Pioneers, Elks, Moose, and the statewide associations for Firefighters, Fire Chiefs and Fire Investigators.

In Petersburg, Naomi babysat other children while raising their own. As the kids grew older, she worked at several different businesses around town. Today she is co-owner of the Cubby Hole, an arts and crafts supply store and painting studio.

Naomi is active in Norwegian rosemaling and tole painting. She is a member of the Lutheran Church, Muskeg Maleriers (painters), and Emblem Club.

Naomi and Doug have three children: Stacy Ann, Rachel Elaine and Ryan Francis.

Dave and Caroline Westerberg

By Carol Enge

Dave Westerberg was a well loved pioneer. He was born in Texas on August 12, 1912. When he was very young, Dave's family moved to Ohio and later to Seattle, Washington.

Being related to Peter Jorgenson, the family had come to Petersburg by the time Dave was in the first grade. He enjoyed talking about his first grade teacher, Edna Miller, who was a well known early resident in the town.

Dave's family returned to Seattle, but he had Alaska in his blood and returned to Ketchikan in 1919. He met his wife, Caroline, when she visiting a girl friend in Ketchikan.

Caroline Powell was born March 25, 1904, in Seattle, Washington. She worked for Seattle Hardware Co. before coming to Ketchikan and meeting Dave. They were married April 16, 1938.

At that time, Dave was the projectionist at the Ketchikan Theater. They were transferred to Petersburg's Coliseum Theater where Dave was the projectionist and Caroline the cashier. The young couple lived in an apartment above the theater and managed the apartments.

Dave Westerberg

Caroline Westerberg and Marit Fuglvog

In 1939, Dave started work at the Petersburg Cold Storage where he remained for 12 years. His last job was in the hardware department at The Trading Union.

Dave was active in the Elks Lodge and, at one time, was Exalted Ruler. As a charter member of Pioneers of Alaska, Igloo 26, he served as president and secretary-treasurer. His enthusiasm and expertise were credited for the large membership in those early years. He died in July of 1986.

After years of working as cashier at the local theater, in 1960, Caroline went to work for the Alaska Department of Fish and Game in Petersburg.

She was an active and enthusiastic member of Toastmistress, Emblem Club, and Auxiliary 10 of Pioneers of Alaska.

Caroline loved to play cards and socialize with her friends. She enjoyed their home on North Nordic Drive, watching both the ever-changing scene of boats and the mountains across Frederick Sound. Caroline passed away in May of 1999.

Lars and Laura Westre

By Bruce Westre

Leaving Alesund, Norway, in 1920, Lars Westre (1889-1964) and Laura Berg Westre (1893-1940) boarded the M/V *Empress* of Britain, sailing from Liverpool, England, with their two sons, Casper "Cap" (1917) and Anton "Tony" (1919-1992). Landing in St. John's Harbor, Canada, they traveled the rest of their journey across Canada by train.

Lars and Laura lived in Vancouver for a short time and then relocated to Prince Rupert. In 1923, traveling by steamer, Lars moved his family to Petersburg. They added two more members to their family, Lawrence "Larry" (1924-1980) and Marian (1928-2002).

Lars opened a boat repair shop that was located close to where The Trading Union is today. He purchased an old scow, in the area by the current Dockside Apartments, and built a 28-foot troller.

The troller was named after a Norwegian island, the F/V *Svarboard*. It was this boat that transported the family to Port Alexander every summer to fish. Lars bought a piece of property in Port Alexander, building a small cabin for his family.

In the winter, they would move back into Petersburg where Lars would repair and build boats. Some of the boats that Lars built are the *Marian*, *Arden* and *Balder*. These boats were constructed in a warehouse located on the beach south of the cemetery.

Just prior to 1940, Casper helped Lars build a warehouse where the Petersburg Shipwrights is now located. He would also help Lars around the shipyard and recalls working on the *Happy* and the *Peggy*.

Laura, while raising four children, was active in the Daughters of Norway. She enjoyed knitting, crocheting and working with embroidery.

Casper enlisted in the U.S. Navy in 1941. He met Sadie Galeson (1919-1986) at a dance in Seattle. They were married on June 10, 1944.

After his discharge in 1945, Casper brought his bride back to Petersburg where they commercial fished for a living. Sadie was Casper's right hand and his first mate. Casper owned the *Judith* and the *Faithful*.

Sadie was active in the Sons of Norway, Emblem Club, and the Hospital Guild. She enjoyed gardening, berry picking and hunting. Casper is currently a member of the Elks, Pioneers of Alaska and the Sons of Norway.

Anton "Tony" Westre also enlisted in the U.S. Navy in 1941, and was discharged in 1945. Tony married Vivian E. Close on September 22, 1947.

Tony owned and operated the local grocery store, the Sanitary Market, for 20 years. He was a member of the Masons, Elks, Pioneers of Alaska and the Sons of Norway.

Vivian kept the books for their business and raised their three children: Daniel, Sylvia and Bruce. Tony later sold the grocery store to Hack White and went commercial fishing for his semi-retirement.

Sylvia married Robert C. Larson of Ketchikan in August 1976, and she is a homemaker. They have three

Laura and Lars Westre

Lars and Laura Westre cont'd

children: Eric (1980), Troy (1983) and Sean (1987). Robert worked as a biologist for the Alaska Department of Fish and Game in both Ketchikan and Petersburg for 26 years. He is currently working for the U.S. Forest Service in Petersburg.

Casper, Anton and Lawrence
stand behind their sister, Marian

Bruce married Wendy Hammer in Petersburg in January 1979. They have two children, James Tyrell (1980) and Krystlyn (1982). Bruce started working for the Petersburg Police Department in September 1979, and is currently the Captain of Police.

Lars and Laura's third child, Larry, joined the U.S. Merchant Marine during the war. He married Ruth Jones (1930-1964) in Petersburg.

About 1954, Larry and Ruth moved to New Mexico to be closer to Ruth's family. Larry fished during the summers. During the off-season, he drove an oil truck in New Mexico.

Larry eventually moved to Seattle and continued fishing the summers in Alaska. He fished on the F/V *Pamela Rae* with Magnus Martens for many years.

As a hobby, Larry enjoyed building and fixing things. Family recalls that whenever Larry ran out of things to fix at home, he would go to garage sales and look for items to fix up. Larry was a member of the Elks, Sons of Norway and the Masons.

Larry and Ruth had two children, Michael (1949) and Karen (1950).

Mike was career military, retiring from the U.S. Navy in 2001. He is currently living in Tennessee.

Karen has two children, Trea Dumas (1975) and Jennifer Case (1972). Karen works as an administrative assistant for a realty company and is currently living in Myrtle Beach, South Carolina.

After high school, Lars and Laura's daughter, Marian, moved to Ballard, Washington. She met and married Robert Svendsen in Seattle in 1953. Marian worked many years in retail. She loved to travel with friends and family. One of her favorite pastimes was to dance.

Robert and Marian raised three children, Greg (1958), Joy (1954) and Jeff (1956).

Greg has one daughter Katie (1987) and is currently working as a longshoreman in Tacoma, Washington.

Joy married Reid Brown in Puyallup, Washington, in 1979. They have two children, Kyle (1981) and Keri (1983). Reid is a roofing contractor in Orting, Washington. Joy works for Boeing.

Jeff married Linea Benoy in September of 1990. They have two children, Jeremy (1982) and Kailyn (1993). Jeff currently conducts maintenance on fuel systems and resides in Fircrest, Washington.

Snowy scene

James and Frances Wheeler

By Lois Wheeler Rutledge

My father, James H. Wheeler, was born in New Orleans, Louisiana, on July 25, 1871, one of eight children. His family moved to San Antonio, Texas, while he was still a young boy. The children helped their father in his business at Overland Freight — horse-drawn wagons hauling supplies between Texas and Louisiana.

James H. Wheeler

He attended St. Mary's College for several years in San Antonio, which concluded his formal education.

Sometime in the late 1800s, he left the family home and worked at various jobs throughout the country. After returning home, he was soon hired by the Chicago Portrait Co. as a salesman. He traveled along the West Coast from San Francisco to Alaska, with his base of operations being the city of Portland, Oregon. His main job was to contact potential customers, show them completed portraits from his sample case, and send customers' photos back to Chicago, which were then copied in color onto canvas.

It was during this period that he met a beautiful young lady, Frances Thomas, who worked for the Northern Pacific Railway in Portland.

My father shared many stories about his travels. Here are two of them: Father William Duncan was a white Anglican minister who established a Tsimshian Indian village, called Metlakatla, on what is now known as Annette Island. Because of a friendship with Roderic Davies, an Indian man at Ketchikan, my father was able to meet with Father Duncan, who arranged a vote of the Indian elders, giving my father the honorary privilege of being the first white man to stay overnight in the village to conduct his business.

Another interesting anecdote that he liked to tell occurred during the days of "Gold Rush Fever." While south, he would buy up stray cats for 50 cents each, cage them, and take them to Skagway. He then would sell the cats as pets to the dance hall girls, receiving as much as $300 each! Thus he became known as the "Cat Man of the Yukon."

On one of his trips to Alaska, Father became acquainted with a Dr. O.F. Stanton, who owned a drugstore in Fort Wrangell. He decided to make his home there and leased the Fort Wrangell Hotel from the Sylvester estate, from 1903-1905.

He sent for Miss Fannie Thomas to come and work for him in the hotel dining room. After the hotel was sold, they were married. They worked for Dr. Stanton in the drugstore and later purchased the store from him.

In 1909, my mother, Fannie Wheeler, was the first of our family to become a registered pharmacist, receiving her certificate from the National Institute of Pharmacy correspondence school, in Chicago. The Alaska Territorial Board of Pharmacy granted Father a license through a grandfather clause for being a drugstore owner of long-standing, relying on family members to fill prescriptions.

While still operating the drugstore at Fort Wrangell, Father was talked into taking over a store in Petersburg next to the old Brennan building. He had a man named McFarland running the store. It turned out to be an unsuccessful venture and he sold out.

During all those difficult years, my mother maintained the pharmacy in Wrangell and raised our family. Several years passed and, in 1916, the Wheelers got an opportunity to expand their business interests. E. Schoenwald, superintendent of Pacific Coast and Norway Packing Co. (later Pacific American Fisheries), offered Father land if he would return to Petersburg

James and Frances Wheeler cont'd

Frances "Fannie" Wheeler

and set up another store.

The store was never built in that location because of the marine ways for the cannery. The windlass for pulling the boats occupied the lot intended for a drugstore. Instead, the new Wheeler drugstore was built at the intersection of Main Street and Sing Lee Alley. In 1926, fire gutted the upper floor where Dr. Dan Standard's office was located.

In the early 1930s, at an entirely different location on Main Street, a three-story building was completed. It housed the old post office, the Lillian Shop, and Dr. Smith's office to the rear. The building was later demolished, making way for a new bank.

Another fire destroyed the original drugstore in the 1940s. Business continued at a temporary location until Father moved into a newly remodeled building at the corner of Main and Fram streets, formerly owned by pioneer Chris Lang. He considered this his home until his death in 1974.

My father was the first secretary of the Petersburg Commercial Club, later the Chamber of Commerce. Being the largest landowner in the Petersburg-Wrangell area at that time, he donated land to various organizations such as the Moose Lodge in Petersburg and a playground in the town of Wrangell.

He and Ed Locken were major stockholders in the Bank of Petersburg. At different times, he served as president, vice-president and chairman of the board. My parents were both active in the Republican party and my father acted as committeeman for the Eisenhower campaign, and organized the Women's Republican Club in town. He was instrumental in attempting to get the Canadian Pacific Railway's steamships to make the town one if its ports of call — but, since Petersburg did not have a customs office, Canadian ships bypassed it.

James and Fannie raised four children: Eugene, James Jr., Raymond and Lois. We all served early apprenticeships as clerks in both Wrangell and Petersburg stores, doing the daily chores of dusting, washing windows and showcases, unpacking freight (packed with excelsior in large wooden crates), stocking shelves, and waiting on customers.

Childhood days, while growing up in two small Alaska towns, were carefree and wonderful. The basketball games between Petersburg High School and Wrangell High School were eagerly anticipated, highly competitive, and lots of fun!

As for education, Eugene graduated from North Pacific Dental College in Portland. He established his first dental practice in Petersburg, and then in Wrangell, practicing for over 30 years. Jim Jr. studied

Wheeler Building, 1930s

pharmacy for two years at the University of Washington and returned to clerk in the Petersburg store. Ray received a pharmacy degree from the University of Washington in 1936. He was stationed

James and Frances Wheeler cont'd

on Shemya Island in the Aleutians during World War II for the Army as head pharmacist.

I attended both Washington State College and University of Washington and was a clerk at both stores. I moved to Seattle during World War II, where I met and married Robert Rutledge, my husband of 57 years. He was serving in the U.S. Navy.

Besides our four children — Shelley, Rory, Rob and Zane — we have nine grandchildren and three great-grandchildren.

My brother Ray is survived by his daughter, Shemya, of Tacoma, Washington. Jim III, son of Jim Jr., is deceased. My mother met a tragic end due to a pedestrian accident in Seattle in 1955. My father also died in Seattle, in 1974, at the young age of 103 — a full life indeed!

As the last surviving member of the Wheeler family, I have recorded these memories and history to the best of my knowledge. I am writing this down, so we will all stop crying.

To this end, everyone it seems, sooner or later in their lifetime, returns to their ROOTS — and thus, part of my heart will always remain in Alaska.

James and Ray Wheeler

Interior of the Wheeler drug store.

Elias Wikan

By Nancy Lamb

Elias "Ed" Wikan was the first born and oldest son of Johan Fætten and Marie Vikan. He was born in Rissa, Norway, in 1887. As a young man, he fished for cod with his father in northern Norway. Later, he enrolled in a trade school and finished as a carpenter.

In 1911, he immigrated to the United States, joining a younger brother who had immigrated earlier. The two brothers took the Americanized version of their mother's maiden name, as it was easier to spell in English. The two brothers lived and worked in both Seattle and Everett, Washington.

In 1916, he met and married a Swedish lady by the name of Nanny Grubstrum. Their son, Harold, was born in Seattle on February 21, 1917. Their daughter, Edna, was born on November 28, 1919.

Nan and the children lived in Seattle, while Ed fished in Alaska, but came to Petersburg in the summer. Ed and Nan divorced in the early 1930s.

Ed owned the fishing vessel *Harold*. He fished for salmon in Alaskan waters and for salmon and tuna off the coast of Washington.

After his divorce, he lived in Petersburg for a time and built a home on Lumber Street. After selling his home in the early 1940s, he returned to Seattle, where he remarried. He continued to fish in the summer and worked as a carpenter in the winter.

He died in Seattle in April of 1959 and lies in rest in North Seattle.

Both of his children are now deceased. Harold Wikan died in 1991 and Edna Wikan died in 1993.

Eiler Wikan

By Jane Slater

Eiler Wikan was born Johan Eiler Faetten on August 26, 1899, in Rissa, Norway. He was the son of Johan and Marie Fætten.

Eiler came to America on the *Stavangerfjord* with his brothers Oscar and Olaf. They landed at Ellis Island, New York, on May 1, 1923.

The brothers took the train to Seattle, and then an Admiral Line ship to Petersburg, where their brother Andrew met them. Ed Wikan, who lived in Seattle, financed Eiler's trip.

Eiler's first job was on a boat that went to Le Conte Bay for glacier ice. The ice was chopped and brought to the cold storage.

His first fishing job was on the *Lenore* with Andrew Mathisen. Along with deckhanding, Eiler was always the cook. He spent many years on the F/V *Edgecomb* and the F/V *Zarembo*.

His first winter job was delivering milk for Hammer & Wikan. The milk was brought over from Brown Cove. When not fishing, Eiler also worked as a carpenter on many of the buildings in town.

Eiler was a life member of the Moose, a 30-year member of the Elks, and a member of the Sons of Norway Fedrelandet 23 Lodge. He was known as one of the best dancers in Alaska and taught many people the Scandinavian dances. He was "Grandpa" to many who were not related. He gave love and received it from those who knew him.

Eiler Wikan married Dagny Lian of Hasselvika, Norway, in Petersburg on March 30, 1929. They had met in 1928 at a cannery, where Eiler was making barrels for herring. Dagny worked as a waitress for a while at a café above the old Hammer and Wikan store.

Dagny had come to Petersburg through Canada. She had a sister, Marie, living in Petersburg, who was married to Arne Fenswick.

Dagny and Eiler Wikan had three children. David was born May 22, 1933; Jane was born May 3, 1936; and Robert was born September 23, 1938.

Dagny was a great baker and always made extra bread for Eiler's bachelor friends. Dagny and Eiler entertained friends at parties by singing together.

In 1958, Eiler married Loyla Ohmer.

He died in 1984 and is buried in Petersburg.

Besides his two sons and daughter, Eiler had two stepchildren, seven grandchildren, thirteen step-grandchildren, eight great-grandchildren, and eleven step-great-grandchildren.

Andrew and Margaret Wikan

By Sharon Wikan

Marit Kaasen was born March 19, 1890, in Alvdal, Norway. She lived on a very small farm in the mountains. In 1908, she immigrated to Spring Valley, Wisconsin, with one of her uncles, changing her name to Margaret, the Americanized version of Marit. She came to clean house and take care of children.

Later, she and her Uncle Simon moved to Everett, Washington, where she met Andrew J. Wikan. They were married December 26, 1912, in Everett.

In March 1913, Margaret went to Petersburg on the steamship *Jefferson* to join Andrew. They lived in a 10-by-12-foot shack, made of 1-foot-by-10-inch planks, which they rented from Knute Hestness for $6 a month. It was equipped with a cast-iron boat stove and wooden crates for furniture. Their first child, Marie, was born in this house on July 22, 1913.

Gudolf was born April 18, 1915; Andrew M. was born February 4, 1920; and Johan Bojer was born September 16, 1921. Andrew and Margaret also had a baby boy born July 12, 1917, who passed away July 15, 1917. Gudolf died of tuberculosis November 18, 1932, at the age of 17.

Margaret was content to stay at home, while Andrew was social and political. Margaret loved the outdoors and always took the children and grandchildren on picnics.

Margaret passed away on December 28, 1962, in Petersburg.

Andrew Wikan was born Andreas Johansen Fætten in Rissa, South Trøndelag, Norway, on September 5, 1888. Rissa was a small town on the Trondheim Fjord. Andrew fished in the fjord and the Lofoten Islands.

In April of 1909, 21-year-old Andreas left Trondheim for the United States on the *Saxonia*, a converted 18,000-ton cattle ship. On the way over, the passengers teased Andrew about his last name, Fætten. They told him what fat meant in English, so he ended up taking the name Wikan, the Americanized version of his mother's maiden name, Vikan.

Andrew had a train ticket to La Crosse, Wisconsin, where he remained for two months. He then traveled on to North Dakota, where he had relatives.

In October 1909, he went on to Everett, Washington, where he stayed for three and a half years, working in the sawmills and fishing.

In the fall of 1912, Andrew made up his mind to go to Petersburg, where he heard there were lots of fish. He and Sivert Ronning were partners in a fishing boat, a troller named the *Hovit*. It was 30 feet long, with a 5 hp engine and a sail.

They sailed out of Seattle and arrived in Petersburg seven days later, on March 15, 1913.

When Andrew arrived he had no money. When he talked to Skyler Duryea, the manager of the Pacific Coast and Norway Packing Co. store, about supplies, Duryea said, "You come and take what you want." Andrew did. As he made money, he paid off his bill.

Andrew and Margaret Wikan, with children Andy, Bojer, Gudolf and Marie

Andrew built himself a skiff and fished at Cape Ommaney in May and June. Andrew and Sivert hand trolled with three lines and three hooks. Andrew also worked for Pacific Coast and Norway Packing Co., as a trap watchman on their Point Colpoys trap.

In 1921, Andrew talked to John Hammer about

Andrew and Margaret Wikan cont'd

going in together to bring milk to town from Point Agassiz. They bought milk from the farmers for 10¢ a quart and sold it in town for 15¢. They didn't make any money, but it was something to do.

Later in 1921, they rented a building from Pacific Packing Co., successor to Pacific Coast and Norway Packing Co., and outfitted it as a bottle-washing shed. At that time, Andrew and John called their business the Petersburg Dairy.

In 1924, the partners bought the lot where the original Hammer & Wikan building still stands. They borrowed $1000 from the bank and built a 24-by-60-foot structure and moved their dairy business there.

During the early years, John gillnetted in the summer, while Andrew and Mrs. Hammer ran the business. In the fall, John ran the business and Andrew used his boat, the *Lund*, to troll and haul gravel.

Andrew hauled gravel for the grade school and high school buildings, and the first part of the road to Scow Bay. Everything they made was split 50/50. The partners added a few groceries to their business. By 1926, they were able to drop the milk business and concentrate on the grocery line.

They changed the name of the business to its present-day Hammer & Wikan, Inc., and, in 1934, finished adding on to the building.

The store offered home delivery of groceries and Andrew was the deliveryman. If no one was home, he would carry the groceries to the kitchen. If he knew the family well enough, he would put the perishables in the refrigerator.

In 1960, construction on a new store began that adjoined the original Hammer & Wikan store. The new building was 85 by 100 feet, with two stories. Throughout the years, they added hardware and housewares, as well as various other items. In 1971, they added to the 1960 structure, expanding the building again. In 1994, a new grocery store complex was built up the hill off Haugen Drive.

Andrew and John would be very pleased to see that Hammer & Wikan is still a very important part of the community.

Andrew and John never had a formal written agreement. The two families still own the business 50/50. The ownership has passed on to their children, grandchildren, and great-grandchildren.

In 1924, Andrew had a very special guest come from Norway for a visit. It was his godfather, Johan Bojer, who was a famous Norwegian author. His most famous book was *The Emigrants,* which has been translated to English. Johan Bojer was a foster child of Andrew's grandparents and was raised on the same farm in Norway as Andrew.

Community activities were a big part of Andrew's life. He served on the Petersburg Hospital Board, the school board, Thomas Bay Power Authority, city council, and was mayor for three years.

In 1976, he gave a gift of $24,000 to the Petersburg General Hospital to purchase the land adjoining the old hospital, so the hospital could expand to its present-day location. At the time, it was the largest single donation to the City of Petersburg. He stated that Petersburg had always been good to him, and he wanted to express his appreciation to the town.

Andrew was also an avid skier. Behind the current airport, there used to be a ski hill with a jump. There were many ski jumping competitions held there in the early years. Andrew won many competitions and also won one in Juneau.

In 1969, Andrew received the Norwegian-American Award at the Little Norway Festival. This was the second year the award had been presented.

In the '60s, Andrew purchased a Norwegian costume in Oslo for himself. He wore this proudly to every Norwegian function.

In 1975, Andrew made a trip to Anchorage to meet King Olav, King of Norway. This was a re-acquaintance, as Andrew had first met the king when they were children.

Andrew made many trips back to the old country, but his home was Petersburg. He loved it here and his memories and accomplishments live on.

The family still operates the business that he started. His granddaughter has refurbished the family home and lives there. His Norwegian outfit is worn every Little Norway Festival by a Wikan, and the family still keep the many ties to Norway.

Andrew passed away in Petersburg on November 14, 1976. Andrew, Margaret and their three sons are buried in Petersburg.

Marie Wikan Jensen lives in Stanwood, Washington. *(See Marie Jensen story.)*

Andy and Noca Wikan

By Vava Wikan and Audrey Samuelson

Andrew M. Wikan was the fourth child of Norwegian immigrants Andreas and Margit Wikan. Born on February 4, 1920, he lived with his family on South Nordic Drive in the house his father built.

As a boy, Andy brought milk daily from the Point Agassiz dairy to town with his father. Educated in the Petersburg schools, he was a member of the Petersburg High School basketball team that won the regional championship title.

Andy was also a skier and, in 1938, won a second place trophy at a tournament in Petersburg.

Andy fished with Leif Stromdahl during his teenage years, gillnetting for salmon on the Stikine River. During that time he owned a boat called the *Ramona*. By age 17, he was gillnetting with his second boat, the *Noseum*.

At 21, Andy entered the U.S. Navy and served from 1941 until the end of World War II. He was stationed mainly in Alaska on Shumagin Island. He wasn't allowed leave from his ship, as the captain was from the Midwest and didn't know much about boats. When Andy finally did get leave, he came straight to Petersburg and was storm-bound for several days.

After the war in 1945, Andy met his future wife, Noca, at the Sons of Norway dance hall in Petersburg.

Noca May McCutchan was born to Pearl and Beulah McCutchan in Belle Fourche, South Dakota, on November 11, 1916. She was their only child.

Noca's early years were spent on an "extraordinary" piece of land in Wyoming, where her father ranched. She had memories of a sleigh pulled by a team of black horses. At one Fourth of July rodeo, President Hoover shared his chair with her.

Noca became an experienced rider with her own handmade saddle. She recalled being extremely happy those six years at the ranch.

In 1922, her father was diagnosed with diabetes and Brights disease. The family was forced to auction off all of their possessions and move to South Sioux City, Iowa, where there was better medical care. Pearl died in 1924. Beulah and Noca continued to live in South Sioux City.

Shortly after her father died, Noca began having arthritis in her shoulders. After seeing doctors in Iowa City, she was diagnosed with rheumatoid arthritis. Her arthritis would eventually spread to her elbows, wrists and ankles. She was forced to wear braces attached to her shoes during her school days; she was actually walking on her knees. She still recalled her school days as fun.

The Great Depression came. They would remark about how lucky they were. Her mother was a seamstress, and they were "poor as church mice," but they still had each other.

Andy and Noca Wikan

Noca graduated from high school in 1936, and continued her education at Wayne State Teachers College. Still in braces, she graduated in 1938 with her teacher's certificate. Noca was one of 96 to apply for a teaching job. She was chosen as a first grade teacher in South Dakota.

After applying to teach in Petersburg, August of

Andy and Noca Wikan cont'd

1945, Noca left South Sioux City by train for Alaska. From Seattle, she arrived in Petersburg via steamship. Superintendent Les Wingard met her at the dock. He gave her a room in his home.

She later lodged at the Wasvik's home and ate in their café. She finally found a room of her own at the Mitkof Hotel, which was fairly nice, but the bathroom was clear down the hall!

After school, she enjoyed her hand sewing, being outdoors — she loved the beauty of the mountains and the water — clam digging, and the Sons of Norway dances that lasted until dawn. It was at one of these dances she met Andy Wikan.

When they were a new item, Noca went with Andy to Wrangell to have work done to his boat. Andy asked Noca to steer the boat while he ran to the engine room. "Just stay between these two markers," Andy said. But being a girl from the Midwest, she stayed between the markers and promptly ran the boat right up Petersburg Creek! Andy didn't utter a word. Not even so much as a boo. But, Noca was sure he got teased a lot by his friends.

Andy and Noca were married October 29, 1946. They had two daughters. Vava was born in 1947, and Audrey was born in 1949.

Family life was very important. There were many picnics, skating and skiing adventures.

As young girls, Vava and Audrey have many memories of going with their dad to places such as the coffee shop and down to work on the boat. They would fish for herring and play until it was time for lunch. The family always ate together at noon for lunch and at 5 p.m. for supper.

As she got older, Audrey would go seining with Andy. Andy could often be seen riding his childhood bike on the dock, as he rode it back and forth to the boat every day.

Eventually, Andy and Noca would purchase a house across the bay on Kupreanof Island. Andy worked on repairs, but as Noca's arthritis worsened, the house was sold to Harold Bergmann.

In winters, Andy worked construction, while Noca taught at the elementary school.

They built their home in 1956 on South Nordic, near the old Wikan residence. Andy dug a full basement for the 3,000 square foot home by hand, wheelbarrow after wheelbarrow. The cement for the basement was also mixed by hand in a cement mixer. Andy and friends poured and cured the cement. Due to Noca's special requests, he also worked along with carpenter Oliver Olsen, doing lots of tearing out and rebuilding at night.

Andy and his brother Bojer had bought the *Curlew* together to fish halibut and salmon. By 1965, Andy and Bojer decided they needed a bigger boat, so they purchased the *Pacific Sea*. After two years, Andy became sole owner. He continued to fish halibut and salmon, and was a pioneer of the crab fisheries along with Neal MacDonald, Lloyd Pederson and Phil Clausen. In 1966, Andy was the highliner, when he spent more days laying up (eight days per trip) than fishing days, as he loaded up the boat so quickly. He spent more time in town than fishing that summer.

Andy was also one of the original investors in Icicle Seafoods. Before individual fishing quotas began, halibut fishing trips lasted either until the boat was full, the fishing was slow, or the season closed. In the 1985 season, Andy delivered 56,000 pounds of halibut on the *Pacific Sea* with crew Knute Fredricksen, Louie Vessel and Bojer Wikan. They were honored at the Little Norway Festival for the largest delivery to the cold storage that year.

Noca taught school until 1973, when she retired. There were as many as 60 students a day in her kindergarten classes, which consisted of two classes per day. This was before there were teacher's aides! Many of her students recall sitting on a chair behind the piano for what we call today "time out." She always had kindergarten graduation, which started with *Not At The Top But Climbing*, and many students still have the shadow pictures Noca did of each child for Mother's Day.

Andy was always willing to help people. While in Eliza Harbor, he helped several women secure a log raft. All of the men had gone to town and left the women, so Andy got the log raft together. As he was waving goodbye, he fell off a huge log, right into the mucky beach, and was the stickiest mess you ever saw!

Andy also went out into stormy weather at Cape St. Elias and rescued three men in a small cruiser that had broken down. The crew had to go hand over hand from the cruiser to the *Pacific Sea*, one man weighing

Andy and Noca Wikan cont'd

well over 300 pounds. Louie Vessel broke three ribs, as the *Pacific Sea* crew helped pull this large man aboard. The irony of this story is that the cruiser's owner wanted to sue for the loss of his boat!

With the inception of limited entry for salmon, fishermen were adding up their points. Being a diversified fisherman, Andy could not get enough points for salmon no matter what he did. Finally, he got on a plane and went to Juneau, straight to the limited entry office, paperwork in hand. He told the gentleman there that he had seined for many years and they could just do the calculations and come up with the correct points, while he went to breakfast. Sure enough, when Andy returned, the points were there.

In 1976, Andy and Noca purchased a townhouse located at Vista Del Valle in Yuma, Arizona. They spent many summers there with their grandchildren, and partial winters with each other. Andy would walk about a mile to Noca's cousins' home and eat fresh oranges from their trees before breakfast. He would also swim several times a day in the pool at the townhouse. He was a dark Norwegian and tanned at the drop of a hat! They spent one Christmas there and decided never again, as they missed the snow and their grandchildren during that holiday.

Noca did beautiful embroidery work throughout her life and crocheted many items, including blankets as the new grandchildren came along. Her beautiful embroidery will be enjoyed for generations to come, as she made Norwegian bunads for herself, daughters and granddaughters. Her embroidery is as fine on the inside as the outside.

Noca also traveled, not only with Andy, but also with good friend Hixie Sunde. She received teaching credits for some of her travels. She saw such places as Spain, Norway, Ireland, North Africa, Italy, Portugal, China, and northern parts of Alaska. Noca would take her grandchildren on trips to Europe and the Bahamas, always with education in mind.

Noca was a member of the Lutheran Church, American Legion Auxiliary, Emblem Club and Sons of Norway.

She held and attended many elegant parties. They all had a theme — one was a hat party and all of the women made and decorated hats.

Andy was active in the Sons of Norway, VFW, Elks, Moose, Petersburg Vessel Owners, Hammer & Wikan board, Icicle Seafood board, Pioneers of Alaska and Petersburg Lutheran Church.

Andy passed away on August 8, 1986, after fighting cancer.

Noca finally gave in to her arthritis and was bedridden at home after breaking her hip. She had home health care for several years. Her caregiver continued with the style of living Noca had always enjoyed. There were always family dinners and theme parties. The family was always welcome and another place could always be set at the table.

Noca passed away on May 5, 1999, at Petersburg Medical Center. She left behind her daughters, Vava and Audrey; grandchildren Michael, Gwynne, Andreas and Steven; and her great-grandchildren, Andrew, Matthew, Bud, Tore, Gunnar and Alexxis.

Andy Wikan's *Ramona* lays beside the *San Juan*.

Johan "Bojer" and Carlene Wikan

By Sharon Wikan

Johan Bojer Wikan was born September 16, 1921, at the family home in Petersburg. He was the youngest of Andrew and Margaret Wikan's five children and was named after Johan Bojer, the famous writer in Norway. Johan was Andrew's godfather.

Bojer's father owned Hammer & Wikan, Inc., so he had many opportunities to help out in his younger years. He remembered delivering milk with a two-wheeled wagon. When he was a bit older, he also delivered groceries.

Bojer started fishing when he was 17 years old. His first chance on a halibut boat was as a cook. When he told Lloyd Pederson, the skipper, "I can't boil water," Pederson replied that he "betta learn to cook or they all would starve."

Pederson told the story of the time when Bojer had an entire meal on the table, and the boat took a nasty roll — all the dishes landed on the floor. Bojer surveyed the mess and said "Hammer & Wikan has lots of dishes."

During World War II, Bojer enlisted in the U.S. Navy and served two years on the battleship *Nevada*. The *Nevada* had been moored directly behind the *Arizona* during the bombing of Pearl Harbor. The *Nevada* had been damaged, so it was towed to San Diego for repairs. Bojer was assigned to it once the repairs were completed.

He took part in the invasion of Attu in the Aleutians and worked aboard a minesweeper, preparing for the invasion of Okinawa. Upon his return to the states, Bojer became a naval instructor, based in Chicago. After his discharge in 1945, he returned to Petersburg.

Always preferring fishing to working in the family store, Bojer fished sardines in California. Next, he signed on the *Iceland* and went to the Bering Sea.

While fishing in the Seattle area, he met Carlene Helen Thorsen at a dance.

Carlene Thorsen was born in Arlington, Washington, on October 25, 1925, to Carl and Josie Thorsen, a logging family. She had an older sister and younger brother. During the war, Carlene worked in Seattle, at Boeing, as a riveter. She was building airplanes for World War II.

Carlene and Bojer were married February 5, 1948, in Lakewood, Washington. The day after the wedding, they sailed to Petersburg on the *Princess Louise*.

After arriving in Petersburg, Bojer continued fishing on various boats. In the winter he delivered groceries for Hammer & Wikan and also worked on various construction projects.

Carlene and Bojer had two children. Sharon was born August 19, 1948. John was born October 18, 1949.

They purchased a piece of property about 200 feet away from his parent's family home. Bojer moved the house from the upper part of the lot down to the waterfront and remodeled it. There, he and Carlene lived the rest of their lives. Bojer always used to say, "I have lived not more than 200 feet from the home I was born in, except when I was in the service."

Carleen and Bojer Wikan

In 1950, he and his brother Andy formed a partnership and bought the *Curlew*, longlining, seining and crabbing with the boat. Once in the late 1950s, they were heading for either Ketchikan or Prince Rupert with a deck-load of halibut. They hit a rock in the Snow Pass area. Luckily, they managed to save the boat and the fish.

In 1965, they bought the *Pacific Sea*. Together they longlined, seined and fished crab aboard the vessel. Shortly thereafter, they chose to each take a boat and go out on their own.

Bojer skippered the *Curlew* until the early 1970s. He then went back fishing with his brother Andy.

After the children went to school, Carlene started working as a clerk at Hammer & Wikan. She just went

Johan "Bojer" and Carlene Wikan cont'd

to help out for a few days and ended up working until 1990, when she turned 65 years old.

As the store expanded, Carlene helped initiate new departments and was responsible for starting the housewares department. It started out slowly with Lusterware dishes and Revere kettles to a complete housewares department. She was very proud of all the giftware, especially the Norwegian items. She also was responsible for selling live plants each spring.

Bojer retired from fishing in 1984. He continued to make a few halibut trips with his grandson Jon to show him a few tricks of the trade. He also helped his daughter, Sharon, and her children to set their Dungeness crab pots in the correct spots.

Wikan Brothers, from left: Olaf, Eiler, Andrew, Ed and Oscar. Andrew is Bojer's father.

He was instrumental in helping with several remodeling projects at Hammer & Wikan and was especially proud to see the new store built up the hill off Haugen Drive.

Bojer was the driving force in getting the Sons of Norway Hall listed as a National Historic Site and procuring grant monies to remodel the building in the 1980s.

In 1987, he was given the Norwegian-American Award at the Little Norway Festival.

Bojer had built Carlene a greenhouse in the early 1970s. Carlene loved her flowers and Bojer liked the vegetables. Carlene had it overflowing all the time, and they were always very generous with the seedlings. Many were the lucky recipients of flowers. Boaters would stop by and want to buy flowers, as they thought it was a nursery.

Carlene was very active in the Emblem Club in the 1950s and 1960s. She was a past president of the organization. She had many stories to pass on of all the goods times they had in the club and the many trips they went on throughout Southeast Alaska. She especially remembered the camaraderie between the Petersburg and Wrangell clubs.

Boyer and Carlene traveled extensively to see the world, but Petersburg was their home. They both loved the people here and loved living next to the harbor where they could see all of the goings on.

Bojer was known as a friend to everyone, and is remembered for always having something positive to say, no matter how gloomy things appeared. He always had a hug or a kiss for the girls. He was a very fun-loving person and liked to be called "Boyaye," after the movie actor, Charles Boyer.

Bojer passed away January 28, 1996.

At the time of his death, Bojer was active in the Sons of Norway, Elks Lodge, Pioneers of Alaska, Moose Lodge, Veterans of Foreign War, and the Petersburg Lutheran Church.

After his death, the Sons of Norway honored him with the Johan Bojer Wikan Fishermen's Memorial Park. His wish had been to see a park honoring all of the lost fishermen at sea and others that were related to the fishing industry. We now have a lovely park and a statue of Bojer overlooking the harbor.

Carlene passed away December 28, 2002.

At the time of her death, she was active in the Sons of Norway, Emblem Club, Pioneers of Alaska and the Petersburg Lutheran Church.

Olaf and Mette Wikan

By Leif Wikan

Olaf Wikan was born in Rissa, Norway, on August 4, 1893. His wife, Mette Molsknes, was born April 8, 1888, in Stjordal, Norway. They both had an eighth grade education, typical of the times in Norway.

Olaf was one of five brothers who immigrated to this country. At one time, all five lived in Petersburg. The other brothers were Ed, Andrew, Oscar and Eiler. On arrival at Ellis Island in New York, the brothers changed their last name to that of their mother's maiden name, as one could not spell their Norwegian name in English. This was not an uncommon practice.

Three of the brothers, Olaf, Oscar and Eiler, arrived at Ellis Island in April 1923, unable to speak the language. When they indicated their destination as Seattle, the agent put a baggage tag around one of their necks — on it was written "Olaf Wikan Seattle." The agent then directed them to the train station and the brothers wore the tag until they reached Seattle.

Their brother Andrew had jobs for them in Petersburg, so they took passage on the steamship to Alaska. The jobs were as lumberjacks, working in the woods for a local logger by the name of Jack Hanseth. The pay, including room and board, was $30 a month, paid in gold coin. They worked seven days a week.

In 1925, Olaf wrote to his sweetheart in Norway, asking her to come to the United States and marry him. His future wife, Mette, arrived in Halifax, Canada, and crossed Canada by train, arriving in Price Rupert in November of 1925. Mette's lasting impression of the train trip was how great the distances were on this continent, as the trip took nearly a week.

Olaf's brother Oscar met her in Prince Rupert, since Olaf was out fishing. Olaf and Mette were married on December l, 1925, at the home of Andrew Wikan. Shortly thereafter, Olaf bought their home on Lumber Street, where they lived for over 40 years.

The home they moved into was a one-bedroom house, heated by wood and coal. It had no washing machine, dryer, dishwasher, refrigerator, telephone or radio. The only utilities were electricity and water. For entertainment, they had a hand-wound phonograph. Clothes were washed in the bathtub with a scrub board and hung to dry on a clothesline.

In 1931, their son, Leif, was born. Leif grew up in Petersburg, finishing high school in 1949. In the fall, he moved to Washington to further his education.

Olaf was primarily a halibut and blackcod fisherman, fishing as a crewman on the boats *Teddy J*, *Zarembo*, and *Balder*. In the late '40s and '50s, he fished for salmon as a seiner, when the halibut boats

Leif, Mette and Olaf Wikan

converted to salmon seining for the summer season. In 1932, Olaf kept a diary of his fishing trips — he made 11 halibut trips selling fish in Petersburg, Ketchikan, Prince Rupert, and Seattle. Fish sold for as much as four cents and as low as one cent a pound. His earnings for the year were $430.

In 1947, he took his family back to Norway for the first time since leaving. They spent three months visiting friends and relatives. In 1960, he and his wife returned to Norway for their last time.

Olaf's wife, Mette, was a homemaker. She worked in the PAF cannery in the summers, during the 1950s, for what she called "extra spending money."

Their son, Leif, finished his education in Washington State, served in the military during the later part of the Korean War. He married in Seattle and established his home there. During the 1950s and 1960s, Olaf and Mette would leave Petersburg in the late fall and spend Christmas and the early part of the New Year in Seattle, near their son and his family.

Olaf retired from fishing in the early 1960s. In 1966 he sold his home in Petersburg, and he and his wife moved to Seattle. Olaf passed away in 1975 and Mette in 1976. Both are laid to rest in Seattle.

Oscar Wikan

By Sharon Wikan

Oscar was the fifth child, and fourth son, born to Johan Fætten and Marie Vikan Fætten on February 11, 1896, in Rissa, Norway. As a young man, he fished for cod with his father in the North Sea. In later years, he worked onshore in Trondheim.

In 1923, he immigrated to the United States with two other brothers, Olaf and Eiler, who would raise families in Petersburg. Oscar, like all the brothers, changed his last name to that of his mother's maiden name, changing the V to a W. The U.S. sponsor for the three brothers was their older brother, Andrew. He and his family were well established in Petersburg.

Andrew had arranged jobs for the brothers. They worked for Jack Hanseth, as lumberjacks in the forests near Petersburg. They worked seven days a week for $30 a month, including room and board. When not in the woods, the brothers lived in a cabin of Andrew's, located on the waterfront west of his home. The cabin is now a rental property. Two of the three brothers married and moved into homes of their own. Oscar remained in the cabin for many years, later moving into a larger home near Eagle's Roost.

After a few years in the woods, Oscar became a fisherman, fishing for halibut, blackcod and salmon. He was always a crewman and fished on local boats by the names of *Betty*, *Edgecomb*, *Balder*, and his brother Ed's boat, *Harold*.

Oscar had left a girlfriend in Norway, who was not interested in moving to the United States. He never married. Oscar was the godfather to his brother's son, Leif, to whom he was very generous with gifts for birthdays, Christmas and other occasions.

When fishing was profitable, Oscar would go south to Seattle for a month or two in the winter.

In 1952 when the Winter Olympics were held in Norway, he visited Norway, taking in the games and visiting his father, brothers, and sisters, who had remained in the old country.

Oscar was a loyal member of the Sons of Norway and the Petersburg Elks Club. With no children of his own, he catered to young children in the community, many of whom called him Okey, for uncle.

Oscar was still actively fishing, when he died on May 6, 1963. He lies at rest in the Petersburg Cemetery.

Wikan Family, about 1937. Sitting, from left: Edna, Marie, Margaret, Mette, Leif, Dagny (holding Jane) and David. Standing: Oscar, Elias, Harold, Andy, Andrew, Bojer, Olaf and Eiler.

Lester and Dorothy Wingard

By Beverly Wingard Concannon

Lester Wingard was born in Tacoma, Washington, in 1904. His father, William Wingard, went to Alaska during the gold rush. Family lore claims that, on his way back from the gold fields, he cached a considerable amount of gold in the Chilkat Pass. An avalanche later buried the gold forever.

In 1922, Les took a year off from his studies at Tacoma's Stadium High School to work in Alaska. In 1928, he married Dorothy "Dory" Lee Megquier, who had also attended Stadium High School. Les earned his BS at Washington State College (WSC) in Pullman, Washington, in 1929.

In the '30s, Les operated a speedboat, patrolling Southeastern Alaska waters for the Alaska Bureau of Fisheries. One day, he docked his speedboat in Petersburg and stopped by to ask Superintendent George V. Beck if he needed a coach/teacher. Les was hired on the spot. Dory, who was in Montana, headed for Alaska after receiving his telegram. She and their 3-year-old daughter, Beverly, arrived in Petersburg in August 1935.

Les was given multiple assignments at school. He was principal of the high school, as well as instructor of social sciences and athletics. He also coached the Petersburg High School basketball team. During his teaching career, he taught many courses: physics, chemistry — and what were to become his forte — civics, world history and U.S. history.

The athletic program had been chronically short of funds before Les' arrival. Soon, he set up the "Athletic Benefit," which became a very popular annual fall event, making a significant donation to the sports program. He also organized more than one "standing room only smoker" (boxing event), functioning as coach, referee and boxer.

Although Les had never played basketball, and had done relatively little basketball coaching, it wasn't long before the Vikings regularly brought home the trophies. He stopped coaching in 1950, in order to devote his time to administrative duties.

In the early '40s, Lem Wingard, Les' brother, started a two-line cannery in Ugashik, Alaska. Until the mid-'50s, Les spent the greater part of every

Southeastern Alaska basketball championship team, 1940. Standing, from left to right: Palmer Pederson, Alfred Johnson, Erling Jensen, captain Tom Wanberg, Tom Thompson, George Nicholson and coach Les Wingard. Front, from left: Bill Johnson, Nels Otness, Roy Lund and Norman Holm.

summer "out westward" as warehouse foreman for the company. Dory accompanied him a few times, and Beverly went along twice.

In 1944, the school board offered Les the position of superintendent of schools, on the condition that he earn his master's degree. The Wingard family spent a sabbatical year, 1947-1948, at Les' alma mater, WSC, where he earned his Master of Educational Administration.

Les took an active part in politics, both as an educator and as a private citizen. After becoming

Lester and Dorothy Wingard cont'd

superintendent, Les spent many evenings at school board and city council meetings. He argued forcefully for a new school building, believing the town would soon need more school space for the post-war baby boom. Les' efforts were successful; the eighth graders and high school students moved into a new building in 1951.

The Wingards and their close friends, the Dick Brennans, bought the Allen Camp on Woewodski Island in the '40s, renaming the cabin "Brenwin." The camp lives in the memory of almost every Petersburg community member of that time — the log cabin was never locked and groups were allowed to stay there. The only rule was "leave it the way you found it."

It was later sold to the Roundtree family.

During the early '50s, Dory and her good friend, Bunny Mathisen, were pivotal in making Petersburg part of the Alaska Music Trail concert series. Bunny had become acquainted with Jane and Maxim Shapiro. Maxim was a concert pianist and Jane played the cello. The Shapiros knew many musicians and decided to form an Alaska concert circuit. They sought up-and-coming artists and persuaded them to venture north. These artists adapted admirably to less than perfect acoustics and pianos that were not state-of-the-art. But, they were cheerful and giving people. Many of these artists became world-renowned — Lucine Amara and Nicanor Zabaleta — to name just two.

Les served as Rotary Club president, Exalted Ruler of the Elks, and advanced through the highest degree in Masons. Dory was a member of the Emblem Club and Worthy Matron of the Eastern Star. In 1951, Dory received an award for her "distinguished service" for the American Cancer Society. Some remember Dory for her dancing lessons at the school, where she taught several classes of high school students the rudiments of social dancing.

Dory and Les' 25th Anniversary, 1953, with daughter Beverly.

Les loved hunting, fishing and boating — and was no mean poker player. Dory often went along on duck hunting and fishing trips. She excelled at bridge and went to a weekly bridge club sessions.

After moving to the Seattle area in 1956, Les accepted a position as history teacher in Renton, Washington. He continued to inspire his students, who in the school paper named him *"The Bard of the Yukon...a distinguished gentleman who has led as colorful an existence as any pioneer."* Lester died in February 1968.

Dory married Joe Koenig in 1971. Both Dory and Les had known Joe from WSC.

Dory and Joe enjoyed traveling and going to his beach place in the San Juan Islands. Their happiness was cut short when Dory died in 1973.

Les and Dory's daughter, Beverly, was born in 1932, in Yakima, Washington. She grew up in Petersburg, where she attended grades one through 12, except for her sophomore year at Pullman High School. She received her BA at WSC in 1954. She was employed by the CIA in Washington D.C. for two years, spent two years in Paris working for the Foreign Service, and then worked for the CIA in San Francisco.

By 1961, she had earned her master's degree at the University of California at Berkley. She then became a French and Spanish teacher at Redwood High School in Marin County, California. She lives in Oakland with Jim Street, a writer, mathematician and computer scientist. Beverly has a daughter, Katherine Lee Concannon, born in 1968.

Old school

Eigel and Marie Winther

By Bunny Winther Conlon

Two young women in their early teens departed a ship in Halifax, after a long voyage from Norway, the first leg of a journey that would take them to their new home. Not being able to speak English, they had their names printed on tags pinned to their coats. These young travelers were my mother, Marie Pileberg, and her sister Kristen.

They traveled by train across Canada to a small Indian village on the west coast of British Columbia, where a fishing vessel was to take them to Petersburg, Alaska. Their widowed mother, Hannah Pileberg, had gone before them with their three siblings.

Marie and Kristen had stayed behind in Aulesund to work for a year as maids to make enough money for one-way passage.

Marie was 20 years old when she met Egil Winther. They were married December 7, 1926, at the home of his sister, Liv Husvik.

Together they lived busy and productive lives, but they always had time for fun. Whenever the sun was out and the tide was good, they would row up Petersburg Creek or go to Sandy Beach for a picnic. We have fond memories of pulling a wagon along the boardwalk to Sandy Beach.

Egil and Marie had four children: Elinor, Katherine "Bunny," Sven and Barbro.

They were members of the Sons of Norway and the Lutheran Church.

After she was widowed, Marie found many ways to keep busy. Her hands were never idle — she knitted socks and mittens for many children in her neighborhood. She was known for her homemade bread and fish cakes, which she took to people who were ill.

Her Bible study group, "Gleaners," was an important part of her life, as she was a student of the Bible. She was a babysitter and substitute grandmother for several little children. One mother commented that her son learned to talk with a Norwegian accent. Marie liked having friends over for coffee.

Berry picking was a special pleasure. She would go with Gudrun Thynes and later with Maxine Husvik. They had their special spots that they never revealed. While taking a break, they would sit on a log in the muskeg and drink coffee or build a bonfire.

Marie was instrumental in starting the local children's Norwegian folk dances, which are now a beautiful tradition during the May 17th Festival.

Marie passed away in January 1974.

My father, Egil Winther, was born in 1891, in Vaagen, Domes, Norway. By the time he was 15, he had graduated from school. His handwritten diploma stated that he was an outstanding student.

For the next two years, he was engaged in fishing near his homeland. He began to sail out of Liverpool, England, mainly on square-rigger sailing ships, to as far away as Australia.

During the First World War, German U-boats found the square-riggers to be easy targets.

Egil traveled to America in order to sail the much safer waters of the Pacific, out of San Francisco. Winters were spent sailing to South America and the Orient, while summers meant going to Bristol Bay in Alaska on Alaska Packer vessels. These were the last of the square-riggers, carrying 30-foot gillnetters onboard that were used for fishing sockeye.

Among Egil's papers was found the following recommendation: *"This are to introduce Egil Winther. From 1920 to 1925 he were a seaman First Class, attentive to his duties and obedient to orders. He were engaged as Seaman and fisherman in roundtrip from San Francisco to Bristol Bay each year. I take great pleasure in making this recommendation. —H.M. Mortensen, Master Bark"*

On his last trip, Egil took a Pacific American Fisheries tender to Petersburg in order to visit his sister, Liv Husvik. There, he met Marie Pileberg.

Egil was engaged in fishing halibut, serving as crewman on a number of local boats. At one time he was on the *Augusta* with Martin Enge. In mid-May of 1935, while taking on fuel in Sitka, the boat blew up. One man was killed and Egil was badly burned. This resulted in a lengthy recovery.

When he later became able, Egil fished on the *Unimak*, jointly owned by Ole Husvik and Ole Rosvold. Early in the 1940s, Egil took over the *Unimak*. Halibut and blackcod fishing kept him busy until the late 1940s, when sockeye returned to Port Snettisham and Egil was there to greet them.

Gillnetting became a family affair with Sven as

Egil and Marie Winther cont'd

deckhand, Marie as cook, and Barbro as mascot. They enjoyed some wonderful summers.

When winter came and there was no fishing, many other activities took its place. Eigel hunted, put up deer meat, made meatballs, fish cakes, salted herring, and helped make lefse for the holidays.

He worked for the Civilian Conservation Corps during the construction of Sandy Beach road. We would tramp through the muskeg to bring him his lunch, locating him only by the huge bonfire that could be seen through the trees.

One of his other chores was cutting enough wood to see the family through the winter. Our house, at that time, was heated by a woodstove in the kitchen. He had a big wood sled that was painted green. When the snow was deep, he would take us out in the woods and fill the sled with logs that he had marked earlier in the fall. Aided by a rope and us pushing from the back, we would get the sled to the top of Thynes' hill.

All the kids would pile on and the death-defying ride would begin. The only means of steering the sled was for Egil to stand on the runners with a big stick as a rudder, and the only means of stopping was heading straight for a snow bank. Everyone would all fall off into the hospital lawn. It was a thrilling ride for all of us youngsters.

He was an avid reader and read our schoolbooks. We learned much geography and history from stories of his early shipping days.

Egil passed away in April 1953. Both he and Marie are buried in Petersburg's cemetery, the final resting place for many of Petersburg's early pioneers. It is a beautiful spot with its green rolling lawn, overlooking the quiet waters of Wrangell Narrows flowing by.

Here he lies where he longed to be;
Home is the sailor, home from the sea,
And the hunter home from the hill.
By Robert Louis Stevenson

Pier 2 in Seattle
Alaska State Library, Skinner Foundation Collection, PCA 44-3-180

For many of Petersburg's Pioneers, the last leg of their journey north began at Seattle's Pier 2, home of the Alaska Steamship Company. Established in 1895, Alaska Steamship provided passenger service to Southeast Alaska until 1954. The last sailing from Petersburg was in September of 1954, on the *Denali*.

Russell and Gussie York

By Carol Enge

Russell and Gussie York are fondly remembered in Petersburg for their many acts of generosity. They were owners and operators of Citizen's Steam Laundry, and during the Depression, they helped many young families get a start. If anyone needed money, they went to Gussie and Russell.

The York's had no children of their own, but Russell often took young friends trout fishing and on other boat trips. John Enge remembers Russell giving him his first gun — a Remington 20 long rifle.

He had one of the few trucks in town and all the kids liked to ride with him when he delivered laundry.

Gussie was born in Sweden in 1886. At the age of 9, an uncle brought her to the United States. They first made their way to Minneapolis, arriving during a big fair. She recalls the men getting drunk and being left in the train depot. She said that ever since she walked out of that depot, she had been on her own.

She was taken in by a family that needed help with housework and caring for their young son. She stayed with the family for 12 years, accumulating $1,200 for her work.

Gussie met and married Russell in 1907, and together they moved to Petersburg, Alaska.

The Yorks operated the Citizen's Steam Laundry for over 40 years. The men did the washing and the women ironed.

On Saturday night, Gussie often made beds in the boiler room for the kids staying overnight, while their mothers went to the dance. The business was sold to Bob and Charlotte Schwartz in 1952.

John Enge, Gussie York and Arnold Enge

After toiling hard from an early age through many years as owner of a laundry, Gussie lived to celebrate her 100th birthday.

Her last years were spent at the Riverton Heights Convalescent Home in Seattle.

Steamship

Other Early Settlers

This group of men in the photo below met to record as much information, as possible, about settlers who no longer have any descendants in Petersburg. All lifelong residents, they remember the individuals who are included in this section.

For many of these early settlers, little more than the name of the boat the person owned, or where he or she worked, can be recalled. Some were residents for only a short time. They were shipmates or friends. All had an influence on the developing community.

Forgive us for the many omissions. This is solely because there was no information available.

ADAMS John Adams was a Mexican who ran a taxi. It is remembered that he and his wife had 20 children. They later moved to Yakutat where he beach seined, and could lay in his tent, watching the net.

ALLEN Bob Allen came to Petersburg around 1916. He was a machinist and had a scow built down south and brought to Petersburg. Moored to the approach to Citizen's Dock, it housed a machine shop on the lower floor and living quarters above. After many years, Bob sold the business to Art Peterson. Later sold to Dave Ellis, it is now owned by Mike Luhr, who operates Piston and Rudder on the premises. Bob Allen was married and had one son.

ASK Andrew Ask and his wife lived at Point Agassiz and ran a dairy farm. They had three children. Andrew also fished for halibut on the *Sherman*.

BELL Helen Bell was born and raised in Kake. She belonged to the Shanqykedi clan. (Thunderbird/Eagle) She attended school at Pius X Mission in Skagway. Helen and Merlin Bell were married on August 11, 1946. During the years, she worked at the cannery, as a waitress, and as a nurse's aide. Helen was known for her beautiful smile that was enjoyed by all who met her. Her love for her family and friends was the focus of her life.

BIRCH Dick Birch and his wife lived on Hammer Slough. They had three children: Mike, Mildred and Nellie. He fished for trout and seined for salmon on his boat *Sunrise*.

BIRCH Fred Birch and his wife lived across the bay and had a mink ranch. He later became a welder and worked on the refrigeration systems at both cold storages. They had two sons: Fred Jr. and Ted.

BIRCH George and Ann Birch moved to Petersburg in 1910. He built a cabin for his family on Hammer Slough. Three children were born to the family: Dick, Fred and Gertrude. Soon after Gertrude's birth, the family moved to a fox farm near Level Island where they led a subsistence life. Gertrude helped by gillnetting fish for the foxes and raked herring for the family, as well as the animals. In 1929, because of the crash and Russians flooding the fur market, the family moved back to Petersburg. Attending school was a challenge. The kids had to walk a single-board walkway

Nels Evens, Lloyd Pederson, Leo Ness, Don Nelson, Erling Husvik and John Enge reminisced to compile the list of early settlers on the following pages.

Other Early Settlers cont'd

down to the Wrangell Narrows bridge and cross the slough. (Later, the Miller family built the first bridge across the slough.)

BLATCHFORD Arthur Blatchford served in the British Army before leaving England. His ship pulled out of the English Channel the day the *Titanic* was sunk. He was a shrimp fisherman for many years. His wife's name was Pauline and they had five children.

BRUCE John Bruce took an active interest in developing the town after he arrived in 1907. He ran a tailor shop and a restaurant and promoted the Citizen's Steam Laundry. He was founder of the Sons of Norway Hall. Serving on the town council, he helped blaze the proposed trail from Scow Bay. During World War I, as chairman of the Red Cross, he worked diligently to care for the victims of the influenza epidemic. In 1920, he moved to Everett, Washington.

DAHL Heinie Dahl came from Minnesota to Juneau to work at the Treadwell mine. He spent some time in Sitka before coming to Petersburg in 1916. He worked for Soft and Refling and Hogue & Tveten. He was married to Elsie and they had one daughter, Henrietta.

DAHL I.M. Dahl was among the early settlers in Petersburg who contributed much to the welfare of the community. Arriving in 1912, he fished for several years before homesteading at Point Agassiz. He was one of the pioneer prospectors in the community, contributing much to the discovery of mineral deposits in this area. In 1927, he started the People's Drug Store.

DeZORDO Jack DeZordo ran the Civilian Conservation Corps at Twin Creek before becoming superintendent of public works. At that time, all sewers in town ran into the Narrows and the streets were wooden planks. He married Vi Weyrick.

DUVALL George Duvall was born July 16, 1903, in Shell Lake, Wisconsin. At the age of 16, he traveled west, working on farms and in logging camps. In 1931, he arrived in Petersburg and worked in the local canneries and cold storages. When World War II was declared, he enlisted in the Navy and served aboard the USS *St. Lewis*. After the war, he worked for the City of Petersburg tending the cemetery. He had one son, Richard.

ELLIOT Charles Elliot was a Scotsman of noble birth. He came to America in 1926 and lived across the Narrows. Rumor has it that he was a disgrace to his family and was excommunicated. He was known as a remittance man.

ELSMORE Tom Elsmore was a co-founder of the Bank of Petersburg and the American Legion Post. He was active in the political life of the early settlement.

ENOS Charles Enos was a colorful and familiar figure on Petersburg streets in the early days. He came to Petersburg from Washington State and owned the troller *Thunderbird*, which he fished until suffering a stroke. He is remembered as a musician, playing the saxophone and clarinet.

GAUFFIN Sam Gauffin was the son of a saloon owner. In about 1921, he was skipper of the *Marion* for Petersburg Packing Co., and was later manager of the cold storage. He and his wife, the former Barbara Wharfanger, moved to Seattle in 1935. During World War I, he served in the Army Transport Service.

GJERDE Andrew Gjerde arrived in Petersburg in 1910 and started trolling near Forrester Island. He bought the *Happy*, which had a 20 hp engine. He got sons Melvin and Halvor involved in fishing, so he could count on a good crew. Son Andrew also became a fisherman. With his wife, Marie, they built a home on North Nordic Drive where Albie Hofstad now lives.

GJERDE Hofter Gjerde Sr. was a longline fisherman. He first had the boat *Rambler* and then the *Midway*, which he later passed on to his son, Andrew. Hofter Sr. died of a brain tumor. His son, Andrew, graduated from high school, in 1937, and attended the University of Alaska and Seattle Pacific College. When war was declared on December 7, 1941, he joined the Army and was subsequently stationed at Paine Field, near Seattle; Hikam Field, Hawaii; and Victorville Army Air Base, in California. He served as a laboratory technician. He met and married Catherine King in Long Beach, California in 1943. Following the war, they returned to Petersburg, where he first worked as a police officer. He fished the *Midway* until his retirement. They had two children: Hofter Jr. and Ava. Andrew currently resides at the long-term care facility in Petersburg.

GOODMAN Tom Goodman had a men's clothing store on Main Street.

GRANDQUIST Oscar Grandquist came to Petersburg, as a bookkeeper for Petersburg Packing

Other Early Settlers cont'd

Co., a subsidiary of Pacific American Fisheries in Bellingham, Washington. Coming to Alaska to work at the San Juan cannery in Latouche, he was later hired as manager of The Trading Union. He was married to the former Lillian Morrow.

GREBSTAD John Grebstad was married to Eileen Nelson and they had two children, Jenning and Eileen. He was foreman for a floating fish trap with partners Oscar Granquist and Oscar Nicholson.

GRIBBLE William Gribble came to Petersburg about 1910 from Colorado, where he worked as a hard rock miner. He was employed at the Treadwell mine in Juneau until it closed. He arrived in Petersburg, in 1917, and was first employed as a driver for the Hogue & Tveten store, which owned the only automobile in Petersburg. Later, he ran the mail boats *Trygve* and *Americ* to all the small bays in the area. He married Gertrude Biech and they had three children: Alma, Bill Jr. and Dick. Bill Jr. fished halibut, first out of Petersburg, then out of Seattle. He was married to Caroline Ekrum. Alma, married to Harold Sisson, worked for Hammer & Wikan before moving to Seattle. Dick worked at The Trading Union and Sanitary Market before working on the Alaska state ferries for 18 years. He married Vera Weyrick and they had two daughters, Ginger and Sharon.

HADLAND Jacob Hadland built the first saloon in town, on what is currently the site of Viking Travel. When prohibition closed saloons in 1918, he turned it into a restaurant known as the Grand Café. He built a house on North Nordic Drive that was later owned by Nick and Nette Martinsen. That house has now been moved to Papke's Landing. He was one of the first men to gillnet on the Stikine River.

HADLAND Tom Hadland came from Bayfield, Wisconsin, in 1906. He ran a fox farm in Beecher's Pass and tried his hand at fishing. He and his wife had a large family of 11 children. Their oldest daughter, Mamie, married Chris Tveten. Another daughter, Gertrude, married Andrew Heimdahl.

HALL Ralph Hall is best remembered as manager of Petersburg Cold Storage. He was born in Oklahoma. During the Depression, he came across country as a hobo to the Puget Sound area. Going down the streets of Seattle, he saw an advertisement saying "Go To Alaska." Alaskan jobs available for $5. Pawning his gold watch for $22, he paid $15 for a ticket to Wrangell and $5 for a job. While doing odd jobs in Wrangell, he was able to stake a claim and prospected for 10 to 15 years above Telegraph Creek. Prospecting was not lucrative, as gold was selling for $22 an ounce. When his gold claim played out, he came to Petersburg and fished halibut. He and his wife, Clara, and had one son, Arden. One of his Ralph's jobs was driving the laundry truck for Citizen's Steam Laundry. He was also fire chief for many years. In retirement, he and his second wife, Alex, built a beautiful house at Hungry Point.

HANSON Dick and Edith Hanson had six children: Andy, Dorothy, Joanne, Peter, Jim and Katherine. He was a commercial trout fisherman and a World War I veteran. Old timers remember him playing the drums in a band at the Sons of Norway Hall. Dick was an avid basketball fan and referee and was awarded a lifetime pass to local games. He retired to Ballard, where he died.

HEMNES Magnus Hemnes came to Petersburg in 1922, as port engineer at the cold storage. He married Gertrude Hallingstad and they had two daughters, Mildred and Jackie. They built a home on North Nordic Drive, where John Winther now lives.

Other Early Settlers cont'd

HENTZE Bue Hentze was born in Chicago on November 8, 1892. He moved to Portland, Oregon, at a young age and graduated from Benson Polytechnic High School. He was a veteran of the U.S. Army in World War I. When he came to Petersburg, he ran a metal and plumbing business for 34 years. In 1949, he married Jane Greely, who is recalled as being a limousine driver in San Francisco during the founding of the United Nations. Jane died in 1986 and Bue in 1996. He was 104 year old.

JAMES Marie James was a wonderful, warm Tlingit woman who founded Marie's Beauty Salon in 1964. Marie was born in Juneau. She described her Native background, as "I am wolf, eagle and thunderbird." She was never ashamed of being an Indian. She used to do a lot of fighting when someone called her something else. Marie lived most of her life in Petersburg and has been active in community affairs, as well as in the Alaska Native Sisterhood. Business and Professional Women was an organization she really believed in because it helped her to get started in her own business. Once, when some friends stopped in to visit Marie, she had just finished cutting one daughter's hair and giving another daughter a permanent. The friends asked, "Why don't you go to beauty school?" She had never thought about it, but with the help of the BPW, the school superintendent, and another teacher, she was able to go. After finishing beauty school, she returned and started her beauty shop. She continued operating the shop until her health failed and she sold it to Ellie Hegar.

JOHNSON Chester Johnson was married to Winnie Greinier, and they had two children, Bill and Barney. Together with Andrew Heimdahl, he started a grocery store. A few years later, he became a traveling salesman, representing grocery companies between Seattle and Alaska.

JOHNSON Jacob Johnson had come from Wisconsin with Erick Ness, and started a saltery in Washington Bay for salt and bait herring. Together with Jacob Hadland, he had operated a store and fishermen's outfitting store in Wisconsin. He owned the *Teddy J* and the *Betty*.

JOHNSON Ted Johnson was a halibut fisherman, besides seining on his boat the *Ankle Deep*. He married Miriam Benson, widow of Dr. Benson.

JORGENSON Peter Jorgenson arrived with Buschmann's original crew in 1898. He returned to Denmark to marry, returning with his bride in 1901. Peter fished halibut on his boat *Hohop*. They built a large two-story house located at First and Excel streets, where Alaska Power and Telephone is now located now. They had four sons and two daughters. Their daughter, Alaska, married John Varnes and raised their family in town. Two of the sons, Harve and Albert, also remained in Petersburg. Peter was very active in Petersburg politics, serving as mayor several times.

KNUTSEN Ole Knutsen had a barrel factory across the Narrows at the mouth of Petersburg Creek. Pete Knutsen had the boat *Charm* that he found drifting in Frederick Sound and salvaged. ("Charm" is a section between the hoops of a barrel.) They also had a sawmill that they ran until 1947.

KRAUSE Edward Krause is remembered by some Petersburg residents as an upstanding man, a gentleman who wrote poems, and a fine boat builder. Another side of Krause was discovered after an FBI investigation led to his conviction of the murder of James Plunkett of Juneau and the kidnapping of William Christie, who worked at the Treadmill mine. Krause was thought to have murdered others, including O.M. Moe, a Petersburg fisherman. Krause escaped from jail in April of 1917, only to be killed by Arvid Franzen on Admiralty Island.

LANG Chris Lang was a tailor who ran a men's department store before selling out to Tom Goodman.

LERO Pete Lero ran the *Jugoslav* before buying the troller *Fosna*. He was a nephew of Severin Lero and a cousin of Bertha, who was a well-known schoolteacher and died of a brain tumor. Pete's wife was named Ann.

McKECKNIE Joe McKecknie and his wife, Lulu, came to Petersburg with the U.S. Forest Service. As superintendent of Power and Light, they lived at Blind Slough. They had three children: Joe, Bruce and Don.

NILSEN Eivart Nilsen was born in Haugesund, Norway, April 15, 1884. He came to America as a young man and worked as a farmhand in South Dakota and Nebraska for Jake Hallingstad. He migrated to Petersburg in 1912 and worked as a fisherman and carpenter. He built a home on Lumber Street for Jacob Hallingstad. Ed was one of Petersburg's earliest fire

Other Early Settlers cont'd

chiefs. He was also a street superintendent for many years and a policeman. The streets were made of planks and in constant need a repair. A two-wheeled cart was the conveyance used to move material and tools to the place of repair. Jack DeZordo and William Gribble Sr. were his right-hand men.

NORBERG Peter and Charlie Norberg first came to Alaska in 1897 with the Buschmann cannery company. They sailed on the steamer *White Wing* from Tacoma, Washington. They arrived in the future settlement of Petersburg the summer of 1898. Peter was married and had four children. He filed on an 80-acre homestead across the Narrows on Kupreanof. Mrs. Peter Norberg died in 1900. Their oldest daughter took over the household management. In May 1902, Peter and Louis Miller constructed adjoining cabins connected with a large porch. Peter's son Duffy operated a saloon next to the old Salvation Army Hall in Sing Lee Alley. He married Jack O'Donnell's mother and later Astrid Stromdahl. Charlie Norberg later married and had two daughters, one of whom moved to Hollywood and became the actress known as Terry Walker. Charlie was a first-class lumberman. As operator of Buschmann's first sawmill, he

Pacific Coast & Norway Packing Co.
"Good for 50¢ in trade"

cut lumber to construct the first homes and docks in Petersburg. After his first wife died, he married Charlie Mann's niece. They built a large home in West Petersburg on the site of the present City of Kupreanof community center.

PHILBIN Pete Philbin came to Alaska with his brother and sister in 1933, starting their new life on a fox ranch on Midway Island. He enlisted in the Army in 1943 and served in the 208th National Guard with several others from Petersburg. He was stationed on Attu Island in the Aleutians and also saw service in India. He was discharged in 1946 in California. Upon returning to Alaska, he fished with his brother Don on the *Progress*. Involved in construction for many years, he was also employed by the Alaska Department of Fish and Game on the vessel *Stellar*, retiring in 1991. In 1960, he married Betty Trudeau.

RANDRUP Wes Randrup first came to Alaska in 1948, as a machinist for Pacific American Fisheries at King Cove. In 1949, he was transferred to the same position at Petersburg's PAF plant. Besides his summer job in the cannery, he opened a machine shop adjacent to Alaskan Glacier Sea Food under Earl Ohmer. With only a handshake, they agreed he would use the machine shop and, in return, do maintenance work in the plant. This arrangement existed for over 20 years without a penny exchanging hands. In retirement, he has served as secretary of the Elks Lodge and Pioneers of Alaska, and Master of the Masonic Lodge. His favorite avocation is his annual moose-hunting trip with his sons. He has two sons, two daughters, 13 grandchildren and many great-grandchildren.

RICHARDS Frank Richards, known as Shakey Frank, lived on North Nordic Drive. His wife died of cancer, and he sent his son, Debs, south to school. In later years, he lived in a cabin at the mouth of Petersburg Creek. He pioneered oyster farming in Wrangell Narrows.

SARFF Ernest Sarff served in the field artillery in France, in World War I. In 1925, he and his wife, Delia, first came to Ketchikan, where he began fishing. Seeing an advertisement for a clerk at The Trading Union in Petersburg, he applied and was hired. He worked there until his retirement in 1988. Ernest was active in the American Legion and was commander at one time. Delia was a homemaker during the years the children were home. She was a very accomplished poet and worked diligently in the American Legion Auxiliary, serving as president. In later years, she was city librarian. Ernie and Delia had three children: Edward, Frances and Ronald. Ed served in World War II and Korea. He retired after serving 20 years in the Army. He moved to San Francisco and sold insurance. He currently lives in Petersburg and is married to the former Marian Paddock. Frances married Clayton Fleek and lived in Juneau. Ron worked as an administrative officer for the U.S. Forest Service and Park Service. His last years were spent with the Park Service at Mt. Rainier.

SING LEE emigrated from China to Alaska in 1892. He came to Petersburg about 1909 and owned a

Other Early Settlers cont'd

large store on what is now Sing Lee Alley. It was a gathering place for fishermen and bachelors. John Enge remembers going to his store frequently with his grandfather, Rasmus. Sing Lee always gave John candy. In November 1932, he was murdered in an upstairs apartment. His death was never solved. He had always been known for his kindness and generosity.

Sing Lee's name was really Mar Goey. After he married, he changed his name to Mar Chan Len, keeping with the Chinese custom.

SIMONSET Elias Simonset gillnetted on the Stikine River with the boat *Rapid* and lived on Hammer Slough.

SONSTHAGEN A.H. Sonsthagen came to Petersburg to work in the office, when the cannery started in 1900. He was an expert in fish splitting and mild curing. He also bought fish. He had one of the major Napoleonic book collections in North America. The collection, nearly 2,000 volumes recording the grandeur and martial splendor of Napoleon's life and campaigns, is housed at Seattle University.

STEBERG Knut Steberg and Tom Elsmore formed the Bank of Petersburg on September 12, 1912. Knut was the first bookkeeper for the bank. He was agent for Standard Oil before moving to Ketchikan where he became Standard Oil's general manager for Southeast Alaska.

STEPHEN Jack Stephen was born in Morgan County, Indiana, on September 4, 1902, one of 11 children. He served in the U.S. Marine Corps, although the date of his enlistment is unknown. Also unknown is how, or why, he moved to Alaska. Jack worked out at the Brothers Islands, fox farming with the Zimmermans during the early 1940s. He also worked fox farming on Elliot Island. Jack married Agnes Hammer on September 18, 1943. They had one son, Jon Arthur Stephen, born June 22, 1944. Agnes died June 6, 1948. Jack fished on many boats as a crewman, engineer or captain. The boats he worked on over the years include the *Roetta*, *Collete*, *Bernice A*, *Bernice*, *Pirate*, *Laddie* and the *Vesta*. He also packed salmon from the seiniers and shrimp from the shrimpers. Jack was very versatile. He also worked at Processors cannery on the boilers and as a cooker. Over the years, Jack delivered home heating oil in the winters. He also worked on home heating boilers, furnaces, and plumbing for both homes and businesses. Jack was a member of the Elks, Masons, and the local fire department.

Sing Lee

STOLL Hugo Stoll left St. Michaels, Alaska, in 1918, because of the flu epidemic. He had been refrigeration engineer on a ship in Bristol Bay. He had also been on a mail run from Nome to Ruby by dog sled, before moving to Seward. He and his son Fred brought the *Jugoslav* to Petersburg in 1923. Here, he worked as engineer at the cold storage for the remainder of his life. He and his wife had five children: Fred, Bill, Andy, Anita and Eleanor.

SWANSON Carl Elmer Swanson was born and raised at Point Agassiz. He worked for the Bureau of Public Works and was transferred to Hawaii in May 1941. After narrowly escaping death during the bombing of Pearl Harbor, he volunteered for an emergency assignment at Christmas Island for construction of an airfield. The airfield would provide the only means for aircraft to cross the Pacific at that time. Upon returning to Hawaii, he became chief engineer, responsible for engineering, and the inspection of, construction in Hawaii. In December 1945, he joined the staff of the Supreme Commander Allied Powers in Japan for two years. He then transferred to the Eastern Ocean Division of the Corps and was project manager for Goose Bay, Labrador and Newfoundland. Later assignments took him to French Morocco, Karachi, Pakistan and Korea. He retired to Honolulu with his wife, Betty, and three children.

SWANSON Raymond Swanson was born in Petersburg in 1913. He moved to Point Agassiz with his family, where they raised cattle, sheep and silver fox. After graduating from Petersburg High School, he attended Hemphill Diesel Engineering School. He was chief engineer on the *Mildred* for Pacific American Fisheries for three years. He went to work for Standard Oil in Edmonds, Washington, and then Petersburg. He

Sing Lee photo courtesy Clausen Memorial Museum

Other Early Settlers cont'd

and Mildred Heimdahl married. They had two children, Ray Jr. and Jeanette. After a lingering case of cancer, Raymond died in 1963.

SZTUK Felix Sztuk was a tough old guy, who built a 40-foot boat on a gridiron in front of his home using a curved pine tree trunk for the bow stem. He would fish halibut with the far-from-seaworthy boat, the *Gertrude*, out in the rough waters off Cape Spencer. In the winter seasons, he would trim halibut in the cold storage, barehanded. Felix's hands were as big as hams, he never used mitts, and he was never without a pipe in his mouth.

TENFJORD Olaf Tenfjord sent for a mail-order bride, Marie. They had one daughter, Norma. Olaf fished halibut on the *Mira*. Louis Tenfjord was a World War I veteran who had a fox farm at Tebenkoff Bay.

URSIN John Ursin was related to Andrew Mathisen's wife. He built the original Mathisen home. His oldest son, Axle, moved to Seldovia to run cannery tenders. Erling Ursin moved to Bristol Bay. Reider Ursin fished halibut before moving to Seattle to fish on the *Norrona*. John and his wife moved back to Seldovia to live.

WANBERG Jack Wanberg first arrived in Petersburg from Aalesund, Norway, in April of 1905. Arriving on the *City of Seattle* with one dollar in his pocket, he got a job at a sawmill and later with the Olympic mine at Beecher's Pass. John Knutsen asked him to come back to work at the sawmill as an edger. He died in Washington in 1971.

VEVELSTAD Carl Vevelstad worked the Yakobi mine, and also had the mail run to Wrangell.

YOUNG Ralph Young was born in Hammond, Oregon, in 1906. His love of the outdoors began with fishing trips with his father. Losing his parents after World War I, he became a wanderer. In Seattle, and disliking his life, he signed on as a crewman on the *Dellwood*. During the trip, he learned to like Alaska and returned to Kodiak in 1931. Even though his thoughts were with Alaska and the big grizzlies he had seen, he spent the next few years in Montana, where he married Jo and had a son, Bill. In 1934, he boarded the SS *North Sea* for Alaska and began his career as a professional guide, lasting 30 years. Jo soon joined him and came along as cook. By now, he was making his living doing what he was meant to do — hunter, big game guide, trapper, commercial fisherman, bounty hunter, and wildlife photographer. Before long, daughter Julie joined the family. In later years, he put his experiences on paper. His books have been called the greatest hunting autobiographies of all time. Ralph died November 23, 1985, at the age of 70.

ZAVODNIK Joe Zavodnik was born in Soudan, Minnesota, on March 3, 1922. He volunteered for the Army, along with his friend, Louie Vessel, in 1939. He served in the Aleutians and Germany during World War II. He came to Alaska, in 1948, with Louie Vessel and worked in the cannery and for the Reid Brothers Logging Co. He moved to Pelican where he bought his troller, the *Diana*. Returning to Petersburg, he sold his troller to Ed Wood. Joe was married to Nellie Birch. He died December 25, 2000.

Al and Alma Zuver

ZUVER Al Zuver gillnetted with the *Priority* in Kah Sheets Bay. He and his wife, Alma, had two boys and two girls. Bert Zuver fished shrimp for Earl Ohmer.

Epilogue

Alaska gains statehood
January 3, 1959

June 30, 1958
*Photo by Dr. R.C. Smith courtesy of Petersburg High School
From the 1960* Flood Tide *annual*

June 30, 1958, was a day of celebration across Alaska. The United States Senate passed the Alaska Statehood bill by a vote of 64-20, culminating many years of effort by Alaskans across the territory. Petersburg residents joined the celebration, pinning the 49th star on the American flag.

President Dwight D. Eisenhower signed the Alaska Statehood Act into law on July 7, 1958. On January 3, 1959, he then signed the Alaska Statehood Proclamation, officially bringing Alaska into the Union as the 49th state.

The following year, the 1600 Petersburg residents had another celebration — the commemoration of Petersburg's golden anniversary. Fifty years before, on February 28, 1910, Petersburg voters elected to incorporate the town.

Petersburg waterfront and Wrangell Narrows
*Photo courtesy of the Alaska State Library, Historical Collections
ASL-Petersburg-Waterfront-10 VILDA*

Index

The following index contains the names that appear on the top of each Family Page. Names in our "Other Early Settlers" section are not included here. A list of those names, along with a list of organizations and businesses, immediately follows this Family Page list.

Family Pages
Allen, John and Minnie, 11
Andersen, Charles and Jessie, 13
Anderson, Bert and Helen, 14
Anderson, Carl, 15
Arness, Olaf and Constance, 16
Baggen, Ed and Ingeborg, 18
Bailey, Warren and Ann, 19
Bennett, Farrell and Alda, 21
Bergmann, Harold and Ethel, 22
Bollen, Frank and Annie, 25
Brennan, Dick and Helen, 28
Brennan, Jim and Edna, 26
Buschmann, Peter, 29
Clausen, Carroll and Elsie, 39
Close, Gifford and Agnes, 41
Colp, Harry and Minnie, 42
Cornelius, Bert and Myrtle, 45
Counter, Vernon and Mildred, 46
Dahl, Chris and Nina, 48
Dawes, Harold and Minnie, 50
Delegard, Esther, 51
Durbin, Mike and Margaret, 52
Duval, Royal and Clara, 53
Eide, Lars and Meredith, 55
Elkins, Lester and Mildred, 56
Elstad-Rayner Family, 57
Enge, Arnold and Barbara, 63
Enge, Ernest and Ethel, 64
Enge, John and Carol, 60
Enge, Martin and Augusta, 59
Enge, Rasmus and Anna, 58
Engstrom, Inez, 66
Espeseth, Arvid and Bea, 70
Espeseth, Bert and Larine, 68
Espeseth Family, 67
Evens, Nels and Mildred, 71
Fenn, Cliff and Helen, 72
Fernandez, Francisco and Pauline, 75
File, Claude and Elizabeth, 76
Fredricksen, Knute and Dorothy, 77
Frink, Marion and Geraldine, 79
Fryer, Forrest and Christine, 80
Fuglvog, Ed and Mildred, 84
Fuglvog, Erik and Marit, 81
Greinier, Andrew and Zella, 85
Greinier, Bill and Barbara, 86
Gronseth, Chris and Petra, 87
Hallingstad, Jacob and Gertrude, 88
Haltiner, Fred and Beulah, 89
Hammer, Jim and Bev, 94
Hammer, John and Marie, 92
Hansen, Trygve and Esther, 95
Hanseth, Jacob, 98
Hanson, Peter and Anna, 99
Harris, Hugh and Alice, 100
Hasbrouck, Henry and Ellen, 101
Hasbrouck, Leon and Sarah, 102
Haube, Max and Rose, 105
Haugen, Ernie and Ruby, 106
Heimdahl, Norman and Marjorie, 107
Henderson, Robert and Wilma, 109
Hofstad, Myhre and Birgitte, 111
Hofstad, Morten and Valborg, 114
Hofstad, Oliver and Angie, 116
Hofstad, Richard and Dorothy, 112
Hungerford, Edgar and Caroline, 118
Husvik, Ole and Liv, 119
Israelson, Andrew and Anne, 124
Israelson, Louis and Alex, 122
Jensen, John and Gina, 127
Jensen, Howard and Marie, 129
Johansen, Sverre and Alma, 130
Johnson, Andrew and Laura, 131
Johnson, James A., 135
Johnson, Joe and Cora, 133
Johnson, John and Dell, 138
Jones, Hugh and Eva, 139
Jordan, Wilhelm and Marilyn, 140
Kaino, Shunichi and Hana, 143
Kawashima, Joe and Fran, 144
Kayler, Dean and Mabel, 145
Kildall Family, 147
Kito, Tom and Lucy, 149
Klabo, Sig and Jensine, 150
Kuwata, 144

Index cont'd

Lando Family, 151
Lee, Eldor and Pauline, 157
Lee, Harold, 160
Lee, Harold and Magnhild, 153
Lee, Roxane, 161
Leekley, James and Anne, 162
LeRoy, Paul and Florence, 164
Lind, Justin and Magda, 165
Locken, Ed and Sibyl, 167
Longworth, Jack and Mary Alice, 169
Lopez, Art and Ethelyn, 172
Loseth, John and Dora, 173
Luhr, Don and Beulah, 175
Luhr, Frank and Laura, 174
Lund, Peder and Anna, 177
Lyons, George and Mary, 178
MacDonald, Gordon and Georgia, 180
Magill, Frederick and Enid, 181
Marifern, Lon and Camille, 182
Martens, Leonard and Emily, 187
Martens, Loui and Ragnhild, 184
Martin, Robert and Margaret, 188
Martinsen's Dairy, 189
Mathisen, Adolph and Frances, 200
Mathisen, Andrew, 201
Mathisen, Andrew and Tora, 196
McGilton, Alexander and Anna, 203
Miller, Louis and Annea, 209
Miller, Louis and Marie, 205
Miller, Richard and Verne, 207
Mjorud Family, 210
Molver, John and Asbjorg, 211
Molver, Laurence and Twila, 213
Mortensen, George and Alice, 214
Nelson, Donald and Betty, 218
Nelson, Frederick and Edna, 216
Ness, Erick and Agnes, 220
Newlun, Neil and Margaret, 222
Nicholson, Erling and Colleen, 224
Nicholson, George and Gusta, 223
Nicholson, Oscar and Alma, 226
Nordgren, Kurt and Clara, 228
Noreide, Anton and Sophie, 229
Norheim, Jorgen and Tora, 231
Odegaard, Kristian and Agnes, 232
O'Donnell, Jack and Vera, 233

Ohmer, David Paul, 239
Ohmer, Earl Nicholas, 235
Ohmer, Gloria Lucille, 241
Ohmer, Loyla, 237
Oines, Willmer and Sylvia, 243
Olsen, Chris and Agnes, 244
Olsen, Jack, 246
Olsen, Melvin, Ilene and Irene, 249
Other Early Settlers, 368
Otness, John and Ragna, 250
Otness, Oscar and Rikka, 251
Papke, Herman, 252
Parr, Gordon and Polly, 253
Pautzke, Charlie and Anna, 254
Pederson, Lloyd and Betty, 255
Peterson, Arthur and Frances, 257
Powels, Ruth Lee, 259
Preuschoff, Edmund and Louise, 260
Ramstead, Edward and Ida, 262
Rastad, Elise Hofstad, 264
Rayner (Elstad-Rayner), 57
Reid Brothers, 265
Reid, Glenn and Martha, 268
Reid, Gordon and Connie, 267
Reid, John and Bernice, 267
Reid, Robert and Vena, 266
Reid, Stan and Elda, 270
Rhoden, Dorsey and Ruth, 271
Rogers, Carl and Elizabeth, 273
Rosvold, Ole and Ellen, 274
Roundtree, Claude and Isabella, 277
Roundtree, Guy, 276
Roundtree, Lloyd and Irene, 281
Roundtree, Lyle and D.J., 279
Roundtree, Melvin and Connie, 283
Rude, Joseph and Amy, 285
Runstad, Harold, 289
Sales, Johnny, 290
Samuelson, Chris and Inga, 291
Sandvik, Nils and Malla, 293
Sandvik, Oscar and Ruth, 295
Sasby, John, 298
Sather, Per and Louise, 299
Schwartz, Bob and Charlotte, 300
Severson, Louis and Ida, 304
Severson, Louis and Ragna, 303

Index cont'd

Silva, John and Maria, 305
Smith, Ben and Margit, 306
Stafford, Jim and Alice, 308
Stedman, Charles and Hester, 309
Stedman, William and Elvina, 310
Stedman, William Kenneth, 313
Stenslid, Knud and Ragna, 314
Stolpe, Harold and Pat, 315
Strand, Erling and Claire, 316
Stromdahl, Leif and Alta, 317
Swanson, Carl and Aurora, 318
Swanson, Lillian L., 321
Swanson, Norris and Mary Anne, 324
Swanson, Wally and Colleen, 322
Tate, Norman and Vange, 325
Taylor, Jim and Billie, 326
Thomassen, Haakon and Eleanor, 327
Thompson, Knut and Ann, 328
Thompson, Tom and Lorraine, 329
Thorsen, Ed and Ingeborg, 331
Thorstenson, Bob and Pam, 332
Thynes, Carl and Gudrun, 334
Thynes, Carl and Molly, 336
Thynes, Pete and Tora, 335
Torwick, Roy and Thelma, 338
Tveten, Chris and Mamie, 340
Vallestad, Gus and Perla, 341
Wasvick, Arnold and Evelyn, 343
Wasvick, Berger and Petra, 342
Welde, Peder and Ragna, 345
Westerberg, Dave and Caroline, 347
Westre, Lars and Laura, 348
Wheeler, James and Frances, 350
Wikan, Andrew and Margaret, 354
Wikan, Andy and Noca, 356
Wikan, Eiler, 353
Wikan, Elias, 353
Wikan, Johan and Carlene, 359
Wikan, Olaf and Mette, 361
Wikan, Oscar, 362
Wingard, Lester and Dorothy, 363
Winther, Eigel and Marie, 365
York, Russell and Gussie, 367

Other Early Settlers, beginning on page 368

Adams, John
Allen, Bob
Ask, Andrew
Bell, Helen
Birch, Dick
Birch, Fred
Birch, George
Blatchford, Arthur
Bruce, John
Dahl, Heinie
Dahl, I.M.
DeZordo, Jack
Duvall, George
Elliott, Charles
Elsmore, Tom
Enos, Charles
Gauffin, Sam
Gjerde, Andrew
Gjerde, Hofter Sr.
Goodman, Tom
Grandquist, Oscar
Grebstad, John
Gribble, William
Hadland, Jacob
Hadland, Tom
Hall, Ralph
Hanson, Dick
Hemnes, Magnus
Hentze, Bue
James, Marie
Johnson, Chester
Johnson, Jacob
Johnson, Ted
Jorgenson, Peter
Knutsen, Ole & Peter
Krause, Edward
Lang, Chris
Lero, Pete
McKecknie, Joe
Nilsen, Eivart
Norberg, Peter & Charlie
Philbin, Pete
Randrup, Wes
Richards, Frank
Sarff, Ernest
Sing Lee
Simonset, Elias
Sonsthagen, A.H.
Steberg, Knut
Stephen, Jack
Stoll, Hugo
Swanson, Carl Elmer
Swanson, Raymond
Sztuk, Felix
Tenfjord, Olaf
Ursin Family
Wanberg, Jack
Vevelstad, Carl
Young, Ralph
Zavodnik, Joe
Zuver, Al

Businesses and Organizations

Alaskan Glacier Sea Food Co., 238, 240
American Legion, 12
Hammer & Wikan, Inc., 93
Lee's Clothing, Inc., 161
Masonic Lodge No. 262, 194
People's Drug Store, 69
Petersburg Fisheries, 333
Petersburg Motors, Inc., 78
Sons of Norway, 307
The Trading Union, Inc., 248
Wells Fargo, 168

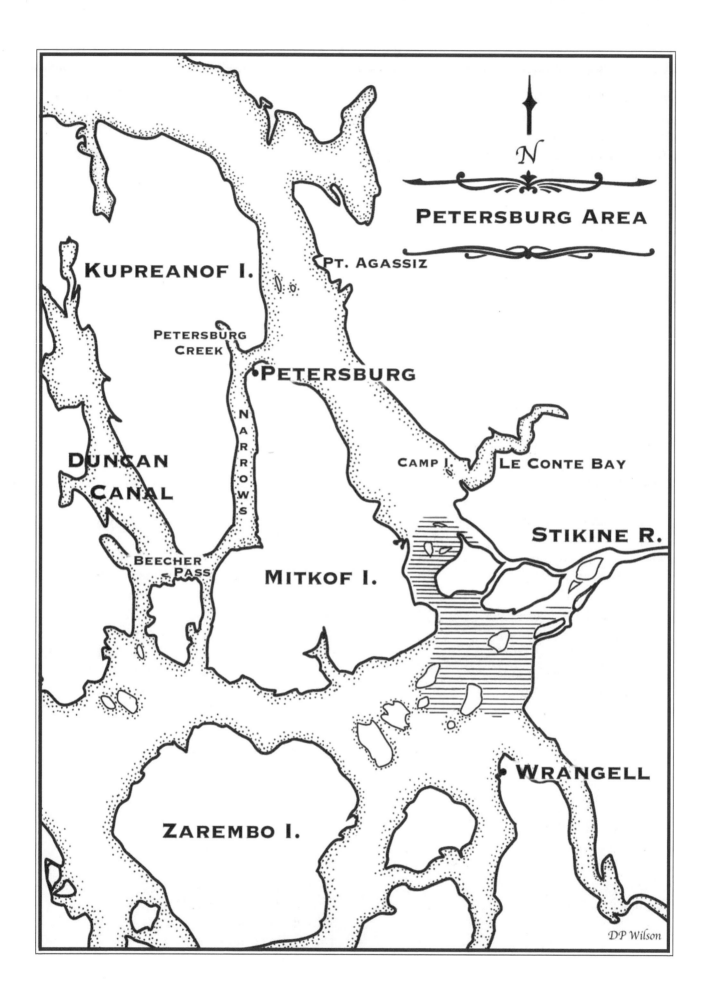

Made in United States
Troutdale, OR
11/08/2024

24576555R00213